TUDOR CONSTITUTIONAL DOCUMENTS

Tudor Constitutional Documents
A.D. 1485–1603
with an historical commentary

by

J. R. TANNER

Cambridge
at the University Press
1951

CAMBRIDGE UNIVERSITY PRESS
Cambridge, New York, Melbourne, Madrid, Cape Town,
Singapore, São Paulo, Delhi, Mexico City

Cambridge University Press
The Edinburgh Building, Cambridge CB2 8RU, UK

Published in the United States of America by Cambridge University Press, New York

www.cambridge.org
Information on this title: www.cambridge.org/9781107679405

First Edition 1922
Second Edition 1930
Reprinted 1940
„   1948
„   1951
First published 1930
First paperback edition 2013

A catalogue record for this publication is available from the British Library

ISBN 978-1-107-67940-5 Paperback

PREFACE

TEACHERS of experience would probably agree that English Constitutional History should be studied in close connexion with documents. These serve a high educational purpose, for they supply materials for constructing a proper historical background and creating the real historical atmosphere. With their aid it is possible for the student to test for himself the generalisations and epigrams of historians, and to find out what is really behind them. Instead of relying entirely upon eloquent modern statements in praise or in condemnation of the Tudor ecclesiastical policy, he can follow the genuine movement of Reformation thought expressed in the language of the great churchmen of that age, and can trace in the Royal Injunctions[1] and in Hooker's *Ecclesiastical Polity* the reasonableness, moderation, and learning which came to be characteristic of the Anglican Church. The dry bones of Star Chamber history clothe themselves with flesh and blood in the records of actual cases in which human beings are concerned; and arid legal propositions about the Law of Treason take on a new character in the story of things that really happened in a treason trial. Ready-made summaries of the great constitutional statutes, memorised for examination purposes, cease to satisfy the student who has access to the statutes themselves, and can extract from their resounding phrases and interminable verbiage his own idea of their essential meaning.

An experience of nearly forty years in preparing candidates for the Cambridge Historical Tripos has, however, convinced the present writer that the documents will never be properly studied while they are divorced from the history and relegated to separate collections, often only to be read up in a hurry on the eve of an examination. To the collection of Tudor documents here printed there has therefore been

---

[1] *E.g.* the Injunction of 1536 concerning pilgrimages (p. 93 below).

added a full historical commentary, dealing with the more important problems of the constitutional history of the 16th century. The work is based upon a course of lectures on Later Constitutional History delivered to Tripos candidates at Cambridge.

The texts of the documents selected are chosen mainly for their accessibility to the student in the University and College Libraries.

Thanks are due to the following for permission to print copyright material. To the Controller of His Majesty's Stationery Office for extracts from the *Calendar of Patent Rolls; Letters and Papers, Foreign and Domestic, Henry VIII; Calendar of State Papers (Domestic)*; and *Acts of the Privy Council*, edited by Sir J. R. Dasent. To the President and Council of the Selden Society, for extracts from *Select Cases in the Court of Requests* and *Select Cases in the Court of Star Chamber*, both edited by Mr I. S. Leadam. To the Somerset Record Society for permission to print cases from *Proceedings in the Court of Star Chamber in the reigns of Henry VII and Henry VIII*, edited by Miss G. Bradford. To the Early English Text Society for extracts from *The Supplication of Beggars*, by Simon Fish, edited by Dr F. J. Furnivall; and *England in the reign of King Henry VIII*, by Thomas Starkey, edited by Mr J. M. Cowper and by Mr S. J. Herrtage. To Mr J. E. Neale, and the editor and publishers of the *English Historical Review* for permission to print better versions of two Elizabethan speeches than those given by D'Ewes. To Messrs G. Bell & Sons for quotations from a sermon printed in Lupton's *Life of Colet*. To Messrs Macmillan & Co. for permission to quote freely from the Royal Injunctions printed in Messrs Gee and Hardy's collection of *Documents illustrative of English Church History*. Finally, to the Syndics of the Cambridge University Press for leave to use Mr L. Alston's edition of Sir Thomas Smith's *De Republica Anglorum*.

The writer also desires gratefully to acknowledge the kindness of two personal friends, G. G. Coulton, M.A., Fellow of St John's College, Cambridge, who read the section on the Dissolution of the Monasteries and made some valuable suggestions; and H. D. Hazeltine, Litt.D., Downing Professor of the Laws of England, who went through the whole work in proof, and did all that a friend could do to rescue its author from the snares which beset the feet of a constitutional historian who is not also a lawyer.

15 *December* 1921   J. R. T.

PREFACE TO THE SECOND EDITION

IN this Second Edition the opportunity has been taken to correct a few errors of detail which were pointed out by reviewers[1] when it was first published. Among the works which have appeared since, attention may be called to the following: (1) THE STATUTE OF TREASON, 1495 (p. 5 f. below), see A. F. Pollard in 'Tudor Gleanings' (*Bulletin of the Institute of Historical Research*, vii, No. 19, June 1929); (2) THE CHURCH SETTLEMENT OF HENRY VIII (p. 13 ff.), A. F. Pollard, 'Wolsey' (1929); (3) THE CHURCH SETTLEMENT OF ELIZABETH (p. 163 ff.), A. F. Scott-Pearson, 'Thomas Cartwright and Elizabethan Puritanism, 1535–1603' (1928); (4) THE KING'S SECRETARY (p. 202 ff.), Miss F. M. G. Evans, 'The Principal Secretary of State... 1558 to 1680' (1923); (5) PRIVY COUNCIL AND STAR CHAMBER (p. 213 ff., p. 249 ff.), A. F. Pollard, 'Council, Star Chamber, and Privy Council under the Tudors,' in *English Historical Review*, xxxvii, 337, 516, xxxviii, 42; (6) PRIVILEGE OF PARLIAMENT (p. 554 ff.), J. E. Neale, 'Peter Wentworth,' in *English Historical Review*, xxxix, 36 and 175; (7) FINANCE (p. 598 ff.), Local government and finance in E. P. Cheyney, *A History of England from the Defeat of the Armada to the Death of Elizabeth* (1926)[2].

The editor has received from Mr P. E. Roberts, of Worcester College, Oxford, an interesting suggestion for an emendation in the extract from Sir Thomas Smith printed on pp. 284–285 below: 'For that is the effect of this Court, to bridle such stout noblemen or gentlemen which would offer wrong by force to any manner men.' He points out that the extract has already referred to 'mean gentlemen,'

---

[1] In this connexion the editor acknowledges special indebtedness to the review in *The Times Literary Supplement*.

[2] See also F. C. Dietz, *English Government Finance*, 1485–1558 (University of Illinois, 1920).

and that the reading 'to any meaner men' fits in better with the sense of the text; as also with the Latin version, the *De Republica Anglorum*, which reads: 'Scopus quippe hujus fori praecipuus hic est fastum et arrogantiam nobiliorum mitigare, qui quod *plebeios* opibus longe fortassis superant, jura et leges sibi natas valde indignantur.'

J. R. T.

1 *July* 1929

CONTENTS

		PAGE
PREFACE		v
LIST OF DOCUMENTS		xii
LIST OF BOOKS		xx
THE FOUNDATIONS OF THE TUDOR MONARCHY		1
THE CHURCH SETTLEMENT OF HENRY VIII		13
§ 1 Minor Ecclesiastical Reforms		13
§ 2 Submission of the Clergy		16
§ 3 Cessation of Payments to the See of Rome		25
§ 4 Prohibition of Appeals to Rome		40
§ 5 Dissolution of the Monasteries		50
§ 6 The Injunctions of 1536 and 1538		93
§ 7 The Six Articles		95
THE CHURCH SETTLEMENT OF EDWARD VI		99
§ 1 The Injunctions of 1547		100
§ 2 Statutes of the Protectorate		102
§ 3 Later Religious Changes, 1550–53		113
THE CHURCH SETTLEMENT OF MARY		121
THE CHURCH SETTLEMENT OF ELIZABETH		130
§ 1 The Acts of Supremacy and Uniformity		130
§ 2 The Injunctions of 1559		140
§ 3 The Penal Laws against the Catholics		141
§ 4 The Puritan Movement		163
THE KING'S SECRETARY		202
THE PRIVY COUNCIL		213
§ 1 Composition and Procedure		216
§ 2 Business of the Council		225
THE STAR CHAMBER		249
§ 1 Composition		254
§ 2 Procedure		255
§ 3 Business of the Star Chamber		257

PAGE

THE COURT OF REQUESTS 299

  § 1 PROCEDURE 300
  § 2 BUSINESS 301
  § 3 DECLINE OF THE COURT 301

COUNCIL COURTS 314

  § 1 THE COUNCIL OF THE NORTH 314
  § 2 THE COUNCIL OF WALES 331
  § 3 THE COUNCIL OF THE WEST 335

FINANCIAL COURTS 336

  § 1 COURT OF AUGMENTATIONS 336
  § 2 COURT OF FIRST FRUITS AND TENTHS . . . 340
  § 3 COURT OF WARDS AND LIVERIES . . . 340
  § 4 COURT OF SURVEYORS 341

ANCIENT COURTS 342

  § 1 THE COURTS OF COMMON LAW 342
  § 2 COURT OF ADMIRALTY 346
  § 3 COURT OF THE CONSTABLE AND MARSHAL . . 348

FRANCHISE COURTS 350

  § 1 THE PALATINE COURTS 350
  § 2 THE STANNARY COURTS 354

ECCLESIASTICAL COURTS 357

  § 1 THE ARCHDEACON'S COURT 358
  § 2 COURT OF THE BISHOP 358
  § 3 COURTS OF THE ARCHBISHOP 358
  § 4 HIGH COURT OF DELEGATES 359
  § 5 COURT OF HIGH COMMISSION 360

THE LAW OF TREASON 375

  § 1 CONSTRUCTIVE TREASONS 376
  § 2 STATUTORY TREASONS 378
  § 3 PROCEDURE IN TRIALS FOR TREASON . . . 421
  § 4 ATTAINDER 423
  § 5 COURT OF THE LORD STEWARD . . . 427
  § 6 PUNISHMENT OF TREASON 432
  § 7 TRIALS FOR TREASON 433

PAGE

LOCAL GOVERNMENT 452
  § 1 The Commission of the Peace 453
  § 2 Judicial Functions of the Justices of the Peace . 463
  § 3 Vagabonds, Beggars, and Poor Relief . . . 469
  § 4 Roads and Bridges 495
  § 5 Licensing of Ale-houses 500
  § 6 Regulation of Labour and Wages 502
  § 7 Miscellaneous Police Duties 506
  § 8 The Ecclesiastical Parish 508

PARLIAMENT 511
  § 1 Composition of Parliament 513
  § 2 Sessions of Parliament 515
  § 3 Franchise and Qualifications 517
  § 4 Influence of the Crown on Parliament . . . 518
    (a) Interference in Elections 518
    (b) Choice of a Speaker 527
    (c) Influence of the Crown upon Legislation . . 529
  § 5 Parliamentary Procedure 541
  § 6 Privilege of Parliament 550
    (a) The Speaker's claim of Privilege 550
    (b) The Privilege of Freedom of Speech . . . 554
    (c) The Privilege of Freedom from Arrest . . . 578
    (d) The right of either House to commit to prison . 589
    (e) The right to determine questions connected with
        membership of the House of Commons . . . 595

FINANCE 598
  § 1 Permanent Revenue 598
  § 2 Parliamentary Revenue 603
  § 3 Extraordinary Revenue 619
  § 4 Expenditure 625

INDEX 627

LIST OF DOCUMENTS

(A) STATUTES

DATE		PAGE
1487	Star Chamber Act (3 Henr. VII, c. 1)	258
1487	Bail Act (3 Henr. VII, c. 4)	464
1489	Justices Act (4 Henr. VII, c. 12)	465
1495	Statute of Treason (11 Henr. VII, c. 1)	5
1495	Beggars Act (11 Henr. VII, c. 2)	473
1504	Act concerning Corporations (19 Henr. VII, c. 7) . .	7
1504	Statute of Liveries (19 Henr. VII, c. 14) . .	7
1504	Act for the Feudal Aid (19 Henr. VII, c. 32) . . .	600
1510	Tonnage and Poundage Act (1 Henr. VIII, c. 20) . .	601
1512	Strode's Act (4 Henr. VIII, c. 8)	558
1512	Poll Tax Act (4 Henr. VIII, c. 19)	606
1523	Act for the Attainder of the Duke of Buckingham (14 & 15 Henr. VIII, c. 20)	423
1529	Star Chamber Act (21 Henr. VIII, c. 20) . . .	259
1531	Statute of Bridges (22 Henr. VIII, c. 5) . . .	495
1531	Act against Poisoners (22 Henr. VIII, c. 9) . . .	381
1531	Beggars Act (22 Henr. VIII, c. 12)	475
1531	Act for the Pardon of the Clergy of Canterbury (22 Henr. VIII, c. 15)	16
1532	Act in Conditional Restraint of Annates (23 Henr. VIII, c. 20)	25
1533	Act in Restraint of Appeals (24 Henr. VIII, c. 12) . .	40
1534	Act for the Submission of the Clergy (25 Henr. VIII, c. 19)	22
1534	Act in Absolute Restraint of Annates (25 Henr. VIII, c. 20)	29
1534	Dispensations Act (25 Henr. VIII, c. 21) . . .	31
1534	First Succession Act (25 Henr. VIII, c. 22) . . .	382
1534	Act of Supremacy (26 Henr. VIII, c. 1) . . .	46
1534	Act annexing First-fruits and Tenths to the Crown (26 Henr. VIII, c. 3)	36
1534	Act concerning the Marches of Wales (26 Henr. VIII, c. 6)	334
1534	Treasons Act of Henry VIII (26 Henr. VIII, c. 13) .	388
1536	Act annexing certain Franchises to the Crown (27 Henr. VIII, c. 24).	352
1536	Beggars Act (27 Henr. VIII, c. 25)	479
1536	Act for the Court of Augmentations (27 Henr. VIII, c. 27)	336

DATE   PAGE

1536 Act for the Dissolution of the Lesser Monasteries (27 Henr. VIII, c. 28) 58
1536 Second Succession Act (28 Henr. VIII, c. 7) . . . 389
1536 Act against the Papal Authority (28 Henr. VIII, c. 10) . 48
1536 Act for the Court of Admiralty (28 Henr. VIII, c. 15) . 347
1539 Statute of Proclamations (31 Henr. VIII, c. 8) . . 532
1539 Bishoprics Act (31 Henr. VIII, c. 9) 68
1539 Act of Precedence (31 Henr. VIII, c. 10) . . . 204
1539 Act for the Dissolution of the Greater Monasteries (31 Henry VIII, c. 13) 63
1539 Statute of Six Articles (31 Henr. VIII, c. 14) . . 95
1540 Act concerning Liberties (32 Henr. VIII, c. 20) . . 339
1540 Act dissolving the Cleves Marriage (32 Henr. VIII, c. 25) 395
1540 Subsidy Act (32 Henr. VIII, c. 50) 328
1542 Act for the Attainder of Queen Catherine Howard (33 Henr. VIII, c. 21) 425
1542 Act for the Court of Surveyors (33 Henr. VIII, c. 39) . 340
1543 Act concerning the Principality of Wales (34 & 35 Henr. VIII, c. 26). 335
1543 Third Succession Act (35 Henr. VIII, c. 1) . . . 397
1547 First Treasons Act of Edward VI (1 Edw. VI, c. 12) . 401
1547 Act for the Dissolution of the Chantries (1 Edw. VI, c. 14) 103
1549 First Act of Uniformity (2 & 3 Edw. VI, c. 1) . . 107
1550 Act against Superstitious Books and Images (3 & 4 Edw. VI, c. 10) 113
1552 Second Act of Uniformity (5 & 6 Edw. VI, c. 1) . . 116
1552 Second Treasons Act of Edward VI (5 & 6 Edw. VI, c. 11) 405
1552 Licensing Act (5 & 6 Edw. VI, c. 25) 501
1553 First Treasons Act of Mary (1 Mary, st. 1, c. 1) . . 406
1553 Mary's First Statute of Repeal (1 Mary, st. 2, c. 2) . 121
1554 Act concerning the Regal Power (1 Mary, st. 3, c. 1) . 122
1554 Act reviving the Heresy Laws (1 & 2 P. & M. c. 6) . 124
1555 Mary's Second Statute of Repeal (1 & 2 P. & M. c. 8) . 125
1555 Act against Traitorous Words (1 & 2 P. & M. c. 9) . 407
1555 Second Treasons Act of Mary (1 & 2 P. & M. c. 10) . 408
1555 Bail Act (1 & 2 P. & M. c. 13) 468
1555 First Statute of Highways (2 & 3 P. & M. c. 8) . . 498
1559 Act of Supremacy (1 Eliz. c. 1) 130
1559 Act of Uniformity (1 Eliz. c. 2) 135
1559 First Treasons Act of Elizabeth (1 Eliz. c. 5) . . 411
1559 Act against Smuggling (1 Eliz. c. 11) 602
1563 Statute of Labour (5 Eliz. c. 4) 502

DATE		PAGE
1563	Second Statute of Highways (5 Eliz. c. 13) . . .	499
1571	Second Treasons Act of Elizabeth (13 Eliz. c. 1) . .	413
1571	Act against Bulls from Rome (13 Eliz. c. 2) . . .	146
1571	Tillage Act (13 Eliz. c. 13)	329
1576	Poor Relief Act (18 Eliz. c. 3)	481
1581	Act against Reconciliation to Rome (23 Eliz. c. 1) .	150
1585	Act for the Surety of the Queen's Person (27 Eliz. c. 1) .	417
1585	Act against Jesuits and Seminary Priests (27 Eliz. c. 2)	154
1585	Act for Redress of Erroneous Judgments (27 Eliz. c. 8) .	343
1589	Act for Appeals (31 Eliz. c. 1)	345
1593	Act against Seditious Sectaries (35 Eliz. c. 1) . .	197
1593	Act against Popish Recusants (35 Eliz. c. 2) . .	159
1598	Poor Relief Act (39 Eliz. c. 3)	488
1598	Beggars Act (39 Eliz. c. 4)	484
1601	Blackmail Act (43 Eliz. c. 13)	329
1601	Clerical Subsidy Act (43 Eliz. c. 17)	616
1601	Lay Subsidy Act (43 Eliz. c. 18)	610

(B) CASES

Privy Council

Cases from the Council Register (1540–1603) 229–42

Star Chamber

Attorney-General v. Parre and others (fining of juries, 1489)	263
Cooper v. Gervaux and others (unjust tolls, 1493) . .	276
Vale v. Broke (slander, 1493)	275
Abbot of Eynesham v. Harcourt and others (riot, 1503) . .	265
Walterkyn v. Lettice (trespass, 1503)	272
Merchant Adventurers v. Staplers (1504)	260
Dobell v. Soley and others (assault, 1533)	269
Cappis v. Cappis (assault, c. 1547)	270

Court of Requests

Amadas v. Williams and another (1519)	303
Peterson v. Frederick and others (1521)	304
Burges v. Lacy (c. 1540)	305

Stannary Courts

Trewynard's case in the Court of Chancery (1562) . . .	355
Trewynard's case in the Star Chamber (1564) . .	356

PAGE

Ecclesiastical Courts

Select cases 362–7
Cawdrey's case (1591) 372

Treason Trials

Sir Thomas More (1535) 433
The Duke of Norfolk (1572) 440
Mary Queen of Scots (1586) 443
The Earl of Essex (1601) 448

Privilege of Parliament: Freedom from arrest

Ferrers's case (1543) 580
Wickham's case (1571) 583
Lord Cromwell's case (1572) 583
Smalley's case (1576) 584
Digges's case (1584) 585
Case of Robert Finnies (1584) 585
Richard Cook's case (1585) 586
Kyrle's case (1585) 586
Martin's case (1587) 587
Fitzherbert's case (1593) 588
Tracy's case (1597) 588
Hogan's case (1601) 589

Privilege of Parliament: The right to commit

Case of Arthur Hall (1581) 592
Case of Dr Parry (1584) 593
Case of John Bland (1586) 594

Privilege of Parliament: Membership

Russell's case (1550) 596
Nowell's case (1553) 596
Case of the County of Norfolk (1586) 596

(C) EXTRACTS

Anonymous writer (c. 1600):
    on the Court of Requests 311
Francis Bacon, Viscount St Albans (1621):
    on Henry VII's Council 229
    on the Star Chamber 288
Henry Barrow (1590):
    on Independency 186
Nicholas Bownd (1595):
    on the Sabbatarian Controversy 200

	PAGE
Sir Julius Caesar (*c.* 1597):	
on the Court of Requests	308
Thomas Cartwright (1572):	
on Church government	167
Sir Edward Coke (*c.* 1628):	
on the Star Chamber	289
on the Court of Requests	311
on the Council of the North	318
on the Duchy Chamber of Lancaster	351
on Treason	377
on the Court of the Lord Steward	428
on the election of the Speaker	527
John Colet, Dean of St Paul's (1511):	
on clerical abuses	70
Simon Fish (1528):	
on clerical abuses	76
Richard Hooker (1594–7):	
on Church government	170
William Hudson (*c.* 1633):	
on the Star Chamber	294
William Lambarde:	
on the Justices of the Peace (1581)	457
on the Star Chamber (1591)	285
on the Court of Requests (1591)	306
Hugh Latimer (1548):	
in criticism of the Bishops	88
Martin Marprelate (1588):	
in criticism of the Bishops	195
Sir Thomas More:	
on clerical abuses (1528)	73
in defence of the Church (1529)	79
Francis Osborne (1658):	
on the Star Chamber	296
John Rushworth (1680):	
on the Star Chamber	297
Sir Thomas Smith (1565):	
on the Star Chamber	284
on the Justices of the Peace	455
on the procedure of the House of Commons . . .	547
on the claim of Privilege	554
Thomas Starkey (1535–6):	
on clerical abuses	82

(D) MISCELLANEOUS DOCUMENTS

DATE   PAGE

Dissolution of the Monasteries

1537 Confession of St Andrew's Priory, Northampton   .   89

Church Settlement of Edward VI

1550 Ridley's Injunction concerning the Altar   .   .   .   115

Elizabeth and the Catholics

1570 The Bull of Excommunication   143

Elizabeth and the Puritans

1563 Puritan Articles in Convocation   164
1574 Regulations for the Diocese of Lincoln concerning
      Prophesyings   179
1576 Archbishop Grindal's Letter concerning Prophesyings .   182
1577 Queen Elizabeth's Letter for the suppression of Prophesyings 184
1584 Petition of the House of Commons for Ecclesiastical Reform 190

The King's Secretary

1518 Letter from Henry VIII to Wolsey (relation of the Secretary
      to the King)   211
1521 Letter from Richard Pace to Wolsey (relation of the Secretary
      to the King)   211
1526 Ordinances of Eltham   207
1540 Warrant for two Secretaries   206
c. 1544 Secretaries' 'Bouche of Court'   208
c. 1578 Queen Elizabeth's Annual Expenses (stipends of officials) 208
1600 Dr John Herbert's Memorandum (duties of the Secretary) .   212

Privy Council

1526 Council Ordinances of Henry VIII   220
1553 Council Ordinances of Edward VI   221
1554 Committees of the Council under Mary   224
1558 Committees of the Council under Elizabeth   .   .   . 224
1566 Order against Seditious Books   245
1570 The Oath of a Privy Councillor   225
1582, 1589 Orders concerning Private Suits   243
1600 Dr John Herbert's Memorandum (concerning the distribu-
      tion of Council business)   247

Star Chamber

1509–90 The Lords' Diet in the Star Chamber   .   .   .   263
1570 Letter from the Council to Sir William Paulet   .   .   261

DATE		PAGE
1586	Star Chamber Decree concerning Printers	279
1597	Letter from Sir John Smyth to Lord Burghley	262
1600	Speech in the Star Chamber	278

Court of Requests

c. 1518	Establishment of the Court of Requests at Westminster	302

Council of the North

1545	Instructions for the Council of the North	320

High Commission

1559	Ecclesiastical Commission	367
1584	Lord Burghley's criticism of the Ecclesiastical Commission	373

Justices of the Peace

1590	Commission of the Peace	461
1598, 1604	Testimonials for a Sturdy Rogue	494

Parliament

1529–1601	Interference in Elections	520–6
1542	Petition for Privilege	551
1548	Passing of the Chantries Act	535
1549	Seymour's case	513
1559	Petition for Privilege	551
1559, 1597	Election of a Speaker	528
1563	The Opening of Parliament	542
1563	Proxies in the House of Lords	545
1563–93	The Queen's Marriage and the Succession to the Throne	559
1571	First case of Bribery	526
1571	Lord Keeper's speech at the Dissolution of Parliament	536
1571–89	Privacy of Debate	590
1571–1601	Ecclesiastical affairs in Parliament	565
1572–1601	Attendance at the House of Commons	546
1576	Case of Peter Wentworth	537
1576	Punishment of Assault	591
1581	Repression of Disorder	592
1581	Fining of Absentees	593
1589	Procedure by writ of *Supersedeas*	587
1593	Answer to the Petition of Privilege	552
1593	Divisions in the House of Commons	547
1593–1601	Change of tone in later Parliaments	578
1597	*Subpoenas* from the Chancery and the Star Chamber	589

DATE   PAGE

1597 The Chaplain of the House of Commons   .   .   .   546
1601 Answer to the Petition of Privilege   553
1601 Trade Questions in Parliament   573

Finance

1491 The Benevolence of 1491   621
1523 The Subsidy of 1523   608
1525 The 'Amicable Loan'   621
1556 The Loan of 1556   624
1593 Subsidy Debate of 1593   610

LIST OF BOOKS

₊ *The following are the full titles and editions of the works referred to in an abbreviated form in the foot-notes.*

AMOS, A. Observations on the Statutes of the Reformation Parliament...
(1859).

ANDREWS, W. Bygone Lincolnshire (1891).

ANSON, Sir W. R. The Law and Custom of the Constitution: vol. i, Parliament (4th edition, 1909); vol. ii, The Crown, pts i and ii (3rd edition, 1907–8).

ARBER, E. The English Scholar's Library (1880–4).

Archaeologia...(1770–   ).

ARCHBOLD, W. A. J. The Somerset Religious Houses (Cambridge Historical Essays, No. 6, 1892).

ASCHROTT, P. F. The English Poor Law System...trans. H. Preston-Thomas (1st edition, 1888).

BACON, FRANCIS. Works, ed. J. Spedding (1857–9), 7 vols.

BALDWIN, J. F. The King's Council in England during the Middle Ages (1913).
See also Select Cases before the King's Council, 1243–1482, ed. I. S. Leadam and J. F. Baldwin (Selden Society, 1918).

BARNARD, F. P. Companion to English History: The Middle Ages (1902).
A revised edition, under the title *Mediaeval England* is about to be published by the Oxford University Press.

BATESON, Miss M. Preface to the Camden Miscellany, vol. ix (1893).

BEARD, C. The Reformation of the Sixteenth Century...(Hibbert Lectures, 1883).

BEARD, C. A. The Office of Justice of the Peace in England...(Columbia University Studies, vol. xx, no. 1, 1904).

BENHAM, E. The Prayer Book of Queen Elizabeth.

BIRT, H. N. The Elizabethan Religious Settlement (1907).

BRADFORD, Miss G. (Mrs Temperley). Proceedings in the Court of the Star Chamber in the reigns of Henry VII and Henry VIII (Somerset Record Society, vol. 27, 1911).

BREWER, J. S. The Reign of Henry VIII...to the death of Wolsey (1884), 2 vols.

Bullarium Romanum (1727–53), 18 vols.

BURN, J. S. The High Commission (1865).

—— The Star Chamber (1870).

BUSCH, W. England under the Tudors, vol. i (Henry VII): trans. Alice M. Todd (1895).

CAESAR, Sir JULIUS. The Ancient State...of the Court of Requests (1597).

Calendar of Patent Rolls, Henry VII, 1494–1509 (1916).

—— State Papers, Domestic [contracted as *Cal. S. P. Dom.*]

Cambridge Modern History [contracted as *C.M.H.*]

CARDWELL, E. The two Books of Common Prayer set forth...in the reign of Edward VI compared (1838).

CARDWELL, E. Documentary Annals of the Reformed Church of England, 1546–1716 (1839), 2 vols.

Catholic Encyclopedia (1907), 15 vols.

CHAUCER, GEOFFREY. The Canterbury Tales.

COKE, Sir EDWARD. The third and fourth parts of the Institutes of the Laws of England (c. 1628: edition of 1669).

Collectanea Anglo-Praemonstratensia, ed. F. A. Gasquet (Camden Society, 1904–6), 3 vols.

COULTON, G. G. Medieval Studies (2nd revised edition, 1915).

CRAIES, W. F. A Treatise on Statute Law (edition of 1907).

DASENT, Sir J. R. Acts of the Privy Council of England, 1542– (1890–   ).

DENTON, W. England in the Fifteenth Century (1888).

D'EWES, Sir SIMONDS. A complete Journal of…both of the House of Lords and House of Commons throughout the whole reign of Queen Elizabeth…(1682: edition of 1693).

DICEY, A. V. The Privy Council (Arnold Prize Essay, 1860: 2nd edition, 1887)

—— The Law of the Constitution (1st edition, 1885).

Dictionary of National Biography (1st edition, 1885–   ) [contracted as D.N.B.]

DIXON, R. W. History of the Church of England, 1529–70 (1878–1902), 6 vols.

DOWELL, S. A History of Taxation and Taxes in England (2nd edition, 1888), 4 vols.

English Historical Review [contracted as E.H.R.]

FISHER, H. A. L. The History of England, 1485–1547 (The Political History of England, vol. v, 1906).

FORTESCUE, Sir JOHN. The Governance of England…(1471–6: ed. C. Plummer, 1885).

FOSS, E. The Judges of England (1848–64), 9 vols.

FREEMAN, E. A. The History of the Norman Conquest (3rd edition, 1877), 3 vols.

FRERE, W. H. The Use of Sarum (1898).

—— The Principles of Religious Ceremonial (Oxford Library of Practical Theology, 1906).

FRIEDMANN, P. Anne Boleyne…(1884), 2 vols.

FROUDE, J. A. The Reign of Elizabeth (Everyman Library, 1911), 5 vols.

FULLER, THOMAS. The Church History of Britain (1655: edition of 1837), 3 vols.

GAIRDNER, J. Lollardy and the Reformation in England (1908–   ), 4 vols.

GARDINER, S. R. Reports of cases in the Courts of Star Chamber and High Commission (Camden Society, 1886).

GASCOIGNE, THOMAS. Loci e Libro Veritatum, ed. Thorold Rogers (1881). Extracts from the Dictionarium Theologicum, Gascoigne's principal work, written at various times between 1434 and 1457.

GASQUET, F. A. Henry VIII and the English Monasteries (edition of 1889), 2 vols.

—— Hampshire Recusants (1896).

Gasquet, F. A. *Collectanea Anglo-Praemonstratensia* [*q.v.*]

Gee, H. and Hardy, W. J. Documents illustrative of English Church History (1896).

Gneist, R. The History of the English Constitution, trans. P. A. Ashworth (1st edition, 1886), 2 vols.

Goldwin Smith, *see* Smith.

Gwatkin, H. M. Church and State in England to the death of Queen Anne (1917).

Hall, Edward. Henry VIII (1542: ed. C. Whibley, 1904), 2 vols.

Hallam, Henry. The Constitutional History of England...(1827: 7th edition, 1854), 3 vols.

Harcourt, L. W. V. His Grace the Steward and Trial of Peers (1907).

Harrison, William. Description of England (1577), ed. F. J. Furnivall (New Shakspere Society, 1877).

Hayward, Sir John (*d.* 1627). Annals of the first four years of the reign of Queen Elizabeth, ed. J. Bruce (Camden Society, 1840).

Hearn, W. E. The Government of England (2nd edition, 1887)

Herbert of Cherbury, Lord. The Life and Reign of King Henry VIII (1649: edition of 1672).

Hibbert, F. A. Monasticism in Staffordshire (1909).

—— The Dissolution of the Monasteries as illustrated by the suppression of the Religious Houses of Staffordshire (1910).

Holdsworth, W. S. A History of English Law (1903), 3 vols.

Holinshed, Raphael. Chronicles (1577: edition of 1807–8), 6 vols.

Hudson, William. Treatise of the Court of Star Chamber (written *c.* 1633: printed in *Collectanea Juridica*, 1792).

Jacob, Giles. Law Dictionary (1729: 7th edition, 1756).

Jessopp, A. Visitations of the Diocese of Norwich, 1492–1532 (Camden Society, 1888).

Jusserand, J. A. A. J. English Wayfaring Life in the Middle Ages, trans. L. Toulmin Smith (1st edition, 1889).

Kempe (Archbishop). York Visitations, ed. A. H. Thompson (Surtees Society, vol. cxxvii, 1916).

Kenny, C. S. Outlines of Criminal Law (4th edition, 1909).

Lambarde, William. Eirenarcha, or of the office of the Justices of Peace (1581: edition of 1610).

—— Archeion, or a commentary upon the High Courts of Justice in England (1591: edition of 1635).

Lapsley, G. T. The County Palatine of Durham (Harvard Historical Studies, viii, 1900).

Latimer, Hugh. Sermons (1548: Parker Society, 1844–5), 2 vols.

Law, T. G. The Archpriest Controversy (Camden Society, 1896).

Law Quarterly Review

Lea, H. C. History of Sacerdotal Celibacy in the Christian Church (1867: 3rd edition, 1907).

Leach, A. F. Visitations...of Southwell Minster (Camden Society, 1891).

Leadam, I. S. Select Cases in the Court of Requests, 1497–1569 (Selden Society, vol. xii, 1898).

—— Select Cases...in the Star Chamber, 1477–1544. (Selden Society, vols. xvi, xxv, 1902, 1910), 2 vols.

Letters and Papers, Foreign and Domestic, Henry VIII [contracted as *L. and P.*]

LEWIS, J. The Life of John Fisher...(1855), 2 vols.

Lincoln Visitations, *see* Thompson, A. H.

McILWAIN, C. H. The High Court of Parliament and its Supremacy (1910).

MACY, J. The English Constitution...(1897).

MAITLAND, F. W. Roman Canon Law in the Church of England (1898).

—— The Constitutional History of England (1908).

MARSDEN, R. G. Select Pleas in the Court of Admiralty (Selden Society, vol. vi, 1894).

MAY, Sir T. E. A treatise on the law, privileges, proceedings, and usage of Parliament (9th edition, 1883).

MEREWETHER, H. A. and STEPHENS, A. J. History of...Boroughs... (1835), 3 vols.

MERRIMAN, R. B. Life and Letters of Thomas Cromwell (1902), 2 vols.

MOORE, A. L. Lectures...on the history of the Reformation...(1890).

MORE, CRESACRE. The Life of Sir Thomas More (*c.* 1631: edn of 1828).

NAUNTON, Sir ROBERT. *Fragmenta Regalia* (written *c.* 1630: edn of 1653).

NEAL, D. History of the Puritans (1732–8: edition of 1822), 5 vols.

NICOLAS, Sir NICHOLAS HARRIS. Proceedings and Ordinances of the Privy Council of England (1834–7), 7 vols.

—— Observations on the offices of Secretary of State, etc. (1837).

Norwich Visitations, *see* JESSOPP, A.

OMAN, [Sir] C. W. C. Warwick the Kingmaker (English Men of Action Series, 1891).

Oxford English Dictionary.

Paston Letters, 1422–1509: ed. J. Gairdner (1896), 3 vols.

PERCY, Lord EUSTACE. The Privy Council under the Tudors (Stanhope Essay, 1907).

PIKE, L. O. A Constitutional History of the House of Lords (1894).

POLLARD, A. F. Thomas Cranmer and the English Reformation, 1489–1556 (Heroes of the Reformation, 1904).

—— Henry VIII (new edition, 1905).

—— Factors in Modern History (1907).

—— The Reign of Henry VII from contemporary sources (1919), 3 vols.

—— The Evolution of Parliament (1920).

POLLOCK, Sir F. and MAITLAND, F. W. The History of English Law before the time of Edward I (2nd edition, 1898), 2 vols.

PORRITT, E. The Unreformed House of Commons (1903), 2 vols.

PROTHERO, [Sir] G. W. Select Statutes and other Constitutional Documents illustrative of the reigns of Elizabeth and James I (3rd edn, 1906).

REDLICH, J. The Procedure of the House of Commons, trans. A. E. Steinthal (1908), 3 vols.

REID, Miss R. R. The King's Council in the North (1921).

RUSHWORTH, JOHN. Historical Collections (1659–   ), 8 vols.

SANDERS, NICHOLAS. *De Origine ac Progressu Schismatis Anglicani* (1585): trans. D. Lewis (1877).

SAVINE, A. English Monasteries on the eve of the Dissolution (Oxford Studies in Social and Legal History, vol. i, 1909).

SCOFIELD, Miss C. L. A Study of the Court of Star Chamber (1900).

Scottish Historical Review.

SEELEY, Sir J. R. The Growth of British Policy (1895), 2 vols.

SINCLAIR, Sir JOHN. The History of the Public Revenue of the British Empire (2nd edition, 1790).

SKEEL, Miss C. A. J. The Council in the Marches of Wales (Girton College Studies, ii, 1904).

SMITH, GOLDWIN. The United Kingdom: a political history (1899), 2 vols.

SMITH, Sir THOMAS, De Republica Anglorum: a discourse on the Commonwealth of England (written 1565; first published, 1583; edition by L. Alston, 1906).

Spectator, The.

SPELMAN, Sir HENRY. The History and Fate of Sacrilege (c. 1633; first published, 1698; edition of 1853).

State Papers...King Henry the Eighth (1830–52), 11 vols.

State Trials, ed. William Cobbett and T. B. Howell (1809), 34 vols.

STEPHEN, Sir J. F. A History of the Criminal Law...(1883), 3 vols.

STEPHENS, W. R. W. and HUNT, W. A History of the English Church (1899–ﾠ), 6 vols.

STRYPE, JOHN. Annals of the Reformation...(1708–9: edition of 1725–31), 4 vols.

—— The History of the Life and Acts of Edmund Grindal, Archbishop of Canterbury (edition of 1710).

STUBBS, W. The Constitutional History of England (Clarendon Press Series, 1874–8; vol. i, 3rd edition, 1880), 3 vols.

—— Report of the Ecclesiastical Courts Commission (1883).

—— Lectures on the Study of Medieval and Modern History (edition of 1886).

TANNER, THOMAS. Notitia Monastica, or a short History of the Religious Houses in England and Wales (1695).

TEMPERLEY, Mrs G. Henry VII (Kings and Queens of England, 1914).

TERRY, C. S. John Graham of Claverhouse, Viscount of Dundee (1905).

THOMPSON, A. H. (ed.). Visitations of Religious Houses in the Diocese of Lincoln...(Canterbury and York Series, vol. xvii–ﾠ, 1915–ﾠ), vol. i–ﾠ.

TRAILL, H. D. Social England (edition of 1898), 6 vols.

Transactions of the Royal Historical Society.

TROTTER, Miss E. Seventeenth century life in the Country Parish; with special reference to local government (1919).

USHER, R. G. The Rise and Fall of the High Commission (1913).

Valor Ecclesiasticus, ed. J. Hunter (Rolls Series, 1810–34), 6 vols.

WAKEMAN, H. O. The Church and the Puritans, 1570–1660 (Epochs of Church History, 1887).

WALTON, IZAAK. Lives (1670: edition of 1796).

West Riding Sessions Rolls, ed. J. Lister (Yorkshire Archaeological... Record Series, vol. iii, 1888).

WILKINS, D. Concilia Magnae Britanniae et Hiberniae...446–1717... (1737), 4 vols.

WILLIS-BUND, J. W. Trials for Treason, vol. i, 1327–1660 (1879).

WINFIELD, P. H. The History of Conspiracy and Abuse of Legal Procedure (Cambridge Studies in English Legal History, 1921).

York Visitations, see KEMPE.

TUDOR CONSTITUTIONAL DOCUMENTS
A.D. 1485–1603

The Foundations of the Tudor Monarchy

In his treatise *The Governance of England*[1], Sir John Fortescue, who lived under Henry VI, recommends a policy which is not unlike that adopted and pursued with striking ability by Henry VII, the first of the Tudor kings The two main evils present to Fortescue's mind are the power of the great nobles and the poverty of the Crown. He entitles one of his chapters, 'Here he sheweth the perils that may come to the King by overmighty subjects'[2]; another, 'The harm that cometh of a King's poverty'[3]; and a third, 'How great good will grow of the firm endowing of the Crown.'[4]

As Fortescue's editor points out, 'Many of the lords were...enormously rich. Their estates were concentrated in fewer hands, and the lands of a man like Warwick represented the accumulations of two or three wealthy families. They engrossed offices as greedily as lands, their pensions and annuities exhausted the revenues of the Crown, they made large fortunes out of the French wars which drained the royal exchequer, and they were among the chief wool-growers and sometimes wool-merchants in the kingdom.'[5] They were rich enough to keep on foot small armies of retainers, and their influence in their localities was sufficient to enable them to control the nomination of local officers, and to pervert to their own ends the administration of justice. The justices of the peace and even the royal judges could be corrupted, juries bribed or intimidated, and claims to property maintained by force. Thus came about the condition of things described in the *Paston Letters*, in which the law was powerless against great offenders, and open violence reigned supreme[6].

For this state of things Fortescue has remedies to propose. It is important that 'the King's livelihood, above such revenues as shall be assigned for his ordinary charges, be greater than the livelihood of the greatest lord in England,'[7] for it is necessary 'that the King have great possessions and peculiar livelihood for his own surety, namely, when any of his lords shall happen to be so excessively great as there might thereby grow peril to his estate. For certainly there may no greater peril grow to a prince than to have a subject

---

[1] Plummer's edition. The full titles of the works referred to in the footnotes are printed on pp. xviii to xxii above.

[2] Ch. ix.   [3] Ch. v.   [4] Ch. xix.   [5] Fortescue, p. 17.

[6] The *Paston Letters* assume that it is useless to institute legal proceedings unless the sheriff and the jury can be secured beforehand. For instance, 'extorcious amerciaments' were taken of the Prior of Westacre; he was also robbed of 'a flock of hogs,' and his man was set 'openly and shamefully' and with 'great oppression' in the stocks. But 'of these,' the letter-writer goes on to say, 'and of many more worse, it is a great folly to labour in as for any indictments but if ye be right sure of the sheriff's office' (*Letters*, i, 191).   [7] p. 128.

equipollent to himself.'[1] To this end there should be 'a general resumption, made by authority of Parliament,'[2] of lands alienated or given away by the Crown, and the establishment of 'a worshipful and a notable council' which could prevent fresh alienations and control future rewards. The council was no longer to be composed 'of great princes and of the greatest lords of the land,'[3] but almost entirely of persons chosen because of their business capacity[4]. The King should also reclaim the patronage of the Crown and appoint to all offices himself, and no man should 'have any office of the King's gift, but he be first sworn that he is servant to none other man, or will serve any other man or take his clothing or fee while he serveth the King.'[5] The accumulation of offices is to be prevented, for no man is to have 'more offices than one, except that the King's brethren may have two offices.'[6] 'And when the King, by the means aforesaid or otherwise, hath gotten again his livelihood, if then it would like his most noble Grace to establish, and as who saith, amortise the same livelihood to his Crown, so as it may never be aliened therefrom without the assent of his Parliament, which then would be as a new foundation of his crown, he shall be thereby the greatest founder of the world.'[7] The Crown will then be endowed, as if it were a bishopric, an abbey, or a university, and the King will no longer have overmighty subjects 'equipollent to himself.'

We are scarcely justified in supposing that Henry VII consciously appropriated Fortescue's ideas, but circumstances, aided by his own policy, placed him in the position where Fortescue had desired the King to be. The conditions at his accession favoured a king who sought to build up a strong monarchy and went to work in the right way. There had been a change in the balance of power within the kingdom, for the great houses had been exhausted and impoverished under the economic strain of the Civil Wars. And the impoverishment of the houses had been associated with the enrichment of the Crown, for both Yorkists and Lancastrians had confiscated the estates of their respective traitors and the gains of both dynasties had fallen to the Tudors. The humiliation of the baronage had left the Church in isolation, and a secularised Papacy could no longer give it effective support. Finally, the Crown was now steadily supported by the people at large, for a strong monarchy was a guarantee against a recrudescence of private war, and private war interfered in all kinds of ways with their common everyday happiness. The nation as a whole was weary of dynastic quarrels and eager for internal peace; and moreover it was now that Englishmen were finding new opportunities for commerce, and were beginning to open up the new worlds that lay on the other side of the sea.

Given these favourable conditions, Henry VII was the kind of king who could appreciate them, and use them for the building up of a strong monarchy. He was 'one of the best sort of wonders,' says Bacon, 'a wonder

---

[1] p. 130.   [2] p. 143.   [3] p. 145.
[4] 'xii spiritual men and xii temporal men, of the wisest and best disposed men that can be found in all the parts of this land' (p. 146). These were to have a permanent tenure, and to them were to be added four lords spiritual and four lords temporal to be chosen every year.
[5] p. 153. 'Clothing' is a reference to 'livery': see p. 8 n. below.
[6] p 153.   [7] p. 154.

for wise men'[1]; and he classes him with Louis XI and Ferdinand of Aragon as 'the three Magi of kings of those ages.'[2] Bacon was not a contemporary, but Bishop Fisher, in a sermon preached on the occasion of the King's funeral, is quite as appreciative. 'His politic wisdom in governance it was singular; his wit always quick and ready; his reason pithy and substantial; his memory fresh and holding; his experience notable; his counsels fortunate and taken by wise deliberation; his speech gracious in diverse languages; his person goodly and amiable, his natural complexion of the purest mixture; his issue fair and in good number... his dealing in times of perils and dangers was cold and sober with great hardiness.'[3] He was deemed abroad one of the wisest of European princes; and his policy was his own—it was not minister-made. 'He was of an high mind, and loved his own will and his own way; as one that revered himself, and would reign indeed,... not admitting any near or full approach either to his power or to his secrets.'[4] And, like the other members of his house, he knew how to establish and maintain full personal control of the business of government. 'He was a prince sad, serious, and full of thoughts and secret observations; and full of notes and memorials of his own hand, especially touching persons; as whom to employ, whom to reward, whom to inquire of, whom to beware of, what were the dependencies, what were the factions, and the like; keeping (as it were) a journal of his thoughts.'[5] This industrious, skilful, secretive statesman is the founder of the Tudor character; and when Henry VIII, Mary, and Elizabeth gave so much time to the mastery of the principles and details of government, they were only following in his steps.

The policy of such a king would be characterised by precision, effective-ness, a careful adaptation of adequate means to an end clearly conceived and well understood. Henry VII perceived that what England needed in his day was an efficient central administration controlled by a strong and wealthy royal house; and he set his policy steadily in this direction. It is true that avarice grew upon him with advancing years, but the experience of the Lancastrians had shewn that royal power depended upon wealth, and behind his 'miserliness' lay a principle of policy. He aimed at making the Crown richer than any noble or group of nobles. As Fortescue had advised, there was a resumption by Parliamentary authority of alienated Crown lands[6].

Benevolences, heavy compositions from royal wards, the revival of dis-used feudal tenures, the exaction of large sums for the removal of outlawry in personal actions, fines for breaches of obsolete statutes, the systematic pressing of legal technicalities against individuals, a wholesale abuse of the ordinary process of law—all these methods, steadily and systematically prac-tised, brought vast sums into the King's treasury. The rebellions of the reign also served to enrich the Crown with forfeitures. 'The less blood he drew,' says Bacon, 'the more he took of treasure'[7]; and so treason became a pro-fitable part of the royal revenue. But all this was not common greed; it was statesmanship pursuing an intelligible purpose. Empson and Dudley,

---

[1] *Works*, vi, 238.   [2] *Ib.* vi, 244.
[3] Quoted from *The English Works of John Fisher* in H. A. L. Fisher, *Polit. Hist.* p. 125.
[4] *Works*, vi, 240.   [5] *Ib.* vi, 243.
[6] Fisher, *Polit. Hist.* p. 126.   [7] *Works*, vi, 239.

the 'ravening wolves,' were not simply the agents of an extortioner; they were impoverishing the great houses with a definite end in view.

In another way also Empson and Dudley stand for a deliberate policy foreshadowed by Fortescue—the exclusion of the noble houses from the administration. Henry VII, as far as he was able to do so, employed only churchmen and lawyers; and churchmen were cheap, for they could be paid by ecclesiastical promotion. 'He chose his ministers from churchmen, and made bishops of his ministers.'[1] The leading men of the reign were not the 'great princes' and 'the greatest lords of the land' referred to by Fortescue[2], but churchmen like Morton, Fox, and Warham, or laymen of the official class, such as Sir Reginald Bray, the son of a physician, Sir Thomas Lovell, whose mother was a Norwich alderman's daughter, or Sir Edward Poynings, the son of Jack Cade's carver and sword-bearer. Dudley was at any rate 'of a good family,'[3] but he was not a great noble, and Bacon's phrase concerning Empson, that he was 'the son of a sieve-maker,'[4] indicates his antecedents although it may not be literally true. The growth of this class of royal officials, entirely dependent upon the king, and serving as his protection against the revival in the government of the power of the houses, is a fact of considerable importance in the Tudor period. The remedy of the nobles against a policy which they hated was conspiracy; but against successful conspiracy the king was protected by his officials, who first entrapped his traitors for him and then secured their condemnation under the forms of law. This was made all the easier by Henry VII's secret service, an institution which Bacon is disposed to justify. 'As for his secret spials which he did employ both at home and abroad, by them to discover what practices and conspiracies were against him, surely his case required it; he had such moles perpetually working and casting to undermine him.'[5] This system passed as an heirloom to his successors. It was of the greatest service both to Henry VIII and to the government of Edward VI; and it was carried to high efficiency by Burghley and Walsingham, who were able by its aid to protect the life of Elizabeth against the assassination plots by which it was so continually threatened.

The reign of Henry VII suffers by contrast with the reigns that succeeded it, and its importance is sometimes underrated. There is little in the period that is stirring and picturesque; the story is confused and difficult to understand; and there is a remarkable deficiency of the original material of history. But if the reign is studied from the constitutional standpoint it will be seen that the massive foundations of the Tudor monarchy are being silently but well and truly laid. The great position of Henry VIII and his successors is, in part at any rate, of the nature of an inheritance.

Henry VII had done much to establish a new tradition for the English monarchy and to set it in a place apart. He arranged royal marriages for his children instead of allowing them to marry among the English nobility, and although a king careful of money he deliberately spent money in keeping up a splendid court. Thus 'the Crown withdrew to a position of splendid isolation.'[6] But he was hampered by unpopularity and by a defective title, and he

---

[1] Stubbs, *Lectures*, p. 342.   [2] p. 145.
[3] Bacon, *Works*, vi, 217.   [4] *Ib.*   [5] *Ib.* vi, 241.
[6] Temperley, p. 249; see also note on p. 12 below.

had to face a series of rebellions before his authority was assured. For Henry VIII these difficulties scarcely existed. His title was never questioned, for he was 'of the progeny of the race of kings,' and in his person the Yorkist and Lancastrian claims were blended. Bacon in one of his *Fragments* notes of his accession that there was now 'no such thing as any great or mighty subject who might eclipse or overshade the imperial power.'[1] And the beginning of the new King's reign is 'the birthday of loyalty, in the sense of personal devotion to the Crown.'[2] Foreign ambassadors in their private despatches to their governments had no motive for flattering Henry VIII, but they comment with something approaching enthusiasm upon his beauty of person, his horsemanship, his skill as a jouster and tennis-player, and his knowledge of music and languages[3]. This young, gracious, magnificent figure struck the imagination of his subjects, and the sovereign was no longer unpopular. Thus although the foundations of the Tudor monarchy were laid by his father, Henry VIII made his own contribution to their stability and permanence.

The constitutional documents of the reign of Henry VII[4] which are important for the present purpose are the Star Chamber Statute, the Statute of Treason, the Act concerning Corporations, and the Statute of Liveries. The first of these is printed in another section [p. 258]; it should however be noted here that the preamble, indicating the offences and abuses with which the persons named in the statute were specially commissioned to deal, enumerates exactly those which were characteristic of the social disorder described in the *Paston Letters* and alluded to by Fortescue—'unlawful maintenances, giving of liveries, signs, and tokens, and retainders by indenture,' 'untrue demeanings of sheriffs in making of panels, and other untrue returns,' 'taking of money by juries,' and 'great riots and unlawful assemblies.' The statute is intended to furnish fresh facilities for dealing effectively with disorder, and clearing up the troublesome situation which a period of civil war had created.

(1) Statute of Treason, 1495

This statute ordained, as Bacon puts it, 'that no person that did assist in arms or otherwise the king for the time being, should after be impeached therefore or attainted...but if any such act of attainder did hap to be made, it should be void and of none effect.'[5] Henry VII took the precaution of excluding from the benefits of the Act all who should in future desert himself, but the intention was to do away with the dynastic proscriptions of the Civil Wars by protecting from the vengeance of the king *de jure*, when he came to his own again, those who adhered to the king *de facto* and the existing social order. It was 'a kind of *eirenikon*, founded upon the rough practical common-sense which generally commends itself to the English nation.'[6] The statute has been described as 'the earliest recognition to be found in English law of a possible difference between the person and the office of the King, though nothing can be more vague and indirect than the way in which the distinction is hinted at.'[7]

[1] *Works*, vi, 270. [2] Goldwin Smith, i, 297.
[3] Pollard, *Henry VIII*, p. 39; cf. also *Factors*, p. 89.
[4] See also Pollard, *Sources*, ii, 3–208.
[5] *Works*, vi, 159. But see note on p. 6 below.
[6] Fisher, *Polit. Hist.* p. 63. [7] Stephen, quoted in Holdsworth, iii, 359.

An Act that no person going with the King to the Wars
shall be attaint of treason

The King our Sovereign Lord, calling to his remembrance the duty of allegiance of his subjects of this his realm, and that they by reason of the same are bounden to serve their Prince and Sovereign Lord for the time being in his Wars for the defence of him and the land against every rebellion, power, and might reared against him, and with him to enter and abide in service in battle if the case so require; And that for the same service what fortune ever fall by chance in the same battle against the mind and weal of the Prince, as in this land sometime past hath been seen, That it is not reasonable but against all laws, reason, and good conscience that the said subjects going with their Sovereign Lord in Wars, attending upon him in his person, or being in other places by his commandment within this land or without, any thing should lose or forfeit for doing their true duty and service of allegiance: It be therefore ordained, enacted, and established... that from henceforth no manner of person nor persons, whatsoever he or they be, that attend upon the King and Sovereign Lord of this land for the time being in his person, and do him true and faithful service of allegiance in the same, or be in other places by his commandment, in his Wars within this land or without, that for the same deed and true service of allegiance he or they be in no wise convict or attaint of high treason nor of other offences for that cause by Act of Parliament or otherwise by any process of law, whereby he or any of them shall mowe[1] forfeit life, lands, tenements, rents, possessions, hereditaments, goods, chattels, or any other things, but to be for that deed and service utterly discharged of any vexation, trouble, or loss; And if any Act or Acts or other process of the law hereafter thereupon for the same happen to be made contrary to this ordinance, that then that Act or Acts or other processes of the law, whatsoever they shall be, stand and be utterly void[2].

II. Provided alway that no person nor persons shall take any benefit or advantage by this Act which shall hereafter decline from his or their said allegiance.

11 Henr. VII, c. 1: *Statutes of the Realm*, ii, 568.

[1] See note on p. 24 below.

[2] Bacon points out that this provision is valueless: 'But the force and obligation of this law was in itself illusory, as to the latter part of it (by a precedent act of Parliament to bind or frustrate a future). For a supreme and absolute power cannot conclude itself, nor can that which is in nature revocable be made fixed; no more than if a man should appoint or declare by his will that if he made any later will it should be void.' But he adds the astute remark: 'But things that do not bind may satisfy for the time' (*Works*, vi, 160).

(2) Act concerning Corporations, 1504

Bacon says of Henry VII: 'In that part, both of justice and policy, which is the most durable part, and cut as it were in brass or marble—the making of good laws—he did excel'; and the new commercial development of Tudor England in particular is suggested by a mass of commercial and trade legislation[1]. Among these statutes the Act concerning Corporations is of constitutional rather than economic importance, for it asserts the right of the central government to complete industrial control. The exactions of the guilds, called by Bacon 'fraternities in evil,'[2] had been a principal cause of the decay of the towns. These exactions were now to pass under the supervision and limitation of the government. The statute may therefore be regarded as a contribution to the Tudor policy of asserting in all spheres the supremacy of the central authority.

The preamble recites an Act of 1437[3] 'which Act is now expired, and since the expiring of the same divers and many ordinances have been made by many and divers private bodies corporate within cities, towns, and boroughs, contrary to the King's prerogative, his laws, and to the common weal of his subjects'; and the substance of the statute re-enacts the earlier provisions with an important difference. The Act of 1437 had subjected guild ordinances to the review of the local administration—'the justices of the peace or the chief governors of cities'; the Act of 1504 brings into operation the central authority.

De privatis et illicitis statutis non faciendis

...Be it therefore ordained, established, and enacted...that no Masters, Wardens, and Fellowships of crafts or mysteries, nor any of them, nor any rulers of guilds or fraternities, take upon them to make any acts or ordinances, nor to execute any acts or ordinances by them here afore made, in disheritance or diminution of the prerogative of the King, nor of other, nor against the common profit of the people, but if the same acts or ordinances be examined and approved by the Chancellor, Treasurer of England, and Chief Justices of either Bench, or three of them, or before both the Justices of Assizes in their circuit or progress in that shire where such acts or ordinances be made, upon the pain of forfeiture of £40 for every time that they do the contrary[4]...

19 Henr. VII, c. 7: *Statutes of the Realm*, ii, 652.

(3) Statute of Liveries, 1504

The evils connected with livery and maintenance and the keeping of retainers find their original source in the Hundred Years War with France.

---

[1] An account of Henry VII's commercial policy is given in Fisher, pp. 96–109; see also Temperley, ch. v.   [2] *Works*, vi, 223.   [3] 15 Henr. VI, c. 6.

[4] The Act also contains a clause forbidding corporations to make acts or ordinances 'to restrain any person or persons to sue to the King's Highness or to any of his Courts.'

From the time of Stephen onwards the feudal levies of the realm had been frequently supplemented by mercenaries drawn from the adventurers of Europe. The forty days of feudal service did not meet the case of a regular campaign oversea, and it was necessary for government to fall back on the professional soldier. In the reign of Edward III the Crown adopted the practice of contracting—or in the technical phrase, 'indenting'[1]—with great lords and others, for the supply of men. By a further development of the system smaller men commanding levies of their own would bind themselves by indentures to place themselves and their men at the disposal of a greater lord in peace and war. Thus the military power at the disposal of a wealthy lord might be very great. As long as this military power was employed abroad it raised no dangerous questions, but when the English were driven from France, and the country was filled with disbanded soldiers, ready to indent or be indented, the way was prepared for the growth of the perilous practice of keeping retainers. These wore their lord's badge[2]; they received their lord's livery[3] and enjoyed his hospitality[4]; they were paid wages in money, varying from a mark to £4 or £5 a year according to their services and standing; and they could rely upon their lord's protection in the courts of law from the legal consequences of crimes committed in his service[5].

Great lords who thus controlled military power were under a standing temptation to employ it in private war or in other acts of violence. In 1411 Sir Robert Tirwhit, himself a royal judge, with 500 men at his back, set an ambush for Lord Roos, with whom he had a dispute about common of pasture, and when called in question, pleaded in his defence that he did not know that he had broken the law[6]. In 1455 the Earl of Devon, at the head of 4000 foot and 800 horse, plundered the cathedral at Exeter, held the canons to ransom, and committed 'many other great and heinous inconveniences.'[7] In 1469 Sir John Fastolf's castle of Caister, which was claimed by the Duke of Norfolk, was besieged by him in due form with a train of artillery and a force of 3000 men. The *Paston Letters*[8] give an account of the progress of the siege, which lasted for five weeks. At the end of that time provisions began to fail, and the place was 'sore broken with guns,' so the garrison surrendered and the Duke acquired the property. No mention is made of any appeal to the courts of law; yet the claimant who adopted this method of enforcing his rights was Earl Marshal, Constable of the Tower of London, and a Knight of the Garter[9].

The Statute of Liveries of 1504 is only one in a series of statutes[10]

---

[1] See Plummer's Introduction to Fortescue, *The Governance of England*, p. 15.

[2] The bear and the ragged staff, the badge of the Kingmaker, is still borne by the inmates of the Leycester Hospital at Warwick.

[3] 'Livery' was whatever was delivered to the retainer—livery of food or livery of ale, as well as livery of cloth. The term was not limited to a reward for the service of retainers; for instance litigants sometimes paid counsel in kind by livery of cloth and robes (Holdsworth, ii, 412).

[4] When Warwick the Kingmaker came to London, six oxen were eaten at a breakfast, and there was free food for all comers (Holinshed, iii, 301).

[5] This is what is technically known as 'maintenance.'

[6] Holdsworth, ii, 347.   [7] Denton, p. 275.

[8] ii, pp. xlv, l–liii, 371 ff.   [9] Denton, p. 299.

[10] See note on p. 9 below.

designed to put down private war, their number being evidence, not of the vigour of the law but of its ineffectiveness. Henry VII's Act inflicts a penalty upon persons giving or taking livery, and by making indentures ot retainers void it destroys the legal foundation upon which the system was based. The Act was limited to the life-time of the king, but larger causes were at work to end the abuse. The Tudor period supplied new outlets for lawless energy in the development of commerce and maritime enterprise, in the opening up of the New World, and finally in the war with Spain; and the retainers of the fifteenth century became the adventurers and mariner-pirates of the sixteenth. There were also new openings for the employment of capital, and great lords who had once spent their substance in the profuse hospitality which kept the private armies together, now found that they had something better to do with their money. Thus the problem of liveries solved itself.

De Retentionibus illicitis

The King our Sovereign Lord calleth to his remembrance that where before this time divers statutes[1] for punishment of such persons that give or receive liveries, or that retain any person or persons or be retained with any person or persons...have been made and established, and that notwithstanding divers persons have taken upon them some to give and some to receive liveries and to retain and be retained...and little or nothing is or hath been done for the punishment of the offenders in that behalf, Wherefore our Sovereign Lord the King, by the advice [etc.]...hath ordained, stablished, and enacted that all his statutes and ordinances afore this time made against such as make unlawful retainers and such as so be retained, or that give or receive livery, be plainly observed and kept and put in due execution.

II. And over that, our said Sovereign Lord the King ordaineth, stablisheth, and enacteth by the said authority, that no person, of what estate or degree or condition he be,...privily or openly give any livery or sign or retain any person, other than such as he giveth household wages unto without fraud or colour, or that he by his manual servant[2] or his officer or man learned in the one law or in the other[3], by any writing, oath, promise, livery, sign, badge, token, or in any other manner wise unlawfully retain; and if any do the contrary, that then he run and fall in the pain and forfeiture for every such livery and sign, badge or token, so accepted, 100s., and the taker and acceptor of every such livery, badge, token, or sign, to forfeit and pay for every such livery and sign, badge or token, so accepted, 100s., and for every month that

---

[1] Statutes were passed in 1399, 1401, 1406, 1411, 1414, 1429, and 1468; see Fortescue, pp. 27–8.

[2] *I.e.* a servant who works with his hands.

[3] *I.e.* learned either in the civil or in the canon law.

he useth or keepeth such livery or sign, badge or token, after that he hath taken or accepted the same, to forfeit and pay 100s., and every person that [shall] by oath, writing, or promise, or in any other wise unlawfully retain, privily or openly, and also every such person that is so retained, to forfeit and pay for every such time 100s., and as well every person that so retaineth as every person that is so retained to forfeit and pay for every month that such retainer is continued, 100s....

III. And also it is ordained and enacted that no person of what estate [or] condition he be...name or cause himself to be named servant or retained to or with any person, or buy or cause to be bought or wear any gown as a livery gown, sign, or token of the suit or livery of any person, or any badge, token, or sign of any person, upon pain of forfeiture for every day or time that he doth, 40s., and also to have imprisonment by the discretion of the judges or persons afore whom he shall be thereof convicted, and that without bail or mainprize[1].

* * * * * *

VI. Moreover the King our Sovereign Lord, by the advice, assent, and authority aforesaid, hath ordained, stablished, and enacted, that every person that will sue or complain before the Chancellor of England or the Keeper of the King's Great Seal in the Star Chamber[2], or before the King in his Bench, or before the King and his Council attending upon his most royal person wheresoever he be, so that there be 3 of the same Council at the least of the which two shall be lords spiritual or temporal, against any person or persons offending or doing against the form of this ordinance or any other of the premises, be admitted by their discretion to give information...And that upon the same all such persons be called by writ, subpoena, privy seal, or otherwise, And the said Chancellor or Keeper of the Seal, the King in his Bench, or the said Council to have power to examine all persons defendants and every of them, as well by oath as otherwise, and to adjudge him or them convict or attaint, as well by such examination as otherwise, in such penalties as is aforesaid as the case shall require;...And also the same party, plaintiff, or informer shall have such reasonable reward of that that by his complaint shall grow to the King as shall be thought reasonable by the discretion of the said Chancellor or Keeper of the Great Seal, Justices, or Council.

VII. And also it is enacted by the said authority that the said

---

[1] The old law drew a subtle distinction between mainprize and bail; see Jacob, *Law Dictionary*, under 'mainprize.'   [2] See p. 249 below.

Chancellor or Keeper of the Great Seal, Justices, or Council have full authority and power by this Statute to do send by writ, sub-poena, privy seal, warrant, or otherwise by their discretion, for any person or persons offending or doing contrary to the premises, without any suit or information made or put before them or any of them, and the same person or persons to examine by oath or otherwise by their discretions, and to adjudge all such persons as shall be found guilty in the premises by verdict, confession, ex-amination, proofs, or otherwise, in the said forfeitures and pains as the case shall require, as though they were condemned therein after the course of the common law, and to commit such offenders to ward and to award execution accordingly.

VIII. ...And that all manner of writings or indentures between any person herebefore made, whereby any person is re-tained contrary to this Act, that indenture or writing, as touching any such retainder only and no further, be void and of none effect: This Act to take his effect and beginning for such retainers and offences and other misdemeanours as shall be done, had, or made contrary to the form of this Act after the Feast of Pentecost next coming only, and the same Act to continue and endure during the life of our said Sovereign Lord the King that now is and no longer.

* * * * * *

X. Provided also that this Act extend not to the punishment of any person or persons the which by the virtue of the King's placard[1] or writing, signed with his hand and sealed with his privy seal or signet, shall take, appoint, or indent with any persons to do and to be in a readiness to do the King service in War, or otherwise at his commandment, so that they that shall have such placard or writing for their part use not by that retainer, service, attendance, or any other wise the person or persons that they shall take, appoint, or indent with, nor the persons that so do in-dent to do the King service use not themselves for their part in doing service or giving attendance to them that shall have author-ity by reason of the King's writing to take, appoint, or indent with them, in any thing concerning the said Act otherwise than shall be comprised in the same the King's placard or writing, and that placard or writing to endure during the King's pleasure and no longer.

XI. Provided also that this Act extend not to any livery to be given by any serjeants at the law at their making or creation, or to be given by any executors at the interment of any person for

---

[1] *I.e.* warrant or licence.

any mourning array, or to be given by any guild, fraternity, or craft corporate, or by the Mayor and Sheriffs of the City of London, or by any other mayor or sheriff or chief officers of any city, borough, town, or port of this realm of England, during the time of his office and by reason of the same, or to be given by any abbot or prior of or other chief head or governor or officer of any monastery, abbey, or priory, or other places corporate, given to their farmers or tenants or otherwise, according as it hath been used and accustomed in the same monastery, abbey, or priory.

19 Henr. VII, c. 14: *Statutes of the Realm*, ii, 658.

NOTE

The exaltation of the Sovereign in Acts of Parliament begins with Henry VII. In 11 Henr. VII, c. 12, there is a reference to his 'most gracious disposition' (cf. also c. 24), and in 19 Henr. VII, c. 19, to his 'most noble Grace and great wisdoms.' Under Henry VIII the references become more laudatory. In 1534 the King is a 'most dread, benign, and gracious,' a 'most rightful and dreadful Sovereign Lord' (pp. 38, 382 below), who in 1536 is 'daily finding and devising the increase, advancement, and exaltation of true doctrine and virtue,' and 'the total extirping and destruction of vice and sin' (p. 59 below). Thus the Tudor doctrine of indivisible sovereignty finds expression, even in formal legal documents. The glorification of Elizabeth, as in her Treasons Act of 1571 (p. 413 below), rests upon a different consideration. As her threatened life alone stood between England and a Catholic reaction—a return under Mary Stuart to the evil days of Mary Tudor—it seemed infinitely precious; and we find Elizabethan lawyers saying in prose what the great Elizabethan writers say in poetry. It is after all a political situation which accounts for Queen Elizabeth's place in literature.

The Church Settlement of Henry VIII

The English Reformation was accomplished in two stages; for the Papal authority was rejected first and doctrine and ritual were modified afterwards. The rejection of the Pope was the work of Henry VIII, and he effected important constitutional changes. The permanent doctrinal changes were postponed for nearly a generation, and belong to the reign of Elizabeth. These two episodes of vast importance are separated by two minor movements—the premature doctrinal reformation of the reign of Edward VI, and the temporary reconciliation with Rome carried through in the reign of Mary.

§ 1. Minor Ecclesiastical Reforms

It is characteristic of Tudor policy that the religious changes of Henry VIII were effected mainly by statute, for it was the king's 'masterpiece' to 'make use of his Parliaments.'[1] The 'Reformation Parliament' met on November 3, 1529, and the English Reformation began in a way peculiarly English —'not with the enunciation of some new truth, but with an attack on clerical fees.'[2] An Act of 1529[3] established a scale of fees to be charged by the Church courts for the probate of wills: nothing where the effects of the deceased were of the value of £5 and under, 'except only to the scribe to have for writing of the probate,' 6d.; 3s. 6d. if over £5, but not exceeding £40; 5s. if over £40.

Another Act of 1529[4] accomplished a similar reform in the case of 'mortuaries, otherwise called corpse-presents.' No mortuary is to be demanded where the goods of the deceased at the time of death are less than ten marks. If their value is ten marks or more and under £30 the fee is fixed at 3s. 4d.; if £30 or more and under £40, at 6s. 8d.; if £40 or over, at 10s.

A third statute of 1529[5] restrains pluralities, deals with the clerical non-residence which the system of pluralities encouraged[6], and forbids farming and trading by the clergy. The statute also deals with the special kind of absenteeism practised by parish priests who served chantries[7], forbidding spiritual persons, secular or regular, beneficed with cure, to 'take any particular stipend' to 'sing for any soul.' The Act is linked up with the greater Reformation statutes by a clause providing that dispensations from its terms should be void, but that in certain circumstances dispensations might be

---

[1] Lord Herbert of Cherbury, p. 539.
[2] Pollard, *Henry VIII*, p. 272.   [3] 21 Henr. VIII, c. 5.
[4] 21 Henr. VIII, c. 6.   [5] 21 Henr. VIII, c. 13.
[6] Latimer had nicknamed the absentees 'strawberries, which come but once a year, and tarry not long.'
[7] Cf. Chaucer's good parson in the Prologue to the *Canterbury Tales*, l. 507 ff.:
        'He set not his benefice to hire
        And left his sheep encumbered in the mire,
        And ran to London unto Saint Poulès,
        To seeken him a chaunterie for soulès.'

purchased—the prohibition being aimed at dispensations from Rome, and the permission contemplating dispensations from the Crown[1].

The policy of the Tudors which struck at the liberties of overmighty subjects was also directed against the immunities of an overmighty corporation. Both Henry VII and Henry VIII attempted to deal with benefit of clergy and sanctuary—two evils by which 'all over England the arm of justice was paralysed.'[2]

'Privilege of clergy,' says Sir J. F. Stephen[3], 'consisted originally in the right of the clergy to be free from the jurisdiction of lay courts.' This principle had in course of time been extended (1) by including among clerks entitled to the privilege 'secular clerks,' such as doorkeepers, exorcists, readers, and subdeacons; and (2) by allowing clergy to all who were capable of taking orders, *i.e.* to persons who could read Latin and were therefore able to go through a mass if required. In practice this latter extension meant that clergy could be claimed by anyone who could stumble through the 'neck-verse.' On the other hand, at the beginning of the Tudor period there were three classes of persons who could not claim clergy: (1) high treason was not clergyable[4]; (2) felons committing highway robbery or the wilful burning of houses were excluded from benefit of clergy at common law[5]; (3) women could have no clergy because they were not capable of being ordained[6]. Nor was it the case that a criminal claiming clergy was allowed to go free. He was delivered after conviction to the representative of the bishop and detained in the bishop's prison until he could make his purgation by the oath of witnesses[7]. If he was unable to purge himself, he might be degraded or put to penance. If he was a notorious offender, the secular court might hand him over to the bishop *absque purgatione*, in which case he forfeited his lands, goods, and chattels, and was imprisoned in the bishop's prison for life. Tudor legislation on this question begins with an Act of 1488–9[8], which provided that a felon who claimed clergy should be branded, and that if he claimed it a second time he should be denied it, unless he could prove that he was actually in orders. An Act of 1496–7[9] had deprived of clergy laymen committing petty treason by 'prepensedly' murdering their 'lord, master, or sovereign immediate.' A temporary Act of 1512[10] took away benefit of clergy from persons 'such as be within holy orders only except' committing murder or felony 'in any church, chapel, or hallowed place,' or who murder or rob any 'in the King's highway' or 'any person in his house.' The Reformation Parliament, by an Act of 1531–2[11], provided that everyone convicted of petty treason, or 'for any wilful murder of malice prepensed,' or for 'robbing of any churches, chapels, or other holy places,' or for burglary, or highway robbery, or for 'wilful burning of any dwelling-houses or barns wherein any grain of corns shall happen to be' should lose his clergy, 'such as

---

[1] Two such licences from the Crown, of 27 Henr. VIII, are quoted in Amos, p. 239.
[2] Fisher, p. 19.   [3] i, 459.   [4] Stephen, i, 464.
[5] *Ib.*   [6] *Ib.* i, 461.
[7] See Miss C. B. Firth in the *English Historical Review*, xxxii, 187; also Stephen, i, 460–1.   [8] 4 Henr. VII, c. 13.   [9] 12 Henr. VII, c. 7.
[10] 4 Henr. VIII, c. 2. This Act was to last only until the next Parliament.
[11] 23 Henr. VIII, c. 1.

be within holy orders, that is to say of the orders of sub-deacon or above, only except.' Clerks convicted of these offences, and then admitted to clergy and delivered to the ordinary, were to remain in the bishop's prison, and were not to be admitted to purgation and liberated unless they could find sufficient sureties for good behaviour; and they could be degraded by the ordinaries to whose custody they were committed, and handed over to the Justices of the King's Bench to be dealt with as if they had not been in orders. This Act, and later legislation of the reign[1], effected considerable improvements in the law, but it is noteworthy that no attempt was made to repudiate the principle of benefit of clergy. In a way characteristic of English legislation one statute after another took away the privilege from particular crimes, until it was finally abolished in 1827[2].

The system of sanctuary had grown up out of the fact that in early times a criminal who took refuge in a church could not be taken from it, but was allowed to take before the coroner an 'oath of abjuration,'[3] by which he admitted his offence and swore to abjure the realm for life, proceeding for that purpose to a port appointed by the coroner. He was to go 'un-girt, un-shod, bare-headed, in his bare shirt, as if he were to be hanged on the gallows, having received a cross in his hands.'[4] In the case of the greater chartered sanctuaries, such as Beverley and Durham, an alternative to abjuration was residence within the precincts of the sanctuary as a 'sanctuary man.' The first restriction upon sanctuary was established by the case of Humphrey Stafford in 1487, when the judges held that sanctuary could not afford protection in cases of high treason; and the position of the Crown in this matter was subsequently supported by bulls from the Pope which imposed other limitations also upon the privilege. In the reign of Henry VIII further restrictions were established by legislation. An Act of 1529[5] provided that a criminal taking sanctuary for felony or murder should, 'immediately after his confession and before his abjuration,' be branded upon the thumb of the right hand 'with the sign of an A, to the intent that he may the better be known among the king's subjects that he was abjured.' Should he refuse to 'take his passage' out of sanctuary on the day appointed by the coroner for his abjuration, he was to lose the benefit of sanctuary altogether. Two years later an Act of 1531[6] entirely revolutionised the law of sanctuary by abolishing abjuration. The preamble of the statute recites that sundry offenders abjuring the realm are 'very expert mariners,' and others 'very able and apt men for the wars,' who not only instruct the inhabitants of 'outward realms and countries' in archery, but 'have disclosed their knowledges of the commodities and secrets of this realm, to no little damage and prejudice of the same.' The Act therefore provides that persons abjuring are no longer to be directed by the coroner to a port of embarkation but to

---

[1] 23 Henr. VIII, c. 11; 27 Henr. VIII, c. 17; 28 Henr. VIII, c. 1.

[2] By 7 and 8 Geo. IV, c. 28. An Act of 1547 (1 Edw. VI, c. 12) gave every peer of the realm, 'though he cannot read,' a privilege equivalent to, though not identical with, benefit of clergy. This was overlooked when the Act of 1827 was passed, and was not abolished until 4 and 5 Vict. c. 22 (Stephen, i, 462).

[3] The form of oath *temp.* Edw. II is quoted in Jusserand, p. 160.

[4] Quoted from Fleta in Jusserand, p. 161 *n.*

[5] 21 Henr. VIII, c. 2.　　　　　　[6] 22 Henr. VIII, c. 14.

a sanctuary within the realm, where they are to remain under penalty of death. An Act of 1534[1] puts into statutory form the decision in Stafford's case; and an Act of 1536[2] devises improved regulations for the control of 'sanctuary men.' Finally, by an Act of 1540[3] all sanctuaries were abolished except churches and churchyards and certain places named in the Act[4]; and sanctuary was not in future to protect persons guilty of murder, rape, burglary, robbery, arson, or sacrilege. Sanctuary was abolished in 1623[5], but 'in a modified form sanctuaries continued, apparently in defiance of the law, for another century, so far at least as regards the execution of civil process'[6]; and debtors continued to find protection in Whitefriars, the Savoy, and the Rules of the Fleet.

The last of the minor ecclesiastical reforms of the Reformation Parliament was effected by the Act of 1532 'in restraint of citations.'[7] As the Court of the Archbishop was a court of first instance as well as of appeal for the whole province, it was possible for proceedings to be begun there, and for the person proceeded against to be cited out of his own diocese to Canterbury, London, or York, there to 'answer to surmised and feigned causes.' If the person so cited failed to appear, he might be excommunicated, or at the least suspended from all divine service, and before he was absolved he was compelled to pay the fees of the court and the 'summoner, apparitor, or other light literate person'[8] by whom the citation was served, at the rate of 2d. a mile. If on the other hand he elected to appear before the court, he had to meet the expenses of the journey; and his absence, in days of poor communication, gave 'great occasion of misbehaviour and misliving' of his servants and household, 'to the great impairment and diminution of their good names and honesties.' To meet this grievance the statute provided that no one should be cited out of his own diocese, unless for a spiritual offence, except on appeal from his own bishop's court, saving the right of the archbishop to cite any person for heresy or in cases of probate of wills. Fees for citations were limited to 'three pence sterling.'

§ 2. Submission of the Clergy

Before he opened his main attack upon the Papal jurisdiction, it was necessary for the King to secure himself in the rear by silencing Convocation. The documents associated with these operations may be grouped together under the head of 'the submission of the clergy.'

(1) Act for the Pardon of the Clergy of Canterbury, 1531

Before the opening of the second session of the Reformation Parliament in January, 1531, the Attorney-General had been instructed to proceed against the bishops on the ground that by acknowledging Wolsey's jurisdic-

---

[1] 26 Henr. VIII, c. 13.   [2] 27 Henr. VIII, c. 19.
[3] 32 Henr. VIII, c. 12.
[4] Wells, Westminster, Manchester, Northampton, Norwich, York, Derby, and Launceston. An account of each of the important chartered sanctuaries will be found in J. C. Cox, *Sanctuaries and Sanctuary Seekers.*
[5] By 21 Jac. I, c. 28.   [6] Stephen, i, 492.   [7] 23 Henr. VIII, c. 9.
[8] Cf. the description of the 'somonour' in the Prologue to Chaucer's *Canterbury Tales.*

tion as papal legate the whole body of the clergy had incurred the penalties of *praemunire*. The Great Statute of Praemunire of 1393[1] had provided, in language at once comprehensive and vague, 'that if any purchase or pursue ...in the Court of Rome or elsewhere...translations, processes, and sentences of excommunication, bulls, instruments, or any things whatsoever, which touch our Lord the King, against him, his crown, and his royalty, or his realm,' and 'they which bring the same within the realm or make thereof notification...that they, their notaries, procurators, maintainers, abettors, favourers, and counsellors, shall be put out of the king's protection, and their lands, tenements, goods, and chattels forfeited to our Lord the King, and that they be attached by their bodies...and brought before the King and his Council...or that process be made against them by *praemunire facias*.'[2] Under a writ of *praemunire* issued in accordance with this statute, the King had been able to confiscate Wolsey's vast possessions, on the ground that his exercise of authority as papal legate was a breach of the law, and this in spite of the fact that he had received that authority with the King's consent and had used it to carry out the King's policy. It was now contended that the whole body of the English clergy because they had accepted the legatine authority had shared as maintainers and abettors in Wolsey's offence. The Act of 1531 granted the clergy of Canterbury pardon for the past on payment of a ransom or fine of £100,000[3]. Before he would accept the subsidy and promote the bill of pardon, the King also required an acknowledgment from Convocation that he was 'sole protector and Supreme Head of the Church and clergy of England.' This form of words was eventually altered by Convocation to 'their singular protector, only and supreme lord, and, as far as the law of Christ allows, even Supreme Head'[4]; but this, as the Emperor's ambassador pointed out, was only an empty phrase, as no one would venture to dispute with the King where his supremacy ended and that of Christ began[5].

An Act concerning the pardon granted to the King's Spiritual Subjects of the Province of Canterbury for the Praemunire

The King our Sovereign Lord, calling to his blessed and most gracious remembrance that his good and loving subjects the most Reverend Father in God the Archbishop of Canterbury and other bishops, suffragans, prelates, and other spiritual persons of the Province of the Archbishopric of Canterbury of this his realm of England, and the ministers underwritten which have exercised, practised, or executed in spiritual courts and other spiritual jurisdictions within the said Province, have fallen and incurred into divers dangers of his laws by things done, perpetrated, and com-

---

[1] 16 Rich. II, c. 5.   [2] Gee and Hardy, p. 125.
[3] Another Act (23 Henr. VIII, c. 19) passed in 1532, granted a similar pardon to the clergy of the Province of York, on payment of a sum of £18,840. 0s. 10d.
[4] Fisher, p. 308. This qualification was afterwards omitted when the Act of Supremacy came to be drawn.
[5] Pollard, *Cranmer*, p. 70.

mitted contrary to the order of his laws, and specially contrary to the form of the statutes of provisors, provisions, and praemunire[1]; and his Highness, having alway tender eye with mercy and pity and compassion towards his said spiritual subjects, minding of his high goodness and great benignity so always to impart the same unto them as justice being daily administered all rigour be excluded, and the great and benevolent minds of his said subjects largely and many times approved towards his Highness, and specially in their Convocation and Synod now presently being in the Chapter House of the Monastery of Westminster, by correspondence of gratitude to them to be requited: Of his mere motion, benignity, and liberality, by authority of this his Parliament, hath given and granted his liberal and free pardon to his said good and loving spiritual subjects and the said ministers and to every of them, to be had, taken, and enjoyed to and by them and every of them by virtue of this present Act in manner and form ensuing, that is to wit: The King's Highness, of his said benignity and high liberality, in consideration that the said Archbishop, Bishops, and Clergy of the said Province of Canterbury in their said Convocation now being, have given and granted to him a subsidy of one hundred thousand pounds of lawful money current in this realm, to be levied and collected by the said clergy at their proper costs and charges and to be paid in certain form specified in their said grant thereof, is fully and resolutely contented and pleased that it be ordained, established, and enacted by authority of this his said Parliament, That the most Reverend Father in God, William[2], Archbishop of Canterbury, Metropolitan and Primate of All England, and all other bishops and suffragans, prelates, abbots, priors, and their convents and every person of the same convents, and convents corporate and every person, [etc.]...abbesses, prioresses, and religious nuns, and all other religious and spiritual persons, deans and chapters and other dignities of cathedral and collegiate churches, prebendaries, canons and petty

---

1 'Provisions' are appointments to sees or benefices not yet vacant, made by the Pope in derogation of the rights of the regular patrons. 'Provisors' are the holders of such provisions.

'Praemunire' is derived from the name of the writ, *praemunire facias*, by which the sheriff is charged to summon a person accused of prosecuting in a foreign court a suit cognisable by the law of England. The term is also applied to an offence against the Statute of Praemunire, the penalty being imprisonment and loss of goods.

The first Statute of Provisors was passed in 1351, and the second in 1390. The first Statute of Praemunire was passed in 1353, and the second in 1393. For the terms of these statutes see Gee and Hardy, pp. 103, 112, 122.

2 Archbishop Warham.

canons, vicars and clerks of the same and every person of the same, all archdeacons, masters, provosts, presidents, wardens of colleges and of collegiate churches, masters and wardens of hospitals, all fellows, brethren, scholars, priests, and spiritual conducts[1], and every of the same, and all vicars-general of dioceses, chancellors, commissaries, officials, and deans rurals, and all ministers hereafter generally rehearsed of any spiritual court or courts within the said Province of Canterbury, that is to say: All judges, advocates, registers and scribes, proctors[2] constituted to judgments and apparitors[3], and all other which within the said Province of the Archbishopric of Canterbury at any time heretofore have administered, exercised, practised, or executed in any jurisdictions within the said Province as officers or ministers of the said courts or have been ministers or executors to the exercise or administration of the same; and all and singular politic bodies spiritual in any manner wise corporated, and all parsons, vicars, curates, chantry priests, stipendiaries, and all and every person and persons spiritual of the clergy of the said Province of Canterbury in this present Act of pardon hereafter not excepted or to the contrary not provided for, by whatsoever name or surname, name of dignity, preeminence, or office they or any of them be or is named or called, the successors, heirs, executors, and administrators of them and of every of them, shall be by authority of this present pardon acquitted, pardoned, released, and discharged against his Highness, his heirs, successors, and executors, and every of them, of all and all manner offences, contempts, and trespasses committed or done against all and singular statute and statutes of provisors, provisions, and praemunire, and every of them, and of all forfeitures and titles that may grow to the King's Highness by any of the same statutes, and of all and singular trespasses, wrongs, deceits, misdemeanors, forfeitures, penalties and profits, sums of money, pains of death, pains corporal and pecuniary, as generally of all other things, causes, quarrels, suits, judgments, and executions in this present Act hereafter not excepted nor forprised[4], which may or can be by his Highness in any wise or by any means pardoned, before and to the tenth day of the month of March in the twenty-second year of his most noble reign, to every of his said loving subjects, that

---

[1] *I.e.* spiritual guides or directors.

[2] Proctors in courts administering civil or canon law correspond to attorneys or solicitors in courts of common law or equity.

[3] Officers or messengers of an ecclesiastical court. Cf. the Act of Citations (see p. 16 above).   [4] Reserved.

is to say: To the said archbishop and other the said bishops, suffragans, prelates, abbots, priors, and convents and every person of the same convents, and convents corporate and every person of the same convents corporate, abbesses, prioresses, nuns, and spiritual persons in dignity, and all other religious and spiritual persons, deans, chapters, prebendaries, canons, petty canons, vicars choral and clerks, archdeacons, masters, provosts, presidents, wardens, fellows, brethren, scholars, priests and spiritual conducts, chancellors, vicars-general of dioceses, commissaries, officials, deans rurals, all judges, advocates, registers and scribes, proctors and apparitors, which have administered, practised, or executed any jurisdiction in any spiritual court within the said Province, and to the said politic bodies, spiritual persons, vicars, curates, chantry priests, stipendiaries, and to all and every person and persons spiritual of the clergy of the said Province, and to all and every other person or persons before named....

*   *   *   *   *   *

22 Henr. VIII, c. 15: Statutes of the Realm, iii, 334.

When the bill for the pardon of the clergy of Canterbury was read in the Lower House, 'divers froward persons would in no wise assent to it except all men were pardoned, saying that all men which had anything to do with the Cardinal were in the same case.' The result was an Act of 1531[1] by which the King, 'moved with most tender pity, love, and compassion,' 'of his mere motion and of his high benignity, special grace, pity, and liberality,' gave 'to all and singular his temporal and lay subjects' 'his most gracious, general, and free pardon' for all offences by them committed against the Statutes of Provisors and Praemunire before March 30 in the twenty-second year of his reign. A statutory pardon of a whole people has no parallel in history.

The moral effect of these proceedings can scarcely be exaggerated. Convocation in particular, which had shewn signs of resisting the King's ecclesiastical policy, now lay at his mercy. The clergy and laity were pardoned for the past, but what guarantee was there for the future? The Statute of Praemunire was vague; there were daily dealings with Rome; who could say at what point these became illegal? Until the religious changes of Henry VIII were finally accomplished, the clergy lay under the sinister shadow of praemunire, and all power of concentrated constitutional resistance to the King was broken down[2].

---

[1] 22 Henr. VIII, c. 16.

[2] 'Henry, like a mighty hunter, resolved to subject to his authority the first-born of the kingdom of heaven.... By an act of tyranny never heard of before he had all the clergy indicted.... The terror inspired by this most iniquitous charge crushed' them and 'bowed them down to the ground.... Seeing no hope of relief anywhere, they gave up the battle as lost and allowed themselves to be trodden under foot, as salt that has lost its strength' (Nicholas Sanders, De origine ac progressu schismatis Anglicani, 1585, trans. D. Lewis, p. 90).

(2) Supplication against the Ordinaries, 1532

In March, 1532, the Commons presented to the King their 'Supplication against the Ordinaries.'[1] After complaining in general terms of 'much discord, variance, and debate' of late arisen in the realm, 'as well through new, fantastical, and erroneous opinions, grown by occasion of frantic, seditious, and overthwartly framed books, compiled, imprinted, published, and made into the English tongue, contrary and against the very true Catholic and Christian faith, as also by the extreme and uncharitable behaviour and dealing of divers ordinaries' which 'have the examination in and upon the said errors and heretical opinions,' the document goes on to enumerate certain 'special particular griefs.' Of these the most important are: (1) the power of Convocation to make 'laws, constitutions, and ordinances' without the royal assent or the assent of the laity; (2) the delays of the Canterbury courts of Arches and Audience[2], and the vexatious exactions of the ordinaries and the ecclesiastical courts; (3) the ordinaries 'do daily confer and give sundry benefices unto certain young folks, calling them their nephews or kinsfolk, being in their minority and within age, not apt nor able to serve the cure of any such benefice,' whereby 'the poor silly souls' of the king's subjects, 'for lack of good curates, do perish without doctrine or any good teaching'; (4) the excessive number of holy days kept 'with very small devotion'; (5) in cases of heresy the ordinaries or their ministers put to the accused 'such subtle interrogatories concerning the high mysteries of our faith as are able quickly to trap a simple, unlearned, or yet a well-witted layman without learning, and bring them by such sinister introduction soon to his own confusion.' The importance of this document lies in what it omits rather than in what it contains. If other grievances had been seriously felt, they would probably have found their way into it. As it stands it may be regarded as representing the worst that the more responsible critics of the bishops could say in public against them.

The 'Answer of the Ordinaries'[3] to these accusations was approved by Convocation in April, 1532, and presented to the King at the end of the month. The ordinaries, who describe themselves as the King's 'orators and daily bounden bedesmen,' begin by denying that there is any such 'discord, debate, variance, or breach of peace' as had been alleged against the King's subjects, their 'brethren in God and ghostly children,' and then proceed to deal with the detailed accusations *seriatim* in vague terms and at inordinate length. The general line of argument adopted is, that if the things complained of really happen, it is the fault of individuals and not of the whole order of the clergy. On April 30 the King delivered the document to the Speaker and a deputation of the Commons for their consideration, with a hint of his own opinion. 'We think,' he said, 'their answer will smally please you, for it seemeth to us very slender. You be a great sort of wise

---

[1] The fact that there are in the Record Office four corrected drafts of the 'supplication,' with corrections in Cromwell's own hand, has been taken as evidence that it really emanated from the Court (Stephens and Hunt, iv, 114; but see Pollard, *Henry VIII*, p. 291). The 'supplication' is printed in full in Gee and Hardy, pp. 145–153.   [2] On these courts, see pp. 358–9 below.
[3] Printed in Gee and Hardy, pp. 154–176.

men. I doubt not but you will look circumspectly on the matter, and we will be indifferent between you.'[1] In a second answer Convocation offered not to publish canons henceforth without the King's consent, unless it were for the maintenance of the faith[2]. This also failed to satisfy the King; on May 10 he sent to Convocation three articles for their acceptance, and on the following day he sent for the Speaker and twelve of the Commons, and addressed them in words which shewed that to his mind the real issue was one of sovereignty. 'Well-beloved subjects, we thought that the clergy of our realm had been our subjects wholly; but now we have well perceived that they be but half our subjects—yea, and scarce our subjects. For all the prelates at their consecration make an oath to the Pope clean contrary to the oath they make to us, so that they seem his subjects and not ours.'[3] On May 15 Convocation surrendered and accepted the three articles[4], undertaking (1) not to make any new canons unless the King should license them to make such canons, and thereto should give his royal assent and authority; and (2) to submit all canons heretofore enacted to the King and a commission of 32 persons chosen by him; (3) canons determined by the majority of the commission 'not to stand with God's laws' and the laws of the realm, to be 'abrogated and taken away by your grace and the clergy,' and those approved by the commission 'to stand in full strength and power, your grace's most royal assent and authority once impetrate[5] and fully given to the same.' On May 16, the day on which this submission was presented to the King, Sir Thomas More resigned the Chancellorship and retired into private life. The proposed reform of ecclesiastical law was never carried into effect, but the first of the three articles gave the King all that he really wanted. The question of sovereignty was settled in his favour, and he was now secure against any attempt on the part of Convocation to protest against the steps which he was proposing to take in the matter of the divorce. The permanent constitutional importance of the submission lies in this, that it put an end to the autonomy of the English Church. Chapuys, the Imperial ambassador, wrote: 'Churchmen will be of less account than shoemakers, who have the power of assembling and making their own statutes.'[6]

(3) Act for the Submission of the Clergy, 1534

This Act embodied in statutory form the substance of the submission made by Convocation in 1532. It also modified the system of appeals set up by the Act of 1533 'for the restraint of appeals.'[7]

An Act for the submission of the Clergy to the King's Majesty

Where the King's humble and obedient subjects the clergy of this realm of England have not only knowledged[8] according to the truth that the Convocations of the same clergy is always, hath

---

[1] Quoted in Stephens and Hunt, iv, 118.   [2] *Ib.* iv, 119.   [3] *Ib.* iv, 120.
[4] Their submission is printed in Gee and Hardy, p. 176.
[5] *I.e.* obtained. The word is used especially of anything obtained by request to an authority (*Oxford Dictionary*).
[6] Quoted in Gairdner, i, 450.   [7] 24 Henr. VIII, c. 12; see p. 41 below.
[8] Used in the sense of 'acknowledged.'

been, and ought to be assembled only by the King's writ, but also submitting themselves to the King's Majesty hath promised *in verbo sacerdotii* that they will never from henceforth presume to attempt, allege, claim, or put in ure[1], or enact, promulge, or execute any new canons, constitutions, ordinance provincial, or other, or by whatsoever other name they shall be called, in the Convocation, unless the King's most royal assent and licence may to them be had to make, promulge, and execute the same, and that his Majesty do give his most royal assent and authority in that behalf: And where divers constitutions, ordinance, and canons, provincial or synodal, which heretofore have been enacted, and be thought not only to be much prejudicial to the King's prerogative royal and repugnant to the laws and statutes of this realm, but also overmuch onerous to his Highness and his subjects, the said clergy hath most humbly besought the King's Highness that the said constitutions and canons may be committed to the examination and judgment of his Highness and of 32 persons of the King's subjects....Be it therefore now enacted by authority of this present Parliament, according to the said submission and petition of the said clergy, that they nor any of them from henceforth shall presume to attempt, allege, claim, or put in ure any constitutions or ordinances, provincial or synodal, or any other canons, nor shall enact, promulge, or execute any such canons, constitutions, or ordinance provincial, by whatsoever name or names they may be called, in their Convocations in time coming, which alway shall be assembled by authority of the King's writ, unless the same clergy may have the King's most royal assent and licence to make, promulge, and execute such canons, constitutions, and ordinances, provincial or synodal; upon pain of every one of the said clergy doing contrary to this Act and being thereof convict, to suffer imprisonment and make fine at the King's will.

* * * * * *

III. Provided alway that no canons, constitution, or ordinance shall be made or put in execution within this realm by authority of the Convocation of the Clergy which shall be contrariant or repugnant to the King's prerogative royal, or the customs, laws, or statutes of this realm; anything contained in this Act to the contrary hereof notwithstanding.

IV. And be it further enacted...that...no manner of appeals shall be had, provoked, or made out of this realm or out of any of the King's dominions to the Bishop of Rome nor to the see of

---

[1] *I.e.* 'put in practice.' The word 'ure,' though now obsolete, was at this time in common use.

Rome in any causes or matters happening to be in contention and having their commencement and beginning in any of the courts within this realm or within any of the King's dominions, ...but that all manner of appeals...shall be made and had.... after such manner, form, and condition as is limited for appeals to be had and prosecuted within this realm in causes of matrimony, tithes, oblations, and obventions, by a statute thereof made and established since the beginning of this present Parliament[1]....

And for lack of justice at or in any of the courts of the archbishops of this realm or in any the King's dominions, it shall be lawful to the parties grieved to appeal to the King's Majesty in the King's Court of Chancery, and that upon every such appeal a commission shall be directed under the great seal to such persons as shall be named by the King's Highness, his heirs and successors, like as in case of appeal from the Admiral Court[2], to hear and definitively determine such appeals and the causes concerning the same....

V. And if any person or persons...provoke or sue any manner of appeals...to the said Bishop of Rome or to the see of Rome, or do procure or execute any manner of process from the see of Rome or by authority thereof to the derogation or let of the due execution of this Act or contrary to the same, that then every such person or persons so doing, their aiders, counsellors, and abettors, shall incur and run into the dangers, pains, and penalties contained and limited in the Act of Provision and Praemunire made in the sixteenth year of...King Richard the second against such as sue to the Court of Rome against the King's crown and prerogative royal.

VI. Provided always that all manner of provocations and appeals hereafter to be had, made, or taken from the jurisdiction of any abbots, priors, and other heads and governors of monasteries, abbeys, priories, and other houses and places exempt[3], in such cases as they were wont or might afore the making of this Act, by reason of grants or liberties of such places exempt to have or make immediately any appeal or provocation to the Bishop of Rome, otherwise called the Pope, or to the see of Rome, that in all these cases every person and persons having cause of appeal or provocation shall may[4] take and make their appeals and pro-

---

[1] 24 Henr. VIII, c. 12; see p. 41 below.   [2] See p. 347 below.
[3] See p. 36 n. below.
[4] Cf. 'shall mowe,' on p. 6 above. 'Mowe' is an obsolete form of 'may': cf. 11 Henr. VII, c. 5, 'No ship of great burden shall mowe come...in the said haven' (*Oxford Dictionary*).

vocations immediately to the King's Majesty of this realm into the Court of Chancery, in like manner and form as they used afore to do to the see of Rome; which appeals and provocations so made shall be definitively determined by authority of the King's commission in such manner and form as in this Act is above mentioned; so that no archbishop nor bishop of this realm shall intermit[1] or meddle with any such appeals otherwise or in any other manner than they might have done afore the making of this Act; any thing in this Act to the contrary thereof notwithstanding.   ⁎   ⁎   ⁎   ⁎   ⁎   ⁎

25 Henr. VIII, c. 19: *Statutes of the Realm*, iii, 460.

§ 3. Cessation of payments to the See of Rome

(1) Act in conditional Restraint of Annates, 1532

The first statute of the Reformation Parliament bearing upon Papal finance is of the nature of a diplomatic manœuvre. By withholding the 'payments due and accustomed,' the King sought to bring pressure to bear on the Pope to grant him a divorce from Catharine of Aragon[2].

Annates had long been regarded as a grievance, and a statute of the reign of Henry IV[3] had referred to them as a 'horrible mischief and damnable custom,' but the preamble of Henry VIII's statute exaggerates the grievance. It has been pointed out that the object of Tudor preambles is not to tell the truth but to make out a case, and the reference to 'great and inestimable sums of money' 'daily conveyed out of this realm to the impoverishment of the same' goes far beyond the facts. The King is authorised to compound with the Pope for annates, and pending some settlement, to declare by letters patent any time before the feast of Easter, 1533, or at any time before the beginning of the next Parliament, whether the Act should take effect or not. But in spite of its provisional character this legislation was opposed by all the bishops in the House of Lords, and by a considerable party in the House of Commons[4]. The most important feature in the Act, regarded as a step towards the separation of the Church of England from the Church of Rome, is that it sets up provisional machinery for the consecration of archbishops and bishops without the necessary bulls from Rome, and defies interdict and excommunication in advance, requiring the clergy to administer the sacraments 'or any other thing or things necessary for the health of the soul of mankind,' interdict or excommunication notwithstanding. Nevertheless the King is careful to assert that he and all his subjects 'be as obedient, devout,

---

[1] Interfere.

[2] The manœuvre failed as far as the Divorce was concerned, but it succeeded at another point, for the hope that the King would suspend the Act was one of the considerations which obtained from Rome the bulls for Cranmer's consecration as Archbishop (Fisher, p. 317).

[3] 6 Henr. IV, c. 1.

[4] Fisher, p. 315.

Catholic, and humble children of God and Holy Church as any people be within any realm christened.'

As soon as it became clear that concessions from Rome would not be forthcoming, the Act was allowed to take effect by letters patent dated 9 July, 1533.

An Act concerning restraint of payment of Annates[1] to the See of Rome

Forasmuch as it is well perceived by long approved experience that great and inestimable sums of money be daily conveyed out of this realm to the impoverishment of the same, and specially such sums of money as the Pope's Holiness, his predecessors, and the Court of Rome by long time have heretofore taken of all and singular those spiritual persons which have been named, elected, presented, or postulated to be archbishops or bishops within this realm of England, under the title of Annates, otherwise called firstfruits; which Annates or firstfruits heretofore have been taken of every archbishopric or bishopric within this realm by restraint of the Pope's bulls for confirmations, elections, admissions, postulations, provisions, collations, dispositions, institutions, installations, investitures, orders holy, benedictions, palls[2], or other things requisite and necessary to the attaining of those their promotions, and have been compelled to pay before they could attain the same great sums of money, before they might receive any part of the fruits of the said archbishopric or bishopric whereunto they were named, elected, presented, or postulated; By occasion whereof not only the treasure of this realm hath been greatly conveyed out of the same, but also it hath happened many times by occasion of death unto such archbishops and bishops so newly promoted within two or three years after his or their consecration, that his or their friends by whom he or they have been holpen to advance and make payment of the said Annates or firstfruits have been thereby utterly undone and impoverished; And for because the said Annates have risen, grown, and increased by an uncharitable custom grounded upon no just or good title, and the payments thereof obtained by restraint of bulls until the same Annates or firstfruits have been paid or surety made for the same, which declareth the said payments to be ex-

---

[1] 'Annates' are the entire revenues of one year, and are here identical with firstfruits.

[2] The *pallium* was a woollen vestment worn by the Pope, and conferred by him on certain ecclesiastics as a necessary preliminary to their exercising the functions of their office. Cf. Fuller's description of it: 'The breadth exceeded not three fingers (one of our Bachelor's lamb-skin hoods in Cambridge would make three of them) having two labels hanging down before and behind' (i, 107).

acted and taken by constraint, against all equity and justice; The noblemen therefore of this realm and the wise, sage, politic commons of the same assembled in this present Parliament, considering that the Court of Rome ceaseth not to tax, take, and exact the said great sums of money under the title of Annates or firstfruits as is aforesaid to the great damage of the said prelates and this realm, which Annates or firstfruits were first suffered to be taken within the same realm for the only defence of Christian people against the infidels[1], and now they be claimed and demanded as mere duty, only for lucre, against all right and conscience, insomuch that it is evidently known that there hath passed out of this realm unto the Court of Rome since the second year of the reign of the most noble Prince of famous memory King Henry the vijth unto this present time, under the name of Annates or firstfruits paid for the expedition of bulls of archbishoprics and bishoprics, the sum of eight hundred thousand ducats, amounting in sterling money at the least to eight score thousand pounds, besides other great and intolerable sums which have yearly been conveyed to the said Court of Rome by many other ways and means, to the great impoverishment of this realm; And albeit that our said Sovereign Lord the King and all his natural subjects as well spiritual as temporal be as obedient, devout, Catholic, and humble children of God and Holy Church as any people be within any realm christened, yet the said exactions of Annates or firstfruits be so intolerable and importable to this realm that it is considered and declared by the whole body of this realm now represented by all the estates of the same assembled in this present Parliament that the King's Highness before Almighty God is bound as by the duty of a good Christian prince, for the conservation and preservation of the good estate and commonwealth of this his realm, to do all that in him is to obviate, repress, and redress the said abusions and exactions of Annates or firstfruits; And because that divers prelates of this realm be now in extreme age and in other debilities of their bodies, so that of likelihood bodily death in short time shall or may succeed unto them; by reason whereof great sums of money shall shortly after their deaths be conveyed unto the Court of Rome for the unreasonable and uncharitable causes abovesaid, to the universal damage, prejudice, and impoverishment of this

[1] Cf. Dr Thomas Gascoigne (*ob.* 1458): 'Pope John XXII obtained' annates 'for the See of Rome to rescue the Land of Promise from the hands of Pagans and Gentiles, and since then these moneys remain to the Pope's Chamber, to be distributed among cardinals and chamberlains of the Pope....' Quoted in Gairdner (i, 256). Annates really originated, however, in voluntary gifts made to the authorities by bishops receiving episcopal consecration at Rome.

realm, if speedy remedy be not in due time provided; It is therefore ordained, established, and enacted by authority of this present
Parliament that the unlawful payments of Annates or firstfruits...
shall from henceforth utterly cease...and that no manner person or persons hereafter to be named, elected, presented, or postulated to any archbishopric or bishopric within this realm shall
pay the said Annates or firstfruits...upon pain to forfeit to our
said Sovereign Lord the King, his heirs and successors, all manner
his goods and chattels for ever, and all the temporal lands and
possessions of the same archbishopric or bishopric during the
time that he or they which shall offend contrary to this present
Act shall have, possess, or enjoy the archbishopric or bishopric
wherefore he shall so offend contrary to the form aforesaid.

[II. If the Court of Rome should delay or deny the 'bulls apostolic and
other things requisite' for the consecration of any prelate to be hereafter appointed by the Crown, he is to be consecrated without them; if a bishop,
by the archbishop in whose province the bishopric happens to be, and if an
archbishop, by a commission of two bishops appointed by the King.]

*   *   *   *   *   *

V. And if that upon the foresaid reasonable, amicable, and
charitable ways and means by the King's Highness to be experi-
mented, moved, and compounded or otherwise approved, it shall
and may appear or be seen unto his Grace that this realm shall be
continually burdened and charged with this and such other intolerable exactions and demands as heretofore it hath been; And
that thereupon for continuance of the same our said Holy Father
the Pope or any of his successors or the Court of Rome will or do
or cause to be done at any time hereafter so is as above rehearsed,
unjustly, uncharitably, and unreasonably vex, inquiet, molest,
trouble, or grieve our said Sovereign Lord, his heirs or successors
kings of England, or any of his or their spiritual or lay subjects
of this his realm, by excommunication, excommengement[1], interdiction, or by any other process, censures, compulsories, ways, or
means; Be it enacted by the authority aforesaid that the King's
Highness, his heirs and successors kings of England, and all his
spiritual and lay subjects of the same, without any scruple of conscience[2] shall and may lawfully to the honour of Almighty God,
the increase and continuance of virtue and good example within
this realm, the said censures, excommunications, interdictions,
compulsories, or any of them notwithstanding, minister or cause

---

[1] Excommunication.

[2] For the State to be absolving scruples of conscience is a novel invasion of the
province of the Church.

to be ministered throughout this said realm and all other the dominions and territories belonging or appertaining thereunto, all and all manner sacraments, sacramentals, ceremonies, or other divine service of Holy Church, or any other thing or things necessary for the health of the soul of mankind, as they heretofore at any time or times have been virtuously used or accustomed to do within the same....

23 Henr VIII, c. 20: Statutes of the Realm, iii, 385.

(2) Act in absolute restraint of Annates, 1534

This Act recites and confirms the Act of 1532 and provides that, since the 'gentle ways' contemplated in that Act had proved ineffectual, no man should hereafter be presented to the 'Bishop of Rome, otherwise called the Pope,' for the dignity of an archbishop or bishop, nor should procure from Rome 'bulls, briefs, palls, or other things requisite for an archbishop or bishop,' nor should 'pay any sums of money for annates, firstfruits, or otherwise, for expedition of such bulls, briefs, or palls,' but that 'such bulls, briefs, palls, annates, firstfruits' and other payments to Rome 'shall utterly cease and no longer be used' within the realm. But this Act of 1534 also deals with the more important question of the election of bishops. It had been the custom in the case of a vacant abbey for the abbey chapter to apply to the founder or founder's heir for 'leave to elect' a new abbot; and in such a case the founder would sometimes send with the congé d'élire a 'letter missive' recommending a particular candidate to the consideration of the chapter. As the kings of England claimed to be the founders of the English bishoprics, the same procedure was followed in the case of a vacant see. In theory the choice of the cathedral chapter was free, but in practice any recommendation in a royal 'letter missive' would be received with great respect. What the Act of 1534 does is to make occasional royal interference habitual and to subject the dean and chapter to the penalties of praemunire if they fail to elect the King's nominee[1]. Should they defer or delay the election for more than twelve days, the King is empowered to appoint by letters patent. Under the same penalties the archbishop is required to proceed to consecration.

An Act restraining the payment of Annates, etc.

[I. Recites 23 Henr. VIII, c. 20, and its confirmation by the King's letters patent.]

II. And forasmuch as in the said Act it is not plainly and certainly expressed in what manner and fashion archbishops and

---

[1] The legal position is exactly defined in Lord John Russell's reply to a member of the Cathedral Chapter of Hereford, who wrote to him in 1848 to say that he could not conscientiously vote for Dr Hampden: 'Sir,—I have the honour to acknowledge your letter of the 20th instant in which you announce your intention of breaking the law.'

bishops shall be elected, presented, invested, and consecrated within this realm and in all other the King's dominions: Be it now therefore enacted...that the said Act and everything therein contained shall be and stand in strength, virtue, and effect; except only that no person nor persons hereafter shall be presented, nominated, or commended to the said Bishop of Rome, otherwise called the Pope, or to the see of Rome, to or for the dignity or office of any archbishop or bishop within this realm or in any other the King's dominions, nor shall send nor procure the e for any manner of bulls, briefs, palls, or other things requisite for an archbishop or bishop, nor shall pay any sums of money for Annates, firstfruits, or otherwise, for expedition of any such bulls, briefs, or palls; but that by the authority of this Act such presenting, nominating, or commending to the said Bishop of Rome or to the see of Rome, and such bulls, briefs, palls, annates, firstfruits, and every other sums of money heretofore limited, accustomed, or used to be paid at the said see of Rome for procuration or expedition of any such bulls, briefs, or palls, or other thing concerning the same, shall utterly cease and no longer be used within this realm or within any the King's dominions; anything contained in the said Act aforementioned, or any use, custom, or prescription to the contrary thereof notwithstanding.

III. And furthermore be it ordained and established by the authority aforesaid, that at every avoidance of any archbishopric or bishopric within this realm or in any other the King's dominions, the King our Sovereign Lord, his heirs and successors, may grant unto the prior and convent or the dean and chapter of the cathedral churches or monasteries where the see of such archbishopric or bishopric shall happen to be void, a licence under the great seal[1], as of old time hath been accustomed, to proceed to election of an archbishop or bishop of the see so being void, with a letter missive[1] containing the name of the person which they shall elect and choose; By virtue of which licence the said dean and chapter or prior and convent to whom any such licence and letters missives shall be directed, shall with all speed and celerity in due form elect and choose the said person named in the said letters missives to the dignity and office of the archbishopric or bishopric so being void, and none other; and if they do defer or delay their election above 12 days next after such licence and letters missives to them delivered, that then for every

---

[1] A *congé d'élire* for an election to the Bishopric of Ely, dated 18 July, 1559, and a letter missive recommending Dr Herbert Westphaling for election to the Bishopric of Hereford, dated 23 November, 1585, are printed in Prothero, p. 242.

such default the King's Highness, his heirs and successors, at their liberty and pleasure shall nominate and present, by their letters patents under their great seal, such a person to the said office and dignity so being void as they shall think able and convenient for the same....

* * * * * *

VI. And be it further enacted by the authority aforesaid, that if the prior and convent of any monastery or dean and chapter of any cathedral church where the see of any archbishop or bishop is within any of the King's dominions, after such licence as is afore rehearsed shall be delivered to them, proceed not to election and signify the same according to the tenor of this Act within the space of 20 days next after such licence shall come to their hands, or else if any archbishop or bishop within any the King's dominions, after any such election, nomination, or presentation shall be signified unto them by the King's letters patents[1], shall refuse and do not confirm, invest, and consecrate with all due circumstance as is aforesaid every such person as shall be so elected, nominate, or presented and to them signified as is above mentioned, within 20 days next after the King's letters patents of such signification or presentation shall come to their hands; or else if any of them or any other person or persons admit, maintain, allow, obey, do, or execute any censures, excommunications, interdictions, inhibitions, or any other process or act of what nature, name, or quality soever it be, to the contrary or let of due execution of this Act, that then every prior and particular person of his convent, and every dean and particular person of the chapter, and every archbishop and bishop and all other persons so offending and doing contrary to this Act or any part thereof, and their aiders, counsellors, and abettors, shall run into the dangers, pains, and penalties of the statute of the provision and praemunire made in the twenty-fifth year of the reign of King Edward the Third[2] and in the sixteenth year of King Richard the Second[3].

25 Henr. VIII, c. 20: *Statutes of the Realm*, iii, 462.

(3) The Dispensations Act, 1534

This Act forbade the payment to Rome of Peter's Pence 'or any other impositions.' Peter's Pence was an annual tribute to Rome, first paid in England, which originally took the form of a penny from each householder owning land of a certain value[4]. It has been variously attributed to

---

[1] *I.e.* in the event of the Dean and Chapter failing to elect the King's nominee.
[2] The First Statute of Provisors, 1351.
[3] The Second Statute o. Praemunire, 1393.
[4] See *The Catholic Encyclopedia*.

Ine, King of Wessex (688–726), to Offa, King of Mercia (in 787), and to Ethelwulf, King of Kent (*c.* 855). It was regularly paid from the reign of William I, but some time in the twelfth century the English bishops compounded with the Papacy for a fixed annual payment of £200; it was therefore only a small part of the revenue paid to Rome.

The Act further provides that dispensations, hitherto obtained from Rome at a price, are in future to be granted by the Archbishop of Canterbury on terms set forth in the Act. But the visitation of monasteries 'exempt,' hitherto visited only by the Papacy, is not assigned to the archbishop, but to 'the King's Highness' 'by commission under the great seal.' It is in this Act that a phrase occurs which suggests how little Henry VIII's Reformation was intended to be doctrinal—that the King and realm do not intend 'to decline or vary from the congregation of Christ's Church in any things concerning the very articles of the Catholic faith of Christendom.'

An Act for the exoneration from exactions paid to the See of Rome

Most humbly beseech your most Royal Majesty your obedient and faithful subjects the Commons of this your present Parliament assembled by your most dread commandment; That where your subjects of this your realm, and of other countries and dominions being under your obeisance, by many years past have been and yet be greatly decayed and impoverished by such intolerable exactions of great sums of money as have been claimed and taken and yet continually be claimed to be taken out of this your realm, and other your said countries and dominions, by the Bishop of Rome called the Pope, and the see of Rome, as well in pensions, censes[1], Peter pence, procurations, fruits, suits for provisions, and expeditions of bulls for archbishoprics and bishoprics, and for delegacies, and rescripts in causes of contentions and appeals, jurisdictions legatine, and also for dispensations, licences, faculties, grants, relaxations, writs called *perinde valere*, rehabilitations, abolitions, and other infinite sorts of bulls, briefs, and instruments of sundry natures, names, and kinds in great numbers heretofore practised and obtained otherwise than by the laws, laudable uses, and customs of this realm should be permitted, the specialities whereof be over long, large in number, and tedious here particularly to be inserted; wherein the Bishop of Rome aforesaid hath not been only to be blamed for his usurpation in the premises but also for his abusing and beguiling your subjects, pretending and persuading to them that he hath full power to dispense with all human laws, uses, and customs of all realms in all causes which be called spiritual, which matter hath been usurped and practised by him and his predecessors by many

---

[1] *Census* was a term applied to any kind of tribute or tax.

years in great derogation of your imperial Crown and authority royal, contrary to right and conscience; For where this your Grace's realm, recognising no superior under God but only your Grace, hath been and is free from subjection to any man's laws, but only to such as have been devised, made, and ordained within this realm for the wealth[1] of the same, or to such other as by sufferance of your Grace and your progenitors the people of this your realm have taken at their free liberty by their own consent to be used amongst them, and have bound themselves by long use and custom to the observance of the same, not as to the observance of the laws of any foreign prince, potentate, or prelate, but as to the accustomed and ancient laws of this realm originally established as laws of the same by the said sufferance, consents, and custom, and none otherwise: It standeth therefore with natural equity and good reason that in all and every such laws human, made within this realm or induced into this realm by the said sufferance, consents, and custom, your Royal Majesty and your Lords spiritual and temporal and Commons, representing the whole state of your realm in this your most high Court of Parliament, have full power and authority not only to dispense but also to authorise some elect person or persons to dispense with those and all other human laws of this your realm and with every one of them, as the quality of the persons and matter shall require: And also the said laws and every of them to abrogate, annul, amplify, or diminish, as it shall be seen unto your Majesty and the Nobles and Commons of your realm present in your Parliament meet and convenient for the wealth of your realm, as by divers good and wholesome Acts of Parliament made and established as well in your time as in the time of your most noble progenitors it may plainly and evidently appear; And by cause that it is now in these days present seen that the state, dignity, superiority, reputation, and authority of the said imperial Crown of this realm, by the long sufferance of the said unreasonable and uncharitable usurpations and exactions practised in the times of your most noble progenitors, is much and sore decayed and diminished, and the people of this realm thereby impoverished and so worse be like to continue if remedy be not therefor shortly provided:

It may therefore please your most noble Majesty for the honour of Almighty God and for the tender love, zeal, and affection that you bear and always have borne to the wealth of this your

---

[1] 'Wealth' in the sense of welfare: cf. 'commonwealth' in the sense of 'commonweal.'

realm and subjects of the same, forasmuch as your Majesty is Supreme Head of the Church of England, as the prelates and clergy of your realm representing the said Church in their synods and convocations have recognised[1], in whom consisteth full power and authority upon all such laws as have been made and used within this realm, to ordain and enact by the assent of your Lords spiritual and temporal and the Commons in this your present Parliament assembled and by authority of the same, that no person or persons of this your realm or of any other your dominions shall from henceforth pay any pensions, censes, portions, Peter pence, or any other impositions to the use of the said Bishop or of the see of Rome, like as heretofore they have used by usurpation of the said Bishop of Rome and his predecessors and sufferance of your Highness and your most noble progenitors to do; but that all such pensions, censes, portions, and Peter pence, which the said Bishop of Rome otherwise called the Pope hath heretofore taken and perceived[2] or caused to be taken and perceived to his use and his chambers which he calleth apostolic[3] by usurpation and sufferance as is abovesaid within this your realm or any other your dominions, shall from henceforth clearly surcease and never more be levied, taken, perceived, nor paid to any person or persons in any manner of wise; any constitution, use, prescription, or custom to the contrary thereof notwithstanding.

II. And be it further enacted by the authority aforesaid that neither your Highness, your heirs nor successors, kings of this realm, nor any your subjects of this realm nor of any other your dominions, shall from henceforth sue to the said Bishop of Rome called the Pope, or to the see of Rome, or to any person or persons having or pretending any authority by the same, for licences, dispensations, compositions, faculties, grants, rescripts, delegacies, or any other instruments or writings of what kind, name, nature, or quality so ever they be of, for any cause or matter for the which any licence, dispensation, [etc.]...heretofore hath been used and accustomed to be had and obtained at the see of Rome or by authority thereof, or of any prelate of this realm, nor for any manner of other licences, dispensations, [etc.]...that in causes of necessity may lawfully be granted without offending of the Holy Scriptures and laws of God: But that from henceforth every such

---

[1] By the Submission of the Clergy: see p. 17 above.
[2] 'Perceive' is used in the sense of taking into possession: it was often applied to the recovering of rents or dues.
[3] The Apostolic Camera was the central board of finance in the Papal administrative system. To this Peter's pence and other alms of the faithful were paid.

licence, dispensation [etc.]...necessary for your Highness, your heirs and successors, and your and their people and subjects, upon the due examinations of the causes and qualities of the persons procuring such dispensations, licences, [etc.]...shall be granted, had, and obtained from time to time within this your realm and other your dominions and not elsewhere in manner and form following and none otherwise, that is to say; the Archbishop of Canterbury for the time being and his successors shall have power and authority from time to time by their discretions to give, grant, and dispose by an instrument under the seal of the said Archbishop unto your Majesty and to your heirs and successors kings of this realm, as well all manner such licences, dispensations, [etc.]...for causes not being contrary or repugnant to the Holy Scriptures and laws of God, as heretofore hath been used and accustomed to be had and obtained by your Highness or any your most noble progenitors, or any of yours or their subjects, at the see of Rome or any person or persons by authority of the same, and all other licences, dispensations, [etc.]...in, for, and upon all such causes and matters as shall be convenient and necessary to be had for the honour and surety of your Highness, your heirs and successors, and the wealth and profit of this your realm; so that the said Archbishop or any his successors in no manner of wise shall grant any dispensation, licence, rescript, or any other writing afore rehearsed for any cause or matter repugnant to the law of Almighty God.

* * * * * *

XIII. Provided always that this Act nor any thing or things therein contained shall be hereafter interpreted or expounded that your Grace, your nobles and subjects, intend by the same to decline or vary from the congregation of Christ's Church in any things concerning the very articles of the Catholic Faith of Christendom; or in any other things declared by Holy Scripture and the word of God necessary for your and their salvations; but only to make an ordinance by policies necessary and convenient to repress vice and for good conservation of this realm in peace, unity, and tranquillity from ravin and spoil, ensuing much the old ancient customs of this realm in that behalf, not minding to seek for any reliefs, succours, or remedies for any worldly things or human laws in any cause of necessity but within this realm at the hands of your Highness, your heirs and successors kings of this realm, which have and ought to have an imperial power and authority in the same and not obliged in any worldly causes to any other superior.

XIV. Provided alway that the said Archbishop of Canterbury or any other person or persons shall have no power or authority by reason of this Act to visit or vex any monasteries, abbeys, priories, colleges, hospitals, houses, or other places religious which be or were exempt[1] before the making of this Act, anything in this Act to the contrary thereof notwithstanding; but that redress, visitation, and confirmation shall be had by the King's Highness, his heirs and successors, by commission under the great seal to be directed to such persons as shall be appointed requisite for the same, in such monasteries, colleges, hospitals, priories, houses, and places religious exempt; So that no visitation nor confirmation shall from henceforth be had nor made in or at any such monasteries, colleges, hospitals, priories, houses, and places religious exempt, by the said Bishop of Rome nor by any of his authority nor by any out of the King's dominions; Nor that any person religious or other resiant[2] in any the King's dominions shall from henceforth depart out of the King's dominions to or for any visitation, congregation, or assembly for religion, but that all such visitations, congregations, and assemblies shall be within the King's dominions.

* * * * * *

XXI. And be it enacted by authority of this present Parliament, that the King our Sovereign Lord by the advice of his honourable Council shall have power and authority from time to time for the ordering, redress, and reformation of all manner of indulgences and privileges thereof within this realm or within any the King's dominions heretofore obtained at the see of Rome or by authority thereof, and of the abuses of such indulgences and privileges thereof, as shall seem good, wholesome, and reasonable for the honour of God and weal of his people. And that such order and redress as shall be taken by his Highness in that behalf shall be observed and firmly kept upon the pains limited in this Act for the offending of the contents of the same.

* * * * * *

25 Henr. VIII, c. 21: *Statutes of the Realm*, iii, 464.

(4) Act annexing Firstfruits and Tenths to the Crown, 1534

In March, 1533, the King had told Chapuys that he held himself bound by his coronation oath to unite to the Crown the goods which churchmen held of it[3], and an extensive scheme of secularisation was prepared; but the

---

[1] *I.e.* exempt from visitation by the Bishop of the diocese; see note on p. 51 below.

[2] Resident. [3] Fisher, p. 345.

only part of it which was carried into effect was the appropriation of first-fruits and tenths[1]. The Act in conditional restraint of annates had referred to firstfruits as now 'intolerable and importable,' having 'risen, grown, and increased by an uncharitable custom grounded upon no just or good title,' and had represented the realm as impoverished, and the bishops and their friends as 'utterly undone' by the burden laid upon them. Thus in annexing them to the Crown the King was in a position of some delicacy, and the pre-amble of the statute is a triumph of rhetorical skill and ingenuity.

In 1703 firstfruits and tenths were assigned by the Crown to trustees, called the Governors of Queen Anne's Bounty, for the augmentation of poor livings. The burden is one now easily borne by the clergy, as firstfruits and tenths are calculated, not in modern values but in those fixed by the *Valor Ecclesiasticus*, a survey of ecclesiastical property throughout England and Wales compiled by Henry VIII's direction in 1535[2].

An Act concerning the payment of First Fruits of all dignities, benefices, and promotions spiritual; and also concerning one annual pension of the tenth part of all the possessions of the Church, spiritual and tem-poral, granted to the King's Highness and his heirs

Forasmuch as it is and of very duty ought to be the natural inclination of all good people, like most faithful, loving, and obedient subjects, sincerely and willingly to desire to provide not only for the public weal of their native country but also for the

---

[1] A later statute, 27 Henr. VIII, c. 42 (1536), exempts the Universities and Colleges of Oxford and Cambridge and the Colleges of Eton and Winchester, and the officers and students of the same, from the payment of firstfruits and tenths, out of the King's 'most excellent goodness and divine charity, with the fervent zeal which his Majesty hath conceived and beareth, as well principally to the advance-ment of the sincere and pure doctrine of God's Word and Holy Testament, as to the increase of the knowledge in the seven liberal sciences, and the three tongues of Latin, Greek, and Hebrew, to be by his people applied and learned.' The 'seven liberal sciences' were those of the *trivium* (Grammar, Logic, and Rhetoric) and the *quadrivium* (Arithmetic, Geometry, Music, and Astronomy). In consideration of this, each University was to maintain 'one discreet and learned personage to read one open and public lecture' in 'any such science or tongue' as the King might appoint, and the Chancellors of the Universities, the Provost of Eton, and the Warden of Winchester were to cause two masses to be sung yearly, on May 8 and October 8, and after the King's death to keep these days as 'solemn anniversaries, that is to say, *dirige* overnight and mass of requiem in the next morrow.'

[2] The survey was the work of a Commission, appointed 30 January, 1535, under Sections 9 and 10 of the Act, and was completed in about six months. It superseded the *Taxatio* of Pope Nicholas IV, made in 1291. It is printed in the Rolls Series, but see the criticism of this edition by Dr A. Savine (*Oxford Studies*, i, 22). The difference between this valuation and modern figures may be illustrated by the case of the Rectory of Hockwold in Norfolk, now worth about £500 a year. This is valued in the *Valor Ecclesiasticus* at £9. 13s. 11½d.; the Rector therefore pays £9. 13s. 11d. to the Governors of Queen Anne's Bounty as firstfruits on insti-tution, and 19s. 4d. every year as tenths.

supportation, maintenance, and defence of the royal estate of their most dread, benign, and gracious Sovereign Lord, upon whom and in whom dependeth all their joy and wealth[1], in whom also is united and knit so princely a heart and courage, mixed with mercy, wisdom, and justice, and also a natural affection joined to the same, as by the great, inestimable, and benevolent arguments thereof being most bountifully, largely, and many times shewed, ministered, and approved towards his loving and obedient subjects hath well appeared, which requireth a like correspondence of gratitude to be considered according to their most bounden duties; Wherefore his said humble and obedient subjects, as well the Lords spiritual and temporal as the Commons in this present Parliament assembled, calling to their remembrance not only the manifold and innumerable benefits daily administered by his Highness to them all, and to the residue of all other his subjects of this realm, but also how long time his Majesty hath most victoriously by his high wisdom and policy protected, defended, and governed this his realm and maintained his people and subjects of the same in tranquillity, peace, unity, quietness, and wealth[2]; And also considering what great, excessive, and inestimable charges his Highness hath heretofore been at and sustained by the space of five and twenty whole years, and also daily sustaineth for the maintenance, tuition, and defence of this his realm and his loving subjects of the same, which cannot be sustained and borne without some honourable provision and remedy may be found, provided, and ordained for maintenance thereof, do therefore desire and most humbly pray that for the more surety of continuance and augmentation of his Highness's royal estate, being not only now recognised (as he always in deed heretofore hath been) the only Supreme Head in earth next and immediately under God of the Church of England, but also their most assured and undoubted natural sovereign liege Lord and King, having the whole governance, tuition, defence, and maintenance of this his realm and most loving, obedient subjects of the same: It may therefore be ordained and enacted by his Highness and the Lords spiritual and temporal and the Commons in this present Parliament assembled and by authority of the same in manner and form following; That is to say, that the King's Highness, his heirs and successors kings of

---

[1] See note on p. 33 above.

[2] Cf. 37 Henr. VIII, c. 25. 'We, the people of this his realm, have for the most part of us so lived under his Majesty's sure protection...even as the small fishes of the sea, in the most tempestuous and stormy weather, do lie quietly under the rock or bank side, and are not moved with the surges of the water, nor stirred out of their quiet place, howsoever the wind bloweth.'

this realm, shall have and enjoy from time to time, to endure for
ever, of every such person and persons which at any time after the
first day of January next coming shall be nominated, elected, prefected, presented, collated, or by any other means appointed to
have any archbishopric, bishopric, abbacy, monastery, priory,
college, hospital, archdeaconry, deanery, provostship, prebend,
parsonage, vicarage, chantry, free chapel, or other dignity, benefice, office, or promotion spiritual within this realm or elsewhere
within any of the King's dominions, of what name, nature, or
quality soever they be or to whose foundation, patronage, or gift
soever they belong, the firstfruits, revenues, and profits for one year
of every such archbishopric, bishopric [etc.]...whereunto any such
person or persons shall after the said first day of January be nominated, elected, prefected, presented, collated, or by any other
means appointed; and that every such person and persons, before
any actual or real possession or meddling with the profits of any
such archbishopric, bishopric, [etc.]...shall satisfy, content, and pay,
or compound or agree to pay to the King's use at reasonable days
upon good sureties the said firstfruits and profits for one year.

*　*　*　*　*　*

VIII. And over this be it enacted by authority aforesaid that
the King's Majesty, his heirs and successors kings of this realm,
for more augmentation and maintenance of the royal estate of his
imperial Crown and dignity of Supreme Head of the Church of
England, shall yearly have, take, enjoy, and perceive[1], united and
knit to his imperial Crown for ever, one yearly rent or pension
amounting to the value of the tenth part of all the revenues, rents,
ferms[2], tithes, offerings, emoluments, and of all other profits, as
well called spiritual as temporal, now appertaining or belonging
or that hereafter shall belong to any archbishopric, bishopric,
abbacy, monastery, priory, archdeaconry, deanery, hospital, college, house collegiate, prebend, cathedral church, collegiate church,
conventual church, parsonage, vicarage, chantry, free chapel, or
other benefice or promotion spiritual, of what name, nature, or
quality soever they be, within any diocese of this realm or in
Wales; the said pension or annual rent to be yearly paid for ever
to our said Sovereign Lord....

*　*　*　*　*　*

26 Henr. VIII, c. 3: *Statutes of the Realm*, iii, 493.

[1] See note on p. 34 above.
[2] A 'ferm' or 'farm' is a fixed annual rent.

§ 4. Prohibition of Appeals to Rome

The prohibition of appeals to Rome grew inevitably out of the Divorce Case. In January, 1533, the King had been secretly married to Anne Boleyn, in anticipation of a judgment in his favour to be pronounced by the English ecclesiastical courts; and it was important in that event to prevent the case of Queen Catharine being carried to Rome by way of appeal.

(1) Act in Restraint of Appeals, 1533

This Act, which was passed through Parliament in spite of some opposition in the Lower House, is an historical landmark of great importance, for the preamble embodies a view of the relations of Church and State on which all subsequent legislation has proceeded, down to modern times[1]. It declares the realm of England to be an empire, and asserts in the most formal manner the insular independence of the nation-church within the nation-state. It should be noted that the word 'empire' is not here used in the modern sense, still less in the sense in which we speak of the 'empire' of the Caesars. The British Empire and the Roman Empire differ in important respects, but they are alike in this that they were built up from within outwards by means of a great expansion. The 'empire' of Henry VIII is the result of the opposite process; it is the nation-state contracting itself upon its insularity. The object of the statute is to deny the subjection of the insular power to any external authority, temporal or spiritual, and it thus embodies the fundamental principle of Henry VIII's Reformation. All spiritual causes concerning wills, marriage, and tithe are to be finally adjudged and determined within the realm, appeals being carried from the archdeacon to the bishop of the diocese, and from the bishop to the archbishop of the province, save in causes touching the King, which might be carried to 'the spiritual prelates and other abbots and priors' of the Upper House of Convocation. This Act was subsequently modified by the Act for the Submission of the Clergy of 1534 (p. 22), which provided that a final appeal from the Archbishop's Court should lie to the King in Chancery, who should appoint a special commission, 'like as in case of appeal from the Admiral Court,' to hear and determine each case; and the same procedure was to be adopted in the case of appeals from monasteries exempt, which had hitherto been entitled to appeal direct to the see of Rome. These special commissions appointed *ad hoc* were called 'Courts of Delegates,' the term being taken from the corresponding procedure of the Admiral's Court[2]. While the Act of Appeals was pending, Convocation was persuaded or driven to admit that the Pope could not by dispensation sanction a marriage with a brother's widow, and on May 23, 1533, Cranmer, sitting in his archiepiscopal court at Dunstable, pronounced the marriage with Catharine of Aragon to be null and void. At Lambeth, five days later, after a secret enquiry, he found the marriage already contracted with Anne Boleyn to be valid, and on Whitsunday, June 1, she was crowned queen.

---

[1] Stephen, ii, 477.
[2] See p. 347 below.

An Act that the Appeals in such cases as have been used to be pursued to the See of Rome shall not be from henceforth had nor used but within this Realm

Where by divers sundry old authentic histories and chronicles it is manifestly declared and expressed that this realm of England is an empire[1], and so hath been accepted in the world, governed by one Supreme Head and King having the dignity and royal estate of the imperial Crown of the same, unto whom a body politic, compact of all sorts and degrees of people divided in terms and by names of Spiritualty and Temporalty, be bounden and owe to bear next to God a natural and humble obedience; he being also institute and furnished by the goodness and sufferance of Almighty God with plenary, whole, and entire power, preeminence, authority, prerogative, and jurisdiction to render and yield justice and final determination to all manner of folk resiants[2] or subjects within this his realm, in all causes, matters, debates, and contentions happening to occur, insurge, or begin within the limits thereof, without restraint or provocation[3] to any foreign princes or potentates of the world: the body spiritual whereof having power when any cause of the law divine happened to come in question or of spiritual learning, then it was declared, interpreted, and shewed by that part of the said body politic called the Spiritualty, now being usually called the English Church, which always hath been reputed and also found of that sort that both for knowledge, integrity, and sufficiency of number, it hath been always thought and is also at this hour sufficient and meet of itself, without the intermeddling of any exterior person or persons, to declare and determine all such doubts and to administer all such offices and duties as to their rooms spiritual doth appertain; For the due administration whereof and to keep them from corruption and sinister affection the King's most noble progenitors, and the antecessors of the nobles of this realm, have sufficiently endowed the said Church both with honour and possessions: And the laws temporal for trial of propriety of lands and goods, and for the conservation of the people of this realm in unity and peace without ravin or spoil, was and yet is administered, adjudged, and executed by sundry judges and administers[4] of the other part of the

---

[1] The Anglo-Saxon kings from Athelstan to Canute claimed and used imperial titles, such as *imperator* (see Freeman, i, 133–147); and the term 'emperor' is used of Edward I, Richard II, and Henry V. See also an article by Professor C. H. Firth in the *Scottish Historical Review*, xv, 185, on the use of the phrase 'British Empire.'

[2] Residents.   [3] See note on p. 45.

[4] *I.e.* ministers or administrators.

said body politic called the Temporalty, and both their authorities and jurisdictions do conjoin together in the due administration of justice the one to help the other: And whereas the King his most noble progenitors, and the Nobility and Commons of this said realm, at divers and sundry Parliaments as well in the time of King Edward the First[1], Edward the Third[2], Richard the Second[3], Henry the Fourth[4], and other noble kings of this realm, made sundry ordinances, laws, statutes, and provisions for the entire and sure conservation of the prerogatives, liberties, and preeminences of the said imperial Crown of this realm, and of the jurisdictions spiritual and temporal of the same, to keep it from the annoyance as well of the see of Rome as from the authority of other foreign potentates attempting the diminution or violation thereof as often and from time to time as any such annoyance or attempt might be known or espied: And notwithstanding the said good estatutes and ordinances made in the time of the King's most noble progenitors in preservation of the authority and prerogative of the said imperial Crown as is aforesaid, yet nevertheless since the making of the said good statutes and ordinances divers and sundry inconveniences and dangers not provided for plainly by the said former acts, statutes, and ordinances have risen and sprung by reason of appeals sued out of this realm to the see of Rome, in causes testamentary, causes of matrimony and divorces, right of tithes, oblations, and obventions[5], not only to the great inquietation, vexation, trouble, costs, and charges of the King's Highness and many of his subjects and resiants in this his realm, but also to the great delay and let to the true and speedy determination of the said causes, for so much as the parties appealing to the said court of Rome most commonly do the same for the delay of justice: And forasmuch as the great distance of way is so far out of this realm, so that the necessary proofs nor the true knowledge of the cause can neither there be so well known nor the witnesses there so well examined as within this realm, so that the parties grieved by

[1] The Statute of Carlisle, 1307 (35 Edw. I, st. 1), an Act against the abuses of papal patronage (Gee and Hardy, p. 92).
[2] The First Statute of Provisors, 1351 (25 Edw. III, st. 4) and the First Statute of Praemunire, 1353 (27 Edw. III, st. 1).
[3] The Second Statute of Provisors, 1390 (13 Rich. II, st. 2) and the Second Statute of Praemunire, 1393 (16 Rich. II, c. 5).
[4] 2 Henr. IV, c. 3, confirmed and extended the Second Statute of Provisors and this was again confirmed by 9 Henr. IV, c. 8; 2 Henr. IV, c. 4, forbade bulls from Rome for exemption from tithe.
[5] 'Oblations' here include whatever is assigned to pious uses; 'obventions' in ecclesiastical law are fees occasionally received.

means of the said appeals be most times without remedy: In consideration whereof the King's Highness, his Nobles and Commons, considering the great enormities, dangers, long delays, and hurts that as well to his Highness as to his said nobles, subjects, commons, and resiants of this his realm in the said causes testamentary, causes of matrimony and divorces, tithes, oblations, and obventions do daily ensue, doth therefore by his royal assent and by the assent of the Lords spiritual and temporal and the Commons in this present Parliament assembled and by authority of the same, enact, establish, and ordain that all causes testamentary, causes of matrimony and divorces, rights of tithes, oblations, and obventions, the knowledge whereof by the goodness of princes of this realm and by the laws and customs of the same appertaineth to the spiritual jurisdiction of this realm already commenced, moved, depending, being, happening, or hereafter coming in contention, debate, or question within this realm or within any the King's dominions or marches of the same or elsewhere, whether they concern the King our Sovereign Lord, his heirs or successors, or any other subjects or resiants within the same of what degree soever they be, shall be from henceforth heard, examined, discussed, clearly finally and definitively adjudged and determined, within the King's jurisdiction and authority and not elsewhere, in such courts spiritual and temporal of the same as the natures, conditions, and qualities of the causes and matters aforesaid in contention or hereafter happening in contention shall require, without having any respect to any custom, use, or sufferance in hindrance, let, or prejudice of the same or to any other thing used or suffered to the contrary thereof by any other manner person or persons in any manner of wise; any foreign inhibitions, appeals, sentences, summons, citations, suspensions, interdictions, excommunications, restraints, judgments, or any other process or impediments of what natures, names, qualities, or conditions soever they be, from the see of Rome or any other foreign courts or potentates of the world, or from and out of this realm or any other the King's dominions or marches of the same to the see of Rome or to any other foreign courts or potentates, to the let or impediment thereof in any wise notwithstanding. And that it shall be lawful to the King our Sovereign Lord and to his heirs and successors, and to all other subjects or resiants within this realm or within any the King's dominions or marches of the same, notwithstanding that hereafter it should happen any excommengement[1], excommunications, interdictions, citations, or any other

[1] Excommunication.

censures or foreign process out of any outward parties to be ful-
minate, provulged[1], declared, or put in execution within this said
realm or in any other place or places for any of the causes before
rehearsed, in prejudice, derogation, or contempt of this said Act
and the very true meaning and execution thereof, may and shall
nevertheless as well pursue, execute, have, and enjoy the effects,
profits, benefits, and commodities of all such processes, sentences,
judgments, and determinations, done or hereafter to be done in
any of the said courts spiritual or temporal as the cases shall require,
within the limits, power, and authority of this the King's said
realm and dominions and marches of the same, and those only
and none other to take place and to be firmly observed and obeyed
within the same: As also that all spiritual prelates, pastors, ministers, and curates within this realm and the dominions of the same
shall and may use, minister, execute, and do, or cause to be used,
ministered, executed, and done, all sacraments, sacramentals[2], divine
services, and all other things within the said realm and dominions
unto all the subjects of the same as Catholic and Christian men
owe to do; Any foreign citations, processes, inhibitions, suspensions, interdictions, excommunications, or appeals for or touching
any of the causes aforesaid from or to the see of Rome or any
other foreign prince or foreign courts to the let or contrary thereof
in any wise notwithstanding. And if any of the said spiritual persons, by the occasion of the said fulminations of any of the same
interdictions, censures, inhibitions, excommunications, appeals,
suspensions, summons, or other foreign citations for the causes
beforesaid or for any of them, do at any time hereafter refuse to
minister or to cause to be ministered the said sacraments and sacramentals and other divine services in form as is aforesaid, shall for
every such time or times that they or any of them do refuse so to
do or to cause to be done, have one year's imprisonment and to
make fine and ransom at the King's pleasure.

II. And it is further enacted...that if any person or persons
...do attempt, move, purchase, or procure, from or to the see of
Rome or from or to any other foreign court or courts out of this
realm, any manner foreign process, inhibitions, appeals, sentences,
summons, citations, suspensions, interdictions, excommunications,
restraints, or judgments, of what nature, kind, or quality soever
they be, or execute any of the same process, or do any act or acts
to the let, impediment, hindrance, or derogation of any process,

---

[1] Published.
[2] Rites or ceremonies analogous to a sacrament but not reckoned among the
sacraments, *e.g.* the sign of the cross or the use of holy water.

sentence, judgment, or determination had, made, done, or hereafter to be had, done, or made in any courts of this realm or the
King's said dominions or marches of the same for any of the
causes aforesaid...that then every person or persons so doing,
and their fautors[1], comforters, abettors, procurers, executors, and
counsellors, and every of them being convict of the same, for every
such default shall incur and run in the same pains, penalties, and
forfeitures ordained and provided by the statute of provision and
praemunire made in the sixteenth year of the reign of...King
Richard the Second[2]....

III. And furthermore in eschewing the said great enormities,
inquietations, delays, charges, and expenses hereafter to be sustained in pursuing of such appeals and foreign process...do
therefore...ordain and enact that in such cases where heretofore
any of the King's subjects or resiants[3] have used to pursue, provoke, or procure any appeal to the see of Rome...they...shall
from henceforth take, have, and use their appeals within this
realm and not elsewhere, in manner and form as hereafter ensueth
and not otherwise; that is to say, First from the archdeacon or
his official, if the matter or cause be there begun, to the bishop
diocesan of the said see...; And likewise, if it be commenced
before the bishop diocesan or his commissary, from the bishop
diocesan or his commissary, within fifteen days next ensuing the
judgment or sentence thereof there given, to the archbishop of the
province of Canterbury, if it be within his province, and if it be
within the province of York then to the archbishop of York; and
so likewise to all other archbishops in other the King's dominions
as the case by the order of justice shall require; and there to be
definitively and finally ordered, decreed, and adjudged according
to justice, without any other appellation or provocation[4] to any
other person or persons, court or courts: And if the matter or
contention for any of the causes aforesaid be or shall be commenced...before the archdeacon of any archbishop or his commissary, then the party grieved shall or may take his appeal, within
fifteen days next after judgment or sentence there given, to the
Court of the Arches or Audience[5] of the same archbishop or archbishops, and from the said Court of the Arches or Audience, within fifteen days then next ensuing after judgment or sentence there
given, to the archbishop of the same province, there to be de-

---

[1] *I.e.* favourers, in the sense of adherents or abettors.
[2] The Second Statute of Praemunire, 1393.   [3] Residents.
[4] 'Provocation' is a term technically applied to an appeal from a lower to a
higher ecclesiastical court.   [5] On these courts see pp. 358–9 below.

finitively and finally determined without any other or further process or appeal thereupon to be had or sued.

IV. ...And in case any cause, matter, or contention... which hath, doth, shall, or may touch the King, his heirs or successors kings of this realm, that in all and every such case or cases the party grieved...shall or may appeal...to the spiritual prelates and other abbots and priors of the Upper House assembled and convocate by the King's writ in the Convocation being or next ensuing within the province or provinces where the same matter of contention is or shall be begun; so that every such appeal be taken by the party grieved within fifteen days next after the judgment or sentence thereupon given or to be given. And that whatsoever be done or shall be done and affirmed, determined, decreed, and adjudged by the foresaid prelates, abbots, and priors of the Upper House of the said Convocation as is aforesaid, appertaining, concerning, or belonging to the King, his heirs or successors, in any of these foresaid causes of appeals, shall stand and be taken for a final decree, sentence, judgment, definition, and determination, and the same matter so determined never after to come in question and debate to be examined in any other court or courts: And if it shall happen any person or persons hereafter to pursue or provoke any appeal contrary to the effect of this Act, or refuse to obey, execute, and observe all things comprised within the same...that then every person and persons so doing, refusing, or offending, ...their procurers, fautors, advocates, counsellors, and abettors, and every of them, shall incur into the pains, forfeitures, and penalties ordained and provided in the said statute made in the said sixteenth year of King Richard the Second[1]....

24 Henr. VIII, c. 12: *Statutes of the Realm*, iii, 427.

(2) Act of Supremacy, 1534

If the Act of Appeals declares English independence of all external authority, the Act of Supremacy declares the authority of the Crown of England over all persons and all causes within the realm. The idea of the Supremacy was nothing new. It had found expression as early as 1515, when Wolsey had urged the King to allow the case of Standish to be referred to Rome Henry's reply anticipated his later policy: 'We are, by the sufferance of God, King of England; and the Kings of England in times past never had any superior but God. Know, therefore, that we will maintain the rights of the Crown in this matter like our progenitors.'[2] The Act now recognises the Supreme Headship as something already existing, and assigns to the Crown the power of ecclesiastical visitation. It has been remarked that Wolsey's legatine autocracy had prepared the way for Henry's Supreme

[1] The Second Statute of Praemunire, 1393. [2] Quoted in Gairdner, i, 283.

Headship[1], but the Act itself, except for the clause relating to visitation, is not of the first importance. What the Pope claimed in England was not Supreme Headship, except in virtue of his Supreme Headship of the whole of Christendom, but a practical jurisdiction controlling a large part of the daily life of men. Of this he had been deprived already by the far more important Act of Appeals. The King places on his work an ornamental coping-stone, but the foundations had been already laid and the building erected. The view of the statesmen who supported the Supremacy is indicated by Cranmer. 'The Bishop of Rome,' he said, 'treadeth under foot God's laws and the King's'[2]; and a little later he declared that the clergy maintained the Pope 'to the intent they might have as it were a kingdom and laws within themselves, distinct from the laws of the Crown, and wherewith the Crown may not meddle; and so being exempt from the laws of the realm, might live in this realm like lords and kings without damage or fear of any man, so that they please their high and supreme head at Rome.'[3]

An Act concerning the King's Highness to be Supreme Head of the Church of England and to have authority to reform and redress all errors, heresies, and abuses in the same

Albeit the King's Majesty justly and rightfully is and ought to be the Supreme Head of the Church of England, and so is recognised by the clergy of this realm in their Convocations; yet nevertheless for corroboration and confirmation thereof, and for increase of virtue in Christ's religion within this realm of England, and to repress and extirp all errors, heresies, and other enormities and abuses heretofore used in the same, Be it enacted by authority of this present Parliament that the King our Sovereign Lord, his heirs and successors kings of this realm, shall be taken, accepted, and reputed the only Supreme Head in earth of the Church of England called *Anglicana Ecclesia*, and shall have and enjoy annexed and united to the imperial Crown of this realm as well the title and style thereof, as all honours, dignities, preeminences, jurisdictions, privileges, authorities, immunities, profits, and commodities, to the said dignity of Supreme Head of the same Church belonging and appertaining: And that our said Sovereign Lord, his heirs and successors kings of this realm, shall have full power and authority from time to time to visit, repress, redress, reform, order, correct, restrain, and amend all such errors, heresies, abuses, offences, contempts, and enormities, whatsoever they be, which by any manner spiritual authority or jurisdiction ought or may lawfully be reformed, repressed, ordered, redressed, corrected, restrained, or amended, most to the pleasure of Almighty God, the increase of virtue in Christ's religion, and

[1] *C. M. H.* i, 646.   [2] Pollard, *Cranmer*, p. 351.
[3] *Ib.* p. 352.

for the conservation of the peace, unity, and tranquillity of this realm: any usage, custom, foreign laws, foreign authority, prescription, or any other thing or things to the contrary hereof notwithstanding.

26 Henr. VIII, c. 1: *Statutes of the Realm*, iii, 492.

(3) Act against the Papal Authority, 1536

In connexion with the Act of Supremacy should be studied the rather full-blooded preamble of the Act against the Papal Authority. It marks another stage in the progressive rudeness to the Pope which can be traced throughout the Reformation of Henry VIII[1].

An Act extinguishing the authority of the Bishop of Rome

Forasmuch as notwithstanding the good and wholesome laws, ordinances, and statutes heretofore enacted, made, and established ...for the extirpation, abolition, and extinguishment, out of this realm and other his Grace's dominions, seignories, and countries, of the pretended power and usurped authority of the Bishop of Rome, by some called the Pope, used within the same or elsewhere concerning the same realm, dominions, seignories, or countries, which did obfuscate and wrest God's holy word and testament a long season from the spiritual and true meaning thereof, to his worldly and carnal affections, as pomp, glory, avarice, ambition, and tyranny, covering and shadowing the same with his human and politic devices, traditions, and inventions, set forth to promote and stablish his only dominion, both upon the souls and also the bodies and goods of all Christian people, excluding Christ out of his kingdom and rule of man his soul as much as he may, and all other temporal kings and princes out of their dominions which they ought to have by God's law upon the bodies and goods of their subjects; whereby he did not only rob the King's Majesty, being only the Supreme Head of this his realm of England immediately under God, of his honour, right, and preeminence due unto him by the law of God, but spoiled this his realm yearly of innumerable treasure, and with the loss of the same deceived the King's loving and obedient subjects, persuading to them, by his laws, bulls, and other his de-

[1] In 1527 Henry, writing to Cardinal Cibo concerning the sack of Rome, refers to the Pope as 'our most holy Lord, the true and only Vicar of Jesus Christ upon earth.' In the Act of Annates he becomes 'the Bishop of Rome, otherwise called the Pope.' In the Dispensations Act he is charged with 'abusing and beguiling' the King's subjects; and this charge is amplified in the Act against the Papal authority. Finally, in a letter written shortly after the passing of the Act of Supremacy, the Pope is referred to as 'the pestilent idol, enemy of all truth, and usurpator of princes.'

ceivable means, such dreams, vanities, and phantasies as by the same many of them were seduced and conveyed unto superstitious and erroneous opinions; so that the King's Majesty, the Lords spiritual and temporal, and the Commons in this realm, being overwearied and fatigated with the experience of the infinite abominations and mischiefs proceeding of his impostures and craftily colouring of his deceits, to the great damages of souls, bodies, and goods, were forced of necessity for the public weal of this realm to exclude that foreign pretended power, jurisdiction, and authority, used and usurped within this realm, and to devise such remedies for their relief in the same as doth not only redound to the honour of God, the high praise and advancement of the King's Majesty and of his realm, but also to the great and inestimable utility of the same; and notwithstanding the said wholesome laws so made and heretofore established, yet it is come to the knowledge of the King's Highness and also to divers and many his loving, faithful, and obedient subjects, how that divers seditious and contentious persons, being imps[1] of the said Bishop of Rome and his see, and in heart members of his pretended monarchy, do in corners and elsewhere, as they dare, whisper, inculce[2], preach, and persuade, and from time to time instil into the ears and heads of the poor, simple, and unlettered people the advancement and continuance of the said Bishop's feigned and pretended authority, pretending the same to have his ground and original of God's law, whereby the opinions of many be suspended, their judgments corrupted and deceived, and diversity in opinions augmented and increased, to the great displeasure of Almighty God, the high discontentation of our said most dread Sovereign Lord, and the interruption of the unity, love, charity, concord, and agreement that ought to be in a Christian region and congregation: For avoiding whereof, and repression of the follies of such seditious persons as be the means and authors of such inconveniences, Be it enacted, ordained, and established. . . . That if any person or persons, dwelling, demurring[3], inhabiting, or resiant[4] within this realm or within any other the King's dominions, seignories, or countries, or the marches of the same, or elsewhere within or under his obeisance[5] and power, of what estate, dignity, preeminence, order, degree, or condition soever he or

---

[1] 'Imp' is here used in the sense of 'offshoot.' The sense of the term is not necessarily bad, as the expression 'an imp of Glory' occurs in Quarles, 1621 (*Oxford Dictionary*).

[2] A form of 'inculk,' a word in frequent use in the sense of 'inculcate.'

[3] In the sense of staying or remaining.   [4] Resident.   [5] Jurisdiction.

they be, after the last day of July which shall be in the year of our Lord God 1536 shall, by writing, ciphering, printing, preaching, or teaching, deed, or act, obstinately or maliciously hold or stand with to extol, set forth, maintain, or defend the authority, jurisdiction, or power of the Bishop of Rome or of his see, heretofore used, claimed, or usurped within this realm or in any dominion or country being of, within, or under the King's power or obeisance, or by any pretence obstinately or maliciously invent anything for the extolling, advancement, setting forth, maintenance, or defence of the same or any part thereof, or by any pretence obstinately or maliciously attribute any manner of jurisdiction, authority, or preeminence to the said see of Rome, or to any Bishop of the same see for the time being, within this realm or in any the King's dominions or countries, that then every such person or persons so doing or offending, their aiders, assistants, comforters, abettors, procurers, maintainers, fautors[1], counsellors, concealors, and every of them, being thereof lawfully convicted according to the laws of this realm, for every such default and offence shall incur and run into the dangers, penalties, pains, and forfeitures ordained and provided by the Statute of Provision and Praemunire made in the sixteenth year of the reign of the noble and valiant prince King Richard the Second[1] against such as attempt, procure, or make provision to the see of Rome or elsewhere for any thing or things to the derogation, or contrary to the prerogative royal or jurisdiction, of the Crown and dignity of this realm.

*   *   *   *   *   *

28 Henr. VIII, c. 10: *Statutes of the Realm*, iii, 663.

§ 5. Dissolution of the Monasteries

The problem of the moral condition of the English monasteries at the time of the Dissolution has not yet been completely solved. It is clear that in certain houses 'vicious, carnal, and abominable living' had 'shamelessly increased and augmented'[2]; but the study of particular cases may give a false impression, and it is only by a survey of large groups of monasteries that a charge of general corruption can be sustained. For this purpose the episcopal registers are of great importance, but even these do not contain detailed

[1] The Second Statute of Praemunire, 1393.

[2] For instance, Archbishop Morton's letter to the Abbot of St Albans in 1490 is a terrible indictment (Wilkins, iii, 632; see also Gairdner, i, 269). The visitation of the Abbey of Thame, a 'monastery exempt,' in 1526 discloses grave disorders (*English Historical Review*, iii, 704). The condition of the house of secular canons at Southwell (1469–1542) was simply shocking, not only for the multitude and gravity of the offences but for the trivial nature of the punishments inflicted (Leach, pp. lxxiv–lxxxvii), and both the offences and the lack of punishment are characteristic of other houses under regular monastic rule.

accounts of the visitations, but only references to the *comperta* or records of evidence. The actual visitation records have seldom survived. Nevertheless, the episcopal injunctions which are entered in the registers, being founded on the *comperta* and directed to delinquencies proved to the Bishop, serve as reliable evidence, as far as they go, about the internal condition of a monastery[1]. In the worst cases, however, the criticisms of the Bishop are likely to be within the mark, owing to the difficulty of obtaining evidence in a corrupt community[2], and to the tendency of some episcopal pronouncements to avoid scandal by minimising evils and hushing up the facts.

In approaching the problem it is necessary also to bear in mind that long before the Reformation the kind of public opinion which expressed itself in medieval literature had pronounced an adverse judgment upon monasticism as it then appeared. In this connexion ordinary satirists may be neglected, but the charges are made by some of the greater churchmen. In one of his fragments, written in 1271 or 1272, Roger Bacon had attacked the clergy and the monastic orders as the enemies of true learning. In 1414 the University of Oxford, at the request of Henry V, put forward articles for the reformation of the Church, in which the open profligacy of ecclesiastics is declared to be a scandal, and it is urged that priests guilty of immorality should be suspended or severely punished, instead of being sentenced to pecuniary fines too paltry to act as a deterrent[3]. Thomas Gascoigne, Chancellor of Oxford in 1434, a vehement opponent of the teaching of Wycliffe, is as vigorous as Wycliffe in his denunciation of clerical abuses—pluralities, non-residence, ignorant, worldly, and luxurious bishops[4] and clergy, who lived at Court or in the household of great nobles; the avarice of the bishops' officials; the idleness and gluttony of the monks, who have ceased to be chroniclers or scribes or to labour with their hands, and neglect their duty; and last of all, the crowning abuse of the Church, the Papacy itself[5]. The same points are made by John Colet, Sir Thomas More, and Thomas Starkey [pp. 69, 73, 82], all writing on the eve of the Dissolution.

The evidence of the episcopal visitations can be conveniently studied in

[1] All religious houses were liable to periodical visitation by the Bishop, except those of the 'exempt' orders—the Cistercian, Praemonstratensian, and Gilbertine —the friaries, and individual monasteries which were influential enough to obtain exemption from episcopal jurisdiction. These exempt houses were not necessarily unvisited, for the exempt orders held their own visitations, and other houses were liable to visitation by the Papacy. The Praemonstratensian order had its own Visitor, who held triennial visitations. An account of the procedure at an episcopal visitation will be found in the Introduction to the *Lincoln Visitations*, vol. i, pp. ix–xiii. The Bishop of Norwich visited the non-exempt houses in his diocese once in every six years.

[2] In the Norwich visitations there is a reference to a conspiracy among the brethren of St Benet's, Hulme, to report nothing to the Bishop (Jessopp, p. 126).

[3] Lea, ii, 9.

[4] 'Alas, how unlucky are the times in which we live, when the prelates give themselves up to delights...' (Gascoigne, p. lxviii). See also Gairdner, i, 243–67.

[5] 'Rome, as a special and principal wild beast, has laid waste the vineyard of the Church' (quoted in Gairdner, i, 255). See also Coulton, pp. 14–17, 57.

three groups[1] which are now easily accessible—those of Lincoln, Norwich, and of the Praemonstratensian order throughout England.

The great diocese of Lincoln possessed no less than 136 religious houses, exclusive of hospitals and houses of friars, but the exempt orders were largely represented, especially the Cistercians. The visitations at present published extend only from 1420 to 1449, but even a hundred years before the Dissolution the decay of religious zeal is manifest. The injunctions[2] printed in the first volume relate to 27 houses, and in four cases, Caldwell, Daventry, Huntingdon, and St Neots[3], the preamble selected by the Bishop as most appropriate to the facts disclosed by his visitation is 'a sweeping indictment of a state of utter slackness and degeneracy.' The rule of the order is no longer observed, the divine offices are neglected, alms are wasted, and hospitality is not kept. 'There is nothing else here but drunkenness and surfeit, disobedience and contempt, private aggrandisement and apostasy, drowsiness—we do not say incontinence—but sloth, and every other thing which is on the downward path to evil and drags man to hell.'[4] In three other cases also the injunctions suggest a bad state of things. At Ramsey[5] the open injunctions were accompanied by others, sealed up, dealing with certain 'defaults, transgressions, and offences' discovered to the Bishop, 'concerning the which,' he says, 'we here keep silence, that we may spare your fame and honesty.' At Godstow nunnery[5] it was found that 'certain things forbidden and contrary to holy religion' were 'shamelessly committed therein'; and, in particular, there was trouble with 'the scholars of Oxford.' At Elstow nunnery[5] the Bishop found it necessary to provide that 'no nun convicted, publicly defamed, or manifestly suspect of the crime of incontinency, be deputed to any office within the monastery, and especially to that of gatekeeper.' At the nunneries of Heynings and Markyate[6] there were scandals affecting individuals—in the latter case no less a person than the prioress herself. At Sewardsley[7] the Bishop authorised an enquiry into general charges of a formidable kind, but the result does not appear. Three houses receive good reports: Fineshade, Missenden, and the nunnery of St Mary Delapré, near Northampton[8]. In the case of the remaining houses the injunctions

---

[1] See also Hibbert, Kempe, and Coulton. The last-named gives notes on some of the visitations of Exeter (p. 4), and the Sussex Cluniacs (p. 57); also on particular visitations of Wigmore (p. 88) and Sinningthwaite (p. 90).

[2] As these injunctions are based upon the *comperta*, or matters actually discovered by the Bishop on his visitation, they are reliable evidence of the internal condition of a monastery, and not, as is sometimes supposed, mere formal exhortations that have no relation to actual facts. On this see the editor's Introduction to vol. i, pp. xi and xii, and to vol. ii, p. xlviii.

[3] Daventry belonged to the Cluniacs, St Neot's to the Benedictines, and Caldwell and Huntingdon were houses of Augustinian canons. They were all small houses with 9 or 10 inmates.   [4] p. 76 and *n.*

[5] Ramsey was one of the larger abbeys and had 44 monks in 1439; Godstow and Elstow, though well known, could not at this time have had more than 20 inmates each. They were all Benedictine houses.

[6] Heynings was a small Cistercian house of 13 nuns, and Markyate a still smaller Benedictine priory of only 7 nuns.   [7] Sewardsley was Cistercian.

[8] Fineshade and Missenden were houses of Augustinian canons, and the 'Nuns of the Meadows, Northampton,' was the only house of Cluniac nuns in England.

point rather to laxity and general secularisation. They refer to 'the frequent access of secular folk, especially women' to the cloister; to absence from divine service without due cause; to 'talkings together' and 'drinkings' after compline. There is a hint of quarrelling[1], and the use of 'disdainful and despiteful words of insolence and reproach.' The monks possess private property in violation of the rule of their order. There is trouble at several houses because the inmates 'gad about and wander' and visit the neighbouring towns; and at Newnham Priory the Bishop forbids it altogether except with proper permission, and then only with someone 'of ripe age and discretion' and 'other honest company,' care being taken that 'in such towns they have no leisure for eatings, drinkings, or trifles, nor wander or gad about through the streets or open places, nor haunt the public taverns, but that, having despatched their affairs and the reasons of their coming, they return at once to the cloister without delay.' References also occur to 'unseemly games,' 'hunting[2], hawking, and other lawless wanderings abroad,' and 'archery with secular folk' without proper permission. The ostentatious Prior of Canons Ashby wore 'short and tight doublets' with several ties to his hose, and rode abroad in a showy and gaudy habit; he was advised to practise 'a devout gait or manner of riding.' At Elstow the nuns wore silver head-pins and silken gowns, with several rings on their fingers[3]. At Humberstone the monks were addicted to flesh-meat at prohibited seasons; and at St Frideswide's, Oxford, the Prior was instructed no longer to allow 'the superfluous and luxurious expenses whereby your house has been brought to poverty.' The 'common barber' at Croyland was to be 'obedient and more ready to do service to the monks in his art with all humility, putting aside all his rebelliousness and sauciness'; and the corresponding functionary at Bardney was to 'shave at a fitting season all the monks, both old and young, so that the juniors, while their elders are being shaved, may give their time meanwhile to books and study, and no wise to idleness or frivolities'; and the young monks were warned 'in no wise' to 'shave one another, as has been their wont, on account of the serious dangers which may arise from want of skill in that art.'

The second volume of the Lincoln visitations, containing the visitations of Bishop Alnwick from 1436 to 1449, confirms the conclusions suggested by the first volume, but the delinquencies now appear rather more frequent and the complaints of waste and dilapidation more insistent. The penalties inflicted appear, as before, to be inadequate, but the documents illustrate the difficulties with which the Bishop had to contend. A secular canon at Irthlingborough who was threatened with deprivation produced letters of absolution from the agent of the Pope, and the Bishop could go no further; and in another case proceedings were stayed by an appeal to the Court of Arches. Thus the Bishop was not always master in his own house, and in

---

[1] At Newnham Priory an encounter between two of the canons had led to the 'forcible shedding of blood' (p. 92).

[2] At St Frideswide's, Oxford, 'hounds for hunting' are not to be 'nourished' within the precincts of the monastery (p. 97).

[3] Cf. also vol. ii, p. 3, recording the proceedings of the Prioress of Ankerwyke in 1441, who wore 'golden rings exceeding costly with divers precious stones, and also girdles silvered and gilded over, and silken veils' and 'furs of vair.'

exercising authority he had to proceed with caution, lest he should find himself in conflict with external powers.

The Norwich visitations, 1492–1532[1], are much later in date and cover a good deal of ground, as there were only seven exempt houses in the diocese, and the number reported on is 42. Bishop Goldwell's visitation of Wymondham in 1492 discloses dilapidation and an utter decay of discipline. The abbot was got rid of, but there was no improvement, and on Bishop Nicke's visitation in 1514 the condition of the house was disgraceful. Although the community consisted only of eleven monks, there were cases of insubordination, free fights in the cloister, drunkenness, peculation, dilapidation, and immorality. The prior had abstracted documents; had tried to kill two fellow monks with a sword; had thrown a stone at another in the presence of the abbot; and had not been to confession for 12 months. But a better abbot took the place in hand; in 1520 there were only complaints of drinking, and in 1526 there were no serious charges. The visitation of Norwich Priory in 1514 shews that the house was in a scandalous state, both morally and financially. Westacre was in an unsatisfactory state in 1514, and greatly in debt; in 1520 things were worse on the financial side; and in 1526 the Bishop had to deal with a serious scandal. The famous Priory of Walsingham was the worst of all. In 1514 the prior was a dissolute and scandalous person who dressed as a layman and kept a jester; he appropriated money and jewels; and he was suspected of immorality. The canons were dissipated and noisy; they frequented taverns, hawked and hunted, and stole the prior's wine. A new prior effected an improvement, but the numbers declined and there was no pretence of piety or learning.

The rest of the evidence in these visitations points mainly to secularisation. Some Augustinian communities were living harmlessly as resident landlords or country gentlemen, keeping up the services in the church regularly and doing a certain amount of educational work. Some of the smaller and poorer houses with half-a-dozen inmates or less were merely useless, as they had hard work to live at all. The nunneries appear to have been on the whole decent but poor. At Carrow Priory the nuns wear silk waistbands, go outside the precincts without veils, and the younger sort are addicted to gossip. At Campsey the prioress is described as austere, mean, and stingy, and too strict with her nuns; and the cooking is bad. But in a period of 40 years only one serious scandal comes to light at the visitations, although there are cases of suspicion. In Bishop Nicke's visitations altogether 33 monks or nuns are suspected of immorality, and in 15 of these cases the charge was held to be well-founded[2]. But the great majority of the complaints recorded are of a different kind. The rule of silence is broken; there is quarrelling and ill-feeling among the brethren; the psalms are sung badly, the mass is said and not sung, and certain of the monks are so ignorant that they can scarcely read or sing; the vestments are dilapidated and the service-books out of repair. The monks go out without leave; they are lazy and get up late; agriculture is neglected. There is disobedience; the servants of the monastery are insolent; the faults of the brethren are not sufficiently punished; the common seal of one monastery is not properly kept. It is complained of several houses that there is no schoolmaster, and at two that there is no convent tailor. At

[1] Ed. A. Jessopp.　　　　　[2] Coulton, p. 3.

Woodbridge there is disorder and drunkenness; at St Benet's, Hulme, the third prior is addicted to hunting, and too many dogs are kept, which devour the food that ought to have been distributed to the poor; at Buckenham one of the canons insisted on wearing pointed shoes; and at Redlingfield Priory the sisters complain that there are no curtains in the dormitory.

Even if many of the houses are to be acquitted of the graver vices, everything points to a relaxation of discipline and a notable decay of high religious feeling. Another consideration which suggests a general lowering of the tone of monastic life is the inadequacy of the punishments inflicted. One of the nuns of Crabhouse, who confessed to a breach of her vow of chastity, was ordered by the Bishop to sit for a month below the other nuns and to repeat the Psalter seven times[1]. The Prior of Walsingham, who had embezzled money, stolen jewels and plate, and committed both manslaughter and adultery, was allowed to retire from office on a pension for life[2].

The Praemonstratensian visitations (1475–1503)[3] disclose a condition of things in some respects scarcely better than in the monasteries of the Norwich diocese. The visitations cover the last 25 years of the fifteenth century and include all the 35 English houses of the order, which were supposed to be visited by the commissary of the Abbot of Prémontré every three years. These visitations are regular from 1488 onwards, but before that date there are only two general visitations recorded—in 1478 and in 1482; although visitations of particular houses occur. It is also the case as elsewhere that part of the visitation material is missing[4]. The total number of the inmates of the houses at any particular time was about 420. Out of these 48 were accused of immorality, 29 of them being undoubtedly guilty, and the rest, though not actually convicted, were suspect[5]. Other serious offences were theft, embezzlement, apostasy, and murderous assaults. The standing abuse of the inadequacy of the punishments inflicted appears in these visitations also. A canon who had pawned three books was condemned to recite seven penitential psalms[6]. Four canons who went out at night without leave to frequent taverns, were each to recite the whole Psalter within a week. The abbot of Langley, a very scandalous person, was deposed but received a large pension for life. The abbot of St Radegund's in 1500 was accused by the brethren of immorality, of frequenting taverns on Sundays and holy days, there indulging in evil conversation, and of wasting the goods of his house upon women of bad character. The Visitor contents himself with forbidding him to frequent taverns or assemblies of the laity. In this case there is always the possibility that the other charges were regarded as not proved; but in 1488 he had been excommunicated as an apostate and a sower of discord, and at the visitation of 1497 the whole convent had brought serious charges against him. About 38 sentences of banishment to other abbeys were pronounced, but 28 of these were mitigated, and in some cases where there

---

[1] Cf. the visitations of Southwell, where immorality was punished in 1478 by suspension for *three days* from office and benefice (Leach, p. 37); and in 1503 by a fine of 2 lb. of wax. (p. 72.)

[2] See also Coulton, p. 3.

[3] *Collectanea Anglo-Praemonstratensia*. In connexion with these should be read Dr G. G. Coulton's criticisms in *Medieval Studies* (2nd edition), pp. 92 and 126.

[4] Coulton, p. 127.   [5] *Ib.*

[6] See also Coulton, p. 129.

was no such mitigation the sentence was not actually carried out. In 1489 a canon of Cockersand was sentenced to be banished to Croxton for three years for immorality, but in 1491 he was still at Cockersand, and was now sub-prior. Another Cockersand canon was sentenced for the same offence to banishment to Sulby for seven years; in 1491 he was still at Cockersand, and in 1502 he became abbot[1].

The minor complaints indicating secularisation and relaxation of discipline are frequent, although less so than in the Norwich visitations. The most common breach of discipline relates to the rule of silence, which the Visitor describes as the key of religious life. Another is the practice of going out of bounds without leave—sometimes for the purpose of drinking at the neighbouring town, and in one case in order to 'attend spectacles.' There is also eating and drinking in the dormitory, and Saturday suppers have to be forbidden. Cases of quarrelling and fighting occur; the canons of Tupholme are not to be allowed to carry long knives, and at West Dereham one brother had struck another with a weapon and had then thrown him into a pond. Injunctions are issued against hunting, fishing, the keeping of birds, dogs, and rabbits, and games for money, especially dice and cards. In some houses it is difficult to get all the brethren up in time for matins. The Visitor has also something to say about the introduction of new fashions in dress, of habits not worn long enough, of large sleeves and slippers[2], of the shape of the tonsure, and of the use of skull caps.

On the other hand at many visitations the Visitor commends the house for its good order.

It should be observed that the evil of secularisation was not confined to the monasteries; the clergy generally were infected by it. On the eve of the Reformation the bishops were either ministers managing affairs of state, or courtiers waiting for livings to be held *in commendam* with their bishopric or for translation to a richer see. It was not learning, or eloquence, or a saintly life that obtained promotion, but administrative ability applied to the King's service. The type is Morton or Wolsey—the statesman who is in orders and can be rewarded with church preferment. Under this system the bishops were many of them non-resident[3], and delegated their duties to suffragans; the higher clergy tended to become mere country gentlemen; and the parish priests were often idle and ineffective. Indications of contemporary opinion on this question will be found in the extracts printed below [pp. 69–88].

To this general secularisation must be added another evil which was itself a contributory cause of it. The Norwich visitations suggest a widespread dilapidation of monastic buildings and property. In several of the Lincoln visitations an injunction forbids the abbot to grant corrodies, liveries, pensions, or annuities, or to sell or cut down 'the old copses of the monastery which are not in decay' without the licence of the bishop and the consent of the whole convent. There are also references to jewels in pawn

---

[1] Coulton, p. 130.

[2] These 'slippers' were the long fashionable pointed shoe—a standing offence to the medieval moralist.

[3] Richard Fox, consecrated Bishop of Exeter in 1487, translated to Bath and Wells in 1491, and to Durham in 1494, 'never saw his cathedral at Exeter, nor set foot in his diocese of Bath and Wells' (Gasquet, i, 24).

and to a burden of debt. This raises the important question of the financial condition of the houses. It has been said that the monasteries in general were heavily in debt at the time of the Dissolution; but a recent investigation[1] suggests a different conclusion. The details given in the *Valor Ecclesiasticus* shew that few houses owed more than one year's gross income[2], but as it was difficult for them to obtain credit when the Dissolution was known to be impending, a great stimulus was given to an earlier tendency towards 'waste' of monastic goods. The monks were obliged to sell their moveables in order to raise money, and in that way insolvency came very near[3]. This was specially the case with the smaller monasteries, the convents of nuns[4], and the houses of friars[5]. They were without resources, either of money or of administrative ability, and had, as a rule, been badly managed. The preamble of the first Dissolution Statute [p. 59], although it begins with morality, makes almost as strong a point of 'waste.' The loss of public faith in monasticism due to secularisation also influenced finance in another way, for voluntary offerings almost ceased. In 1535 they only amounted to £7. 19s. 8d. for the whole county of Stafford[6]. In the 30 years before Henry VIII's accession no new monastery had been founded in England[7], for the more advanced thinkers were beginning to use their money in a different way. Bishop Smythe, the founder of Brasenose College, Oxford, in 1495 converted the Austin Priory at Lichfield into a grammar school and almshouses[8]. Bishop Alcock in 1497 suppressed the Cambridge nunnery of St Radegund in order to found Jesus College; and Wolsey dissolved 29 of the smaller houses for the benefit of his new colleges at Oxford and Ipswich[9]—whereby he 'made all the forest of religious foundations in England to shake, justly fearing the King would finish to fell the oaks, seeing the Cardinal began to cut the underwood.'[10] The attitude of enlightened opinion towards monasticism in the early part of the sixteenth century is expressed by Bishop Oldham: 'Shall we build houses and provide livelihoods for a company of bussing monks, whose end and fall we ourselves may live to see? No, no: it is meet to provide for the increase of learning, and for such as by learning shall do good to Church and commonwealth.'[11] To the greater churchmen of the time monastic life was out of date; the future lay with collegiate life and the New Learning.

It has been argued in defence of the monasteries that they never really recovered from the shock of the Black Death. This not only affected numbers, but also discipline, tradition, and learning. But serious as the blow was, the decline went steadily on after the effects of the plague should have worn off, and the houses could only be kept up by reducing the number of their inmates. Losses which in earlier times would have been repaired by the abundant vitality of monasticism, proved fatal to a movement which had already spent itself.

[1] Savine in *Oxford Studies*, vol. i.
[2] *Ib.* i, 217; cf. also Hibbert, *Dissolutions*, pp. 185–7.
[3] Savine, p. 211.
[4] Gasquet, ii, 213.
[5] *Ib.* ii, 256.
[6] Hibbert, *Monasticism*, p. 102.
[7] Traill, iii, 35 *n.*
[8] Hibbert, *Dissolution*, p. 20.
[9] Gwatkin, p. 167. On Wolsey's dissolutions see also Hibbert, *Dissolution*, pp. 20–29.
[10] Fuller, ii, 202.
[11] Quoted in Creighton, *Wolsey*, p. 141.

(1) Act for the Dissolution of the Lesser
Monasteries, 1536

As early as March, 1533, the King was beginning to contemplate an extensive secularisation of Church property, and a scheme of 1534 included the confiscation of the lands of monasteries with fewer than 13 inmates[1]. It was, however, decided to proceed by visitation, and in July, 1535, the commissioners began their work. They proceeded on the lines of the episcopal visitations, which were suspended during the royal visitation[2], accumulating data, formulating *comperta*, and issuing injunctions. The result was an indictment of the most formidable kind, which would have furnished ample justification for the harshest measures against the monks[3]. There are still extant results of this visitation of three kinds: (1) some of the informal letters written to Cromwell by the Visitors; (2) a formal *compendium compertorum* for the Province of York, and for the diocese of Coventry and Lichfield, and the diocese of Norwich; and (3) seven 'confessions,' or perhaps more properly surrenders, the fullest of which is that from St Andrew's Priory, Northampton [p. 89]. These not only accuse the monks of the vilest practices, but they incriminate the 'great, honourable, and solemn monasteries' of the realm quite as seriously as the smaller houses, and so expose the bad faith of the preamble of the first Dissolution Statute. All this evidence is in fact worthless. The Visitors were men of doubtful character. 'They were men who well understood the message they went on,' says Fuller, himself no friend to the monks, 'and would not come back without a satisfactory answer to him that sent them, knowing themselves were likely to be no losers thereby.'[4] The number of houses actually visited was not one-third of the whole number[5]; and the rapidity of the visitation deprived it of all claim to be regarded as a judicial proceeding[6]. Again, the *comperta* do not always agree with the reports of the local commissions of country gentry appointed to superintend the actual process of dissolution. It should also be noticed that a number of monasteries purchased temporary exemption from the Act, and among these were some houses which the visitation had professed to convict of serious vice. In one way, however, the work of Cromwell's commissioners throws light upon the monastic problem. It shews that in the current state of opinion about monasticism, the most damaging statements did not appear utterly incredible.

[1] Fisher, p. 345. Thirteen had long been the nominal 'conventual' quorum.

[2] Authority to visit exempt monasteries had been vested in the King by 25 Henry VIII, c. 21 (see p. 36 above). The visitation of those not exempt was undertaken by Cromwell in his capacity of the King's vicegerent.

[3] 'When their enormities were first read in the Parliament House they were so great and abominable that there was nothing but "Down with them"' (Latimer, *Sermons*, ed. Parker Society, 1844–5), i, 123. It is, however, an open question whether the 'Black Book' ever really existed.

[4] ii, 214.

[5] Gairdner, ii, 87.

[6] *E.g.* for the pace of the Staffordshire visitations see Hibbert, *Dissolution*, p. 136. Cf. also Fisher, p. 374.

An Act whereby all Religious Houses of monks, canons, and nuns which may not dispend manors, lands, tenements, and hereditaments above the clear yearly value of £200 are given to the King's Highness, his heirs and successors, for ever

Forasmuch as manifest sin, vicious, carnal, and abominable living, is daily used and committed amongst the little and small abbeys, priories, and other religious houses of monks, canons, and nuns, where the congregation of such religious persons is under the number of 12 persons, whereby the governors of such religious houses and their convent[1] spoil, destroy, consume, and utterly waste, as well their churches, monasteries, priories, principal houses, farms, granges, lands, tenements, and hereditaments, as the ornaments of their churches and their goods and chattels[2], to the high displeasure of Almighty God, slander of good religion, and to the great infamy of the King's Highness and the realm if redress should not be had thereof; And albeit that many continual visitations hath been heretofore had by the space of two hundred years and more[3] for an honest and charitable reformation of such unthrifty, carnal, and abominable living, yet nevertheless little or none amendment is hitherto had, but their vicious living shamelessly increaseth and augmenteth, and by a cursed custom so rooted and infested[4] that a great multitude of the religious persons in such small houses do rather choose to rove abroad in apostasy than to conform them to the observation of good religion; so that without such small houses be utterly suppressed and the religious persons therein committed to great and honourable monasteries of religion in this realm, where they may be compelled to live religiously for reformation of their lives, there can else be no reformation in this behalf: In consideration whereof the King's most Royal Majesty, being Supreme Head in earth under God of the Church of England, daily finding and devising the increase, advancement, and exaltation of true doctrine and virtue in the said Church, to the only glory and honour of God and the total extirping and destruction of vice and sin, having knowledge that the premises be true, as well by the compts[5] of his late visitations as by sundry credible informations, considering also that divers and great solemn monasteries of this realm wherein, thanks be to

---

[1] See note on p. 62 below.

[2] On the charge of waste, see p. 57 above.

[3] Grosseteste had visited the monasteries of his diocese of Lincoln as far back as 1235.

[4] Fixed, rooted, inveterate. The printed copies of the statute usually amend this, quite unnecessarily, into 'infected.'   [5] Accounts.

God, religion is right well kept and observed, be destitute of such
full numbers of religious persons as they ought and may keep,
hath thought good that a plain declaration should be made of the
premises as well to the Lords spiritual and temporal as to other
his loving subjects the Commons in this present Parliament assembled; whereupon the said Lords and Commons by a great
deliberation finally be resolved that it is and shall be much more
to the pleasure of Almighty God and for the honour of this his
realm that the possessions of such spiritual religious houses, now
being spent, spoiled, and wasted for increase and maintenance of
sin, should be used and converted to better uses, and the unthrifty
religious persons so spending the same to be compelled to reform
their lives; And thereupon most humbly desire the King's Highness that it may be enacted by authority of this present Parliament,
that his Majesty shall have and enjoy to him and to his heirs for
ever all and singular such monasteries, priories, and other religious
houses of monks, canons, and nuns, of what kinds or diversities
of habits, rules, or orders so ever they be called or named, which
have not in lands and tenements, rents, tithes, portions, and other
hereditaments, above the clear yearly value of two hundred pounds;
And in like manner shall have and enjoy all the sites and circuits
of every such religious houses, and all and singular the manors,
granges, meses[1], lands, tenements, reversions, rents, services,
tithes, pensions, portions, churches, chapels, advowsons, patronages, annuities, rights, entries, conditions, and other hereditaments appertaining or belonging to every such monastery, priory,
or other religious house, not having as is aforesaid above the said
clear yearly value of two hundred pounds, in as large and ample
manner as the abbots, priors, abbesses, prioresses, or other
governors of such monasteries, priories, and other religious houses
now have or ought to have the same in the right of their houses;
And that also his Highness shall have to him and to his heirs all
and singular such monasteries, abbeys, and priories which, at
any time within one year next afore the making of this Act, hath
been given and granted to his Majesty by any abbot, prior, abbess,
or prioress under their convent seals, or that otherwise hath been
suppressed or dissolved; And all and singular the manors, lands,
[etc.]. . . to the same monasteries, abbeys, and priories or to any of
them appertaining or belonging; To have and to hold all and
singular the premises with all their rights, profits, jurisdictions,
and commodities, unto the King's Majesty and to his heirs and

---

[1] Messuages.

assigns for ever, to do and use therewith his or their own wills to the pleasure of Almighty God and to the honour and profit of this realm. * * * * * *

IV. Provided always and be it enacted that forasmuch as divers of the chief governors of such religious houses, determining[1] the utter spoil and destruction of their houses, and dreading the suppressing thereof, for the maintenance of their detestable lives have lately fraudulently and craftily made feoffments[2], estates, gifts, grants, and leases under their convent seals, or suffered recoveries[3] of their manors, lands, tenements, and hereditaments in fee simple, fee tail, for term of life or lives, or for years, or charged the same with rents or corrodies[4], to the great decay and diminution of their houses, that all such crafty and fraudulent recoveries, feoffments, estates, gifts, grants, and leases, and every of them, made by any of the said chief governors of such religious houses under the convent seals within one year next afore the making of this Act, shall be utterly void and of none effect. . . .

V. And it is also enacted by authority aforesaid, that the King's Highness shall have and enjoy to his own proper use all the ornaments, jewels, goods, chattels, and debts which appertained to any of the chief governors of the said monasteries or religious houses in the right of their said monasteries or houses at the first day of March in the year of our Lord God 1535[–6] or any time since, wheresoever and to whose possession soever they shall come or be found: Except only such beasts, grain, and woods, and such like other chattels and revenues, as have been sold in the said first day of March or since for the necessary or reasonable expenses or charges of any of the said monasteries or houses. . . . * * * * * *

VIII. In consideration of which premises to be had to his Highness and to his heirs as is aforesaid, his Majesty is pleased and contented of his most excellent charity to provide to every

[1] Deciding.

[2] A 'feoffment' is a mode of conveyance by which a person is invested with freehold land by livery of seisin. It could be used to effect a mortgage.

[3] A 'recovery' was a method of alienating land by a collusive action. By the Tudor period it had become a regular method of conveyance.

[4] 'Corrody' was 'originally the right of free quarters due from the vassal to the lord on his circuit; but later applied especially to certain contributions of food, provisions, etc., paid annually by religious houses. . . . Sometimes the contribution might be commuted, and then it would be practically undistinguishable from an annuity or pension' (Fortescue, p. 337).

chief head and governor of every such religious house during their lives such yearly pensions or benefices as for their degrees and qualities shall be reasonable and convenient; wherein his Highness will have most tender respect to such of the said chief governors as well and truly conserve and keep the goods and ornaments of their houses to the use of his Majesty, without spoil, waste, or embezzling the same; And also his Majesty will ordain and provide that the convents[1] of every such religious house shall have their capacities, if they will, to live honestly and virtuously abroad, and some convenient charity disposed to them toward their living, or else shall be committed to such honourable great monasteries of this realm wherein good religion is observed as shall be limited by his Highness, there to live religiously during their lives.

IX. And it is ordained by authority aforesaid that the chief governors and convents of such honourable great monasteries shall take and accept into their houses from time to time such number of the persons of the said convents as shall be assigned and appointed by the King's Highness, and keep them religiously during their lives within their said monasteries in like manner and form as the convents of such great monasteries be ordered and kept.   *   *   *   *   *   *

XIII. Provided always that the King's Highness, at any time after the making of this Act, may at his pleasure ordain and declare, by his letters patents under his great seal, that such of the said religious houses which his Highness shall not be disposed to have suppressed nor dissolved by authority of this Act shall still continue, remain, and be in the same body corporate and in the said essential estate, quality, and condition, as well in possessions as otherwise, as they were afore the making of this Act, without any suppression or dissolution thereof or any part of the same by authority of this Act....

*   *   *   *   *   *

XVII. And further be it enacted, ordained, and established by authority aforesaid, that all and singular persons, bodies politic, and corporate, to whom the King's Majesty, his heirs or successors, hereafter shall give, grant, let, or demise any site or precinct, with the houses thereupon builded, together with the

---

[1] The word 'convent' was applied in the Middle Ages to the whole community of monks, friars, or nuns living in a single house, not to the building in which they lived. It is only by a later usage that it has been specially assigned to a house of nuns.

demesnes of any monasteries, priories, or other religious houses
that shall be dissolved or given to the King's Highness by this
Act, And the heirs, successors, executors, and assigns of every
such person, body politic, and corporate, shall be bounden by
authority of this Act, under the penalties hereafter ensuing, to
keep or cause to be kept an honest continual house and household
in the same site or precinct, and to occupy yearly as much of the
same demesnes in ploughing and tillage of husbandry, that is to
say, as much of the said demesnes which hath been commonly
used to be kept in tillage by the governors, abbots, or priors of
the same houses, monasteries, or priories, or by their farmer or
farmers occupying the same, within the time of 20 years next
before this Act: And if any person or persons, bodies politic or
corporate, that shall be bounden by this Act do not keep an honest
house, household, husbandry, and tillage in manner and form as
is aforesaid, that then he or they so offending shall forfeit to the
King's Highness for every month so offending £6. 13s. 4d. to be
recovered to his use in any of his Courts of Record.

*   *   *   *   *   *

27 Henr. VIII, c. 28: Statutes of the Realm, iii, 575.

(2) Act for the Dissolution of the Greater Monasteries, 1539

'The fourth day of February' [1536], says the chronicler Hall, 'the
King held his High Court of Parliament at Westminster, in the which was
many good and wholesome statutes and laws made and concluded. And in
this time was given unto the King by the consent of the great and fat abbots
all religious houses that were of the value of 300 mark and under, in hope
that their great monasteries should have continued still. But even at that
time one said in the Parliament House that these were as thorns, but the
great abbots were putrified old oaks, and they must needs follow....'[1] But
in the case of the greater abbeys, many of whose mitred abbots sat in the
House of Lords, it was desirable that all appearance of confiscation should
be avoided. The houses were approached singly by Cromwell, and either

---

[1] Hall, ii, 267. The same point is put in a fictitious speech in Convocation
attributed to Bishop Fisher: 'Wherefore the manner of these proceedings puts me
in mind of a fable, how the axe which wanted a handle came upon a time unto the
wood making his moan to the great trees how he wanted a handle to work withal,
and for that cause was constrained to sit idle. Wherefore he made it his request unto
them, that they would be pleased to grant him one of their small saplings within the
wood to make him a handle, who, mistrusting no guile, granted him one of the
smaller trees, wherewith he made himself a handle; so becoming a complete axe, he
so fell to work within the same wood that in process of time there was neither great
nor small tree to be found in the place where the wood stood. And so, my Lords, if
you grant the King these smaller monasteries, you do but make him a handle,
whereby at his own pleasure he may cut down all the cedars within your Libanus,
and then you may thank yourselves after ye have incurred the heavy displeasure of
Almighty God' (Lewis, ii, 42).

bullied or persuaded into signing deeds of voluntary surrender. Some houses concealed their valuables; others made over their lands to laymen in the hope of saving them; some offered gifts to Cromwell and the King. But these were determined, as Cromwell said, 'to taste the fat priests,' and although there was no legal power to suppress, between 1537 and 1539 a large number of the greater monasteries surrendered to the King[1]. The movement was stimulated by another visitation of January, 1538, and steps were also taken against the friaries[2]. Twelve of the more powerful houses still held out, and these were involved in charges of treason. The abbots were accused of complicity in rebellion, and by a novel interpretation of the law, their abbeys were declared forfeited to the Crown by their attainder, as if they had been their private estates. Thus, in connexion with the Pilgrimage of Grace, Jervaux, Whalley, Barlings, Kirkstead, and Bridlington were dissolved; the abbot of Furness was forced to surrender; and the Cistercian abbey of Holm Cultram was involved in the Lincolnshire rebellion[3]. The abbots of Glastonbury, Reading, and Colchester, three of the most famous houses in England, were all hanged. The last abbey to surrender was Waltham—on March 23, 1540. The Act of 1539 for the Dissolution of the Greater Monasteries recognised what had been done, and to prevent any doubts as to legal titles, vested the surrendered houses, and such as should hereafter be surrendered, in the King, his heirs and successors, for ever.

An Act for dissolution of Abbeys

Where divers and sundry abbots, priors, abbesses, prioresses, and other ecclesiastical governors and governesses of divers monasteries, abbacies, priories, nunneries, colleges, hospitals, houses of friars, and other religious and ecclesiastical houses and places within this our Sovereign Lord the King's realm of England and Wales, of their own free and voluntary minds, good wills, and assents, without constraint, coaction, or compulsion of any manner of person or persons, since the fourth day of February, the 27th year[4] of the reign of our now most dread Sovereign Lord, by the due order and course of the common laws of this his realm of England, and by their sufficient writings of record under their convent and common seals, have severally given, granted, and by the same their writings severally confirmed all their said monasteries, abbacies [etc.]...and all their sites, circuits, and precincts of the same, and all and singular their manors, lordships, granges, meses[5], lands, tenements, meadows, pastures, rents, reversions, services, woods, tithes, pensions, portions, churches, chapels, advowsons, patronages, annuities, rights, entries, conditions, commons, leets[6], courts,

---

[1] Between 1537 and 1540 surrenders were obtained from 158 abbeys and 30 nunneries (Gwatkin, p. 166).

[2] Fisher, p. 425.   [3] *Ib.* p. 416.

[4] February 4, 1536.   [5] Messuages.   [6] Jurisdictions of court leet

liberties, privileges, and franchises, appertaining or in any wise belonging to any such monastery, abbacy [etc.]. . . or to any of them, by whatsoever name or corporation they or any of them were then named or called, and of what order, habit, religion, or other kind or quality soever they or any of them then were reputed, known, or taken; To have and to hold all the said monasteries, abbacies [etc.]. . . sites, circuits [etc.]. . . and all other the premises to our said Sovereign Lord, his heirs and successors, for ever; and the same their said monasteries, abbacies, [etc.]. . . sites, circuits [etc.]. . . and other the premises, voluntarily as is aforesaid have renounced, left, and forsaken, and every of them hath renounced, left, and forsaken: Be it therefore enacted. . . That the King our Sovereign Lord shall have, hold, possess, and enjoy to him, his heirs and successors, for ever all and singular such late monasteries, abbacies [etc.]. . . which since the said fourth day of February the 27th year of the reign of our said Sovereign Lord have been dissolved, suppressed, renounced, relinquished, forfeited, given up, or by any other mean[1] come to his Highness; and by the same authority and in like manner shall have, hold, possess, and enjoy all the sites, circuits [etc.]. . . and other whatsoever hereditaments which appertained or belonged to the said late monasteries, abbacies [etc.]. . . or to any of them, in as large and ample manner and form as the late abbots, priors, abbesses, prioresses, and other ecclesiastical governors and governesses of such late monasteries, abbacies [etc.]. . . had, held, or occupied, or of right ought to have had, holden, or occupied, in the rights of their said late monasteries, abbacies [etc.]. . . at the time of the said dissolution, suppression, renouncing, relinquishing, forfeiting, giving up, or by any other manner of mean coming of the same to the King's Highness, since the fourth day of February above specified.

II. And it is further enacted by the authority abovesaid, that not only all the said late monasteries, abbacies [etc.]. . . sites, circuits [etc.]. . . and all other the premises, forthwith, immediately, and presently[2], but also all other monasteries, abbacies [etc.]. . . which hereafter shall happen to be dissolved, suppressed, [etc.]. . . and also all the sites, circuits [etc.]. . . and other hereditaments, whatsoever they be, belonging or appertaining to the same or any of them, whensoever and as soon as they shall be dissolved, suppressed, [etc.]. . . shall be vested, deemed, and adjudged by authority of this present Parliament in the very actual and real seisin

---

[1] 'Mean' in the singular was in common use.
[2] Immediately.

and possession of the King our Sovereign Lord, his heirs and successors, for ever, in the state and condition as they now be and as though all the said late monasteries, abbacies [etc.]. . . so dissolved, suppressed [etc.]. . . as also the said monasteries, abbacies [etc.]. . . which hereafter shall happen to be dissolved, suppressed [etc.]. . . sites, circuits [etc.]. . . and other the premises whatsoever they be and every of them, were in this present Act specially and particularly rehearsed, named, and expressed, by express words, names, titles, and faculties, and in their natures, kinds, and qualities.

III. And be it also enacted by authority aforesaid, that all the said late monasteries, abbacies [etc.]. . . which be dissolved, suppressed [etc.]. . . and all the manors, lordships, granges, lands, tenements, and other the premises, Except such thereof as be come to the King's hands by attainder or attainders of treason, And all the said monasteries, abbacies [etc.]. . . which hereafter shall happen to be dissolved, suppressed [etc.]. . . and all the manors, lordships, granges, lands, tenements, meadows, pastures, rents, reversions, services, woods, tithes, portions, pensions, parsonages, appropriate vicarages[1], churches, chapels, advowsons, nominations, patronages, annuities, rights, interests, entries, conditions, commons, leets, courts, liberties, privileges, franchises, and other hereditaments whatsoever they be, belonging to the same or to any of them (except such thereof which shall happen to come to the King's Highness by attainder or attainders of treason), shall be in the order, survey, and governance of our said Sovereign Lord the King's Court of Augmentations of the Revenues of his Crown. . . .

*   *   *   *   *   *

XVIII. And be it further enacted by authority of this present Parliament, that such of the said late monasteries, abbacies [etc.] . . . and all churches and chapels to them or any of them belonging, which before the dissolution, suppression [etc.]. . . were exempted from the visitation or visitations and all other jurisdiction of the ordinary or ordinaries[2] within whose diocese they were situate or set, shall from henceforth be within the jurisdiction or visitation of the ordinary or ordinaries within whose diocese they or any of them be situate and set, or within the jurisdiction and visitation

---

[1] The word 'appropriate' is here used in a technical ecclesiastical sense, of a benefice annexed to a religious corporation.

[2] In ecclesiastical law the 'ordinary' is one who has of his own right, and not by special deputation, immediate jurisdiction in ecclesiastical causes. In practice this would usually, but not invariably, be the bishop of the diocese.

of such person or persons as by the King's Highness shall be limited or appointed; This Act or any other exemption, liberty, or jurisdiction to the contrary notwithstanding.

*　　*　　*　　*　　*

31 Henr. VIII, c. 13: *Statutes of the Realm*, iii, 733.

The number of the smaller religious houses affected by the First Act of Dissolution was 376. Under the Second Act about 200 greater houses[1] and 200 friaries were acquired by the King. From the *Valor Ecclesiasticus* particulars of the income of 553 monasteries can be obtained, and this works out at a total of £160,000 gross or £135,000 net[2]. This income was derived from a variety of sources—tithe, voluntary offerings, glebe, leases of benefices, rents, minerals (salt-works, quarries, and mines), mills, markets, fisheries, fines and fees and the income from manorial courts, rights of common, cattle and sheep farming, and the sale of timber. In addition to the monastic income and the landed and other property which produced it, the Crown acquired under the Dissolution Acts a considerable quantity of plate, ornaments, vestments, and other moveable property, in spite of the fact that as the Dissolution drew near the monks sold off their cattle, grain, and timber, and tried to conceal their jewels and plate[3]. Further, although they ceased to spend money on keeping up their buildings, which tended to fall into decay, it was found when the architectural tragedy of the Dissolution was consummated that a good deal of money could be realised by the sale of building materials, bells, and lead from the roofs. Of the value of this miscellaneous property no very satisfactory calculation has yet been made[4].

The effects of the Dissolution upon education, the poor, and social life belong properly to the province of economic and social history. The most important result from the point of view of constitutional history was the endowment of a new nobility out of the spoils. The approximate yearly value of lands granted by free gift, or by sale, sometimes at a nominal price, was £90,000, the number of grantees being about 1000[5]. A great part of what remained was let out by the Crown on lease. The largest grantees— those receiving lands worth more than £200 a year—were 15 peers and 30 commoners, nearly all of the latter being in the service of the King[6]. Thus

---

[1] Professor Savine (pp. 114–15) points out that this classification into 'smaller' and 'greater' houses is of the roughest kind. The houses really fall into five groups— 53 with less than £20 a year; 188 from £20 to £100; 199 from £100 to £300; 89 from £300 to £1000; and 24 with more than £1000—reckoning by the net income. The monasteries with a net income from £20 to £300 are almost 2½ times the number of all the rest.

[2] Savine, p. 100.　　　　　　　[3] Savine, p. 189.

[4] Gasquet (ii, 438) gives £1,423,500, as the cash value of the spoils to the King, of which £85,000 was the melting-price of gold and silver plate.

[5] These figures, from Dr Savine's researches, are given in Fisher, p. 497. They do not include grants of monastic land in Wales. The sales and leases greatly preponderated over the gifts (p. 482).

[6] 'If ever the poet's fiction of a golden shower rained into Danae's lap found a moral or real performance, it was now, at the dissipation of abbeys-lands...it is certain that in this age small merits of courtiers met with a prodigious recompense for their service' (Fuller, ii, 248).

an influential class of English society was committed to the support of the King's ecclesiastical policy[1], and the arrangement was not upset, even in the reign of Mary.

(3) Bishoprics Act, 1539

The preamble of this statute, which passed through all its stages in both Houses in one day, suggests various ways in which the spoils of the monasteries might have been employed for the benefit of the Church and of education. The need for new bishoprics was urgent, and the first scheme, that of 1534, provided for 26 new suffragan sees[2]. In 1539 the number of new bishoprics contemplated was 18. The number actually founded was only six —Chester, Peterborough, Gloucester, Oxford, Bristol, and Westminster; and the last did not long survive its foundation.

An Act for the King to make Bishops

Forasmuch as it is not unknown the slothful and ungodly life which hath been used amongst all those sort which have borne the name of religious folk, and to the intent that from henceforth many of them might be turned to better use as hereafter shall follow, whereby God's word might the better be set forth, children brought up in learning, clerks nourished in the Universities, old servants decayed to have livings, almshouses for poor folk to be sustained in, Readers of Greek, Hebrew, and Latin to have good stipend, daily alms to be ministered, mending of highways, exhibition[3] for ministers of the Church; It is thought therefore unto the King's Highness most expedient and necessary that more bishoprics, collegiate and cathedral churches shall be established, instead of these foresaid religious houses, within the foundation whereof these other titles afore rehearsed shall be established; Be it therefore enacted by authority of this present Parliament that his Highness shall have full power and authority from time to time to declare and nominate, by his letters patents or other writings to be made under his great seal, such number of bishops, such number of cities sees for bishops, cathedral churches, and dioceses, by meets[4] and bounds for the exercise and ministration of their episcopal offices and administration as shall appertain, and to endow them with such possessions after such manner, form, and condition as to his most excellent wisdom

---

[1] Bishop Creighton suggested that many of the grants were disposed by design so as to form a barrier to protect London from the rebels of the North and West (Gwatkin, p. 169).

[2] Traill, iii, 65.

[3] 'Exhibition' could be applied to any kind of maintenance or support; it was not limited to that assigned to students at the Universities.

[4] 'Mete' is a boundary or limit. 'Meets and bounds' is a common legal phrase.

shall be thought necessary and convenient; and also shall have power and authority to make and devise translations, ordinances, rules, and statutes concerning them all and every of them, and further to do all and every other thing and things whatsoever it shall be which shall be devised and thought requisite, convenient, and necessary by his most excellent wisdom and discretion for the good perfection and accomplishment of all and singular his said most godly and gracious purposes and intents touching the premises, or any other charitable or godly deeds to be devised by his Highness concerning the same; And that all and singular such translations, nominations of bishops cities sees and limitation of dioceses for bishops, erections, establishments, foundations, ordinances, statutes, rules, and all and every other thing and things which shall be devised, comprised, and expressed by his Grace's sundry and several letters patents or other writings under his great seal touching and concerning the premises or any of them, or any circumstances or dependences thereof necessary and requisite for the perfection of the premises or any of them, shall be of as good strength, force, value, and effect to all intents and purposes as if such things that shall so be devised, expressed, and mentioned in his letters patents or other writings under his great seal had been done, made, and had by authority of Parliament.

31 Henr. VIII, c. 9: *Statutes of the Realm*, iii, 728.

(4) Extracts

The extracts which follow indicate the attitude with regard to ecclesiastical abuses adopted by the greater contemporary churchmen, and a distinguished layman like Sir Thomas More. The *Supplication of Beggars* has been included to show the worst that hostile critics said of the Church.

1. JOHN COLET, 1511

John Colet, the friend of Erasmus, Dean of St Paul's and founder of St Paul's School, was an unsparing critic of clerical abuses. The sermon of 1511, preached before Convocation in St Paul's, is directed against the shortcomings of the secular clergy; but something must be allowed for the rhetorical form naturally adopted by a preacher. Colet's attitude towards monasticism is shewn by the quotation from Erasmus printed below (p. 73).

...To exhort you, reverend fathers, to the endeavour of reformation of the Church's estate (because that nothing hath so disfigured the face of the Church as hath the fashion of secular and worldly living in clerks and priests) I know not where more conveniently to take beginning of my tale than of the Apostle Paul, in whose temple ye are gathered together...'Be you not' (saith he) 'conformable to this world.'

The apostle calleth the world the ways and manner of secular living, the which chiefly doth rest in four evils of this world: that is to say, in devilish pride, in carnal concupiscence, in worldly covetousness, in secular business. These are in the world, as St John the apostle witnesseth in his epistle canonical. For he saith: 'All thing that is in the world' is either the 'concupiscence of the flesh' or the 'concupiscence of the eyes,' or 'pride of life.' The same are now and reign in the Church, and in men of the Church; that we may seem truly to say, all thing that is in the Church is either concupiscence of flesh or eyes, or pride of life.

And first for to speak of pride of life: how much greediness and appetite of honour and dignity is now-a-days in men of the Church? How run they, yea, almost out of breath, from one benefice to another; from the less to the more, from the lower to the higher? Who seeth not this? Who seeing this sorroweth not? Moreover, these that are in the same dignities, the most part of them doth go with so stately a countenance and with so high looks, that they seem not to be put in the humble bishopric of Christ, but rather in the high lordship and power of the world....

The second secular evil is carnal concupiscence. Hath not this vice so growen and waxen in the Church as a flood of their lust, so that there is nothing looked for more diligently in this most busy time of the most part of priests than that that doth delight and please the senses? They give themselves to feasts and banquetting; they spend themselves in vain babbling; they give themselves to sports and plays; they apply themselves to hunting and hawking; they drown themselves in the delights of this world. Procurers and finders of lusts they set by....

Covetousness is the third secular evil, the which St John the apostle calleth concupiscence of the eyes. St Paul calleth it idolatry. This abominable pestilence hath so entered in the mind almost of all priests, and so hath blinded the eyes of the mind, that we are blind to all things but only unto those which seem to bring unto us some gains. For what other thing seek we now-a-days in the Church than fat benefices and high promotions? Yea, and in the same promotions, of what other thing do we pass upon than of our tithes and rents? that we care not how many, how chargeful, how great benefices we take, so that they be of great value. O covetousness! St Paul justly called thee the root of all evil. Of thee cometh this heaping of benefices upon benefices. Of thee, so great pensions assigned of many benefices resigned. Of thee, all the suing for tithes, for offering, for mortuaries, for dilapidations, by the right and title of the Church. For the which thing we strive no less than for our own life. O covetousness! of thee cometh these chargeful visitations of bishops. Of thee cometh the corruptness of courts, and these daily new inventions wherewith the silly[1] people are so sore vexed. Of thee cometh the busyty[2] and wantonness of officials. O covetousness! mother of all iniquity, of thee cometh this fervent study of ordinaries to dilate their jurisdictions. Of thee cometh this wood[3] and raging contention in ordinaries; of thee, insinuation[4] of testaments; of thee cometh the undue sequestration of fruits; of thee cometh the superstitious observing of all those laws that sound[5] to any lucre, setting aside and despising those that concern the amendment of manners. What should I rehearse the rest? To be short, and to conclude at one word: all corruptness, all the decay of the Church, all the offences of the world, come of the covetousness of priests; according to that of St Paul, that here I repeat again and beat into your ears, 'Covetousness is the root of all evil.'

The fourth secular evil that spotteth and maketh ill-favoured the face of the Church, is the continual secular occupation wherein priests and bishops now-a-days doth busy themselves, the servants rather of men than of God; the warriors rather of this world than of Christ....

...In this time also we perceive contradiction of the lay people. But they are not so much contrary unto us as we are our-selves; nor their contrariness hurteth not us so much as the con-trariness of our evil life, the which is contrary both to God and Christ....

...The way whereby the Church may be reformed into better fashion is not for to make new laws. For there be laws many enough and out of number....Therefore it is no need that new laws and constitutions be made, but that those that are made already be kept....

First, let those laws be rehearsed that do warn you fathers that ye put not over soon your hands on every man, or admit unto holy orders. For there is the well of evils, that, the broad gate of holy orders opened, every man that offereth himself is allwhere[6] admitted without pulling back. Thereof springeth and cometh out the people that are in the Church both of unlearned and evil priests[7]....

Let the laws be rehearsed that command that benefices of the

---

[1] Unlearned, simple, ignorant.   [2] Officiousness, fussiness.   [3] Mad.
[4] In the legal sense, the production of a will for registration with a view to obtaining probate.   [5] Tend.
[6] Everywhere.   [7] Cf. Sir Thomas More, p. 74 below.

Church be given to those that are worthy; and that promotions be made in the Church by the right balance of virtue, not by carnal affection, not by the acception of persons[1]; whereby it happeneth now-a-days that boys for old men, fools for wise men, evil for good, do reign and rule.

Let the laws be rehearsed that warreth against the spot of simony. The which corruption, the which infection, the which cruel and odible[2] pestilence, so creepeth now abroad, as the canker evil in the minds of priests, that many of them are not afraid now-a-days both by prayer and service, rewards and promises, to get them great dignities.

Let the laws be rehearsed that command personal residence of curates in their churches. For of this many evils grow, because all things now-a-days are done by vicars and parish priests; yea, and those foolish also and unmeet, and oftentimes wicked; that seek none other thing in the people than foul lucre, whereof cometh occasion of evil heresies and ill christendom[3] in the people.

Let be rehearsed the laws and holy rules given of fathers, of the life and honesty of clerks; that forbid that a clerk be no merchant, that he be no usurer, that he be no hunter, that he be no common player, that he bear no weapon; the laws that forbid clerks to haunt taverns, that forbid them to have suspect familiarity with women; the laws that command soberness, and a measure-ableness in apparel, and temperance in adorning of the body.

Let be rehearsed also to my lords these monks, canons, and religious men the laws that command them to go the strait way that leadeth unto Heaven, leaving the broad way of the world; that commandeth them not to turmoil themselves in business, neither secular nor other; that command that they sow not in princes' courts for earthly things. For it is in the Council of Chalcedon that monks ought only to give themselves to prayer and fasting, and to the chastening of their flesh, and observing of their rules.

Above all things, let the laws be rehearsed that pertain and concern you, my reverend fathers and lords bishops, laws of your just and canonical election in the chapters of your churches with the calling of the Holy Ghost. For because that is not done now-a-days, and because prelates are chosen oftentimes more by favour of men than by the grace of God, therefore truly have we not a few times bishops full little spiritual men, rather worldly than

---

[1] Corrupt acceptance, or favouritism.   [2] Hateful.
[3] Christianity.

heavenly, savouring more the spirit of this world than the spirit of Christ.

Let the laws be rehearsed of the residence of bishops in their dioceses; that command that they look diligently and take heed to the health of souls; that they sow the word of God; that they shew themselves in their churches at the least on great holy days; that they do sacrifice for their people; that they hear the causes and matters of poor men; that they sustain fatherless children and widows; that they exercise themselves in works of virtue.

Let the laws be rehearsed of the good bestowing of the patrimony of Christ: the laws that command that the goods of the Church be spent, not in costly building, not in sumptuous apparel and pomps, not in feasting and banquetting, not in excess and wantonness, not in enriching of kinsfolk, not in keeping of dogs, but in things profitable and necessary to the Church....

J. H. Lupton, *Life of John Colet* (1887), pp. 293–304.

Erasmus

...Though no one approved of Christian devotion more than [Colet], yet he had but very little liking for monasteries—undeserving of the name as many of them now are. The gifts he bestowed upon them were either none, or the smallest possible; and he left them no share of his property even at his death. The reason was not that he disliked religious orders, but that those who took them did not come up to their profession. It was, in fact, his own wish to disconnect himself entirely from the world, if he could only have found a fraternity anywhere really bound together for a Gospel life....

Quoted in J. H. Lupton, *Life of John Colet*, p. 216.

2. SIR THOMAS MORE, 1528

More's *Dialogue*, completed in 1528, is chiefly directed against Luther and Tindal. He was hostile to Luther's attempt to reform the Church from without, but he admitted the existence of abuses.

...But yet where ye speak of other countries, making an argument that our clergy is the worst of all other, I wot well the whole world is so wretched that spiritual and temporal everywhere all be bad enough, God make us all better. But yet for that I have myself seen and by credible folk have heard, like as ye say by our temporalty that we be as good and as honest as anywhere else, so dare I boldly say that the spiritualty of England, and specially that part in which ye find most fault, that is to wit that part which we commonly call the secular clergy, is in learning

and honest living well able to match, and (saving the comparisons
be odious, I would say farther) far able to overmatch, number for
number, the spiritualty of any nation christened. I wot well there
be therein many very lewd and naught; and surely wheresoever
there is a multitude it is not without miracle well possible to be
otherwise. But now if the bishops would once take unto priesthood better laymen and fewer (for of us be they made) all the
matter were more than half amended. Now where ye say that ye
see more vice in them than in ourselves, truth it is that everything
in them is greater because they be more bounden to be better[1].
But else the things that they misdo be the selfsame that we sin
in ourselves, which vices that, as ye say, we see more in them
than in ourselves; the cause is, I suppose, for we look more upon
theirs than on our own.... Would God we were all of the mind
that every man thought no man so bad as himself, for that were
the way to mend both them and us. Now, they blame us, and we
blame them, and both blameworthy, and either part more ready
to find others' faults than to mend their own. For in reproach of
them we be so studious that neither good nor bad passeth unre-
proved. If they be familiar, we call them light. If they be solitary,
we call them fantastic[2]. If they be sad, we call them solemn. If
they be merry, we call them mad. If they be comprynable[3], we
call them vicious. If they be holy, we call them hypocrites. If
they keep few servants, we call them niggards. If they keep many,
we call them pompous. If a lewd priest do a lewd deed, then we
say, lo! see what sample the clergy giveth us, as though that
priest were the clergy. But then forget we to look what good
men be therein, and what good counsel they give us, and what
good ensample they shew us. But we fare as do the ravens and
the carrion crows, that never meddle with any quick flesh, but
where they may find a dead dog in a ditch thereto they flee and
thereon they feed apace. So where we see a good man, and hear
and see a good thing, there we take little heed. But when we see
once an evil deed, thereon we gape, thereof we talk, and feed
ourselves all day with the filthy delight of evil communication.
Let a good man preach, a short tale shall serve us thereof, and we
shall neither much regard his exhortation nor his good examples.
But let a lewd friar be taken with a wench, we will jest and rail

---

[1] This point is also taken by Thomas Starkey; see p. 84 below.
[2] Fanciful or capricious; the sixteenth century sense of the word is much less
strong than the modern sense.
[3] Probably an error for 'compynable,' a variant of 'companable' = sociable,
friendly.

upon the whole order all the year after, and say, lo! what sample they give us...(p. 225).

...And whereof is there now such plenty as of priests?... Now runneth every rascal and boldly offereth himself for able. And where the dignity passeth all prince's, and they that lewd[1] be desireth it for worldly winning, yet cometh that sort thereto with such a mad mind that they reckon almost God much bounden to them that they vouchsafe to take it. But were I Pope—

By my soul, quoth he[2], I would ye were, and my lady your wife Popess too.

Well, quoth I, then should she devise for nuns. And as for me, touching the choice of priests, I could not well devise better provisions than are by the laws of the Church provided already, if they were as well kept as they be well made. But for the number, I would surely see such a way therein that we should not have such a rabble that every mean man must have a priest in his house to wait upon his wife, which no man almost lacketh now, to the contempt of priesthood in as vile office as his horse-keeper.

That is, quoth he, truth indeed—and in worse too, for they keep hawks and dogs. And yet meseemeth surely a more honest service to wait on an horse than on a dog.

And yet I suppose, quoth I, if the laws of the Church which Luther and Tindal would have all broken were all well observed and kept, this gear should not be thus, but the number of priests would be much minished and the remnant much better. For it is by the laws of the Church provided, to the intent no priest should unto the slander of the priesthood be driven to live in such lewd manner or worse, there should none be admitted unto priesthood until he have a title of a sufficient yearly living, either of his own patrimony or otherwise. Nor at this day they be none otherwise accepted.

Why, quoth he, wherefore go there then so many of them a begging?

Marry, quoth I, for they delude the law and themselves also. For they never have grant of a living that may serve them in

---

[1] 'Lewd' here='lay'—used in the common medieval sense of *laicus*, 'unlearned.' Probably the sense is that the dignity of the priesthood is so high that laymen ('they that lewd be') seek it for worldly advantage.

[2] The other party to the dialogue is supposed to be a young university student who had been attracted by the teaching of Tindal, and is now sent by 'a worshipful friend' of More's, 'with certain credence,' to discuss with him the matters to which the book refers and so to be won back from error. The whole conversation is imaginary, but it is a vehicle for More's views. The scene of the dialogue is his library at Chelsea.

sight for that purpose but they secretly discharge it ere they have
it, or else they could not get it. And thus the Bishop is blinded
by the sight of the writing, and the priest goeth a-begging for all
his grant of a good living, and the law is deluded, and the order
is rebuked by the priest's begging and lewd living, which either
is fain to walk at rovers[1] and live upon trentals[2] or worse, or else
to serve in a secular man's house, which should not need if this
gap were stopped. For ye should have priests few enough if the
law were truly observed that none were made but he that were
without collusion sure of a living already.

Then might it hap, quoth he, that ye might have too few to
serve the rooms and livings that be provided for them, except the
prelates would provide that orders were not so commonly given,
but alway receive into orders as rooms and livings fall void to
bestow them in, and no faster.

Surely, quoth I, for aught I see suddenly[3], that would not be
much amiss. For so should they need no such titles at all, nor
should need neither run at rovers nor live in laymen's houses, by
reason whereof there groweth among[4] no little corruption in the
priests' manners by the conversation of lay people and company of
women in their houses.

Nay, by our Lady, quoth he, I will not agree with you therein.
For I think they cannot lightly[5] meet with much worse company
than themselves, and that they rather corrupt us than we them...
(pp. 227–8).

Sir Thomas More, *A Dialogue concerning Heresies* (*Works*, ed. 1557).

3. SIMON FISH, 1528

A Supplication for the Beggars, written in 1528, is one of the most violent
attacks upon the Church and the clergy that the Reformation produced—indeed,
it is so violent as to suggest deliberate exaggeration with humorous intent. Many
copies of it were circulated in London just before the meeting of the Reformation
Parliament, as it was excellent propaganda, and expressed in a popular form the
general dissatisfaction with the Church which was prevailing at the time. It
is impossible to accept the statements of the author, but the interest of his work
lies in the fact that there was something in the public mind which responded to it.
The *Supplication for the Beggars* was of sufficient importance to draw a reply from
Sir Thomas More entitled *A Supplication of Souls* (p. 79), and it served as a model
for a series of pamphleteers[6].

Most lamentably complaineth their woeful misery unto your
Highness your poor daily bedemen, the wretched, hideous mon-

---

[1] At random, without any definite object.
[2] *I.e.* live by saying requiem masses. See note on p. 104 below.
[3] *I.e.* on the spur of the moment.
[4] Meanwhile.   [5] Easily.   [6] *D.N.B.* xix, 51.

sters (on whom scarcely for horror any eye dare look), the foul, unhappy sort of lepers and other sore people, needy, impotent, blind, lame, and sick, that live only by alms, how that their number is daily so sore increased that all the alms of all the well-disposed people of this your realm is not half enough for to sustain them, but that for very constraint they die for hunger. And this most pestilent mischief is come upon your said poor bedemen by the reason for that there is, in the times of your noble predecessors passed, craftily crept into this your realm another sort, not of impotent, but of strong, puissant, and counterfeit holy and idle beggars and vagabonds, which, since the time of their first entry by all the craft and wiliness of Satan, are now increased under your sight, not only into a great number but also into a kingdom. These are not the herds[1] but the ravenous wolves going in herds' clothing devouring the flock—the bishops, abbots, priors, deacons, archdeacons, suffragans, priests, monks, canons, friars, pardoners, and sumners[2]. And who is able to number this idle, ravenous sort, which (setting all labour aside) have begged so importunately that they have gotten into their hands more than the third part of all your realm. The goodliest lordships, manors, lands, and territories are theirs. Besides this they have the tenth part of all the corn, meadow, pasture, grass, wool, colts, calves, lambs, pigs, geese, and chickens. Over and besides, the tenth part of every servant's wages, the tenth part of the wool, milk, honey, wax, cheese, and butter. Yea, and they look so narrowly upon their profits that the poor wives must be countable to them of every tenth egg, or else she getteth not her rights at Easter, shall be taken as an heretic. . . . What money pull they in by probates of testaments, privy tithes, and by men's offerings to their pilgrimages and at their first masses? Every man and child that is buried must pay somewhat for masses and *diriges* to be sung for him, or else they will accuse the dead's friends and executors of heresy. What money get they by mortuaries[3], by hearing of confessions (and yet they will keep thereof no counsel), by hallowing of churches, altars, super-altars[4], chapels, and bells, by cursing of men and absolving them again for money? What a multitude of money gather the pardoners in a year? How much money get the sumners by extortion in a year, by citing the people to the commissary's court[5] and afterwards releasing the appearance for money? Finally, the

[1] Shepherds.   [2] A summoning officer in an ecclesiastical court.
[3] See p. 13 above.
[4] A portable stone slab consecrated for use upon an unconsecrated altar or table.
[5] The court of a bishop's commissary; see p. 358 below.

infinite number of begging friars; what get they in a year?...Is
it any marvel that the taxes, fifteenths, and subsidies that your
Grace most tenderly of great compassion hath taken among your
people to defend them from the threatened ruin of their commonwealth have been so slothfully, yea, painfully levied, seeing that
almost the utmost penny that might have been levied hath been
gathered before yearly by this ravenous, cruel, and insatiable
generation?...(pp. 1–3).

And what do all these greedy sort of sturdy, idle, holy thieves
with these yearly exactions that they take of the people? Truly
nothing but exempt themselves from the obedience of your Grace.
Nothing but translate all rule, power, lordship, authority, obedience, and dignity from your Grace unto them. Nothing but that
all your subjects should fall into disobedience and rebellion
against your Grace, and be under them. As they did unto your
noble predecessor, King John; which for because that he would
have punished certain traitors that had conspired with the French
king to have deposed him from his crown and dignity,...inter-
dicted his land. For the which matter your most noble realm
wrongfully (alas, for shame!) hath stood tributary, not unto any
kind temporal prince but unto a cruel, devilish bloodsupper,
drunken in the blood of the saints and martyrs of Christ, ever
since. Here were an holy sort of prelates, that thus cruelly could
punish such a righteous King, all his realm and succession, for
doing right!...(pp. 4–5)

...Yea, and what do they more? Truly nothing but apply themselves, by all the sleights they may, to have to do with every man's
wife, every man's daughter, and every man's maid....These be
they that by their abstaining from marriage do let[1] the generation
of the people, whereby all the realm at length, if it should be continued, shall be made desert and inhabitable[2]....(p. 6).

What remedy make laws against them? I am in doubt
whether ye be able. Are they not stronger in your own Parliament
House than yourself? What a number of bishops, abbots, and
priors are Lords of your Parliament?...Who is he (though he
be grieved never so sore)...dare lay it to their charge by any
way of action? And if he do, then is he by-and-by[3] by their wiliness
accused of heresy....So captive are your laws unto them, that no
man that they list to excommunicate may be admitted to sue any
action in any of your courts[4]. If any man in your sessions dare be
so hardy to indict a priest,...he hath, ere the year go out, such

---

[1] Hinder.   [2] Uninhabited.   [3] Immediately.   [4] See p. 357 below.

a yoke of heresy laid in his neck that it maketh him wish he had not done it.... (p. 8).

...This is the great scab[1] why they will not let the New Testament go abroad in your mother tongue, lest men should espy that they by their cloaked hypocrisy do translate thus fast your kingdom into their hands, that they are not obedient unto your high power[2], that they are cruel, unclean, unmerciful, and hypocrites, that they seek not the honour of Christ but their own, that remission of sins are not given by the Pope's pardon but by Christ, for the sure faith and truth that we have in him.... Set these sturdy loobies[3] abroad in the world... to get their living with their labour in the sweat of their faces according to the commandment of God, Gen. iii, to give other idle people by their example occasion to go to labour. Tie these holy, idle thieves to the carts to be whipped naked about every market town till they will fall to labour, that they by their importunate begging take not away the alms that the good Christian people would give unto us sore, impotent, miserable people your bedemen. Then shall as well the number of our foresaid monstrous sort, as of the bawds, whores, thieves, and idle people decrease. Then shall these great yearly exactions cease. Then shall not your sword, power, crown, dignity, and obedience of your people be translated from you. Then shall you have full obedience of your people. Then shall the idle people be set to work. Then shall matrimony be much better kept. Then shall the generation of your people be increased. Then shall your commons increase in riches. Then shall the gospel be preached. Then shall none beg our alms from us. Then shall we have enough and more than shall suffice us; which shall be the best hospital that ever was founded for us. Then shall we daily pray to God for your most noble estate long to endure. (pp. 11, 14–15.)

> Simon Fish, *A Supplication for the Beggars* (ed. F. J. Furnivall, Early English Text Society, 1871, extra series, No. 13, pp. 1–15). Also printed in Arber's *English Scholar's Library*, No. 4, 1878.

4. SIR THOMAS MORE, 1529

More's *Supplication of Souls* is a reply to Fish. The souls in purgatory discuss various questions, and among them the arguments of Fish in favour of a general confiscation of the property of the Church.

...And yet as though because he hath said it he had therefore proved it, he runneth forth in his railing rhetoric against the

---

[1] Here applied figuratively, as to moral or spiritual disease.
[2] Cf. Henry VIII's speech to the Commons (p. 22 above). [3] Louts.

whole clergy, and that in such a sort and fashion that very hard it were to discern whether it be more false and more foolish. For first, all the faults that any lewd priest or friar doeth, all that layeth he to the whole clergy, as well and as wisely as though he would lay the faults of some lewd lay people to the default and blame of all the whole temporalty. But this way liketh him so well, that thus laying to the whole clergy the faults of such as be simple and faulty therein, and yet not only laying to their charge the breach of chastity and abuse in fleshly living of such as be naught, but also madly like a fond[1] fellow laying much more to their charge, and much more earnestly reproving the good and honest living of those that be good, whom he rebuketh and abhorreth because they keep their vows and persevere in chastity (for he sayeth that they be the marrers and destroyers of the realm, bringing the land into wilderness for lack of generation by their abstaining from wedding) then aggrieveth[2] he his great crimes with heinous words, gay repetitions, and grievous exclamations, calling them bloodsuppers, and drunken in the blood of holy martyrs and saints, which he meaneth for the condemning of holy heretics. Greedy golophers[3] he calleth them and insatiable whirlpools, because the temporalty hath given them possessions and give to the friars their alms...(p. 295).

...Like truth is there in this that he saith, if any man trouble a priest for any temporal suit, the clergy forthwith will make him an heretic and burn him, but if he be content to bear a faggot for their pleasure. The falsehood of this cannot be unknown. For men know well in many a shire how often that many folk indict priests of rape at the sessions[4]. And as there is sometime a rape committed in deed, so is there ever a rape surmised were the woman never so willing, and oftentime where there was nothing done at all. And yet of any such that so procured priests to be indicted, how many have men heard taken and accused for heretics...(p. 297).

...He layeth unto the charge of the clergy that they live idle all, and that they be all bound to labour and get their living in the sweat of their faces by the precept that God gave to Adam in the first chapter of Genesis...(p. 303).

...But it is good to look betime what this beggar's proctor[5] meaneth by this commandment of hand labour that he speaketh of. For if he confess that it bindeth not every man, then is it laid to no purpose against the clergy; for there was a small clergy

---

[1] Foolish.   [2] Aggravates.   [3] Gluttons.
[4] In successfully meeting the argument that the law of heresy is used to protect the priests, More here makes an important admission.   [5] Advocate.

when that word was said to our first father Adam. But now if ye call it a precept, as he doth, and then will that it extend unto all the whole kind[1] of man, as a thing by God commanded unto Adam and all his offspring, then, though he say little now, he meaneth to go farther hereafter than he speaketh of yet. For if he might first have the clergy put out of their living and all that they have clean taken from them, and might have them joined to these beggars that be now, and over that added unto them and send a-begging too all those that the clergy find[2] now full honestly— this pageant once played, and his beggars' bill so well sped, then when the beggars should have so much less living and be so many more in multitude, surely likewise as for the beggars he now maketh his bill[3] to the King's Highness against bishops, abbots, priors, prelates, and priests, so would he then within a while after make another bill to the people against merchants, gentlemen, kings, lords, and princes, and complain that they have all, and say that they do nothing for it but live idle, and that they be commanded in Genesis to live by the labour of their hands in the sweat of their faces, as he saith by the clergy now. Wherein if they ween that they shall stand in other case than the clergy doth now, they may peradventure sore deceive themselves. For if they will think that their case shall not be called all one because they have lands and goods to live upon, they must consider so hath the clergy too. But that is the thing that this beggars' proctor complaineth upon, and would have them taken away. Now if the landed men suppose that their case shall not seem one with the case of the clergy, because they shall haply think that the Church hath their possessions given them for causes which they fulfil not, and that if their possessions happen to be taken from them it shall be done upon that ground, and so the lay landed men out of that fear, because they think that such like occasion and ground and consideration faileth and cannot be found in them and their inheritance—surely if any man, clerk or lay, have lands in the gift whereof hath been any condition adjoined which he fulfilleth not, the giver may well with reason use therein such advantage as the law giveth him. But on the other side, whoso will advise princes or lay people to take from the clergy their possessions, alleging matters at large, as laying to their charge that they live not as they should nor use not well their possessions, and therefore it were well done to take them from them by force and dispose them better—we dare boldly say, whoso giveth this device, as

---

[1] Race.   [2] Provide for.   [3] Plea or indictment.

now doth this beggar's proctor, we would give you counsel to look well what will follow. For he shall not fail, as we said before, if this bill of his were sped, to find you soon after in a new supplication new bald[1] reasons enough that should please the people's ears, wherewith he would labour to have lords' lands and all honest men's goods to be pulled from them by force and distributed among beggars...(p. 304–5).

Sir Thomas More, *A Supplication of Souls* (*Works*, ed. 1557).

5. THOMAS STARKEY, 1535 AND 1536

With the diatribes of Simon Fish should be compared the judicious, statesman-like, and temperately-expressed views of Thomas Starkey. These are contained in an imaginary dialogue between Thomas Lupset and Cardinal Pole, probably written in the early part of 1535[2] for the satisfaction of Henry VIII, and also in a letter addressed to the King in 1536[3]. Lupset, a friend of Pole, and also of More and Erasmus, died in 1530, five years before the dialogue was written.

Pole. ....A great part of these people which we have here in our country is either idle or ill occupied.... First, look what an idle rout our noblemen keep and nourish in their houses, which do nothing else but carry dishes to the table and eat them when they have done; and after, giving themselves to hunting, hawking, dicing, carding, and all other idle pastimes and vain, as though they were born to nothing else at all. Look to our bishops and prelates of the realm, whether they follow not the same trade in nourishing such an idle sort, spending their possessions and goods, which were to them given to be distributed among them which were oppressed with poverty and necessity. Look, furthermore, to priests, monks, friars, and canons, with all their adherents and idle train, and you shall find also among them no small number idle and unprofitable, which be nothing but burdens to the earth. Insomuch that if you after this manner examine the multitude in every order and degree, you shall find, as I think, the third part of our people living in idleness, as persons to the common weal utterly unprofitable; and to all good civility much like unto the drone bees in a hive, which do nothing else but consume and devour all such thing as the busy and good bee with diligence and labour gathereth together...(pp. 76–7).

...Princes and lords seldom look to the good order and wealth of their subjects; only they look to the receiving of their rents and revenues of their lands, with great study of enhancing thereof to the further maintaining of their pompous state.... Bishops also and prelates of the Church, you see how little regard

[1] Trivial, paltry.　　　　[2] Gairdner, iii, p. xxxvii.
[3] *D.N.B.* liv, 110.

they have of their flock. So that they may have the wool, they little care for the simple sheep, but let them wander in wild forests in danger of wolves daily to be devoured...(p. 85).

...And how think you by the law which admitteth to religion[1] of all sorts, youth of all age almost; insomuch that you shall see some friars whom you would judge to be born in the habit, they are so little and young admitted thereto?...(p. 127).

...How think you by the manner used with our bishops, abbots, and priors touching the nourishing also of a great sort of idle abbey-lubbers which are apt to nothing but, as the bishops and abbots be, only to eat and drink? Think you this a laudable custom and to be admitted in any good policy?

Lupset. Nay, surely this I cannot allow, it is so evident a fault to every man's eye; for by this mean[2] all the possessions of the Church are spent as ill as the possessions of temporal men, contrary to the institution of the law and all good civility....

Pole. There is another great fault which is the ground of all other almost, and that is concerning the education of them which appoint themselves to be men of the Church. They are not brought up in virtue and learning, as they should be, nor well approved therein before they be admitted to such high dignity. It is not convenient men without learning to occupy the place of them which should preach the word of God, and teach the people the laws of religion, of the which commonly they are most ignorant themselves; for commonly you shall find that they can nothing do but patter up their matins and mass, mumbling up a certain number of words nothing understood.

Lupset. Sir, you say in this plain truth; I cannot nor will not this deny.

Pole. Yea, and yet another thing. Let it be that the priests were unlearned, yet if they were of perfect life and studious of virtue, that by their example they might teach other, this ignorance yet might be the better suffered; but now to that ignorance is joined all kind of vice, all mischief and vanity, insomuch that they are example of all vicious life to the lay people. How say you, Master Lupset, is not this also a plain truth and manifest?

Lupset. Yes, truly, insomuch that almost the infants now born into the light perceive it plainly. There is no man that looketh into our manner of living that may doubt of this...(pp. 131–3).

Pole. And as for this ignorance and vicious life of the clergy, no man can it deny but he that, perverting the order of all things,

[1] *I.e.* to the cloister.   [2] See note on p. 65 above.

6—2

will take vice for virtue and virtue for vice. And though it be so
that the temporalty live much after the same trade, yet meseemeth
they are not so much to be blamed as they which for the purity
of life are called spiritual[1]; forasmuch as they should be the light,
as it is said in the Gospel, unto the other, and not only by word, but
much more by example of life, whereby chiefly they should induce
the rude people to the train of virtue[2]. Wherefore surely this is
no small fault in our custom of life. To the which we may join
also another ill custom, that priests be not resident upon their
benefices, but either be in the Court or in great men's houses,
there taking their pleasure; by the reason whereof the people
lack their pastors, which gather the wool diligently without
regard of the profit of their sheep.

Lupset. Sir, this is as clear as the light of the sun. Wherefore
I will not repugn therein; but I would wish that you might as
easily hereafter see the way to amend such fault as we may see
it...(p. 133).

Lupset. ....I have thought long and many a day a great let
to the increase of Christian people the law of chastity ordained by
the Church, which bindeth so great a multitude of men to live
thereafter; as all secular priests, monks, friars, canons, and nuns,
of the which, as you know, there is no small number, by the
reason whereof the generation of man is marvellously let and
minished[3]. Wherefore, except the ordinance of the Church were
(to the which I would never gladly rebel) I would plainly judge
that it should be very convenient something to release the band
of this law...(p. 148).

Pole. ....In this matter I think it were necessary to temper
this law, and, at the least, to give and admit all secular priests to
marry at their liberty, considering now the great multitude and
number of them. But as touching monks, canons, friars, and nuns,
I hold for a thing very convenient and meet, in all well-ordained
commonweals, to have certain monasteries and abbeys, to the
which all such as after lawful proof of chastity before had may
retire, and from the business and vanity of the world may withdraw themselves, wholly giving their minds to prayer, study, and
high contemplation...(pp. 149–150).

Lupset. Sir, of this there is no doubt but that this ordinance[4]

---

[1] Cf. Sir Thomas More, p. 74 above.   [2] The way of virtue.

[3] The slow growth of population in the Middle Ages was not infrequently
ascribed to the ascetic teaching of the Church. See Lea, i, 449.

[4] The appointment of officers in every town 'for the taking away' of 'ill-occupied persons in vain crafts,' and providing for the employment of the people 'in
honest and profitable crafts to the common weal' (p. 155).

should be very profitable. But yet you have left the one half of
the ill-occupied persons and nothing touched them at all. That is
to say, these religious persons in monasteries and abbeys.

Pole. Surely you say truth. Of them there is a great number
and unprofitable; but, Master Lupset, as touching them, as I said
before, I would not that these religious men with their monasteries should utterly be taken away but only some good reformation to be had of them. And, shortly to say, I would think in that
behalf chiefly this to be a good remedy, that youth should have
no place therein at all, but only such men as by fervent love of
religion moved thereto, flying the dangers and snares of the world,
should there have place. And if that gap were once stopped I
dare well say their number would not be over-great: we should
have fewer in number religious men but better in life....I cannot tell how you brought them in and numbered them among
idle and ill-occupied persons. Howbeit, to say the truth, they are
neither idle, as they say, neither yet well occupied...(p. 156).

Lupset. Sir,...I pray you tell me one thing that I shall ask
of you here. What difference is in this matter to send the firstfruits to Rome, and spend it in triumph[1] here at home among
whores and harlots and idle lubbers serving to the same purpose
in our own nation?[2]

Pole. Difference there is; for yet this it is spent at home in
our own country. Howbeit, Master Lupset, here you touch
another great fault which we noted also before in our bishops and
abbots, which triumph no less than the temporal lords....And,
briefly to say, I would nothing in this matter but only provision
that the order of the common law of the Church might have
place; that is to say, that bishops should divide their possessions
in four parts to the use appointed by the authority of the law: the
first to build churches and temples ruinate in their dioceses; the
second to maintain the poor youth in study; the third to the poor
maids and other poverty; and the fourth to find himself and his
household with a mean[3] number convenient to his dignity. Other
provision than this needeth not at all, saving that I would have
them to be resident upon their sees, except such as were necessary
about the prince. And as touching abbots and priors in our
country, I would none other but only the order of the monks of

---

[1] Pomp or show.
[2] This is the only reference to the more serious charges brought against some of
the clergy, but it regards them as something notorious, and Pole is represented as
offering no contradiction.
[3] Moderate.

Italy[1]; that is to say, that every three years to choose their abbots and priors, and there to give reckoning of their offices commonly, and to live among his brethren and not to triumph in their chambers as they do, which causeth all the envy in the cloisters and is the occasion of the great expense of the intrate[2] of the monastery, for to his table resorteth the idle company dwelling about him. This manner surely should be a great reformation in the monasteries of England...(p. 200).

Thomas Starkey, England in the Reign of King Henry VIII
(Early English Text Society, extra series, No. 32, 1878,
Part II ed. J. M. Cowper).

To the King's Highness

...And first herein this is certain, that many there be which are moved to judge plainly this Act of Suppression of certain abbeys both to be against the order of charity and injurious to them which be dead, because the founders thereof and the souls departed seem thereby to be defrauded of the benefit of prayer and almsdeeds there appointed to be done for their relief by their last will and testament; and also the common weal and politic order appeareth to be much hindered and troubled by the same, because many poor men thereby are like to be deprived of their living and quietness, wherein lieth, as they think, no small injury: howbeit, as touching these causes commonly alleged, though they seem to be of no small weight, yet they are objected in this matter by manifest lack of judgment and consideration, for to me a little considering with myself the nature of this Act, it appeareth plainly neither to be utterly against the order of charity neither yet the founders' wills to be broken thereby with any notable injury, for this is a sure ground by the order of all laws and by the consent of all men of learning and judgment approved, that though great respect ever hath been had of the last will of testators and much privilege granted thereto, specially when it pertained and tended to matters of religion, yet this I trow was never thought of any men of wisdom and prudence that all their posterity should be bounden of high necessity to the sure accomplishment and full observation of their wills prescribed in testament, and that by no means they might be changed and ordered to other purpose, for this is a sure truth that the will and deed of every private man for a common weal may be altered by the supreme authority in every country and kind of policy, forasmuch

---

[1] This is a reference to the great reform of the Congregation of Sta. Giustina at Padua.   [2] Income.

as every man by the order of God is subject thereto and his will ever presupposed to be obedient to the same, insomuch that though he be either absent or dead yet it is alway by reason thought that if he were present he would give his consent to all such things as be judged by common authority to be expedient to the public weal, to the which no private will may be lawfully repugnant. Wherefore albeit the last will of the testator's be by this Act altered with authority yet it is not broken with injury, because the consent of the testator is presupposed to be contained therein. Insomuch that it may surely be thought that if they were now living again and saw the present state of this world now in our days, how under the pretence of prayer much vice and idleness is nourished in these monasteries institute and founded of them, and how little learning and religion is taught in the same, yea, and how little Christian hospitality is used therein, they would peradventure cry out with one voice, saying after this manner to princes of the world,—'Alter these foundations which we of long time before did institute, and turn them to some better use and commodity. We never gave our possessions to this end and purpose to the which by abuse they be now applied. We thought to stablish houses of virtue, learning, and religion, the which now by the malice of man in process of time we see turned to vice, blindness, and superstition. We thought to stablish certain companies to live together in pure and Christian charity, wherein we see now reigneth much hate, rancour, and envy, much sloth, idleness, and gluttony, much ignorance, blindness, and hypocrisy, wherefore we cry, alter these foundations and turn them to better use; provide they may be as common schools to the education of youth in virtue and religion, out of the which you may pick men apt to be ordained bishops and prelates for their perfection; provide they may be some ornament to the common weal and not as they be now, slanderous and therewith great detriment.' This peradventure they would say unto your Highness, requiring your wisdom to call this matter to some like consideration, whereby it may appear that their wills are not utterly frustrate and broken by your Grace's acts....

Thomas Starkey, *England in the Reign of King Henry VIII*
(Early English Text Society, extra series, No. 32, 1878,
Part 1 ed. S. J. Herrtage), p. lv.

6. HUGH LATIMER, 1548

Latimer's *Sermon on the Plough* was preached at St Paul's before Edward VI, 18 January, 1548. Latimer was an honest partisan, and in his denunciation of current abuses he was carried away by the fervour of the preacher and the lure of alliteration; but the evils to which he refers were real, and in general he represents the attitude of the reformers towards them.

...This much I dare say, that since lording and loitering hath come up, preaching hath come down, contrary to the apostles' times, for they preached and lorded not, and now they lord and preach not....For ever since the prelates were made lords and nobles the plough standeth; there is no work done, the people starve. They hawk, they hunt, they card, they dice; they pastime in their prelacies with gallant gentlemen, with their dancing minions, and with their fresh companions, so that ploughing is set aside; and by their lording and loitering, preaching and ploughing is clean gone...(p. 66).

...And now I would ask a strange question: who is the most diligentest bishop and prelate in all England, that passeth all the rest in doing his office? I can tell for I know him who it is; I know him well. But now I think I see you listening and hearkening that I should name him. There is one that passeth all the other, and is the most diligent prelate and preacher in all England. And will ye know who it is? I will tell you: it is the Devil. He is the most diligent preacher of all other; he is never out of his diocese; he is never from his cure; ye shall never find him unoccupied; he is ever in his parish; he keepeth residence at all times; ye shall never find him out of the way, call for him when you will he is ever at home; the diligentest preacher in all the realm; he is ever at his plough; no lording nor loitering can hinder him; he is ever applying his business, ye shall never find him idle, I warrant you. And his office is to hinder religion, to maintain superstition, to set up idolatry, to teach all kind of popery. He is ready as he can be wished for to set forth his plough; to devise as many ways as can be to deface and obscure God's glory....O that our prelates would be as diligent to sow the corn of good doctrine as Satan is to sow cockle and darnel...(p. 70).

...But in the mean time the prelates take their pleasures. They are lords and no labourers; but the Devil is diligent at his plough. He is no unpreaching prelate; he is no lordly loiterer from his cure, but a busy ploughman; so that among all the prelates, and among all the pack of them that have cure, the Devil shall go for my money, for he still applieth his business. Therefore, ye unpreaching prelates, learn of the Devil...(p. 77).

Latimer, *Sermons* (ed. G. E. Corrie, Parker Society, 1844).

(5) Confessions of the Monks

The language of these confessions is quite inconsistent with the theory that they were genuine 'confessions' in the ordinary sense of the term. They were more probably the work of some expert draughtsman in Cromwell's office, and were placed before the monks for signature ready-drawn. In form they are reasoned surrenders rather than confessions.

St Andrew's Priory, Northampton, 1537

The following extracts are from the longer form of confession. One in the short form, that of the Friary of St Francis, Stamford, is also printed in Weever, *Funeral Monuments*, p. 110.

Most noble and virtuous Prince, our most righteous and gracious Sovereign Lord and undoubted Founder, and in earth, next under God, Supreme Head of this English Church. We, your Grace's poor and most unworthy subjects, Francis, Prior of your Grace's Monastery of Saint Andrew the Apostle within your Grace's town of Northampton, and the whole convent of the same[1], being stirred by the grief of our conscience unto great contrition for the manifold negligence, enormities, and abuses of long time by us and other our predecessors, under the pretence and shadow of perfect religion, used and committed, to the grievous displeasure of Almighty God, the crafty deception and subtle seduction of the pure and simple minds of the good Christian people of this your noble realm, knowledgen[2] ourselves to have grievously offended God and your Highness our Sovereign Lord and Founder, as well in corrupting the conscience of your good Christian subjects with vain, superstitious, and other unprofitable ceremonies, the very means and plain inductions[3] to the abominable sin of idolatry, as in omitting the execution of such devout and due observances and charitable acts as we were bounden to do by the promises and avows[4] made by us and our predecessors unto Almighty God, and to your Grace's most noble progenitors, original founders of your said monastery; for the which observances and deeds of charity only your said monastery was endowed with sundry possessions, jewels, ornaments, and other goods, moveable and unmoveable, by your Grace's said noble progenitors. The revenues of which possessions we, the said Prior and convent, voluntarily only by our proper conscience compelled, do recognise neither by us nor our predecessors to have been employed according to the original intent of the founders of your said monastery, that is to say, in the pure observ-

---

[1] See note on p. 62 above.   [2] Confessing, acknowledging.
[3] Inducements.   [4] *I.e.* vows.

ance of Christ's Religion, according to the devout rule and doctrine of holy Saint Benedict, in virtuous exercise and study according to our profession and avow, nor yet in the charitable sustaining,
comforting, and relieving of the poor people by the keeping of
good and necessary hospitality. But as well we as others our predecessors called religious persons within your said monastery,
taking on us the habit or outward vesture of the said rule only to
the intent to lead our lives in an idle quietness and not in virtuous
exercise, in a stately estimation and not in obedient humility,
have under the shadow or colour of the said rule and habit vainly,
detestably, and also ungodly employed, yea rather devoured, the
yearly revenues issuing and coming of the said possessions in continual ingurgitations[1] and farcings[2] of our carayne[3] bodies, and
of others the supporters of our voluptuous and carnal appetite,
with other vain and ungodly expenses, to the manifest subversion
of devotion and cleanness of living, and to the most notable
slander of Christ's holy Evangel, which in the form of our profession we did ostentate[4] and openly advaunt[5] to keep most exactly; withdrawing thereby from the simple and pure minds of
your Grace's subjects the only truth and comfort which they
ought to have by the true faith of Christ, and also the divine
honour and glory only due to the glorious majesty of God Almighty, steering them with all persuasions, engines[6], and policy,
to dead images and counterfeit relics for our damnable lucre.
Which our most horrible abominations and execrable persuasions
of your Grace's people to detestable errors, and our long covered
hypocrisy cloaked with feigned sanctity, we revolving daily and
continually pondering in our sorrowful hearts, and thereby perceiving the bottomless gulf of everlasting fire ready to devour us
if persisting in this state of living we should depart from this
uncertain and transitory life; constrained by the intolerable
anguish of our conscience; called as we trust by the grace of God,
who would have no man to perish in sin; with hearts most con-
trite and repentant, prostrate at the noble feet of your most royal
Majesty, most lamentably do crave of your Highness, of your
abundant mercy, to grant unto us most grievous against God and
your Highness your most gracious pardon for our said sundry
offences, omissions, and negligences committed as before by us
is confessed against your Highness and your most noble progenitors.

---

[1] 'Ingurgitation' is used of excessive eating or drinking in the sense of greedy
swallowing.   [2] Stuffing or cramming.   [3] An obsolete form of 'carrion.'
  [4] In the sense of displaying ostentatiously.   [5] Boast.   [6] Tricks or artifices.

And, where your Highness, being Supreme Head, immediately next after Christ, of his Church in this your realm of England, so consequently general and only reformator of all religious persons there, have full authority to correct or dissolve at your Grace's pleasure and liberty all convents and religious companies abusing the rules of their profession; and, moreover, to your Highness, being our Sovereign Lord and undoubted founder of your said monastery, by dissolution whereof appertaineth only the original title and proper inheritance, as well of all other goods, moveable and unmoveable, to the said monastery in any wise appertaining or belonging, to be disposed and employed as to your Grace's most excellent wisdom shall seem expedient and necessary; all which possessions and goods your Highness, for our said offences, abuses, omissions, and negligences, being to all men obedient[1] and by us plainly confessed, now hath, and of long time past hath had, just and lawful cause to resume into your Grace's hands and possession at your Grace's pleasure; the resumption whereof your Highness nevertheless, like a most natural, loving Prince and clement governor over us your Grace's poor and for our offences most unworthy subjects, hath of long season deferred, and yet doth, in hope and trust of our voluntary reconciliation and amendment, by your Grace's manifold, loving, and gentle admonishments shewed unto us by divers and sundry means. We therefore considering with ourselves your Grace's exceeding goodness and mercy extended at all times unto us most miserable trespassers against God and your Highness, for a perfect declaration of our unfeigned contrition and repentance, feeling ourselves very weak and unable to observe and perform our aforesaid avows and promises made by us and our predecessors to God and your Grace's noble progenitors, and to employ the possessions of your said monastery according to the first will and intent of the original founders; And to the intent that your Highness, your noble heirs and successors, with the true Christian people of this your Grace's realm of England, be not from henceforth eftsoons[2] abused with such feigned devotion and devilish persuasions, under the pretext and habit of religion, by us or any other which should happen to bear the name of religious within your said monastery; And, moreover, that the said possessions and goods should be no longer restrained from a better or more necessary employment; Most humbly beseechen your Highness our most gracious Sovereign Lord and Founder that it might

---

[1] The sense would appear to be 'evident.' 'Obedient' may be a misreading.
[2] A second time.

like your Majesty, for the discharging and exonerating us of the most grievous burden of our pained conscience to the imminent peril and danger of our own damnation that we should be in if by persisting in the state that we now rest in we should be the let[1] of a more godly and necessary employment, graciously to accept our free gifts without coercion, persuasion, or procurement of any creature living other than of our voluntary free will, of all such possessions, right, title, or interest as we the said Prior and convent hath or ever had or are supposed to have had in or to your said Monastery of Northampton aforesaid; And all and every parcel[2] of the lands, advowsons, commodities, and other revenues, whatsoever they be, belonging to the same; And all manner of goods, jewels, ornaments, with all other manner of chattels, moveable and unmoveable, to the said monastery in any wise appertaining or belonging, into whose hands or possession soever they be come into, to be employed and disposed as to your Grace's most excellent wisdom shall seem expedient and necessary. And although, most gracious Sovereign Lord, that the thing by us given unto your Highness is properly and of right ought to be your Grace's own, as well by the merits of our offences as by the order of your Grace's laws, yet, notwithstanding, we eftsoons most humbly beseechen your Highness graciously and benevolently to accept our free will with the gift thereof, nothing requiring of your Majesty therefor other than your most gracious pardon, with some piece of your Grace's alms, and abundant charity towards the maintenance of our poor living, and licence henceforth to live in such form in correcting the rest of our lives as we hope to make satisfaction thereby to God and your Highness for our hypocrisy and other our grievous offences by us committed as well against his Deity as your Majesty....

...And finally we most humbly and reverently, with abundant tears proceeding from our hearts, having before our eyes our detestable offences, submit ourselves totally to the order of God and your merciful and benign Majesty, most heartily beseeching Almighty God to grant your Highness, with the noble Prince Edward your Grace's most noble and natural son, next unto your Grace the most precious jewel and chief comfort of this your Grace's realm, long to live among us your natural and true subjects, with prosperous and fortunate success of all your Grace's honourable and devout proceedings, which hitherto through your

---

[1] In the scriptural sense of 'hindrance.'

[2] 'Parcel of land,' in the sense of a piece of land, is a technical legal expression well known in conveyancing.

Grace's most excellent wisdom and wonderful industry, assidu-ally[1] solicited about the confirming and stablishing men's conscience, continually vexed with sundry doubtful opinions and vain ceremonies, have taken both good and laudable effect, to the undoubted contentation[2] of Almighty God, the great renown and immortal memory of your Grace's high wisdom and excellent knowledge, and to the spiritual weal of all your Grace's subjects. Dated and subscribed in our Chapter the first day of March in the 29th year of your Grace's reign. By the hands of your Grace's poor and unworthy subjects [*The confession is signed by the Prior, the Sub-prior, and eleven brethren*].

Weever, *Funeral Monuments* (1631), p. 106.

§ 6. The Injunctions of 1536 and 1538

In August, 1536, Cromwell, as the King's vice-gerent, issued the first Tudor Injunctions in matters of religion. 'This,' says Wriothesley[3], 'was the first act of pure supremacy done by the King, for in all that had gone before he had acted with the concurrence of Convocation.'

Some of the Injunctions are only administrative, and have small historical importance, although one of them reflects the revolt from Rome, since it requires the clergy 'to the uttermost of their wit, knowledge, and learning, purely, sincerely, and without any colour or dissimulation' to preach once every Sunday for the next three months, 'and after that at the leastwise twice every quarter,' against 'the Bishop of Rome's usurped power and jurisdiction.' At two points, however, the Injunctions exhibit in a remarkable way the influence of the New Learning. (1) In language that is in striking reaction against medieval superstition, they forbid the clergy to 'set forth or extol any images, relics, or miracles for any superstition or lucre, nor allure the people by any enticements to the pilgrimage of any saint,... as though it were proper or peculiar to that saint to give this commodity or that, seeing all goodness, health, and grace ought to be both asked and looked for only of God, as of the very Author of the same, and of none other, for without Him that cannot be given; but they shall exhort as well their parishioners as other pilgrims that they do rather apply themselves to the keeping of God's commandments and fulfilling of His works of charity, persuading them that they shall please God more by the true exercising of their bodily labour, travail, or occupation, and providing for their families, than if they went about to the said pilgrimages; and that it shall profit more their soul's health if they do bestow that on the poor and needy which they would have bestowed upon the said images or relics.' (2) The clergy are required 'diligently' to 'admonish the fathers and mothers, masters and governors of youth, being within their cure, to teach or cause to be taught their children and servants, even from their infancy, their *Pater noster*, the Articles of our

---

[1] Constantly, continually.   [2] Pleasure, satisfaction.

[3] Quoted in Gee and Hardy, p. 269, where the Injunctions of 1536 will be found printed in full. These include the famous Injunction for the keeping of a register of births, deaths, and marriages.

faith, and the Ten Commandments in their mother tongue; and the same so taught, shall cause the said youth oft to repeat and understand.'

In October, 1538, Cromwell issued, with the authorisation and approval of Cranmer, a second set of Injunctions[1], in which the reaction against medieval superstition was carried still further. The clergy once a quarter were to warn their hearers from the pulpit 'not to repose their trust or affiance in any other works devised by men's phantasies beside Scripture; as in wandering to pilgrimages, offering of money, candles, or tapers to images or relics,... saying over a number of beads not understood or minded on, or in such-like superstition.' 'For avoiding that most detestable offence of idolatry,' images were to be taken down, and the clergy were to 'suffer from henceforth no candles, tapers, or images of wax to be set afore any image or picture, but only the light that commonly goeth across the church by the rood loft, the light before the Sacrament of the Altar, and the light about the sepulchre, which for the adorning of the church and divine service you shall suffer to remain; still admonishing your parishioners that images serve for none other purpose but as to be books of unlearned men that cannot know letters, whereby they might be otherwise admonished of the lives and conversation of them that the said images do represent; which images if they abuse for any other intent than for such remembrances, they commit idolatry in the same to the great danger of their souls....' The Injunctions require the clergy to provide 'on this side the Feast of Easter next coming, one book of the whole Bible of the largest volume in English[2], and the same set up in some convenient place within the said church that you have cure of, whereas your parishioners may most commodiously resort to the same and read it'[3]; and they are to 'discourage no man' from 'the reading or hearing of the said Bible, but shall expressly provoke, stir, and exhort every person to read the same, as that which is the very lively word of God, that every Christian man is bound to embrace, believe, and follow, if he look to be saved.'

It is probable that when Henry VIII authorised the reading of the Bible, he was thinking mainly of the support which he might obtain from the fact that it did not mention monasticism and said nothing to sustain the claims of the Papacy. But consequences followed which he had not foreseen. The Bible promoted diversity of belief, and the general permission to read it could be represented as encouraging the promulgation of 'strange and contradictory doctrines.' By an Act of 1543[4] 'for the advancement of true religion and for the abolishment of the contrary' this general permission was withdrawn. Noblemen, gentlemen, and merchant householders might read it privately, but women, artificers, apprentices, and others were forbidden to read it either privately or openly. Noblewomen or gentlewomen might read it to themselves, but not to others.

---

[1] Printed in Gee and Hardy, p. 275.

[2] This 'Bible of the largest volume' was the 'Great Bible' which Coverdale was now passing through the press at Paris. It was completed in haste in 1539 for use as required by the Injunctions (Gairdner, ii, 287). It is familiar as the source of the Prayer-Book version of the Psalms.

[3] A similar provision had appeared in the Injunctions of 1536 as first drafted, but it was eventually omitted (ib. ii, 277).

[4] 34 & 35 Henr. VIII, c. 1.

§ 7. The Six Articles

Although the Injunctions of 1536 and 1538 suggest that Henry VIII, like most educated laymen of his day, was influenced by the New Learning, the Statute of Six Articles [below], passed in 1539, shews that he was nevertheless prepared to enforce under heavy penalties the fundamental doctrines of the Church.

The constitutional importance of the statute lies in the fact that it modifies and consolidates the existing laws against heresy. The rule of the canon law punished heretics by burning, and the case of Sawtrey in 1401 shews that the common law recognised the rule of the canon law, and therefore that a writ *de haeretico comburendo* could be issued at common law[1]. This was reinforced by the Heresy Acts of 1401[2] and 1414[3], the first of which provided that heretics might be arrested on suspicion by the bishop, and those refusing to abjure or relapsing after abjuration were to be burned; and the second enabled the bishops to call upon the civil power for assistance, and authorised courts of quarter sessions to receive indictments for heresy and to deliver persons so indicted to the bishops to be tried[4]. The law against heresy was, however, considerably modified by Henry VIII. An Act of 1533[5] repealed the Act of 1401, and so deprived the bishops of their power to arrest on suspicion; but it confirmed the Act of 1414, and so made it necessary for proceedings in heresy cases to begin by indictment. This had the effect of discouraging prosecutions, and between 1533 and 1539 the cases were not numerous[6]. But the Act of 1533 also furnishes 'a kind of negative definition of heresy,' for it provides that speaking against the authority of the Pope, or against spiritual laws made by the see of Rome repugnant to the laws of the realm or the authority of the King, shall not be deemed heresy. The Statute of Six Articles should be read in close connexion with this Act of 1533, to which it is supplementary. It provides a positive definition of heresy, and establishes a special procedure for the prosecution of heretics, for commissions were to be issued in every diocese to the bishop and others to enquire into offences against the Act, and the commissioners were empowered to compel the attendance of accused persons before them and to try them with a jury. The effect of these two Acts taken together was to make heresy 'in great measure a secular offence,'[7] and to mitigate the severity of the older laws against it. Nothing was made heresy by the Statute of Six Articles which the bishop would not have held to be heresy under the Act of 1401, and the procedure was far less oppressive than that established by the Acts of 1401 and 1414.

Statute of Six Articles, 1539

An Act abolishing diversity in Opinions

Where the King's most excellent Majesty is by God's law Supreme Head immediately under him of this whole Church and

---

[1] Holdsworth, i, 385.
[2] 2 Henr. IV, c. 15.
[3] 2 Henr. V, st. 1, c. 7.
[4] Stephen, ii, 450.
[5] 25 Henr. VIII, c. 14.
[6] Stephen, ii, 455.
[7] Hale, quoted in Stephen, ii, 458.

Congregation of England, intending the conservation of the same Church and Congregation in a true, sincere, and uniform doctrine of Christ's Religion, calling also to his blessed and most gracious remembrance as well the great and quiet assurance, prosperous increase, and other innumerable commodities which have ever ensued, come, and followed of concord, agreement, and unity in opinions, as also the manifold perils, dangers, and inconveniences which have heretofore in many places and regions grown, sprung, and arisen of the diversities of minds and opinions, especially of matters of Christian Religion; And therefore desiring that such an unity might and should be charitably established in all things touching and concerning the same, as the same so being established might chiefly be to the honour of Almighty God, the very author and fountain of all true unity and sincere concord, and consequently redound to the common wealth of this his Highness's most noble realm and of all his loving subjects and other resiants and inhabitants of or in the same: Hath therefore caused and commanded this his most high Court of Parliament, for sundry and many urgent causes and considerations, to be at this time summoned, and also a Synod and Convocation of all the archbishops, bishops, and other learned men of the clergy of this his realm to be in like manner assembled; And forasmuch as in the said Parliament, Synod, and Convocation there were certain articles, matters, and questions proponed[1] and set forth touching Christian Religion....The King's most royal Majesty, most prudently pondering and considering that by occasion of variable and sundry opinions and judgments of the said articles, great discord and variance hath arisen as well amongst the clergy of this his realm as amongst a great number of vulgar people his loving subjects of the same, and being in a full hope and trust that a full and perfect resolution of the said articles should make a perfect concord and unity generally amongst all his loving and obedient subjects; Of his most excellent goodness not only commanded that the said articles should deliberately and advisedly by his said archbishops, bishops, and other learned men of his clergy be debated, argued, and reasoned, and their opinions therein to be understood, declared, and known, but also most graciously vouchsafed in his own princely person to descend and come into his said high Court of Parliament[2] and Council, and

---

[1] Put forward.

[2] The King had come into the House of Lords to argue against the reformers. Cranmer afterwards stated that but for this the bill would not have been passed (Fisher, p. 435).

there like a prince of most high prudence and no less learning opened and declared many things of high learning and great knowledge touching the said articles, matters, and questions, for an unity to be had in the same; Whereupon, after a great and long deliberate and advised disputation and consultation had and made concerning the said articles, as well by the consent of the King's Highness as by the assent of the Lords spiritual and temporal and other learned men of his clergy in their Convocation and by the consent of the Commons in this present Parliament assembled, it was and is finally resolved, accorded, and agreed in manner and form following, that is to say; First, that in the most blessed Sacrament of the Altar, by the strength and efficacy of Christ's mighty word, it being spoken by the priest, is present really, under the form of bread and wine, the natural body and blood of our Saviour Jesu Christ, conceived of the Virgin Mary, and that after the consecration there remaineth no substance of bread and wine, nor any other substance but the substance of Christ, God and man; Secondly, that communion in both kinds is not neces sary *ad salutem* by the law of God to all persons; And that it is to be believed and not doubted of but that in the flesh under form of bread is the very blood, and with the blood under form of wine is the very flesh, as well apart as though they were both together; Thirdly, that priests after the order of priesthood received as afore may not marry by the law of God; Fourthly, that vows of chastity or widowhood by man or woman made to God advisedly ought to be observed by the law of God, and that it exempteth them from other liberties of Christian people which without that they might enjoy; Fifthly, that it is meet and necessary that private masses be continued and admitted in this the King's English Church and Congregation as whereby good Christian people ordering themselves accordingly do receive both godly and goodly consolations and benefits, and it is agreeable also to God's law; Sixthly, that auricular confession is expedient and necessary to be retained and continued, used, and frequented, in the Church of God:... It is therefore ordained and enacted....

* * * * * *

The enacting clauses provided (1) that persons who 'by word, writing, imprinting, ciphering[1], or in any other wise, do publish, preach, teach, say, affirm, declare, dispute, argue, or hold,' any opinion contrary to the first article, together with 'their aiders, comforters, counsellors, consenters, and abettors therein,' shall be 'deemed and adjudged heretics,' and 'shall therefor have and suffer judgment, execution, pain, and pains of death by way of burning'; (2) that persons who preach in any

[1] *I.e.* by writing in cipher.

public sermon or 'teach in any common school or to other congregation of people' or 'do obstinately affirm' opinions contrary to the other five articles, shall be 'deemed and adjudged' felons, and shall 'suffer pains of death as in cases of felony' with forfeiture of lands and goods; (3) persons publishing, declaring, or holding such opinions 'by word, writing, printing, ciphering, or otherwise than is above rehearsed,' were to forfeit their goods and chattels and the profits of their lands, offices, and benefices during life, and to be imprisoned during the King's pleasure, and on a second offence to suffer death as felons with forfeiture of lands and goods.

VI. And be it further enacted...that if any person or persons...contemn[1] or contemptuously refuse, deny, or abstain to be confessed at the time commonly accustomed within this realm and Church of England, or contemn or contemptuously refuse, deny, or abstain to receive the holy and blessed sacrament abovesaid at the time commonly used and accustomed for the same, that then every such offender...shall suffer such imprisonment and make such fine and ransom to the King our Sovereign Lord and his heirs as by his Highness or by his or their Council shall be ordered and adjudged in that behalf; And if any such offender...do eftsoons[2]...refuse...to be confessed or to be communicate...that then every such offence shall be deemed and adjudged felony, and the offender...shall suffer pains of death and lose and forfeit all his...goods, lands, and tenements, as in cases of felony.

*   *   *   *   *   *

31 Henr. VIII, c. 14: *Statutes of the Realm*, iii, 739.

[1] Scorn.   [2] A second time.

The Church Settlement of Edward VI

The Tudor Monarchy assumed that the Sovereign exercised a personal control over the business of government, and on the death of Henry VIII this personal control passed into the hands of a boy of nine, who would be likely to become what older people cared to make him. The religious policy of the future was therefore closely bound up with the question of the young King's education. It is possible that Henry VIII did not intend his own Church settlement to be final. At any rate he chose men of the New Learning to be his son's tutors—Richard Cox, with John Cheke 'as a supplement to Mr Cox,' and afterwards Anthony Cooke, while Roger Ascham gave lessons in penmanship[1] And when he made provision in his will for a Council of Regency the majority of the members were of the same way of thinking, and the name of Gardiner, Bishop of Winchester, the strongest man on the other side, was left out. The King's chief preoccupation may have been to take guarantees that his own religious policy would not be reversed, but he must have foreseen other possibilities; indeed, according to Cranmer, he was actually engaged, during the last few months of his life, in devising a scheme for destroying roods, suppressing bell-ringing, and turning the mass into a communion service[2]. And when he died, circumstances favoured the reformers, for it was found necessary to choose a Protector, and the tradition of the English constitution indicated the person on whom the choice must fall. The young King's uncle[3], the Earl of Hertford, afterwards Duke of Somerset, brother to Queen Jane Seymour, was appointed by the Privy Council on the day of the King's proclamation, and in his hands all power was soon afterwards gathered, for the Protector took out a new patent for his office which made him independent of the Council, and the executors and assistant-executors appointed by Henry were amalgamated into a single privy council appointed by Edward VI[4]. It was known that Hertford was 'well disposed to pious doctrine, and abominated the fond inventions of the Papists,'[5] and after Henry's death he soon opened up a correspondence with Geneva[6].

At the beginning of Edward VI's reign sharp lines between Protestant and Catholic had not been drawn, for the Council of Trent had not yet defined heresy. There was only a confused welter of embittered controversy out of which various doctrinal views were beginning to emerge. The fundamental division was that between the Old Learning and the New—the one appealing to the decisions of an infallible Church, and the other resting upon

---

[1] *D.N.B.* xvii, 85.　　　　　　　　[2] *C.M.H.* ii, 479.

[3] Cf. *Richard III*, ii, iii, where Shakespeare makes the third citizen say of the minority of Henry VI

　　　'For then this land was famously enriched
　　　With politic, grave counsel; then the King
　　　Had virtuous uncles to protect his Grace.'

[4] Pollard, *Polit. Hist.* p. 8.　　　　　[5] See Pollard, *Cranmer*, p. 187.

[6] *D.N.B.* li, 303.

the private interpretation of an infallible Book. The Sacrament of the Altar was the centre of controversy, but out of this there grew the question of the celibacy of the consecrating priesthood, and the proper amount of reverence to be paid in worship to images, and relics, and to the sacred elements themselves. There was also a further question of a highly abstract character, whether justification was by faith alone, or by faith and charity together. On all these vital matters the Protector and those who were associated with him held advanced views and were prepared to carry through further religious changes, but the precise form which these were to take was mainly determined by Cranmer, who in the Church Settlement of Edward VI plays a most important part. He was not, like many of those who surrounded him, a greedy and unscrupulous politician, but a learned and conscientious theologian, whose study of theological questions had led him to change his opinions. From one point of view the importance of Henry's death and Edward's minority was that it gave Cranmer a free hand.

The Church Settlement of Henry VIII and that of Edward VI were based on different constitutional principles. The point established by Henry VIII was simply the Royal Supremacy—that the Church, like the State, is independent of any foreign jurisdiction, and is under the constitutional government of the King. But the changes contemplated by Somerset and Cranmer went much further than this. They proposed to use the Royal Supremacy itself, during a minority, to make alterations in religion which could not afterwards be reversed. Thus when Bonner refused to declare at Paul's Cross that the King's authority was as great during his minority as if he were thirty or forty years old[1], and when Gardiner protested that the Council had no right to make alterations in religion until the King came of age[2], they were taking up a strong position and defending the Royal Supremacy as Henry VIII had understood it[3]. But unfortunately for them the power was in the hands of their opponents, and Gardiner went to the Tower and Bonner to the Marshalsea prison.

§ 1. The Injunctions of 1547

As long as Somerset was in power the process of doctrinal change was carried out gradually and with caution, and it may be regarded as a natural development of what had gone before. The method, a combination of injunction and statute, was the method of Henry VIII.

The Injunctions of 1547 were moderate in tone, and contain little which is not 'in keeping with that aspiration for a purging of the practice of

---

[1] *D.N.B.* v, 359.   [2] Gairdner, iii, 55.

[3] 28 Henr. VIII, c. 17, taking the view that the personal authority of the sovereign was necessary to the validity of legislation, had provided that 'as laws and statutes may happen hereafter to be made within this realm as Parliaments holden at such times as the kings of the same shall happen to be within age, having small knowledge and experience of their affairs,' successors who came to the throne under 24 years of age should have power to annul by letters patent statutes passed during their minority as soon as they reached that age. This statute would have checked religious changes by making them only provisional, but it was repealed in the first Parliament of the reign.

INJUNCTIONS OF 1547 101

the Church which supplied the moral force of the Reformation.'[1] They followed closely the Injunctions of 1536 and 1538[2], adopting at many points the same phrases, but they also contain certain features that are new.

(1) The policy of discouraging a superstitious use of images and ceremonies is carried much further than heretofore. The Dissolution of the Monasteries had been accompanied by a crusade against relics and shrines, and the images with which shrines were adorned, for Henry VIII was not unwilling to destroy the popular reverence for anything which brought credit to the monks. The Injunctions of 1538 had ordered the destruction of 'such feigned images' as were 'abused with pilgrimages, or offerings of anything made thereunto,' and had forbidden 'candles, tapers, or images of wax' being 'set afore any image or picture.' The Injunctions of 1547[3] repeat these precepts and prohibitions, and further instruct the clergy to 'take away, utterly extinct, and destroy' all shrines, candlesticks, pictures, and 'all other monuments of feigned miracles, pilgrimages, idolatry, and superstition,' and to warn their parishioners against misuse of 'the laudable ceremonies of the Church,' 'as in casting holy water upon his bed, upon images, and other dead things, or bearing about him holy bread, or St John's Gospel ...or blessing with the holy candle, to the intent thereby to be discharged of the burden of sin, or to drive away devils.' The injunction against images was found difficult to enforce, as it was not easy to say what came into the category of images 'abused,' and in February, 1548, the Council ordered the bishops to give instructions for removing them all[4]. The Act of 1550, against Books and Images [p. 113], should be read in connexion with this. It orders the destruction of all images under penalties by a given date, except those of 'any king, prince, nobleman, or other dead person, which hath not been commonly reputed and taken for a saint.'[5]

(2) The Injunctions of 1547 also further develop the study of the Scriptures and the use of the vulgar tongue in the services of the Church. The Injunctions of 1536 had required children and servants to be taught the Paternoster, the Articles of Faith, and the Ten Commandments in English, and those of 1538 had extended this to all parishioners and had included the Creed. They had also provided for the setting up of the Great Bible in the churches. The Injunctions of 1547 associate with the Bible the *Paraphrase* of Erasmus, and require 'every parson, vicar, curate, chantry priest, and stipendiary, being under the degree of a Bachelor of Divinity' to 'provide and have of his own' the *Paraphrase* and the New Testament 'both in Latin and in English'; and they are to be examined by the bishops on their visitations 'how they have profited in the study of Holy Scripture.' The Epistle and Gospel for the day are to be read in English and not in Latin; and a chapter of the New Testament in English is to be read at matins and a chapter of the Old Testament at evensong. Processions 'about the church or churchyard' are forbidden, but 'immediately before high mass the priests, with other of the choir, shall kneel in the midst of the church and sing or

[1] Pollard, *Cranmer*, p. 196.   [2] See p. 93 above.
[3] See Cardwell (i, 4–23), where these Injunctions are printed in full.
[4] Cardwell, i, 38.
[5] 'Thus Oswald and Wulfstan vanished from Worcester cathedral, while King John remained' (Gwatkin, p. 185).

say plainly and distinctly the Litany which is set forth in English.'[1] Another
injunction requires the churchwardens, at the common charge of the parishioners, to provide 'a comely and honest pulpit' for the preaching of God's
word.

It should, however, be observed that the Injunctions of 1547 do not
interfere with the use of the confessional as an habitual practice; the termin-
ology of the old order, 'high mass,' 'matins,' and 'evensong,' is still employed;
and prayers for the dead are expressly retained.

§ 2. Statutes of the Protectorate

So far the government had acted without Parliament, but in November,
1547, Edward VI's first Parliament met, and the next innovations were
made by statute.

The Statute of Treasons, which repealed the heresy laws and the Statute
of Six Articles, and removed all restrictions upon the use of the Bible, is
discussed below [p. 380] in a different connexion.

The Act of 1547 against reviling the Sacrament and for communion
in both kinds[2] declared that the Sacrament of the Altar 'hath been of late
marvellously abused' by those who 'of wickedness or else of ignorance and
want of learning, for certain abuses heretofore committed of some in misusing
thereof, have condemned in their hearts and speech the whole thing, and
contemptuously depraved, despised, or reviled the same most holy and
blessed Sacrament, and not only disputed and reasoned unreverently and
ungodly of that most high mystery, but also in their sermons, preachings,
readings, lectures, communications, arguments, talks, rhymes, songs, plays,
or gests[3], name or call it by such vile and unseemly words as Christian ears
do abhor to hear rehearsed'; it was therefore provided that persons who
'shall deprave, despise, or contemn' the Sacrament, shall 'suffer imprisonment of...their bodies and make fine and ransom at the King's will and
pleasure.' The same Act declared it to be 'more agreeable both to the first
institution of the said Sacrament...and also more conformable to the common use and practice both of the Apostles and of the primitive Church by
the space of five hundred years and more after Christ's Ascension' that the
Sacrament should be 'ministered to all Christian people under both the kinds
of bread and wine than under the form of bread only'; it was therefore provided that the Sacrament should be administered in both kinds, and should
not be denied 'to any person that will devoutly and humbly desire it.'[4]

The Act of 1547 'for the election of Bishops'[5] substitutes for *congé*

---

[1] The English Litany had been printed in 1545, and had been first sung in St
Paul's on Sunday October 18 of that year (Pollard, *Cranmer*, p. 174). At the date of
the Injunctions it was already in use in the churches; the novelty lay in the requirement
that it should no longer be sung in procession but kneeling. On the relation of this
to our present Litany see Gwatkin, p. 177.   [2] 1 Edw. VI, c. 1.

[3] 'Gest,' in the sense of a story or romance in verse, was beginning to be used in
the later sense of a satirical utterance or lampoon.

[4] 'This made the whole of the Canon Law inoperative, and put a stop to any
requirement of fasting or confession as a condition of communion' (Gwatkin, p. 183).

[5] 1 Edw. VI, c. 2.

d'élire nomination by the King's letters patent, on the ground that elections to archbishoprics and bishoprics are long delayed, and involve those appointed to them in 'great costs and charges,' and also that such elections 'be in very deed no elections but only by a writ of *congé d'élire* have colours, shadows, or pretences of elections, serving nevertheless to no purpose and seeming also derogatory . . . to the King's prerogative royal, to whom only appertaineth the collation and gift.' Henry VIII had at any rate retained the form of an election. Appointment by the King's letters patent reduced the bishops to the position of mere state officials liable to summary deprivation, for letters patent could be at any time withdrawn. The Act represents the most advanced conception of the Royal Supremacy which appears in any of the Reformation statutes.

(1) Act for the Dissolution of the Chantries, 1547

This Act not only carried through the dissolution of 2374 chantries or small foundations endowing a priest or priests to say masses for ever for the repose of the founder's soul, but it also confiscated that part of the funds of guilds and corporations assigned to superstitious objects, the payments hither-to made for these purposes being now converted into a rent-charge payable to the Crown. The preamble of the Act speaks of the erection of grammar schools, the augmentation of the Universities, and the relief of the poor; but the first use of the funds produced by the sale of chantry lands under the Act was 'specially for the relief of the King's Majesty's charges and expenses, which do daily grow and increase by reason of divers and sundry fortifications, garrisons, levying of men and soldiers,' etc.[1] Schools kept by chantry priests were continued by the commissioners appointed under the Act, but a bill to found grammar schools, introduced a year later, disappeared after its first reading in the Lords on February 18, 1549[2]. A large part of the chantry endowments eventually went to the harpies who surrounded the young king[3].

An Act whereby certain Chantries, Colleges, Free Chapels, and the possessions of the same, be given to the King's Majesty

The King's most loving subjects, the Lords spiritual and temporal and the Commons, in this present Parliament assembled, considering that a great part of superstition and errors in Christian Religion hath been brought into the minds and estimation of men by reason of the ignorance of their very true and perfect salvation through the death of Jesus Christ, and by devising and phantasing vain opinions of purgatory and masses satisfactory[4] to

---

[1] Dasent, ii, 184–5.   [2] *C.M.H.* ii, 482.

[3] 'Now, all scruples removed, chantry-land went down without any regret. Yea, such who mannerly expected till the King carved for them out of abbey-lands, scrambled for themselves out of chantry-revenues, as knowing this was the last dish of the last course, and after chantries as after cheese, nothing to be expected' (Fuller, ii, 275).

[4] *I.e.* making satisfaction or atonement for sin.

be done for them which be departed, the which doctrine and vain opinion by nothing more is maintained and upholden than by the abuse of trentals[1], chantries, and other provisions made for the continuance of the said blindness and ignorance; And further considering and understanding that the alteration, change, and amendment of the same, and converting to good and godly uses, as in erecting of grammar schools to the education of youth in virtue and godliness, the further augmenting of the Universities, and better provision for the poor and needy, cannot in this present Parliament be provided and conveniently done, nor cannot nor ought to any other manner person be committed than to the King's Highness, whose Majesty with and by the advice of his Highness's most prudent Council can and will most wisely and beneficially, both for the honour of God and the weal of this his Majesty's realm, order, alter, convert, and dispose the same; And calling further to their remembrance... [*here follows a recital of 37 Henr. VIII, c. 4, for the Dissolution of the Chantries*[2]]. It is now ordained and enacted...that all manner of colleges, free chapels, and chantries, having being or *in esse*[3] within five years next before the first day of this present Parliament, which were not in actual and real possession of the said late King, nor in the actual and real possession of the King our Sovereign Lord that now is, nor excepted in the said former Act....And all manors, lands, tenements, rents, tithes, pensions, portions, and other hereditaments and things above mentioned belonging to them or any of them, and also all manors, lands, tenements, rents, and other hereditaments and things above mentioned, by any manner of assurance, conveyance, will, devise[4], or otherwise had, made, suffered, knowledged, or declared, given, assigned, limited, or appointed to the finding of any priest to have continuance for ever, and wherewith or whereby any priest was sustained, maintained, or found within five years next before the first day of this present Parliament, which were not in the actual and real possession of the said late King nor in the actual and real possession of our Sovereign Lord the King that now is, and also all annual rents, profits, and emolu-

---

[1] 'Trentals' are requiem masses, usually collected in sets of thirty.

[2] Commissioners were appointed under this Act to survey the possessions of the chantries, but although there were some voluntary surrenders, it is doubtful if any dissolutions took place under it (Gee and Hardy, p. 328; but see Dixon, ii, 381). This Act had now expired, so it was necessary to deal with the question afresh by a new statute.

[3] 'In actual existence,' as opposed to *in posse*, 'in potentiality' (*Oxford Dictionary*).

[4] A testamentary disposition, usually of real property.

ments at any time within five years next before the beginning of
this present Parliament employed, paid, or bestowed toward or
for the maintenance, supportation, or finding of any stipendiary
priest intended by any act or writing to have continuance for
ever, shall by authority of this present Parliament, immediately
after the Feast of Easter next coming, be adjudged and deemed
and also be in the very actual and real possession and seisin of the
King our Sovereign Lord and his heirs and successors for ever;
without any office[1] or other inquisition thereof to be had or found,
and in as large and ample manner and form as the priests, wardens,
masters, ministers, governors, rulers, or other incumbents of
them or any of them at any time within five years next before the
beginning of this present Parliament had occupied or enjoyed, or
now hath, occupieth, and enjoyeth the same; and as though all
and singular the said colleges, free chapels, chantries, stipends,
salaries of priests, and the said manors, lands, tenements, hereditaments, and other the premises whatsoever they be, and every
of them, were in this present Act specially, peculiarly, and certainly rehearsed, named, and expressed, by express words, names,
surnames, corporations, titles, and faculties, and in their natures,
kinds, and qualities.

*   *   *   *   *   *

VII. And furthermore be it ordained and enacted by the
authority aforesaid, that the King our Sovereign Lord shall from
the said Feast of Easter next coming have and enjoy to him, his
heirs and successors, for ever, all fraternities, brotherhoods, and
guilds being within the realm of England and Wales and other
the King's dominions, and all manors, lands, tenements, and
other hereditaments belonging to them or any of them, other than
such corporations, guilds, fraternities, companies, and fellowships
of mysteries or crafts, and the manors, lands, tenements, and other
hereditaments pertaining to the said corporations, guilds, fraternities, companies, and fellowships of mysteries[2] or crafts above
mentioned, and shall by virtue of this Act be judged and deemed
in actual and real possession of our said Sovereign Lord the King,
his heirs and successors, from the said Feast of Easter next coming
for ever, without any inquisitions or office thereof to be had or
found.

[VIII–XII. The King may appoint commissioners under the great
seal with power to survey all 'lay corporations, guilds, fraternities, companies,

---

[1] This term is used of an official enquiry concerning any matter that entitles the
Crown to the possession of lands or goods.
[2] Handicrafts or trades.

and fellowships of mysteries or crafts incorporate' as well as 'all other the said fraternities, brotherhoods, and guilds within the limits of their commission,' 'to the intent thereby to know what money and other things was paid or bestowed to the finding or maintenance of any priest or priests, anniversary or obit[1], or other like thing, light or lamp[2], by them or any of them,' and also to enquire what lands, etc., are vested in the King by this Act. The commissioners are also empowered to assign, 'in every such place where guild, fraternity, the priest or incumbent of any chantry *in esse* the first day of this present Parliament, by the foundation, ordinance, or first institution thereof should or ought to have kept a grammar school or a preacher, and so hath done since the Feast of St Michael the Archangel last past,' the lands of every such chantry or guild 'to remain and continue in succession to a schoolmaster or preacher for ever, for and toward the keeping of a grammar school or preaching.' They are also empowered 'to make and ordain a vicar to have perpetuity in every parish church the first day of this present Parliament being a college, free chapel, or chantry, or appropriated and annexed ... to any college, free chapel, or chantry' coming to the King's hands by virtue of the Act, and 'to endow every such vicar sufficiently, having respect to his cure and charge.' They are further empowered to assign chantry lands for the maintenance of additional priests in any parish; to make rules 'concerning the service, user, and demeanours' of priests or schoolmasters appointed by them; and to grant pensions to the priests of dissolved chantries and to poor persons hitherto dependent on them for 'yearly relief.']

XIII. And also be it ordained and enacted by the authority of this present Parliament, that our Sovereign Lord the King shall have and enjoy all such goods, chattels, jewels, plate, ornaments, and other moveables as were or be the common goods of every such college, chantry, free chapel, or stipendiary priest, belonging or annexed to the furniture or service of their several foundations, or abused of any of the said corporations in the abuses aforesaid, the property whereof was not altered or changed before the 8th day of December in the year of our Lord God 1547.

* * * * * *

XV. Provided always and be it ordained and enacted by the authority aforesaid, That this Act or any article, clause, or matter contained in the same, shall not in any wise extend to any college, hostel, or hall being within either of the Universities of Cambridge and Oxford; nor to any chantry founded in any of the colleges, hostels, or halls being in the same universities; nor to the free chapel of St George the Martyr, situate in the Castle of Windsor; nor to the college called St Mary College of Winchester

---

[1] An 'obit' is a mass said for the soul of a deceased founder or benefactor on the anniversary of his death.

[2] *E.g.* the chantry at Burton-on-Trent paid 2*s.* a year towards the maintenance of a lamp in the church of Allestree (Hibbert, *Dissolution*, p. 69).

besides Winchester of the foundation of Bishop Wykeham; nor to the College of Eton; nor to the parish church commonly called the Chapel in the Sea[1], in Newton within the Isle of Ely in the county of Cambridge; nor to any manors, lands, tenements, or hereditaments to them or any of them pertaining or belonging; nor to any chapel made or ordained for the ease of the people dwelling distant from the parish church, or such like chapel whereunto no more lands or tenements than the churchyard or a little house or close doth belong or pertain; nor to any cathedral church or college where a bishop's see is within this realm of England or Wales, nor to the manors, lands, tenements, or other hereditaments of any of them, other than to such chantries, obits, lights, and lamps, or any of them, as at any time within five years next before the beginning of this present Parliament have been had, used, or maintained within the said cathedral churches or within any of them, or of the issues, revenues, or profits of any of the said cathedral churches; to which chantries, obits, lights, and lamps it is enacted by the authority aforesaid that this Act shall extend.

*　　*　　*　　*　　*　　*

1 Edw. VI, c. 14: Statutes of the Realm, iv, 24.

(2) First Act of Uniformity, 1549

The revolution in national worship which this Act accomplished is mainly due to three changes effected by it. (1) The abandonment of various local and diocesan uses in favour of a single form of prayer for the whole kingdom. The most widely known of the old uses was the Use of Sarum, and this was adopted as the basis of the new prayer-book; but the drafting commission had before it much other material, including in particular the reformed Breviary published by Cardinal Quignon in 1535. Cranmer had made a profound study of existing liturgies, Eastern as well as Western[2], and thus it was from a variety of sources that the compilers of the first English Prayer-Book drew their inspiration. (2) The use of the vernacular throughout the service[3]. (3) The novel character of the Prayer-Book imposed by the Act. This was on the whole Lutheran rather than Roman, resembling in some respects Luther's Latin Mass of 1523 and his German

---

[1] This was a college or large chantry, consisting of a warden and several chaplains, founded by Sir John Colvill in the reign of Henry IV (Tanner, *Notitia Monastica*, p. 54). The lands of the chantry were afterwards annexed to the rectory of Newton.

[2] A catalogue of Cranmer's library has been reconstructed which shews that it contained a number of books on the eucharistic controversy and was rich in works bearing on liturgical questions. These books shew signs of having been carefully studied, and many are underlined and annotated with marginal notes.

[3] Where the vernacular is a translation from the Latin it is often much more than a mere translation. See Gwatkin, p. 186.

Mass of 1526; and the reduction of the Roman daily service arranged in Hours to Matins and Evensong is in particular characteristically Lutheran. The influence is also apparent of the liturgy prepared by Hermann von Wied, the deprived Archbishop-Elector of Cologne, with the assistance of Luther himself. But the resemblances are due 'not so much to conscious imitation as to the common conservatism which characterised the Lutheran and Anglican service-books, and led to the retention in them of many Catholic usages which Reformed churches in Europe rejected.'[1]

An Act for the Uniformity of Service and Administration of the Sacraments throughout the Realm

Where of long time there hath been had in this realm of England and Wales divers forms of common prayer commonly called the service of the Church, that is to say, the use of Sarum, of York, of Bangor, and of Lincoln[2]; And besides the same now of late much more divers and sundry forms and fashions have been used in the cathedral and parish churches of England and Wales, as well concerning the matins or morning prayer and the evensong, as also concerning the Holy Communion commonly called the Mass, with divers and sundry rites and ceremonies concerning the same, and in the administration of other sacraments of the Church; And as the doers and executors of the said rites and ceremonies in other form than of late years they have been used were pleased therewith, so other not using the same rites and ceremonies were thereby greatly offended; And albeit the King's Majesty, with the advice of his most entirely beloved uncle the Lord Protector and other of his Highness's Council, hath heretofore divers times assayed to stay innovations or new rites concerning the premises, yet the same hath not had such good success as his Highness required in that behalf; whereupon his Highness by the most prudent advice aforesaid, being pleased to bear with the frailty and weakness of his subjects in that behalf, of his great clemency hath not been only content to abstain from punishment of those that have offended in that behalf, for that his Highness taketh that they did it of a good zeal, but also to the intent a uniform, quiet, and godly order should be had concerning the premises, hath appointed the Archbishop of Canterbury and certain of the most learned and discreet bishops and other learned

---

[1] Pollard, *Cranmer*, p. 220.

[2] The Use of Sarum prevailed in the south of England and over the greater part of Scotland and Ireland. The not very dissimilar uses of York, Lincoln, Bangor, and Hereford were adopted in the north of England and in Wales. The Sarum Use represents the Roman rite of the eleventh century, before the changes introduced by Gregory VII and his successors (*Catholic Encyclopedia*; see also W. H. Frere, *The Use of Sarum*).

men of this realm to consider and ponder the premises, and thereupon having as well eye and respect to the most sincere and pure Christian Religion taught by the Scripture as to the usages in the primitive Church, should draw and make one convenient and meet order, rite, and fashion of common and open prayer and administration of the sacraments, to be had and used in his Majesty's realm of England and in Wales; the which at this time, by the aid of the Holy Ghost, with one uniform agreement is of them concluded, set forth, and delivered to his Highness, to his great comfort and quietness of mind, in a book entitled The Book of the Common Prayer and Administration of the Sacraments and other Rites and Ceremonies of the Church after the Use of the Church of England: Wherefore the Lords spiritual and temporal and the Commons in this present Parliament assembled, considering as well the most godly travail of the King's Highness, of the Lord Protector, and other of his Highness's Council, in gathering and collecting the said archbishop, bishops, and learned men together, as the godly prayers, orders, rites, and ceremonies in the said book mentioned, and the considerations of altering those things which be altered and retaining those things which be retained in the said book, but also the honour of God, and great quietness which by the grace of God shall ensue upon the one and uniform rite and order in such common prayer and rites and extern ceremonies[1], to be used throughout England and in Wales, at Calais, and the marches of the same, do give to his Highness most hearty and lowly thanks for the same, and humbly pray that it may be ordained and enacted by his Majesty, with the assent of the Lords and Commons in this present Parliament assembled and by the authority of the same, that all and singular person and persons that have offended concerning the premises, other than such person and persons as now be and remain in ward in the Tower of London or in the Fleet, may be pardoned thereof: and that all and singular ministers in any cathedral or parish church, or other place within this realm of England, Wales, Calais, and marches of the same, or other the King's dominions, shall from and after the Feast of Pentecost next coming be bounden to say and use the matins, evensong, celebration of the Lord's Supper commonly called the Mass, and administration of each of the sacraments, and all their common and open prayer, in such order and form as is mentioned in the said book and none other or otherwise.

II. And albeit that the same be so godly and good that they

[1] Outward ceremonies.

give occasion to every honest and conformable man most willingly
to embrace them, yet lest any obstinate person who willingly
would disturb so godly order and quiet in this realm should not
go unpunished, that it may also be ordained and enacted by the
authority aforesaid, that if any manner of parson, vicar, or other
whatsoever minister that ought or should sing or say common
prayer mentioned in the said book or minister the sacraments,
shall after the said Feast of Pentecost next coming refuse to use
the said common prayers or to minister the sacraments in such
cathedral or parish church or other places as he should use or
minister the same, in such order and form as they be mentioned
and set forth in the said book, or shall use, wilfully and obstinately
standing in the same, any other rite, ceremony, order, form, or
manner of mass, openly or privily, or matins, evensong, administration of the sacraments, or other open prayer than is mentioned
and set forth in the said book; open prayer in and throughout
this Act is meant that prayer which is for other to come unto and
hear, either in common churches or private chapels or oratories,
commonly called the Service of the Church; or shall preach, declare, or speak anything in the derogation or depraving[1] of the
said book or anything therein contained or of any part thereof,
and shall be thereof lawfully convicted according to the laws of
this realm by verdict of twelve men, or by his own confession,
or by the notorious evidence of the fact, shall lose and forfeit to
the King's Highness, his heirs and successors, for his first offence
the profit of such one of his spiritual benefices or promotions as
it shall please the King's Highness to assign or appoint coming
and arising in one whole year next after his conviction; and also
that the same person so convicted shall for the same offence suffer
imprisonment by the space of six months without bail or mainprize[2]; and if any such person once convict of any offence concerning the premises shall after his first conviction eftsoons[3] offend
and be thereof in form aforesaid lawfully convict, that then the
same person shall for his second offence suffer imprisonment by
the space of one whole year, and also shall therefor be deprived
ipso facto of all his spiritual promotions; and that it shall be lawful
to all patrons, donors, and grantees of all and singular the same
spiritual promotions to present to the same any other able clerk
in like manner and form as though the party so offending were
dead: And that if any such person or persons, after he shall be
twice convicted in form aforesaid, shall offend against any of the

---

[1] Vilifying or disparaging.   [2] See note on p. 10 above.
[3] A second time.

premises the third time and shall be thereof in form aforesaid lawfully convicted, that then the person so offending and convicted
the third time shall suffer imprisonment during his life: And if
the person that shall offend or be convict in form aforesaid concerning any of the premises shall not be beneficed nor have any
spiritual promotion, that then the same person so offending and
convict shall for the first offence suffer imprisonment during six
months without bail or mainprize; and if any such person not
having any spiritual promotion after his first conviction shall
eftsoons offend in anything concerning the premises and shall
in form aforesaid be thereof lawfully convicted, that then the
same person shall for his second offence suffer imprisonment
during his life.

III. And it is ordained and enacted by the authority above-said,
that if any person or persons whatsoever, after the said Feast of
Pentecost next coming, shall in any interludes, plays, songs, rhymes,
or by other open words, declare or speak anything in the derogation,
depraving, or despising of the same book or of anything therein
contained or any part thereof, or shall by open fact[1], deed, or by
open threatenings compel or cause or otherwise procure or maintain any parson, vicar, or other minister, in any cathedral or
parish church or in any chapel or other place, to sing or say any
common and open prayer or to minister any sacrament otherwise
or in any other manner or form than is mentioned in the said
book, or that by any of the said means shall unlawfully interrupt
or let[2] any parson, vicar, or other ministers in any cathedral or
parish church, chapel, or any other place to sing or say common
and open prayer or to minister the sacraments or any of them in
any such manner and form as is mentioned in the said book, That
then every person being thereof lawfully convicted in form abovesaid shall forfeit to the King our Sovereign Lord, his heirs and
successors, for the first offence ten pounds; And if any person or
persons, being once convict of any such offence, eftsoons offend
against any of the premises and shall in form aforesaid be thereof
lawfully convict, that then the same person so offending and convict shall for the second offence forfeit to the King our Sovereign
Lord, his heirs and successors, twenty pounds; And if any person,
after he in form aforesaid shall have been twice convict of any
offence concerning any of the premises, shall offend the third
time and be thereof in form aforesaid lawfully convict, that then
every person so offending and convict shall for his third offence

---

[1] In the sixteenth century the commonest sense of 'fact' was an evil deed or
crime. [2] Hinder or obstruct.

forfeit to our Sovereign Lord the King all his goods and chattels and shall suffer imprisonment during his life: And if any person or persons that for his first offence concerning the premises shall be convict in form aforesaid do not pay the sum to be paid by virtue of his conviction, in such manner and form as the same ought to be paid, within six weeks next after his conviction, That then every person so convict and so not paying the same shall for the same first offence, instead of the said ten pounds, suffer imprisonment by the space of three months without bail or main-prize; And if any person or persons that for his second offence concerning the premises shall be convict in form aforesaid do not pay the sum to be paid by virtue of his conviction, in such manner and form as the same ought to be paid, within six weeks next after his said second conviction, That then every person so convict and not so paying the same shall for the same second offence, instead of the said twenty pounds, suffer imprisonment during six months without bail or mainprize.

*   *   *   *   *   *

VI. Provided always that it shall be lawful to any man that understandeth the Greek, Latin, and Hebrew tongue, or other strange tongue, to say and have the said prayers heretofore speci-fied of matins and evensong in Latin or any such other tongue, saying the same privately as they do understand: And for the further encouraging of learning in the tongues in the Universities of Cambridge and Oxford, to use and exercise in their common and open prayer in their chapels, being no parish churches or other places of prayer, the matins, evensong, litany, and all other prayers, the Holy Communion commonly called the Mass ex-cepted, prescribed in the said book, in Greek, Latin, or Hebrew; Anything in this present Act to the contrary notwithstanding.

*   *   *   *   *   *

2 & 3 Edw. VI, c. 1: *Statutes of the Realm,* iv, 37.

The year 1549 also saw the passing of an Act[1] legalising the marriage of priests. This had been approved by Convocation as early as December, 1547, and Parliament now gave statutory authority to the change. The preamble of the Act affirms the desirability of celibacy for the clergy but admits its difficulties, and all positive laws prohibiting the marriage of ecclesi-astical or spiritual persons are therefore declared void. A proviso was, how-ever, inserted that nothing in the Act should 'extend to give any liberty to any person to marry without asking in church or without any other cere-mony being appointed' in the Book of Common Prayer.

[1] 2 & 3 Edw. VI, c. 21. The Act is printed in Gee and Hardy, p. 366.

§ 3. Later Religious Changes, 1550–53

The first phase of Edward VI's reign was now drawing to an end. In October 1549 Somerset fell, the Protectorate was abolished, and the preponderant influence in the government passed to the Earl of Warwick, afterwards Duke of Northumberland—a statesman as rapacious and more unscrupulous than Somerset, and without his largeness of view. The result was a complete change of policy. In the constitutional sphere Warwick gradually supplanted the Regency which the will of Henry VIII had set up, and brought the young King himself to the front in the government. In the sphere of religion he abandoned the more cautious policy of the Protector, and greatly accelerated the pace of the Reformation. He played the part assigned to him by Hooper of a 'faithful and intrepid soldier of Christ' and a 'most holy and fearless instrument of the word of God'[1]; and when his policy had disclosed itself John ab Ulmis wrote of him two years later, 'He is manifestly the thunderbolt and terror of the papists.'[2] As far as religion is concerned, Cranmer is the link between the two periods, but Cranmer had been carrying his theological speculations farther, and was prepared to travel on the road of innovation far beyond the point which he had reached under the Protectorate.

(1) Act against superstitious Books and Images, 1550

This Act is one of the consequences of the First Act of Uniformity. As the use of the new Prayer Book was now established by law, the older service-books were unnecessary and were to be given up to be destroyed, and the opportunity was taken to continue the crusade against superstitious images in churches.

An Act for the abolishing and putting away of divers Books and mages

Where the King's most excellent Majesty hath of late set forth and established by authority of Parliament an uniform, quiet, and godly order for common and open prayer, in a book entitled, The Book of Common Prayer and Administration of the Sacraments and other Rites and Ceremonies of the Church after the Church of England, to be used and observed in the said Church of England, agreeable to the order of the primitive Church, much more conformable[3] unto his loving subjects than other diversity of service as heretofore of long time hath been used, being in the said book ordained nothing to be read but the very pure word of God, or which is evidently grounded upon the same, And in the other things corrupt, untrue, vain, and superstitious, and as it were a preparation to superstition, which for that they be not called in but permitted to remain undefaced, do not only give occasion to such perverse persons as do impugn

---

[1] Pollard, *Polit. Hist.* p. 46.   [2] Gairdner, iii, 294.   [3] Suitable.

the order and godly meaning of the King's said Book of Common
Prayer to continue in their old accustomed superstitious service,
but also minister great occasion to diversity of opinions, rites,
ceremonies, and services: Be it therefore enacted . . . that all books
called antiphoners[1], missals, grails[2], processionals, manuals, leg-
ends[3], pies[4], portuises[5], primers[6] in Latin or English, couchers[7],
journals[8], ordinals[9], or other books or writings whatsoever heretofore used for service of the Church, written or printed in the
English or Latin tongue, other than such as are or shall be set
forth by the King's Majesty, shall be by authority of this present
Act clearly and utterly abolished, extinguished, and forbidden
for ever to be used or kept in this realm or elsewhere within any
the King's dominions.

II. And be it further enacted by the authority aforesaid, that
if any person or persons of what estate, degree, or condition soever
he, she, or they be, body politic or corporate, that now have or
hereafter shall have in his, her, or their custody any the books
or writings of the sorts aforesaid, or any images of stone, timber,
alabaster, or earth[10], graven, carved, or painted, which heretofore
have been taken out of any church or chapel, or yet stand in any
church or chapel, and do not before the last day of June next
ensuing deface and destroy or cause to be defaced and destroyed
the same images and every of them, and deliver or cause to be
delivered all and every the same books to the mayor, bailiff, constable, or churchwardens of the town where such books shall then
be, to be by them delivered over openly within three months next
following after the said delivery to the archbishop, bishop, chancellor, or commissary of the same diocese, to the intent the said
archbishop, bishop, chancellor, or commissary and every of them

[1] Chant-books.
[2] A 'grail' or 'gradual' was an antiphon sung between the Epistle and the Gospel
at the Eucharist from the steps of the altar. The reference here is to books of such
antiphons.
[3] Books of lessons, containing passages from Scripture or from the lives of the
saints, for use at divine service.
[4] 'Pies' were collections of rules for dealing with the concurrence of more than
one office on the same day in consequence of the variations of Easter (*Oxford Dictionary*).
[5] 'Portuises' were portable breviaries.
[6] 'Primers' were prayer-books or devotional manuals.
[7] 'Couchers' were large breviaries which could not be held in the hand but had
to be kept lying down on a desk or table.
[8] Service-books containing the canonical day-hours.
[9] 'Ordinals' are here service-books setting forth the order of the service.
[10] Clay.

cause them immediately either to be openly burnt or otherways defaced and destroyed, shall for every such book or books willingly retained in his, her, or their hands or custody within this realm or elsewhere within any the King's dominions, and not delivered as is aforesaid after the said last day of June, and be thereof lawfully convict, forfeit and lose to the King our Sovereign Lord for the first offence twenty shillings, and for the second offence shall forfeit and lose being thereof lawfully convict four pounds, and for the third offence shall suffer imprisonment at the King's will.

*   *   *   *   *   *

V. Provided alway and be it enacted by the authority aforesaid, That any person or persons may use, keep, have, and retain any primers in the English or Latin tongue set forth by the late King of famous memory, King Henry the Eighth[1]; so that the sentences of invocation or prayer to saints in the same primers be blotted or clearly put out of the same; anything in this Act to the contrary notwithstanding.

VI. Provided always, That this Act or anything therein contained shall not extend to any image or picture set or graven upon any tomb in any church, chapel, or churchyard only for a monument of any king, prince, nobleman, or other dead person, which hath not been commonly reputed and taken for a saint; but that such pictures and images may stand and continue in like manner and form as if this Act had never been had or made; anything in this Act to the contrary in any wise notwithstanding.

3 & 4 Edw. VI, c. 10: *Statutes of the Realm*, iv, 110.

(2) Ridley's Injunction concerning the Altar, 1550

The Injunction concerning the Altar, included among the injunctions issued by Ridley at his visitation 'for an uniformity in his Diocese of London,' effected a visible change in public worship. The demolition of the altars had begun as early as 1548, when the altars of the dissolved chantries had been taken down; and now a general destruction of altars in the diocese took place, beginning with the removal of the High Altar in St Paul's Cathedral.

. . . Whereas in divers places some use the Lord's board after the form of a table, and some of an altar, whereby dissension is perceived to arise among the unlearned; therefore, wishing a godly unity to be preserved in all our diocese, and for that the form of a table may more move and turn the simple from the old superstitious opinions of the Popish Mass, and to the right use of the Lord's Supper, we exhort the curates, churchwardens, and questmen[2] here present, to erect and set up the Lord's board after

[1] Henry VIII's Primer, a private prayer-book, had been set forth by authority in 1545.   [2] Sidesmen.

the form of an honest table decently covered, in such place of the choir or chancel as shall be thought most meet by their discretion and agreement, so that the ministers with the communicants may have their place separated from the rest of the people; and to take down and abolish all other by-altars or tables....

Burnet, *History of the Reformation*, pt ii, bk. i, no. lii.

The policy of Ridley was finally adopted by the Council and applied to the whole kingdom. On November 24, 1550, an instruction was sent in the King's name to every bishop 'to give substantial order' that 'with all diligence all the altars in every church or chapel...within your said diocese to be taken down, and instead of them a table to be set up in some convenient part of the chancel within every such church or chapel, to serve for the ministration of the blessed communion.'[1]

(3) Second Act of Uniformity, 1552

This Act imposed upon the clergy under penalties a revised Prayer Book, and subjected to imprisonment laymen who should attend services other than those contained in the new book. The Second Prayer Book of Edward VI was mainly the work of Cranmer, assisted by Ridley. Bucer and Peter Martyr gave advice and criticism, but it is probable that the influence of foreign divines in its compilation has been much exaggerated. It is neither Lutheran, nor Calvinistic, nor even Zwinglian, although the alterations in the Communion Service brought it very near to the Zwinglian conception of the Lord's Supper as a rite that was merely commemorative[2]. As Convocation was not consulted and the book was not modified by Parliament, it may be regarded as reflecting a genuine development in Cranmer's own views.

If the Second Prayer Book of Edward VI is compared with the First[3], a number of differences will be observed, but the following are perhaps the most significant: (1) In the First Prayer Book Matins and Evensong had begun with the Lord's Prayer; in the Second Book in Morning and Evening Prayer there are inserted before it the Sentences, the Exhortation, the General Confession, and the Absolution, as they stand in the Prayer Book now—for the First Book had contemplated auricular confession, and the General Confession in the Second Book is the reformers' substitute for it. (2) In the First Book, in the service for 'The Supper of the Lord and the Holy Communion commonly called the Mass,' the priest had been instructed to stand 'humbly afore the midst of the altar'; in the Second Book, in 'The Order for Administration of the Lord's Supper or Holy Communion,' he is to stand 'at the north side of the table,' and the word 'altar' is changed wherever it occurs. Further, it was only by the resistance of Cranmer to a determined effort on the part of Knox and Hooper that the rubric was retained which required the communicants to receive the sacrament kneeling.

---

[1] This instruction is printed in Cardwell, i, 89.

[2] 'It is clear that whatever foreign inspiration there may have been was Zwinglian rather than Calvinistic, and that the point of view adopted was not exactly that of any foreign church or any foreign divine in England' (Pollard, *Polit. Hist.* p. 69).

[3] See Cardwell, *The two Books...compared.* Cheap reprints of both books have been published by Messrs Griffith, Farran, Browne & Co., 35, Bow Street, E.C.

These changes shew how far Cranmer had moved from the doctrine of the Real Presence which he formerly held, towards a communion of simple remembrance[1]. (3) The First Book, in a rubric concerning vestments prefixed to the Communion Service, had required the officiating priest to wear 'a white alb plain, with a vestment or cope'; the Second Book, in a rubric prefixed to the Order for Morning Prayer, had ordered 'that the minister at the time of the Communion and at all other times in his ministration shall use neither alb, vestment, nor cope; but being archbishop or bishop, he shall have and wear a rochet; and being a priest or deacon, he shall have and wear a surplice only.' (4) The First Book retained while the second excluded prayers for the dead. In the First Book the prayer for all men in the Communion Service had been introduced by the words 'Let us pray for the whole state of Christ's Church,' and it had offered 'most high praise and hearty thanks for the wonderful grace and virtue declared in all Thy saints from the beginning of the world: And chiefly in the glorious and most blessed Virgin Mary, Mother of Thy Son Jesu Christ our Lord and God, and in the holy Patriarchs, Prophets, Apostles, and Martyrs.' It also contained the petition, 'We commend unto Thy mercy, O Lord, all other Thy servants which are departed hence from us with the sign of faith, and now do rest in the sleep of peace.' In the Second Book these passages are omitted[2], and in order to give no colour to the idea that prayers for the dead are intended, the opening phrase is amended so as to read: 'Let us pray for the whole state of Christ's Church militant here in earth.' (5) The direction to reserve the Sacrament for the sick is withdrawn; the anointing of the child in Baptism is abolished; and the Bishop is no longer to sign with the cross in confirmation.

An Act for the Uniformity of Common Prayer and Administration of the Sacraments

Where there hath been a very godly order set forth by authority of Parliament for common prayer and the administration of the sacraments, to be used in the mother tongue within the Church of England, agreeable to the word of God and the primitive Church, very comfortable to all good people desiring to live in Christian conversation, and most profitable to the estate of this realm, upon the which the mercy, favour, and blessing of Almighty God is in no wise so readily and plenteously poured as by common prayers, due using of the sacraments, and often

---

[1] 'The best summing up of Cranmer's views may...be given in his own words: "figuratively He is the bread and wine, and spiritually He is in them that worthily eat and drink the bread and wine; but really, carnally, and corporally He is only in Heaven, from whence He shall come to judge the quick and the dead." These words represent Cranmer's mature opinion, from which he only varied during some six weeks in 1556; and when that moment of weakness had passed he returned to the position here indicated...' (Pollard, *Cranmer*, p. 243).

[2] The sentence beginning 'We bless Thy most Holy name for all Thy servants departed this life in Thy faith and fear' was not inserted in the Prayer Book until 1662.

preaching of Gospel, with the devotion of the hearers; And yet this notwithstanding, a great number of people in divers parts of this realm, following their own sensuality and living either without knowledge or due fear of God, do wilfully and damnably before Almighty God abstain and refuse to come to their parish churches and other places where common prayer, administration of the sacraments, and preaching of the word of God is used, upon the Sundays and other days ordained to be holy days: For reformation hereof be it enacted...that from and after the Feast of All Saints next coming, all and every person and persons inhabiting within this realm or any other the King's Majesty's dominions, shall diligently and faithfully, having no lawful or reasonable excuse to be absent, endeavour themselves to resort to their parish church or chapel accustomed, or upon reasonable let[1] thereof to some usual place where common prayer and such service of God shall be used in such time of let, upon every Sunday and other days ordained and used to be kept as holy days, and then and there to abide orderly and soberly during the time of the common prayer, preachings, or other service of God there to be used and ministered; upon pain of punishment by the censures of the Church.

II. And for the due execution hereof the King's most excellent Majesty, the Lords temporal, and all the Commons in this present assembled, doth in God's name earnestly require and charge all the archbishops, bishops, and other ordinaries[2] that they shall endeavour themselves to the uttermost of their knowledge that the due and true execution hereof may be had throughout their dioceses and charges, as they will answer before God for such evils and plagues wherewith Almighty God may justly punish his people for neglecting this good and wholesome law.

III. And for their authority in this behalf, be it further likewise enacted by the authority aforesaid, that all and singular the same archbishops, bishops, and all other their officers exercising ecclesiastical jurisdiction, as well in place exempt as not exempt[3] within their diocese, shall have full power and authority by this Act to reform, correct, and punish by censures of the Church all and singular persons which shall offend within any their jurisdictions or dioceses after the said Feast of All Saints next coming against this Act and Statute; any other law, statute, privilege, liberty, or provision heretofore made, had, or suffered to the contrary notwithstanding.

[1] Hindrance.   [2] See note on p. 66 above.
[3] See note on p. 51 above.

IV. And because there hath arisen in the use and exercise of the foresaid common service in the Church heretofore set forth, divers doubts for the fashion and manner of the ministration of the same, rather by the curiosity of the minister, and mistakers, than of any other worthy cause; therefore as well for the more plain and manifest explanation hereof as for the more perfection of the said order of common service, in some places where it is necessary to make the same prayers and fashion of service more earnest and fit to stir Christian people to the true honouring of Almighty God; The King's most excellent Majesty, with the assent of the Lords and Commons in this present Parliament assembled and by the authority of the same, hath caused the foresaid order of common service entitled The Book of Common Prayer to be faithfully and godly perused, explained, and made fully perfect; and by the foresaid authority hath annexed and joined it so explained and perfected to this present Statute[1], adding also a form and manner of making and consecrating archbishops, bishops, priests, and deacons, to be of like force, authority, and value as the same like foresaid book entitled The Book of Common Prayer was before, and to be accepted, received, used, and esteemed in like sort and manner, and with the same clauses of provisions and exceptions to all intents, constructions, and purposes, as by the Act of Parliament made in the second year of the King's Majesty's reign was ordained and limited, expressed and appointed, for the Uniformity of Service and Administration of the Sacraments throughout the Realm[2], upon such several pains as in the said Act of Parliament is expressed: And the said former Act to stand in full force and strength to all intents and constructions, and to be applied, practised, and put in ure[3] to and for the establishing of the Book of Common Prayer now explained and hereunto annexed[1], and also the said form of making of archbishops, bishops, priests, and deacons hereunto annexed, as it was for the former book.

V. And by the authority aforesaid it is now further enacted, that if any manner of person or persons inhabiting and being within this realm or any other the King's Majesty's dominions shall after the said Feast of All Saints willingly and wittingly hear and be present at any other manner or form of common prayer, of administration of the sacraments, of making of ministers in the churches, or of any other rites contained in the book annexed to this Act[1] than is mentioned and set forth in the said book or that

---

[1] The Book is not on the Parliament Roll nor in the Parliament Office.
[2] See p. 108 above.   [3] See note on p. 23 above.

is contrary to the form of sundry provisions and exceptions contained in the foresaid former Statute, and shall be thereof convicted according to the laws of this realm before the Justices of Assize, Justices of Oyer and Terminer, Justices of Peace in their sessions, or any of them, by the verdict of twelve men or by his or their own confession or otherwise, shall for the first offence suffer imprisonment for six months without bail or mainprize[1], and for the second offence being likewise convicted as is abovesaid imprisonment for one whole year, and for the third offence in like manner imprisonment during his or their lives.

VI. And for the more knowledge to be given hereof and better observation of this law, be it enacted by the authority aforesaid that all and singular curates shall upon one Sunday every quarter of the year, during one whole year next following the foresaid Feast of All Saints next coming, read this present Act in the church at the time of the most assembly, and likewise once in every year following; At the same time declaring unto the people by the authority of the Scripture how the mercy and goodness of God hath in all ages been shewed to his people in their necessities and extremities by means of hearty and faithful prayers made to Almighty God; especially where people be gathered together with one faith and mind to offer up their hearts by prayer, as the best sacrifices that Christian men can yield.

5 & 6 Edw. VI, c. 1: *Statutes of the Realm*, iv, 130.

---

[1] See note on p. 10 above.

The Church Settlement of Mary

The religious history of Mary's reign falls into two phases. The first, from 1553 to 1554, was presided over by Stephen Gardiner, Bishop of Winchester, who in the reign of the Queen's predecessor had specially represented the policy of Henry VIII. The second, from 1554 to 1558, saw the Spanish marriage, and the eclipse of Gardiner's influence by that of the Emperor Charles V. In the first phase the work of Edward VI was undone—not by the Papal authority operating by means of bulls from Rome, but by the same constitutional process which had accomplished it in the first instance—partly by statutes passed in Parliament, and partly by the Royal Supremacy working by visitation and injunction. The second or Spanish phase witnessed the undoing of the work of Henry VIII, and the reconciliation to Rome of the schismatic state.

(1) Mary's First Statute of Repeal, 1553

This Act 'involved the renunciation of the chief results of Cranmer's efforts during the preceding reign—the Reformed Liturgy, the First and Second Books of Common Prayer, the administration of the Sacrament in both kinds, and the recognition of a married clergy,—and was consequently not allowed to pass without considerable opposition.'[1]

An Act for the Repeal of certain Statutes made in the time of the Reign of King Edward the Sixth

Forasmuch as by divers and several Acts hereafter mentioned, as well the divine service and good administration of the sacraments as divers other matters of religion which we and our forefathers found in this Church of England to us left by the authority of the Catholic Church, be partly altered and in some part taken from us, and in place thereof new things imagined and set forth by the said Acts, such as a few of singularity have of themselves devised, whereof hath ensued amongst us in very short time numbers of divers and strange opinions and diversities of sects, and thereby grown great unquietness and much discord, to the great disturbance of the common wealth[2] of this realm, and in very short time like to grow to extreme peril and utter confusion of the same, unless some remedy be in that behalf provided, which thing all true, loving, and obedient subjects ought and are bounden to foresee and provide to the uttermost of their power: In consideration whereof Be it enacted [*here follows the repeal of* 1 Edw. VI, c. 1, *concerning the Sacrament of the Altar;*

---

[1] *C.M.H.* ii, 522.   [2] See note on p. 33 above.

1 Edw. VI, c. 2, *concerning the Election of Bishops;* 2 & 3 Edw. VI, c. 1, *the First Act of Uniformity;* 2 & 3 Edw. VI, c. 21, *concerning the Marriage of Priests;* 3 & 4 Edw. VI, c. 10, *concerning Images;* 3 & 4 Edw. VI, c. 12, '*An Act for the ordering of Ecclesiastical Ministers*'; 5 & 6 Edw. VI, c. 1, *the Second Act of Uniformity;* 5 & 6 Edw. VI, c. 3, '*An Act for the Keeping of Holy Days and Fasting Days*'; and 5 & 6 Edw. VI, c. 12, *a declaratory Act concerning the Marriage of Priests*].

II. And Be it further enacted by the authority aforesaid, that all such Divine Service and Administration of Sacraments as were most commonly used in the realm of England in the last year of the reign of our late Sovereign Lord King Henry the Eighth, shall be, from and after the 20th day of December in this present year of our Lord God one thousand five hundred fifty and three, used and frequented through the whole realm of England and all other the Queen's Majesty's dominions; And that no other kind nor order of Divine Service nor Administration of Sacraments be after the said 20th day of December used or ministered in any other manner, form, or degree within the said realm of England or other the Queen's dominions than was most commonly used, ministered, and frequented in the said last year of the reign of the said late King Henry the Eighth.

*   *   *   *   *   *

1 Mary, st. 2, c. 2: *Statutes of the Realm,* iv, 202.

The Statute of Repeal was followed by the Marian Injunctions of 1554[1], which are probably the work of Bonner. They were sent by the Queen to the bishops for enforcement in March. Unlike the important constructive injunctions of Henry VIII and Edward VI, these merely require the bishops to restore the old order within their respective jurisdictions. They are to 'have a vigilant eye and use special diligence and foresight' to see that heretics are not admitted to benefices; they are 'diligently' to 'travail for the repressing of heresies and notable crimes, especially in the clergy' and 'for the condemning and repressing of corrupt and naughty opinions, unlawful books, ballads, and other pernicious and hurtful devices, engendering hatred among the people and discord among the same'; and they are to punish and remove 'schoolmasters, preachers, and teachers' who set forth 'any evil or corrupt doctrine.' Married priests are to be deprived 'with all celerity and speed'; Latin processions are to be revived; such holy days and fasting days are to be kept as in 'the latter time of King Henry VIII'; and 'laudable and honest ceremonies' are to be revived.

(2) Act concerning the Regal Power, 1554

The Spanish marriage was everywhere most unpopular. The marriage treaty was signed at Westminster on January 12, 1554, and was immediately

[1] Printed in Gee and Hardy, p. 380.

followed by Sir Peter Carew's insurrection in Devonshire, and by the much
more formidable rising under Sir Thomas Wyatt in Kent. When Parliament met on April 2 to confirm the treaty, the precaution was taken of
vesting the regal power by statute in the Queen as fully as it had ever been
vested in a king, so as to remove all excuse for foreign meddling. The constitutional importance of this statute lies in the fact that it finally disposed of
the doctrine that a woman could not succeed to the throne of England in
her own right.

*An Act declaring that the Regal Power of this Realm is in the Queen's
    Majesty as fully and absolutely as ever it was in any of her most
    noble Progenitors, Kings of this Realm*

Forasmuch as the imperial Crown of this realm, with all
dignities, honours, prerogatives, authorities, jurisdictions, and
preeminences thereunto annexed, united, and belonging, by the
Divine Providence of Almighty God is most lawfully, justly, and
rightfully descended and come unto the Queen's Highness that
now is, being the very true and undoubted heir and inheritrix
thereof, and invested in her most Royal Person, according unto
the laws of this realm; And by force and virtue of the same all
regal power, dignity, honour, authority, prerogative, preeminence, and jurisdictions doth appertain, and of right ought to appertain and belong unto her Highness, as to the sovereign supreme
Governor and Queen of this realm and the dominions thereof,
in as full, large, and ample manner as it hath done heretofore to
any other her most noble progenitors, kings of this realm: Nevertheless the most ancient statutes of this realm being made by
Kings then reigning, do not only attribute and refer all prerogative, preeminence, power, and jurisdiction royal unto the name
of King, but also do give, assign, and appoint the correction and
punishment of all offenders against the regality and dignity of
the Crown and the laws of this realm unto the King; By occasion
whereof the malicious and ignorant persons may be hereafter induced and persuaded unto this error and folly, to think that her
Highness could nor should have, enjoy, and use such like royal
authority, power, preeminence, prerogative, and jurisdiction, nor
do nor execute and use all things concerning the said statutes,
and take the benefit and privilege of the same, nor correct and
punish offenders against her most Royal Person and the regality
and dignity of the Crown of this realm and the dominions thereof,
as the kings of this realm her most noble progenitors have heretofore done, enjoyed, used, and exercised: For the avoiding and
clear extinguishment of which said error or doubt, and for a plain
declaration of the laws of this realm in that behalf; Be it declared

and enacted by the authority of this present Parliament, that the
law of this realm is and ever hath been and ought to be understood, that the kingly or regal office of the realm, and all
dignities, prerogative royal, power, preeminences, privileges,
authorities, and jurisdictions thereunto annexed, united, or belonging, being invested either in male or female, are and be and
ought to be as fully, wholly, absolutely, and entirely deemed,
judged, accepted, invested, and taken in the one as in the other;
so that what and whensoever statute or law doth limit and appoint
that the King of this realm may or shall have, execute, and do
anything as King, or doth give any profit or commodity to the
King, or doth limit or appoint any pains or punishment for the
correction of offenders or transgressors against the regality and
dignity of the King or of the Crown, The same the Queen (being
supreme Governess, possessor, and inheritor to the imperial
Crown of this realm as our said Sovereign Lady the Queen most
justly presently is) may by the same authority and power likewise have, exercise, execute, punish, correct, and do, to all intents,
constructions, and purposes, without doubt, ambiguity, scruple,
or question: Any custom, use, or scruple, or any other thing
whatsoever to be made to the contrary notwithstanding.

1 Mary, st. 3, c. 1: *Statutes of the Realm*, iv, 222.

(3) Act reviving the Heresy Laws, 1554

An attempt to restore the heresy laws had already been made in the
Queen's second Parliament, where two bills, one reviving the statutes against
the Lollards and the other the Act of Six Articles, had passed the Commons,
but had failed to pass the Lords. In the third Parliament this question gave
little trouble and thus the way was prepared for the Marian persecution.

*An Act for the renewing of three Statutes made for the
punishment of Heresies*

For the eschewing and avoiding of errors and heresies which
of late have risen, grown, and much increased within this realm,
for that the ordinaries[1] have wanted authority to proceed against
those that were infected therewith: Be it therefore ordained and
enacted by the authority of this present Parliament, That the
Statute made in the fifth year of the reign of King Richard the
Second concerning the arresting and apprehension of erroneous
and heretical preachers[2], And one other Statute made in the

[1] See note on p. 67.
[2] 5 Rich. II, c. 5, the Act of 1382, authorising the secular authorities, on the
certificate of the bishops, to arrest heretical preachers. For an account of this Act see
Stephen, ii, 443.

second year of the reign of King Henry the Fourth concerning the repressing of heresies and punishment of heretics[1], And also one other Statute made in the second year of the reign of King Henry the Fifth concerning the suppression of heresy and Lollardy[2], and every article, branch, and sentence contained in the same three several Acts and every of them, shall from the 20th day of January next coming be revived and be in full force, strength, and effect, to all intents, constructions, and purposes for ever.

1 & 2 Philip & Mary, c. 6: *Statutes of the Realm*, iv, 244.

(4) Mary's Second Statute of Repeal, 1555

On November 29, 1554, Mary's third Parliament passed a petition for reconciliation with Rome, and on St Andrew's Day (November 30) the King and Queen in Parliament assembled received at Whitehall solemn absolution at the hands of Cardinal Pole as Papal Legate. On the following Sunday, being the First Sunday in Advent, even Gardiner abandoned his position as the defender of the work of Henry VIII in a sermon at St Paul's from the text, 'Now it is high time to awake out of sleep.' The Second Statute of Repeal may be regarded as embodying the terms of the bargain with the Papacy. It made a clean sweep of all the Acts passed against Rome since the year 1528, with an important exception—it did not repeal the Dissolution Acts. Indeed, a considerable part of the enacting clauses of the Statute is devoted to securing the rights of the holders of the abbey lands. This was the price which Mary had to pay to the English nobility for the reconciliation with Rome.

An Act repealing all Statutes, Articles, and Provisions made against the See Apostolic of Rome since the 20th year of King Henry the Eighth, and also for the establishment of all Spiritual and Ecclesiastical Possessions and Hereditaments conveyed to the Laity

Whereas since the 20th year of King Henry the Eighth of famous memory, father unto your Majesty our most natural Sovereign and gracious Lady and Queen, much false and erroneous doctrine hath been taught, preached, and written, partly by divers the natural-born subjects of this realm, and partly being brought in hither from sundry other foreign countries, hath been sown and spread abroad within the same; By reason whereof as well the spiritualty as the temporalty of your Highness's realms and dominions have swerved from the obedience of the See Apostolic and declined from the unity of Christ's Church, and so have continued, until such time as your Majesty being first raised up by God and set in the seat royal over us, and then by

[1] 2 Henr. IV, c. 15 (1401): see p. 95 above.
[2] 2 Henr. V, st. 1, c. 7 (1414): see p. 95 above.

his divine and gracious Providence knit in marriage with the
most noble and virtuous prince, the King our Sovereign Lord
your husband, the Pope's Holiness and the See Apostolic sent
hither unto your Majesties (as unto persons undefiled and by
God's goodness preserved from the common infection aforesaid)
and to the whole realm, The most Reverend Father in God the
Lord Cardinal Pole, Legate *de latere*, to call us home again into
the right way, from whence we have all this long while wandered
and strayed abroad: And we after sundry long and grievous
plagues and calamities, seeing by the goodness of God our own
errors, have acknowledged the same unto the said most Reverend
Father, and by him have been and are the rather at the contemplation of your Majesties received and embraced into the
unity and bosom of Christ's Church; and upon our humble submission and promise made, for a declaration of our repentance,
to repeal and abrogate such acts and statutes as had been made in
Parliament since the said 20th year of the said King Henry the
Eighth against the Supremacy of the See Apostolic, as in our
submission exhibited to the said most Reverend Father in God
by your Majesties appeareth: The tenor whereof ensueth:

We the Lords spiritual and temporal and the Commons
assembled in this present Parliament, representing the whole body
of the realm of England and the dominions of the same, In the
name of ourselves particularly and also of the said body universally in this our supplication directed to your Majesties, with
most humble suit that it may by your Graces' intercession and
mean[1] be exhibited to the most Reverend Father in God the Lord
Cardinal Pole, Legate sent specially hither from our most Holy
Father the Pope Julius the Third and the See Apostolic of Rome,
Do declare ourselves very sorry and repentant of the schism and
disobedience committed in this realm and dominions aforesaid
against the said See Apostolic, either by making, agreeing, or
executing any laws, ordinances, or commandments against the
Supremacy of the said See, or otherwise doing or speaking that
might impugn the same; offering ourselves and promising by
this our supplication that for a token and knowledge of our said
repentance we be and shall be always ready, under and with the
authorities of your Majesties, to the utmost of our powers, to do
that shall lie in us for the abrogation and repealing of the said
laws and ordinances in this present Parliament as well for ourselves as for the whole body whom we represent: Whereupon we
most humbly desire your Majesties, as personages undefiled in

_____
[1] See note on p. 65 above.

the offence of this body towards the said See, which nevertheless God by his Providence hath made subject to you, To set forth this our most humble suit that we may obtain from the See Apostolic by the said most Reverend Father, as well particularly as generally, absolution, release, and discharge from all danger of such censures and sentences[1] as by the laws of the Church we be fallen into: And that we may as children repentant be received into the bosom and unity of Christ's Church, so as this noble realm with all the members thereof may in this unity and perfect obedience to the See Apostolic and Popes for the time being serve God and your Majesties to the furtherance and advancement of his honour and glory, We are at the intercession of your Majesties by the authority of our Holy Father Pope Julius the Third and of the See Apostolic assoiled, discharged, and delivered from excommunication, interdictions, and other censures ecclesiastical which hath hanged over our heads for our said defaults since the time of the said schism mentioned in our supplication. It may now like your Majesties that for the accomplishment of our promise made in the said supplication, that is to repeal all laws and statutes made contrary to the said Supremacy and See Apostolic during the said schism, the which is to be understood since the 20th year of the reign of the said late King Henry the Eighth, and so the said Lord Legate doth accept and recognise the same.

[II repeals the clauses of 21 Henr. VIII, c. 13 (in restraint of pluralities) which forbade the procuring from Rome of dispensations for pluralities or non-residence.]

[III repeals 23 Henr. VIII, c. 9, in restraint of citations; 24 Henr. VIII, c. 12, in restraint of appeals; 23 Henr. VIII, c. 20, for the conditional restraint of annates; 25 Henr. VIII, c. 19, for the submission of the clergy; 25 Henr. VIII, c. 20, in absolute restraint of annates and for the election of bishops; and 25 Henr. VIII, c. 21, the Dispensations Act.]

[IV repeals 26 Henr. VIII, c. 1, the Act of Supremacy; 26 Henr. VIII, c. 14, for the consecration of suffragans; 27 Henr. VIII, c. 15, for the appointment of a commission of 32 persons for the making of ecclesiastical laws; 28 Henr. VIII, c. 10, 'extinguishing the authority of the Bishop of Rome'; 28 Henr. VIII, c. 16, 'for the release of such as have obtained pretended licences and dispensations from the see of Rome'; 28 Henr. VIII, c. 7, § 7, i.e. that part of the Second Succession Act which 'concerneth a prohibition to marry within the degrees expressed in the said Act'[2]; 31 Henr. VIII, c. 9, authorising the King to erect new bishoprics and to appoint bishops to them by letters patent; 32 Henr. VIII, c. 38, 'concerning

---

[1] 'Sentence' is applied technically to the judgment of an ecclesiastical court.

[2] This had contained a provision that persons marrying within the prohibited degrees should be separated by judgment of the Bishop's Court, without any appeal to Rome.

pre-contracts of marriages and degrees of consanguinity'[1]; and 35 Henr. VIII, c. 3, concerning the King's style[2].]

[V repeals § 7 of 35 Henr. VIII, c. 1, the Third Succession Act, which had imposed an oath of supremacy.]

[VI repeals 37 Henr. VIII, c. 17, entitled 'An Act that the Doctors of the Civil Law may exercise ecclesiastical jurisdiction.'[3]]

[VII repeals §§ 5 and 6 of 1 Edw. VI, c. 12[4], which had assigned penalties for preaching against the Royal Supremacy or affirming that the Bishop of Rome is Supreme Head.]

VIII. And be it further enacted by the authority aforesaid, That all clauses, sentences, and articles of every other statute or Act of Parliament made since the said 20th year of the reign of King Henry the Eighth against the supreme authority of the Pope's Holiness or See Apostolic of Rome, or containing any other matter of the same effect only, that is repealed in any of the statutes aforesaid, shall be also by authority hereof from henceforth utterly void, frustrate, and of none effect.

*   *   *   *   *   *

[IX.] ...And finally, where certain acts and statutes have been made in the time of the late schism concerning the lands and hereditaments of archbishoprics and bishoprics, the suppression and dissolution of monasteries, abbeys, priories, chantries, colleges, and all other the goods and chattels of religious houses, Since the which time the right and dominion of certain lands and hereditaments, goods and chattels, belonging to the same be dispersed abroad and come to the hands and possessions of divers and sundry persons who by gift, purchase, exchange, and other means, according to the order of the laws and statutes of this realm for the time being, have the same: For the avoiding of all scruples that might grow by any the occasions aforesaid or by any other ways or means whatsoever, It may please your Majesties to be intercessors and mediators to the said most Reverend Father Cardinal Pole, That all such causes and quarrels as by pretence of the said schism or by any other occasion or mean

[1] This Act had denounced 'the usurped power of the Bishop of Rome' by which lawful marriages had been dissolved on pretence of pre-contract, and had forbidden such dissolution.

[2] This Act, declaring the King's style, had described him as 'of the Church of England and also of Ireland in earth the Supreme Head.'

[3] This Act, after again declaring the King to be Supreme Head, repudiated the ordinances of 'the Bishop of Rome and his adherents,' whereby, in order that 'they might gather and get to themselves the government and rule of the world,' they had prohibited the exercising of spiritual jurisdiction by married men or laymen, and allowed doctors of the civil law being laymen or married to exercise such jurisdiction.

[4] 'An Act for the repeal of certain statutes concerning treasons, felonies, etc.'

whatsoever might be moved, by the Pope's Holiness or See Apostolic or by any other jurisdiction ecclesiastical, may be utterly removed and taken away; so as all persons having sufficient conveyance of the said lands and hereditaments, goods and chattels, as is aforesaid by the common laws, acts, or statutes of this realm, may without scruple of conscience enjoy them, without impeachment or trouble by pretence of any General Council, canons, or ecclesiastical laws, and clear from all dangers of the censures of the Church.

*　　*　　*　　*　　*　　*

[XIII–XXVI are mainly concerned with saving the rights of the holders of the abbey lands.]

1 & 2 Philip & Mary, c. 8: *Statutes of the Realm,* iv, 246.

The Church Settlement of Elizabeth

§ 1. THE ACTS OF SUPREMACY AND UNIFORMITY

The Elizabethan Church Settlement was founded upon two important statutes, the Act of Supremacy and the Act of Uniformity. These were entirely the work of the laity, as Convocation was not consulted[1], and the Parliament which passed them was not packed[2]. The spiritual peers opposed the Act of Supremacy in the House of Lords, but they stood alone. In their opposition to the Act of Uniformity they were, however, reinforced by some of the temporal lords, and the bill only escaped shipwreck in the Upper House by a majority of three[3].

(1) Act of Supremacy, 1559

The Act of Supremacy repealed Mary's Second Statute of Repeal, and so brought into force again the statutes of Henry VIII's Reformation and restored the Henrician relation to Rome; but it treated the Supremacy after a fashion of its own. It was doubtful if the title of Supreme Head could properly be borne by a woman, and Elizabeth was content to retain the substance of the Supremacy as 'Supreme Governor of this realm...as well in all spiritual or ecclesiastical things or causes as temporal.' The Act also required 'a corporal oath[4] upon the Evangelist,' acknowledging the Queen's ecclesiastical authority and renouncing all foreign jurisdiction, to be taken by all ecclesiastical and lay officials. This oath was used to deprive the Marian bishops and to assure the government a majority in the House of Lords.

An Act restoring to the Crown the ancient Jurisdiction over the State Ecclesiastical and Spiritual, and abolishing all Foreign Power repugnant to the same

Most humbly beseech your most excellent Majesty your faithful and obedient subjects the Lords spiritual and temporal and the Commons in this your present Parliament assembled; That where in time of the reign of your most dear Father of worthy memory, King Henry the Eighth, divers good laws and statutes were made and established, as well for the utter extinguishment and putting away of all usurped and foreign powers and authorities out of this your realm and other your Highness's dominions and countries, as also for the restoring and uniting to the imperial Crown of this realm the ancient jurisdictions, authorities, superiorities, and preeminences to the same of right belonging and appertaining; by reason whereof we your most

---

[1] Gwatkin, p. 224. [2] Pollard, *Polit. Hist.* p. 199. [3] *Ib.* p. 208.
[4] A corporal oath is an oath ratified by corporally touching a sacred object, *e.g.* the Gospels (*Oxford Dictionary*).

humble and obedient subjects, from the five and twentieth year of the reign of your said dear Father, were continually kept in good order, and were disburdened of divers great and intolerable charges and exactions before that time unlawfully taken and exacted by such foreign power and authority as before that was usurped, until such time as all the said good laws and statutes by one Act of Parliament made in the first and second years of the reigns of the late King Philip and Queen Mary, your Highness's sister, entitled An Act repealing all Statutes, Articles, and Provisions made against the See Apostolic of Rome since the twentieth year of King Henry the Eighth, and also for the Establishment of all Spiritual and Ecclesiastical Possessions and Hereditaments conveyed to the Laity[1], were all clearly repealed and made void, as by the same Act of Repeal more at large doth and may appear: By reason of which Act of Repeal your said humble subjects were eftsoons[2] brought under an usurped foreign power and authority, and yet do remain in that bondage, to the intolerable charges of your loving subjects if some redress by the authority of this your High Court of Parliament with the assent of your Highness be not had and provided; May it therefore please your Highness, for the repressing of the said usurped foreign power and the restoring of the rights, jurisdictions, and preeminences appertaining to the imperial Crown of this your realm, That it may be enacted by the authority of this present Parliament, That the said Act...and all and every branch, clauses, and articles therein contained (other than such branches, clauses, and sentences as hereafter shall be excepted) may from the last day of this session of Parliament, by authority of this present Parliament, be repealed, and shall from thenceforth be utterly void and of none effect.

II. And that also for the reviving of divers of the said good laws and statutes made in the time of your said dear Father, It may also please your Highness...[*the following statutes are then revived: 23 Henr. VIII, c. 9, Foreign Citations; 24 Henr. VIII, c. 12, Appeals to Rome; 23 Henr. VIII, c. 20, Payment of Annates; 25 Henr. VIII, c. 19, Submission of the Clergy; 25 Henr. VIII, c. 20, Consecration of Bishops; 25 Henr. VIII, c. 21, Exactions from Rome; 26 Henr. VIII, c. 14, Suffragans; 28 Henr. VIII, c. 16, Dispensations*]...And all and every branches, words, and sentences in the said several Acts and Statutes contained, by authority of this present Parliament from and at all times after the last day of this session of Parliament, shall be revived and shall stand and

[1] 1 & 2 Philip & Mary, c. 8 (Mary's Second Statute of Repeal): see p. 125 above.   [2] A second time.

be in full force and strength to all intents, constructions, and purposes; And that the branches, sentences, and words of the said several Acts and every of them from thenceforth shall and may be judged, deemed, and taken to extend to your Highness, your heirs and successors, as fully and largely as ever the same Acts or any of them did extend to the said late King Henry the Eighth, your Highness's Father.

*   *   *   *   *   *

IV. And that it may also please your Highness that it may be further enacted by the authority aforesaid, That all other laws and statutes, and the branches and clauses of any act or statute, repealed and made void by the said Act of Repeal...and not in this present Act specially mentioned and revived, shall stand, remain, and be repealed and void, in such like manner and form as they were before the making of this Act; Anything herein contained to the contrary notwithstanding.

[V revives 1 Edw. VI, c. 1, concerning communion in both kinds.]

[VI repeals the heresy laws revived by Mary, and the Act which revived them.]

VII. And to the intent that all usurped and foreign power and authority, spiritual and temporal, may for ever be clearly extinguished and never to be used nor obeyed within this realm or any other your Majesty's dominions or countries: May it please your Highness that it may be further enacted by the authority aforesaid, That no foreign prince, person, prelate, state, or potentate, spiritual or temporal, shall at any time after the last day of this session of Parliament use, enjoy, or exercise any manner of power, jurisdiction, superiority, authority, preeminence, or privilege, spiritual or ecclesiastical, within this realm or within any other your Majesty's dominions or countries that now be or hereafter shall be, but from thenceforth the same shall be clearly abolished out of this realm and all other your Highness's dominions for ever; Any statute, ordinance, custom, constitutions, or any other matter or cause whatsoever to the contrary in any wise notwithstanding.

VIII. And also that it may likewise please your Highness that it may be established and enacted by the authority aforesaid, That such jurisdictions, privileges, superiorities, and preeminences, spiritual and ecclesiastical, as by any spiritual or ecclesiastical power or authority hath heretofore been or may lawfully be exercised or used for the visitation of the ecclesiastical state and persons, and for reformation, order, and correction of the same, and of all manner of errors, heresies, schisms, abuses, offences, contempts, and enormities, shall for ever by authority of this present Parliament be united and annexed to the imperial Crown of this realm; And that your Highness, your heirs and successors, kings or queens of this realm, shall have full power and authority, by virtue of this Act, by letters patents under the great seal of England to assign, name, and authorise, when and as often as your Highness, your heirs or successors, shall think meet and convenient, and for such and so long time as shall please your Highness, your heirs or successors, such person or persons being natural born subjects to your Highness, your heirs or successors, as your Majesty, your heirs or successors, shall think meet, to exercise, use, occupy, and execute under your Highness, your heirs and successors, all manner of jurisdictions, privileges, and preeminences in any wise touching or concerning any spiritual or ecclesiastical jurisdiction within these your realms...and to visit, reform, re-dress, order, correct, and amend all such errors, heresies, schisms, abuses, offences, contempts, and enormities whatsoever which by any manner spiritual or ecclesiastical power, authority, or jurisdic-tion can or may lawfully be reformed, ordered, redressed, corrected, restrained, or amended, to the pleasure of Almighty God, the in-crease of virtue, and the conservation of the peace and unity of this realm; And that such person or persons so to be named, assigned, authorised, and appointed by your Highness, your heirs or suc-cessors, after the said letters patents to him or them made and de-livered as is aforesaid, shall have full power and authority, by virtue of this Act and of the said letters patents, under your Highness, your heirs or successors, to exercise, use, and execute all the pre-mises according to the tenor and effect of the said letters patents; Any matter or cause to the contrary in any wise notwithstanding.

IX. And for the better observation and maintenance of this Act, may it please your Highness that it may be further enacted by the authority aforesaid, That all and every archbishop, bishop, and all and every other ecclesiastical person and other ecclesias-tical officer and minister, of what estate, dignity, preeminence, or degree soever he or they be or shall be, and all and every temporal judge, justicer, mayor, and other lay or temporal officer and minis-ter, and every other person having your Highness's fee or wages within this realm or any your Highness's dominions, shall make, take, and receive a corporal oath[1] upon the Evangelist, before such person or persons as shall please your Highness, your heirs or successors, under the great seal of England to assign and name to accept and take the same, according to the tenor and effect

[1] See note on p. 130 above.

hereafter following, that is to say: I, *A. B.*, do utterly testify and declare in my conscience that the Queen's Highness is the only Supreme Governor of this realm and of all other her Highness's dominions and countries, as well in all spiritual or ecclesiastical things or causes as temporal, and that no foreign prince, person, prelate, state, or potentate hath or ought to have any jurisdiction, power, superiority, preeminence, or authority, ecclesiastical or spiritual, within this realm, and therefore I do utterly renounce and forsake all foreign jurisdictions, powers, superiorities, and authorities, and do promise that from henceforth I shall bear faith and true allegiance to the Queen's Highness, her heirs and lawful successors, and to my power shall assist and defend all jurisdictions, preeminences, privileges, and authorities granted or belonging to the Queen's Highness, her heirs and successors, or united or annexed to the imperial Crown of this realm: So help me God and by the contents of this Book.

[X attaches to refusal to take the oath the penalty of loss of 'every ecclesiastical and spiritual promotion, benefice, and office, and every temporal and lay promotion and office' which the person so refusing holds 'at the time of such refusal made,' 'and that also all and every such person and persons so refusing to take the said oath shall immediately after such refusal be from thenceforth during his life disabled to retain or exercise any office or other promotion which he at the time of such refusal hath jointly or in common with any other person or persons.' Persons hereafter preferred 'to any archbishopric or bishopric, or to any other spiritual or ecclesiastical benefice, promotion, dignity, office or ministry, or...to any temporal or lay office, ministry, or service,' are required to take the oath before they 'receive, use, exercise, supply, or occupy' such office.]

*   *   *   *   *   *

XIV. And for the more sure observation of this Act and the utter extinguishment of all foreign and usurped power and authority, May it please your Highness that it may be further enacted by the authority aforesaid, That if any person or persons dwelling or inhabiting within this your realm or in any other your Highness's realms or dominions, of what estate, dignity, or degree soever he or they be, after the end of thirty days next after the determination of this session of this present Parliament, shall by writing, printing, teaching, preaching, express words, deed, or act, advisedly, maliciously, and directly affirm, hold, stand with, set forth, maintain, or defend the authority, preeminence, power, or jurisdiction, spiritual or ecclesiastical, of any foreign prince, prelate, person, state, or potentate whatsoever, heretofore claimed, used, or usurped within this realm or any dominion or country being within or under the power, dominion, or obeisance of your

Highness, or shall advisedly, maliciously, or directly put in ure[1] or execute anything for the extolling, advancement, setting forth, maintenance, or defence of any such pretended or usurped jurisdiction, power, preeminence, or authority, or any part thereof, that then every such person and persons so doing and offending, their abettors, aiders, procurers, and counsellors, being thereof lawfully convicted and attainted according to the due order and course of the common laws of this realm, [*shall be subject to the following penalties: for the first offence, forfeiture of goods, or if these are not worth £20, one year's imprisonment, the benefices and promotions of ecclesiastics becoming void; for the second offence, the penalties of praemunire; the third offence is to be deemed high treason*].

*   *   *   *   *   *

XX. Provided always and be it enacted by the authority aforesaid, That such person or persons to whom your Highness, your heirs or successors, shall hereafter by letters patents under the great seal of England give authority to have or execute any jurisdiction, power, or authority spiritual, or to visit, reform, order, or correct any errors, heresies, schisms, abuses, or enormities by virtue of this Act, shall not in any wise have authority or power to order, determine, or adjudge any matter or cause to be heresy but only such as heretofore have been determined, ordered, or adjudged to be heresy by the authority of the canonical Scriptures, or by the first four General Councils[2] or any of them, or by any other General Council wherein the same was declared heresy by the express and plain words of the said canonical Scriptures, or such as hereafter shall be ordered, judged, or determined to be heresy by the High Court of Parliament of this realm with the assent of the Clergy in their Convocation; Anything in this Act contained to the contrary notwithstanding.

*   *   *   *   *   *

1 Eliz. c. 1: *Statutes of the Realm*, iv, 350.

(2) Act of Uniformity, 1559

The Act of Uniformity passes beyond the position of Henry VIII and travels far towards the standpoint of Edward VI and Cranmer, placing the Church of England definitely on the side of the Reformation in Europe. It

---

[1] See note on p. 23 above.
[2] 1, The Council of Nicaea (325), which dealt with the Arian heresy; 2, the Council of Constantinople (381), directed against the followers of Macedonius, who impugned the Divinity of the Holy Ghost; 3, the Council of Ephesus (431), which pronounced against the Nestorian and Pelagian heresies; 4, the Council of Chalcedon (451), which defined the two natures, divine and human, in Christ against Eutyches, who was excommunicated (*Catholic Encyclopedia*, iv, 425).

authorises one form of public worship and prohibits all others under penalties—the form thus authorised being that contained in Edward VI's Second Prayer Book, now cautiously modified so as to minimise opposition, and to comprehend as many as possible. The two most important changes are: (1) the substitution for Edward VI's rubric about vestments, which had enjoined the use of the surplice only, the difficult and ambiguous Ornaments Rubric, reverting to the practice of the First Prayer Book of 1549[1]; and (2) the compromise established with regard to the Sacrament. The First Prayer Book had affirmed the doctrine of the Real Presence, in the words 'The Body of our Lord Jesus Christ which was given for thee, preserve thy body and soul unto everlasting life.' The Second Prayer Book had denied it, substituting a phrase which implied the Zwinglian doctrine of a communion of simple remembrance—'Take and eat this in remembrance that Christ died for thee, and feed on Him in thy heart by faith with thanksgiving.' The Prayer Book of Elizabeth combined both clauses in the form in which they stand to-day. (3) It should also be noticed that the Act requires attendance at the parish church on Sundays and Holy Days under pain of a fine—a policy which was to find further development later on.

Although the process of general conversion to the new order was slow, the form of service appointed by the Act was accepted by the great body of the English clergy[2].

An Act for the Uniformity of Common Prayer and Divine Service in the Church, and the Administration of the Sacraments

Where at the death of our late Sovereign Lord King Edward the Sixth there remained one uniform order of common service and prayer and of the administration of sacraments, rites, and ceremonies in the Church of England, which was set forth in one book entitled The Book of Common Prayer and Administration of Sacraments and other Rites and Ceremonies in the Church of England[3], authorised by Act of Parliament holden

[1] For a discussion of the Ornaments Rubric see W. H. Frere, *Principles of Religious Ceremonial*, ch. xiv. The question is also treated from the opposite point of view in Gwatkin, *Church and State in England*, pp. 232–6. The Elizabethan Prayer Book has been printed with an historical introduction by Dr Benham (Edinburgh: John Grant, 1909).

[2] It is commonly said, on the authority of Camden, that out of 9400 clergy in England only 187 refused to conform (E. Benham, *The Prayer Book of Queen Elizabeth*, p. ix). These figures have, however, been criticised. Camden speaks of 9400 'ecclesiastical preferments' and not of 'clergy,' and it is suggested that the number of parishes in England and Wales was at this time only 8911 (H. N. Birt, *The Elizabethan Religious Settlement*, pp. 124, 161). Owing partly to the difficulty of finding clergy for the vacant cures, some of them were pluralists, holding more than one benefice by special dispensation (p. 414). Returns of 1560–3 shew a great lack of clergy and many vacant livings and ruinous churches (Stephens and Hunt, v. 104). But these deductions, even if justified, do not substantially affect the statement in the text.

[3] The Second Prayer Book of Edward VI, 1552.

in the fifth and sixth years of our said late Sovereign Lord King
Edward the Sixth, entitled An Act for the Uniformity of Common
Prayer and Administration of the Sacraments[1]; the which was
repealed and taken away by Act of Parliament in the first year of
the reign of our late Sovereign Lady Queen Mary[2], to the great
decay of the due honour of God and discomfort to the professors
of the truth of Christ's Religion: Be it therefore enacted by the
authority of this present Parliament, That the said Statute of
Repeal and everything therein contained only concerning the said
book and the service, administration of sacraments, rites, and
ceremonies contained or appointed in or by the said book shall
be void and of none effect from and after the Feast of the   ativity
of St John Baptist next coming; and that the said book with the
order of service and of the administration of sacraments, rites,
and ceremonies, with the alteration and additions therein added
and appointed by this Statute shall stand and be from and after
the said Feast...in full force and effect according to the tenor
and effect of this Statute; Anything in the aforesaid Statute of
Repeal to the contrary notwithstanding.

II. And further be it enacted by the Queen's Highness, with
the assent of the Lords[3] and Commons in this present Parliament
assembled and by authority of the same, That all and singular
ministers in any cathedral or parish church or other place within
this realm of England, Wales, and the marches of the same, or
other the Queen's dominions, shall, from and after the Feast of
the Nativity of St John Baptist next coming, be bounden to say
and use the matins, evensong, celebration of the Lord's Supper
and administration of each of the sacraments, and all their common and open prayer, in such order and form as is mentioned in
the said book so authorised by Parliament in the said fifth and
sixth year of the reign of King Edward the Sixth, with one alteration or addition of certain lessons to be used on every Sunday in
the year, and the form of the Litany altered and corrected, and
two sentences only added in the delivery of the sacrament to the
communicants[4], and none other or otherwise: And that if any
manner of parson, vicar, or other whatsoever minister that ought
or should sing or say common prayer mentioned in the said
book, or minister the sacraments, from and after the Feast of the
Nativity of St John Baptist next coming, refuse to use the said

---

[1] The Second Act of Uniformity, 1552.   [2] Mary's First Statute of Repeal.
[3] On the narrowness of the majority by which the Bill escaped rejection in the
House of Lords see Pollard, *Polit. Hist.* p. 208.
[4] For these alterations see p. 136 above.

common prayers or to minister the sacraments in such cathedral or parish church or other places as he should use to minister the same, in such order and form as they be mentioned and set forth in the said book, or shall wilfully or obstinately (standing in the same) use any other rite, ceremony, order, form, or manner of celebrating of the Lord's Supper openly or privily, or matins, evensong, administration of the sacraments, or other open prayers than is mentioned and set forth in the said book (open prayer in and throughout this Act is meant that prayer which is for other to come unto or hear, either in common churches or private chapels or oratories, commonly called the Service of the Church) or shall preach, declare, or speak anything in the derogation or depraving of the said book or anything therein contained, or of any part thereof, and shall be thereof lawfully convicted according to the laws of this realm by verdict of twelve men, or by his own confession, or by the notorious evidence of the fact [*he shall suffer penalties as follows: First offence, forfeiture of one year's profit of his 'spiritual benefices or promotions' and six months' imprisonment; Second offence, one year's imprisonment and deprivation; Third offence, deprivation and imprisonment for life. If not beneficed, for the first offence, one year's imprisonment, and for the second, imprisonment for life*].

III. And it is ordained and enacted by the authority above-said, That if any person or persons whatsoever after the said Feast... shall in any interludes, plays, songs, rhymes, or by other open words, declare or speak anything in the derogation, de-praving, or despising of the same book, or of anything therein contained, or any part thereof, or shall by open fact, deed, or by open threatenings, compel or cause or otherwise procure or main-tain any parson, vicar, or other minister in any cathedral or parish church or in chapel or in any other place to sing or say any com-mon or open prayer or to minister any sacrament otherwise or in any other manner and form than is mentioned in the said book, or that by any of the said means shall unlawfully interrupt or let any parson, vicar, or other minister in any cathedral or parish church, chapel, or any other place to sing or say common and open prayer, or to minister the sacraments or any of them, in such manner and form as is mentioned in the said book, that then every such person being thereof lawfully convicted in form above-said [*shall be subject to penalties as follows: First offence, 100 marks; Second offence, 400 marks; Third offence, forfeiture of goods and im-prisonment for life; on non-payment of fines for the first and second offences, imprisonment for six and twelve months respectively*]: And that from and after the said Feast...all and every person and persons inhabiting within this realm or any other the Queen's Majesty's dominions, shall diligently and faithfully, having no lawful or reasonable excuse to be absent, endeavour themselves to resort to their parish church or chapel accustomed, or upon reasonable let[1] thereof, to some usual place where common prayer and such service of God shall be used in such time of let, upon every Sunday and other days ordained and used to be kept as Holy Days, and then and there to abide orderly and soberly during the time of the common prayer, preachings, or other service of God there to be used and ministered; upon pain of punishment by the censures of the Church, and also upon pain that every person so offending shall forfeit for every such offence twelve pence, to be levied by the churchwardens of the parish where such offence shall be done, to the use of the poor of the same parish, of the goods, lands, and tenements of such offender by way of distress[2].

* * * * * *

XIII. Provided always and be it enacted, That such ornaments of the church and of the ministers thereof shall be retained and be in use as was in the Church of England by authority of Parliament in the second year of the reign of King Edward the Sixth until other order shall be therein taken by the authority of the Queen's Majesty, with the advice of her commissioners appointed and authorised under the great seal of England for causes ecclesiastical or of the metropolitan of this realm; And also that if there shall happen any contempt or irreverence to be used in the ceremonies or rites of the Church by the misusing of the orders appointed in this book, the Queen's Majesty may, by the like advice of the said commissioners or metropolitan, ordain and publish such further ceremonies or rites as may be most for the advancement of God's glory, the edifying of his Church, and the due reverence of Christ's holy mysteries and sacraments.

XIV. And be it further enacted by the authority aforesaid, That all laws, statutes, and ordinances wherein or whereby any other service, administration of sacraments, or common prayer is limited, established, or set forth to be used within this realm or any other the Queen's dominions or countries, shall from henceforth be utterly void and of none effect.

1 Eliz. c. 2: *Statutes of the Realm*, iv, 355.

---

[1] Hindrance.

[2] There is reason for thinking that fines for non-attendance at church were regularly enforced throughout the reign (*E.H.R.* xxxiii, 528).

§ 2. THE INJUNCTIONS OF 1559

The Act of Uniformity came into force on June 24, and the Injunctions[1] which had been already prepared, were issued immediately afterwards. In some respects they follow closely the Injunctions of 1547; but there are alterations and many important additions. Among these the following occur: (1) The marriage of priests, although lawful, was discouraged by injunction, in view of the 'lack of discreet and sober behaviour in many ministers of the Church, both in choosing of their wives and indiscreet living with them.' To remedy this it was provided 'that no manner of priest or deacon shall hereafter take to his wife any manner of woman without the advice and allowance first had upon good examination by the bishop of the same diocese and two justices of the peace of the same shire.' The marriages of bishops were to be 'allowed and approved' by the metropolitan of the province and also by 'such commissioners as the Queen's Majesty thereunto shall appoint.' Masters of Colleges wishing to marry were to apply to the Visitor of the College, 'who shall in any wise provide that the same tend not to the hindrance of their House.' This curious provision was in actual operation at least until the middle of the reign. (2) The dress of the clergy was regulated by an injunction requiring 'such seemly habits, garments, and such square caps as were most commonly and orderly received in the latter year of the reign of King Edward VI.' (3) 'In time of the Litany and all other collects and common supplications to Almighty God' the congregation was required to kneel; and 'whensoever the name of Jesus shall be in any lesson, sermon, or otherwise in the church pronounced,' 'due reverence' is to be made 'of all persons young and old, with lowliness of courtesy, and uncovering of heads of the menkind, as thereunto doth necessarily belong and heretofore hath been accustomed.' (4) In an appendix to the Injunctions, under the title 'An admonition to simple men deceived by malicious,' the oath of supremacy is explained as not intended to require 'any other duty, allegiance, or bond' than 'was acknowledged to be due to the most noble kings of famous memory, King Henry VIII, her Majesty's father, or King Edward VI, her Majesty's brother.' The Queen accordingly forbids 'all manner her subjects to give ear or credit to such perverse and malicious persons which most sinisterly and maliciously labour to notify to her loving subjects how by the words of the said oath it may be collected that the kings or queens of this realm, possessors of the Crown, may challenge authority and power of ministry of divine offices in the Church.... For certainly her Majesty neither doth nor ever will challenge any other authority than that was challenged and lately used by the said noble kings of famous memory, King Henry VIII and King Edward VI, which is and was of ancient time due to the imperial Crown of this realm; that is, under God to have the sovereignty and rule over all manner persons born within these her realms, dominions, and countries, of what estate, either ecclesiastical or temporal, soever they be, so as no other foreign power shall or ought to have any superiority over them.' (5) Another appendix to the Injunctions, entitled 'For tables in the church,' treats in a spirit of compromise the difficult controversy concerning

---

[1] These are printed in Cardwell, i, 178; also in Gee and Hardy, p. 417, where they are compared with the Edwardian Injunctions.

the altar. It provides 'that the holy table in every church be decently made, and set in the place where the altar stood, and there commonly covered. . . . and so to stand, saving when the communion of the Sacrament is to be distributed; at which time the same shall be so placed in good sort within the chancel as whereby the minister may be more conveniently heard of the communicants in his prayer and ministration. . . . And after the communion done, from time to time the same holy table to be placed where it stood before.'

The most important part of the Supremacy as claimed by Elizabeth was the right of visitation, and the Injunctions were drawn up for use in the course of a royal visitation which lasted from June to October, 1559. The Visitors were also instructed to administer the oath of supremacy required by the Act of Supremacy and to enforce the use of the Prayer Book under the Act of Uniformity. On the completion of their work the permanent ecclesiastical commission contemplated by the Supremacy Act was called into existence by letters patent dated 19 July, 1559.

§ 3. THE PENAL LAWS AGAINST THE CATHOLICS

It has often been pointed out that the Church of the Elizabethan Settlement was an island-church. The English Prayer Book was drawn from ancient sources, and the whole tone of its devotion was widely different from that of the reformed continental worship. Episcopal succession also maintained an 'organic relation with catholic antiquity'[1] about which the continental Churches cared little. On the other hand, the Church of England was separated by a great gulf from the Church of Rome, for England rejected the Papal Supremacy and was declared by the Papacy itself to be in schism. Thus 'she was not Catholic, as countries which accepted the decrees of the Council of Trent understood Catholicism; still less was she Protestant, as Calvin and William the Silent understood Protestantism.'[2] But on the whole the compromise was in the long run successful. It is true that in spite of iconoclastic riots the new order did not at first command the undivided allegiance of the people. Returns of 1564 relating to the attitude of the justices of the peace towards the proceedings of the government in matters of religion shew 431 described as favourable, 264 indifferent, neuter, or not favourable, and 157 'hinderers or adversaries.'[3] The dioceses in the north and west were the most hostile, and the towns more hostile than the counties[4]. A list of the principal gentlemen of Yorkshire sent to Lord Burghley in 1572 gave 43 as Protestants, 19 of the 'worst sort,' 22 as 'mean or less evil,' and 39 as 'doubtful,' with the significant addition at the end of the list, 'many more evil and doubtful.'[5] Even as late as 1578 the Council complained that 'sundry persons being in commission of the peace within divers counties have of late years forborne to come to the church to any common prayer and divine service; whereby not only is God dishonoured and the laws infringed, but very evil example given to the common sort of people.'[6] But under the steady pressure of the Act of Uniformity the great majority

---

[1] Moore, p. 229.   [2] Wakeman, p. 12.
[3] Miss M. Bateson, Preface to *Camden Miscellany*, vol. ix (1895), p. iii.
[4] Birt, p. 339.   [5] *Ib.* p 327.   [6] *Ib.* p. 522.

gradually conformed, and the younger generation was brought up in a different tradition.

It is, however, doubtful whether the Elizabethan compromise would have been so successful, had not the events which followed connected the reformed Church very closely with the idea of national independence. The Bull of Excommunication in 1570, the Jesuit Invasion in 1580, and the Spanish Armada in 1588 identified the Papacy with a dangerous attack upon the national life, and the Church of England now appeared, not only as a bulwark against Rome, but also as part of England's defences against Spain. There were political reasons why patriotic Englishmen should hate the Pope, and from this it was only a short step to hatred of the whole religious system which the Pope represented. Men who were in violent hostility to Rome on political grounds soon found themselves in opposition to the worship and practices of the Roman Church on religious grounds; and thus religion and politics combined to strengthen the position of the Elizabethan Settlement.

It was also the case that in the sphere of thought the Church of England found able defenders, and their effective statement of the case against Rome was bound in time to influence the younger generation. The Anglican position was developed with moderation and reasonableness as well as with sound learning, and the work of the Elizabethan divines did much to transform what was at first a reluctant conformity to the Church of England into loyal and filial devotion.

Although the Church of the Elizabethan Settlement thus came by degrees to include the majority of Englishmen, it never succeeded in including all; and it was liable to attack from two sides at once. On the one hand, in spite of the Queen's concessions to the English Catholics, her quarrel with the Papacy exposed her to onslaughts from Rome; on the other hand, by her attempt to include the English Catholics she herself created Puritanism. Thus she had to deal not only with 'sedition, privy conspiracy, and rebellion,' but also with 'false doctrine, heresy, and schism.'

The Church of the Elizabethan Settlement was not intended to be a persecuting Church. The English Catholics themselves at first thought of the Queen as open to conviction, and as late as 1565 Richard Shacklock, who had fled from Cambridge to Louvain, was inviting her to 'come out of the cockering boat of schismatical noisomeness into the stedfast ark of Noah.'[1] It is true that an Act of 1563[2] 'for the assurance of the Queen's royal power' recognised the 'perils, dishonours, and inconveniences' that have resulted from the usurped power of the see of Rome, and 'the dangers by the fautors of the said usurped power, at this time grown to marvellous outrage and licentious boldness, and now requiring more sharp restraint and correction of laws than hitherto in the time of the Queen's Majesty's most mild and merciful reign have been had, used, or established,' and provided (1) that all who maintained the authority of the Pope within the realm should incur the penalties of *praemunire*, and (2) that the oath of supremacy should be tendered under penalties to all members of the House of Commons; to persons admitted into Holy Orders or to any University degree; to all schoolmasters and teachers; and to all barristers, attorneys, officers of the Inns of Court, and

---

[1] Stephens and Hunt, v. 82.   [2] 5 Eliz. c. 1.

other persons engaged in the execution of the law. But for the first ten years of the reign there was no systematic or active persecution of the Catholics[1]. New factors were, however, being introduced into the problem of the relations between the Queen and her Roman Catholic subjects. These begin in 1564 with the Council of Trent and the regeneration of the Papacy. 'The regenerated Catholic Church is for a while the mistress of the world, as in the time of the Crusades. It is felt that the Council of Trent ought to be followed by the suppression of heresy everywhere, as of a thing no longer excusable.'[2] A principal European question comes to be the suppression of heresy in France and the Low Countries, to be followed later on by its suppression in England and Scotland. In 1568 the arrival of Mary Queen of Scots in England profoundly affected the attitude of the leading English Catholics towards the government. Her title appeared to them a better one than that of Elizabeth, who only represented Anne Boleyn, and might be regarded as a kind of Lady Jane Grey who had temporarily seized the throne[3]. Mary was able to negotiate from her prison at Tutbury with the great Catholic houses of the north, and out of these negotiations grew the dangerous Northern Insurrection of 1569, which, though partly feudal, turned mainly on matters of religion[4]. Last of all came the Papal Bull of 1570, which John Felton nailed to the door of the Bishop of London's palace in St Paul's Churchyard.

(1) The Bull of Excommunication, 1570

The Papal Bull of 1570 'rendered treason a necessary part of the religious duties of every English Romanist.'[5] It was no longer possible for anyone to be at the same time a Roman Catholic and a patriot, for loyalty to the Papacy was now brought into conflict with loyalty to the Queen. 'Do you renounce the Pope?' said Sir Francis Knollys to Campion at his execution. 'I am a Catholic,' he replied; whereupon a bystander cried out, 'In your Catholicism all treason is contained.'[6] This view came to be widely and not unnaturally held; and the Papal Bull enabled the government to justify further penal legislation[7].

[1] 'Until the tenth of her reign her times were calm and serene, though sometimes a little overcast, as the most glorious sunrisings are subject to shadowings and droppings-in; for the clouds of Spain and the vapours of the Holy League began then to disperse and threaten her serenity' (Naunton, *Fragmenta Regalia*, p. 31).
[2] Seeley, i, 81.   [3] *Ib.* i, 39.
[4] Sir Ralph Sadler at the time wrote of the North, 'there be not ten gentlemen in all this country that do favour and allow of her Majesty's proceedings in the cause of religion,' and described the common people as 'ignorant, superstitious, and altogether blinded with the old Popish doctrine' (Birt, p. 489).
[5] Pollard, *Polit. Hist.* p. 377.
[6] Froude, *Elizabeth*, c. xxviii (vol. iv, p. 312).
[7] 'Indeed hitherto the English Papists slept in a whole skin; and so might have continued, had they not wilfully torn it themselves. For the late rebellion in the North, and the Pope thundering out his excommunication against the Queen, with many scandalous and pernicious pamphlets daily dispersed, made her Majesty about this time first to frown on Papists, then to chide, then to strike them with penalties, and last to draw life-blood from them by the severity of her laws' (Fuller, ii, 497).

Regnans in Excelsis[1]

Pius Bishop, servant to God's servants, for a future memorial of the matter.

He that reigneth on high, to whom is given all power in Heaven and in Earth, hath committed his One, Holy, Catholic, and Apostolic Church, out of which there is no salvation, to one alone upon earth, namely to Peter the chief of the Apostles, and to Peter's successor the Bishop of Rome, to be by him governed with plenary authority. Him alone hath he made prince over all people and all kingdoms, to pluck up, destroy, scatter, consume, plant, and build; that he may preserve his faithful people (knit together with the band of charity) in the unity of the Spirit, and present them spotless and unblameable to their Saviour. In discharge of which function, We, who are by God's goodness called to the government of the aforesaid Church, do spare no pains, labouring with all earnestness that unity and the Catholic Religion (which the Author thereof hath, for the trial of his children's faith and for our amendment, suffered to be tossed with so great afflictions) might be preserved sincere. But the number of the ungodly hath gotten such power that there is now no place in the whole world left which they have not essayed to corrupt with their most wicked doctrines; and amongst others, Elizabeth, the pretended Queen of England, the servant of wickedness, lendeth thereunto her helping hand, with whom, as in a sanctuary, the most pernicious persons have found a refuge. This very woman, having seized on the kingdom and monstrously usurped the place of Supreme Head of the Church in all England and the chief authority and jurisdiction thereof, hath again reduced the said kingdom into a miserable and ruinous condition, which was so lately reclaimed to the Catholic faith and a thriving condition.

For having by strong hand prohibited the exercise of the true religion which Mary, the lawful Queen of famous memory had by the help of this See restored, after it had been formerly overthrown by Henry the Eighth a revolter therefrom, and following and embracing the errors of heretics, she hath changed the royal Council consisting of the English nobility and filled it up with obscure men being heretics; suppressed the embracers of the Catholic faith; constituted lewd preachers and ministers of impiety; abolished the sacrifice of the mass, prayers, fastings, choice

---

[1] Translation printed in Camden, *Elizabeth*, p. 146. The original Latin Bull is in *Bullarium Romanum*, ii, 324; and the greater part of it will be found in Prothero, p. 195.

of meats, unmarried life, and the Catholic rites and ceremonies; commanded books to be read through the whole realm containing manifest heresy, and appointed impious rites and institutions, by herself entertained and observed according to the prescript of Calvin, to be likewise observed by her subjects; presumed to eject bishops, parsons of churches, and other Catholic priests, out of their churches and benefices, and to bestow them and other church livings upon heretics, and to determine church causes; prohibited the prelates, clergy, and people to acknowledge the Church of Rome or obey the precepts and canonical sanctions thereof; compelled most of them to condescend to her wicked laws, and to abjure the authority and obedience of the Bishop of Rome, and to acknowledge her to be sole Lady in temporal and spiritual matters, and this by oath; imposed penalties and punishments upon those which obeyed not, and exacted them of those which persevered in the unity of the faith and their obedience aforesaid; cast the Catholic prelates and rectors of churches into prison, where many of them, being worn out with long languishing and sorrow, miserably ended their lives. All which things being so manifest and notorious to all nations, and by the serious testimony of so very many so substantially proved that there is no place at all left for excuse, defence, or evasion: We seeing that impieties and wicked actions are multiplied one upon another, as also that the persecution of the faithful and affliction for religion groweth every day heavier and heavier, through the instigation and by means of the said Elizabeth, and since We understand her heart to be so hardened and obdurate that she hath not only contemned the godly requests and admonitions of Catholic Princes concerning her cure and conversion but also hath not so much as suffered the Nuncios of this See to cross the seas for this purpose into England, are constrained of necessity to betake ourselves to the weapons of justice against her, being heartily grieved and sorry that we are compelled thus to punish one to whose ancestors the whole state of Christendom hath been so much beholden. Being therefore supported with His authority whose pleasure it was to place Us (though unable for so great a burden) in this Supreme Throne of Justice, We do out of the fulness of our Apostolic power declare the aforesaid Elizabeth as being an heretic and a favourer of heretics, and her adherents in the matters aforesaid, to have incurred the sentence of excommunication, and to be cut off from the unity of the Body of Christ. And moreover We do declare her to be deprived of her pretended title to the kingdom aforesaid, and of all dominion, dignity, and privilege whatsoever; and also the nobility, subjects, and people of the said kingdom, and all others who have in any sort sworn unto her, to be for ever absolved from any such oath, and all manner of duty of dominion, allegiance, and obedience: and We also do by authority of these presents absolve them, and do deprive the said Elizabeth of her pretended title to the kingdom, and all other things before named. And We do command and charge all and every the noblemen, subjects, people, and others aforesaid that they presume not to obey her or her orders, mandates, and laws; and those which shall do the contrary We do include them in the like sentence of anathema.. . .

Camden, Elizabeth (4th edition, 1688), p. 146.

(2) Act against Bulls from Rome, 1571

The Act of 1571 was the rejoinder of the government to the Bull of Excommunication. Not only this, but the Act of Uniformity also was now strictly enforced, and something of the nature of a crusade against the recusants began. But the first act of aggression came from the Papacy; and behind the Papal Bull the Queen saw a league of foreign powers against her. Thus the attitude of the government towards the English Catholics was changed, and the policy of the first ten years of the reign reversed. Men were beginning to fear, as Bishop Challoner put it, 'lest the Romans should come, and take away both their place and nation.'

An Act against the bringing in and putting in execution of Bulls and other Instruments from the See of Rome

Where in the Parliament holden at Westminster in the fifth year of the reign of our Sovereign Lady the Queen's Majesty that now is, by one act and statute then and there made, entitled An Act for the Assurance of the Queen's Majesty's Royal Power over all States and Subjects within her Highness's Dominions[1], it is among other things very well ordained and provided, for the abolishing of the usurped power and jurisdiction of the Bishop of Rome and of the See of Rome heretofore unlawfully claimed and usurped within this realm and other the dominions to the Queen's Majesty belonging, that no person or persons shall hold or stand with to set forth, maintain, defend, or extol the same usurped power, or attribute any manner jurisdiction, authority, or preeminence to the same, to be had or used within this realm or any the said dominions, upon pain to incur the danger, penalties, and forfeitures ordained and provided by the Statute of Provision and Praemunire made in the sixteenth year of the reign of King Richard the Second, as by the same Act more at large it doth and

---

[1] 5 Eliz. c. 1 (1563): see p. 142 above.

may appear; And yet nevertheless divers seditious and very evil
disposed people, without respect of their duty to Almighty God
or of the faith and allegiance which they ought to bear and have
to our said Sovereign Lady the Queen, and without all fear or
regard had to the said good law and statute or the pains therein
limited; but minding as it should seem, very seditiously and unnaturally, not only to bring this realm and the imperial Crown
thereof (being in very deed of itself most free) into the thraldom
and subjection of that foreign, usurped, and unlawful jurisdiction,
preeminence, and authority claimed by the said See of Rome,
but also to estrange and alienate the minds and hearts of sundry
her Majesty's subjects from their dutiful obedience, and to raise
and stir sedition and rebellion within this realm, to the disturbance of the most happy peace thereof, have lately procured and
obtained to themselves from the said Bishop of Rome and his said
See divers bulls and writings, the effect whereof hath been and
is to absolve and reconcile all those that will be contented to forsake their due obedience to our most gracious Sovereign Lady the
Queen's Majesty, and to yield and subject themselves to the said
feigned, unlawful, and usurped authority, and by colour of the
said bulls and writings the said wicked persons very secretly and
most seditiously in such parts of this realm where the people for
want of good instruction are most weak, simple, and ignorant,
and thereby farthest from the good understanding of their duties
towards God and the Queen's Majesty, have by their lewd and
subtle practices and persuasions so far forth wrought that sundry
simple and ignorant persons have been contented to be reconciled
to the said usurped authority of the See of Rome and to take
absolution at the hands of the said naughty and subtle practisers,
whereby hath grown great disobedience and boldness in many,
not only to withdraw and absent themselves from all Divine
Service now most godly set forth and used within this realm, but
also have thought themselves discharged of and from all obedience, duty, and allegiance to her Majesty, whereby most wicked
and unnatural rebellion hath ensued, and to the further danger of
this realm is hereafter very like to be renewed if the ungodly and
wicked attempts in that behalf be not by severity of laws in time
restrained and bridled; For remedy and redress whereof, and to
prevent the great mischiefs and inconveniences that thereby may
ensue, Be it enacted...That if any person or persons after the first
day of July next coming shall use or put in ure[1] in any place
within this realm or in any the Queen's dominions any such bull,

[1] See note on p. 23 above.

writing, or instrument written or printed, of absolution or reconciliation at any time heretofore obtained and gotten, or at any
time hereafter to be obtained and gotten, from the said Bishop of
Rome or any his successors, or from any other person or persons authorised or claiming authority by or from the said Bishop
of Rome, his predecessors or successors, or See of Rome; Or if
any person or persons after the said first day of July shall take
upon him or them by colour of any such bull, writing, instrument,
or authority to absolve or reconcile any person or persons, or to
grant or promise to any person or persons within this realm or
any other the Queen's Majesty's dominions any such absolution
or reconciliation by any speech, preaching, teaching, writing, or
any other open deed; Or if any person or persons within this
realm or any the Queen's dominions after the said first day of
July shall willingly receive and take any such absolution or reconciliation; Or else if any person or persons have obtained or
gotten since the last day of the Parliament holden in the first
year of the Queen's Majesty's reign, or after the said first day of
July shall obtain or get from the said Bishop of Rome or any his
successors or See of Rome any manner of bull, writing, or instrument written or printed, containing any thing, matter, or cause
whatsoever; Or shall publish or by any ways or means put in ure
any such bull, writing, or instrument, That then all and every
such act and acts, offence and offences, shall be deemed and adjudged by the authority of this Act to be high treason, and the
offender and offenders therein, their procurers, abettors, and
counsellors to the fact and committing of the said offence or
offences, shall be deemed and adjudged high traitors to the Queen
and the realm; and being thereof lawfully indicted and attainted,
according to the course of the laws of this realm, shall suffer
pains of death, and also lose and forfeit all their lands, tenements,
hereditaments, goods, and chattels, as in cases of high treason by
the laws of this realm ought to be lost and forfeited.

[II. 'Aiders, comforters, or maintainers' after the fact are to be subject
to the penalties of *praemunire*.]

III. Provided always and be it further enacted by the authority aforesaid, That if any person or persons to whom any such
absolution, reconciliation, bull, writing, or instrument as is aforesaid shall after the said first day of July be offered, moved, or
persuaded to be used, put in ure, or executed, shall conceal the
same offer, motion, or persuasion, and not disclose and signify
the same by writing or otherwise within six weeks then next
following to some of the Queen's Majesty's Privy Council or

else to the President or Vice-President of the Queen's Majesty's Council established in the North Parts[1] or in the Marches of Wales[2] for the time being, That then the same person or persons so concealing and not disclosing or not signifying the said offer, motion, or persuasion, shall incur the loss, danger, penalty, and forfeiture of misprision of high treason[3]: And that no person or persons shall at any time hereafter be impeached, molested, or troubled in or for misprision of treason for any offence or offences made treason by this Act other than such as by this Act are before declared to be in case of misprision of high treason.

IV. And be it further enacted by the authority aforesaid, That if any person or persons shall at any time after the said first day of July bring into this realm of England or any the dominions of the same any token or tokens, thing or things, called by the name of an *Agnus Dei*, or any crosses, pictures, beads, or suchlike vain and superstitious things from the Bishop or See of Rome, or from any person or persons authorised or claiming authority by or from the said Bishop or See of Rome to consecrate or hallow the same, which said *Agnus Dei* is used to be specially hallowed and consecrated, as it is termed, by the said Bishop in his own person, and the said crosses, pictures, beads, and suchlike superstitious things be also hallowed either by the said Bishop or by others having power or pretending to have power for the same, by or from him or his said See, and divers pardons, immunities, and exemptions granted by the authority of the said See to such as shall receive and use the same, and that if the same person or persons so bringing in as is aforesaid such *Agnus Dei* and other like things as be before specified shall deliver or offer or cause to be delivered the same or any of them to any subject of this realm or any of the dominions of the same to be worn or used in any wise, that then as well the same person and persons so doing, as also all and every other person or persons which shall receive and take the same to the intent to use or wear the same, being thereof lawfully convicted and attainted by the order of the common laws of this realm, shall incur into the dangers, penalties, pains, and forfeitures ordained and provided by the Statute of Praemunire

---

[1] On the Council of the North, see p. 314.

[2] On the Council of Wales, see p. 331.

[3] Originally an offence akin to treason, but involving a lesser degree of guilt and not liable to the penalty of death. As concealment of a knowledge of treasonable actions was made misprision of treason by statute, this came to be a common interpretation of the term.

and Provision made in the sixteenth year of the reign of King Richard the Second.

*   *   *   *   *   *

13 Eliz. c. 2: *Statutes of the Realm*, iv, 528.

(3) Act against Reconciliation to Rome, 1581

The Act of 1571 governed for ten years the relations between the Queen and the English Catholics, but in 1581 there is fresh penal legislation; for the seminary priests 'depraved and soured with a new leaven of malignity the whole lump of Catholics, which had before been more sweet and harmless.'[1] The movement which had led to the invasion of the seminary priests had been originated by William Allen, one of the ablest and most courageous of the English Catholics. In 1568 he opened a seminary in the University town of Douay, with a view to educating a body of learned priests who should be ready to assist in the restoration of Catholicism in England whenever circumstances should permit, fearing, as he himself said some years afterwards, 'that if the schism should last much longer, owing to the death of the few who at its beginning had been cast out of the English Universities for the faith, no seed would be left hereafter for the restoration of religion, and that heresy would thus obtain a perpetual and peaceful possession of the realm.'[2] As an afterthought there grew out of this scheme a plan for immediate and active missionary work under existing conditions, and in 1574 priests from Douay began to land in England. In 1578 the college was moved from Douay to Rheims, where it was placed under the patronage of the Guises and received an annual allowance from Philip of Spain. In 1579 the Pope founded another college at Rome. Thus the Seminarist movement was in a manner a symbol of the union of the Catholic powers against the English Reformation.

The establishment of English colleges beyond the seas struck a deadly blow at the Elizabethan Church Settlement. The Bull of Excommunication had checked conformity; the seminary priests succeeded for a time in stopping conformity altogether. Under their influence the Catholic families ceased to bow themselves in the house of Rimmon, and a marked revival of active Catholicism took place in England. And in 1579 the seminarists were reinforced from a new quarter. Allen succeeded in inducing the order of Jesuits to take part in the English Mission, and in 1580 the first two Jesuit priests, Edmund Campion and Robert Parsons, landed at an English port.

This invasion of learned priests was the more dangerous because of the low level of learning among the English clergy. The deprivations had made

[1] Bacon, vi, 315.

[2] *D.N.B.* i, 316. Cf. Fuller, 'The old store of Papists in England began now very much to diminish and decay; insomuch that the Romanists perceived they could not spend at this rate out of the main stock, but it would quickly make them bankrupt. Prisons consumed many, age more of their priests; and they had no place in England whence to recruit themselves. The largest cistern with long drawing will grow dry, if wanting a fountain to feed the daily decay thereof. Hereupon they resolved to erect colleges beyond the seas for English youth to have their education therein' (ii, 485).

it necessary to admit a large number of men to holy orders, and the Universities could not cope with the demand. Thus many older men 'being grave and sober persons, though no scholars, but perhaps tradesmen before, were thought convenient to be admitted into orders to supply the present necessity of the Church.'[1] Cartwright charges Archbishop Whitgift with the fact that 'there be admitted into the ministry of the basest sort,...such as are suddenly changed out of a serving-man's coat into a minister's cloak, making for the most part the ministry their last refuge.' These men were no match for the trained dialecticians of the seminary, and they were often inefficient defenders of the Church which they represented.

It was also the case that some of the seminarists were dangerous to the state[2]. The failure of the Northern Insurrection had shewn that the enemies of Elizabeth had little to hope from rebellion, and they were thrown back upon assassination. The first conspiracy was hatched in 1571, and from that time onward siege was laid to the Queen's life. A writer of the time makes the Pope's allies say to each other, 'Come, let us kill her, and the inheritance shall be ours.' In the schemes against the Queen's life only some of the seminarists were involved, and several of them were not even prepared to allow the validity of her deposition by the Pope; but it was not easy either for the Privy Council or for public opinion to distinguish between the innocent and the guilty. It was assumed that all Roman Catholics were traitors until they proved their loyalty by explicitly denying the Pope's power to depose the Queen. It was not until the end of the reign that the idea of 'a distinction between priests politically safe and priests politically unsafe' could be entertained at all, and even as late as the reign of James I this distinction was again obscured by the discovery of Gunpowder Plot.

The Act of 1581 was mainly intended to make the work of the seminarists in reconciling individuals and families to the Church of Rome as difficult and dangerous as possible, but at one point it bore heavily upon the English Catholics as a whole, for the shilling fine for non-attendance at church imposed by the Act of Uniformity was now raised to £20 a month[3].

[1] Strype, *Life of Grindal*, p. 40.

[2] 'Now began priests and Jesuits to flock faster into England than ever before; having exchange of clothes, and names, and professions. He who on Sunday was a priest or Jesuit was on Monday a merchant, on Tuesday a soldier, on Wednesday a courtier, etc., and with the shears of equivocation (constantly carried about him) he could cut himself into any shape he pleased. But under all their new shapes they retained their old nature; being akin in their turbulent spirits to the wind pent in the subterranean concavities, which will never be quiet until it hath vented itself with a state-quake of those countries wherein they abide. These distilled traitorous principles into all people wheresoever they came, and endeavoured to render them disaffected to her Majesty; maintaining that she neither had nor ought to have any dominion over her subjects whilst she persisted in a heretical distance from the Church of Rome' (Fuller, iii, 19).

[3] 'Twenty pounds a month! a vast sum...enough to shatter the containment of a rich man's estate. They commended the moderation of the former statute... that did smart, yet did not fetch blood; at the worst, did not break bones. Whereas now twenty pounds a month, paid severally by every recusant for himself and as much for his wife (which though one flesh in divinity yet are two persons in law) held so heavy as to cripple their estates' (*ib.* iii, 20).

There is evidence to shew that late in the reign these fines were being enforced[1], except in remoter parts of the country where feeling was strongly Roman Catholic and the local squire was omnipotent.

An Act to retain the Queen's Majesty's Subjects in their due Obedience

Where since the Statute made in the thirteenth year of the reign of the Queen our Sovereign Lady, entitled An Act against the bringing in and putting in execution of Bulls, Writings, and Instruments, and other superstitious things from the See of Rome[2], divers evil affected persons have practised[3], contrary to the meaning of the said Statute, by other means than by bulls or instruments written or printed, to withdraw divers the Queen's Majesty's subjects from their natural obedience to her Majesty to obey the said usurped authority of Rome, and in respect of the same to persuade great numbers to withdraw their due obedience to her Majesty's laws established for the due service of Almighty God: For reformation whereof, and to declare the true meaning of the said law, Be it declared and enacted by the authority of this present Parliament, That all persons whatsoever which have, or shall have, or shall pretend to have power, or shall by any ways or means put in practice to absolve, persuade, or withdraw any of the Queen's Majesty's subjects or any within her Highness's realms and dominions from their natural obedience to her Majesty, or to withdraw them for that intent from the religion now by her Highness's authority established within her Highness's dominions to the Romish religion, or to move them or any of them to promise any obedience to any pretended authority of the See of Rome, or of any other prince, state, or potentate, to be had or used within her dominions, or shall do any overt act to that intent or purpose, and every of them, shall be to all intents adjudged to be traitors, and being thereof lawfully convicted shall have judgment, suffer, and forfeit as in case of high treason: And if any person shall, after the end of this session of Parliament, by any means be willingly absolved or withdrawn as aforesaid, or willingly be reconciled, or shall promise any obedience to any such pretended authority, prince, state, or potentate as is aforesaid, that then every such person, their procurers and counsellors thereunto, being thereof lawfully convicted, shall be taken, tried, and judged, and shall suffer and forfeit as in cases of high treason.

---

[1] Gasquet, *Hampshire Recusants*, p. 27; but cf. *West Riding Sessions Rolls*, ed. Lister, pp. xx–xxiii, where it is suggested that they were often not levied in full.
[2] 13 Eliz. c. 2 (1571).   [3] Plotted or conspired.

II. And be it likewise enacted and declared, That all and every person and persons that shall wittingly be aiders or maintainers of such persons so offending as is above expressed, or of any of them knowing the same, or which shall conceal any offence aforesaid and shall not, within twenty days at the furthest after such person's knowledge of such offence, disclose the same to some justice of peace or other higher officer, shall be taken, tried, and judged, and shall suffer and forfeit as offenders in misprision of treason.

III. And be it likewise enacted, That every person which shall say or sing mass, being thereof lawfully convicted, shall forfeit the sum of two hundred marks and be committed to prison in the next gaol, there to remain by the space of one year, and from thenceforth till he have paid the said sum of 200 marks: and that every person which shall willingly hear mass shall forfeit the sum of one hundred marks and suffer imprisonment for a year.

IV. Be it also further enacted by the authority aforesaid, That every person above the age of 16 years which shall not repair to some church, chapel, or usual place of common prayer, but forbear the same contrary to the tenor of a statute made in the first year of her Majesty's reign for Uniformity of Common Prayer, and being thereof lawfully convicted, shall forfeit to the Queen's Majesty for every month after the end of this session of Parliament which he or she shall so forbear, twenty pounds of lawful English money: and that over and besides the said forfeitures, every person so forbearing by the space of 12 months as aforesaid shall for his or her obstinacy, after certificate thereof in writing made into the Court commonly called the King's Bench by the ordinary of the diocese, a justice of assize and gaol delivery, or a justice of peace of the county where such offender shall dwell or be, be bound with two sufficient sureties in the sum of two hundred pound at the least to the good behaviour, and so to continue bound until such time as the persons so bound do conform themselves and come to the church, according to the true meaning of the said Statute made in the said first year of the Queen's Majesty's reign.

* * * * * *

IX. Provided also, That every person which usually on the Sunday shall have in his or their house the Divine Service which is established by the law in this realm, and be thereat himself or herself usually or most commonly present, and shall not obstinately refuse to come to church and there to do as is aforesaid, and shall also four times in the year at the least be present at the Divine Service in the church of the parish where he or she shall be resident, or in some other open common church or such chapel of ease, shall not incur any pain or penalty limited by this Act for not repairing to church.

*　　*　　*　　*　　*

XII. Provided also, That neither this Act nor anything therein contained shall extend to take away or abridge the authority or jurisdiction of the ecclesiastical censures for any cause or matter, but that the archbishops and bishops and other ecclesiastical judges may do and proceed as before the making of this Act they lawfully did or might have done; Anything in this Act to the contrary notwithstanding.

23 Eliz. c. 1: Statutes of the Realm, iv, 657.

(4) Act against Jesuits and Seminary Priests, 1585

The Act of 1585 arose out of the Throckmorton Plot, which brought home to the Queen's subjects in October, 1583, the danger in which she stood. This was followed by the murder of William the Silent, 'upon whose Atlantean shoulders the whole insurrection of the Low Countries rested,'[1] on July 10, 1584, and by the discovery in September of that year of the formidable designs of the Guises against her. The effect of these plots was to rouse the most serious apprehensions in the minds of all those who were loyal to the Queen and to the Elizabethan Church Settlement. The English Protestants knew their weakness, for if Elizabeth should die she would be succeeded by Mary Stuart, since they had no Lady Jane Grey ready as an alternative candidate for the throne. Parliament would be dissolved by the demise of the Crown, the Privy Council would cease to exist, and the law of treason would change sides, for it would be the reformers who would be the rebels if they should resist the restoration of the mass. Thus when Parliament met in November, its first Act achieved the new departure in the law of treason described below [pp. 381, 417], and its second Act banished all Jesuits and seminary priests. This legislation was specially aimed at priests educated and ordained abroad, and thus distinguished between the disloyal seminarist and the old Marian priest, who was, generally speaking, loyal[2].

An Act against Jesuits, Seminary Priests, and such other like disobedient Persons

Whereas divers persons called or professed Jesuits, seminary priests, and other priests, which have been and from time to time are made in the parts beyond the seas by or according to the order and rites of the Romish Church, have of late years come and been sent, and daily do come and are sent, into this realm of

---

[1] Seeley, i, 168.
[2] See Law, *The Archpriest Controversy* (Camden Society).

England and other the Queen's Majesty's dominions, of purpose (as hath appeared as well by sundry of their own examinations and confessions as by divers other manifest means and proofs) not only to withdraw her Highness's subjects from their due obedience to her Majesty but also to stir up and move sedition, rebellion, and open hostility within her Highness's realms and dominions, to the great dangering of the safety of her most royal person and to the utter ruin, desolation, and overthrow of the whole realm, if the same be not the sooner by some good means foreseen and prevented: For reformation whereof be it ordained, established, and enacted by the Queen's most excellent Majesty and the Lords spiritual and temporal and the Commons in this present Parliament assembled and by the authority of the same Parliament, That all and every Jesuits, seminary priests, and other priests whatsoever, made or ordained out of the realm of England or other her Highness's dominions or within any of her Majesty's realms or dominions by any authority, power, or jurisdiction derived, challenged, or pretended from the See of Rome since the Feast of the Nativity of St John Baptist in the first year of her Highness's reign, shall within forty days next after the end of this present session of Parliament depart out of this realm of England and out of all other her Highness's realms and dominions, if the wind, weather, and passage shall serve for the same; or else so soon after the end of the said forty days as the wind, weather, and passage shall so serve.

II. And be it further enacted by the authority aforesaid, That it shall not be lawful to or for any Jesuit, seminary priest, or other such priest, deacon, or any religious or ecclesiastical person whatsoever, being born within this realm or any other her Highness's dominions, and heretofore since the said Feast of the Nativity of St John Baptist in the first year of her Majesty's reign made, ordained, or professed, or hereafter to be made, ordained, or professed, by any authority or jurisdiction derived, challenged, or pretended from the See of Rome, by or of what name, title, or degree soever the same shall be called or known, to come into, be, or remain in any part of this realm or any other her Highness's dominions after the end of the same forty days, other than in such special cases and upon such special occasions only and for such time only as is expressed in this Act; and if he do, that then every such offence shall be taken and adjudged to be high treason; And every person so offending shall for his offence be adjudged a traitor, and shall suffer, lose, and forfeit as in case of high treason: And every person which after the end of the same forty days, and after such time of departure as is before limited and appointed, shall wittingly and willingly receive, relieve, comfort, aid, or maintain any such Jesuit, seminary priest, or other priest, deacon, or religious or ecclesiastical person as is aforesaid, being at liberty or out of hold, knowing him to be a Jesuit, seminary priest, or other such priest, deacon, or religious or ecclesiastical person as is aforesaid, shall also for such offence be adjudged a felon without benefit of clergy, and suffer death, lose, and forfeit as in case of one attainted of felony.

III. And be it further enacted by the authority aforesaid, If any of her Majesty's subjects (not being a Jesuit, seminary priest, or other such priest, deacon, or religious or ecclesiastical person as is before mentioned) now being or which hereafter shall be of or brought up in any college of Jesuits or seminary already erected or ordained or hereafter to be erected or ordained in the parts beyond the seas or out of this realm in any foreign parts, shall not, within six months next after proclamation in that behalf to be made in the City of London under the great seal of England, return into this realm, and thereupon, within two days next after such return, before the bishop of the diocese or two justices of peace of the county where he shall arrive, submit himself to her Majesty and her laws, and take the oath set forth by Act in the first year of her reign[1]; that then every such person which shall otherwise return, come into, or be in this realm or any other her Highness's dominions, for such offence of returning or being in this realm or any other her Highness's dominions without submission as aforesaid, shall also be adjudged a traitor, and shall suffer, lose, and forfeit as in case of high treason.

IV. And be it further enacted by the authority aforesaid, If any person under her Majesty's subjection or obedience shall at any time after the end of the said forty days by way of exchange or by any other shift, way, or means whatsoever, wittingly and willingly, either directly or indirectly, convey, deliver, or send, or cause or procure to be conveyed or delivered to be sent, over the seas or out of this realm or out of any other her Majesty's dominions or territories into any foreign parts, or shall otherwise wittingly and willingly yield, give, or contribute any money or other relief to or for any Jesuit, seminary priest, or such other priest, deacon, or religious or ecclesiastical person as is aforesaid, or to or for the maintenance or relief of any college of Jesuits or seminary already erected or ordained or hereafter to be erected or ordained in any the parts beyond the seas or out of this realm

---

[1] *I.e.* the oath of Supremacy imposed by 1 Eliz. c. 1, § 9 (the Act of Supremacy).

in any foreign parts, or of any person then being of or in any the same colleges or seminaries and not returned into this realm with submission as in this Act is expressed, and continuing in the same realm; That then every such person so offending, for the same offence shall incur the danger and penalty of *praemunire* mentioned in the Statute of Praemunire made in the 16th year of the reign of King Richard the Second.

V. And be it further enacted by the authority aforesaid, That it shall not be lawful for any person of or under her Highness's obedience, at any time after the said forty days, during her Majesty's life (which God long preserve) to send his or her child or other person being under his or her government into any the parts beyond the seas out of her Highness's obedience without the special license of her Majesty, or of four of her Highness's Privy Council, under their hands in that behalf first had or obtained; (except merchants, for such only as they or any of them shall send over the seas only for or about his, her, or their trade of merchandise, or to serve as mariners, and not otherwise); upon pain to forfeit and lose for every such their offence the sum of one hundred pounds.

* * * * * *

VIII. Provided also, That this Act or anything therein contained shall not in any wise extend to any such Jesuit, seminary priest, or other such priest, deacon, or religious or ecclesiastical person as is before mentioned, as shall at any time within the said forty days, or within three days after that he shall hereafter come into this realm or any other her Highness's dominions, submit himself to some archbishop or bishop of this realm, or to some justice of peace within the county where he shall arrive or land, and do thereupon truly and sincerely before the same archbishop, bishop, or such justice of peace, take the said oath set forth *in anno primo*, and by writing under his hand confess and acknowledge and from thenceforth continue his due obedience unto her Highness's laws, statutes, and ordinances made and provided, or to be made or provided, in causes of religion.

* * * * * *

X. Provided nevertheless, and it is declared by authority aforesaid, That if any such Jesuit, seminary priest, or other priests abovesaid shall fortune to be so weak or infirm of body that he or they may not pass out of the realm by the time herein limited without imminent danger of life, and this understood, as well by the corporal oath of the party as by other good means, unto the bishop of the diocese and two justices of peace of the same county where such person or persons do dwell or abide; that then upon good and sufficient bond of the person or persons, with sureties of the sum of two hundred pounds at the least, with condition that he or they shall be of good behaviour towards our Sovereign Lady the Queen and all her liege people, then he or they so licensed and doing as is aforesaid shall and may remain and be still within this realm, without any loss or danger to fall on him or them by this Act, for so long time as by the same bishop and justices shall be limited and appointed, so as the same time of abode exceed not the space of six months at the most; and that no person or persons shall sustain any loss or incur any danger by this Act for the receiving or maintaining of any such person or persons so licensed as is aforesaid, for and during such time only as such person or persons shall be so licensed to tarry within this realm; Anything contained in this Act to the contrary notwithstanding.

XI. And be it also further enacted by authority aforesaid, That every person or persons being subject of this realm which after the said forty days shall know and understand that any such Jesuit, seminary priest, or other priest abovesaid shall abide, stay, tarry, or be within this realm or other the Queen's dominions and countries, contrary to the true meaning of this Act, and shall not discover the same unto some justice of peace or other higher officer within twelve days next after his said knowledge, but willingly conceal his knowledge therein; that every such offender shall make fine and be imprisoned at the Queen's pleasure: And that if such justice of peace or other such officer to whom such matter shall be so discovered do not within 28 days then next following give information thereof to some of the Queen's Privy Council or to the President or Vice-President of the Queen's Council established in the North[1] or in the Marches of Wales[2] for the time being, that then he or they so offending shall for every such offence forfeit the sum of two hundred marks.

*   *   *   *   *   *

XIII. And be it also enacted, That all such oaths, bonds, and submissions as shall be made by force of this Act as aforesaid, shall be certified into the Chancery by such parties before whom the same shall be made, within three months after such submission, upon pain to forfeit and lose for every such offence an hundred pounds of lawful English money, the said forfeiture to be to the Queen, her heirs and successors: And that if any person submitting himself as aforesaid do at any time within the space

1 See p. 314 below.   2 See p. 331 below.

of ten years after such submission made come within ten miles of such place where her Majesty shall be, without especial license from her Majesty in that behalf to be obtained in writing under her hand, that then and from thenceforth such person shall take no benefit of the said submission, but that the said submission shall be void as if the same had never been.

27 Eliz. c. 2: *Statutes of the Realm*, iv, 706

(5) Act against Popish Recusants, 1593

The Parliament of 1593 was summoned to deal with religion, and the ecclesiastical question occupied much of its time. It was chiefly concerned with the repression of the extremer forms of Puritanism, and an Act was passed against the separatist sectaries [p. 197]; but these were now for the first time differently treated from the Romanists, who were dealt with in a separate Act.

An Act against Popish Recusants

For the better discovering and avoiding of all such traitorous and most dangerous conspiracies and attempts as are daily devised and practised against our most gracious Sovereign Lady the Queen's Majesty and the happy estate of this common weal by sundry wicked and seditious persons, who terming themselves Catholics and being indeed spies and intelligencers, not only for her Majesty's foreign enemies but also for rebellious and traitorous subjects born within her Highness's realms and dominions, and hiding their most detestable and devilish purposes under a false pretext of religion and conscience do secretly wander and shift from place to place within this realm to corrupt and seduce her Majesty's subjects and to stir them to sedition and rebellion: Be it ordained and enacted by our Sovereign Lady the Queen's Majesty and the Lords spiritual and temporal and the Commons in this present Parliament assembled and by the authority of the same, That every person above the age of sixteen years, born within any the Queen's Majesty's realms or dominions or made denizen, being a Popish recusant and before the end of this session of Parliament convicted for not repairing to some church, chapel, or usual place of common prayer to hear Divine Service there, but forbearing the same contrary to the tenor of the laws and statutes heretofore made and provided in that behalf, and having any certain place of dwelling and abode within this realm, shall within forty days next after the end of this session of Parliament (if they be within this realm and not restrained or stayed, either by imprisonment, or by her Majesty's commandment, or by order and direction of some six or more of the Privy Council, or by such sickness or infirmity of body as they shall not be able to travel without imminent danger of life, and in such cases of absence out of the realm, restraint, or stay, then within twenty days next after they shall return into the realm, and be enlarged of such imprisonment or restraint, and shall be able to travel) repair to their place of dwelling where they usually heretofore made their common abode, and shall not any time after pass or remove above five miles from thence: And also that every person being above the age of sixteen years born within any her Majesty's realms or dominions or made denizen, and having or which hereafter shall have any certain place of dwelling and abode within this realm, which being then a Popish recusant shall at any time hereafter be lawfully convicted for not repairing to some church, chapel, or usual place of common prayer to hear Divine Service there, but forbearing the same contrary to the said laws and statutes, and being within this realm at the time that they shall be convicted, shall within forty days next after the same conviction, (if they be not restrained or stayed by imprisonment or otherwise as is aforesaid, and in such cases of restraint and stay then within twenty days next after they shall be enlarged of such imprisonment or restraint and shall be able to travel,) repair to their place of usual dwelling and abode, and shall not at any time after pass or remove above five miles from thence: upon pain that every person and persons that shall offend against the tenor and intent of this Act in any thing before mentioned shall lose and forfeit all his and their goods and chattels, and shall also forfeit to the Queen's Majesty all the lands, tenements, and hereditaments, and all the rents and annuities of every such person so doing or offending, during the life of the same offender.

[II. Recusants 'not having any certain place of dwelling and abode' are to 'repair to the place where such person was born, or where the father or mother of such person shall then be dwelling,' and under like penalty 'shall not at any time after remove or pass above five miles from thence.']

*   *   *   *   *   *

IV. Provided always and be it further enacted by the authority aforesaid, That all such persons as by the intent and true meaning of this Act are to make their repair to their place of dwelling and abode, or to the place where they were born, or where their father or mother shall be dwelling, and not to remove or pass above five miles from thence as is aforesaid, shall within twenty days next after their coming to any of the said places, as the case shall happen, notify their coming thither and present themselves and deliver their true names in writing to the minister or curate of the same parish and to the constable, headborough[1], or tithingman[2] of the town; and thereupon the said minister or curate shall presently enter the same into a book to be kept in every parish for that purpose; And afterward the said minister or curate and the said constable, headborough, or tithingman shall certify the same in writing to the justices of the peace of the same county at the next general or quarter sessions to be holden in the said county; and the said justices shall cause the same to be entered by the clerk of the peace in the rolls of the same sessions.

V. And to the end that the realm be not pestered and over-charged with the multitude of such seditious and dangerous people as is aforesaid, who having little or no ability to answer or satisfy any competent penalty for their contempt and disobedience of the said laws and statutes, and being committed to prison for the same do live for the most part in better case there than they could if they were abroad at their own liberty; The Lords spiritual and temporal and the Commons in this present Parliament assembled do most humbly and instantly[3] beseech the Queen's Majesty that it may be further enacted, That if any such person or persons being a Popish recusant, not being a *feme covert*, and not having lands, tenements, rents, or annuities of an absolute estate of inheritance or freehold of the clear yearly value of twenty marks above all charges, to their own use and behoof and not upon any secret trust or confidence for any other, or goods and chattels in their own right and to their own proper use and behoof, and not upon any secret trust or confidence for any other, above the value of forty pounds, shall not within the time before in this Act in that behalf limited and appointed repair to their place of usual dwelling and abode, if they have any, or else to the place where they were born or where their father or mother shall be dwelling, according to the tenor... of this present Act. And thereupon notify their coming and present themselves and deliver their true names in writing to the minister or curate of the parish and to the constable, headborough, or tithingman of the town within such time and in such manner and form as is aforesaid; or at any time after such their repairing to any such place as is before appointed shall pass or remove above five miles from the same, and shall not within three months next after such person shall be apprehended or taken for offending as is aforesaid conform themselves to the obedience of the laws and statutes of this realm in coming usually

---

[1] 'Originally the head of a *friðborh*, tithing, or frankpledge: afterwards a parish officer identical in functions with the petty constable' (*Oxford Dictionary*).

[2] The head of a tithing; see note 1.   [3] *I.e.* urgently, persistently.

to the church to hear Divine Service, and in making such public confession and submission as hereafter in this Act is appointed and expressed, being thereunto required by the bishop of the diocese, or any justice of peace of the county where the said person shall happen to be, or by the minister or curate of the parish; that in every such case every such offender, being thereunto warned or required by any two justices of the peace or coroner of the same county where such offender shall then be, shall upon his or their corporal oath[1] before any two justices of the peace or coroner of the same county abjure[2] this realm of England and all other the Queen's Majesty's dominions for ever; And thereupon shall depart out of this realm at such haven and port and within such time as shall in that behalf be assigned and appointed by the said justices of peace or coroner before whom such abjuration shall be made, unless the same offenders be letted or stayed by such lawful and reasonable means or causes as by the common laws of this realm are permitted and allowed in cases of abjuration for felony, and in such cases of let or stay, then within such reasonable and convenient time after as the common law requireth in case of abjuration for felony as is aforesaid; And that every justice of peace and coroner before whom any such abjuration shall happen to be made as is aforesaid, shall cause the same presently to be entered of record before them, and shall certify the same to the justices of assizes and gaol delivery of the said county at the next assizes or gaol delivery to be holden in the same county: and if any such offender which by the tenor and intent of this Act is to be abjured as is aforesaid shall refuse to make such abjuration as is aforesaid, or after such abjuration made shall not go to such haven and within such time as is before appointed and from thence depart out of this realm according to this present Act, or after such his departure shall return or come again into any her Majesty's realms or dominions without her Majesty's special license in that behalf first had and obtained, That then in every such case the person so offending shall be adjudged a felon and shall suffer and lose as in case of felony without benefit of clergy.

VI. And be it further enacted and ordained by the authority aforesaid, That if any person which shall be suspected to be a Jesuit, seminary, or massing priest, being examined by any person having lawful authority in that behalf to examine such person which shall be so suspected, shall refuse to answer directly and

---

[1] See note on p. 130 above.
[2] On abjuration of the realm, see p. 15 above.

truly whether he be a Jesuit or a seminary or massing priest as is aforesaid, every such person so refusing to answer shall for his disobedience and contempt in that behalf be committed to prison by such as shall examine him as is aforesaid, and thereupon shall remain and continue in prison without bail or mainprize[1] until he shall make direct and true answer to the said questions whereupon he shall be so examined.

VII. Provided nevertheless and be it further enacted by the authority aforesaid, That if any of the persons which are hereby limited and appointed to continue and abide within five miles of their usual dwelling place, or of such place where they were born or where their father or mother shall be dwelling as is aforesaid, shall have necessary occasion or business to go and travel out of the compass of the said five miles, That then and in every such case upon license in that behalf to be gotten under the hands of two of the justices of the peace of the same county, with the privity and assent in writing of the bishop of the diocese, or of the lieutenant or of any deputy lieutenant of the same county, under their hands, it shall and may be lawful for every such person to go and travel about such their necessary business, and for such time only for their travelling, attending, and returning as shall be comprised in the same license; anything before in this Act to the contrary notwithstanding.

* * * * * *

[X provides that offenders against the Act may, before conviction, 'come to some parish church on some Sunday or other festival day and then and there hear divine service, and at service time before the sermon or reading of the gospel make public and open submission' according to a form provided, and so escape the penalties of the Act; the minister of the parish being required to enter such submission 'into a book to be kept in every parish for that purpose,' and also within ten days to 'certify the same in writing to the bishop of the diocese.']

* * * * * *

35 Eliz. c. 2: *Statutes of the Realm*, iv, 843.

§ 4. THE PURITAN MOVEMENT

In the Tudor period foreign influences were potent in English ecclesiastical affairs. During the reign of Edward VI exiles from the continent took refuge in England and lavished advice upon the English reformers, and although the criticisms of Martin Bucer and Peter Martyr upon the Prayer Book of 1549 did not deflect the course of the English Reformation, which remained insular and not continental, they influenced individuals like Hooper and Ridley. During the reign of Mary the process was reversed, and exiles from England took refuge on the continent, where they came

---

[1] See note on p. 10 above.

under the influence of continental religious thought, establishing direct contact both with the movement of the first generation, which Luther had founded, and that of the second generation which Calvin still controlled—the one as typical of the German mind as the other of the mind of France[1]. The attraction of Geneva proved the stronger, and when the exiles returned to England on the death of Mary, the majority of them profoundly impressed with the coherent system of doctrine and discipline which Calvin had established, they sought a closer conformity to the Genevan model, and advocated further changes in doctrine and worship which the Act of Uniformity would not allow.

Their chief criticisms of the Act fall into two groups: (1) the simpler controversy concerning vestments, and (2) the more complicated controversy about the service-book and ceremonies.

The Puritan party in the Church held that vestments were a relic of Popery, to which the common people were apt to attach undue and superstitious importance, and they urged that they should be entirely abandoned in divine service. Even Bishop Jewel called them the 'habits of the stage' and the 'relics of the Amorites,' and urged that they should be 'extirpated to the roots';[2] while Grindal hesitated to accept a bishopric because it would involve the obligation of wearing them.

In connexion with the service-book and ceremonies a number of points were raised. The Puritans objected to cathedral worship[3], partly because it involved the use of musical instruments. They also objected to the responses in the service; to the frequent use there of the Lord's Prayer, as 'vain repetition'; to the reading of the Apocrypha in the lessons; to the sign of the cross in baptism; to the institution of godfathers and godmothers; to the imposition of hands by the bishop at confirmation; to bowing at the name of Jesus; and to the use of the ring in marriage.

(1) Puritan Articles in Convocation, 1563

The objections of the Puritans to what they regarded as abuses in worship received strong support in the Lower House of Convocation, when articles embodying their criticisms were brought in, and after 'a great contest in the House,' were rejected by 59 votes to 58. The proposers were prepared to tolerate the surplice, but on most of the other points at issue they supported the Puritan view; although they were prepared to compromise on the question of kneeling at the sacrament.

I. That all the Sundays in the year and principal feasts of Christ be kept holy days; and all other holy days to be abrogated.

II. That in all parish churches the minister in common prayer turn his face towards the people; and there distinctly read the

---

[1] *C.M.H.* ii, 349.   [2] Neal, i, 159.

[3] 'Where the service of God is grievously abused by piping with organs; singing, ringing, and trowling of psalms from one side of the choir to another; with the squeaking of chanting choristers, disguised...in white surplices...imitating the fashion and manner of Antichrist the Pope, that man of sin and child of perdition, with his other rabble of miscreants and shavelings' (pamphlet quoted in Neal, i, 384). But see Hooker's defence of music in worship, quoted on p. 177 below.

divine service appointed, where all the people assembled may hear and be edified.

III. That in ministering the sacrament of baptism, the ceremony of making the cross in the child's forehead may be omitted, as tending to superstition.

IV. That forasmuch as divers communicants are not able to kneel during the time of the communion, for age, sickness, and sundry other infirmities, and some also superstitiously both kneel and knock[1]; that order of kneeling may be left to the discretion of the ordinary within his jurisdiction.

V. That it be sufficient for the minister, in time of saying divine service and ministering of the sacraments, to use a surplice; and that no minister say service or minister the sacraments but in a comely garment or habit.

VI. That the use of organs be removed.

Strype, *Annals of the Reformation* (edn of 1725), i, 337.

During the first few years of Elizabeth's reign uniformity in public worship was not actively enforced, and great diversity of practice prevailed. An inquiry of 1565 shewed that the service was sometimes said in the chancel and sometimes in the nave, in some places from the lectern and in others from the pulpit; that the surplice was not invariably used; that the communion table was sometimes placed 'altar-wise' at the east end of the church, and sometimes 'table-wise' in the middle of the church or against the wall; and that the communicants stood, sat, or knelt, as they pleased. But the Puritan clergy first came into collision with authority, not over any fundamental question of doctrine or worship, but over what kind of dress the clergy were to wear.

The Injunctions of 1559 had prescribed 'such seemly habits, garments, and such square caps as were most commonly and orderly received in the latter year of the reign of King Edward VI,' and the minimum requirement of the rubrics was the surplice in ministration. 'Many well-meaning men,' says Strype[2], 'chiefly such as had lived in the churches abroad (where they were not used) utterly refused these habits, upon these grounds, that they were popish, and used by the priests in the idolatrous church of Rome, and invented by the Pope, and a note of Antichrist.' At Cambridge, in particular at St John's College, 'the fellows and scholars...chiefly the younger sort...threw off the surplice with one consent...and many in other colleges were ready to follow their example...such a persuasion of the superstition of it had some of their guides...beat into the heads of the younger; for the elder were generally more steady.'[3] The movement spread, and soon all the colleges were affected by it, with one exception—'King's College, in this hubbub among the rest of the colleges about the habits, remained obedient and quiet in the wearing of them.'[4]

---

[1] In the sense of smiting upon the breast.   [2] *Annals*, i, 459.   [3] *Ib.* i, 478.

[4] *Ib.* i, 482. Even in King's there was a faithful remnant. A certain 'sophister' came into the choir and 'placed himself among the thickest of the rest of the company,

Archbishop Parker was anxious to deal with these disorders, but he was hampered by the unwillingness of Grindal, who sympathised with the Puritans, to act in his diocese of London, and by the refusal of the Queen to take a responsibility which she regarded as the business of the bishops. He was therefore obliged to proceed alone. He issued articles on the points in dispute, opened an ecclesiastical commission at Lambeth on March 26, 1566, summoned before it nearly a hundred of the London clergy who refused to conform, admonished them, and threatened them with deprivation unless they consented to wear the gown and square cap, and in their ministration the surplice. Thirty-seven refused to conform, and some of them were eventually deprived; but they continued to conduct services and to preach in spite of their deprivation. These may be regarded as the first English Nonconformists. The Archbishop's articles were twice unsuccessfully submitted to the Queen for her signature, but they never received the royal sanction. They were therefore published under the unobtrusive title of 'Advertisements.'[1]

(2) The Controversy concerning Church Government, 1572

Hitherto the Puritan attack upon the Elizabethan Church Settlement had been confined to doctrine and worship. In 1572, however, a fresh line of controversy was developed when Thomas Cartwright and his followers opened an assault upon Church government and organisation. This at first took the comparatively innocent form of professorial lectures. In 1569 Cartwright had been appointed Lady Margaret's Professor of Divinity in the University of Cambridge, and in lecturing upon the Acts of the Apostles he took occasion to compare the hierarchical constitution of the Church of England with what he conceived to be the organisation of the primitive Church. This led to his deprivation and withdrawal to Geneva, but he returned to England in 1572 to publish the *Second Admonition to Parliament* [p. 167], in support of the *First Admonition* already issued by John Field and Thomas Wilcox, two London clergymen. In 1574 Walter Travers published his *Disciplina Ecclesiastica*, which Cartwright translated under the title *A full and plain Declaration of Ecclesiastical Discipline out of the Word of God, and of the declining of the Church of England from the same*. This work became the text-book of English Puritan discipline, for it attempted to adapt to English life the Presbyterian system which Calvin had set up at Geneva.

These writings broke new ground, and, for a time at least, changed the whole character of English Puritanism. 'Hitherto,' says Strype[2], 'the quarrel was only about wearing the cap and the surplice and such-like apparel, and the

all with their surplices on but he alone without one. And when the Censor of the College had called him and questioned him for this irregularity, he answered modestly, laying the cause upon his conscience, which would not suffer him to let loose the reins to such things; when at length the true cause was known to be that he had pawned his surplice to a cook, with whom he had run in debt for his belly' (p. 483).

[1] These are printed in full in Gee and Hardy, p. 467, and with omissions in Prothero, p. 191.

[2] *Annals*, i, 623.

posture in receiving the sacrament; but now they attempt to move another and a more dangerous matter in assaulting the hierarchy of the Church, and disproving and condemning the ancient, wholesome government used in it by archbishops and bishops, deans and archdeacons, and other ecclesiastical officers.' In thus criticising the system of Church government, the Puritans were attacking the Royal Supremacy—the corner-stone of the Elizabethan Settlement.

Cartwright and his followers anticipated the position of the later Puritans, that the Bible is not only infallible but also literally inspired, affording the sole authoritative rule of conduct in matters public and political as well as private and personal. They also professed to find in the New Testament a system of government clearly laid down for the Church of Christ, which ordered all the details of Christian worship with as much precision as the government and worship of the Jewish Church had been ordered in the Old Testament. This was not the episcopal system of the reign of Elizabeth, but a Presbyterian system like that set up by Calvin at Geneva. They therefore advocated the abolition of bishops, the popular election of clergy to livings, and the government of the Church by synods and presbyteries.

1. THOMAS CARTWRIGHT, 1572

The *Second Admonition* was entirely the work of Cartwright, and was mainly concerned in developing the views which he had already expressed. He had argued that a reformation in Church government was needed; he now proceeds to indicate the lines on which it should be carried out.

The life of the Word is the ministry of the same.... The former treatises therefore have rightly spoken against the bastard, idle, and unpreaching ministry of this Church.... Also there must be orders taken and looked unto for the bestowing of the livings provided in the Universities (now dens of many thievish non-residents), not to the greedy use of many cormorant Masters of Colleges and at their wicked pleasure, as they are, but to the bringing up for the most part of such as will be content to be employed upon the charge of the ministry whenas the Church shall have need of them, and to take from them that have more livings all save one, and that too, except they will be resident, and be able and willing to discharge it...(pp. 12, 13).

...Next, you must repeal your statute or statutes whereby you have authorised that ministry that now is, making your estate partly to consist of Lords spiritual (as you call them), and making one minister higher than another, appointing also an order to ordain ministers, which order is clean differing from the Scriptures; wherefore you must have the order for these things drawn out of the Scriptures, which order is this. When any parish is destitute of a pastor or of a teacher, the same parish may have recourse to the next conference, and to them make it known,

that they may procure chiefly from the one of the Universities, or, if otherwise, a man learned and of good report, whom, after trial of his gifts had in their conference, they may present unto the parish which before had been with them about that matter, but yet so that the same parish have him a certain time amongst them, that they may be acquainted with his gifts and behaviour, and give their consents for his stay amongst them if they can allege no just cause to the contrary; for he may not be sent away again which is so sent to a parish except a just cause of misliking, the cause alleged being justly proved against him either amongst themselves in their own consistory, so that he will appeal no further for his trial, or else in the next conference, or council provincial, or national, unto which from one to another he may appeal if he find himself clear; and if he give over they may proceed as afore for another. And when such an one is found to whom the parish must give consent because there is no just cause to be alleged against him, the next conference by whose means he was procured shall be certified of the parish's liking, whereupon they shall amongst themselves agree upon one of the ministers which shall be sent by them to the same parish, and after a sermon made according to the occasion, and earnest prayer to God, with fasting according to the example of the Scriptures, made by that congregation to God that it would please him to direct them in their choice and to bless that man whom they choose, he shall require to know their consent, which being granted he and the elders shall lay their hands on him, to signify to him that he is lawfully called to that parish to be pastor there or teacher...
(pp. 13–15).

...If to read the Scriptures, the Homilies, and the course of our Book of Common Prayers were enough...then a boy of ten years old may do the minister's office, for the substance of their office is not in the years but in the reading. And indeed boys and senseless asses are our common ministers for the most part, for but common reason may serve this turn and do this feat well enough. It is indeed less busy[1] than popish priests' service because the calendar and the rubrics of the book are fewer and plainer...so that less clerks than popish priests which had but some blind Latin in their belly may serve for our store; and therefore indeed the blindest buzzard of them, if he will keep his conscience to himself...if he will subscribe to our Articles of Christian Religion before his ordinary and blindly read them at his benefices, he shall not only be serving priest, (I use their own

[1] Elaborate.

terms), but he may have one benefice or more and nothing shall nor may be said against him, and, so he provide his quarter sermons or pay his ordinary for that default and such-like, he is as good a pastor as the best.... No, no, this is not that ministry which we have need of, and which God erected in his Church... (pp. 20, 21).

... This is the right way to bring the ministry into credit and estimation—their gifts given them of God and their painfulness and honest life amongst their congregations, and not to make some of them Lords, Graces, Earls, Prelate and Register of the Garter, Barons, Suffragans, some of them rich Deans, Archdeacons, Masters of Colleges, Chancellors, Prebends, rich parsons and vicars, and though some of them be poor enough to get them credit by their rochets, hoods, caps, cloaks, tippets, and gowns, or such-like implements used by the Pharisees, which claimed high rooms and made large borders on their garments and loved to be greeted and to be called Rabbi, which things by our Saviour are forbidden his ministers and an order enjoined that they which look for it should not have it but be least esteemed ...(p. 22).

... The Book [of Common Prayer] is such a piece of work as it is strange we will use it; besides I cannot account it praying as they use it commonly, but only reading or saying of prayers, even as a child that learneth to read, if his lesson be a prayer he readeth a prayer, he doth not pray.... For though they have many guises, now to kneel and now to stand, these be of course, and not of any prick of conscience or piercing of the heart most commonly. One he kneeleth on his knees, and this way he looketh and that way he looketh; another he kneeleth himself asleep; another kneeleth with such devotion that he is so far in talk that he forgetteth to arise till his knee ache or his talk endeth or service is done. And why is all this but that there is no such praying as should touch the heart?... Is this praying? God grant us to feel our lacks better than this, and to take a better order than this for prayer; it is and will be all naught else...(pp. 39, 40).

... I have already made mention of a consistory which were to be had in every congregation. That consisteth first of the ministers of the same congregation, as the guides and mouth of the rest, to direct them by the Scriptures, and to speak at their appointment that which shall be consented upon amongst them all, because of their gifts and place amongst them, which maketh them more fit for those purposes. The assistants are they whom the parish shall consent upon and choose for their good judgment in religion and godliness,...using the advice of their ministers therein chiefly...and also using earnest prayers with fasting, as in the choice of the minister; and having made their choice, thereafter they shall publish their agreement in their parish, and, after a sermon by their minister, at their appointment and upon their consent the minister may lay his hands upon every of them to testify to them their admission.... This consistory... shall examine all disordered ceremonies used in place of prayer and abolish those which they find evil or unprofitable, and bring in such orders as their congregation shall have need of, so they be few and apparent[1], necessary both for edifying and profit and decent order, proving it plainly to the whole church that it is so.... These shall receive the informations of the deacons for the relief of the poor and their accounts for that which they shall lay out that way and of their diligence in visiting them, that the congregations may by the consistory be certified of all things concerning the poor, both that there may be made provision accordingly, and that the provision made may be well husbanded, and the poor may by the deacons be visited, comforted, and relieved according to their lack. Lastly, one or more of these assistants, with one of the ministers and a deacon or deacons, shall be those that shall at their church's charges meet at the provincial council, or national, if there be any business that concerneth their church.... A deacon is an officer of the church for the behoof of the poor, chosen to this office by the congregation by such means as afore is prescribed in the choice of elders, by advice and consent, being a noted man for godly judgment and faithfulness.... (pp. 44–9).

Cartwright, *Second Admonition to Parliament*, 1572.

2. RICHARD HOOKER, 1594–7

The Elizabethan Church Settlement was not without able defenders. The task of answering the Puritans fell first upon Whitgift, but it was taken up later with far greater dignity and power by Richard Hooker, at first in sermons, which he preached as Master of the Temple in controversy with Travers, who was afternoon lecturer there, and afterwards in the book on which his fame securely rests. Hooker had been educated and sent to Oxford at Jewel's expense; thus the connexion is curiously close between the champion of Anglicanism against the Puritans and the champion of Anglicanism against Rome. But unlike Jewel, who had to administer the diocese of Salisbury, Hooker was a student and not a man of affairs. Walton describes him as 'an obscure, harmless man,...of a mean stature and stooping,'[2] and Fuller refers to his 'dove-like simplicity.'[3] Yet in spite of these drawbacks the author of the *Ecclesiastical Polity* is destined to immortal fame. The Preface and

---

[1] Clear, obvious.   [2] Walton, p. 272.
[3] Fuller, iii, 155.

the first Four Books probably appeared in 1594; the Fifth Book, which is longer than the first four put together, in 1597. The remaining three books did not appear until long after his death, when they were unsatisfactorily edited from his rough notes, and their genuineness has been disputed.

The purpose of the *Ecclesiastical Polity* was to provide the Elizabethan Church Settlement with 'a philosophical and logical basis,'[1] by a systematic investigation of the general principles of Church government; and the enterprise is undertaken in the largest possible spirit. Cartwright and his followers maintained that all ecclesiastical institutions derived their authority from Scripture alone, and therefore that any institution not mentioned in Scripture was erroneous, and ought to be abolished. Hooker argued that human conduct was not to be guided by Scripture alone, but by 'all the sources of light and truth with which man finds himself encompassed.'[2] The Church had not been stereotyped for all time in the pages of the New Testament; it was a living body, able to adapt its institutions from time to time to the varying needs of different ages. His doctrine, if stated in modern terms, is that of the organism adapting itself to its environment; and it was developed by a style as massive and rich as that of Bacon himself.

The Preface

... Under the happy reign of her Majesty which now is, the greatest matter awhile contended for was the wearing of the cap and surplice, till there came Admonitions directed unto the High Court of Parliament[3] by men who, concealing their names, thought it glory enough to discover their minds and affections, which now were universally bent even against all the orders and laws wherein this Church is found unconformable to the platform of Geneva. Concerning the defender of which Admonitions all that I mean to say is but this: *There will come a time when three words uttered with charity and meekness shall receive a far more blessed reward than three thousand volumes written with disdainful sharpness of wit.* But the manner of men's writing must not alienate our hearts from the truth, if it appear they have the truth.... (§ 2).

... Weigh what doth move the common sort so much to favour this innovation, and it shall soon appear unto you that the force of particular reasons which for your several opinions are alleged is a thing whereof the multitude never did nor could so consider as to be therewith wholly carried; but certain general inducements are used to make saleable your cause in gross, and when once men have cast a fancy towards it any slight declaration of specialties will serve to lead forward men's inclinable and prepared minds. The method of winning the people's affection unto a general liking of the cause (for so ye term it) hath been this. First, in the hearing of the multitude the faults especially of higher callings are ripped up with marvellous exceeding severity

---

[1] *D.N.B.* xxvii, 293.   [2] *Ib.*
[3] The First and Second Admonitions referred to on p. 166 above.

and sharpness of reproof; which being oftentimes done, begetteth a great good opinion of integrity, zeal, and holiness to such constant reprovers of sin, as by likelihood would never be so much offended at that which is evil unless themselves were singularly good. The next thing hereunto is to impute all faults and corruptions wherewith the world aboundeth unto the kind of ecclesiastical government established. Wherein, as before by reproving faults they purchased unto themselves with the multitude a name to be virtuous, so by finding out this kind of cause they obtain to be judged wise above others.... Having gotten thus much sway in the hearts of men, a third step is to propose their own form of church government as the only sovereign remedy of all evils, and to adorn it with all the glorious titles that may be. And the nature, as of men that have sick bodies so likewise of the people in the crazedness of their minds, possessed with dislike and discontentment at things present, is to imagine that anything (the virtue whereof they hear commended) would help them, but that most which they least have tried. The fourth degree of inducements is by fashioning the very notions and conceits of men's minds in such sort that when they read the Scripture they may think that everything soundeth towards the advancement of that discipline and to the utter disgrace of the contrary.... (§ 3).

The First Book: concerning Laws and their several kinds in
general

He that goeth about to persuade a multitude that they are not so well governed as they ought to be, shall never want attentive and favourable hearers; because they know the manifold defects whereunto every kind of regiment is subject, but the secret lets and difficulties, which in public proceedings are innumerable and inevitable, they have not ordinarily the judgment to consider. And because such as openly reprove supposed disorders of state are taken for principal friends to the common benefit of all, and for men that carry singular freedom of mind, under this fair and plausible colour whatsoever they utter passeth for good and current. That which wanteth in the weight of their speech is supplied by the aptness of men's minds to accept and believe it. Whereas on the other side, if we maintain things that are established, we have not only to strive with a number of heavy prejudices deeply rooted in the hearts of men, who think that herein we serve the time and speak in favour of the present state because thereby we either hold or seek preferment, but also to bear such exceptions and minds so averted beforehand usually take against that which they are loath should be poured into them...(p. 2).

The Second Book: concerning their first position who urge reformation in the Church of England, namely, That Scripture is the only rule of all things which in this life may be done by men.

...There is no necessity that if I confess I ought not to do that which the Scripture forbiddeth me, I should thereby acknowledge myself bound to do nothing which the Scripture commandeth me not. For many inducements besides Scripture may lead me to that which, if Scripture be against, they all give place and are of no value, yet otherwise are strong and effectual to persuade...(p. 65).

The Third Book: concerning their second assertion, that in Scripture there must be of necessity contained a form of Church polity the laws whereof may in no wise be altered.

...Now as it can be to Nature no injury that of her we say the same which diligent beholders of her works have observed, namely, that she provideth for all living creatures nourishment which may suffice, that she bringeth forth no kind of creature whereto she is wanting in that which is needful; although we do not so far magnify her exceeding bounty as to affirm that she bringeth into the world the sons of men adorned with gorgeous attire or maketh costly buildings to spring up out of the earth for them. So I trust that to mention what the Scripture of God leaveth unto the Church's discretion in some things is not in anything to impair the honour which the Church of God yieldeth to the sacred Scriptures' perfection. Wherein seeing that no more is by us maintained than only that Scripture must needs teach the Church whatsoever is in such sort necessary as hath been set down, and that it is no more disgrace for Scripture to have left a number of other things free to be ordered at the discretion of the Church than for Nature to have left it unto the wit of man to devise his own attire and not to look for it as the beasts of the field have theirs...(p. 92).

...They which first gave out that *Nothing ought to be established in the Church which is not commanded by the Word of God,* thought this principle plainly warranted by the manifest words of the Law....Wherefore having an eye to a number of rites and orders in the Church of England, as marrying with a ring, crossing in the one Sacrament, kneeling at the other, observing of festival days more than only that which is called the Lord's Day, enjoining abstinence at certain times from some kinds of meat, churching of women after childbirth, degrees taken by divines in Universities, sundry Church offices, dignities, and callings, for which they found no commandment in the Holy Scripture, they thought by the one only stroke of that axiom to have cut them off. But that which they took for an oracle, being sifted was repelled... (p. 93).

...In the Church of the Jews is it not granted that the appointment of the hour for daily sacrifices, the building of synagogues throughout the land to hear the Word of God and to pray in when they came not up to Jerusalem, the erecting of pulpits and chairs to teach in, the order of burial, the rites of marriage, with such like, being matters appertaining to the Church, yet are not anywhere prescribed in the Law but were by the Church's discretion instituted? What then shall we think? Did they hereby add to the Law, and so displease God by that which they did? None so hardly persuaded of them....Sundry things may be lawfully done in the Church, so as they be not done against the Scripture, although no Scripture do command them, but the Church, only following the light of reason, judge them to be in discretion meet...so that free and lawful it is to devise any ceremony, to receive any order, and to authorise any kind of regiment, no special commandment being thereby violated, and the same being thought such by them to whom the judgment thereof appertaineth, as that it is not scandalous but decent, tending unto edification, and setting forth the glory of God...(p. 95).

The Fourth Book: concerning their third assertion, that our form of Church polity is corrupted with Popish orders, rites, and ceremonies, banished out of certain reformed Churches, whose example therein we ought to have followed.

...Concerning rites and ceremonies, there may be fault either in the kind or in the number and multitude of them. The first thing blamed about the kind of ours is that in many things we have departed from the ancient simplicity of Christ and his Apostles, we have embraced more outward stateliness, we have those orders in the exercise of religion which they who best pleased God and served him most devoutly never had. For it is out of doubt that the first state of things was best, that in the prime of the Christian religion faith was soundest, the Scriptures of God were then best understood by all men, all parts of godliness did then most abound; and therefore it must needs follow that customs, laws, and ordinances devised since are not so good for the Church of Christ, but the best way is to cut off later inventions and to reduce things unto the ancient state wherein at the first they were. Which rule or canon we hold to be either uncertain or at least wise insufficient, if not both. For in case it be certain, hard it cannot be for them to shew us where we shall find it so exactly set down that we may say without controversy, *These were the orders of the Apostles' times, these wholly and only, neither fewer nor more than these....* So that in tying the Church to the orders of the Apostles' times they tie it to a marvellous uncertain rule, unless they require the observation of no orders but only those which are known to be apostolical by the Apostles' own writings. But then is not this their rule of such sufficiency that we should use it as a touchstone to try the orders of the Church by for ever. Our end ought always to be the same; our ways and means thereunto not so. The glory of God and the good of his Church was the thing which the Apostles aimed at and therefore ought to be the mark whereat we also level. But seeing those rites and orders may be at one time more which at another time are less available unto that purpose, what reason is there in these things to urge the state of our only age as a pattern for all to follow? It is not, I am right sure, their meaning that we should now assemble our people to serve God in close and secret meetings; or that common brooks or rivers should be used for places of baptism; or that the Eucharist should be ministered after meat; or that the custom of church-feasting should be renewed; or that all kinds of standing provision for the ministry should be utterly taken away and their estate made again dependent upon the voluntary devotion of men. In these things they easily perceive how unfit that were for the present, which was for the first age convenient enough... (pp. 130, 131).

> *The Fifth Book: Of their fourth assertion, that touching the several public duties of Christian Religion there is amongst us much superstition retained in them; and concerning persons which for performance of those duties are endued with the power of Ecclesiastical Order, our laws and proceedings according thereunto are many ways herein also corrupted.*

...But howsoever superstition do grow, that wherein unsounder times have done amiss the better ages ensuing must rectify as they may. I now come therefore to those accusations brought against us by pretenders of reformation....For so it is judged, our prayers, our sacraments, our fasts, our times and places of public worship,...our marriages, our burials, our functions, elections, and ordinations ecclesiastical, almost whatsoever we do in the exercise of our religion according to laws for that purpose established, all things are some way or other thought faulty, all things stained with superstition...(p. 192).

...That which inwardly each man should be, the Church outwardly ought to testify. And therefore the duties of our religion which are seen must be such as that affection which is unseen ought to be. Signs must resemble the things they signify. If religion bear the greatest sway in our hearts, our outward religious duties must shew it as far as the Church hath outward ability. Duties of religion performed by whole societies of men ought to have in them according to our power a sensible excellency correspondent to the Majesty of him whom we worship. Yea, then are the public duties of religion best ordered when the militant Church doth resemble by sensible means, as it may in such cases, that hidden dignity and glory wherewith the Church triumphant in heaven is beautified....Let our first demand be therefore that in the external form of religion such things as are apparently, or can be sufficiently, proved effectual and generally fit to set forward godliness, either as betokening the greatness of God, or as beseeming the dignity of religion, or as concurring with celestial impressions in the minds of men, may be reverently thought of, some few, rare, casual, and tolerable or otherwise curable inconveniences notwithstanding.

Neither may we in this case lightly esteem what hath been allowed as fit in the judgment of antiquity and by the long continued practice of the whole Church, from which unnecessarily to swerve, experience hath never as yet found it safe....In which consideration there is cause why we should be slow and unwilling to change, without very urgent necessity, the ancient ordinances, rites, and long approved customs of our venerable predecessors. The love of things ancient doth argue stayedness; but levity and want of experience maketh apt unto innovations....All things cannot be of ancient continuance which are expedient and needful for the ordering of spiritual affairs; but the Church, being a body which dieth not, hath always power, as occasion requireth, no less to ordain that which never was than to ratify what hath been before...(pp. 194–6).

In the rest of the Fifth Book, which is longer than the first four Books taken together, Hooker takes those ceremonies and orders of the Church of England to which the Puritans took exception, and defends them one by one. The extracts that follow will serve to illustrate his method.

...No doubt from God it hath proceeded, and by us it must

be acknowledged a work of his singular care and providence, that the Church hath evermore held a prescript form of Common Prayer, although not in all things everywhere the same yet for the most part retaining still the same analogy. So that if the liturgies of all ancient Churches throughout the world be compared amongst themselves, it may be easily perceived they had all one original mould, and that the public prayers of the people of God in Churches thoroughly settled did never use to be voluntary dictates, proceeding from any man's extemporal wit. To him which considereth the grievous and scandalous inconveniences whereunto they make themselves daily subject with whom any blind and secret corner is judged a fit house of Common Prayer; the manifold confusions which they fall into where every man's private spirit and gift (as they term it) is the only Bishop that ordaineth him to this ministry; the irksome deformities whereby, through endless and senseless effusions of indigested prayers, they oftentimes disgrace in most unsufferable manner the worthiest part of Christian duty towards God who herein are subject to no certain order but pray both what and how they list; to him, I say, which weigheth duly all these things, the reasons cannot be obscure why God doth in public prayer so much respect the solemnity of places where, the authority and calling of persons by whom, and the precise appointment even with what words and sentences his Name should be called on amongst his people.

No man hath hitherto been so impious as plainly and directly to condemn prayer. The best stratagem that Satan hath, who knoweth his kingdom to be no one way more shaken than by the public devout prayers of God's Church, is by traducing the form and manner of them, to bring them unto contempt and so to shake the force of all men's devotion towards them. From this and from no other forge hath proceeded a strange conceit, that to serve God with any set form of Common Prayer is superstitious. As though God himself did not frame to his priests the very speech wherewith they were charged to bless the people; or as if our Lord, even of purpose to prevent this fancy of extemporal and voluntary prayers, had not left us of his own framing one which might both remain as a part of the Church Liturgy and serve as a pattern whereby to frame all other prayers with efficacy yet without superfluity of words...(pp. 239–40).

...Touching musical harmony, whether by instrument or by voice, it being but of high and low in sounds a due proportionable disposition, such notwithstanding is the force thereof, and so pleasing effects it hath in that very part of man which is most divine, that some have been thereby induced to think that the soul itself by nature is or hath in it harmony. A thing which delighteth all ages and beseemeth all states; a thing as seasonable in grief as in joy; as decent being added unto actions of greatest weight and solemnity as being used when men most sequester themselves from action. The reason hereof is an admirable facility which music hath to express and represent to the mind, more inwardly than any other sensible mean, the very standing, rising, and falling, the very steps and inflections every way, the turns and varieties of all passions whereunto the mind is subject; yea, so to imitate them that, whether it resemble unto us the same state wherein our minds already are or the clean contrary, we are not more contentedly by the one confirmed than changed and led away by the other. In harmony the very image and character of virtue and vice is perceived, the mind delighted with their resemblances, and brought, by having them often iterated, into a love of the things themselves. For which cause there is nothing more contagious and pestilent than some kinds of harmony; than some nothing more strong and potent unto good. And that there is such a difference of one kind from another we need no proof but our own experience, inasmuch as we are at the hearing of some more inclined unto sorrow and heaviness; of some more mollified and softened in mind; one kind apter to stay and settle us, another to move and stir our affections; there is that draweth to a marvellous grave and sober mediocrity, there is also that carrieth as it were into extasies, filling the mind with an heavenly joy and for the time in a manner severing it from the body. So that although we lay altogether aside the consideration of ditty or matter, the very harmony of sounds being framed in due sort and carried from the ear to the spiritual faculties of our souls, is by a native puissance and efficacy greatly available to bring to a perfect temper whatsoever is there troubled, apt as well to quicken the spirits as to allay that which is too eager, sovereign against melancholy and despair, forcible to draw forth tears of devotion if the mind be such as can yield them, able both to move and to moderate all affections.... They which, under pretence of the law ceremonial abrogated, require the abrogation of instrumental music, approving nevertheless the use of vocal melody to remain, must shew some reason wherefore the one should be thought a legal ceremony and not the other. In church music curiosity and ostentation of art, wanton or light or unsuitable harmony, such as only pleaseth the ear and doth not naturally serve to the very kind and degree of those impressions which the matter that goeth with it leaveth or is apt to leave in men's minds, doth rather blemish and disgrace that we do than add either beauty or furtherance unto it. On the other side, these faults prevented, the force and efficacy of the thing itself, when it drowneth not utterly but fitly suiteth with matter altogether sounding to the praise of God, is in truth most admirable, and doth much edify, if not the understanding because it teacheth not, yet surely the affection because therein it worketh much. They must have hearts very dry and tough from whom the melody of psalms doth not sometime draw that wherein a mind religiously affected delighteth...(pp. 258–9).

Hooker, *Ecclesiastical Polity* (edition of 1620).

(3) The Controversy concerning Prophesyings, 1574–7

The emphasis laid on the ordinance of preaching by the Puritan party within the Church had led to the development of a means of edification by the systematic study and discussion of the Scriptures which passed under the name of 'Prophesyings.'[1] At Northampton in 1571 these exercises were established 'by the consent of the Bishop of Peterborough,...the Mayor of the town,...and other the Queen's Majesty's Justices of the Peace within the county and town,'[2] and they included exposition of a text in the presence of the laity, followed by a private conference of ministers 'as well touching doctrine, as good life, manners, and other orders meet for them.'[3] A similar system was set up at Bury St Edmunds in 1572, 'as was used in some other places of this and other dioceses, to the profit and edification in the knowledge of the Scripture both of the clergy and laity.'[4] The regulations for the diocese of Lincoln, set forth with the express sanction of the Bishop in 1574, exhibit in detail the character and aims of these exercises.

1. Regulations for the Diocese of Lincoln, 1574

The reasoned approval of the Bishop is given at the end of the document.

...Exercises among the ministers and curates of churches ...were now used in most dioceses....In order to these exercises, the clergy were sorted into divers competent companies or societies by subscription of their names, and particular churches and days appointed, and the persons named to exercise and perform in their order, and the rest, after the exercise was over, were to judge of what had been spoken, and a moderator to be present to determine and conclude all....The moderator was nominated by the bishop of the diocese, as likewise the order of the whole allowed by him.

This was practised to the great benefit and improvement of

[1] So called from 1 Corinthians, xiv: 'Follow after charity, and desire spiritual gifts, but rather that ye may prophesy....He that prophesieth speaketh...to edification, and exhortation, and comfort....Even so ye, forasmuch as ye are zealous of spiritual gifts, seek that ye may excel to the edifying of the church.'

[2] Strype, *Annals* (edition of 1725), ii, 90.   [3] *Ib.* ii, 91.   [4] *Ib.* ii, 219.

the clergy, many of whom in those times were ignorant both in Scripture and Divinity. In October this year the Bishop of Lincoln settled orders and moderators for these prophesyings in that part of Hertfordshire that lay in his diocese...and the like, no question, in the other parts of his see.

[Regulations offered to the Bishop]

First, It is thought meet your exercises shall be kept every other week upon the Thursdays, from nine of the clock in the forenoon until eleven, and not past. So that the first speaker exceed not three quarters of an hour, nor the two last half an hour between them both. The remnant of the time to be left for the moderator....

A table of the names of the speakers being made, it may easily be known who should speak, whereof, at what time, and in what place, what course every man is bound to keep in his own person, except upon urgent occasion he be hindered. And then may he substitute a sufficient deputy, yet such an one as belongeth to our exercise, whose name shall be signified to the moderator before. So that the place be never destitute, and the brethren may know whom to look for.

All the speakers ought carefully to keep them to the text; abstaining from heaping up of many testimonies, allegations of profane histories, exhortations, applications, commonplaces, and divisions, not aptly grounded upon the text; not falling into controversies of our present time or state, neither glancing closely or openly at any persons, public or private, much less confuting one another....

After the first speaker hath ended, the second is to speak of the same text and in the same order, having a careful respect to add and not to repeat, to beware as much as in him lieth that he utter no contradiction to the former speaker. If it fall out the former shall give out any false doctrine, the public confutation and qualifying of the words is to be left to the moderator, and the matter itself further to be handled privately by the brethren. The same order in the same text hath the third speaker to keep. And both of them, as the rest, are bound not to exceed the time.

Prayers ought to be made by the first speaker for the whole state of the Church at the beginning of the exercise shortly; and at the end by the moderator, namely, for the Queen's Majesty, by whose good means God hath granted us liberty to proceed cheerfully in such exercises. Especially we have to pray for the grace of God's Holy Spirit, for truth, unity, reverence, discretion, and diligence in our ministry. The form of prayer is further to be prescribed.

Our exercise shall be had only and wholly in the English tongue, avoiding allegation of Scripture, Fathers, profane authors, etc. in the Latin, for spending of time; unless the force of some Latin or Greek word for further instruction be shewed as a thing most necessarily to be noted where ability will serve.

The exercise ended, the brethren coming together (the assembly being dismissed), and the first speaker for that time put apart, and all, so many as have not given their names to our exercise, secluded, the moderator shall require of the brethren by order their judgments concerning the first speaker, for whose cause chiefly the day's meeting and assembly hath been. First, how sound his doctrine; how he kept his text or wherein he swerved; how truly Scripture expounded and testimonies alleged; how he hath observed our order of prophesy; how plain or obscure his words; how modest his speech or gesture; how seemly, reverend, and sober his whole action in the exercise hath been; and wherein he failed. Withal is to be considered how some of his words doubtfully spoken may be charitably expounded and construed in the better part. This done, the first speaker must be contented to be admonished by the moderator and the rest of the brethren of such things as shall seem to the company worthy admonition. The same enquiry is to be made of the life of the speakers in their course; that we may all be reformed both in doctrine and in life.

In this consultation and after this admonition to the speakers, shall be moved by any of the brethren any doubt that justly might rise of the text, and not yet answered by any of the speakers. Wherein he is to be resolved by the speakers and moderator; but if he seem not yet so fully satisfied, and the question of importance, by consent of the brethren it shall be deferred until the next exercise, for the first speaker for that time to handle in the entrance of that day's prophesy. Further, none of the speakers shall take upon him publicly to make answer, unless he be able presently[1], pithily, and plainly to answer the same.

No man shall willingly shun the exercise or fail in his course; neither shew himself disordered, or refuse to stomach such brotherly admonition as is to be used; neither speak publicly or privately against any good order taken by the brethren and ratified by our ordinary. And if any shall so do and be found therein incorrigible, we have leave to put out his name in the table till he be reformed. And in the meanwhile we are to signify his fault unto the Bishop.

[1] Immediately.

The appointing of the ministers to our exercises belongeth unto our ordinary. Neither are we to place any to the same but such as shall be admitted by him, and those whosoever shall first yield to the observation of these orders and testify the same by their subscription.

The Bishop's allowance

These orders of exercise offered to me by the learned of the clergy of Hertfordshire I think good and godly, and greatly making to the furtherance of true doctrine and the increase of godly knowledge in them that are not as yet able to preach; specially if the same rules be soberly, with wisdom and discretion, observed. Therefore I earnestly exhort and require all such as will not shew themselves to be backward in religion and hinderers of the truth, diligently to observe the same and resort unto the exercise. Or if they will not, presently upon the warning of the moderators to appear before me, to yield an account why they will not submit themselves to so godly and profitable an exercise.

Nevertheless I require that you admit not any to be president or moderator in that exercise but such as I have allowed by this present subscription, before that I, upon particular trial, shall accept and allow the same. Nor shall you permit any stranger to speak among you but such as you know will stay himself within the compass of these orders, and not break them to the defaming of the present state of the Church of England. Or if any shall so do, be he stranger or other, that presently one of the moderators stay him, that he proceed not therein. This 26th of October, *Anno* 1574.   THOMAS LINCOLN[1].

Strype, *Annals* (edn of 1725), ii, 318.

2. ARCHBISHOP GRINDAL'S LETTER TO THE QUEEN, 1576

'These prophesyings,' says Strype[2], 'were in danger of degenerating into controversies and contentious disputings. And the Puritans took their advantage of it by broaching their doctrines. Which was the cause that...the Queen absolutely required the bishops to put them down.' The trouble began as early as 1574, before the death of Parker, and when Grindal succeeded him as Archbishop of Canterbury in 1575 they soon drew to a head. The Queen, to whom all theological speculation was distasteful, regarded them as dangerous, and desired their suppression, but the primate, whose sympathies lay entirely with the Puritans, sought to regulate them by bringing them directly under the control of the bishops, excluding laity, and declining to allow deprived ministers to take part in them. His letter of protest to the Queen, here printed, is dated December 20, 1576.

[1] Thomas Cooper, appointed Bishop of Lincoln in 1570 and translated to Winchester in 1584, was himself a learned preacher. He afterwards suppressed prophesyings in his diocese when they were forbidden by the Queen.

[2] *Annals*, ii, 219.

...Now for the second point, which is concerning the learned exercise and conference amongst the ministers of the Church. I have consulted with divers of my brethren the Bishops by letters, who think the same as I do, viz.—a thing profitable to the Church and therefore expedient to be continued. And I trust your Majesty will think the like when your Highness shall be informed of the manner and order thereof; what authority it hath of the Scriptures; what commodity it bringeth with it; and what incommodities will follow if it be clear taken away.

The authors of this exercise are the Bishops of the dioceses where the same is used, who, both by the law of God and by the canons and constitutions of the Church now in force, have authority to appoint exercises to their inferior ministers for increase of learning and knowledge in the Scriptures as to them seemeth most expedient....(pp. 79–80).

...These orders following are also observed in the said exercise: First, two or three of the gravest and best learned pastors are appointed of the Bishop to moderate in every assembly. No man may speak unless he be first allowed by the Bishop, with this proviso, that no layman be suffered to speak at any time. No controversy of this present time and state shall be moved or dealt withal. If any attempt the contrary, he is put to silence by the moderator. None is suffered to glance openly or covertly at persons public or private, neither yet anyone to confute another. If any man utter a wrong sense of the Scripture, he is privately admonished thereof, and better instructed by the moderators and other his fellow-ministers. If any man use immodest speech, or irreverent gesture or behaviour, or otherwise be suspected in life, he is likewise admonished as before. If any wilfully do break these orders, he is presented to the Bishop to be by him corrected....(p. 80).

...Howsoever report hath been made to your Majesty concerning these exercises, yet I and others of your Bishops whose names are noted in the margin hereof[1], as they have testified unto me by their letters, having found by experience that these profits and commodities following have ensued of them: 1. The ministers of the Church are more skilful and ready in the Scriptures, and apter to teach their flocks. 2. It withdraweth them from idleness, wandering, gaming, etc. 3. Some afore suspected in doctrine are brought hereby to open confession of the truth. 4. Ignorant ministers are driven to study, if not for conscience yet for shame

---

[1] Canterbury, London, Winchester, Bath, Lichfield, Gloucester, Lincoln, Chichester, Exeter, and St David's.

and fear of discipline. 5. The opinion of laymen touching the idleness of the clergy is hereby removed. 6. Nothing by experience beateth down Popery more than that ministers (as some of my brethren do certify) grow to such a good knowledge by means of these exercises, that where afore were not three able preachers, now are thirty meet to preach at St Paul's Cross, and forty or fifty besides able to instruct their own cures; so as it is found by experience the best means to increase knowledge in the simple and to continue it in the learned. Only backward men in religion and contemners of learning in the countries abroad do fret against it; which in truth doth the more commend it. The dissolution of it would breed triumph to the adversaries, but great sorrow and grief unto the favours of religion.... And although some few have abused this good and necessary exercise, there is no reason that the malice of a few should prejudice all....(p. 81).

Strype, *Life of Grindal* (edn of 1710), Bk. ii, Appendix ix.

3. The Queen's Letter suppressing Prophesyings, 1577

The usual method by which the Queen communicated with her bishops was through the Archbishop; but as Grindal was obdurate on the question of prophesyings, she ordered their suppression by a general letter of May 7, 1577, sent to each bishop direct. The Archbishop was suspended from his ecclesiastical functions, and continued in disgrace for five years; although in 1582, when his spirit was 'enough purged of his proud folly,' the Queen forgave him just before his death.

...We hear to our great grief that in sundry parts of our realm there are no small number of persons, presuming to be teachers and preachers of the Church though neither lawfully thereunto called nor yet fit for the same, which, contrary to our laws established for the public divine service of Almighty God and the administration of his holy sacraments within this Church of England, do daily devise, imagine, propound, and put in execution sundry new rites and forms in the Church, as well by their preaching, reading, and ministering the sacraments, as by procuring unlawful assemblies of a great number of our people out of their ordinary parishes and from places far distant, and that also some of good calling (though therein not well advised) to be hearers of their disputations and new devised opinions upon points of divinity far and unmeet of unlearned people, which manner of invasions they in some places call prophesying and in some other places exercises; by which manner of assemblies great numbers of our people, specially the vulgar sort, meet to be otherwise occupied with honest labour for their living, are brought to idleness and seduced and in a manner schismatically divided amongst themselves into variety of dangerous opinions, not only in towns and parishes but even in some families, and manifestly thereby encouraged to the violation of our laws, and to the breach of common order, and finally to the offence of all our quiet subjects that desire to serve God according to the uniform orders established in the Church, whereof the sequel cannot be but over dangerous to be suffered.... We therefore... charge and command you... to take order through your diocese... that no manner of public and divine service, nor other form of the administration of the holy sacraments, nor any other rites or ceremonies, be in any sort used in the Church but directly according to the orders established by our laws. Neither that any manner of person be suffered within your diocese to preach, teach, read, or any wise exercise any function in the Church but such as shall be lawfully approved and licensed as persons able for their knowledge and conformable to the ministry in the rites and ceremonies of the Church of England; and where there shall not be sufficient able persons for learning in any cures to preach or instruct their cures as were requisite, there you shall limit the curates to read the public Homilies, according to the injunctions heretofore by us given for like causes. And furthermore considering for the great abuses that have been in sundry places of our realm by reason of the foresaid assemblies called exercises... we will and straitly charge you that you also charge the same forthwith to cease and not to be used; but if any shall attempt, or continue, or renew the same, we will you not only to commit them unto prison as maintainers of disorders, but also to advertise us or our Council of the names and qualities of them and of their maintainers and abettors, that thereupon for better example their punishment may be more sharp for their reformation. And in these things we charge you to be so careful and vigilant, as by your negligence, if we shall hear of any person attempting to offend in the premises without your correction or information to us, we be not forced to make some example or reformation of you, according to your deserts....

Cardwell, *Documentary Annals*, i, 373.

In 1585 prophesyings were revived, under careful restrictions, by order of Convocation, in the hope of meeting complaints of an unlearned and unpreaching ministry. The regulations for the Diocese of Chester, dated September 1, 1585, are printed by Strype[1].

[1] See *Annals*, ii, 324, and Appendix 38 (p. 73). Extracts are given in Prothero, p. 206.

(4) The Foundation of Independency, 1580

The deprived ministers and the followers of Cartwright had no desire to abandon the Church of England; they sought rather to reform and revolutionise it. It is true that after deprivation they worshipped in conventicles, and on June 19, 1567, a meeting at Plumbers' Hall had been dispersed and fourteen persons imprisoned; this being the first conventicle that was broken up by force. But conventicle worship was an accident of circumstances and not an essential part of their teaching. Thus, although nonconformists, they were not sectaries. But during Grindal's archbishopric there appeared a new kind of rebellion against the Elizabethan Church Settlement, which, although at present unimportant, was destined to have large consequences in the next century. The essential principle of Independency began to emerge, rejecting the authority of bishop and synod alike, and claiming that every 'congregation of faithful men' is autonomous, able to regulate its own doctrine and worship. Sectarianism in its earlier form was an importation, for in 1568 the Family of Love appeared in London, practising 'love-feasts' and refusing to communicate in the parish churches. In 1575 there are references to Anabaptists, and two Flemings were burned at Smithfield. English Independency, however, begins with Robert Browne, an eccentric Puritan from Cambridge, who about 1580 founded a small Independent congregation at Norwich. In April 1581 this came under the censure of the Bishop, and in the autumn of that year its members emigrated in a body to Middelburg. Another notable name among the Independents is that of Henry Barrow; and the extracts from one of his controversial writings given below will serve to indicate his position. It should be noticed that he attacks Calvin and the Genevan Discipline as well as the episcopal system, and claims for the Church the right to excommunicate kings as well as any other brother in Christ. The early Independents were called Brownists or Barrowists. They were relentlessly put down by the government and their conventicles were broken up; and between 1583 and 1593 five Brownists were put to death, among them men of high character. If authority did not tolerate the conventicles of the deprived ministers, still less would it allow preaching by men who were unordained.

HENRY BARROW, 1590

Barrow's *Brief Discovery of the False Church* was not published until 1590; but an earlier statement of his views appears in his Third Examination before Archbishop Whitgift, Lord Burghley, and others, on July 18, 1588, printed from the Harleian MSS. by E. Arber in *The English Scholar's Library*, No. 8, pp. 40–48. In this he argues that tithes are unlawful; that the presbyter is not a priest, but an elder; and that the archbishop 'is a monster, a miserable compound, I know not what to call him, he is neither ecclesiastical nor civil, even the second beast that is spoken of in the Revelation' who 'arose for anger and gnashed his teeth.'

...The people, upon a superstitious reverence and preposterous estimation unto their teachers and elders, resigned up all things, even their duty, interest, liberty, prerogative, into their hands, suffering them to alter and dispose of all things after their own lusts, without inquiry or controlment; whereupon the true pattern of Christ's Testament, so highly and with so great charge incommended by the Apostles unto the fidelity of the whole Church, was soon neglected and cast aside, especially by these evil workmen these governors, who some of them affecting the preeminence, sought to draw an absolute power into their own hands, perverting those offices of more labour and care into swelling titles of fleshly pomp and worldly dignity.... Then were these called bishops...and had under them inferior...bishops, as also deacons, subdeacons. Thus the whole Church growing remiss and negligent, both people and officers, that heavenly pattern left by the Apostles was soon violate, and upon new pretences more and more innovate.... The pride of some could not herewith be satisfied until they had gotten them a new dignity, namely to be archbishops over all the bishops in a province or country. Here were also new deacons, archdeacons erected; yet was not the ambitious thirst of some thus staunched, but they aspired yet to a more high degree and preeminence, so that there must now be picked out four principal cities which must carry four patriarchs. These had yet higher power than the archbishops, and were erected to see to the government and discipline (as they call it) of all churches, in respect, or rather in despite of those four beasts, which had so many eyes and wings, and stood day and night about the throne of God, but they were rather those four angels, which stood upon the four corners of the earth, holding the four winds of the earth, that the winds should not blow upon the earth, neither on the sea, nor on any tree.

But Satan having yet a further reach, ceased not here, but even amongst those four he still contended to set up one chief, which variably fell out, sometimes to one sometimes to another, until at length the lot rested upon the See of Rome, where the Papacy being upholden by and mixed with the Empire, and in the end swallowing it up, became the very throne of Antichrist, where he sitteth in his exaltation, to whom the key of the bottomless pit was given; which being by him set wide open, the smoke of his canons, devices, trumperies, and abominations darkened the sun, poisoned the air; the locusts and scorpions that came out of this pit and out of this smoke, the multitudes and swarms of monks, friars, canons, vagrant and mendicant preachers, parish priests, etc. so pestered and poisoned every tree, so stung and envenomed every conscience, as they could bear no fruit neither brook any wholesome doctrine...(pp. 3, 4).

...The Prince himself entereth by the same door of faith into the Church, and is bound to the strait observation and obedience of God's laws in his calling as well as any other; and is for any transgression thereof liable and subject to the censures and judgments of Christ in his Church, which are without partiality or respect of persons. Which censures and judgments if the Prince contemn, he contemneth them against his own soul, and is thereupon by the same power of Christ to be disfranchised out of the Church, and to be delivered over unto Satan as well as any other offender. Now though by this sin he loseth his right to be a Christian or member of the Church, yet loseth he not his right to be a king or magistrate, and is so to be held and obeyed of all faithful Christians which are his subjects...(pp. 14, 15).

I hope by this little which hath been said concerning the education and training of these our great divines, it appeareth unto all men (that will judge by the word of God and are indued with the spirit of God) what kind of fellowships these University colleges are, what kind of cages full of unclean birds, of foul and hateful spirits, etc....The Universities of Cambridge and Oxford have the same popish and idolatrous beginning that the colleges of monks, friars, nuns, and those vermin had, and still retain the same unsufferable and incurable abuses, etc.; therefore Queen Elizabeth hath and ought by as good right to abolish them as her progenitor did the abbeys....And sure these University knights are the very guard of Antichrist's throne, the strength of his battle, his instruments to carry forth his wares, to subdue the people unto him, and keep them in his obedience —as bitter enemies of the Church and servants of God and of all righteousness as these Turkish janissaries to these christened regions with whom they have to do...(pp. 55, 56).

Is this old rotten Liturgy their new songs they sing unto the Lord with and for his graces? May such old, written, rotten stuff be called prayer, the odours of the Saints, burnt with that heavenly fire of the Altar, the lively graces of the Spirit, etc.? May reading be said praying? May such apocrypha trumpery be brought into the Church of God and there be read, reverenced, and received as the sacred Word of God?...Is not this presumptuously to undertake to teach the Spirit of God and to take away his office, which (as hath been said) instructeth all the children of God to pray...and giveth both words and utterance?...Is this the unity and uniformity that ought to be in all Churches and is amongst all Christ's servants, to make them agree in a stinking patchery-devised apocrypha Liturgy, good for nothing but for cushions and pillows for the idle priests and profane, carnal atheists to rock them asleep and keep them in security, whereby the conscience is no way either touched, edified, or bettered? Truly I am ashamed to think, much more to write, of so gross and filthy abomination, so generally received, even of all estates of these parts of the world, who have by a popish custom and tradition received that, one of and from another, without any warrant from the Word...(pp. 65, 66).

And indeed we poor persecuted Christians whom you so despise and blaspheme, baptising us into the name of *Browne*, as though we had either derived or hold our faith of him or any mortal man...(p. 113).

The poor parish or congregation where these priests serve may not meddle or have to do with the election, administration, or deposing of these their ministers; for why, they are laymen and have no skill, neither ought to intermeddle with ecclesiastical affairs or with the Word of God. Be their minister never so blind, unsufficient, or vile a wretch, detected of never so horrible sins, yet may not they remove him; their only help is to complain to their Lord Ordinary....Let their minister preach never such damnable or heretical doctrine, wrest, pervert, corrupt, falsify the Scriptures never so violently and heinously, all the Church...hath no authority, nay is by express law forbidden, to reprove this doctrine presently or publicly, or yet to forbid him to deal with the Scriptures; their remedy is still to complain to their Ordinary.... But my purpose is...to shew that every Christian congregation hath power in themselves, and of duty ought, presently and publicly to censure any false or unsound doctrine that is publicly delivered or maintained amongst them, if it be known and discerned unto them; yea, any one member in the Church hath this power, whatsoever he be, pastor or prophet, that uttereth it...(p. 165).

Now remaineth to be shewed that this exercise of prophesy belongeth to the whole Church, and ought not to be shut up in this manner amongst the priests only, the people being shut out either to speak or hear...(p. 172).

...Nothing is more sure than this, the true Church can be established into no other order, it can receive none other officers or laws, than are in Christ's Testament prescribed....O how great then is their wickedness, how pernicious their counsel, who (for filthy lucre's sake) persuade princes that they are not only not subject themselves in person to the laws and spiritual censures of Christ in his Church, but that they are not bound to admit that order of government prescribed in his Testament... in their lands?...(pp. 215, 216).

The public censuring of any member, whether elder or other, is an action of the whole Church, whereunto (if it use the most fit members or officers) should such officers and members hereupon arrogate the whole action, interest, and power to themselves, secluding the whole body the Church, whose officers and members they are?...What a dismembering of the body and rending of the Church would these ambitious priests make, who the one would withdraw all public actions of the Church into their popish courts, the other into their conventicles and synods of priests?

As for reproof by admonition, any member of the Church hath free power also to reprove the greatest elder of the Church according to the quality of his offence; if his offence be private, privately, if public, publicly: yea, he is bound by the law of God so to do...(p. 230).

...We have shewed how this power of excommunication, election, ordination, etc., is not committed into the hands of one particular person, as the Pope and his natural children our Lord Bishops now use it; nor yet into the hands of the eldership only or of the pastors of many particular congregations (as the reforming preachers would have it), so much as it is given and committed to the whole Church, even to every particular congregation, and to every member thereof alike...(p. 242).

Henry Barrow, *A Brief Discovery of the False Church*, 1590.

(5) Petition of the Commons for Ecclesiastical Reform, 1584

On Grindal's death in 1583 John Whitgift succeeded him as Archbishop of Canterbury. Elizabeth was fortunate in her archbishops, and in Whitgift she found an ecclesiastic of high ability and character. Like Grindal he was a Calvinist and accepted Puritan doctrine, but he differed from Grindal in being a disciplinarian by temperament[1], and he did not accept Puritan practice where it conflicted with the Act of Uniformity. He is therefore identified with a vigorous coercive policy against Puritanism, and especially Puritanism among the clergy. In this he conceived himself to be defending the principle of unity against that of division, and preserving the ecclesiastical constitution against dangerous foes.

In 1583 he improved upon Parker's Advertisements by drawing up Articles[2] of his own, which had the effect of stopping conventicles altogether, and preventing the exercise of ecclesiastical functions by clergy who did not conform. Those clergy who refused to assent to the Articles were suspended,

---

[1] As Master of Trinity 'he generally ate his meals with the rest in the College Hall, that he might have the more watchful eye over the scholars, and to keep them in awe and obedience; and to teach them likewise to be satisfied with a moderate, thrifty diet, such as that of the College was whereof he was their pattern before their eyes' (Strype, *Whitgift*, p. 78).

[2] Printed in full in Gee and Hardy, p. 481, and with omissions in Prothero, p. 211.

and the powers of the High Commission Court were greatly enlarged on his advice, to make it easier to deal effectively with schismatics.

The Articles required, among other things, (1) that 'all preaching, reading, catechising, and other suchlike exercises in private places and families, whereunto others do resort being not of the same family' should be 'utterly inhibited'; (2) that ecclesiastics should 'at all times wear and use' the apparel prescribed in the Injunctions of 1559 and the Advertisements of 1566; and (3) that no one should be permitted to exercise ecclesiastical functions unless he subscribed before the bishop of the diocese to the Royal Supremacy, the Book of Common Prayer, and the Thirty-Nine Articles.

The disciplinary action of Whitgift provoked a reaction in Parliament, for the ordinary layman disliked a system which silenced able preachers with sensitive consciences, but did not touch lazy, ignorant, and unconscientious clergy who conformed. Thus in 1584 the House of Commons took up the cause of the ministers whom Whitgift had deprived, and presented to the Lords a Petition for Ecclesiastical Reform with a view to joint action by the two Houses. Nothing came of the petition, but it is significant as an indication of the view taken in these matters by the influential laity.

1. Where by a statute[1]...it was enacted that none should be made minister unless he...have special gift and ability to be a preacher, It may please their honourable Lordships to consider whether it were meet to be ordered that so many as have been taken into the ministry...and be not qualified...be within a competent time suspended from the ministry....

[2. A similar clause relating to 'unlearned ministers.']

3. ...That none hereafter be admitted to the ministry but such as shall be sufficiently furnished with gifts to perform so high and so earnest a charge; and that none be superficially allowed as persons qualified...but with deliberate examination of their knowledge and exercise in the Holy Scriptures....

4. ...Whether it be meet to provide that no Bishop shall ordain any minister of the Word and Sacraments but with assistance of six other ministers at the least,...and that the said ministers do testify their presence at the admission of such ministers by subscription of their hands to some act importing the same. And further, that this admission be had and done publicly, and not in private house or chapel.

5. And where the admission of unnecessary multitudes to the ministry at one time hath been an occasion that the Church is at this day burdened with so great a number of unable ministers; ...whether some provision might be made that none be admitted to be a minister...but in a benefice having cure of souls then

[1] 13 Eliz. c. 12, § 4: 'And that none shall be made minister...unless he be able to answer and render to the Ordinary an account of his faith in Latin...or have special gift and ability to be a preacher.'

vacant in the diocese of such a Bishop as is to admit him; or to some place certain where such minister to be made is offered to be entertained for a preacher; or such graduates as shall be at the time of their admission into the ministry placed in some fellowship or scholarship within the Universities....

6. ...Whether, for the better assurance that none creep into charges and cure being men of corrupt life and not of known diligence, it might be provided that none be instituted...without some competent notice before given to the parish where they shall take their charge, and some reasonable time allowed, wherein it may be lawful to such as can discover any fault in conversation of life in the person who is to be so placed...to come and object the same.

7. That for the encouragement of many desirous to enter the ministry which are kept back by some conditions of oath and subscriptions, whereof they make scruple...hereafter no oath or subscription be tendered...but such only as be expressly prescribed by the statutes of this realm; saving that it shall be lawful for every ordinary to try any minister presented to any benefice within his diocese by his oath, whether he is to enter corruptly or incorruptly into the same.

8. Whereas sundry ministers of this realm, diligent in their calling and of good conversation and life, have of late years been grieved with indictments in temporal courts and molested by some exercising ecclesiastical jurisdiction for omitting small portions or some ceremony prescribed in the Book of Common Prayer, to the great disgrace of their ministry, and emboldening of men either hardly affected in religion or void of all zeal in the same, which also hath ministered no small occasion of discouragement to the forwardness of such as would otherwise enter into the ministry;...that such ministers...be not from henceforth called in question for omissions or changes of some portions or rite,...so their doings therein be void of contempt.

9. That forasmuch as it is no small discouragement to many that they see such as be already in the ministry openly disgraced by officials[1] and commissaries[2], who daily call them to their courts

[1] The presiding judges of the archbishop's, bishop's, or archdeacon's courts.

[2] Officers exercising ecclesiastical jurisdiction as representatives of the bishops in parts of their dioceses.

The ecclesiastical courts were very unpopular, as they were regarded as meddlesome and irritating. The authors of the *First Admonition* had described the Archbishop's Court as 'the filthy quake-mire and poisoned plash of all the abominations that do infect the whole realm,' and the Commissaries' Court as 'a petty little stinking ditch that floweth out of that former great puddle, robbing Christ's Church of lawful pastors, of watchful seniors and elders, and careful deacons' (Prothero, p. 199).

to answer complaints of their doctrine and life, or breach of orders prescribed by the ecclesiastical laws and statutes of this realm; It may please the reverend Fathers our Archbishops and Bishops to take to their own hearings, with such grave assistance as shall be thought meet, the causes of complaint made against any known preacher within their diocese....

10. It may also please the said reverend Fathers to extend their charitable favour to such known godly and learned preachers as have been suspended or deprived for no public offence of life, but only for refusal to subscribe to such articles as lately have been tendered in divers parts of the realm, or for such like things, that they may be restored to their former charges or places of preaching, or at the least set at liberty to preach where they may be hereafter called.

11. Further, that it may please the reverend Fathers aforesaid to forbear their examinations *ex officio mero*[1] of godly and learned preachers not detected[2] unto them for open offence of life, or for public maintaining of apparent error in doctrine, and only to deal with them for such matters as shall be detected in them; and that also her Majesty's Commissioners for Causes Ecclesiastical be required...to forbear the like proceeding against such preachers, and not to call any of them out of the diocese where he dwelleth except for some notable offence for reformation whereof their aid shall be required by the Ordinary of the said preachers.

12. *Item*, That for the better increase of knowledge of such as are employed in the ministry...whether it may be permitted to the ministers of every archdeaconry within every diocese to have some common exercises and conferences amongst themselves, to be limited and prescribed by their Ordinaries both touching the moderation and also the times, places, and manner of the same. So as the moderators of those exercises be preachers resident upon their benefices, having cure of souls, and known to bear good affection to the furtherance of such profit as may grow by the same exercises.

---

[1] In 1584 Whitgift drew up a list of 24 interrogatories to be tendered by the High Commission Court to any clergy suspected of non-conformity who were put on their oath to make true answer as to their practices and so to incriminate themselves. This oath, being tendered, not on any accusation or information but in virtue of the Commissioners' office only and at their pleasure, was known as the oath *ex officio mero*. It was condemned by Lord Burghley as 'too much savouring the Romish Inquisition,' but its legality was upheld. The question is discussed in Stephens and Hunt, v, 279.

[2] Accused. Cf. the use of the term in monastic visitations.

13. Where complaint is made of the abuse of excommunication....Whether some bill might not be conveniently framed to this effect, *viz.* That none having ecclesiastical jurisdiction shall in any matter already moved or hereafter to be moved in their Courts (other than in the cases hereafter mentioned) give or pronounce any sentence of excommunication. And that for the contumacy of any person in causes depending before them, it shall be lawful to pronounce him only *contumax*, and so to denounce him publicly. And if upon such denunciation...the party shall not submit himself...then it shall be lawful to signify his contumacy in such manner and sort and to such court as heretofore hath been used for persons...excommunicate. And that upon such certificate a writ *de contumace capiendo* shall be awarded of like force to all effects and purposes and with the like execution as the writ *de excommunicato capiendo* is.

14. Nevertheless, forasmuch as it seemeth not meet that the Church should be left without this censure of excommunication, it may be provided that for enormous crimes, as incest, adultery, and such like, the same be executed by the reverend Fathers the Bishops themselves, with assistance of grave persons, or else by other persons of calling in the Church, with like assistance, and with such other considerations as upon deliberation shall be herein advised of: and not by chancellors, commissaries, or officials, as hath been used.

15. Where licenses of non-residence are offensive to the Church, and be occasion that a great multitude of this realm do want instruction...whether it were more convenient or necessary that the use of them were utterly removed out of the Church: and so likewise of pluralities.

16. ...That none now having license of non-residence...or which shall hereafter have, be permitted to enjoy the benefit of such license except he depute an able and sufficient preacher to serve the cure....

Strype, *Life of Whitgift*, Appendix to Bk. iii, no. xiii (p. 70).

(6) The Marprelate Controversy, 1588–9

The Marprelate libels[1] against the bishops attracted much public attention, but some writers have taken them too seriously. The charges made were so impossible and the expressions used were so violent that they must be regarded as having a humorous intention, and they were so accepted at the time except by the government and by those whom they attacked. But underlying their satire there was always bitter indignation, and often effec-

---

[1] For a chronological list of the works which comprise the Marprelate Controversy, see E. Arber, *The English Scholar's Library*, No. 8, pp. 197–200.

tive argument. John Penry, the chief author of the tracts, was executed for sedition in 1593, although the indictment against him was not based on his complicity in the libels.

MARTIN MARPRELATE, 1588

The Epistle, 'printed oversea, in Europe, within two furlongs of a Bounsing Priest, at the cost and charges of M. Marprelate, gentleman,' was provoked by the publication in 1587 of *A Defence of the Government Established in the Church of England for Ecclesiastical Matters*, a work of 1412 pages directed against the Calvinists, by Dr John Bridges, Dean of Salisbury, and afterwards Bishop of Oxford. The author's ponderous controversial method made him an easy prey to his nimbler antagonist.

To the right puissant and terrible priests, my clergy masters of the Confocation-house, whether fickers general, worshipful paltripolitan, or any other of the holy league of subscription....

Right poisoned, persecuting, and terrible priests...(p. 1). ...They are petty popes and petty Antichrists whosoever usurp the authority of pastors over them who by the ordinance of God are to be under no pastors. For none but Antichristian popes and popelings ever claimed this authority unto themselves, especially when it was gainsaid and accounted Antichristian generally by the most Churches in the world.... Therefore... our L. Bps... with the rest of that swinish rabble are petty Antichrists, petty popes, proud prelates, intolerable withstanders of reformation, enemies of the gospel, and most covetous, wretched priests...(p. 5).

They usurp their authority who violently and unlawfully retain those under their government that both would and ought (if they might) to shake off that yoke wherewith they are kept under. ...Therefore our Bp. and proud, popish, presumptuous, profane, paltry, pestilent, and pernicious prelates...are first usurpers, to begin the matter withal...(p. 7).

...Therefore all the L. Bishops in England, Ireland, and Wales...are petty popes and petty usurping Antichrists, and I think if they will still continue to be so that they will breed young popes and Antichrists; *per consequens*, neither they nor their brood are to be tolerated in any Christian commonwealth, quoth Martin Marprelate. There is my judgment of you, brethren; make the most of it; I hope it will never be worth a bishopric unto you; reply when you dare, you shall have as good as you bring. And if you durst but dispute with my worship in these points, I doubt not but you should be sent home by weeping cross. I would wish you, my venerable masters, for all that, to answer my reasons, or out of doubt you will prove petty Antichrists. Your corner caps and tippets will do nothing in this point...(p. 10).

Is it any marvel that we have so many swine, dumb dogs, non-residents, with their journeymen the hedge priests, so many lewd livers, as thieves, murderers, adulterers, drunkards, cormorants, rascals, so many ignorant and atheistical dolts, so many covetous popish Bps. in our ministry, and so many and so monstrous corruptions in our Church, and yet likely to have no redress; seeing our impudent, shameless, and wainscot-faced bishops, like beasts, contrary to the knowledge of all men and against their own consciences, dare in the ears of her Majesty affirm all to be well where there is nothing but sores and blisters, yea, where the grief is even deadly at the heart. Nay, says my L. of Winchester[1] (like a monstrous hypocrite, for he is a very dunce, not able to defend an argument, but, till he come to the pinch, he will cog and face it out, for his face is made of seasoned wainscot, and will lie as fast as a dog can trot), I have said it, I do say it, and I have said it. And, say I, you shall one day answer it (without repentance) for abusing the Church of God and her Majesty in this sort. I would wish you to leave this villainy and the rest of your devilish practices against God his saints, lest you answer it where your peevish and choleric simplicity will not excuse you. I am ashamed to think that the Church of England should have these wretches for the eyes thereof, that would have the people content themselves with bare reading only and hold that they may be saved thereby ordinarily. But this is true of our Bp. and they are afraid that anything should be published abroad whereby the common people should learn that the only way to salvation is by the word preached...(p. 42).

...But, brethren bishops, I pray you tell me; hath not your brother London[2] a notable brazen face...? I told you Martin will be proved no liar in that he saith the Bps. are cogging and cozening knaves.... The last Lent there came a commandment from his Grace into Paul's Churchyard that no Bible should be bound without the Apocrypha. Monstrous and ungodly wretches, that to maintain their own outrageous proceedings thus mingle heaven and earth together, and would make the Spirit of God to be the author of profane books...(p. 47).

Martin Marprelate, *The Epistle*, 1588 (reprinted in
Puritan Discipline Tracts[3], 1843).

[1] Thomas Cooper, Bishop of Winchester, according to Wood, was 'much noted for his learning and sanctity of life,' and Godwin refers to him as 'a man from whose praises I can hardly temper my pen' (*D.N.B.* xii, 150).

[2] John Aylmer, Bishop of London, was a man of learning, but his temper was unconciliatory and his policy in his diocese gave special offence to the Puritans.

[3] See also E. Arber's reprint in *The English Scholar's Library*, No. 11.

(7) Act against Seditious Sectaries, 1593

The violence of the Marprelate libels provoked a reaction in favour of the bishops, and the government was able to obtain from Parliament, without much difficulty, statutory powers for dealing with Puritan extremists. The Act of 1593 transferred the odium of repression from the bishops to the courts of common law, and by allowing irreconcileables to leave England it put an end to the troubles of the reign as far as they vexed the surface of politics.

An Act to retain the Queen's Subjects in Obedience

For the preventing and avoiding of such great inconveniences and perils as might happen and grow by the wicked and dangerous practices of seditious sectaries and disloyal persons: Be it enacted by the Queen's most excellent Majesty, and by the Lords spiritual and temporal and the Commons in this present Parliament assembled, and by the authority of the same, That if any person or persons above the age of sixteen years which shall obstinately refuse to repair to some church, chapel, or usual place of common prayer to hear Divine Service established by her Majesty's laws and statutes in that behalf made, and shall forbear to do the same by the space of a month next after without lawful cause, shall at any time after forty days next after the end of this session of Parliament, by printing, writing, or express words or speeches, advisedly and purposely practise or go about to move or persuade any of her Majesty's subjects or any other within her Highness's realms or dominions to deny, withstand, and impugn her Majesty's power and authority in causes ecclesiastical united and annexed to the imperial Crown of this realm; or to that end or purpose shall advisedly and maliciously move or persuade any other person whatsoever to forbear or abstain from coming to church to hear Divine Service or to receive the Communion according to her Majesty's laws and statutes aforesaid, or to come to or to be present at any unlawful assemblies, conventicles, or meetings under colour or pretence of any exercise of religion, contrary to her Majesty's said laws and statutes; Or if any person or persons which shall obstinately refuse to repair to some church, chapel, or usual place of common prayer and shall forbear by the space of a month to hear Divine Service as is aforesaid, shall after the said forty days either of him or themselves, or by the motion, persuasion, enticement, or allurement of any other, willingly join or be present at any such assemblies, conventicles, or meetings under colour or pretence of any such exercise of religion, contrary to the laws and statutes of this realm as is aforesaid; That then every such person so offending as afore-said, and being thereof lawfully convicted, shall be committed to prison, there to remain without bail or mainprize[1] until they shall conform and yield themselves to come to some church, chapel, or usual place of common prayer and hear Divine Service, accord-ing to her Majesty's laws and statutes aforesaid, and to make such open submission and declaration of their said conformity as here-after in this Act is declared and appointed.

II. Provided always and be it further enacted by the autho-rity aforesaid, That if any such person or persons which shall offend against this Act as aforesaid shall not within three months next after they shall be convicted of their said offence conform themselves to the obedience of the laws and statutes of this realm in coming to the church to hear Divine Service and in making such public confession and submission as hereafter in this Act is appointed and expressed, being thereunto required by the bishop of the diocese, or any justice of peace of the county where the same person shall happen to be, or by the minister or curate of the parish, That in every such case every such offender, being thereunto warned or required by any justice of the peace of the same county where such offender shall then be, shall upon his and their corporal oath[2] before the justices of peace in the open quarter sessions of the same county, or at the assizes and gaol delivery of the same county before the justices of the same assizes and gaol delivery, abjure[3] this realm of England and all other the Queen's Majesty's dominions for ever unless her Majesty shall license the party to return, And thereupon shall depart out of this realm at such haven or port and within such time as shall in that behalf be assigned and appointed by the said justices before whom such abjuration shall be made, unless the same offender be letted or stayed by such lawful and reasonable means or causes as by the common laws of this realm are permitted and allowed in cases of abjuration for felony; And in such cases of let or stay, then within such reasonable and convenient time after as the common law requireth in case of abjuration for felony as is aforesaid;...And if any such offender...shall refuse to make such abjuration as is aforesaid, or after such abjuration made shall not go to such haven and within such time as is before appointed and from thence depart out of this realm according to this present Act, or after such his departure shall return or come again into any her Majesty's realms or dominions without her

[1] See note on p. 10 above.   [2] See note on p. 130 above.
[3] On abjuration of the realm, see p. 15 above.

Majesty's special licence in that behalf first had and obtained, That then in every such case the person so offending shall be adjudged a felon, and shall suffer as in case of felony without benefit of clergy.

[III. Offenders who, before they are required to make abjuration, 'repair to some parish church on some Sunday or other festival day and then and there hear divine service, and at service time before the sermon or reading of the gospel make public and open submission,' according to a form prescribed in the Act, are discharged from the penalties inflicted by the Act. Such submissions are to be entered by the curate in a book to be kept for the purpose in every parish, and within 10 days he is to 'certify the same in writing' to the bishop of the diocese.]

* * * * * *

V. And for that every person having house and family is in duty bounden to have special regard of the good government and ordering of the same: Be it enacted by the authority aforesaid, That if any person or persons shall at any time hereafter relieve, maintain, retain, or keep in his or their house or otherwise any person which shall obstinately refuse to come to some church, chapel, or usual place of common prayer to hear Divine Service, and shall forbear the same by the space of a month together, contrary to the laws and statutes of this realm, that then every person which shall so relieve, maintain, retain, or keep any such person offending as aforesaid, after notice thereof to him or them given by the ordinary of the diocese, or any justice of assizes of the circuit, or any justice of peace of the county, or the minister, curate, or churchwardens of the parish where such person shall then be, or by any of them, shall forfeit to the Queen's Majesty for every person so relieved, maintained, retained, or kept after such notice as aforesaid, ten pounds for every month that he or they shall so relieve, maintain, retain, or keep any such person so offending.

VI. Provided nevertheless, That this Act shall not in any wise extend to punish or impeach any person or persons for relieving, maintaining, or keeping his or their wife, father, mother, child or children, ward, brother or sister, or his wife's father or mother, not having any certain place of habitation of their own, or the husbands or wives of any of them; or for relieving, maintaining, or keeping any such person as shall be committed by authority to the custody of any by whom they shall be so relieved, maintained, or kept; Anything in this Act contained to the contrary notwithstanding.

* * * * * *

X. Provided also, That every person that shall abjure by force of this Act, or refuse to abjure being thereunto required as aforesaid, shall forfeit and lose to her Majesty all his goods and chattels for ever, and shall further lose all his lands, tenements, and hereditaments for and during the life only of such offender and no longer; And that the wife of any offender by force of this Act shall not lose her dower; nor that any corruption of blood shall grow or be by reason of any offence mentioned in this Act; but that the heir of every such offender by force of this Act shall and may after the death of every offender have and enjoy the lands, tenements, and hereditaments of such offender as if this Act had not been made; And this Act to continue no longer than to the end of the next session of Parliament.

35 Eliz. c. 1: *Statutes of the Realm*, iv, 841.

(8) The Sabbatarian Controversy, 1595

The Puritans had for some time been pressing for a stricter observance of Sunday, and in 1581 the question of the prohibition of Sunday fairs and of trading before morning prayer had been raised in the Privy Council itself. It was not, however, until towards the close of the reign that the controversy fully developed under the influence of Dr Nicholas Bownd's famous treatise, entitled 'The Doctrine of the Sabbath plainly laid forth and soundly proved by testimonies both of Holy Scripture and also of old and new ecclesiastical writers.... Together with the sundry abuses of our time in both these kinds, and how they ought to be reformed.' Bownd's position was adopted by the Puritan party generally, and it was not long before his strict views concerning the observance of the Sabbath came to be in a special manner the note of the Puritan.

Nicholas Bownd, 1595

Now if Adam, because he might fall, did stand in need of this day to preserve him from falling, how much more we, being so horribly fallen already (as we be) do stand in need of it again... to bring ourselves back into that estate from whence we are fallen, and as it were to recover our first footing?...Yes, surely, unless we be too much lovers of ourselves and overweened with the pride of our nature, must we believe that if the perfect image of God in Adam, not lightly shadowed but drawn out with most lively and orient colours by the finger of God himself, could not continue in his first beauty except by the pure means of God's worship (as it were by the first colours) it were now and then refreshed...then when this goodly image is so foully defaced with sin that not so much as the first draught thereof doth appear, nay all the colours of it are by Satan sullied with iniquity or rather clean put out, have we much more need to sanctify many days by the Word, sacraments, and prayer, etc., that so the image of the first man might be renewed in us...(p. 15).

...It is most certain that we are...commanded to rest...
from...all...things which might hinder us from the sanctifying
of the Sabbath...of which sort are all honest recreations and
lawful pleasures which are permitted unto us upon the other days
to further us in the works of our calling, which we do stand in
need of even as of meat, and drink, and sleep....We must not
think it sufficient that we do no work upon the Sabbath, and in
the mean season be occupied about all manner of delights, but we
must cease as well from the one as from the other....Therefore
upon this day all sorts of men must give over utterly all shooting,
hunting, hawking, tennis, fencing, bowling, or such like, and they
must have no more dealing with them than the artificer with his
trade or husbandman with his plough...(pp. 131–2).

Nicholas Bownd, *The Doctrine of the Sabbath*, 1595.

The King's Secretary

The development of the highly organised and centralised Tudor monarchy involved an increase in the importance of the executive, and this is reflected in the history of the office of King's Secretary—the ancestor of the modern Secretary of State. Under the Tudors government begins to be confronted with modern problems and to adopt modern ways of dealing with them. These new developments are assigned, not to the older departments, the functions of which had become stereotyped, but to an officer whose duties had never been subjected to strict definition. Thus local government, trade and plantations, Ireland, and diplomacy abroad fell to the Principal Secretary to the King, who also acted as Secretary to the Council; for although the King was chiefly responsible it was through the Secretary that he was accustomed to act.

In the Middle Ages[1] the King's Secretary appears as an official of considerable importance, but always as a private Household officer, paid out of the Household funds, and performing his duties of letter-writing close to the person of the King. He is really a confidential clerk, although a clerk who is charged with important functions. And inasmuch as in early times the writer of official letters always sealed them, the King's Secretary had the custody of the King's Privy Seal. But there was a tendency for seals which had been private and miscellaneous to become public and specialised, and in time the privy seal became a public seal in charge of a great officer called the Lord Privy Seal, while the King's Secretary used another private seal called the signet. As early as the reign of Edward II there was a secret seal besides the privy seal, and although the keeper of the privy seal did not at once cease to be the King's Secretary, the letters of privy seal were ceasing to be the King's private letters and the privy seal was becoming an instrument of state, like the great seal. William of Wykeham, appointed in 1364, was probably the last fourteenth century keeper of the privy seal who was also King's Secretary[2]; and by the reign of Richard II the signet had replaced the privy seal for all purposes connected with the private correspondence of the King. In 1433 a second Secretary appears as 'the King's Secretary in his realm of France,' an appointment probably due to the difficulties of language in connexion with the correspondence arising out of the French wars. By an Order in Council of 1443 definite responsibility was assigned to the King's Secretary for the use of the signet in preparing letters authorising the affixing of the privy seal to royal grants[3]; and in 1536 this was extended and confirmed by 'An Act concerning Clerks of the Signet and Privy Seal,'[4] which provided that any grants made under any of the King's seals should be first brought to the King's Principal Secretary or to one of the clerks of the signet 'to be at the said office of the signet passed accord-

---

[1] On the early history of the King's Secretary, see Sir Harris Nicolas, *Observations on the Office of Secretary of State,* ... and Miss L. B. Dibben in *E.H.R.* xxv, 430.
[2] *E.H.R.* xxv, 437.   [3] Anson, ii, i, 159.   [4] 27 Henr. VIII, c. 11.

ingly.' Thus the Secretary acquired and retained definite responsibility for the official expression of the royal will.

At the beginning of his reign Henry VII appointed Richard Fox King's Secretary and re-appointed Stephen Fryon his Secretary of the French Language. In 1487 Fox became Bishop of Exeter and resigned the Secretaryship, but one of his successors, Thomas Ruthall, although made Bishop of Durham in 1509, continued to be King's Secretary until 1516. These proceedings shew that although the office involved nothing of the nature of ministerial responsibility, it was becoming one of high consideration, to be filled by important men.

When Oliver King was appointed in 1476 Secretary for the French Language for life, he was described, like his English colleague, as 'the King's First and Principal Secretary'; thus the term 'Principal' does not necessarily imply that a Principal Secretary was chief of the King's Secretaries, but that he was chief of his own staff of subordinates. One secretary is not 'principal' in relation to the other, but both are 'principal' in relation to their respective staffs. In 1549 a further addition was made to the number of secretaries when Peter Vannes was appointed Latin Secretary for life, but he was not a 'Principal Secretary' in the technical sense. This is the office which Milton afterwards held.

In or about 1540 a curious experiment in reorganisation was attempted. By a royal warrant of April of that year [p. 206] the office of English Secretary was divided between Thomas Wriothesley and Ralph Sadler. They both bore the same title, having 'the name and office of the King's Majesty's Principal Secretaries'; were entrusted with duplicate signets; kept two journals, which were open to each other's inspection; were both lodged in the King's palace; and were entitled, when the Lord Privy Seal was at Court, 'to accompany him at his table.' It was also provided that they should sit in alternate weeks, one in the House of Lords and the other in the House of Commons. No definite date can be assigned to this experiment, for it is possible that the royal warrant of 1540 only gave official confirmation to an arrangement which already existed in practice, for Sadler was conducting the royal correspondence at least as early as July, 1538. Nor is it known whether the experiment succeeded in spite of the dangers of divided responsibility; but there were two Principal Secretaries until the accession of Mary. During her reign and for the earlier part of the reign of Elizabeth there was only one Secretary, but soon after Cecil, now Lord Burghley, became Lord Treasurer, he was succeeded in 1573 by Sir Francis Walsingham and Sir Thomas Smith acting jointly. On Davison's disgrace in 1587 the Queen did not appoint a successor, and there seems to have been only one Secretary for the rest of the reign[1]. Thus the number of Principal Secretaries and their relation to each other was not during the Tudor period definitely fixed, either by regulation or constitutional practice. The modern title of the office, Secretary of State, does not appear until about 1592, and then for a few years in the earlier form, 'Secretary of Estate.'

---

[1] On Walsingham's death in 1590, Robert Cecil, Lord Burghley's son, afterwards Earl of Salisbury, became acting Secretary, but his patent of appointment to the office of Principal Secretary was not granted until 1596. On Dr John Herbert's position as 'second Secretary' see p. 212 below.

During the seventeenth and eighteenth centuries there continued to be as a rule[1] two Secretaries of State, and when the Cabinet displaced the Council as the executive government early in the eighteenth century, the Secretaries became great officers of state with large public responsibilities. But in the Tudor period no such public responsibility attached to the office. It is true that in time the Secretary ceased to be a Household officer, and his salary no longer appeared upon the Household accounts;[2] but his sole duty was to the Sovereign, and he owed no respect to the constitution apart from the King. Although the Secretary was the only channel through which the Crown could be approached or the King's pleasure conveyed, he had nothing to do with the royal decisions. Henry VIII read his own letters and dictated the answers himself [p. 211]; and affairs of a very secret nature he did not trust to his Secretary at all [p. 211]. Nevertheless it was out of this that the modern office grew, and 'the King's Secretary, from being little more than the clerical instrument for conveying his Sovereign's commands, has become one of the most influential ministers of state, whose signature is absolutely requisite to legalise nearly every act of the Crown; whose authority to use the King's name cannot be disputed by any one except the King himself; who is answerable with his liberty and life to Parliament for the constitutional and judicious exercise of the prerogatives of the Crown; and who, in the present distribution of the office among...individuals of co-ordinate authority, performs most of the functions of government with all but undefinable powers and unlimited authority.'[3]

In the Tudor period the stipend of the Secretary was small [p. 210], and Walsingham spent his private fortune in an efficient discharge of the duties of his office; but under James I large allowances, over and above the stipend, were made 'for intelligence and other secret services,' and there were various perquisites and fees[4].

(1) Act of Precedence, 1539

That the office of King's Secretary no longer occupied the comparatively humble position assigned to it in the Middle Ages appears from § 6 of the Act, which provides for the precedence of the Secretary when he is already either a Lord of Parliament or a Bishop.

An Act for the placing of the Lords in Parliament

Forasmuch as in all great councils and congregations of men having sundry degrees and offices in the commonwealth it

[1] The exceptions were in 1616, 1707–46, and 1768–82, when there were three (Anson, II, i, 161).

[2] It was not until 1578 that the Principal Secretary was regularly appointed by patent, although the Secretaries for the French and Latin languages had always been so appointed. He was originally designated by the delivery of the King's signet, not necessarily recorded, or performed before witnesses (Nicolas, *The Office of Secretary*, p. 44).

[3] Nicolas, *The Office of Secretary*, p. 48.

[4] The emoluments of the Secretaries of State in the seventeenth century are fully discussed in *E.H.R.* xxxv, 513–28.

is very requisite and convenient that an order should be had and taken for the placing and sitting of such persons as be bound to resort to the same, to the intent that they knowing their places may use the same without displeasure or let of the Council; Therefore the King's most royal Majesty, although it appertaineth unto his prerogative royal to give such honour, reputation, and placing to his counsellors and other his subjects as shall be seeming to his most excellent wisdom, is nevertheless pleased and contented for an order to be had and taken in this his most high Court of Parliament....

* * * * * *

VI. And it is also enacted by authority aforesaid that the King's Chief Secretary being of the degree of a Baron of Parliament shall sit and be placed afore and above all Barons not having any of the offices aforementioned; and if he be a Bishop, that then he shall sit and be placed above all other Bishops not having any of the offices above remembered.

* * * * * *

VIII. And it is further enacted that if any person or persons which at any time hereafter shall happen to have any of the said offices of Lord Chancellor, Lord Treasurer, Lord President of the King's Council, Lord Privy Seal, or Chief Secretary, shall be under the degree of a Baron of the Parliament, by reason whereof they can have no interest to give any assent or dissent in the said House, that then in every such case such of them as shall happen to be under the said degree of a Baron shall sit and be placed at the uppermost part of the sacks in the midst of the said Parliament Chamber[1], either there to sit upon one form or upon the uppermost sack, the one of them above the other in order as is above rehearsed.

* * * * * *

X. And it is enacted by authority aforesaid that as well in all Parliaments as in the Star Chamber, and in all other assemblies and conferences of Council, the Lord Chancellor, the Lord Treasurer, the Lord President, the Lord Privy Seal, the Great Chamberlain, the Constable, the Marshal, the Lord Admiral, the Grand Master or Lord Steward, the King's Chamberlain, and the King's Chief Secretary, shall sit and be placed in such order and fashion as is above rehearsed and not in any other place, by authority of this present Act.

31 Henr. VIII, c. 10: *Statutes of the Realm*, iii, 729.

---

[1] At this time the Lords sat in the Parliament Chamber, where the Commons also sometimes appeared (see p. 542 below).

(2) Warrant for the appointment of two Secretaries, 1540

The precedence assigned to the Secretaries by this warrant, although it varies from that given them by the Act of Precedence of 1539 [p. 204], is the same as that since held by Secretaries of State when below the rank of peers[1]. Wriothesley was knighted in 1540 soon after his appointment, and eventually became Earl of Southampton. Sadler was knighted in 1542.

First, that Thomas Wriothesley and Ralph Sadler, and every of them, shall have the name and office of the King's Majesty's Principal Secretaries during his Highness's pleasure; and shall receive, to be equally divided between them, all such fees, droits, duties, and commodities, not hereafter specially limited, as have, do, or ought to belong to the office of his Majesty's Principal Secretary.

Item, his Highness hath resolved that every of the said Thomas Wriothesley and Ralph Sadler shall, for the time of their being in the said office, have and keep two his Grace's seals called his signets, and with the same seal all such things, warrants, and writings, both for inward and outward parties, as have been accustomed to be passed heretofore by the same; every of the said Thomas Wriothesley and Ralph Sadler nevertheless to keep a book containing all such things as shall pass by either of their hands, and the one to be made ever privy to the other's register.

Item, his Majesty is contented that every of the said Thomas Wriothesley and Ralph Sadler shall have an ordinary chamber or lodging within the gates of his Grace's house, in all places where the same may be, conveniently furnished; and every of them to have like bouche of court[2] in all things as is appointed to the Secretary.

Item, his Majesty is pleased and ordaineth, that all such times as the Lord Privy Seal shall be present in the Court, the said Thomas Wriothesley and Ralph Sadler shall accompany him at his table; and when he shall be absent out of Court, then they to have his diet for themselves and such other as be appointed to that table.

Item, his Majesty ordaineth that in all Councils, as well in his Majesty's Household as in the Star Chamber and elsewhere, all Lords, both of the temporalty and clergy, shall sit above them; and likewise the Treasurer, Comptroller, Master of the Horse, and Vice-Chamberlain of his Highness's Household; then next after to be placed the said Principal Secretaries, and so after them all such other Councillors as shall resort and have place in

---

[1] Nicolas, *The Office of Secretary*, p. 37.   [2] See pp. 207–8 below.

any of the said Councils. And albeit that by a statute lately made[1], the office of the Principal Secretary should be and sit continually in the Upper House of the Parliament upon one of the woolsacks, yet his Highness, considering the good service that the said Thomas Wriothesley and Ralph Sadler may do him in the Nether House, where they have now places, doth ordain that during his pleasure they shall use themselves as hereafter ensueth; that is to say, on all such days as the Speaker shall be present, or that the King's Majesty shall be present in person, they shall attend on his Highness, and shall both have their places upon the said woolsack according to the said statute; and at all other times the one of them to be one week in the High House and the other in the Low House, and so he that was in the Lower House to be the next week in the Higher House, changing their places by course, unless it be upon some special day for matters to be treated in the Nether House, at which time they shall may[2] both be present there accordingly; and in all other places within his Grace's Household and elsewhere his pleasure is that they and every of them shall have, enjoy, and use the place of Principal Secretary as heretofore hath been accustomed.

State Papers (1830–52), ii, 623.

(3) Status of the Secretary

The position of the Secretary in the official hierarchy is indicated by the extracts from the Ordinances for the Royal Household which follow. See also the Act of Precedence of 1539 printed on p. 204 above.

1. Ordinances made at Eltham, 1526

[Bouche of Court]

The Secretary and two Vice Chamberlains

Every of them being lodged within the Court, in the morning, one cheat[3] loaf, one manchet[3], one gallon ale; for afternoon, one manchet, one gallon ale; for after supper, one cheat loaf, one manchet, one gallon ale, half pitcher wine; and from the last day of October unto the first day of April, three links by the week; by the day, one pricket[4], two sizes[5], half pound white lights, four talshides[6], four faggots... and from the last day of March unto the first day of November to have the moiety of the said wax,

---

[1] The Act of Precedence of 1539: see p. 204 above.
[2] See note on p. 24 above.
[3] 'Cheat' is wheaten bread of the second quality, as contrasted with 'manchet,' which was of the finest quality.   [4] Candlestick.
[5] A kind of candle specially used at court and in churches.
[6] Wood for cutting into billets.

white lights, wood, and coals; which doth amount unto in money by the year the sum of £22. 7s. 11d.....(p. 162).

2. BOUCHE OF COURT[1], c. 1544

Secretaries

The two Secretaries[2] to sit in their own chamber, and to be served with their own servants from all offices; and to have from the Kitchen one double mess and one single; and to have one mess for their supper every Friday at night out of Lent and every Saturday within Lent (p. 172).

... The first mess to the Secretaries, with the
charge of supper ... ... [3]£406 10 3¾
Item, their second mess ... ... [3]£406 8 9¾

(p. 192)

... The King's Secretary, being lodged within the Court, stabling for 8 horses, and 3 beds [for his servants][4]....(p. 198).

The increase of charges in the Household by commandment since the receiving of the King's Book of the Ordinary of his most honourable Household.... *Item*, the bouche of court served to the two Secretaries...£33 19 1...(pp. 208, 210).

Ordinances of the Royal Household (Society of Antiquaries, 1790).

3. QUEEN ELIZABETH'S ANNUAL EXPENSE, CIVIL AND MILITARY, c. 1590

The extracts here given shew the stipends and allowances of other great personages, as well as those of the Secretaries. Thus they furnish a standard for estimating their importance, and indicate the method of payment, partly in money and partly in kind.

(p. 241)

The Lord Chancellor...fee	£419	0	0
For his attendance in the Star Chamber	200	0	0
More, by the names of annuities ...	300	0	0
Robes out of the Wardrobe	40	0	0
Wine out of the Butlerage, 12 tuns ...	72	0	0
Seal	16	0	0

[1] The allowance of victual granted to the Court. On the probable date of this document, which is printed as if it were part of the Ordinances of Eltham of 1526, see *State Papers*, ii, p. 623 *n*.

[2] Presumably the King's Secretary and the Secretary for the French language.

[3] The charges varied from £1520. 12s. 4d. for 'the King's diet by the year' to £66. 7s. 5½d. for the 'Chirurgeons,' who had only one mess.

[4] The same as was allowed to Privy Councillors and to the Vice-Chamberlain. A Duke was allowed stabling for 24 horses and beds for 9 servants, and a Bishop for 16 and 6.

Master of the Rolls; fee out of the Exchequer	34	0	0
Livery out of the Hanaper[1]	8	14	0
Wine, one tun...	6	13	4

(p. 242)

The Privy Seal: The Keeper thereof; fee ...	265	2	6

The King's Bench

Lord Chief Justice of England; fee, reward, and robes	208	6	8
Wine, 2 tuns at £5 the tun	10	0	0
Allowance for being Justice of Assize...	20	0	0
Justices, le piece[2], 3; fee, reward, and robes	128	6	8
Allowance as Justices of Assize ...	20	0	0. ...

The Common Pleas

Lord Chief Justice of the Common Pleas: fee, reward, and robes	141	13	4
Wine, 2 tuns	8	0	0
Allowance as Justice of Assize ...	20	0	0
Fee for keeping the Assize in the Augmentation Court (see p. 336 below)	12	10	8
Justices, 3, to every of them: fee, reward, and robes	128	6	8
Allowance as Justices of Assize ...	20	0	0. ...
Attorney-General: fee	61	0	0
Allowance as Justice of Assize ...	20	0	0
Solicitor: fee	50	0	0. ...

The Council in the North

Lord President: diet for himself and the rest of the Council	1000	0	0
Councillors, 7: fee apiece	50	0	0

The Council in Wales and the Marches...

Lord President: fee, and diet for himself and the rest of the Council	1040	0	0
Councillors, divers: To some	50	0	0
To some	40	0	0
To some	30	0	0. ...

[1] A department of the Chancery which received fees for the sealing and enrolling of documents.   [2] Apiece.

(p. 243)
Justices of Oyer and Terminer

From Trent, southward: fee	100	o	o
From Trent, northward: fee	100	o	o

The Exchequer...

Lord High Treasurer of England: fee ...	368	o	o
Robes out of the Wardrobe	15	7	8
Chancellor of the Exchequer: fee	113	6	8
Livery...	12	17	8
Lord Chief Baron of the Exchequer: fee ...	100	o	o
Livery...	12	17	4
Allowance for being Justice of Assize...	20	o	o
Barons of the Exchequer, 3: fee	46	13	4
Livery, apiece	12	17	4
Allowance as Justice of Assize ...	20	o	o

(p. 250)
The Queen's Court or Household...

Principal Secretary: fee, and a table ...	100	o	o
Secretary in the Latin tongue: fee, and a table	40	o	o
Secretary in the French tongue: fee ...	66	13	4
Clerk of the Council in the Star Chamber: fee	26	13	4
Clerks of the Parliament, 2:			
To the one	40	o	o
To the other	10	o	o...
Clerks of the Privy Council, 4: fee apiece...	50	o	o...

(p. 257)
Other Rewards and Allowances

Chirurgeons, 6:			
To two apiece...	60	o	o
To two apiece...	30	o	o
To two apiece...	20	o	o
Physicians, 3: fee apiece	10	o	o
Apothecaries, 3: fee apiece	26	13	4
Astronomer: fee	20	o	o
Serjeant Painter and other to his appointment:			
fee	100	o	o
Keeper of the Libraries: fee per diem ...		6	8
Master of Requests: fee	100	o	o

Ordinances of the Royal Household (Society of Antiquaries, 1790).

(4) The Secretary's relation to the King

The following extracts shew that the Secretary took no political responsibility, but was only a channel of communication for the King's pleasure. Henry VIII in particular reserved all important decisions to himself, and Elizabeth, although she set store by the advice of Burghley and Walsingham, did not always consult them.

1. *Henry VIII to Wolsey*, 1518

My Lord Cardinal, I recommend unto you as heartily as I can, and I am right glad to hear of your good health, which I pray God may long continue; so it is that I have received your letters, to the which (because they ask long writing) I have made answer by my Secretary: two things there be which be so secret that they cause me at this time to write to you myself....

State Papers (1830–52), i, 1.

2. *Richard Pace to Wolsey*, 29 *October*, 1521

Richard Pace had been appointed King's Secretary in 1516, in succession to Thomas Ruthall, Bishop of Durham. He was made Dean of St Paul's in 1519 and Dean of Exeter in 1522, but he retained the office of Secretary until 1526.

...I never rehearsed your Grace's letters, diminutely or fully, but by the King's express commandment, who readeth all your letters with great diligence, and mine answers made to the same not by my device but by his instructions. And as for one of my letters...I had at that time devised a letter in the same matter far discrepant from that ye received; but the King would not approve the same, and said that he would himself devise an answer to your Grace's letters sent to him at that time; and commanded me to bring your said letters into his privy chamber, with pen and ink, and there he would declare unto me what I should write. And when his Grace had your said letters, he read the same three times, and marked such places as it pleased him to make answer unto, and commanded me to write and to rehearse as liked him, and not further to meddle with that answer. So that I herein nothing did but obeyed the King's commandment as to my duty appertaineth, and especially at such time as he would upon good grounds be obeyed, whosoever spake to the contrary. As touching untrue information to be made by me to the King of your Grace's letters, I am sorry ye do lay that to my charge, for if I did untruly inform his Highness of any part of the same letters which be of so great weight and importance, I should not only deal unkindly and falsely with your Grace but also be a manifest traitor to the King.... Furthermore, if I would

14—2

inform the King otherwise of your Grace's letters than the truth is, I could not so do without great shame and to mine own evident ruin, for his Grace doth read them all himself, and examine the same at leisure with great deliberation, and hath better wit to understand them than I to inform him....

State Papers (1830–52), i, 79.

(5) Duties of the Secretary

The variety and range of the duties of the Secretary are suggested by the following memorandum, written for his own guidance by Dr John Herbert, who was appointed second Secretary[1] in 1600.

Dr John Herbert's Memorandum, 26 *April*, 1600

Titles of matters whereof I am charged to have regard as a Councillor and Secretary.

First, to inform myself of all treaties with foreign princes, France, Burgundy and the Low Countries, Spain, Scotland, Denmark, and the Hanses, etc.

To be acquainted with the particular actions and negotiations of ambassadors to her Majesty and from her.

To inform myself of the power and form of proceeding at the Council of the Marches in Wales and the Council in the North, and to understand the manner of the Warden's[2] government.

To be well informed of the state of Ireland, both the yearly charge of the army and the extraordinary, the state of revenue there, and the state of the undertakers[3].

The charge of the Low Country wars, the charges of the French King, the state of their debts to the Queen, what the assurances are and where they are.

To oversee the order of the Council-book and Muster-book of the realm.

To have the custody of letters from foreign princes to the Queen, and answers made to them.

To have care to the intelligences abroad....

[For the remainder of this memorandum, which refers to the business of the Council, see p. 247 below.]   *State Papers (Domestic), Eliz.* cclxxiv, 118.

[1] A warrant of 17 May, 1600, refers to him as 'late Master of Requests, now admitted second Secretary,' and orders two new signets of gold for him and two signets for the Principal Secretary, 'the others having become unserviceable from long use' (*Calendar of State Papers, Domestic, Eliz.* 1598–1601, p. 437). The Principal Secretary here referred to is Sir Robert Cecil.

[2] Presumably the Lord Warden of the Marches of Scotland, who had charge of the Border.

[3] The English families who had taken over the confiscated lands in Munster after the attainder of the Earl of Desmond in 1586.

The Privy Council

The history of the Tudor Council—its relation to the Council of the Lancastrians on the one hand, and to the Star Chamber on the other—is difficult and obscure. This is partly due to a want of clearness and continuity in the records. The 'Book of the Council' contains a register for the period 1421–35, but it was then either discontinued or lost[1]. Even for this period of fifteen years it consists of copies or abridgments of the more important Council minutes only, and is not a complete record of the whole of its proceedings[2]. In 1487 the 'Book of Entries' (*Liber Intrationum*) was begun, but this also disappeared in the eighteenth century, and its contents are only known from notes and extracts made by antiquarians before the disappearance took place. It was not until August 10, 1540, that a more complete Council Register was begun, and this continues down to the present time. It is, however, only a book of 'conclusions' and not a full record of all matters that came before the Council, for questions of high policy were often reserved for the decision of the Sovereign, or were settled by inner circles of advisers, and so do not appear in the Register at all[3]. It is also the case that gaps occur in the series of records, as certain volumes are missing and have never been traced[4]. Thus the student of the history of the Council works under difficulties, and some of the conclusions arrived at have only a provisional character.

The reason for the failure of the Lancastrian Council had been its exploitation by the great nobles. It was largely concerned with the dispensation of royal patronage, and the great lords had selfishly appropriated the royal resources for the benefit of themselves and their dependents. Thus when Fortescue, Henry VI's Chief Justice, who was fully alive to the abuses of the system with which he was familiar, sketched the ideal Council, he proposed to exclude the great nobles in favour of expert officials chosen entirely because of their business capacity. 'The King's Council,' he says[5], 'was wont to be chosen of great princes and of the greatest lords of the land, both spirituals and temporals, and also of other men that were in great authority and offices, which lords and officers had near hand also[6] many matters of their own to be treated in the Council as had the King. Wherethrough, when they came together, they were so occupied with their own matters, and the

---

[1] Baldwin, pp. 391, 419. The author takes the view that there was not a loss of records, as has been commonly supposed, but that they failed for lack of material, due to a partial suspension of the activities of the Council during the reigns of Edward IV, Edward V, and Richard III (pp. 419–22).

[2] *Ib.* p. 391.

[3] Dasent, IX, p. xxvi and XIV, p. ix.

[4] There is a tradition that the Registers for 1603–12 were destroyed in the fire at Whitehall, January 12, 1619. It has also been suggested that some of the Council Registers were among the papers burned by Charles I, to prevent their falling into the hands of the Parliament, when he left Oxford for the North in 1646 (Dasent, I, p. ix).

[5] ch. XV.   [6] Near hand also = almost as.

matters of their kin, servants, and tenants, that they attended but little and otherwhile nothing to the King's matters.... And what lower man was there sitting in that Council that durst say against the opinion of any of the great lords?' He also complains that nothing treated of in Council could be kept secret, 'for the lords oftentimes told their own counsellors and servants that had sued to them for those matters, how they had sped in them and who was against them'; and that a council of great personages cannot be depended upon to conserve the resources of the Crown. 'How may the King be counselled to restrain giving away of his land, of giving of offices, corrodies, or pensions of abbeys, by such great lords to other men's servants, since they most desire such gifts for themselves and their servants?' To remedy these abuses Fortescue suggested the establishment of a new Council consisting of 'twelve spiritual men and twelve temporal men, of the wisest and best disposed men that can be found in all the parts of this land'; they are to be sworn to take 'no fee, nor clothing, nor no rewards' of any but the King; and they are to have a permanent tenure unless the King by the advice of the majority of the Council sees fit to remove them. To these are to be added as temporary councillors 'four lords spiritual and four lords temporal' to be chosen every year by the King; but these members 'need not to have great wages for their attendance,' so there was no special inducement for them to come to the Council. It was also suggested that the great officers of state, 'as Chancellor, Treasurer, and Privy Seal' might attend 'when they list come thereto, or that they be desired by the said councillors'; and that 'the Judges, the Barons of the Exchequer, the Clerk of the Rolls, and such lords as the foresaid councillors will desire to be with them for matters of great difficulty, may be of this Council when they be so desired, and else not.' The business assigned to the Council was to 'commune and deliberate upon the matters of difficulty that fall to the King, and then upon the matters of the policy of the realm.... How also the laws may be amended in such things as they need reformation in; wherethrough the Parliaments shall mowe[1] do more good in a month to the mending of the law than they shall mowe do in a year, if the amending thereof be not debated and by such Council riped to their hands.' Articles 'for the demeaning and rule of this Council' were to be 'put in a book, and that book kept in this Council as a register or an ordinary[2], how they shall do in everything.'

A scheme based on the exclusion of baronial influence from the Council was not likely to succeed in Lancastrian conditions, and so little is known of the Council under Edward IV, that it is impossible to say whether any attempt was made to carry it out. But in all its main features Fortescue's plan is an anticipation of the Tudor Council. England was now to be governed 'not through peers of ancient lineage, but through the Cromwells, the Sadlers, the Petres, and the Cecils, who constitute the story of the Tudors' rule'[3]; and in other less important respects the machinery is the same. The only striking difference is in the appointment and removal of councillors. Fortescue had proposed that unless for 'any default found in them' they should only be dismissed with the assent of a majority of their

---

[1] See note on p. 24 above.   [2] *I.e.* as a book of rules or precedents.
[3] Dicey, p. 86.

colleagues; but the Tudor sovereigns asserted complete control over the composition of the Council[1].

The change in the relations between the Crown and the Council is one of the fundamental constitutional facts of the Tudor period. In selecting his Council the choice of the medieval monarch had been free in theory but limited in practice. Important officials, like the Marshal and the Chamberlain, could not very well be passed over, and some of these offices were hereditary in certain families. The two Archbishops claimed a prescriptive right to be present at all Councils[2]; and since certain offices, the chief of which was the Chancellorship, could only be filled by ecclesiastics, by reason of their superior education and fitness, the King was to a certain extent dependent upon his bishops, and the medieval bishop was not a humble courtier but often a great independent potentate. Further, Parliament would sometimes intervene, claiming, as under Henry IV, that a Council should be nominated that was acceptable to Parliament; itself appointing the Council of Henry VI's minority; and even compelling the King to take the Council's advice. But if the medieval Council had acted as a check upon the King, and had sometimes become his master, the Tudor Council is the King's slave. The key to the change is the humiliation of the baronage and the growth of the new official class. The central government is now strong enough to rule without the help of local lords, and the King's choice of his advisers, which had always been free in name, becomes also free in fact. He is emancipated from the old nobility, and can fill his Council with 'scant-born gentlemen.' Nor is he any longer limited to ecclesiastics in his choice of competent clerks and diplomatists, for he can find laymen who are at least equally efficient. Thus in the Tudor period certain great offices cease to be a monopoly of the Church[3]. The government of England was transferred from the men of ancient lineage, who could not be removed without arousing the hostility of the great houses with which they were connected by blood or intermarriage, and passed to new men who were wholly dependent upon the royal favour. Thus the independence of the Council disappeared, and it was transformed into an agent of the Tudor despotism—a mere instrument of the royal will. But as the independence of the Council diminished, its powers increased, for as soon as the councillors came to be dependent upon

[1] In 1536 Henry VIII stated the position in emphatic terms: 'It appertaineth nothing to any of our subjects to appoint us our Council, ne will we take it so at your hands; wherefore henceforth remember better the duties of subjects to your King and Sovereign Lord, and meddle no more of those nor such-like things as ye have nothing to do in' (*State Papers*, ii, 508).

[2] Dicey, p. 31.

[3] Down to Wolsey the Lord Chancellors had usually been ecclesiastics, and except for some fourteenth century cases Sir Thomas More was the first layman to hold the office; since the deprivation of Nicholas Heath, Archbishop of York, soon after Elizabeth's accession, they have always been laymen—with the solitary exception of John Williams, Bishop of Lincoln, who was Lord Keeper from 1621 to 1625. Until the reign of Henry VIII the Lord Privy Seal was an ecclesiastic; since 1533 he has always been a layman, and, except when the office was in commission, he was, until Disraeli's appointment in 1876, a temporal lord. The same thing happened with the Clerkship to the Parliament, in the Middle Ages a peculiarly clerical office.

the Crown, it was to the interest of the Crown to enlarge their authority. Thus the Tudor period became in a special sense the period of government by Council, for it was through the Council that the centralised monarchy performed its work[1].

The term 'Privy Council,' in common use during the Tudor period, originates late in the Council's history. As early as the reign of Edward II references appear to *secretum consilium* and *privatum consilium*, but, as in the case of the 'cabinet' later, the words convey a sinister meaning, and they are as far as possible avoided in the official documents[2]. The King might summon a secret council for some special purpose, but there was no regular institution of the nature of a 'privy' council, and the older *consilium regis* still held its position as the body on whose advice the Crown performed public acts. Even the familiar expression 'ordinary councillor' does not appear until the reign of Henry VIII[3]. The term 'privy council' is not employed until the reign of Henry VI, probably to emphasise the distinction between the inner body of sworn and paid councillors, and those nobles, lawyers, and others who were only occasionally summoned[4]. This view is supported by the appearance of special regulations for securing secrecy at the meetings of the Council, such as the Ordinance of 1426, which refers to the 'great inconveniences' ensuing from matters 'spoken and treated in the Council having been published and discovered,' and provides that 'from this time forward no person . . . be suffered to abide in the Council whiles matters of the said Council be treated therein, save only those that be sworn unto the said Council, but if they be specially called thereto by authority of the said Council.'[5]

§ 1. COMPOSITION AND PROCEDURE

The Council of Henry VII appears to have been an indeterminate body of shifting membership, consisting of those persons whom at any particular time he wished to consult. At his accession it consisted of a few members only[6], but the numbers soon increased. In 1486 those actually present varied from 22 to 33; by 1494 the attendance had risen to 39; and in 1501 there were as many as 41[7]. Besides those whose names are actually recorded, a number of men of inferior rank are referred to as *et ceteri*, and not all those present at the Council were sworn members of it.

Under Henry VIII the composition of the Council begins to be systematised. It had long been the custom for the King and his Court to move from place to place, and for a number of Councillors to follow in attendance upon him, but there were no definite regulations. The Council existed that it might advise the King, and its proceedings were governed by the King's convenience, and not by modern considerations of mechanical regularity. In 1526, however, the King, possibly influenced by the increasing volume of business at Westminster, which pointed to a division of labour, included in the Ordinances for the Household issued in that year an 'establishment

---

[1] Prothero, p. ci.   [2] Baldwin, p. 105.   [3] *Ib.* p. 114.
[4] Dicey, p. 43.   [5] *Ib.* p. 44.
[6] Henry VII's first Council consisted of five peers, two bishops, and nine other members (Baldwin, p. 435).   [7] *Ib.* p. 436.

of a Council' [p. 220]. This provided for a Council of twenty 'honourable, virtuous, sad, wise, expert, and discreet persons.' Of these, ten were required to 'give their continual attendance' 'unto what place soever his Highness shall resort,' and the other ten remained in London to transact that part of the Council business, and especially the judicial business, which could be most conveniently dealt with in the capital. The Council of twenty named in the Ordinances contained a large majority of officials[1]. The spiritual peers were represented by Cardinal Wolsey, and the Bishops of London, Lincoln, and Bath. The two parts of the Council were always in close correspondence, and sometimes they were reunited and sat as a single body. The first was known as the 'Council at Court' and the other as the 'King's Council in the Star Chamber,' but the term 'privy council' might be applied to both[2]. The limitation of the number of sworn privy councillors to twenty, did not prevent the summoning on occasion of 'ordinary councillors,' also sworn of the King's Council, but not of the Privy Council, and the judges and serjeants-at-law, who were not sworn of the Council, but were summoned to attend when legal help was required. The preponderance on the Council of the new official class who were superseding the great nobles in the work of administration was attacked by the insurgents in the Pilgrimage of Grace of 1536. They complained that the King 'takes of his Council and has about him persons of low birth and small reputation,' and some of them bound themselves by an oath 'to expulse all villain blood from the King's Grace and his Privy Council, for the common wealth and restoring of Christ's Church.'[3]

Until 1540 the materials for the history of the Council are scanty and difficult of interpretation, but in that year the new Council Register was begun and a clerk was appointed to keep it. This 'Book of the Council' was a record of the proceedings of that part of it only which followed the King's person, but its existence removes much of the uncertainty which had hitherto perplexed historians. Thus in August, 1540, when the new Register begins, the Council numbered nineteen[4], of whom no less than fifteen were officials, nine of these fifteen being great officers of state[5].

Under Edward VI the size of the Council was much increased. In 1553 the young King drew up 'A Method for the Proceedings in the Councils' [p. 221], which provided for a Council of forty persons. Of these, ten were great nobles; five were non-official members of a different kind—the Archbishop of Canterbury, two bishops, and two judges; fifteen were commoners of the official class; and the remaining ten were great officers of state. Thus, as under Henry VIII, the officials were in a clear majority. This increase in the size of the Council involved a change in the method of its procedure,

---

[1] See p. 220 below.   [2] Baldwin, p. 448.

[3] *Letters and Papers, Henry VIII*, xi, no. 892.

[4] The reason why the number is not the prescribed twenty is that the Lord Steward was also at that time Lord President of the Council, and served in a double capacity.

[5] The four non-official members were the Archbishop of Canterbury, the Earl of Hertford (afterwards the Protector Somerset), and the Bishops of Durham and Winchester, both eminent for their knowledge of the civil and canon law (Nicolas, vii, p. ix).

and it was now divided into five 'commissions' or committees[1]: (1) a judicial commission of ten 'for hearing of those suits which were wont to be brought to the whole Board'; (2) a commission of eleven for 'the calling of forfeits done against the laws,' and punishing breaches of proclamations; (3) a commission of twenty-one 'for the state,' on which the King himself was to sit; (4) a commission of seven to investigate the state of the Courts and to consider finance; and (5) a commission of three 'for the bulwarks.' This assignment of duties is followed by regulations as to procedure, but these are on the lines already laid down by earlier sovereigns.

At the accession of Mary the membership of the Council rose to forty-four, and of these a large proportion held no office, and were quite without experience[2]. A further specialisation of duties took place, and no less than ten[3] committees of Council were formed [p. 224]. Of these, four were concerned, directly or indirectly, with finance, and one was 'to consider what laws shall be established in this Parliament, and to name men that shall make the books thereof'; but the objects of all ten committees had a temporary character.

Elizabeth's first Council consisted of eighteen members only, but the subdivision of business among committees persisted. In 1558 five committees were set up [p. 224], but these were all temporary; although one of them, 'for consideration of all things necessary for the Parliament,' carries on from Mary's reign a piece of machinery that might very well be found of permanent value. Organisation by committees was so flexible that it could be easily adapted to the varying needs of different times.

Those members who were sworn of the King's Council had administered to them an oath of secrecy and allegiance, and this served as an indication of the duties of a Councillor. The Councillor's oath is first referred to in 1233, and the earliest form known is that of 1257[4]. The form used in 1570 is given on p. 225 below. The obligation of secrecy required of the modern cabinet depends mainly upon the oath taken by ministers in their capacity of Privy Councillors.

The office of President of the Council does not appear until 1497[5]. The ancient *Curia Regis* was presided over by the King himself, or in his absence by the Justiciar, and when the Justiciar ceased to be a political officer and became the head of the Court of King's Bench, his place for this purpose was taken by the Chancellor. When Fortescue in his scheme for a Council suggested that there should be 'an head or a chief to rule the Council... chosen by the King, having his office at the King's pleasure, which may then be called *Capitalis Consilarius*,'[6] he is probably thinking of the Chancellor, who 'when he is present may be president, and have the supreme rule of all

---

[1] Procedure by committees was not entirely new. On the judicial side the Council had appointed 'committees of examination' to prepare cases as early as the reign of Edward III (Baldwin, p. 300).

[2] 'In their counsel there was little wisdom, and in their multitude no safety' (Pollard, *Polit. Hist.* p. 95).

[3] Or eleven, if the Lord Admiral acting alone counts as a committee.

[4] Baldwin, p. 346.

[5] *Ib.* p. 445.

[6] p. 146.

the Council.'[1] The Tudors adopt Fortescue's suggestion of a president, but they create a new office for the purposes of the Council only, instead of accepting the head of an existing department, in spite of the fact that the Chancellor had the tradition of presidency behind him. This is another assertion of unfettered sovereign power.

The office of Clerk to the Council dates from 1405[2]. Before that time its clerical work was performed by one of the clerks of the privy seal assigned for the purpose and receiving extra pay for his services; but when a separate and permanent office was created it soon became one of great distinction and importance. The permanent salary of the office was only 40 marks a year, but this was supplemented by the fees of suitors and other perquisites, and as the volume of business increased it became very profitable. In 1483 a second Clerk to the Council was appointed[3], and in 1527 there was a Clerk of the Star Chamber also[4] (see p. 254 below). As this last official bore the title of Clerk of the Council of State, enjoyed a salary of 40 marks, and took precedence of the clerks of the Privy Council, he is, in all probability, the holder of the office created in 1405.

In Fortescue's time there was a regular scale of annual payments to Councillors dating from the reigns of Richard II and Henry IV—£200 for a duke or an archbishop, 200 marks for an earl or a bishop, £100 for a baron or a banneret, and £40 for an esquire[5]; but these were subject to a fine of so much a day for absence from the Council without reasonable cause. The Chancellor received £200 and the Treasurer 200 marks. Under the Tudors salaries were only paid in certain cases, and to men of lower rank; but the king rewarded laymen liberally with grants of land and ecclesiastics with church preferment[6]. Another inducement to regular attendance was the hospitality of the Court for those Councillors who followed the king's person; and the ample breakfasts and dinners occasionally served to the Council under the Lancastrians, which had disappeared during the Yorkist reigns, were revived by the Tudors[7].

In the thirteenth century the Council usually met in a small upper room near the receipt of the Exchequer, but in the reign of Edward III a new building was erected for their special use. It was within the precincts of the Palace of Westminster near the river bank, conveniently accessible to suitors whether they came by water or by land[8]. The ceiling of the room was decorated with stars, and from the first it was called the Star Chamber[9]. In this room most of the proceedings of the Council were taking place at the beginning of the Tudor period whenever it met at Westminster, and it continued to meet in the starred room from time to time during the reigns of

---

[1] Fortescue, p. 148; see also p. 300. It had been the case that some particular person was occasionally appointed 'chief Councillor,' but he did not necessarily preside at the Council, and this title of dignity had little in common with the office of President of the Council created by Henry VII (Baldwin, p. 369).

[2] Baldwin, p. 366.   [3] *Ib.* p. 435.

[4] *Ib.* p. 449 *n.* See also Lord Burghley's speech, quoted on p. 250 below.

[5] Fortescue, p. 302.   [6] Baldwin, pp. 452–3.   [7] *Ib.* p. 362.

[8] *Ib.* p. 355; and Stephen, i, 168.

[9] For the alternative explanations see pp. 286, 293 below, but these need not be seriously considered.

Henry VIII, Edward VI, Mary, and Elizabeth[1]. In the first instance, therefore, the Star Chamber is not a court or a tribunal, but simply a Council room. But the Council often met elsewhere. In the fifteenth century it sometimes met at the Black Friars, and also in private houses[2]. In 1540 it met on one occasion at the Duke of Suffolk's house[3], and frequently at Windsor, Greenwich, and Hampton Court. On 3 February, 1547, the oaths to Edward VI were to be taken at the Star Chamber, but the same page in the Register refers to a Council Chamber in the Tower[4]. On 31 January and 7 February, 1550, the Council sits in the Star Chamber, but on 1 February it meets 'in the Withdrawing Chamber next to the Parliament Chamber in the old Palace.'[5] As part of it followed the King on his royal progresses, meetings were also held away from London, wherever the King happened to be[6].

(1) Council Ordinances of Henry VIII, 1526

ESTABLISHMENT OF A COUNCIL

...Cap. 74. And to the intent that as well matters of justice and complaints touching the griefs of the King's subjects and disorder of his realm and otherwise which shall fortune to be made, brought, and presented unto his Highness by his said subjects in his demur[7] or passing from place to place within the same, as also other great occurrences concerning his own particular affairs, may be the better ordered and with his Grace more ripely debated, digested, and resolved from time to time as the case shall require; it is ordered and appointed by his Highness that a good number of honourable, virtuous, sad, wise, expert, and discreet persons of his Council shall give their attendance upon his most royal person, whose names hereafter follow, that is to say

[Here follow 20 names, beginning with 'the Lord Cardinal, Chancellor of England,' and including the Lord Treasurer, the Keeper of the Privy Seal, the Marshal, the Steward of the Household, the Lord Chamberlain, the Treasurer of the Household, the Comptroller, the King's Secretary, the Chancellor of the Duchy of Lancaster (Sir Thomas More), the Dean of the King's Chapel, the Treasurer of the King's Chamber, the Vice-Chamberlain, and the Captain of the Guard. Thus out of the total number of 20, no less than 14 are officials.]

Cap. 75. And forasmuch as the said Lord Cardinal, the Lord Treasurer of England, Lord Privy Seal, Lord Steward, and divers other lords and personages before mentioned, by reason of their attendance at the terms for administration of justice, and exercising of their offices, and other reasonable impediments, shall

---

[1] Dasent, *passim*.   [2] Baldwin, p. 358.   [3] Nicolas, vii, 89.
[4] Dasent, ii, 8.   [5] *Ib.* ii, 376, 377, and 385.
[6] For instance, in 1540 Councils were held successively at Reading, Ewelme, Rycote, Notley, Buckingham, Grafton, Ampthill, Dunstable, and St Albans. On a southern royal progress in 1541 they were held at Dartford, Rochester, Sittingbourne, Canterbury, and Dover (Nicolas, vii *passim*).
[7] Stay, residence.

many seasons fortune to be absent from the King's Court, and specially in the term times; to the intent the King's Highness shall not be at any season unfurnished of an honourable presence of Councillors about his Grace, with whom his Highness may confer upon the premises at his pleasure, it is ordered that the persons hereafter mentioned shall give their continual attendance in the causes of his said Council unto what place soever his Highness shall resort; that is to say, the Lord Chamberlain, the Bishop of Bath, the Treasurer and Comptroller of the King's Household, the Secretary, the Chancellor of the Duchy of Lancaster, the Dean of the King's Chapel, the Vice-Chamberlain, the Captain of the Guard, and for ordering of poor men's complaints and causes, Dr Wolman.

And because, per case, it may chance some of these afore-named persons to be absent for some reasonable cause, be it always provided and foreseen that either the Bishop of Bath, the Secretary, Sir Thomas More, and the Dean of the Chapel, or two of them at the least, always be present, except the King's Grace give licence to any of them of the contrary; which said Councillors being appointed for continual attendance shall apply themselves effectually, diligently, uprightly, and justly in the premises, being every day in the forenoon by ten of the clock at the furthest, and at afternoon by two of the clock, in the King's Dining Chamber, or in such other place as shall fortune to be appointed for the Council chamber, there to be in readiness, not only in case the King's pleasure shall be to commune or confer with them upon any cause or matter, but also for hearing and direction of poor men's complaints on matters of justice; which direction well observed, the King's Highness shall always be well furnished of an honourable presence of Councillors about his Grace, as to his high honour doth appertain....

Ordinances for the Royal Household (Society of Antiquaries, 1790), p. 159.

(2) Council Ordinances of Edward VI, 1553

A Method for the Proceedings in the Councils...[1]

The Names of the whole Council

[Here follow 40 names, beginning with 'the Bishop of Canterbury,' and including the Lord Chancellor, the Lord Treasurer, the Lord Privy Seal, the Lord Admiral, the Lord Chamberlain, 'Mr Comptroller,' 'Mr Treasurer' (of the Household), 'Mr Vice-Chamberlain,' two King's Secretaries, and 'Mr Solicitor,' as well as two other bishops and two judges.]

[1] The first part of the document is written in King Edward's own hand.

The Councillors above-named to be thus divided into several Commissions and Charges

First. For hearing of those suits which were wont to be brought to the whole Board.

[10 names, including the Lord Privy Seal, the Lord Chamberlain, the Bishop of London, and two Masters of Requests.]

Those persons to hear the suits, to answer the parties, to make certificate what suits they think meet to be granted; and upon answer received of their certificate received to dispatch the parties: Also to give full answer of denial to those suits that be not reasonable nor convenient: Also to dispatch all matters of justice, and to send to the common courts those suits that be for them.

[Second.] The calling of forfeits done against the laws, for punishing the offenders and breakers of proclamations that now stand in force.

[11 names, including the Lord Privy Seal, the Lord Chamberlain, 'Mr Solicitor,' and Mr Secretary Petre.]

These shall first see what laws penal and what proclamations standing now in force are most meet to be executed, and shall bring a certificate thereof. Then they shall enquire in the countries how they are disobeyed, and first shall begin with the greatest offenders, and so afterward punish the rest, according to the pains set forth. They shall receive also the letters out of the shires of disorders there done, and punish the offenders.

[Third.]   *For the State*

[21 names, including 'the Bishop of Canterbury,' the Lord Chancellor, the Lord Treasurer, the Lord Privy Seal, the Lord Admiral, the Lord Chamberlain, 'Mr Vice-Chamberlain,' and 'Mr Treasurer and Comptroller.']

These to attend to matters of the state. I will sit with them once a week to hear the debating of things of most importance.

[Fourth.] These persons underwritten shall look to the state of all the Courts, especially of the new erected Courts, as the Augmentation, the First Fruits and Tithes, the Wards; and shall see the revenues answered at the half-year's end, and shall consider with what superfluous charges they be burdened, and thereof shall make a certificate which they shall deliver.

[7 names, including the Lord Chamberlain and the Bishop of Norwich.]

I understand it is a member of the Commission that followeth, but yet those shall do well to do it for the present, because the other shall have no leisure till they have called in the debts; after which done they may sit with them.

Those that now be in Commission for the Debts to take accompts of all payments since the 35th of the King that dead is, after that they have done this Commission they are now in hand with[1].

[Fifth.] Likewise for the Bulwarks, the Lord Chamberlain, Mr Treasurer, and Mr Comptroller to be in Commission in their several jurisdictions.

The rest of the Council, some go home to their countries straight after the Parliament, some be sore sick that they shall not be able to attend anything, which when they come they shall be admitted of the Council. Also that these Councils sit apart. . . .

15 January, 1552[-3]

Certain Articles devised and delivered by the King's Majesty for the quicker, better, and more orderly dispatch of Causes by his Majesty's Privy Council

. . .9. That none of them depart his Court for longer than two days without there be left here at the least eight of the Council, and that not without giving notice thereof to the King's Majesty.

10. That they shall make no manner of assembly or meeting in Council without there be to the number of four at the least.

11. Furthermore, if they be assembled to the number of four and under the number of six, then they shall reason and debate things, examine all inconveniences and dangers and also commodities on each side; make those things plain which seem diffuse at the first opening; and if they agree amongst themselves, then at the next full assembly of six they shall make a perfect conclusion and end with them.

12. Also if there rise such matter of weight as it shall please the King's Majesty himself to be at the debating of, then warning shall be given, whereby the more may be at the debating of it. . . .

. . .15. In matters that be long, tedious, and busy there may be appointed or chosen two or three, more or less as the case shall seem to require, to prepare, set forth, and make plain the matters and to bring report thereof, whereby the things being less cumbrous and diffuse may the easilier be dispatcht. . . .

. . .18. That no private suit be intermeddled with the great affairs, but heard on the Mondays before.

19. If there be under four and a matter of expedition arise,

---

[1] The sense of these two paragraphs appears to be that a sixth Commission 'for the debts' was already in being, and that this, as soon as its special work was finished, was to amalgamate with the Commission for the Courts, the business of both being mainly financial.

they shall declare it to the King's Majesty and before him debate it, but not send answer without it require wonderful haste.

Burnet, *History of the Reformation*, Pt II, Bk. i, no. 6.

(3) Committees of the Council under Mary, 1554

At Westminster, 23 February, 1554

...The names of all such as be appointed for the purposes following:

To call in the debts and provide for money [4 names].

To give order for supply of all wants at Calais, Guisnes, and other pieces of those Marches; to give like order for Berwick and other places upon the Borders of the North; to give the like order for Ireland, Portsmouth, the Isle of Wight, and the islands [9 names].

To give order for the ships, and to appoint captains and others to serve on them: 'My Lord Admiral.'

To give order for victuals necessary to be sent to Calais, Berwick, etc. [3 names].

To consider what laws shall be established in this Parliament, and to name men that shall make the books thereof [7 names].

To appoint men to continue in the examination of the prisoners [no names given].

To consider what lands shall be sold, and who shall be in commission for that purpose [no names given].

To moderate the excessive charges: My Lord Steward, etc., for the Household; My Lord Chamberlain, etc., for the Chamber.

To consider the patents and annuities payable in sundry places, so as the same may be paid all in one place [6 names].

To appoint a Council to attend and remain at London [6 names, including the Lieutenant of the Tower].

To give order for the furniture and victualling of the said Tower: The men aforesaid to give order.

Dasent, *Acts of the Privy Council*, iv, 397.

(4) Committees of the Council under Elizabeth, 1558

At Westminster, 23 December, 1558

For care of the North parts towards Scotland and Berwick [6 names].

To survey the office of the Treasurer of the Chamber, and to assign order of payment [4 names].

For Portsmouth and the Isle of Wight [7 names].

For consideration of all things necessary for the Parliament [7 names].

To understand what lands have been granted from the Crown in the late Queen's time [5 names].

Dasent, *Acts of the Privy Council*, vii, 27.

(5) The Oath of a Privy Councillor, 1570[1]

You shall swear to be a true and faithful councillor to the Queen's Majesty as one of her Highness's Privy Council. You shall not know or understand of any manner thing to be attempted, done, or spoken against her Majesty's person, honour, crown, or dignity royal, but you shall let and withstand the same to the uttermost of your power, and either do or cause it to be forthwith revealed either to her Majesty's self or to the rest of her Privy Council. You shall keep secret all matters committed and revealed to you as her Majesty's councillor or that shall be treated of secretly in council. And if any of the same treaties or counsels shall touch any other of the councillors, you shall not reveal the same to him, but shall keep the same until such time as by the consent of her Majesty or of the rest of the Council publication shall be made thereof. You shall not let to give true, plain, and faithful counsel at all times, without respect either of the cause or of the person, laying apart all favour, meed, affection, and partiality. And you shall to your uttermost bear faith and true allegiance to the Queen's Majesty, her heirs and lawful successors, and shall assist and defend all jurisdictions, preeminences, and authorities granted to her Majesty and annexed to her Crown against all foreign princes, persons, prelates, or potentates, whether by Act of Parliament or otherwise. And generally in all things you shall do as a faithful and true councillor ought to do to her Majesty. So help you God and the holy contents of this book.

State Papers (Domestic), Eliz. lxxxiii, 33.

§ 2. BUSINESS OF THE COUNCIL

It was not the case that the Tudor Council, like the modern Cabinet, had a right to deal with all important matters of state. The Tudors were their own ministers, and decisions on vital questions, and especially on questions of foreign policy, were often taken by the Sovereign without consulting the Council at all. Nor were individual ministers always consulted. Wolsey, and afterwards Cromwell, exercised more influence over Henry VIII, and Burghley and Walsingham over Elizabeth, than any other ministers, but in some cases the royal decision was reached alone.

Nevertheless, the amount of business which came before the Council was enormous, and its variety bewildering[2]. In the Registers for the reign

---

[1] Compare the modern form of the oath, printed in Anson, II, i, 138.
[2] See Prothero, p. ci.

of Henry VIII this falls into five main groups of affairs[1]: the English Pale in France, the Scottish Border, the guardianship of the Narrow Seas, the regulation of trade[2], and finance. After the loss of Calais the first of these disappears, but the increasing volume of the other business more than compensates for this. These are great matters, but it is also the case that nothing was too small for the Council to consider. It surveyed the whole field of administration, and even penetrated into private life. At the beginning of the reign of Elizabeth, especially, much time was absorbed by private quarrels and matrimonial disputes[3], and modern legislation concerning judicial separation was anticipated by Tudor administrative action. Illustrations from the Register of the range of Council interference are given on pp. 229–31 below. The Council also possessed an extensive judicial authority, which was exercised under the name of the Council Table.

The supreme judicial power of the King in Council, dating from a time before the Courts of Law by a differentiation of function had grown out of the ancient *Curia Regis* [pp. 288–9], was carefully reserved through all the changes and developments of the Middle Ages. This jurisdiction had been made a subject of complaint by the House of Commons, and petitions against it were frequently presented, especially in the reign of Edward III; but the principal grievance was the interference of the Council in causes properly cognisable in the Courts of Common Law. Redress given by the Council in cases where it could not be obtained in the ordinary courts was regarded differently. The common law had dangerous defects[4], and in the view of those times it was the positive duty of the King in Council to provide a remedy[5]. Thus in the fourteenth and fifteenth centuries the Council jurisdiction was recognised and supported by Parliament. An Act of 1363[6] provides that persons offending against the Statutes of Provisors and Praemunire are to be 'presented to the King and his Council.' An Act of 1388[7] assigns to it the punishment of justices of the peace who do not hold quarter-sessions for the enforcement of the Statutes of Labourers. Acts of 1411[8] and 1414[9] support its jurisdiction over riots; and an Act of 1453[10] admits the lawfulness of writs directing persons guilty of 'great riots, extortions, oppressions, and grievous offences' to appear before it. Thus the Council

---

[1] Dasent, I, p. xviii.

[2] This, in particular, occupied an immense amount of the Council's time and attention.

[3] Dasent, VII, p. xxvi.

[4] Maitland (pp. 218–19) points out that the procedure of the common law courts was extremely formal, so there were advantages about a tribunal like the Council, which was not fettered by narrow rules. They were also incompetent to punish offences which fell short of felony, such as interference by violence or bribery with the ordinary course of justice. 'It was...felt,' he adds, 'that there were men who were too big for any court but the Council; they would bribe jurors and even judges;...there were men whom no jury would convict.'

[5] 'Shall no help at all be sought for at the hands of the King, when it cannot be found in the common law? That were to stop his ears at the cry of the oppressed, and would draw wrath and punishment from Heaven' (Lambarde, printed on p. 285 below).

[6] 38 Edw. III, st. 2, c. 1.

[7] 12 Rich. II, c. 10.

[8] 13 Henr. IV, c. 7.

[9] 2 Henr. V, st. 1, c. 8.

[10] 31 Henr. VI, c. 2.

jurisdiction as recognised by statute covered wide ground. Further, the rules for the management of causes by the Council, adopted in 1430 with the approval of the Lords and Commons, provide 'that all bills that comprehend matters terminable at the common law shall be remitted there to be determined, but if[1] so be that the discretion of the Council feel too great might on that one party and unmight on that other, or else causes reasonable that shall move them.'[2] In the fifteenth century the Council was overwhelmed with judicial business and possessed the largest powers for dealing with it. Offenders could be summoned before it, fined, imprisoned, and sentenced to the pillory. The legal machinery was fully developed, but the trouble was that it was not effectively employed against great persons. During the reign of Henry VI there is scarcely an instance of a great lord being punished by the Council for a breach of the statutes against maintenance[3]. Where the Tudors differ from the Lancastrians is not that they possessed larger legal powers, by that they used their legal powers with energy and courage against great offenders.

The 'Book of Entries' begins in 1485, and four-fifths of its contents relate to prosecutions and suits[4]. Some of these represent Star Chamber business, but the book is a Council Book, and not a book of Star Chamber decrees. The new Council Register which begins in 1540 shews that the Privy Council attending the King's person, although its character was largely political and administrative, still occupied itself with treason, riots, and breaches of the peace. Mercantile cases, country quarrels, and disputes about land are frequently referred to the Council, probably in order to save the expense of protracted lawsuits, and these would either be determined at the Table, or more often remitted to arbitrators[5]. In dealing with them the power to bind over the parties in recognisances beforehand to accept an award was of the greatest service. As a rule the Council declined to use its equitable jurisdiction in matters determinable by the ordinary courts of law [p 243], but in spite of this it was so 'troubled and pestered' with private suitors that in 1589 special arrangements were made for its relief [p. 243]. Causes 'between party and party' were still, nevertheless, a most important branch of the Council's activities as late as 1603[6]. It also dealt with recusants[7] and political prisoners, and investigated cases of forgery, perjury, and libel.

The Council always acted with promptitude against what were called 'lewd and naughty words'—perhaps the sixteenth-century equivalent of modern political criticism. It was ready to investigate any accusation, however trivial, which could possibly be construed into disaffection to the King. This readiness to receive accusations encouraged the practice of delation,

---

[1] 'But if' = 'unless.'   [2] Nicolas, iv, 60.

[3] Baldwin, p. 305.

[4] *Ib.* p. 437: see also p. 252 below. Extracts from the 'Book of Entries' are printed in Scofield, pp. 6–8, 16–24.

[5] Dasent, xiv, p. xxxii; xv, p. xxxvi; xx, p. xviii; xxi, p. xxxiii; xxii, p. xxxiv.

[6] E.H.R. xxxiv, 589.

[7] Dasent, xviii, pp. xxvii and 414–17. A code of regulations for recusants confined in the Bishop's Palace at Ely and the castle of Banbury, was approved by the Council and entered in the Register.

and cases are on record in which innocent men were charged by their private enemies out of sheer malice[1]; but in dealing with these the Tudor Councils were on the whole remarkably painstaking and fair, although they could not compensate the victims for the trouble and expense to which they were put by the necessity of meeting accusations. Extracts from the Council Register illustrating the range of their judicial activity are printed on pp. 229–242 below.

The use of torture was unknown to the common law of England, except for refusal to plead[2], but it was a recognised prerogative of the King in Council, and orders to torture occur not infrequently in the Council Register [pp. 241–2].

Two points of judicial procedure call for special notice. (1) In some cases the Council, after a preliminary enquiry, would commission persons in the locality to investigate and proceed further, thus delegating their powers for a particular purpose [pp. 232–4]; while other cases would be referred by them to the more public and formal Court of Star Chamber [p. 247]. (2) In 1540 a Commission under the Great Seal was issued to the Council, 'whereby in matters touching the King, they and every of them should have authority to take recognisance of such as appear before them.'[3] This power of taking recognisances was freely used, not only for purposes of bail or of binding men over to keep the peace or to appear in the Star Chamber[4], but also to compel them to do or abstain from doing almost any kind of act[5] [p. 231].

The Council also exercised supreme authority over the Council Courts. It was an ancient legal maxim that 'the King of England never did nor doth grant any jurisdiction to any court in his dominions, but so as he still retaineth in himself and his Council attendant upon his person a supereminent authority and jurisdiction over them all.' Thus in 1559 the Council of Wales was ordered to send up certain principal offenders for trial in London; in 1587 the Lord Deputy of Ireland was required by the Council to liberate a victim of arbitrary imprisonment there[6]; and in 1588 the proceedings of the Irish Castle Chamber were brought under review [p. 240]. Appeals from the Courts of the Channel Islands were also heard by the Council[7].

The rules for the distribution of their judicial business by the Council are given in Dr John Herbert's memorandum printed on p. 247 below.

[1] Nicolas, vii, p. xxvii.

[2] On *peine forte et dure* see Pollock and Maitland, ii, 651–2; see also ii, 659–60.

[3] Nicholas, vii, 27.   [4] Dasent, i, 380; v, 71–2.

[5] 'Disputes between private individuals, between members of corporations, between the City and the University of Oxford, questions as to the legality of captures at sea, as to the ownership of property supposed to belong to the enemy whether French or Scottish, applications for privateering licenses, infractions of trade regulations, charges of rioting in the City, the liability of a gaoler for the escape of a prisoner, commercial disputes of all kinds, and even questions as to the interpretation of the Scriptures, resulted in the binding in recognisances of those who appeared before the Council, with or without sureties, either to obey the decision of the Council or to be ready to appear again before a given date' (Dasent, i, p. xviii).

[6] Percy, p. 46   [7] Dasent, xv, p. xxxv.

(1) Henry VII's Council

...Justice was well administered in his time, save where the King was party; save also that the Council Table intermeddled too much with *meum* and *tuum*. For it was a very court of justice during his time; especially in the beginning....

Bacon, Works (ed. Spedding), vi, 239.

(2) Extracts from the Council Register, 1540–1603

(1) *Personal quarrels*

[At Windsor, 22 November, 1540]

...Sir John Done, knight, and Thomas Holcroft, esquire, were set at one and made friends by arbitrament of the Council; the same judging Sir John Done to pay unto the said Holcroft for amends 100 marks....

The matter between David Vincent and Richard Cecil of the Wardrobe was heard, and after that Robert Browne and Miles Forest, which were sent for concerning the said matter, had deposed what they knew in the same, it appeared that Cecil had used himself evil in the matter, and thereupon giving him an honest monition for his fault, exhorted as well the said Cecil as the said Vincent to be friends, and so dismissed them....

Nicolas, Ordinances of the Privy Council (1834–7), vii, 87.

(2) *Matrimonial disputes*

[At Westminster, 10 March, 1542]

...Upon an humble petition made and exhibited by Joan Bulmer, wife to [John] Bulmer, esquire, that where the said [John] Bulmer enjoyed by the said Joan Bulmer his wife one hundred mark by year, and upon none occasion refusing her company, thereof allowed her nothing, an order was taken by the Council that forasmuch as the said [John] Bulmer alleged himself to be far indebted, he should the Monday next ensuing the date hereof bring and present to the Council the particulars of the same. And nevertheless it was ordained that he should permit the said Joan Bulmer his wife to sojourn for one year at her brother's house...allowing her for the said year 20 marks for her board and 20 other marks for her necessary expenses. And in case he should during the said term haunt and resort to her, and use her after such a convenient sort as it behoveth an honest man to use his wife, then upon relation made of the same at the year's end, an order should be taken as well for the release of the payment of this said money to her as to have her, and to appoint her for her demur[1] where he should think good.

[At Westminster, 3 April, 1542]

...John Bulmer, esquire, for his wilful disobeying of an order taken between him and his wife by the Council, was committed to the Fleet.

Nicolas, vii, 321 and 333.

(3) *Minor administrative business*

[At Hampton Court, 1 March, 1541]

...A letter was sent to — Malt, the King's tailor, to provide at convenient prices and make meet for the Lord Lisle, which remaineth at this time prisoner in the Tower, these parcels of apparel and other necessaries, and thereupon to bring unto the said Council a note of all particulars with the prices of the same, to the intent a warrant might be made for repayment unto him of the same.

In primis, a large gown of damask furred with black coney.

Item, a long nightgown of cloth at 10s. the yard furred with black lamb and faced with budge[2].

Item, two jackets, one of damask, another of satin.

Item, two doublets of satin.

Item, four pair of hose.

Item, six pair of shoes and one pair of slippers.

Item, four shirts.

Item, two nightcaps of velvet and satin.

Item, two upper caps of cloth.

Item, two night-kerchiefs....

Nicolas, vii, 146.

[At Greenwich, 14 May, 1546]

...A letter to the Vice-Chancellor of Cambridge, signifying the despatch unto him of Maxwell that took the Master of Peterhouse's horse, and his and his master's punishment for that act, and contempt in not obeying the Lord Chancellor's letter, being therefore both of them committed to the Counter for a season; and further the Vice-Chancellor was required to see the said Maxwell, if the horse was anything the worse, to make recompense therefore, and to advertise hither thereof accordingly....

Dasent, *Acts of the Privy Council*, i, 416.

[At Greenwich, 15 June, 1546]

...A letter to the Commissioners for the Contribution in Cambridgeshire to surcease from pressing the scholars of Cam-

---

[1] Place of residence.   [2] Lamb-skin fur.

bridge to the same, considering none of them might by his living in the University there despend £10 by the year, which was under the rates in their commission limited.... Dasent, i, 454.

(4) *Recognisances*

[At More Park, Hertfordshire, 7 October, 1540]

Recognisances were taken in £40 of three Hertfordshire yeomen, to observe the following condition:

...The condition of this recognisance is that if the foresaid John Butler do abstain at all time and times from taking or killing in any manner place within the King's realm of England any partridges and pheasants with any nets, setters[1], horses, trammels[2], or other gins, that then, etc.... Nicolas, vii, 56.

[At St James's, 20 July, 1558]

...The condition of this recognisance[3] is such that if the above-bounden Lord Latymer do make his continual attendance upon the Lords of the Council and not depart before licence given unto him by the Lord Chancellor or the rest of the Council, and do also make no part or portion of his land away, neither bestow any of his daughters in marriage, without the Queen's Majesty's special licence so to do, then this recognisance to be void and of none effect, or else, etc.... Dasent, vi, 349.

(5) *Treason*

[At Greenwich, 13 April, 1590]

In this case the Council orders a preliminary examination by the President of the Council of the North, and then takes the case into its own hands for further proceedings.

...A letter to the Earl of Huntingdon, that whereas certain articles had been exhibited unto the Queen's Majesty containing matter of treason and other heinous crimes wherewith Ralph Tankerd, of Arden in the county of York, his sons, servants, and others of his confederacy stand charged, as might appear by the enclosed informations, his Lordship is prayed and required to call before him the said malefactors and to examine the particular points of their accusation, and in case the allegations should appear to be true, and that the same were not prosecuted only of malice to defame the said persons, without any good pretence

---

[1] Nets or traps for catching birds.   [2] Fowling-nets.
[3] The recognisance was in the large sum of 10,000 marks.

whereupon the informations were grounded, then to see the offenders to be forthcoming, and with convenient expedition to certify their Lordships of his travail and the effects thereof, together with the names of the delinquents and the offences by them committed, to the intent they may be proceeded withal according to their deserts....   Dasent, xix, 54.

[6 October, 1598]

In this case the accused actually appears before the Council.

A letter of warrant to Sir John Peyton, knight, Lieutenant of the Tower of London. Whereas one Richard Rolles hath been brought before us for matter of treason wherewith he is charged in such manner as that there is great presumption of his guiltiness, we have therefore thought good to commit him prisoner under your custody to the Tower, and have herewithal sent him unto you under safe guard, requiring you to keep him close prisoner there until you shall receive farther direction from us in that behalf, and this shall be your sufficient warrant....

Dasent, xxix, 219.

(6) *Riot*

[27 August, 1548]

The Council usually proceeded by delegation when dealing with riots, but in this case it acts directly.

...Upon complaint made by Sir Thomas Wrothe, knight, of a riot made against him and his men by divers of the parish of Enfield, certain of the same parish that were the chief authors of the riot were sent for, who being arrived at the Court at Oatlands, and being heard in the Council Chamber there before the Lord Protector's Grace and Council, forasmuch as it did appear to his Grace and Lordships that the matter being between the said Sir Thomas and parishioners in controversy was before that accorded between them in the Duchy Chamber by Sir William Paget, Knight of the Order, Chancellor[1], and the rest of the Council of the same Duchy, and recorded in the same Chamber in writing by an Act and Decree passed upon their making; it was decreed by his Grace and their Lordships that the parties should be referred to the same Decree of the Duchy and should stand thereunto, and that Thomas Asplin [*and others*]...should, as the chief authors of the riot, be committed to prison, and moreover Edmund Moodam [*and others*]...should be bound to the peace,

---

[1] Sir William Paget, afterwards Lord Paget of Beaudesert, had been appointed Chancellor of the Duchy of Lancaster, 1 July, 1547.

and to appear in the Duchy Chamber the first of the next term
to abide such further order as should be then taken for them.

Dasent, ii, 219.

[At Westminster, 31 June, 1571]

In this case the riot is referred by the Council to the Council of the Welsh
Marches.

A letter to the Vice-President and Council in the Marches of
Wales, understanding lately of a great riot and assault made in
the town of Bromyard upon the Bishop of Hereford's officers and
servants, and that the offenders therein be of such insolency as
the Bishop, being lord of the said town, cannot reform the same
but is made afraid to see redress, and, as their Lordships are
informed, dare not well without a great guard travel from his
dwelling-house; for the better meeting of the same they are required to give order that the principal offenders be apprehended
and committed to prison, and thereupon appointing a private
sessions, if the time of their general sessions be not near, to cause
the riot to be enquired of, and to proceed with all due severity
and by corporal punishment and fines, according to the quality
of their offence....

Dasent, viii, 33.

[At Westminster, 9 February, 1558]

This case illustrates delegation to a particular person, who is given full power
to act.

...A letter to the Earl of Shrewsbury, that where a notable
disorder and riot hath been of late committed by one William
Gascoyne of Gawthorpe, who with 12 other persons in his company came to the house of Piers Stanley, presently serving under
the Earl of Westmorland, and there did sore wound one Thomas
Writte, brother to the wife of the said Piers, which disorder he
is willed to examine, and to see the offenders herein punished
according to justice and the qualities of their offences....

Dasent, vi, 265.

[At Greenwich, 30 July, 1581]

This is a typical case of delegation to a few local magnates.

A letter to [Sir] Robert Wingfield, Sir Robert Jermyn, Sir
Nicholas Bacon, knights, Richard Wingfield, Bassingbourn
Gaudy, and John Rivett, esquires, and to any five, four, or three
of them, touching certain outrages and notorious riots committed
by John Crisp, William Bugge, William Barrett, etc., upon certain grounds called the Denes, lying in Gunton in the county of
Suffolk; they are required to call before them and examine the
parties offenders, and such others as they shall think good, for

understanding of the truth of the matter, and to certify the same unto their Lordships, and further to remove the force, if he shall find any there, according to the statute in that behalf....

Dasent, xiii, 143.

(7) Breach of the peace
[At St James's, 1 April, 1543]

The Earl of Surrey being sent for to appear before the Council, was charged by the said presence as well of eating of flesh[1] as of a lewd and unseemly manner of walking in the night about the streets and breaking with stone-bows[2] of certain windows. And touching the eating of flesh, he alleged a licence, albeit he had not so secretly used the same as appertained. And touching the stone-bows, he could not deny but he had very evil done therein[3], submitting himself therefore to such punishment as should to them be thought good. Whereupon he was committed to the Fleet....

Dasent, i, 104.

(8) Assault
[At Greenwich, 4 April, 1546]

...Robert Bonham...for the striking of a priest, and evil behaving of himself in that act, was brought before the Council and admonished of his fault, and recommitted to the Fleet till another season....

[At Westminster, 11 April, 1546]

...This day was Robert Bonham dismissed of his imprisonment of the Fleet, after admonition given unto him for his better behaviour hereafter, and to the end some penalty might make him the warer how to attempt any like deed, it was awarded he should forthwith pay unto the priest for a recompense of his hurt five marks sterling, and to the King's Majesty by way of a fine ten pounds...and further John Maxie and Reignold Hollingworth, gentlemen, were either of them bound in one hundred pounds sterling by recognisance, whereof the condition was that if the said Robert Bonham did keep the peace against all persons, specially against the priest,...between this and the first day of

---

[1] In Lent.   [2] A cross-bow or catapult for shooting stones.

[3] The Earl of Surrey's defence was at any rate ingenious. Observing the corrupt and licentious manners of the citizens, and the deaf ears they turned to the remonstrances of their spiritual pastors, 'I went,' he said, 'at midnight through the streets and shot from my cross-bow at their windows, that the stones, passing noiseless through the air and breaking in suddenly upon their guilty secrecy, might remind them of the suddenness of that punishment which the Scriptures tell us Divine Justice will inflict upon impenitent sinners and so lead them to reformation' (*Archaeologia*, xxv, 382).

Midsummer Term next, and then present himself before the King's Majesty's Council in the Star Chamber and not depart from thence till he shall be dismissed...then, etc., or else, etc.

Dasent, i, 367, 379.

(9) *Seditious words*
[At Westminster, 18 March, 1541]

...Whereas Thomas Dawes, of Ildersley in the county of Derby, labourer, had accused Sir Robert Moore, priest, parson of Bradley in the said county, and a certain woman being in house with the said priest, of sundry heinous and traitorous words supposed by the said Thomas to have been spoken by the said priest and woman, and thereupon certain letters were written from Hampton Court the 3rd of this present to the Earl of Shrewsbury to apprehend the said parties and to examine the matter. Forasmuch it appeareth by the answer of the said Earl and the examinations taken by him that the priest and woman were in no wise culpable of such things as were laid to their charge, the said Earl was required by another letter not only to discharge the said priest and woman in case there could be no further evidence brought against them for the proofs of such matter as was objected unto them, but also to cause the said Thomas Dawes openly in the parish church of the said priest to ask him forgiveness upon his knees, acknowledging that he had falsely and maliciously slandered them; and if he refused so to do, then to cause him to be set upon the pillory the next market day, in example of such malicious, false knaves as might hereafter attempt to do the semblable....

Nicolas, vii, 158.

[At London, 20 December, 1541]

...Sir Robert Welle, curate of Cole church, accused by two several witnesses for the wreaching of the 8th chapter of Daniel to his own imagination, and expounding the same as written of the King's person[1], lewdly and traitorously, therein depraving his Majesty's godly proceedings, duly and evidently convinced[2] thereof, was committed to the Tower.

Nicolas, vii, 285.

(10) *Malicious accusation*
[At Westminster, 25 November, 1541]

...Whereas John Cheyney, son and heir of Sir Thomas Cheyney, Lord Warden of the Five Ports, upon a displeasure

---

[1] 'And in the latter time of their kingdom, when the transgressors are come to the full, a king of fierce countenance, and understanding dark sentences, shall stand up...and shall destroy the mighty and the holy people' (Daniel, viii, 23, 24).

[2] Convicted.

came before the Council, there accusing his said father of treason, and examined of the particularities of the same could allege none other thing but that he had images in his chapel; for that it was thought this accusation proceeded rather of pride than of any just matter, for an example he was committed to the Tower.

Nicolas, vii, 273.

(11) *Maintaining suits*
[At Grafton, 20 July, 1541]

...Nicholas Wentworth, of Livingstone in the county of Northampton, gentleman, exhibited a supplication as well against William Poyner of the said town, yeoman, accusing him to be a procurer of perjury, and a great embracer[1], and maintainer[2] of brabbling matters and suits... whereupon the said Poyner, being convinced by the deposition of sundry witnesses to be guilty of the said crimes, was committed to the porter's ward, and for his further punishment adjudged to be set upon the pillory at Northampton, Stamford, Oxford, and Aylesbury at four several market days, with a paper written in great letters declaring the cause of his punishment....

Nicolas, vii, 217.

(12) *Religious offences*
[At St James's, 5 April, 1543]

...Sir John Clere, [William] Stafford, esquire, Thomas Clere, and — Husey were committed to the Fleet for eating of flesh upon Good Friday....

[At Westminster, 19 April, 1543]

...Whereas Sir John Clere [etc.]...were committed unto the Fleet for eating flesh upon Good Friday last past, there to be kept two and two in a chamber without any farther liberty, this day it was ordered that they should have the liberty of the garden....

Dasent, i, 106 and 114.

[At St James's, 10 April, 1543]

...Certain joiners, to the number of 20, having made a disguising[3] upon the Sunday morning, without respect either of the day or the order which was known openly the King's Highness intended to take for the repressing of plays, were therefore committed to ward, and bestowed some in the Tower, some in Newgate, and some in the Gatehouse....

Dasent, i, 109.

---

[1] See note on p. 258 below.
[2] One who unlawfully supports a suit in which he is not concerned.
[3] A mask or masquerade.

[At St James's, 7 June, 1546]

...Lanam, a prophesier, was committed this day to the Tower for prophesying according to Weston's and Barker's depositions, and a letter was addressed to the Lieutenant for his safe keeping there accordingly.

Dasent, i, 449.

[At Greenwich, 19 June, 1546]

...Thomas Keyme of Lincolnshire, who had married one Anne Ascue, called hither and likewise his wife...was appointed to return to his country till he should be eftsoons[1] sent for; and for that she was very obstinate and heady in reasoning of matters of religion, wherein she shewed herself to be of a naughty opinion, seeing no persuasions of good reasons could take place, she was sent to Newgate to remain there to answer to the law; like as also one — White, who attempted to make an erroneous book, was sent to Newgate after debating with him of the matter, who shewed himself of a wrong opinion concerning the Blessed Sacrament....

Dasent, i, 462.

(13) *Forgery*
[At St James's, 6 December, 1556]

This day one Thomas Browne, nephew unto Justice Browne, being demanded by the Lords whether (as it was complained) he had counterfeited or no certain licences for the carrying from place to place of grain, and counterfeited thereunto the names of divers justices of peace and their seals, he confessed that he so did, and made, he saith, no more of them but six, and all within this twelvemonth, humbly submitting himself and desiring to be punished for the same his lewd doings to the example of others ...thereupon the said Thomas Browne was committed to the Fleet.

Dasent, vi, 28.

(14) *Libel*
[At Westminster, 30 April, 1557]

...Upon consideration of the matter in variance between Richard Michell, esquire, and William Penry, it was this day for a final end between them ordered, by the consent and agreement of the said Richard Michell, that the said Penry should at the next general sessions to be holden within the county of Carmarthen, in open court before the Justices there declare that he knoweth nothing touching the allegiance of the said Michell but honesty and truth, and that he, the same Penry, spake the words

---

[1] A second time.

alleged against him in the action of the case brought by the said Michell rashly and unadvisedly, and that he cannot justify the same, for the which he is sorry and asketh him forgiveness; whereupon it is ordered that the said Michell, his attorneys and deputies, shall surcease from further proceeding against the said Penry in his action or in the execution of the same....

Dasent, vi, 82.

(15) *Perjury*
[At Greenwich, 19 February, 1587]

...A letter to ——, Justices of Peace in the county of Worcester, to take the hearing of a matter in controversy between one Richard Pressey, a poor man of Worcester, and one John Cottrell, whom the said Pressey chargeth with perjury, and if they can to end the same between them; if not, to certify their Lordships in whom the default is....

Dasent, xiv, 335.

(16) *Unlicensed printing*
[At St James's, 8 April, 1543]

...[Eight] printers, for printing of such books as were thought to be unlawful, contrary to the proclamation made on that behalf, were committed unto prison....

Dasent, i, 107.

(17) *Procedure by arbitration*
[At Greenwich, 12 May, 1575]

This case illustrates the machinery of arbitration in private disputes coming before the Council Table, and the share of the Council in determining the final award. It shews also that the Star Chamber could still be used as a Council room.

This day their Lordships having called before them Mr Doctor Humfrey, Vice-Chancellor, and some other of the officers of the University of Oxford, Roger Taylor, Mayor, and some other of the aldermen and burgesses of the said City, caused certain Orders to be openly read before them, the tenor whereof ensueth:

Whereas heretofore there hath been divers controversies, debates, and strifes between the Vice-Chancellor, Masters, and Scholars of the University of Oxford on the one side, and the Mayor, Aldermen, and Commons of the said City on the other side, touching the use and exercise of sundry charters and privileges alleged by both parts for the maintenance of such liberties and other things as were claimed by them, whereby did and was daily more and more like to ensue great disquietness in the said University and Town, not meet to be suffered; wherefore upon the repair hither of Mr Doctor Humfrey, Vice-Chancellor, and certain other officers of the said University, and Roger Taylor, Mayor, with some of the aldermen and the Recorder, Town Clerk, and other burgesses of the said City of Oxford, their Lordships thought it convenient to move both parties to submit the hearing of the causes of their controversies in law to grave and indifferent men learned in the laws of the realm; whereupon both parties did assent that all and singular the said controversies and debates should be committed to the hearing, report, and consideration of Roger Manwood and Roger Monson, two of the Justices of the Common Pleas, Gilbert Gerrard and Thomas Bromley, her Majesty's Attorney- and Solicitor-General, who by order of their Lordships sundry times called before them both parties, with their learned counsel, and fully heard and examined the charters and privileges on each side, with all the allegations and answers of both parts, and thereupon the said four Commissioners set down in writing their opinions concerning the said controversies as agreeable with law and justice, and afterwards their Lordships having had at three several times the said Vice-Chancellor and officers of the University with their learned counsel, the Mayor, aldermen, Recorder, and Town Clerk of the said City before them with their learned counsel, whereof the one time was at the Star Chamber, where the Lord Keeper of the Great Seal of England and some others of the Privy Council, besides those above-named, were present, and with good deliberation considered not only the report of the said committees exhibited in writing, but also particularly in presence of the said committees and all other parties heard the circumstance of the whole matter, the claims, answers, and replies on both sides, what each party could allege, and so with great and advised deliberation their Lordships have according to right and equity for the benefit and quiet both of the said University and City, places necessary to be ordered always by the order and authority of the Privy Council, thought convenient and necessary to have these Orders following set down to be inviolably hereafter observed by both parties, and upon the return of the said Vice-Chancellor and Mayor within 14 days to be published and notified by them in the common places of the assemblies of the said University and City, to be by them appointed and called together for that purpose so as in like solemn acts hath been heretofore accustomed, as Orders enjoined unto them from their Lordships in the Queen's Majesty's name, and there to be registered in the Common Book of the said University and City, to remain as a perpetual memory and record of such Orders between them, as followeth:

Here follow the Orders in Council dealing with the various points in the dispute. One of these raises a curious question. Under a deed of 31 Edw. III the City of Oxford was bound to pay to the University 100 marks yearly 'for a memorial or penance of a slaughter committed by their predecessors in a conflict against the said University,' this memorial taking the usual form of a mass 'for the souls of them that were slain in the said conflict.' The University claimed 1500 marks as arrears, but the City contended that as for the last fifteen years these masses had been illegal, they were no longer bound. The decision of the Council was that in lieu of a mass the City 'shall yearly procure a communion or sermon to be made in St Mary's Church' on the former anniversary, 'and then and there with such number of the City' as were mentioned in the original deed 'make their oblation yearly of a penny apiece at the least to the use of the said University, for a perpetual memory or remembrance of the said slaughter or misdemeanour by them committed as aforesaid, and not for the souls of the parties then slain or for any other superstitious use.'

Dasent, viii, 376.

(18) *Control over courts*

[1 April, 1588]

This extract not only illustrates the control exercised by the English Council over the Star Chamber in Ireland, but shews that in Ireland also the distinction between the Council Board and the Star Chamber was that between a private body and a public court[1].

...A letter to the Lord Deputy of Ireland and the rest of the Council, that whereas Henry Eyland, late Sheriff of the county of Roscommon, exhibited a petition unto their Lordships, herein enclosed, complaining of a hard sentence given against him in the Star Chamber at Dublin, he being absent in her Majesty's service, so as their Lordships could not but much marvel thereat in case both the matter and the manner of proceeding to his condemnation therein were such as he alleged; but because their Lordships thought it not reasonable to give credit to the said Eyland's own allegations, and himself desired no more but that the truth of his cause and the whole proofs touching the said sentence might be re-examined in that realm, refusing no manner of fine or punishment laid upon him already or to be laid on him in case upon re-examination of the matter objected against him he should be found faulty in the same as the same sentence purported, their Lordships could not deny his request in this behalf, and therefore did refer both him and the re-examination of his whole cause and sentence so given as aforesaid unto his Lordship, etc., praying them to look into the same with all indifferency, hearing at large as well what this suppliant personally could answer for himself as that he had been charged withal, and thereupon if they should see no cause to alter the said sentence, then to cause the same to be put in execution, and

[1] See p. 253 below.

contrariwise finding cause why it should not be executed, then to revoke and mitigate the same as the justice or equity of his cause should require; which re-examination and that which was further thereupon by them to be done their Lordships thought meet should be done at the Council Board and not in the Star Chamber, because it could not in their opinions stand with the honour and reputation of any such Court of Justice after a judgment given in the same Court to have it re-examined and altered.. . .

Dasent, xvi, 10.

(19) *The use of torture*

[At Windsor, 16 November, 1540]

. . . Thomas Thwaites was sent to the Tower of London by certain of the guard with a letter to the Lieutenant declaring his confession, and commanding him that in case he would stand still in denial to shew of whom he had heard the things he confessed, he should give him a stretch or two at his discretion upon the brake[1].. . .

Nicolas, vii, 83.

[At Greenwich, 3 June, 1553]

. . . A letter to the Earl of Sussex to cause Man and Gardiner to be sent hither under sure custody, seeing they obstinately refuse to confess the truth of their doings touching their stealing of the hawks out of Winfarthing, to the end they may be here farther examined and put to the torture, if need shall be, to the example of other.. . .

Dasent, iv, 284.

[At Westminster, 27 January, 1555]

A letter of thanksgiving to the Mayor of Bristol, signifying the receipt of his letters to the Lords by the Sheriff there, together with the counterfeit coins and other the coiners' instruments and tools by him lately apprehended; requiring him for the better trial and boulting out[2] of such as be privy with them, and specially the graver of their irons, to put the parties to the rack if he shall so think good by his discretion and to use all other means whereby the truth and whole circumstances thereof may come to light.. . .

Dasent, v, 93.

[3 May, 1581]

. . . A letter unto the Lieutenant of the Tower, Doctor Hamond, and Thomas Norton gentleman, that whereas there hath been of late apprehended among others a certain seminary

---

[1] 'The brake or rack, commonly called the Duke of Exeter's daughter because he was the deviser of that torture' (Stow, quoted in the *Oxford Dictionary*).

[2] *I.e.* sifting out, as of flour.

priest or Jesuit naming himself Bryant, about whom there was taken divers books and writings carrying matter of high treason, and is (as may by good likelihood be conjectured) able to discover matters of good moment for her Majesty's service, it was therefore thought necessary that he should be to that purpose substantially examined upon such interrogatories as may be framed and gathered out of the said books and writings, which their Lordships send them therewith, for the doing whereof especial choice was made of them three, and thereby authority given unto them to draw the interrogatories and to examine the said Bryant accordingly; and if he shall refuse by persuasion to confess such things as they shall find him able to reveal unto them then they shall offer unto him the torture in the Tower, and in case upon the sight thereof he shall obstinately refuse to confess the truth then shall they put him unto the torture, and by the pain and terror of the same wring from [him] the knowledge of such things as shall appertain....

Dasent, xiii, 37

(20) Unusual punishment
[At Hampton Court, 18 January, 1541]

...A letter under the stamp[1] was sent unto the Dean of York and others, that whereas the King's Majesty being advertised by their letters written unto the Master of the Horse and Mr Secretary Wriothesley of two women which had done and committed detestable offences in those parts, his Majesty's pleasure was that they should first cause the woman that burned the house to be indicted of the said fact, and thereupon to be arraigned, and to see her put to execution of such death as by the law is limited and appointed in that behalf, and for the punishment of the other woman to cause her tongue to be pierced and slit through with a burning iron, to the intent she shall never after disclose her vicious and abominable doings....

Nicolas, vii, 117.

Other cases in the Register which serve to illustrate further the range of the Council's activities are the following: Nicolas, vii, 36 (an order for 'the seizing of' the daughters of a certain knight deceased, 'to the use of the King's wardship'); Dasent, xxi, 461 (an order relating to the exportation of pilchards); ib. i, 33 (a letter to the Bishop of Ely 'for the speedy redubbing of certain marsh walls, broken by the rage of water'); ib. x, 92 (treason); ib. vii, 55, 57, 62, and viii, 294 (riot); Nicolas, vii, 153 (robbery); ib. vii, 95 (examination of one Walsh, 'suspect for a naughty person and a vaga-

---

[1] In Henry VIII's reign the royal sign manual was often affixed to public documents by means of a stamp.

bond'); *ib.* vii, 31, 36, 171 (seditious words); *ib.* vii, 179 (a malicious accusation); *ib.* vii, 29 (enhancing victuals); *ib.* vii, 97, 106 (letters to apprehend one Thomas Walpole, 'a seditious fellow and a setter forth of a naughty book made by Philip Melanchthon[1]); *ib.* vii, 213, 224, and Dasent, iv, 252 (religious offences); Nicolas, vii, 41, 74, 77, 81 (further illustrations of the method of delegation); *ib.* vii, 160 (an arrest by order of the Council); Dasent, iii, 407, iv, 201 (torture).

(3) Council Orders concerning Private Suits, 1582, 1589

[15 April, 1582]

...This day the Lords and others of her Majesty's Privy Council considering what multitude of matters concerning private causes and actions between party and party were daily brought unto the Council Board, wherewith their Lordships were greatly troubled and her Majesty's special services oftentimes interrupted, for remedy whereof it was agreed among them that from henceforth no private causes arising between parties for any action whatsoever which may receive order and redress in any of her Majesty's ordinary courts shall be received and preferred to the Board, unless they shall concern the preservation of her Majesty's peace or shall be of some public consequence to touch the government of the realm.... Dasent, *Acts of the Privy Council*, xiii, 394.

[8 October, 1589]

Whereas by reason of the multitude of private suitors resorting daily to her Majesty's Privy Council the Lords and others of the same are continually so troubled and pestered with the said private suitors and their causes as at the times of their assembling for her Majesty's special services they can hardly be suffered (by the importunity of the said suitors) to attend and proceed in such causes as do concern her Majesty and the state of the realm, the said suits and causes being for the most part of such nature as either have been determined in other courts, or else such as ought to receive hearing and trial and order in the several Courts of Justice or of Conscience[2] within the realm ordained for those purposes. Their Lordships therefore considering the inconvenience and hindrances growing to her Majesty's services commonly interrupted by giving audience to such private suitors, and that many times the judges and justices of sundry of the courts aforesaid, to whom the ordering and determining of many of

[1] Melanchthon's *Epistle to Henry VIII*.

[2] 'The Courts of Conscience for civil causes be these: the Chancery, open to all men; the Court of Requests, that specially heareth the suits of poor men and the Prince's servants' (Lambarde, *Archeion*, p. 26).

the said suits do properly and naturally appertain, do thereby
find cause of offence as derogating the lawful authority of the said
courts and places of judgment. For these considerations their
Lordships this day, upon good deliberation, ordered and decreed
that from henceforth no such private causes or suits which by
due and ordinary course of law ought to receive their trial and
determination in any of her Majesty's Courts of Justice or Conscience, or in any court in corporate towns (where by charters
such causes ought to be heard and determined) should be received
and admitted to be heard and determined by the said Privy
Council, and if any suitors shall at any time hereafter resort either
to her Majesty's Principal Secretary, or to the Clerk or Clerks of
the Council for the time attendant, or to the Council Board, as
unacquainted with this Order, whose causes shall manifestly
appear to be of such kind as is aforesaid, that every such suitor
and cause shall be addressed and directed either by her Majesty's
Principal Secretary or in his absence from the Court by any two
of the Council, or when the Council shall not be assembled then
by one of the Clerks of the Council then attendant[1], either to the
Lord Chancellor or Masters of the Court of Requests (if the
order thereof ought to be had in way of equity by course of
those courts), or to such other Courts of the Common Law or
Courts of Equity or the Courts for her Majesty's Revenue where
the said causes are properly determinable; after which directions
according to the nature of the suits, if the parties shall make
complaint that notwithstanding such direction they cannot have
their causes received to be heard and ordered according to the
laudable usage of the courts whereunto they are addressed, then
the parties complaining shall not be denied to be heard and their
griefs remedied, as by proof it shall fall out that justice or usual
help is denied unto them. And to the end that this Order and
decree may be duly and inviolably kept, observed, and maintained,
their Lordships have promised and concluded among themselves
that neither they in general nor any of them in particular will
hereafter in regard of any private person or cause contrary to the
form of this Order move, require, or do anything that shall
impugn or violate the same, and for the better confirmation
thereof they have severally subscribed the said Order and decree,
and commanded the same to be entered into the Council Book,
there to remain of record. Provided nevertheless that hereby is
not meant to seclude any persons with their suits if they shall

---

[1] At this time there were five Clerks of the Council (Dasent, XVIII, p. xxxiii).

complain of any wrong, wilful delay, or denial of justice by any judge or judges in any court, or by any justice of peace in their jurisdictions, where they have made complaint in any ordinary sort, in which cases as their Lordships will be willing to relieve them upon their complaints, so also if it shall be proved they have made their complaints without just cause it shall be reason to punish the said complainants. In like manner no man shall be barred by this Order to give information against any persons for any fact tending to treason or conspiracy, or to any crime that may concern the safety or honour of her Majesty's royal person.

Dasent, xviii, 181.

[At Greenwich, 27 June, 1591]

An addition to the Lords' Order which was written and set down the 8th of October, 1589

We seeing that notwithstanding this Order the multitude of private suitors hath of late increased by reason of some intermission of the due execution of the same, whereby the public services of her Majesty are daily hindered and interrupted, do therefore will and require you, the Masters of Requests, that from henceforth when you shall have received the petitions exhibited at the Council Board you consider of several causes in them contained, and finding them such as by this Order are not to be admitted, that you address the parties to the Courts of Justice and Conscience where they are properly triable, and so provide that we be not troubled therewith, and for your better direction herein we have sent you a copy of our said Order, whereby you may be directed for the nature and quality of the said causes. Hereof fail you not.

Dasent, xxi, 240.

(4) Order against Seditious Books, 1566

This Order is referred to in a plaintiff's bill of complaint in the Star Chamber in 1582 as a decree of that Court[1], but the form of the Order is not that of a Star Chamber decree, and it is more probably an Order in Council which happens to be dated from the Star Chamber room where the Council had been sitting. As the volume of the Council Register for the greater part of 1566 is missing, the point cannot be finally settled.

I. That no person should print, or cause to be printed, or bring or procure to be brought into the realm printed, any book against the force and meaning of any ordinance, prohibition, or commandment, contained or to be contained in any the statutes or laws of this realm, or in any injunctions, letters patents, or

[1] Scofield, p. 52 n.

ordinances passed or set forth, or to be passed or set forth, by the Queen's grant, commission, or authority.

II. That whosoever should offend against the said ordinances should forfeit all such books and copies; and from thenceforth should never use or exercise, or take benefit by any using or exercising, the feat[1] of printing, and to sustain three months imprisonment without bail or mainprize[2].

III. That no person should sell or put to sale, bind, stitch, or sew any such books or copies, upon pain to forfeit all such books and copies, and for every book 20s.

IV. That all books so forfeited should be brought into Stationers' Hall. And there one moiety of the money forfeited to be reserved to the Queen's use, and the other moiety to be delivered to him or them that should first seize the books or make complaint thereof to the Warden of the said Company. And all the books so to be forfeited to be destroyed or made waste paper.

V. That it should be lawful for the Wardens of the Company for the time being or any two of the said Company thereto deputed by the said Wardens, as well in any ports or other suspected places, to open and view all packs, dryfats[3], maunds[4], and other things wherein books or paper shall be contained, brought into this realm, and make search in all work-houses, shops, warehouses, and other places of printers, booksellers, and such as bring books into the realm to be sold, or where they have reasonable cause of suspicion; and all books to be found against the said ordinances to seize and carry to the Hall to the uses abovesaid, and to bring the persons offending before the Queen's Commissioners in Causes Ecclesiastical.

VI. Every stationer, printer, bookseller, merchant, using any trade of book-printing, binding, selling, or bringing into the realm, should before the Commissioners or before any other persons thereto to be assigned by the Queen's Privy Council, enter into several recognisances of reasonable sums of money to her Majesty, with sureties or without, as to the Commissioners should be thought expedient, that he should truly observe all the said ordinances, well and truly yield and pay all such forfeitures, and in no point be resisting but in all things aiding to the said Wardens and their deputies for the true execution of the premises.

---

[1] Art or profession.   [2] See note on p. 10 above.
[3] Cases or barrels for holding dry goods as opposed to liquids.
[4] Wicker baskets.

Upon the consideration before expressed and upon the motion of the Commissioners, we of the Privy Council have agreed this to be observed and kept upon the pains therein contained. At the Star Chamber the 29 June, 1566, and the eighth year of the Queen's Majesty's reign.

[Then follow the signatures of Sir Nicholas Bacon, Keeper of the Great Seal, and seven other Councillors.]

We underwrit think these ordinances meet and necessary to be decreed and observed.

[Then follow the signatures of Matthew Parker, Archbishop of Canterbury, and six other members of the High Commission.]

Strype, *Life of Parker*, Book III, ch. xi.

(5) Memorandum on the distribution of business, 1600

In continuation of Dr John Herbert's Memorandum of 26 April, 1600, on the duties of a Secretary (see p. 212 above).

...Memorandum: That all causes to be treated on in Council and resolved are either only for her Majesty, or betwixt party and party, or betwixt some party (either subject or stranger) and the Queen's Majesty.

The first doth handle principally questions and consultations of state, growing from foreign advertisements or some extraordinary accidents within the realm.

The second (between party and party) are very seldom heard particularly, but rather ended by overruling an obstinate person who is made to acknowledge his fault, or else the parties are remitted to some court of justice or equity, or recommended by some letters to some justices in the country to compound the differences either by consent of the parties or by direction. Or, if the cause be great, then to write letters to some principal persons to have some circumstances better understood and examined concerning matter of fact, whereof the Council cannot be so well informed when they have only the suggestions of one party against another; upon which report it often happeneth that quarrels and differences are taken up by the Council when it appears clearly who is in default.

When there is anything in question wherein the Queen is a party, it is commonly either by the breach of peace or for some other title. If there be breach of peace the Lords do either punish the offender by commitment, or do refer the matter to be further proceeded in in the Star Chamber, where great riots and contempts are punished. If it be matter of title, then the Lords refer it to the Queen's learned counsel, and recommend the same to the Judges' care[1].

If there be some suits to the Queen of poor men, then do the Lords endorse their petitions with their opinions, and recommend the dispatch to the Secretary, or for the poorer sort to the Master of the Requests[2].

State Papers (Domestic), Eliz. cclxxiv, 118.

---

[1] Probably the judges and men learned in the law who were occasional members of the Council. It is from the latter that the modern 'King's Counsel' derive their name.

[2] On the Court of Requests see p. 299 below.

The Star Chamber

The origin of the Court of Star Chamber is a constitutional problem of great difficulty, and its history has been much misunderstood[1]. The famous Star Chamber Statute of Henry VII [p. 258] was interpreted as establishing by statutory authority a new jurisdiction and a new court, and from this initial error a whole series of misconceptions grew.

The Act of 1487 gives authority to seven persons—the Chancellor, the Treasurer, and the Lord Privy Seal (or two of them), a bishop and a temporal lord of the King's Council, and two of the King's judges[2]—to deal with seven offences—maintenance, the giving of liveries, retainers by indenture or otherwise, embracery[3], 'untrue demeanings of sheriffs in making of panels and other untrue returns,' the 'taking of money by juries,' and 'great riots and unlawful assemblies'; these being precisely the offences which most disturbed social order at that time. Proceedings were to be begun by information to the Chancellor, and the Court was empowered to examine the accused. By a Statute of 1529 [p. 259] the Lord President of the Council was added to the members of the Court. The Star Chamber is not mentioned at all in the Act of 1487, but the title *Pro Camera Stellata* is prefixed to it on the Rolls[4].

From the earlier part of the seventeenth century the Court of Star Chamber included all the members of the Council; other persons learned in the law were sworn in to give professional advice in addition to the two judges referred to in the Act of 1487; and the Court was dealing with offences other than those seven enumerated in the Act—*e.g.* sedition, robbery, murder, and especially such crimes as libel, for which the common law provided no punishment.

Out of this discrepancy arose the historical blunder embodied in the Act of 1641[5] 'for the regulating of the Privy Council and for taking away the Court commonly called the Star Chamber.' It was assumed by the Parliamentarian lawyers that the Star Chamber as they knew it derived its authority from the Act of 1487; that it had illegally enlarged the number of the

---

[1] This is partly due to want of material. Although there is a mass of Star Chamber documents in the Record Office, the whole of the decrees and orders of the Court have disappeared. A Committee of the House of Lords reported in 1719 that 'they were last seen in a house in Bartholomew Close, London' (Bradford, p. 14).

[2] It should be observed that the King's judges were not, strictly speaking, judges of the Court, as judgment was not given in their name but in that of members of the Council only. The judges were present as referees upon legal points (Leadam, II, p. xii; cf. also I, pp. xxxvii, xxxviii).

[3] See note on p. 258 below.

[4] The words 'Court of Star Chamber' occur in the title of the Act as printed; but there were no titles to Acts of Parliament until 1495 (Craies, *Statute Law*, ed. of 1907, p. 177); and it was not until 1514 that it became the regular custom to insert them, usually in the margin of the Roll. Further, the titles entered on the original Acts often differ from those on the same Acts as enrolled in Chancery (*Statutes of the Realm*, III, p. v).

[5] 17 Car. I, c. 10.

judges of the Court; and that it had assumed a wider jurisdiction than was allowed to it by law[1]. It was therefore held to be no true Court, and was abolished by statute.

It is now a matter of general agreement among historians that the Court of Star Chamber derived its authority, not from the Act of 1487, but from the far older jurisdiction of the King's Council. The title 'Court of Star Chamber' was not regularly used until comparatively late in its history; and the earliest reference to the Star Chamber in the proceedings before it is not to a Court but to a place[2]. The earlier proceedings refer to the Lords *of the Council* in the Starred Chamber at Westminster (p. 251). The forms of the tribunal followed those of the Council and ran in the Council's name[3]. The clerk of the Star Chamber bore the title of 'Clerk of the Council of State'; and Lord Burghley declared in the Star Chamber 'before all the presence' that 'there was no other Clerk of the Queen's Council of State but only the Clerk of this Court, and that the others were clerks of the Privy Council attendant upon her Majesty's royal person, and those other clerks were to attend at the Council Table.'[4] Again, in 1588 the Clerk of the Star Chamber was recognised as the 'first clerk of the Council in place,'[5] since the King's Council in the Star Chamber, as heir to the medieval Council, took precedence of the Privy Council attendant on the King's person, which might be regarded as a later development[6]. Finally, all the earlier writers on the Star Chamber [pp. 284–96] agree in regarding it as identical with the King's Council, and it is not until Elizabeth's reign that the theory of its statutory origin in 1487 makes its appearance[7].

The effect of the Act of 1487 can perhaps be best described by saying that it established what would now be called a 'statutory committee'[8] of the Council, empowered to act on behalf of the whole Council in respect of certain offences. The Council was large; part of it followed the King; the need of dealing promptly with the kind of disorder referred to in the Act was urgent. It was therefore convenient to have a small body of Councillors authorised to act for the whole Council in these matters; and its statutory character met the criticisms which had been made from time to time on the legality of the Council jurisdiction. But the creation of a statutory committee left the jurisdiction of the Council unimpaired, and it continued to be

[1] 'The said judges have not kept themselves to the points limited by the said statute, but have undertaken to punish where no law doth warrant, and to make decrees for things having no such authority, and to inflict heavier punishments than by any law is warranted' (17 Car. I, c. 10, printed in S. R. Gardiner, *Constitutional Documents*, p. 181).

[2] Hewitt's case, 1500. In the bill filed in this case the Lord Keeper is petitioned to summon the defendants 'to appear before your said Lordship to-morrow in the sterre chamber' (Leadam, 1, pp. lxix and 72).

[3] Leadam, 1, p. xxiv.   [4] Scofield, p. 62. See also p. 219 above.
[5] Hudson, quoted in Scofield, p. 62 *n*.
[6] *Transactions of the Royal Historical Society*, 1918, p. 187.
[7] 5 Eliz. c. 9 refers to 'the power or authority given by Act of Parliament made in the time of King Henry VII to the Lord Chancellor...and others of the King's Council...to examine and punish riots, [etc.]...'
[8] Cf. Henry VIII's Statute of Proclamations, which sets up a statutory committee on similar lines (see p. 530 below).

exercised over the old ground. The Act was intended to increase the efficiency of government and not to diminish it, and it can scarcely be supposed that the general body of the Council would surrender their ancient and unbounded jurisdiction in favour of the Chancellor and his six colleagues working under the limitations set up by the Act.

The view that the Star Chamber is really the King's Council is supported by the documentary records of its proceedings, for these make it clear that the action of the Lords of the Council in the Star Chamber was never limited by the Act of 1487. Down to the year 1500 the form of address with which the plaintiff most commonly prefaces his bill of complaint is either 'To the King our Sovereign Lord' or 'To the King our Sovereign Lord and to the Lords of his most noble Council'; and it is not until after that year that the Chancellor is most commonly addressed[1], and even then the *Council* in the Star Chamber is appealed to not infrequently[2]. In the case of the Merchant Adventurers against the Staplers of Calais, which came before the Council in the 'Sterre Chambre' as early as 1504 [p. 260], there were no less than 41 Councillors present, including the two Chief Justices, three doctors of laws, and both the King's Secretaries. This may have been exceptional, but in a case of 1508 there were nine judges sitting instead of the seven enumerated in the statute; instead of the Chancellor, Treasurer, and Lord Privy Seal, or two of them, only the Chancellor was present; instead of two judges of the courts of law there were six; and there was no bishop[3]. In a case of 1516 there were present not only the Chancellor, Treasurer, and Lord Privy Seal, a bishop, and a temporal lord, as required by the Act, but also nine other members of the Privy Council who all sat as judges and not as mere advisers of the Court[4]. An Act of 1529[5]—the year in which the Lord President of the Council was added to the statutory committee of 1487, and when it was therefore still active—recites a Star Chamber decree 'concerning alien handicraftsmen inhabiting within the realm,' and refers to it as 'ordained, adjudged, and decreed...in our Starred Chamber at Westminster by the most Reverend Father in God, Thomas, Lord Cardinal Legate *de latere* of the Apostolic See, Archbishop of York, Primate and Chancellor of England, and by our nobles and others of our said Council'—a description which might very well fit the King's Council, but could not possibly be applied to the statutory committee of 1487. Again, the *ceteri consularii* sometimes entered as occasionally attending the Court, exceed the whole number of the committee as defined by the Act of 1487[6]. Finally, Hudson, who had been himself the Clerk of the Court and had searched its records, states that the number of the judges in the reigns of Henry VII and Henry VIII was 'well near to forty; at some one time thirty.'[7]

If the composition of the Court was not limited by the Act of 1487, neither was its jurisdiction. The first case heard after the passing of the Act related to the financial affairs of a priory. Other early cases are concerned with defamation, wrongful impounding, violation of royal charters, false

<hr/>

[1] Leadam, i, p. xiv.   [2] *Ib.* ii, p. xvii.   [3] *Ib.* i, p. xxxvi.
[4] *Ib.* ii, p. xi.   [5] 21 Henr. VIII, c. 20.   [6] Leadam, i, p. xxxviii.
[7] *Ib.* i, p. xxxix. A careful discussion of the whole problem will be found on pp. xxiv–l.

imprisonment, abduction, and illegal tolls[1]. It is evident that the tribunal before which these cases were heard regarded itself as possessing the wider jurisdiction of the King in Council, and declined to be kept within the four corners of the Act. It is therefore not surprising to find Hudson describing the later theory that the Star Chamber was founded by the Act of 1487 as 'a doating which no man that had looked upon the records of the Court would have lighted upon.'[2]

If this view is the right one, the Act of 1487 does not lie in the main line of historical evolution, but is a minor episode in the history of the Star Chamber. It is, however, important upon other grounds. (1) It introduced afresh into the practice of the Council, with statutory sanction, the ancient but in part abandoned procedure of examining defendants upon oath[3]. (2) It imposed a statutory duty upon certain members of the Council to attend and hear cases which the general body of the Council, since they received no salary for their attendance, were probably unwilling to discharge[4]. (3) After 1487 the judges and other persons learned in the law do not appear to have been summoned any longer to the Council Table when judicial business was being dealt with, but only to the Star Chamber[5]. (4) The Act gave statutory sanction to the issue of writs of *subpoena* and privy seal, reviving in a different form powers already given in the case of 'great riots, extortions, oppressions, and grievous offences' by the temporary Act of 1453[6] which had expired in 1461. This last was in all probability the main object of the Act[7].

There seems to be little doubt that the Star Chamber was not at first organically distinct from the Council[8]. It is true that the Statute of Liveries of 1504 [p. 9] provides that offenders may be proceeded against by information 'before the Chancellor of England or the Keeper of the King's Great Seal in the Star Chamber, or before the King in his Bench, or before the King and his Council attending upon his most royal person wheresoever he be, so that there be three of the same Council at the least, of the which two shall be lords spiritual or temporal'; but the distinction here drawn is between the Council at Westminster and the Council following the King, and there is nothing to suggest the existence of a separate tribunal of uniform composition called the Star Chamber.

The 'Book of Entries' contains records of Star Chamber proceedings as well as of Council proceedings, and if the Star Chamber had regarded itself as really separate from the Council the elementary principles of business would have required that it should equip itself with a separate book. During Henry VII's reign, at any rate, there could have been no clear distinction between the administrative Council and the judicial Council[9], although the statutory committee of 1487 sometimes acted for the whole Council in the matters assigned to it by the Act. A distinction existed between the Privy Council and the King's Council, for we find Sir Robert Wingfield saying in 1535, 'I have been sworn of [the King's] Council above twenty years and

---

[1] Leadam, I, p. lxvi.
[2] See p. 295 below.
[3] Leadam, I, pp. xxxii and lxiv.
[4] *Ib.* I, p. xlvii.
[5] *Ib.* I, p. lvi.
[6] 31 Henr. VI, c. 2.
[7] Leadam, I, pp. lxiv and lxxi.
[8] *Ib.* I, pp. xlviii, xlix.
[9] Scofield, p. 27.

of his Privy Council above fourteen years'[1]; but the distinction is not between an organ of justice and an organ of administration, nor does it depend upon the place where the business was transacted—it is entirely a matter of composition. A meeting to which only Councillors were summoned, whether it took place at Westminster or elsewhere, and whether it handled judicial or administrative business, was a meeting of the Privy Council; if it included other persons it would be a meeting of the King's Council as a whole.

It is possible that a differentiation begins when the Ordinances of 1526 distinguished between the 'Council at Court' which followed the King and the 'King's Council in the Star Chamber' which remained at Westminster[2]. Even then it was not carried very far, for the two bodies were in close correspondence, and sometimes they were united into a single body[3], the term 'privy council' being often applied to both. In course of time, however, the separation became more complete, the term 'privy council' being exclusively assigned to that branch of the King's Council which, consisting of Privy Councillors only, was becoming increasingly absorbed in politics and administration, while the other branch, which now usually included judges and 'ordinary councillors,' was being specialised to judicial business as the Star Chamber. If this view is correct, the modern Privy Council is not directly descended from the medieval Council, but is a special development of a particular branch of it. The true heir to the medieval Council is the Star Chamber, and that was abolished in 1641 and never restored.

It is not easy to determine the point in time at which the Star Chamber and the Privy Council became organically separate. It was natural that a body exercising judicial functions and sitting regularly at a definite place should acquire the character of a separate tribunal, but the separation was gradual, and was probably not complete until the reign of Elizabeth. Perhaps the earliest indication of this organic separation may be assigned to 1570, when the Council is found asserting its authority against what now appears almost as a rival court [p. 261]. The fundamental distinction between them came to be that the proceedings of the Council Table were private, while the Star Chamber was an 'open' as distinguished from a 'privy' council, and its proceedings had all the formality and publicity of a court of law [p. 262]. Other differences were that after 1487 the judges and other legal experts were summoned to assist at the Star Chamber and not at the Council Table; and that although the Council conducted informal examinations, it did not, like the Star Chamber, possess legal authority to administer interrogatories to be answered upon oath[4].

[1] *L. and P.*, viii, no. 225.　　　　　　　　[2] See p. 217 above.

[3] It is possible that the fluctuations in the numbers attending the Star Chamber are to be explained by the fact that when the King was absent from London, business would be done by the statutory committee or by the part of the Council that did not follow him, but that the larger numbers would reappear when he returned to Westminster (see Bradford, p. 15).

[4] Leadam, i, p. lvi.

§ 1. Composition

The Court of Star Chamber was supposed to be held in the presence of the King, for whom an empty chair was set[1]; but here, as in the Chancery and at the Council Table, the Chancellor was in practice the chief judicial person. He went to the Court in procession with great pomp, the mace and the Great Seal of England being carried before him[2]; and he alone directed the order of proceeding and determined the question of costs. As presiding judge he enjoyed the privilege of speaking with his head covered, and he gave the casting vote if the Court was equally divided. For his attendance in the Star Chamber he received an additional salary of £200 a year. The other judges of the Court were the Privy Councillors *ex officio*; and the two Chief Justices, of the King's Bench and the Common Pleas, together with other judges and persons learned in the law, acted as assessors, being specially sworn in for the Star Chamber although they were not members of the Privy Council. Down to 1529 and probably later, the Court consisted sometimes and for some purposes of the statutory committee named in the Act of 1487, but this imposed no restriction upon the composition of the Court, which often included a much larger number of judges. There are traces of a claim by all members of the House of Lords to attend the Court, but this does not appear to have been sustained[3].

The chief officer of the Court was the Clerk of the Star Chamber, who was originally the Clerk to the Council[4]. This office was in the gift of the Crown, and the holder enjoyed a salary of 40 marks and 'two livery gowns, one of damask, the other of wrought velvet'; but the fees of the suitors made it so lucrative that Bacon estimated its value as £2000 a year, and in 1589 obtained the reversion of it for himself, but it did not fall in to him until 1608. It was the duty of the Clerk to keep the records of the Court, but in later years the actual work of recording was performed by a registrar and a staff of under-clerks. There were also attorneys attached to the Court, at first only two, one for the plaintiff and another for the defendant, but later on a third was appointed, and eventually a fourth. These were paid by fees. The usher, who was usually also usher of the Exchequer, was required 'to keep the place where the Court is kept comely for so great a presence and safe for the records which are there laid,' to summon the suitors, and 'also to make silence and to attend to the Lords for all things they have used.'[5] He enjoyed the use of 'a convenient house for his habitation,' and various fees and perquisites in addition to 'his fee from his Majesty.' There was also a steward 'of the Lords' diet at the Star Chamber,' as well as a butler and a kitchen staff. On Star Chamber days (see p. 255) there were elaborate dinners for the Lords at the public expense[6].

---

[1] Leadam, I, p. lvii. Henry VII and James I often attended the Star Chamber; Henry VIII only once (Bradford, p. 17). On 20 June, 1616, James I made a long speech there, 'to the admiration of the hearers, speaking more like an angel than a man,' and ended by promising 'to frequent that place oftener' (letter of Lord George Carew, quoted in Scofield, p. 58).

[2] On this, and on the other officials of the Star Chamber see Scofield, pp. 61–68.

[3] Leadam, I, pp. xl–xli.   [4] See p. 219 above.

[5] Hudson, quoted in Scofield, p. 67.   [6] See Baldwin, p. 453 and note.

§ 2. Procedure

The Council when dealing with judicial business sat only during the law terms[1]; and the Star Chamber, deriving from the Council and following its practice, maintained the same general rule, although in cases of emergency it would sometimes sit out of term time[2]. The appointed days varied, but under Elizabeth the regular Star Chamber days were Wednesdays and Fridays[3], when the Lords sat to hear cases in public. There was also a good deal of routine business transacted on other days, either by a committee or by the Clerk of the Court[4].

Proceedings in the Star Chamber usually began with a 'bill of complaint' entered by the plaintiff[5], which would be engrossed on parchment and signed by counsel, and then endorsed and filed by the Clerk. This bill would recite his grievances against the defendant, and ask that a writ of subpoena under privy seal might be issued, summoning him to appear before the Court. If he failed to appear, a writ of attachment was issued to the Sheriff of his county to bring him before the Court, and if this failed, he could be apprehended under a commission of rebellion, or in the last resort by a serjeant-at-arms sent from the Court with powers of search[6]. When the defendant appeared before the Court, he was required to make answer upon oath, and this answer was also engrossed on parchment and signed by counsel[7]. If the defendant refused to answer, he was imprisoned, and if he still refused he was held to have confessed. If on the other hand he made answer, as would usually be the case, the plaintiff was allowed four days in which to draw up interrogatories for his examination, and to these he had to make answer upon oath, a refusal being punishable with imprisonment, and if he still refused to answer he was held to be guilty. When answer had been made to the written interrogatories, both sides produced their witnesses, who were usually examined in private[8]. A day was then appointed for a hearing in open court, and the judges, having all the depositions before them, heard the defendant's answers read and then proceeded to a decision. At this public hearing both sides were allowed to be represented by counsel.

[1] 'That out of term time no thing be sped in the Council but such thing as for the good of the King and of his land asketh necessary and hasty speed, and may not goodly be abiden unto the term time' (Order of 1426; Nicolas, iii, 216).
[2] 'If any cause be begun to be heard in the term time, and for length or difficulty cannot be sentenced within the term, it may be continued and sentenced after the term' (Coke; see p. 292 below).
[3] Scofield, p. 69.
[4] *Ib.* p. 70.
[5] The plaintiff might be the Attorney-General acting on behalf of the Crown.
[6] Scofield, pp. 73-4.
[7] Sometimes the plaintiff made a further 'replication' to the defendant's answer, but this occurs rarely, and as he could make no new charges it was in any case a mere formality (Leadam, I, p. xxxiii).
[8] The usual procedure was for the Court to issue a commission to local magnates to examine the witnesses on the spot, in order to avoid the trouble and expense of bringing them up to London, and cases occur in which such a commission would be authorised to come to a final decision (Bradford, p. 14). This method of delegation is specially characteristic of the Council (see p. 228 above).

This was the ordinary procedure of the Court and, in so far as it depended upon the use of an oath, it was based upon the Act of 1487, but sometimes a more summary procedure was adopted which was not authorised by the Act but depended entirely upon the ancient practice of the Council. The Court, acting upon private information or mere suspicion, would send a pursuivant to arrest the defendant without the form of a bill of complaint. He would then be examined in private, although not upon oath, and if in the course of his examination he made any damaging admissions he was liable to be condemned and sentenced at once, *ex ore suo*—on his own confession. This was known as 'the proceeding by *ore tenus*'[1]. This procedure differed fundamentally from that of the courts of common law. In these the mouth of the accused was closed, often to his own salvation, but in the Star Chamber the whole of the proceedings were grounded upon his examination, and if he could be entrapped into admissions, so much the better for the course of justice. The system was much better adapted to catch the guilty than to protect the innocent, and even Mill, the Clerk of the Court, speaking of the summary procedure, admits himself to be 'one that by good experience have found many mischiefs mingled in that manner of dealing'[2].

The punishment of death could not be inflicted by the Star Chamber, but it could fine, imprison, and sentence to corporal punishment such as the pillory, whipping, branding, cutting off the ears, slitting the nose, or undergoing some form of public degradation. Some of the punishments were ingeniously devised to fit the crime, as in the case of a prisoner who, objecting on religious grounds to eating swine's flesh, was ordered to be fed exclusively upon pork[3]. In the reign of Henry VIII John Tyndal and Thomas Patmore were brought before the Court for circulating William Tyndal's translation of the New Testament, and were not only fined the fancy sum of £18,840. 0s. 10d.—the exact equivalent of the ransom paid by the clergy of the Province of York under the Submission Act[4], which had then not long been passed—but were also 'sentenced to ride with their faces to the horse's tail, having papers on their heads and the New Testaments and other books which they had dispersed pinned thick on their clothing: at the Standard in Cheapside they were to throw these books into a fire made for the purpose.'[5] The fines were sometimes out of all proportion to the offender's estate,—£5000, £10,000, and in one case £31,000; but these were imposed rather as an expression of the Court's abhorrence of the offence than with any intention of demanding payment in full. The ordinary fine ranged from £5 to £100, and it was usual twice in the year, at the end of the Trinity Term and again at the end of the Hilary Term, to set apart a day for considering the mitigation of fines. The corporal punishments imposed were often remitted by the Crown[6]. But nothing was done under the Stuarts by

---

[1] Leadam, I, p. lxvii.   [2] Scofield, p. 76 *n*.
[3] A case of 1618; see Burn, p. 79.
[4] See p. 22 above.
[5] Scofield, p. 77. Rushworth (ii, 479) refers to a case of 36 Eliz. in which the defendant was 'sentenced, for beating his grandfather, to be whipt before the picture of his grandfather, he being unable to come to the place where it was to be executed.'
[6] Scofield, p. 79.

way of fine and corporal punishment that had not been already done under the Tudors. The later unpopularity of the Court was due to a change in the popular point of view, and not in the action of the Court.

§ 3. BUSINESS OF THE STAR CHAMBER

The Court of Star Chamber was specially concerned with riots and breaches of the peace, but its jurisdiction covered a far wider field. It punished juries who gave perverse verdicts[1] [p. 263]; and in a case of Henry VII's reign certain lawyers were prosecuted in the Court for giving counsel against the King. Ministers of state were summoned to the Star Chamber to answer for their conduct[2], and religious offences were dealt with there[3]. Cases also occur of murder, robbery, perjury, debt, seduction and abduction, slander, breaches of proclamations, and the enclosure of common lands[4]. In its later days, when disorder had been successfully suppressed, there was a great increase in the activity of the Court in the regulation of trade, and especially in the control of the food supply on which public tranquillity so largely depended[5]. It also supervised guilds and municipalities, and punished breaches of the ordinances relating to printing. Star Chamber cases illustrating some of its activities are printed on pp. 263–78 below.

The Star Chamber not only made a special business of punishing offenders against royal proclamations, but also claimed the right of issuing decrees, some of them of a very comprehensive character, and enforcing them by penalties. These are scarcely distinguishable from Orders in Council, and may be regarded as an exercise of the original authority of the King in Council from which the Court derived so large a part of its powers. There are decrees concerning trading companies, as for instance a decree of 29 January, 1577, deciding a controversy between the Company of Haberdashers and the hat and feltmakers in or near the City of London, and placing the feltmakers under the control of the Haberdashers' Company under penalty of contempt of court[6]. The most important of these decrees were those regulating printing, and so establishing a censorship of the press [p. 279].

Although the Star Chamber was a judicial tribunal, it never quite lost its political character as a council of state, and ambassadors were sometimes

---

[1] Cases of this are referred to in Scofield, p. 45.

[2] William Davison, Elizabeth's Secretary, who was disgraced by her on a charge of having carried out the execution of Mary Queen of Scots without instructions, was brought before the Star Chamber in 1587 for 'misprision and contempt,' and was eventually sentenced to imprisonment in the Tower and a fine of 10,000 marks. Empson also, according to Hudson (p. 16) 'was first blasted in this Court.'

[3] Under Henry VIII the inhabitants of Axminster prosecuted Philip Gammon for heresy, accusing him of having said, among other things, that 'the blessing of a bishop was as good as that of an old horse' (Scofield, p. 47). Cf. a case of 12 Jac. I, where Sir John Yorke was fined £1000 for permitting in his house a play or interlude representing a disputation between a Popish priest and a Protestant minister, in which the priest had the best of the argument and was carried off by an angel, while the minister left the stage in the custody of a fiend from the bottomless pit (*ib.* p. 47 *n*.).

[4] Bradford, p. 33, and Burn, *passim*.   [5] Leadam, II. p. xxi *et passim*.

[6] Scofield, p. 53.

received there and speeches made before the Lords on occasions of special solemnity. For instance, on 28 November, 1567, the Lord Keeper gave an address in the Star Chamber 'before the Council and others' touching seditious books[1]; and a letter of 1600 [p. 278] gives an account of 'a very grave speech' on various matters delivered in the Star Chamber by the Lord Keeper, apparently to the judges of assize about to proceed on circuit[2].

The Star Chamber was tyrannical, because it tended to become 'a court of politicians enforcing a policy, not a court of judges administering the law'[3]; but there can be little doubt that in the Tudor period, at any rate, its jurisdiction was on the whole beneficial. It had two functions of high importance to perform which no tribunal except one composed as this was composed and proceeding as this proceeded could have discharged efficiently. It had to put down anarchy, baronial and other, and to supplement the defects of the common law. The work was well done and the earlier writers are loud in their praise of the Court [pp. 284–98].

(1) The Act of 1487
[Pro Camera Stellata][4]
[An Act giving the Court of Star Chamber Authority to punish divers Misdemeanours]

The King our Sovereign Lord remembereth how by unlawful maintenances, giving of liveries signs and tokens, and retainders by indenture promises oaths writing or otherwise, embraceries[5] of his subjects, untrue demeanings of sheriffs in making of panels and other untrue returns, by taking of money by juries, by great riots and unlawful assemblies, the policy and good rule of this realm is almost subdued, and for the none punishment of this inconvenience and by occasion of the premises nothing or little may be found by inquiry, whereby the laws of the land in execution may take little effect, to the increase of murders, robberies, perjuries, and unsureties of all men living and losses of their lands and goods, to the great displeasure of Almighty God; Be it therefore ordained for reformation of the premises by the authority of this Parliament, That the Chancellor and Treasurer of England for the time being and Keeper of the King's Privy Seal, or two of them, calling to them a bishop and a temporal lord of the King's most honourable Council and the two Chief Justices of the King's Bench and Common Pleas for the time being, or other two

[1] *Cal. S.P. Dom.* 1547–80, p. 302.
[2] Cf. the report of a similar speech of 21 June, 1632, printed in *Cases in the Courts of Star Chamber and High Commission*, ed. S. R. Gardiner (Camden Society, 1886), p. 176. For other illustrations of the ceremonial use of the Star Chamber, see Scofield, pp. 55–60. [3] Maitland, p. 263.
[4] See note 4 on p. 249 above.
[5] 'Embracery' is the 'actual or attempted corrupt or forcible influencing of jurors' (see Winfield, pp. 161–174).

Justices in their absence, upon bill or information put to the said Chancellor for the King or any other against any person for any misbehaving afore rehearsed, have authority to call before them by writ or privy seal the said misdoers, and them and other by their discretions to whom the truth may be known to examine, and such as they find therein defective to punish them after their demerits, after the form and effect of statutes thereof made, in like manner and form as they should and ought to be punished if they were thereof convict after the due order of the law.....

3 Henr. VII, c. 1: Statutes of the Realm, ii, 509.

(2) The Act of 1529

The Privy Council is here referred to as the Council attending the King's person. See p. 217 above.

An Act that the President of the King's Council shall be associate with the Chancellor and Treasurer of England and the Keeper of the King's Privy Seal

[*After reciting* 3 *Henr. VII, c.* 1, *the Act proceeds*] Nevertheless in the same good and profitable statute the President of the King's most honourable Council for the time being attending upon his most noble and royal person is omitted and not named... to be one of the said persons that should have authority to call before them such misdoers so offending the King's laws in any of the premises as is before rehearsed. Be it therefore... enacted, that from henceforth the Chancellor, Treasurer of England, and the President of the King's most honourable Council attending upon his most honourable person for the time being, and the Keeper of the King's Privy Seal, or two of them, calling unto them one bishop and one temporal lord of the King's most honourable Council, and the two Chief Justices of the King's Bench and the Common Pleas for the time being, or other two of the King's Justices in their absence, upon any bill or information hereafter to be put in[1], the Chancellor of England, Treasurer, President of the King's said most honourable Council, or Keeper of the King's Privy Seal for the time being, for any misbehaving before rehearsed, from henceforth have full power and authority to call before them by writ of[2] privy seal such misdoers, and them and other by their discretion by whom the truth

[1] The Act of 1487 had required bills to be put to the Chancellor; this Act allows them to be put, as an alternative to the Chancellor, to any one of the three great officers named (Leadam, II, p. xiii).

[2] The printed copies of the Act read 'or.' The Act of 1487 also reads 'writ or privy seal,' the 'writ' being a writ of *subpoena* under privy seal and the 'privy seal' being letters of privy seal. The effect of reading 'of' would be to exclude the latter, and after 1529 letters of privy seal do not appear to be used. It is possible that 'of' was an error in the first instance which came to be accepted as having authority (*ib.*).

17—2

may be known to examine, and such as they shall find defective to punish them after their demerits after the form and effect of the said former statute and of all other statutes thereof tofore made and not repealed nor expired, in like manner and form as they should and ought to be punished if they were thereof convicted after the due order in the King's laws....

21 Henr. VIII, c. 20: *Statutes of the Realm*, iii, 304.

(3) The Merchant Adventurers *v.* The Staplers, 1504

Here we have a large Council giving judgment in the Star Chamber on a matter not covered by the Act of 1487.

[At Knole, 17 December, 1504]

Exemplification at the request of the society of 'merchauntes adventurers' of:

(1) The tenor of a judgment given by the King and Council in the 'Sterre Chambre' at Westminster, 26 November last, as to certain disputes between the said merchants adventurers and the merchants of the staple of Calais, whereby either party making any use of the privileges of the other, should be subject to all the regulations and penalties by which that other is bound.

(2) The names of the lords spiritual and temporal and others who were present with the King in Council at the giving of the above judgment, to wit: The Archbishop of Canterbury, Chancellor; the Archbishop of York, Treasurer of England; the Bishop of Winchester, the Archbishop of Dublin, the Bishop of Lincoln, the Bishop of Norwich, the Bishop of Coventry and Lichfield, the Bishop of Carlisle, the Bishop of Rochester, the Duke of Buckingham, the Marquis of Dorset, the Earl of Arundel, the Earl of Derby, the Earl of Ormonde; Lord Daubeney, the King's Chamberlain; Lord Abergavenny, Lord Dudley, Lord Hastings, Lord Herbert, Lord Darcy, Lord Willoughby, Lord Dacre of the South; Lord Fyneux, Chief Justice of the King's Bench; Lord Frowyk, Chief Justice of the Common Pleas; Master Routhall[1], the King's Secretary; Thomas Lovell[2], knight; Richard Guildford, knight; Edward Poynings[3], knight; Thomas Bourchier, knight; Edmund Dudley[4]; Master West, Doctor of Laws[5]; Robert Drury[6], knight; Robert Lytton, knight; Gilbert

[1] Bishop of Durham, 1509.
[2] Speaker of the House of Commons, 1485–8; President of the Council, 1502.
[3] Lord Deputy of Ireland, 1494, and the promoter of 'Poynings' Law.'
[4] The notorious Dudley was President of the Council in 1506 (*Calendar of Patent Rolls*, 1494–1509, p. 471).
[5] Probably Nicolas West, LL.D. *c.* 1485; Bishop of Ely, 1515–33.
[6] Sir Robert Drury was a barrister of Lincoln's Inn. He was Speaker of the House of Commons in 1495.

Talbot, knight; Walter Hungerford, knight; Master James
Stanley, Clerk; John Ryseley, knight; Henry Wyatt[1]; Master
Hatton, Doctor of Laws; Master Vaughan[2], Doctor of Laws;
Master Meautis, the King's Secretary in the French tongue.

Calendar of Patent Rolls, 1494–1509, p. 388.

(4) The Council to Sir William Paulet, 1570

This shews that the Star Chamber had become sufficiently separated from the
Council to be regarded as a rival Court.

[At Hampton Court, 21 December, 1570]

A letter to Sir William Paulet[3], knight, in answer of this of
the 4th of this month, whereby he seems to have forgotten or
mistaken their order of proceeding between him and John Yonge
at Chenies, whereat they cannot a little marvel, for as he knows
the cause that moved them to call them both before them grew
upon complaint made by him against the said Yonge, and having
heard what either of them could say for themselves they thought
meet to enjoin him, being the complainant, to put in writing such
matter as he had to charge the said Yonge withal, and to bring
or send the same within 8 or 10 days, to the end they might see
what the said Yonge could answer thereunto, for which purpose
he was commanded to attend about the Court until his bill of
complaint might be brought hither; and perceiving now not only
that he hath not observed the same, but contrary thereunto
means to prosecute the cause in Star Chamber, they cannot but
find this manner of dealing very strange, and think that he hath
therein much forgotten himself; like as[4] they mean not to suffer
the authority of this Table to be so much prejudiced as to endure
that any matter of complaint brought and dealt by them should
by the complainant himself be removed to any other Court before
the same be heard by their Lordships and ordered, so he is required with all speed to exhibit his said bill of complaint to the
intent the said Mr Yonge may answer thereunto. . . .

Dasent, *Acts of the Privy Council*, vii, 404.

[1] Knighted, 1509.
[2] Possibly Edward Vaughan, LL.D. Cambridge; Bishop of St David's, 1509.
[3] Afterwards third Marquis of Winchester.
[4] Since.

(5) Sir John Smyth to Lord Burghley, 1597

This shews that at this time the Star Chamber, unlike the Council Table, was a public and open Court.

[Sir John Smyth's 'railing letter from the Tower' to Lord Burghley,
26 May, 1597]

...I never offended any councillor or nobleman now living, but only you and yours in my drunkenness, and therefore I do not expect any harm by their means but only by yours; so likewise I cannot expect any favour, whatsoever means I should make, although I were at some liberty, without your furtherance, as your authority, as is well known through the kingdom, is exceeding great, and very few dare presume to favour me or any other man contrary to your liking....

...You have divers times asked by what warrant I would lead the people at Colchester; to which I say that at that time it was well known to most of those present that I was not in a case to lead any men, but rather a flock of goslings, I could not tell whither....By all the rest of my drunken doings that afternoon and evening following, till I had sleep, it may be apparent to all men that have any charity in them, and are not carried away with private passion, to consider in what poor estate of brain, through excess of wine, I then stood. All these circumstances considered, I think my petitions to you might have prevailed if you had had any charitable meaning towards me: one was either that you would recover her Majesty's favour towards me; or that I might be called before the Council Table to answer objections against me, and according to the judgment of the Council receive any further punishment; or else, after so long an imprisonment and great affliction, and in a manner my utter undoing, receive greater favour; any of which I think you might in right and without passion have deemed a great deal better for increasing your honour,—with a voluntary satisfaction to be made by me, without any great decay of my good fame, which I esteem more than my life,—rather than bring me into a public audience in the Star Chamber; there, after so long imprisonment and other great afflictions, by the cunning of lawyers to aggravate and turn offences committed in drunkenness as if they had been committed when sober, to increase my imprisonment with unpayable fines and heap afflictions upon afflictions....

Calendar of State Papers (Domestic), Eliz. 1595–7, p. 421.

(6) The Lords' Diet in the Star Chamber

From a paper in Lord Burghley's hand.

Anno, 1559, the ordinary charge of a dinner £4. 10s. or £5. 9s.
    1579   ...   .   £8   or £10
    1590   ...   .   £17   or £18

On Friday, 24 June, 1509, 'Bread, Ale, Beer, Wine, Tryng[1], Blote-fish[2], Pike, Flounders, Soles, Porpoises, Butter and Eggs, Strawberries, Flour, Salt, Herbs, Spices, Peasecods[3]'... ... ... 19 9
Boat-hire and washing of the napery 1 3
Wood and Coals 2 0
Cook's wages 2 4
[Other expenses] ... ... [5 3]

£1 10 7

The charge of a Flesh Dinner at the Star Chamber, 5 Feb. 1588

	s.	d.		s.	d.
Beef, 18 stone at 2s. the stone	37	0	Teals, 18	12	0
			Snipes, 18	9	0
Mutton, 13 joints ...	24	0	Tame Pigeons, 24...	12	0
Veal, 9 joints ...	22	6	Black Birds, 24 ...	6	0
Lamb, ...	15	0	Rabbits, 4	3	0
Three Turkeys ...	20	0	Rabbit Suckers[5], 12	6	0
Ten Capons ...	26	8	Larks, 48	6	8
Pullets of Goose, 9	13	4	Brawn for Collops...	6	8
Pheasants, 3 ...	18	0	Butter	14	0
Hernshaws[4], 3 ...	15	0	Eggs	13	4
Mallards, 8 ...	9	4	With divers other		
Partridges, 11 ...	16	6	things of smaller		
Woodcocks, 11 ...	12	10	rates, so that this		
Plovers, 18 ...	12	0	dinner comes to		

£18. 5s. 2d.

Quoted in J. S. Burn, *The Star Chamber*, pp. 24–5.

(7) Cases in the Star Chamber

(1) *Fining of juries*

ATTORNEY-GENERAL *v.* PARRE AND OTHERS, 1489

This is a case of proceedings against a jury for perjury. The ordinary kind of perjury was a matter for the ecclesiastical courts, and it only came before the royal

[1] 'Tring' is a kind of small plover, but this must be a misreading, perhaps for ling. [2] Bloaters. [3] Pea-pods.
[4] Herons. [5] Very young rabbits.

courts when it affected the King. But as the assizes were a royal ordinance, perjury by a jury there was an offence against the King, and an attaint would lie. In this case the original jury of 12 was tried by another jury of 24 at least, and if the verdict of the 24 was against them, they were arrested and imprisoned, and their lands and goods were forfeited to the Crown. By 11 Henr. VII, c. 24, these tremendous penalties were reduced to a substantial fine. But perjury by juries could also be dealt with by the Council, and later by the Star Chamber; and from perjury by juries its jurisdiction came to be extended to perjuries of all kinds[1].

The original information against the jury is not extant, and only their answer to the information survives.

This is the answer of William Parre [*and eleven others*] to the information put against them by Mr Hobart the King's Attorney.

The said William Parre [*and others*] say that truth it is that they were empanelled upon the acquittal of the said John Wood and William Frank for the matter in the said information specified before the King's Judges and at the time and place in the said information specified; howbeit, they had such evidences given them at that time for the proof that the said John and William were not guilty of that escape whereof before that time they were indicted, that in their consciences they thought plainly they could no otherwise do without they should have been forsworn but to do as they did in the acquittal of the said John and William of the said escape, for they say one ——, the wife of John Edmundes, the under-keeper of the King's Bench, testified to the said William Parre [*etc.*] the said John and William, after the said John Day was arrested for the felony in the said information specified, delivered the said John Day to the keeping of the King's Bench, and there as a prisoner was received, and there he continued by the space of 3 days unto the time he escaped thence after that that the said John Wood and William Frank were lawfully discharged of him; without that[2] the said William Parre [*etc.*] acquitted the said John and William of the said felony by any corrupt mean or that the said William Parre [*etc.*] ever had any such evidence or information given them which should have discharged their conscience to [have] attainted the said John and William of the said escape, and without that the said William Parre [*etc.*] were perjured in giving the said verdict to their knowledge, all which matters the said William Parre [*etc.*] at all times are ready to prove as this Court will award them, and prayeth to be dismissed out of that same with their reasonable costs and damages for their wrong, vexation, and trouble in that behalf.

Leadam, *Select Cases in the Star Chamber* (Selden Society), i, 18.

---

[1] Leadam, I, pp. cxxxiii–cxxxv. [2] See note on p. 274 below.

(2) *Riot*

ABBOT OF EYNESHAM *v.* HARCOURT AND OTHERS, 1503

This case is a good illustration of the social disorder which the Star Chamber under the Tudors did so much to put down. The charges against the defendant include most of the offences referred to in the preamble of the Act of 1487.

To the King our Sovereign Lord

Humbly sheweth unto your noble Highness your daily orator Miles, Abbot of your monastery of Eynesham within the county of Oxford, of divers riots, extortions, wrongs, and injuries done to him and his convent by Sir Robert Harcourt, knight, and divers other evil-disposed persons to him belonging and retained.

First, where one John Walsh, otherwise called Sawyer, a servant to the said Sir Robert, desired and prayed instantly one Dan[1] Roger Wallingford, one of the commons[2] of the said monastery having the rule of the waters and nets of your said monastery, that he might have his draught-net to fish his waters of the Thames side, having therefor as it is accustomed in the country, that is to say the third part; and when the said water was drawed and fished, the said Dan Roger left the poising-stones[3] of the said draught-net in an island pertaining to the farm of the said John, and brought home his net with him again, which was the 19th day of September last past. And the 16th day of February then next following, the said Dan Roger and one Christopher, servant of the said monastery, of the age of 60 years and more, came into the said island with the boat of the said monastery for to fetch the said stones again, and the forsaid John Walsh, perceiving them being there, came privily, while they were in the said island gathering the said stones, and took away their said boat, and seditiously rowed the said boat away, intending to have destroyed them, and so left them there like to have been perished, for it was cold weather and frost. And the said Dan Roger and Christopher were environed with water by the space of half a mile. They perceiving the malice of the said John, cried for help, and so at last one Ralph Murray heard and came to them with a boat and carried them to land, or else that night they had been destroyed for cold and with the water.

Also the 15th day of March the said John Walsh came with another boat of his own into the several[4] water within the orchard

---

[1] For 'dominus'; cf. 'Dom,' still used as a title for monks of the Benedictine order.   [2] *I.e.* co-moynes, fellow-monks.

[3] Stones for weighting the net.   [4] Separate, *i.e.* private.

of the said monastery and there tied his said boat, and then the
officers of your said monastery, perceiving the said boat there,
for the hurt, harm, and great damage done to your said monastery,
as fetting[1] there divers times wiles[2] and nets of your said monastery, took a lock and locked his said boat to a tree; and when the
said John perceived that his boat was fast locked that he could
not have it away, he returned home to his house and fetched a
bill and an hanger and came again forcibly into the said orchard
over an high wall, there meeting with two of the monks menacing
and threatening them, calling them churls and thieves, and upon
that did smite at one of the said monks with the said bill and
smote him down to the ground, and his fellow, perceiving the
malicious disposition of the said John, avoided, and the said John
pursued after him to have slain him.

Also the 23rd day of the said month, at Tenebrae Wednesday[3]
at service time, Martin Whithill [*and others*]...servants retained
with Sir Robert Harcourt, came with force and arms, that is to
say with bills, swords, and daggers, and other weapons, and
entered into the said orchard against the King's peace, coming
over the wall of the said orchard, with other evil-disposed persons
being without the wall ready to assist them, to the number of 11
persons...bringing with them an axe to hew down the said tree
that the boat was locked to, and so forcibly to carry it away and
to be avenged on such persons as did arrest the said boat; and at
such season as they were there was four of the monks walking in
the said orchard, and they seeing them there they returned back
to the Prior and shewed him of the said persons, but what they
intended they knew not. Whereupon the said Prior came to the
said persons and enquired of them why they came there so suspiciously over so high great walls being ditched fifteen foot broad
in such forcible manner, and they answered, 'Whorson churls,
deliver us the boat that ye have arrested, or else we will have it
whether ye will or no, and also be revenged upon you ere we
depart this ground.' And the said Prior, seeing them so wilfully
and unreasonably disposed, satisfied them with good and cold[4]
words. Whereupon they departed.

Also the 10th day of April then next ensuing...came Thomas
Cater [*and others*]...with other persons unknown, servants retained to [the] said Sir Robert Harcourt, into the town of Eynesham with force and arms, that is to say also with bows and
arrows, swords, bucklers, halberds, bills, and daggers, and then

[1] Stealing.   [2] Snares.
[3] The Wednesday before Easter.   [4] Cool.

and there went into divers houses and sought and enquired if any servant pertaining to the Abbey might be found. And so it fortuned that they met with an innocent body, one John Hadley, clerk of the church of the said monastery, having a bottle in his hand to fetch oil for the said church, and there violently the said Thomas Cater smote the said John Hadley with a dagger and sore hurt and wounded him on the head, whereupon the said clerk returned into your said monastery and shewed the Prior and convent, being at supper, how they had beaten and hurt him, and that they were coming after him; upon which shewing, the said Prior did send for the constable and the tithing-men to see the peace kept, and thereupon the said constable and tithing-men charged the said riotous and evil-disposed persons to keep the peace in God's name and the King's, and they defied them and put them in jeopardy of their lives, and so incontinent came to the gates of the said monastery and shot in arrows, putting the Prior and Subprior in jeopardy of their lives, and hewed at the said gates with their bills, and lifted them then out of the hooks with their halberds. Then they within the gates, as the porter with other, set timber against the gate and did under-set it[1] again; and then they took their halberds and hewed at their legs under the gate, and then they made an outcry and called for straw and furzes for to set fire on the gates and on the said monastery. Moreover the said evil-doers afterward went to Stanton and raised up more people that night, and drave the said Prior to ordain men for the safeguard of them and the monastery to watch all night unto the next morrow that they sent for two justices of the peace, Master William Harcourt and Mr Edgecumbe of Oxford. Upon the which Master William Harcourt came to the town of Eynesham beforesaid and charged the constables and tithing-men to see good rule kept, rebuking one John Murray, William Wood, and other, pertaining to Sir Robert Harcourt, to suffer and maintain any such evil-disposed persons, which he would lay to their charge hereafter. And not withstanding the premises, the said Sir Robert Harcourt with his adherents, of very pure malice, without any occasion or lawful cause given unto him or any of his, hath untruly indicted certain of the monks of the said monastery at Islip of felony...to the great hurt and impoverishment of the same monastery, and so utterly he intendeth to undo them, except your good grace to them be shewed in this behalf. And yet after all this the said Sir Robert Harcourt could not be content, but attempted to indict more of the said

---

[1] Prop it up.

monks at the sessions kept at Chipping Norton, and there all the Court knew and perceived that it was of wilful malice, so that at that sessions he could not obtain his malicious purpose.

And moreover the Thursday next following he caused a sessions to be kept at Henley-upon-Thames in the extreme part of the shire of Oxford, which is more than 26 miles from the said monastery, and there caused divers of the said monks to be indicted, some of felony and some of riot and some of both, and hath returned the said indictments into the King's Bench, notwithstanding a *certiorari*[1] to him before delivered.

Also the said Sir Robert Harcourt, contrary to the laudable statutes of this land, maintaineth certain evil-disposed persons in the towns of Eynesham and Charlbury...so that the officers and servants of your said orators, when they shall require any rents or other duties, be so threatened and embraced[2] with the said Sir Robert and his servants that they dare nor may peaceably do your said orator service.

[Then follows an article complaining that Sir Robert Harcourt had taken away 300 of the abbey sheep, and also 16 oxen, so that the Abbot could not sow his lands.]

Also the said Sir Robert at every sessions and assize will not suffer the King's laws peaceably with justice to be executed, and especially when any *nisi prius* should pass between party and party[3]; if the jury be not returned after his mind, with his riotous adherents he stoppeth them with threatening and other means, that the true process of the laws may not pass but after his wilful and unlawful pleasures, insomuch that at the last assize kept upon the bridge[4] besides Abingdon in the county of Oxon he kept certain persons by violence in a chamber, and also letted[5] other persons to come to the said assize, as the Justices then being there can more largely shew....

All which the premises considered, that it may please your good Grace to grant several[6] writs of *subpoena* to be directed as well to the said Sir Robert Harcourt [*as to* 21 *other persons named*] ...commanding them by the same to appear before your Highness and your most honourable Council in the Star Chamber at Westminster to answer as well your Highness as your said orator

---

[1] *Certiorari* was a writ issuing out of the Chancery to an inferior Court calling up to some other Court the record of a pending case, on a complaint from one of the parties that he was not receiving justice or 'not like to have an indifferent trial in the said Court' (Jacob).

[2] See note on p. 258 above; but the term is here used loosely.

[3] *I.e.* 'especially in *nisi prius* cases.'

[4] The Court was probably held in the hall of the abbey, which is close to the bridge.   [5] Hindered.   [6] Separate.

of the said wrongs, riots, and extortions before done; and the same your orator shall alway pray for the preservation of your gracious estate long to endure to God's pleasure.

Then follow the answer of Sir Robert Harcourt and a separate answer on behalf of certain other defendants to the Abbot's bill of complaint.

Leadam, i, 137. The case is also printed in A. F. Pollard, *The Reign of Henry VII from Contemporary Sources*, ii, 90.

(3) *Assault*

This is really a case of aggravated assault, although an attempt is made to represent it as a riot.

DOBELL *v.* SOLEY AND OTHERS, 1533

To the King our Sovereign Lord

In most humble wise sheweth unto your Highness your true and faithful subject, Giles Dobell, that where your said orator is and long time hath been seized...of...one messuage or tenement...in Minehead in your county of Somerset, and by reason thereof hath used to have a seat or pew for him and his wife in the said church of Minehead foresaid, in the which pew one Margery, wife to your said subject...was sitting and hearing her divine service as she ought to do, one Walter Soley [*and others*]...in riotous manner arrayed...with force and arms, that is to say with swords and bucklers, daggers, and other weapons invasive, contrary to your peace...into the said church of Minehead entered, and then and there took out the said Margery...of her said pew where she was kneeling in the said church, and her brought out into an aisle in the said church against her will, and then and there did her beat and ill entreat, by reason whereof, and for such fear as she then stood in, she fell in such a swoon or sickness that she was likely there to have died, if good help of certain of the said parochyns[1] then and there being had not helped her. And the said misruled persons, not with this contented but of their further mischievous mind only intending to have murdered and slain your said subject, the... day...next following in like riotous manner came into the said church...with staves, swords, halberds, and axes, and then and there brake the same pew, where the wife of your said orator then was, and said to her these words following:—'Where is that knave thy husband? And if[2] he were here we would have of him a leg or an arm'; by reason whereof your said subject dare not come to the said church for fear and danger of his life, to the perilous

---

[1] Parishioners.   [2] 'And if' = supposing that.

example of such like offenders in time to come if remedy be not
by your Grace and your most honourable Council the rather provided in this behalf. It may therefore please your Highness, the
premises considered, to grant several writs of *subpoena* to be
directed to the said Robert [*and others*]...commanding them
and every of them by virtue thereof personally to appear before
your Highness and your most honourable Council at Westminster at a certain day to answer to the premises, etc.

Then follow the answer of the defendants to the bill of complaint and the
'replication' of the plaintiff. These shew that the real question at issue was whether
the plaintiff had a right to the pew in virtue of his occupation of his house, or whether
Robert Coke, one of the defendants, had a prior claim, having 'bought the said pew'
from the churchwardens 'for term of his life.' The defendants claimed that they
'brake down the same pew' 'for quieting of the said parish.'

Miss G. Bradford, *Proceedings in the Court of the Star Chamber*
(Somerset Record Society, 1911), pp. 121–5.

CAPPIS *v.* CAPPIS, BEFORE 1548

This is a case of assault arising out of a claim to land, but an attempt is made,
as in the previous case, to treat the incident as if it were a riot.

To the King our Sovereign Lord

In most humble wise complaineth to your Highness your
daily oratrix and poor bedewoman, Philippa Cappis, widow, late
wife of James Cappis, esquire, deceased, That where John Rowe,
serjeant-at-the-law, and other, were and yet be seized of and in
six messuages and 400 acres of land lying in East Whitfield and
West Whitfield in your county of Somerset in their demesne as
of fee to the use of your said oratrix for term of her life as for her
jointure to her by her said late husband willed and put in surety,
which lands and tenements since the decease of her said husband
your said oratrix hath peaceably had, used, and occupied by the
sufferance of the said John Rowe and other....So it is, most
dread Sovereign Lord, that one Robert Cappis, one of the sons
of the said James, being a person of most ragious and wilful condition, nothing dreading the punishment of your laws as concerning his wilful and ragious acts, wrongfully, forcibly, and in
riotous manner, accompanied with three like ragious and riotous
persons apparelled with weapons of warfare defensible...upon
the Feast of St Luke last past came into the town of Wivelscombe
in your said county, and perceiving that your oratrix was at dinner
within an honest man his house within the said town, came into the
said house where your said oratrix was at dinner and seeing her
there suddenly plucked out his sword, saying these words to her
as hereafter followeth, that is to wit: 'Ah, thou stepdame, by

God's Blood I care not though I thrust my sword through thee,'
and he intending so to have done in most eager manner, one of
his said riotous company, being somewhat better advised, plucked
him aback, saying to him these words: 'Master Cappis, beware
what ye do; kill her not.' And furthermore, before the said
riotous persons coming into the said house, the said oratrix had
with her in the said house one of her sons called Sir Roger Cappis,
being a priest, brother to the said Robert Cappis, which Roger
shortly perceiving the sudden coming of the said riotous persons,
unto whom the said Robert had a long time borne his deadly
malice for no other quarrel but for assistance and defence of his
said mother's lawful quarrel and title in the premises, and dreading
the danger of his life or bodily hurt suddenly to be to him done
by the said riotous persons, conveyed himself and avoided from
their presence, before their said coming in, at a back-side of the
said house, and so departed out of their danger; after whose departing and after the said ragious demeanour of the said Robert
to your oratrix as is aforesaid, the said Robert demanded by these
words following: 'Where is that whoreson the priest? If I had
him I would hew him in small gobbets to sell him at the market
ere I went.' And this done, the said riotous persons departed,
leaving your said oratrix in such dread and agony that she was
and hath been since in peril of her body and life, and ever shall
be the worse while she liveth. Yet the said malefactors, not contented with their said ragious demeanour, perceiving your oratrix
to be from home, in like ragious and riotous demeanour incontinent entered into the said lands and there took and drove away
a cow in the name of an heriot[1], saying there and publishing
himself to be very lord and heir of the same lands, and in like
manner he hath used himself upon the premises divers times
before this, and hath received with menacing and threatening of
your oratrix's poor tenants of the said premises divers sums of
money of the rents of right belonging to your oratrix, the said
Robert Cappis having no manner of colour of title to the premises,
neither as heir to the same nor otherwise; which is not only great
dread as well to her person but also of the vexation for her said
poor tenants and danger of their lives, and by occasion whereof
she is in such a confusion, what for lack of receipt of the profits
of the said lands which is her whole living, and what for the wild
and furious rage of the said Robert and his adherents, that she
being a woman in extreme age and impotent, and cannot without

---

[1] A payment due to the lord on the death of a tenant; in the case of copyholds
it usually took the form of the tenant's best live beast.

extreme charges defend herself, knoweth not what to do without the merciful succour of your most gracious Highness in such case requisite to be administered to poor, impotent, and succourless widows; wherefore may it please your Highness of your most abundant grace to grant to your said suppliant your gracious writs of *subpoena* to be directed to the said Robert and other the said riotous persons with him before named, commanding them by virtue of the same to appear before your Highness and your most honourable Council in your High Court of Star Chamber, there to answer to the premises, and further commanding the said Robert by any of the said writs to him to be delivered by way of injunction, to avoid his possession of the premises and to suffer your said oratrix in the mean time peaceably to occupy the same till such time as the title in the premises be tried before your said honourable Council.... Bradford, p. 264.

(4) *Trespass*

WALTERKYN *v.* LETTICE, 1503

In this case the hermit of Highgate proceeds against the Vicar of St Pancras, Kentish Town, for trespass, assault, and loss of goods. The hermit was the successor of a long line of hermits who since 1364 had been charged with the repair of the road from Highgate to Smithfield, with a right of toll. The vicar was claiming the right to take a religious procession through the hermit's garden. As in the two preceding cases an attempt is made to represent the offence as a riot.

To the King our Sovereign Lord

In most humble wise sheweth unto your Highness your poor humble orator and daily bedeman, Thomas Walterkyn, hermit of St Michael besides Highgate in the parish of Hornsey. Whereon Sir Robert Lettice, vicar of the parish of St Pancras in the field called Kentish Town, William Chadwick of the same parish, yeoman, John Hosteler, yeoman, and Richard Taylor, with other divers and many rioters and evil-disposed persons, to the number of 40 persons and more, upon Tuesday last past, the 23rd day of this present month of May, in riotous wise and in manner of war, that is to say with bills and staves and other weapons defensible, came into the house and hermitage of your said orator in the parish of Hornsey aforesaid, your said orator then being in his garden and his servant with him in peaceable manner there labouring, and then and there riotously with divers menacing and threatening words brake and hewed down as well the pale of the orchard of your said orator as the pale of his garden and unlawfully entered into the same, and without cause or occasion given by your said orator the said William Chadwick struck your said orator upon the arm with a bill, and would have murdered him except he had escaped from the said William and his company into the steeple of his said hermitage, wherein he continued by all the time of their being there. And furthermore your said orator saith that the said rioters entered into the dwelling-house of your said orator, and some of them took away two altar-cloths, a surplice, and a book called a grail[1], with other stuff, besides other hurts and harms to him done in his said orchard and garden. And as yet your said orator dare not presume to go home to his said hermitage unless your gracious succour to him be shewed in that behalf. Please it therefore, your said gracious Highness, the premises tenderly considered, grant your gracious letters of privy seal to be directed to the said Sir [Robert], William Chadwick, John Hosteler, and Richard Taylor, or a serjeant-of-arms or some other commandment, them and every of them straitly commanding by the same to appear before your said Highness and the Lords of your most honourable Council at a certain day and under a certain pain to them and to every of them to be limited by the same. And your said orator shall daily pray to God for the preservation of your most noble and royal estate....

> The answer of Sir Robert Lettice, clerk, Vicar of St Pancras, William Chadwick, John Hosteler, and Richard Taylor to the bill of complaint of Thomas Walterkyn of St Michael by Highgate.

The said vicar and the other say that the said bill is not certain nor sufficient to be answered unto, but of great malice untruly feigned and imagined only to slander, vex, and trouble the said vicar and the other, and the matter therein contained determinable at the common law and not in this Court, whereto they pray to be remitted; and, the advantage thereof to them saved, for declaration of truth and answer say that the said vicar and the other beforenamed, with the whole parish of Kentish Town, the said 23rd day of May in the bill of the said hermit specified, which was in the Rogation Week, according to the laudable custom of England went in procession about their said parish in their prayers, as they and their predecessors have used to do time out of mind in God's peace and the King's, till they came to the hermitage of the said hermit at Highgate, which hermit and his predecessors stopped the procession way of your said vicar and of his parishioners by means of making of pales and dykes, and would not suffer them to pass with their procession as they were

[1] See note on p. 114 above.

wont to do, albeit the said hermit was courteously entreated by
the said Chadwick and other to suffer them peaceably to pass
with their procession; and then the said hermit, having a great
club by him in his garden, and two other with him with clubs,
also Richard Yardley and Thomas Marshall, suddenly took the
said clubs and strake at the said Chadwick over the pale, with the
violence of which stroke the said hermit brake divers of his pales;
and afterwards divers of the said parish pulled down certain pales
for the said parish to pass with their procession, and so departed
peaceably that way with their procession without any occasion-
giving or quarrel-making to the said hermit or to any other. And
as to the entering into the dwelling-house of the said hermit and
taking away of certain books thence, they say that they be not
thereof guilty, but they say that the said hermit is a man of ill
conversation and rule, for they say that the said hermit hath laid
to pledge one of the books that he supposeth should be stolen,
that is to say a grail and other stuff, to one John Philip for a certain sum of money, which the said Philip will avow and testify,
which he would now colourably and untruly lay to the charge of
divers of the said parishioners. Without that[1] that the said vicar
and the other before named came riotously into the house and
hermitage of the said hermit in the parish of Hornsey in manner
and form as by the said bill is supposed, and without that that
they be guilty of breaking or hewing any pale otherwise but as
before doth appear, and without that that the said William Chadwick is guilty of striking the said hermit with a bill or otherwise
in manner and form as by the said bill is also supposed, and
without that that the said vicar and the other aforesaid be guilty
of any riot or were of any such misdemeanour in manner and form
as by the bill of the said hermit is supposed. All which matters
the said vicar and the other be ready to prove and make good as
this Court will award, and pray to be dismissed with their reasonable costs and charges for their wrongful vexation and trouble
sustained in this behalf.

> This is the replication of Thomas Walterkyn, hermit of St
> Michael besides Highgate, to the answer of Sir Robert,
> vicar of St Pancras, William Chadwick, and others.

The said hermit saith that his bill of complaint is true in
everything and sufficient to be answered; and he saith that the

---

[1] 'Without that' purports to be a translation of *absque hoc*, a phrase used in
medieval pleadings. The expression is purely formal, but the sense is that the
plaintiff's claim is good 'without that,' *i.e.* 'except' for the defence.

said vicar and other be guilty of the said riot and misbehaving in manner and form as in the said bill is supposed, and moreover he saith that the said hermitage is in the parish of Hornsey out of the parish of St Pancras, and he saith that divers persons, as well of the said parish as of other places, of their devotion have used to enter into the chapel of the said hermitage to hear divine service and to honour God there at times convenient. Without that the said vicar or any of the said parish of St Pancras have or ought to have any procession way there or any there or any other colour or title of entry into the said hermitage or any part thereof other than as he hath before rehearsed; and without that the said hermit or any other for him had any club or staff at the time of the said riot and forcible entry committed by the said vicar and other; and without that the said hermit is a man of misrule or that he pledged any stuff belonging to the said hermitage as the said vicar and other in their answer have supposed. All which matters he is ready to prove as this Court will award, and prayeth as in his bill, etc.

Leadam, i, 164.

(5) *Slander*
VALE v. BROKE, 1493

Proceedings for slander were usually taken in the ecclesiastical courts. In this case the Star Chamber could probably claim to be supplementing the defects of common or statute law[1].

To the King our Sovereign Lord and the discreet Lords of his most noble Council

Lamentably complaining sheweth unto your Highness your humble subject and true liegeman, Simon Vale of Castle Bromwich in your county of Warwick. That where one John Broke and Alice his wife of the same town, of their great malices and evil wills bearing to your said beseecher, and to the intent utterly to shame him and his for ever, hath openly disclandered him amongst his neighbours that he, his wife and children, and all his kin should be strong thieves and common robbers, whereas his neighbours and other inhabitants in his country will record he is a true man and all his household also. And over this the said John Broke of his said malice hath suffered his beasts through his own ground to destroy the grains of your said beseecher, to the intent utterly to destroy and undo him. Considering, gracious Sovereign Lord, that the said John Broke hath said and done these injuries to your said beseecher since an obligation of £40 sealed and delivered by him to your said beseecher was forfeit,

---

[1] Leadam, I, p. cxxxii.

which obligation is ready to be shewed. In consideration of the premises; and that your said orator is not able to sue the said John Broke and his wife for his remedy at your common law; and that also the said John Broke of his great power holdeth great lands in the said parish of his lord there and is his bailiff, for the which he payeth no task[1] to your Grace but compelleth your said beseecher and other his poor neighbours about him to pay his task and tallage to your said Grace for the land he occupieth and holdeth, to their great hurts and impoverishment; and also by his great power the said John and his wife are common receivers of thieves and vagabonds for money to him given; and also is a common receiver, and maintainers of common queans, priests' lemans, and keepeth them for money in his house by 6 or 7 weeks, and will not suffer them for his lucre to come to church to hear God's service, to the great abuse of all his poor neighbours about him and disclander to all the country, so that for dread of him and of such persons adherent to the said thieves and queans he for dread of his death dare not continue in his poor house, but of necessity must inhabit him in other places. And for the true proof of the premises, if need be, all the honest inhabitants of the said parish will, if they be commanded by your Grace, be ready to come afore your Highness and your said Council at their proper costs to report the same. Please it your Highness, the premises graciously considered, and that the said John Broke here now present for his false defamation and other hurts to him done, and also for the said misbehaving, may be punished according to his desert as right requireth. This for the love of God and in the way of charity, and he shall pray to God for the preservation of your full noble and royal estate....   Leadam, i, 38.

(6) *Unjust tolls*

COOPER *v* GERVAUX AND OTHERS, 1493

In this case, as in many others, there is a tendency to associate the real grievance with a suggestion of riot in order to bring it within the special jurisdiction of the Star Chamber.

To the King our Sovereign Lord and the Lords of his most
honourable Council, spiritual and temporal

Sheweth and grievously complaineth unto your most noble Grace your true and faithful subject Hugh Cooper, citizen and draper of your City of London, how that whereas he and many other merchants of your said City have of long continuance used to resort every year unto the Fair of Salisbury there holden and

_____
[1] Tax.

kept at our Lady Day in Lent in the common market-place of that City, and every man to have his convenient room there to utter in such wares and goods as he bringeth thither to and for the same intent during the season that the Fair continueth, and at their departing to reward such officers as be appointed therefor by the same City, every man of his courtesy for the standing, at his pleasure and nothing of duty. Truth it is, gracious Lord, that at our Lady Day was twelvemonth one John Gervaux of the same City, goldsmith, and John Chapman of the same, chapman, came to the booth of your said orator and of him asked 4*d.* for every foot of ground that he occupied...and so because he asked them what authority they had to shew for them whereby to claim the said duty, they all to[1] reviled him and called him knave, with other cruel and despiting words and threats, and there made assault upon him, and finally by the supportation and maintenance of one Blacker, then Mayor there, took from him by force and plain extortion a distress of his goods, and the same carried away with them at their pleasures without his love or leave, expressly against your laws, to his great hurt and wrongs. And furthermore, by the supportation, comfort, and maintenance of one Thomas Coke, Mayor there the last year, your said orator being...at the said Fair, there came to his stall one William Hall, the Bishop's under-bailiff, there and then, and there made a great assault upon him, and him threatened to kill and slay out of hand without he would pay the said money...by mean of which trouble the same bailiff caused your said orator clearly to lose his Fair and feat of merchandise[2] at that time, to his great hurt and loss, fear and jeopardy of his life, insomuch that lest he should have been murdered and slain there amongst them he was fain to get him out of the City as hastily as he could by possibility, and yet as privily as he departed thence the said bailiff, utterly set and disposed to have slain him, lay in a wait upon him with 3 horse and as many men arrayed in manner of war and in riotous wise, that is to say with swords and bucklers, spears, and other defensible weapons, and on horseback, muffled every each one because they would not be known, and so pursued and followed him from the said City of Sarum to Andover....

Please it your good Grace, in consideration of the premises, considering this your said orator has no power to sue your common law for his remedy in this party against the said City, by whom this matter is borne out of wilfulness only, without any lawful ground, of your great bounty to grant hereupon your gracious

---

[1] Utterly.   [2] Feat of merchandise = mercantile business.

letters of privy seal directed to the said Thomas Coke, William
Hall, John Gervaux, goldsmith, and John Chapman, chapman,
charging them straitly by the same to be and appear personally
before your Grace and your said Council at your Palace of Westminster upon a reasonable pain in the utas[1] of the Purification of
our Blessed Lady next coming, to answer unto the premises, and
to such things as then and there shall be objected and laid against
them, at the reverence of God and in the way of charity.. . .

Leadam, i, 36.

A number of seventeenth century cases, printed in *Cases in the Courts
of Star Chamber and High Commission*, ed. S. R. Gardiner (Camden Society,
1886), illustrate the same points. See especially the following: (1) *Attorney-
General* v. *Moody and others*, 1631 (p. 59), dealing with a riot made by
certain persons claiming rights of common against Sir Cornelius Vermuyden's operations for the draining of the fens, in the course of which the
rioters demolished the work, destroyed the spades, wheelbarrows, and planks,
beat the workmen, and 'threw some of them into the water and held them
under a while'; the Court inflicted fines upon the defendants and condemned
them 'to pay for damages unto Sir Cornelius Vermuyden. . .£2000.' (2) In
Attorney-General v. *William Leake and others*, 1631 (p. 79) one defendant
was charged with forging a will leaving a manor and mansion-house to her
son, and the son was charged with organising a riot to enter it by force;
an aggravating circumstance being that he had 'whiffed tobacco' in the
face of the rightful owner; but the Court dismissed the case. (3) In the
Earl of Suffolk v. *Sir Richard Grenville*, 1631 (p. 108) the defendant was
fined £4000 to the King and mulcted in £4000 to the plaintiff for libelling
him by calling him 'a base lord.' (4) In *Attorney-General* v. *Theodore Kelly*,
1632 (p. 112), the defendant was charged with provocation to a breach of
the peace by threatening to cudgel another, which the Court held to tend
to a duel, which, as the Attorney-General pointed out, is 'a most perilous
thing,—it hath in it apparent danger of both their souls and bodies'; the
sentence was a fine of £200 and imprisonment during the King's pleasure,
and the Lord Privy Seal and the Lord Keeper 'found great fault' with Mr
Kelly's 'long, ruffian-like hair,' and 'would have topped him if the vote
of the Court had been for it.'

Rushworth in his *Historical Collections* (ii, 203) also reports a case in
which the Star Chamber in 1633 sentenced an Irish judge to a fine of £2000,
and imprisonment in the Fleet during the King's pleasure, for procuring the
condemnation of an innocent man by means of threats to the jury, with
damages of £1000 to the victim's son.

(8) Speech in the Star Chamber, 1600
[13 June, 1600]

. . . I was yesterday at the Star Chamber upon report of some
special matter that should be delivered touching my Lord of
Essex, where the Lord Keeper made a very grave speech in

[1] Octave.

nature of a charge to the Judges, to look to the overgrowing idle multitude of justices of peace, to maintainers and abettors of causes and suits, to solicitors and pettifoggers, to gentlemen that leave hospitality and housekeeping and hide themselves in cities and borough towns, to the vanity and excess of women's apparel, to forestallers and regraters of markets, to drunkards and disorderly persons, to masterless men and other companions that make profession to live by their sword and by their wit, to discoursers and meddlers in Prince's matters, and lastly to libellers. ...

> John Chamberlain, *Letters during the Reign of Queen Elizabeth* (Camden Society, 1861), p. 77.

(9) Star Chamber Decree concerning Printers, 1586

The Order in Council of 1566 concerning seditious books (see p. 245 above) was followed by a Star Chamber Decree of 23 June, 1584, 'for the redressing the abuses in printing'[1]; and this by the important Decree of 1586 here printed, drafted by Archbishop Whitgift. This follows the order of 1566 in imposing special duties upon the Stationers' Company.

Whereas sundry decrees and ordinances have upon grave advice and deliberation been heretofore made and practised for the repressing of such great enormities and abuses as of late (more than in times past) have been commonly used and practised by divers contemptuous and disorderly persons professing the art or mystery of printing and selling of books; and yet, notwithstanding, the said abuses and enormities are nothing abated, but (as it is found by experience) do rather more and more increase, by the wilful and manifest breach and contempt of the said ordinances, to the great displeasure and offence of the Queen's most excellent Majesty; by reason whereof sundry intolerable offences, troubles, and disturbances have happened, as well in the Church as in the civil government of the State and Commonweal of this realm, which seem to have grown because the pains and penalties contained and set down in the same ordinances and decrees have been too light and small for the correction and punishment of so grievous and heinous offences, and so the offenders and malefactors in that behalf have not been so severely punished as the quality of their offences have deserved:

Her Majesty therefore of her most godly and gracious disposition, being careful that speedy and due reformation be had of the abuses and disorders aforesaid, and that all persons using and professing the art, trade, or mystery of printing or selling of books should from henceforth be ruled and directed therein by

[1] *Cal. S.P. Dom.* 1581–90, p. 184.

some certain or known rules or ordinances which should be inviolably kept and observed and the breakers and offenders of the same to be severely and sharply punished and corrected, hath straitly charged and required the most Reverend Father in God the Archbishop of Canterbury, and the right honourable the Lords and others of her Highness's Privy Council, to see her Majesty's said gracious and godly intention and purpose to be duly and effectually executed and accomplished.

Whereupon the said Reverend Father and the whole Presence sitting in this honourable Court this 23rd day of June in the 28th year of her Majesty's reign, upon grave and mature deliberation, hath ordained and declared that the ordinances and constitution, rules and articles, hereafter following shall from henceforth by all persons be duly and inviolably kept and observed, according to the tenor, purpose, and true intent and meaning of the same, as they tender her Majesty's high displeasure and as they will answer to the contrary at their utmost peril.

I. *Imprimis*, That every printer and other person... which at this time present hath erected... any printing press, roll, or other instrument for imprinting of books, charts, ballads, portraitures, paper called damask paper, or any such things or matters whatsoever, shall bring a true note or certificate of the said presses... already erected, within ten days next coming after the publication hereof, and of the said presses... hereafter to be erected or set up from time to time, within ten days next after the erecting or setting up thereof, unto the Master and Wardens of the Company of Stationers of the City of London for the time being; upon pain that every person failing or offending herein shall have all and every the said presses... utterly defaced and made unserviceable for imprinting for ever, and shall also suffer twelve months imprisonment....

II. *Item*, That no printer of books nor any other person or persons whatsoever shall set up, keep, or maintain any press or presses... for imprinting of books [*etc.*]... but only in the City of London or the suburbs thereof (except one press in the University of Cambridge and one other press in the University of Oxford and no more); and that no person shall hereafter erect, set up, or maintain in any secret or obscure corner or place any such press,... but that the same shall be in such open place or places in his or their houses as the Wardens of the said Company of Stationers for the time being, or such other person or persons as by the said Wardens shall be thereunto appointed, may from time to time have ready access unto to search for and view the same. And that no printer...shall at any time hereafter withstand or make resistance to...any such view or search nor deny, to keep secret, any such press...upon pain that every person so offending in anything contrary to this Article shall have all the said presses...defaced and made unserviceable for imprinting for ever, and shall also suffer imprisonment for one whole year, and be disabled for ever to keep any printing press,...or to be master of any printing-house, or to have any benefit thereby other than only to work as a journeyman for wages.

III. *Item*, That no printer or other person whatsoever that hath set up any press...within six months last passed shall hereafter use or occupy the same, nor any person or persons shall hereafter erect or set up any press...till the excessive multitude of printers having presses already set up be abated, diminished, and by death given over, or otherwise brought to so small a number of masters or owners of printing-houses being of ability and good behaviour as the Archbishop of Canterbury and Bishop of London for the time being shall thereupon think it requisite and convenient, for the good service of the realm, to have some more presses...erected and set up. And that when and as often as the said Archbishop and Bishop...shall so think it requisite and convenient, and shall signify the same to the said Master and Wardens of the said Company of Stationers..., that then and so often as the said Master and Wardens shall (within convenient time after) call the Assistants of the said Company before them, and shall make choice of one or more (as by the opinion of the said Archbishop and Bishop...need shall require) of such persons, being free Stationers, as for their skill, ability, and good behaviour shall be thought by the Master, Wardens, and Assistants, or the more part of them, meet to have the charge and government of a press or printing-house; and that within fourteen days next after such election and choice, the said Master, Wardens, and four other at the least of the Assistants of the said Company shall present before the High Commissioners in Causes Ecclesiastical, or six or more of them whereof the said Archbishop and Bishop to be one, to allow and admit every such person so chosen and presented, to be master and governor of a press and printing-house according to the same election and presentment; upon pain that every person offending contrary to the intent of this Article shall have his press...defaced and made unserviceable and also suffer imprisonment by the space of one whole year....

IV. *Item*, That no person or persons shall imprint or cause to be imprinted or suffer by any means to his knowledge his press, letters, or other instruments to be occupied in printing of any book, work, copy, matter, or thing whatsoever except the same book [etc.]...hath been heretofore allowed, or hereafter shall be allowed, before the imprinting thereof according to the order appointed by the Queen's Majesty's Injunctions[1] and be first seen and perused by the Archbishop of Canterbury and Bishop of London for the time being, or one of them, (the Queen's Majesty's Printer for some special service by her Majesty or by some of her Highness's Privy Council thereunto appointed, and such as are or shall be privileged to print the books of the common law of this realm for such of the same books as shall be allowed of by the two Chief Justices and Chief Baron for the time being, or any two of them, only excepted); nor shall imprint or cause to be imprinted any book, work, or copy against the form or meaning of any restraint or ordinance contained in any statute or laws of this realm, or in any injunction made or set forth by her Majesty or her Highness's Privy Council, or against the true intent and meaning of any letters patents, commissions, or prohibitions under the Great Seal of England, or contrary to any allowed ordinance set down for the good governance of the Company of Stationers within the City of London; upon pain to have all such presses, letters, and instruments as in or about the imprinting of any such books or copies shall be employed or used to be defaced and made unserviceable for imprinting for ever, and upon pain also that every offender and offenders contrary to this present Article or Ordinance shall be disabled (after any such offence) to use or exercise or take benefit by using or exercising of the art or feat of imprinting, and shall moreover sustain six months imprisonment....

V. *Item*, That every such person as shall sell utter or put to sale wittingly, bind stitch or sew, or wittingly cause to be sold uttered put to sale bound stitched or sewed, any books or copies whatsoever printed contrary to the intent and true meaning of any Ordinance or Article aforesaid, shall suffer three months' imprisonment for his or their offence.

VI. *Item*, That it shall be lawful for the Wardens of the said Company for the time being or any two of the said Company thereto deputed by the said Wardens, to make search in all workhouses, shops, warehouses of printers, booksellers, bookbinders, or where they shall have reasonable cause of suspicion, and all books [etc.]...contrary to...these present Ordinances to stay and take to her Majesty's use, and the same to carry into Sta-

[1] The Injunctions of 1559: see Prothero, p. 188.

tioners' Hall in London; and the party or parties offending...to arrest, bring, and present them before the said High Commissioners in Causes Ecclesiastical, or some three or more of them, whereof the said Archbishop of Canterbury or Bishop of London for the time being to be one.

VII. *Item*, That it shall be lawful to or for the said Wardens for the time being, or any two by them appointed,...to enter into any house, work-house, warehouse, shop, or other place or places, and to seize, take, and carry away all presses, letters, and all other printing instruments set up, used, or employed contrary to the true meaning hereof, to be defaced and made unserviceable as aforesaid. And that the said Wardens shall, so often as need shall require, call the Assistants of their said Company, or the more part of them, into their said Hall and there take order for the defacing, burning, breaking, and destroying of all the said presses, letters, and other printing instruments aforesaid; and thereupon shall cause all such printing-presses or other printing instruments to be defaced, melted, sawed in pieces, broken or battered at the smith's forge, or otherwise to be made unserviceable. And the stuff of the same, so defaced, shall re-deliver to the owners thereof again within three months next after the taking or seizing thereof as is aforesaid.

VIII. *Item*, That for the avoiding of the excessive number of printers within this realm, it shall not be lawful for any person or persons being free of the Company of Stationers or using the trade or mystery of printing, bookselling, or bookbinding, to have, take, and keep hereafter at one time any greater number of apprentices than shall be hereafter expressed. That is to say, every person that hath been or shall be Master or Upper Warden of the Company whereof he is free, to keep three apprentices at one time, and not above. And every person that is or shall be Under Warden or of the Livery of the Company whereof he is free, to keep two apprentices, and not above. And every person that is or shall be of the Yeomanry of the Company whereof he is or shall be free, to keep one apprentice (if he himself be not a journeyman) and not above. Provided always, that this Ordinance shall not extend to the Queen's Majesty's Printer for the time being for the service of her Majesty and the realm, but that he be at liberty to keep and have apprentices to the number of six at any one time.

IX. *Item*, That none of the Printers in Cambridge or Oxford for the time being shall be suffered to have any more apprentices than one at one time at the most. But it is and shall be lawful to and for the said Printers and either of them, and their successors, to have and use the help of any journeymen, being freemen of the City of London, without contradiction. Any law, statute, or commandment contrary to the meaning and due execution of these Ordinances or any of them to the contrary notwithstanding.

Strype, *Life of Whitgift*, Book III, ch. xiii, and Appendix to Book III, No. xxiv.

(10) Extracts

1 SIR THOMAS SMITH, 1565

Sir Thomas Smith, the author of *De Republica Anglorum*, was sent as English Ambassador to France by Queen Elizabeth (1562–6), and it was during this absence that the book was written, although it was not published until 1583, six years after the author's death. It has been described as 'the most important description of the constitution and government of England written in the Tudor age.'[1] Sir Thomas Smith was closely connected with Cambridge, as he was a Fellow of Queens', Public Orator, and Regius Professor of Civil Law.

Of the Court of Star Chamber

There is yet in England another Court, of the which that I can understand there is not the like in any other country. In the term time...the Lord Chancellor and the Lords and other of the Privy Council, so many as will, and other lords and barons which be not of the Privy Council and be in the town, and the Judges of England, specially the two Chief Judges, from ix of the clock till it be xi do sit in a place which is called the Star Chamber, either because it is full of windows or because at the first all the roof thereof was decked with images of stars gilted. There is plaints heard of riots. Riot is called in our English term or speech, where any number is assembled with force to do anything.... And further, because such things are not commonly done by mean men, but such as be of power and force, and be not to be dealt withal of every man, nor of mean gentlemen; if the riot be found and certified to the King's Council, or if otherwise it be complained of, the party is sent for, and he must appear in this Star Chamber, where seeing (except the presence of the Prince only) as it were the majesty of the whole realm before him, being never so stout he will be abashed; and being called to answer (as he must come, of what degree soever he be) he shall be so charged with such gravity, with such reason and remonstrance, and of those chief personages of England, one after another handling him on that sort, that, what courage soever he hath, his heart will fall to the ground, and so much the more when if he make not his answer the better, as seldom he can so in open violence,

[1] *D.N.B.* liii, 127.

he shall be commanded to the Fleet, where he shall be kept in prison in such sort as these judges shall appoint him, lie there till he be weary as well of the restraint of his liberty as of the great expenses which he must there sustain, and for a time be forgotten, whilst after long suit of his friends he will be glad to be ordered by reason. Sometime, as his deserts be, he payeth a great fine to the Prince, besides great costs and damages to the party, and yet the matter wherefor he attempteth this riot and violence is remitted to the common law. For that is the effect of this Court, to bridle such stout noblemen or gentlemen which would offer wrong by force to any manner men[1], and cannot be content to demand or defend the right by order of law.

This Court began long before, but took great augmentation and authority at that time that Cardinal Wolsey, Archbishop of York, was Chancellor of England, who of some was thought to have first devised the Court, because that he, after some intermission by negligence of time, augmented the authority of it, which was at that time marvellous necessary to do, to repress the insolency of the noblemen and gentlemen of the north parts of England, who being far from the King and the seat of justice made almost as it were an ordinary war among themselves, and made their force their law, banding themselves with their tenants and servants to do or revenge injury one against another as they listed. This thing seemed not supportable to the noble prince King Henry the Eighth; and sending for them one after another to his Court to answer before the persons beforenamed, after they had had remonstrance shewed them of their evil demeanour and been well disciplined as well by words as by fleeting[2] awhile, and thereby their purse and courage somewhat assuaged, they began to range themselves in order, and to understand that they had a Prince who would rule his subjects by his laws and obedience. Sith that time this Court hath been in more estimation, and is continued to this day in manner as I have said before.

Sir Thomas Smith, *De Republica Anglorum* (ed. L. Alston, 1906), Book III, ch. iv.

2. WILLIAM LAMBARDE, 1591

William Lambarde, the historian of Kent, afterwards a Master in Chancery and Keeper of the Records in the Tower, completed in 1591 *Archeion, or a Commentary upon the High Courts of Justice in England*, in succession to *Eirenarcha, or of the Office of Justices of Peace*, published in 1581 (see p. 457 below). He died in 1601. *Archeion* was not published until 1635.

... Shall no help at all be sought for at the hands of the King when it cannot be found in the Common Law? That were to

---

[1] But see the suggested emendation, 'any meaner men,' referred to in the Preface (p. viii above).   [2] Imprisonment in the Fleet prison.

stop his ears at the cry of the oppressed, and would draw wrath and punishment from Heaven...(p. 141).

It must be true that the King and his Council are not to be tied to any one place, seeing that the place itself neither addeth nor derogateth to or from their authority, and there be many causes of remove and change from place to place; but yet even as the Palace at Westminster hath evermore been reputed the chief royal seat of the realm, as being most frequented with the personal presence of the Kings, and honoured with the solemnity of the coronations and assemblies of estates in Parliament, so the Council Chamber of that Palace hath obtained that dignity to bear a name above all others, and hath been of long time called the Star Chamber (p. 175).

...But from whence this place first purchased the name of Star Chamber there may be divers conjectures: one by derivation from the English word *steoran*, which signifieth to steer or rule, as doth the pilot in a ship, because the King and Council do sit here, as it were at the stern, and do govern the ship of the Commonwealth; then of the Latin word *stellio*, which betokeneth that starry and subtile beast[1] of whose name the fault of crafty cozenage is borrowed by the civilians, which they call *crimen stellionatum*, because the sin is punished in this Court by an extraordinary power, even as it was in the law civil. Lastly, because haply the roof thereof was at the first garnished with gilded stars, as the room itself is starry, or full of windows and light, in which respect some of the Latin records name it *Camera stellata*, the French *le chambre des étoiles*, and the English the Starred Chamber...(p. 183).

But leaving the choice of these, as also all further conjecture therein, to other men, I will proceed to set forth the usage of proceeding in this place before the making of the Statute 3 Henr. VII, c. 1, the which some men (but much deceived) do take to have laid the first stone of this far more ancient and stately erection ...(p. 185).

This Statute as some have thought was made for the restraint of that absolute authority which beforetime was exercised by the King's Council; so as after the making thereof they were to take knowledge of these few causes only, and of none others. But I do rather expound it by way of enlargement of their juridical authority, for insomuch as there is not in it any words prohibitory touching the former manner of proceeding, and the scope of this law is to have those offenders convicted by other means than by

---

[1] See note on p. 289 below.

order of law, as they were before, I gather thereby that the Statute giveth an additament of this sort, *viz.* that whereas before-time the King and the Lords of this Council did not admit any complaint for such only as carried within it a reasonable surmise of maintenance of their jurisdiction,... now by this new Statute, over and besides that ancient authority, only three of the Council, *viz.* the Chancellor, Treasurer, and Keeper of the Privy Seal, using the assistance of some others thereunto appointed, were enabled to hear and determine ordinarily of these eight offences, and that without any manner of such suggestion or surmise at all; and that both King Henry VII and King Henry VIII did, many years after the making of this Statute, sometime in person and very often by their Council, practise by former jurisdictions in Star Chamber without any help of this new law and statute, it doth most certainly appear by the Books of Entries kept there, which is a true journal of the acts of the Court...(p. 197).

...And this was now at the last devised because, as the statutes themselves do report, that ancient and ordinary proceeding at the common law against these maintainers, rioters, and the rest of the common rabble, was hindered by the greatness of the offenders, which were belike so breasted, sided, and backed with a many friends, tenants, and followers in their own countries, that none indictment or trial could make the way to touch them; which thing threatened the utter subversion of the good policy of the realm, if this sovereign and higher hand had not been timely extended for help and remedy.

Howbeit, by the express words of these new laws these offences named in them are in none other degree to be punished in this Court now than they were before upon conviction by judgment and the trial of twelve. And therefore the change that is offered resteth chiefly in the circumstances of place, process, and mean of trial, the very substance itself, (that is to say) the discretion of the fault itself and the distribution of the pain due thereunto, remaining the very same that they were before; from the which appointed pains if the Lords shall at any time think good to vary and depart, then it must be understood to be done by that former authority which they had and have as the Council of the King, and not by virtue of these statutes, which do leave unto them no liberty at all in this behalf, for we may not so conjoin, or rather confound, these authorities, as either of them shall be extinct and drowned in the other, but we must preserve them both separably and distinct, not only in understanding but in execution and practice also, even as when the Justices that ride the circuits do bring with them into the country one Commission of Oyer and Terminer, and another of Gaol Delivery, and a third of the Peace, and do sit upon the trial of felonies, they may lawfully extend their authority by the one where the other will not reach and serve the business, which thing they could not do if by such a conjunction the greater Commission should be said to devour and swallow the less; and this one hold is of sufficient strength to withstand the assaults of all those objections which some are wont to make against certain the proceedings in this Court...(p. 205).

Thus I have made it appear both what hath been the right usage of this Court by the original power thereof, and what access of authority it hath received by these new laws and statutes, the which were, as you see, ordained to apply a most honourable, high, awful, and ordinary remedy for these enormities and excesses, which were at that time grown so exorbitant and high that they might not sufficiently be revenged by the inferior judges and usual stroke of the common law. In which case right necessary it was that the King himself, and such as were nearest in the stair of authority underneath him, should shew themselves, by the majesty and awe of whose personal state and presence both these offenders might be abashed and beaten down, and these offences might be made exemplary and forewarnings to other men.

And therefore this is all that for this time and service I purposed to say in this most noble and praiseworthy Court, the beams of whose bright justice, equal in beauty with Hesperus and Lucifer (as Aristotle said in like case) do blaze and spread themselves as far as the realm is long or wide, and by the influence of whose supereminent authority all other courts of law and justice that we have are both the more surely supported and the more evenly kept and managed...(p. 215).

Lambarde, *Archeion* (1635).

3. FRANCIS BACON, VISCOUNT ST ALBANS, 1621

Bacon's *History of Henry VII* was written in the Long Vacation after his fall in 1621, and it was ready for publication in the following year.

First, the authority of the Star Chamber, which before subsisted by the ancient common laws of the realm, was confirmed in certain cases by Act of Parliament[1]. This Court is one of the sagest and noblest institutions of this kingdom. For, in the distribution of courts of ordinary justice (besides the High Court of Parliament), in which distribution the King's Bench holdeth the

[1] *I. e.* by the Act of 1487.

pleas of the Crown; the Common Pleas, pleas civil; the Exchequer, pleas concerning the King's revenue; and the Chancery, the pretorian power for mitigating the rigour of law in case of extremity by the conscience of a good man; there was nevertheless always reserved a high and preeminent power to the King's Council in causes that might in example or consequence concern the state of the commonwealth; which if they were criminal the Council used to sit in the chamber called the Star Chamber, if civil in the White Chamber or White Hall[1]. And as the Chancery had the pretorian power for equity, so the Star Chamber had the censorian power for offences under the degree of capital. This Court of Star Chamber is compounded of good elements, for it consisteth of four kinds of persons: councillors, peers, prelates, and chief judges; it discerneth also principally of four kinds of causes: forces, frauds, crimes various of stellionate[2], and the inchoations or middle acts towards crimes capital or heinous not actually committed or perpetrated. But that which was principally aimed at by this Act[3] was force, and the two chief supports of force, combination of multitudes and maintenance or headship of great persons.

Bacon, *History of Henry VII* (*Works*, ed. Spedding, vi, 85).

The law giveth that favour to lawful acts that, although they be executed by several authorities, yet the whole act is good....

...So in the Star Chamber a sentence may be good, grounded in part upon the authority given the Court by the Statute of 3 Henr. VII and in part upon that ancient authority which the Court hath by the common law, and so upon several commissions....

Bacon, *Maxims of the Law* (*Works*, ed. Spedding, vii, 379).

4. Sir Edward Coke, c 1628

Sir Edward Coke, Chief Justice of the Common Pleas and afterwards of the King's Bench, had practically completed his *Institutes* by 1628, six years before his death. He was appointed High Steward of the University of Cambridge in 1614. The passages here printed suggest the antiquity of the Star Chamber jurisdiction, and the dignity and usefulness of the Court. The *Fourth Institute* was not published until 1644.

The Honourable Court of Star Chamber

*   *   *   *   *   *

That which now is next to be considered *in serie temporis* is the Statute of 3 H. 7.... Upon this Statute and that which formerly hath been said, these six conclusions do follow. The

---

[1] In the Court of Requests; see p. 300 below.

[2] 'Stellion' is a kind of lizard with star-like spots on its back. 'Stellionate' is a legal term derived from it, to describe all kinds of fraud to which no other special name had been attached.

[3] The Act of 1487.

first conclusion is, that this Act of 3 H. 7 did not raise a new court, for there was a Court of Star Chamber, and all the King's Privy Council judges of the same. For if the said Act did establish a new court, then should those four[1] or any two of them be only judges, and the rest that they should call to them should be but assistants and aidants and no judges: for the Statute of 31 E. 3, cap. 12, which raiseth a new court and before new judges, is introductory of a new law, by having conusance[2] of error in the Exchequer which shall be reversed in the Exchequer Chamber[3] before the Chancellor and Treasurer, or calling to them two Judges, there the Chancellor and Treasurer are only judges in the writ of error, and so in the like[4]. But it is clear that the two Justices in the Star Chamber are judges and have voices, as it hath been often resolved and daily experience teacheth. And further, to clear this point, if the Justices should be but assistants and no judges in the Star Chamber, for that they are to be called, etc., then and for the same reason should neither Lord spiritual nor temporal nor other of the Privy Council be judges nor have voices in the Court of Star Chamber. And therefore the sudden opinion in 8 H. 7 and of others not observing the said distinction between Acts declaratory of proceedings in an ancient court and Acts introductory of a new law in raising of a new Court, is both contrary to law and continual experience.

The second conclusion is, that the Act of 3 H. 7, being in the affirmative, is not in some things pursued. For where that Act directeth that the bill or information should be put to the Lord Chancellor, etc., all bills and informations in that Court are constantly and continually directed to the King's Majesty, as they were before the said Act; and it is a good rule that where the Act of 3 H. 7 is not pursued, there (if there be many judicial precedents in another sort) they must have warrant from the ancient Court, and yet it is good (as much as may be) to pursue this Act, there being no greater assurance of jurisdiction than an Act of Parliament. And where there be no such precedents, then the Statute as to the judges must be pursued; and that was the reason that in default of others, Sir Christopher Wray, Chief

[1] *I.e.* The Chancellor, Treasurer, and Lord Privy Seal mentioned in the original statute, and the Lord President of the Council added in 1529 by 21 Henr. VIII, c. 20 (see p. 259 above).

[2] An early form of 'cognisance' retained as a legal term.

[3] See p. 343 below.

[4] *I.e.* And similarly in the present case. The argument appears difficult at first sight, but a reference to the Act of 1487 (see p. 258 above) makes it clear.

Justice of England, for a time was made Lord Privy Seal to sit in the Star Chamber, *ne Curia deficeret in justitia exhibenda.*

Thirdly, that this Act being (as hath been said) in the affirmative, and enumerating divers particular offences, albeit 'injuries' is a large word, yet that Court hath jurisdiction of many other, as is manifest by authority and daily experience, and this must of necessity be in respect of the former jurisdiction.

Fourthly, this Act in one point is introductory of a new law which the former Court had not, *viz.* to examine the defendant, which being understood after his answer made, to be upon oath upon interrogatories, which this ancient Court proceeding in criminal causes had not nor could have but by Act of Parliament or prescription, the want whereof, especially in matters of frauds and deceits (being like birds closely hatched in hollow trees) was a mean that truth could not be found out, but before the Statute the answer was upon oath.

Fifthly, where it is said in this Act, *And to punish them after their demerits after the form and effect of statutes made, etc.*, the plaintiff may choose whether he will inform upon such statutes as this Act directeth or for the offence at the common law, as he might have done before this Act; which proveth that this Act taketh not away the former jurisdiction.

Lastly, that the jurisdiction of this Court dealeth not with any offence that is not *malum in se*, against the common law, or *malum prohibitum*, against some statute.

    *   *   *   *   *   *

And seeing the proceeding according to the laws and customs of this realm cannot by one rule of law suffice to punish in every case the exorbitancy and enormity of some great, horrible crimes and offences, and especially of great men, this Court dealeth with them, to the end that the medicine may be according to the disease and the punishment according to the offence, *ut poena ad paucos, metus ad omnes perveniat*, without respect of persons, be they public or private, great or small.

As for oppression and other exorbitant offences of great men, whom inferior judges and jurors (though they should not) would in respect of their greatness be afraid to offend, bribery, extortion, maintenance, champerty[1], embracery[2], forgery, perjury, dispersers of false and dangerous rumours, news, and scandalous libelling, false and partial misdemeanours of sheriffs and bailiffs of

---

[1] 'The illegal proceeding whereby a party not naturally concerned in a suit engages to help the plaintiff or defendant to prosecute it on condition that, if it be brought to a successful issue, he is to receive a share of the property in dispute' (*Oxford Dictionary*).   [2] See note on p. 258 above.

liberties, frauds, deceits, great and horrible riots, routs[1], and unlawful assemblies, single combats, challenges, duels, and other
heinous and extraordinary offences and misdemeanours; but
ordinary, and such offences as may be sufficiently and condignly
punished by the proceeding of the common laws, this Court
leaveth to the ordinary courts of justice and dealeth not with them,
ne dignitas hujus Curiae vilesceret, as before is said.

The proceeding in this Court is by bill or information, by
examination of the defendant upon interrogatories, and by examination of witnesses, and rarely *ore tenus*, upon the confession
of the party in writing under his hand, which he again must
freely confess in open court, upon which confession in open
court the Court doth proceed. But if his confession be set down
too short, or otherwise than he meant, he may deny it, and then
they cannot proceed against him but by bill or information, which
is the fairest way.

The informations, bills, answers, replications, etc., and interrogatories are in English, and engrossed in parchment and filed
up. All the writs and process of the Court are under the great
seal: the sentences, decrees, and acts of this Court are engrossed
in a fair book with the names of the Lords and others of the
King's Council and Justices that were present and gave their voices.

* * * * * *

This Court sitteth twice in the week in the term time,
viz. on Wednesdays and Fridays, except either of those days
fall out to be the first or last day of the term and then the Court
sitteth not, but it constantly holdeth the next day after the term
ended; but if any cause be begun to be heard in the term time
and for length or difficulty cannot be sentenced within the term,
it may be continued and sentenced after the term.

It is the most honourable Court (our Parliament excepted)
that is in the Christian world, both in respect of the judges of the
Court and of their honourable proceeding according to their
just jurisdiction and the ancient and just orders of the Court.
For the judges of the same are (as you have heard) the grandees
of the realm, the Lord Chancellor, the Lord Treasurer, the Lord
President of the King's Council, the Lord Privy Seal, all the
Lords spiritual, temporal, and others of the King's most honourable Privy Council and the principal Judges of the realm, and

---

[1] An unlawful assembly becomes a rout as soon as the persons assembled do any
act towards carrying out the illegal purpose which has made their assembly unlawful;
the rout becomes a riot as soon as this illegal purpose is actually put into effect (see
Kenny, p. 283).

such other Lords of Parliament as the King shall name. And they judge upon confession, or deposition of witnesses; and the Court cannot sit for hearing of causes under the number of eight at the least. And it is truly said, *Curia Camerae Stellatae, si vetustatem spectemus, est antiquissima, si dignitatem, honoratissima.* This Court, the right institution and ancient orders thereof being observed, doth keep all England in quiet.

Albeit the style of the Court be *coram Rege et Concilio*, yet the King's Council of that Court hear and determine causes there, and the King in judgment of law is always in court; as in the King's Bench the style of the Court is *coram Rege* and yet his Justices, who are his council of that Court, do hear and determine, and so *coram Rege in Cancellaria*, and the like.

*   *   *   *   *   *

It is now and of ancient time hath been called the Chamber of the Stars, the Star Chamber, the Starred Chamber, in respect the roof of the Court is garnished with golden stars. Some have imagined that it should be called the Star Chamber because *crimina stellionata*[1] are there handled; others of this Saxon word *steeran*, to steer or rule as doth the pilot, because this Court doth steer and govern the ship of the commonwealth. Others because it is full of windows; but the true cause of the name is because, as is afore said, the roof is starred. In all records in Latin it is called *Camera Stellata.*

The process in this Court is *subpoena*, attachment, process of rebellion, etc., all under the great seal.

In this Court there is the Clerk of the Council, which is an office of great account and trust, for he is to receive, endorse, enter, keep, and certify the bills, pleadings, records, orders, rules, sentences, and decrees of the Court; and I find that in former times men of great account have had that office in this Court....

Lastly, it remaineth to be seen what jurisdiction this Court hath in punishment, and where and in what cases this Court may inflict punishment by pillory, papers[2], whipping, loss of ears, tacking of ears, *stigmata* in the face, etc. (For it extendeth not to any offence that concerns the life of man or obtruncation of any member, the ears only excepted, and those rarely and in most heinous and detestable offences). But herein the surest rule is, that seeing it is an ancient Court the precedents of the Court are to be followed, and the rather for that the Court consisteth of such learned and honourable judges. And novelties without war-

---

[1] See note on p. 289 above.

[2] *I.e.* the wearing of papers specifying the offence.

rant of precedents are not to be allowed: generally some certain rules are to be followed, especially where no precedents are extant in the case. *Quod arbitrio Judicis relinquiter, non facile trahit ad effusionem sanguinis:* for general Acts of Parliament which inflict punishment, viz. *sur forfeiture de corps et de avoir*, etc., these are expounded not to extend to life or member, but to imprisonment, etc.. . . .

Coke, *Fourth Institute* (edition of 1669), ch. 5.

5. WILLIAM HUDSON, *c.* 1633

William Hudson had practised in the Court of Star Chamber, and in 1633 he opened the case there against Prynne for publishing *Histriomastix*. He died in or before 1635. His *Treatise of the Court of Star Chamber* was not printed until 1792.

. . . Whosoever will be pleased to look over the records of the reigns of King H. 7 and H. 8 they shall find all the rules and orders there entered in Latin.. . . And in those times matters of smallest moment were observed with a great deal of state; as, that the appearance was recorded before the Lord Chancellor and President of the Council, sometimes in the Chancellor's house, sometimes in the Parliament Chamber, sometimes in the inner Star Chamber, sometimes in the Court; all which gave majesty to the Court and terror to the offenders. It is now descended to so mean a step as that the appearance is taken only by an inferior clerk.. . . Besides, one great inconvenience thereby ensueth, for that in great offences the offender *flagrante crimine* is stricken with amazement, and then coming before a grave and reverend person, truth is easily won from him, which after the party be hardened will never be gained. And this I have observed upon perusal of the records of H. 7 . . . that this Court hath had a certain place or residence in *Camera Stellata*, than which no court of England can be more ascertained in place (p. 7).

Admitting then the King to be supreme judge of all, and sitting in his throne of majesty with his wise men and sages distributing justice in his royal person or by his Council, and that, finding himself and them overcharged, he hath therefore committed the pleas of the crown to certain judges, matters of common right betwixt party and party to other justices, and to others his revenue, all which before they were distributed to others were properly determinable before himself and his Council, it must then follow that all courts of justice have flowed out of this Court as out of a fountain, the King and the Council having distributed these causes to substantial judges for the ease of the subjects and themselves, and then this Court must be the most ancient court of justice and the mother court of this kingdom; which is the more plainly manifested for that almost in man's memory the Court of Requests was instituted by the reference of poor people and of the King's servants out of this Court, whereby a great part of interest betwixt party and party ceased there to be prosecuted. But to prove by judicial acts and records this Court is most ancient as it is now established, I mean in the same manner, place, and all circumstances, and not founded by Act of Parliament in the reign of King II. 7—a doating which no man that had looked upon the records of the Court would have lighted upon...(p. 10).

Order requireth that I should now speak of the dignity of this Court; of which to treat as I ought I shall want the pen of a ready writer, depth of judgment, and the fluent words of a good orator. But yet this I dare say, that since the great Roman Senate, so famous to all ages and nations as that they might be called *jure mirum orbis*, there hath no court come so near them in state, honour, and judicature as this, the judges of this Court being surely in honour, state, and majesty, learning, understanding, justice, piety, and mercy, equal and in many exceeding the Roman Senate by so much, by how much Christian knowledge exceedeth human learning; and surely the causes there handled were of the same nature with those that are handled in this Court...(p. 17).

...Let this then suffice for the dignity of the Court, that in the same it matcheth with the highest that ever was in the world. In justice it is and hath been ever free from the suspicion of injury and corruption; in the execution of justice it is the true servant of the Commonwealth; and whatsoever it takes in hand to reform it bringeth to perfection. And therefore it is well called *Schola Reipublicae*, the discipline whereof doth not only enter all the other courts of justice and ministers thereof, but all the subjects of the kingdom...(p. 22).

It followeth that I should, in the next place, speak of the presence of this Court, that is, the judges thereof, the great senators of this state. And because I have already glanced upon this question, Whether the Treasurer, Chancellor, or Privy Seal, or any of them, be the only judges of this Court, and all the rest but assistants?...It is fit that I leave it charged that the Court...did usually determine causes when neither Treasurer, Chancellor, nor Privy Seal were present; but sometimes the President of the Council alone, and sometimes assisted by others of the Council, above forty times in the 12 and 13 of H. 7. And sometimes, when neither the Treasurer, President, Chancellor, nor Privy Seal were present, other Lords of the Council sat for the determining causes, which proveth that they are all judges of the Court...(p. 22).

...The Court is not alone replenished with noble dukes, marquises, earls, and barons, which surely ought to be frequented with great presence of them, but also with reverend archbishops and prelates, grave counsellors of state, just and learned judges, with a composition for justice, mercy, religion, policy, and government, that it may be well and truly said that *Mercy and Truth are met together, Righteousness and Peace have kissed each other.* The number in the reigns of H. 7 and H. 8 have been well near to 40; at some one time 30; in the reign of Queen Elizabeth oftentimes, but now much lessened since the barons and earls not being Privy Councillors have forborne their attendance. And the Court was in the reign of H. 7 and H. 8 most commonly frequented by seven or eight bishops and prelates every sitting-day; in which times let me without offence observe, that the fines trenched not to the destruction of the offender's estate and utter ruin of him and his posterity as now they do, but to his correction and amendment, the clergy's song being of mercy...(p. 35).

...Fines are new of late imposed *secundum qualitatem delicti*, and not fitted to the estate of the person; so that they are rather *in terrorem populi* than for the true end for the which they were intended when fine and ransom was appointed, the ransom of a beggar and a gentleman being all one to the case of the Crown, the great detriment of the Commonwealth...(p. 224).

> William Hudson, *A Treatise of the Court of Star Chamber* (printed in *Collectanea Juridica*, 1792, vol. ii, pp. 1–240).

6. Francis Osborne, 1658

Francis Osborne was the author of *Advice to a Son* (1656) and *Traditional Memoirs on the Reigns of Elizabeth and James I* (1658). The quotation here given strikes a discordant note in the general chorus of praise of the Star Chamber, but it represents the seventeenth century view.

The Earl of Northumberland[1]...was cast into the Star Chamber, that den of arbitrary justice, where the Keeper for the time being, two bishops, two judges, and as many wise lords and honest great officers sat as were pleased to come. The most of whom, though unable to render a reason, every Wednesday and Friday in term-time concur, like, etc., to tear

[1] Henry Percy, ninth Earl of Northumberland, who was tried in the Star Chamber in 1606 for contempt and misprision of treason in connexion with Gunpowder Plot. He was sentenced to a fine of £30,000 and imprisonment in the Tower for life. He was not released until 1621.

such as refused to worship the minion or to yield to the pretended royal prerogative.

Osborne, *Traditional Memoirs on the Reign of King James* (1658), p. 62.

7. JOHN RUSHWORTH, 1680

The brief *Discourse concerning the High Court of Star Chamber* in Rushworth's *Historical Collections* is in the main an abstract of Hudson (p. 294 above), but the passages on the dignity and utility of the Court, with the reservation with which it concludes, are extracted below. Rushworth claims that during the intermission of Parliaments from 1629 to 1640 he attended all the more important cases in the Star Chamber and before the Council Table. In 1640 he became one of the clerks to the House of Commons.

... It was a glorious sight upon a Star-day, when the Knights of the Garter appear with the stars on their garments, and the Judges in their scarlet; and in that posture they have sat sometimes from nine in the morning till five in the afternoon, before everyone had done speaking their minds in the cause that was before them. And it was usual for those that came to be auditors at the sentence given in weighty causes to be there by three in the morning to get convenient places and standing....

For the dignity of this Court, I find it's said that since the great Roman Senate, so famous to all ages as that they were called *pro jure miraculum orbis*, there hath no court come so near them in state, honour, and judicature; the judges of this Court being surely, in honour, state, and learning, for understanding, justice, piety, and mercy, equal and in many of them exceeding the Roman Senate by so much as Christian knowledge exceedeth humane learning. Nor hath this Court at any time wanted a Cicero or Hortensius to make a defence for such as are there accused; nor is there any bar of pleading which affordeth so large a scope to exercise a good orator, the usual subject being the defence of honour and honesty. But Chancellor Elsmore[1], affecting matter rather than words, tied the same to laconical brevity; an honour to a court of justice to be swayed rather by ponderous reasons than fluent and deceitful speech. It is not the least honour and dignity to this Court that the sentences and judgments of the same are not the opinion of any private person but the judgment of many noble, wise, and learned men conjoined together; so that it is a topic rule[2] for assurance of truth.

Another manifestation of the dignity of it is that the proceedings are *tam lento pede*, without precipitation, but giving time to the defendant to defend or excuse himself, both in pro-

[1] Sir Thomas Egerton, Baron Ellesmere and afterwards Viscount Brackley, was Lord Chancellor from 1603 to 1617.

[2] A general rule, but one which may fail to apply in some particular case.

ducing testimony and in making defence at the bar. And that it taketh hold in judgment only of direct proofs, speaking circumstances, or more than probable presumptions, and these not single but double; which causeth the judgment thereof to be esteemed worthily, like the laws of the Medes and Persians, irrevocable. Besides the reasons of the sentence being succinctly collected and knit together and sagely delivered by grave, learned, and notable personages, whose very countenances add weight to their words, and who tie themselves to certainty and not to conjectural proofs.. . .

The Court for the most part is replenished with dukes, marquises, earls, barons, also with reverend archbishops and prelates, grave councillors of state, learned judges—such a composition for justice, religion, and government as may be well and truly said (whilst so great a presence kept within their bounds), *Mercy and Truth were met together*.. . .

When once this Court began to swell big and was delighted with blood, which sprung out of the ears and shoulders of the punished, and nothing would satisfy the revenge of some clergymen but cropped ears, slit noses, branded faces, whipped backs, gagged mouths, and withal to be thrown into dungeons, and some to be banished, not only from their native country to remote islands[1] but by order of that Court to be separated from wife and children, who were by their order not permitted to come near the prison where their husbands lay in misery; then began the English nation to lay to heart the slavish condition they were like to come unto if this Court continued in its greatness.

Rushworth, *Historical Collections*, ii, 471.

[1] The reference is probably to the cases of Prynne, Burton, and Bastwick, who, after suffering the punishment described in the text, were imprisoned, Prynne in Jersey, Burton in Guernsey, and Bastwick in Scilly.

The Court of Requests

The Court of Requests[1] may be regarded as the jurisdiction of the Council applied to civil matters. Its relation to the Council is very similar to that of the Star Chamber, and the history of one Court throws light upon some doubtful passages in the history of the other. Both are offshoots of the ancient authority of the Council, and in both cases the jurisdiction clothes itself with the form of a court and the court receives a special name; and in both cases the authority of the Council is left unimpaired. Finally, the lawyers of the seventeenth century adopted the same erroneous theory of the origin of both courts, and involved them in a common condemnation.

The origin of the Court of Requests has been assigned either to an Ordinance of 22 Edward III, referring such matters as were of grace to the Chancellor or the Keeper of the Privy Seal, or to an Order of 13 Richard II for regulating the Council which appointed the Keeper of the Privy Seal, with those of the Council who happened to be present, to examine and deal with bills of 'people of the lesser charge.' There seems to be no sufficient authority for presuming such antiquity for the Court, but these orders established a tradition which connected the office of Lord Privy Seal with 'poor men's causes,' and marked him out as the appropriate officer of state to preside over the Court of Requests when it came to be founded. The origin of the Court is rather to be sought for in the reign of Henry VII, although the jurisdiction which it exercised is much older, being a part of the jurisdiction of the King's Council in civil suits. At the beginning of the Tudor period the volume of Council business was so great, that a standing committee of Council of shifting membership was appointed to hear on behalf of the King-in-Council petitions for redress from persons who claimed to be too poor to sue at common law. As the records of proceedings in the Court begin in 1493, it is possible though not certain that this was the date of its establishment. This committee was at first described as 'the Court of Poor Men's Causes' or 'the Poor Men's Court,' but it eventually borrowed a name from a French court representing the patriarchal justice of the King of France and came to be known as the Court of Petitions or Requests. The standing committee was in close relation to the Council, for its sessions were regarded as meetings of the Council, and its judgments were given in the Council's name[2]; the members of the Court were Councillors appointed to hear requests[3] under the presidency of the Lord Privy

---

[1] The most authoritative account of the history of this Court is to be found in the Introduction to I. S. Leadam, *Select Cases in the Court of Requests*.

[2] Baldwin, p. 443.

[3] They were often dignified ecclesiastics and professional lawyers. For instance, on 30 November, 1499, the Bishops of London and Rochester sat with four doctors of law; on 11 March, 1500, the same two bishops, the Dean of the Chapel Royal, the Dean of York, the Prior of the Order of St John of Jerusalem, and Richard Sutton of the Inner Temple, one of the legal members of the Council, well known as Sir Richard Sutton, one of the founders of Brasenose College, Oxford.

Seal; and the Court, like the Council, attended the person of the King and followed the royal progresses[1]. The inconvenience to suitors of a peripatetic Court led Wolsey, either in 1516 or 1517, to establish it in a permanent seat of judgment in the White Hall of the Palace of Westminster[2] [p. 302], although for some years longer it continued occasionally to follow the King. It still regarded itself as the King's Council, and is always so described in the earlier books of orders and decrees. The name 'Court of Requests' does not appear until 1529, and in that reference the judges of the Court are still described as Councillors 'appointed for the hearing of poor men's causes in the King's Court of Requests.'[3]

About 1550 two permanent expert judges called Masters of Requests began to control the business of the Court, and from that time the process was set up, familiar in other spheres, by which the experts gradually drove out or dominated the non-experts, and appropriated all real power. As a consequence of this, procedure hardened and became formal in character, and the historical connexion of the Court of Requests with the Council was obscured. The increase of business, for the honesty of the judges and the comparative simplicity of the procedure made the Court very popular among litigants, led Elizabeth to appoint two 'Masters of Requests Extraordinary' in addition to the two 'Masters of Requests Ordinary,' in order that when she went on royal progresses two Masters could follow the Sovereign without making it necessary to inflict inconvenience upon a crowd of suitors by closing the Court at the White Hall; but true to her policy of economy she only offered to pay them by expectation—the hope of succeeding to one of the salaried Masterships later on. The stipend attached to the office of Master Ordinary was £100 a year. At the accession of James I four Masters Ordinary were appointed, and an immense amount of business was discharged by the Court.

§ 1. Procedure

The Court of Requests did not, like the Star Chamber, keep fixed terms, but was accessible to suitors throughout the year; and provision was made for securing the attendance of a sufficient number of Councillors at all times to hear cases[4].

The procedure of the Court resembled that of the Star Chamber, but it was at first more expeditious and less costly[5]. A suit was begun by a petition addressed to the King, followed by an 'answer' by the defendant, and some-

[1] In 1494 it sat at Sheen, Canterbury, Windsor, Langley, and Woodstock, as well as at Westminster (Leadam, p. xii).

[2] This hall was close to Westminster Hall, and should not be confused with the Palace of Whitehall.

[3] Quoted in Leadam, p. xiv.

[4] Baldwin, p. 443. The arrangements for attendance were contained in an Order of the Court dated 1494, described by Sir Julius Caesar in his *Ancient State ...of the Court of Requests* (1597), p. 1.

[5] But see Leadam, p. xxi. The Court was controlled by civilians and not by the common lawyers, and according to Sir Julius Caesar, its procedure was 'altogether according to the process of summary causes in the civil law' (*Law Quarterly Review*, xxxv, 298).

times by a further 'replication' and 'rejoinder,' and the parties were examined upon interrogatories and could produce witnesses. Appearance was commonly ordered by writ of privy seal, but, if necessary, 'proclamation of rebellion' could be made or a 'commission of rebellion' issued, and the party arrested by a pursuivant or serjeant-at-arms sent out by the Court.

§ 2. BUSINESS

As the Court was 'a court of conscience, appointed to mitigate the rigour of proceeding in law,'[1] it was free to cover a wide field of jurisdiction. It dealt with 'questions of title to and possession of land, especially as to copyholds, fines and commons, tithes, annuities, trusts, extents[2], debt with specialties[3] and without, executorships and administratorships, contracts, villenages, watercourses, leases, covenants generally, highways, wardship, dower, jointure, escape, forfeitures to the King by recognisance or otherwise, riots and routs, forgery and perjury, where goods were seized as forfeited by the lord of any manor or by force, cozenage, or dishonest dealing, questions affecting the conduct of executors, questions of marriage settlements of land or goods, suits for money due upon account or received by the defendant to the plaintiff's use, damages claimed for injuries sustained by violence.'[4]

In theory the benefits of the Court were limited to poor men and to the servants of the King (see p. 307 below), but by a legal fiction suitors sometimes made use of it who could not possibly be regarded as coming within these categories.

A few cases are printed below [pp. 303–6] to illustrate some of these activities; and reference should also be made to Sir Julius Caesar's account of the Court [p. 308].

§ 3. DECLINE OF THE COURT[5]

The lawyers of the seventeenth century agreed in holding that a court of law, to be a true court, must derive its authority either from an ancient royal grant, or from a statute, or from immemorial custom. The Assize Courts were constituted by a Commission under the Great Seal; the Court of the Constable by letters patent under the Great Seal; the King's Bench, Exchequer, and others by ancient ordinances; and these all came under the description of a royal grant. The Courts of Augmentations, Wards and Liveries, and Firstfruits and Tenths derived from statutes. The Courts of the Counties Palatine, the Stannary Court of Cornwall, and the Star Chamber derived from immemorial custom. The Court of Requests, exercising Council jurisdiction, really derived from immemorial custom, like the Star Chamber; but by the end of the sixteenth century the tradition of its origin had ceased to govern the situation. The Masters of Requests were no longer recognised as Privy Councillors, and the Court itself was entirely distinct from the Council. Thus the Judges of the Courts of Common Law disputed the authority of the Court, since it could not produce a royal grant, nor could it refer to a statute, and custom that began with Henry VII or Wolsey was not immemorial custom. From 1590 onwards the Court of

---

[1] Leadam, p. xx.   [2] Valuations of land.
[3] *I.e.* debts based upon written instruments under seal, *e.g.* bonds.
[4] Leadam, p. lxxxix.   [5] See *Ib.* pp. xl–xlv.

Common Pleas began to issue prohibitions to the Masters of Requests, forbidding them to proceed further in cases which came before them, and they were supported by the Court of Queen's Bench. In 1599, in the leading case of Stepney *v.* Flood [p. 312], it was held by the Court of Common Pleas 'that this which was called a Court of Requests or the White Hall was no court that had power of judicature,' and that their arrest of the defendant was therefore false imprisonment. In 1606 Coke, then Lord Chief Justice of the Common Pleas, released from the Fleet one Robotham, who had been imprisoned there by the Court of Requests for contempt, and 'commanded' him 'to bring his action of false imprisonment'; and in 1607 it was held by all the judges that perjury in that Court was not punishable, 'for it is but a vain and idle oath, and not a corrupt oath, because the Court of Requests have nothing to do with nor can examine titles of land, which are real, and are to be discussed and determined in the King's Courts.'

The obstacles thus thrown in their way by the Courts of Common Law placed the Masters of Requests in a position of peculiar difficulty [p. 311], but the Court survived because it was useful, and the statute of 1641 which abolished the Star Chamber did not touch the Court of Requests. In 1642, however, when the Civil War broke out, the Masters of Requests, who were royalists, ceased to sit, and the records of the Court came to an end. We hear of Masters of Requests during the Interregnum, who dealt with petitions and grievances; and at the Restoration Masters of Requests were again appointed, but they now concerned themselves chiefly with the examination of petitions for compensation from subjects who had suffered in the Civil Wars, and no longer exercised jurisdiction as a Court.

It has been pointed out[1] that the crusade of the Common Law Judges against this Court was not altogether inspired by pure zeal for the vindication of the law. They were themselves largely dependent upon fees, and the simpler procedure of the Court of Requests filled it with suitors and made it a formidable competitor for fees. This not only explains the attacks upon it, but shews why it was able to survive them.

There were other Courts of Requests besides the Court at the White Hall. Of these the most important was one established in the City of London in 1518 by the Common Council, 'commonly called the Court of Conscience in the Guild Hall.' This consisted of 'two aldermen and four ancient discreet commoners,' and its jurisdiction extended to debts of 40*s.* and under, due among the citizens of London.

Extracts from early writers bearing on the history of the Court of Requests are printed below [pp. 306–13].

(1) Establishment of the Court of Requests at Westminster, c. 1518

On this see p. 300 above.

For the expedition of poor men's causes depending in the sterred Chambre, It is ordered by the most Reverend Father, etc., Thomas, Lord Cardinal, Chancellor of England, and the other Lords of the King's most honourable [Council] that these

[1] Leadam, p. xlvi.

causes here mentioned shall be heard and determined by the King's Councillors hereunder named. The which Councillors have [been] appointed to sit for the same in the White Hall here at Westminster, unto the which place the pleasure of the said most Reverend Father, etc., and the other etc., is that the said poor suitors shall resort before the said commissioners for the decision and determination of their said causes as appertaineth, where they shall have hearing with expedition.

That is to say
- My Lord of Westminster[1]
- Mr Dean of Paul's
- My Lord of St John's[2]
- Sir Thomas Neville
- Sir Andrew Windsor[3]
- Sir Richard Weston
- Mr Doctor Clerk[4]
- Mr Roper[5]

State Papers (Domestic), Henr. VIII, iii. 571, quoted in Leadam, Select Cases in the Court of Requests, p. lxxxi.

(2) Cases in the Court of Requests

AMADAS v. WILLIAMS AND ANOTHER, 1519

The plaintiff, being a King's servant, was entitled to sue in the Court of Requests.

To the King our Sovereign Lord

Lamentably complaining, sheweth unto your Highness your true and faithful servant, John Amadas, Yeoman of your most honourable Guard. That whereas one John Williams, church-warden of the parish church of Tavistock, in your county of Devon, and other of the substantial persons of the same parish, heretofore instantly[6] desired and required him to buy for them a cross for their church of silver and gilt in London[7], upon whose request and desire, and upon their promise to have payment therefor, that is to say, an old cross of silver and the residue in ready money, your said servant bought for them a cross of silver and gilt weighing twelve score and four ounces at 5s. 1d. the ounce, sum £62, 4d., which cross by your said servant so bought and delivered to the said churchwarden and other the

---

[1] The Abbot of Westminster.
[2] The Prior of the Order of St John of Jerusalem.
[3] Described as 'learned in the temporal law.'
[4] LL.D. of Bologna; afterwards Master of the Rolls and Bishop of Bath and Wells.
[5] William Roper, afterwards Clerk of the Pleas of the Court of King's Bench. He was the son-in-law and biographer of Sir Thomas More. [6] Urgently.
[7] The transaction is perhaps explained by the fact that a certain Robert Amadas, presumably a relation of the plaintiff's, was a London goldsmith.

substantial of the same parish, who promised him the said old cross and payment of the rest in ready money within 8 days after. Howbeit now, most gracious Sovereign Lord, the churchwardens and parishioners now refuse and deny to deliver the said old cross or any part or parcel of the money for the same new cross to your said servant, which amounteth to £62, 4*d.*, to his express wrong and great hindrance unless your grace be unto him mercifully shewed in this behalf. And forasmuch as your said orator can have no remedy against them by your common law, it may therefore please your Highness of your most noble and abundant grace, having tender consideration unto the premises, to address your most gracious letters under your privy seal unto the said John Williams and John Goodstoke, now churchwardens there, commanding them by the same to come and personally appear afore your Highness and your most discreet Council to answer to the premises. And he shall ever pray for your most noble and royal estate....

Leadam, *Select Cases in the Court of Requests*, 1497–1596
(Selden Society, vol. xii, 1898), p. 17.

PETERSON *v.* FREDERICK AND OTHERS, 1521

To my Lord Cardinal's Grace

In most humble wise beseeching your good Grace your humble orator and faithful and [true] bedeman, Cornelius Peterson, Dutchman. That whereas he hath continued brother of the Brotherhood of St Barbara by the space of 10 years, and hath truly paid for his incoming and all other duties and charges as it is yearly ordained for the maintenance of the same Brotherhood according to the rolls and books of the same. And further, gracious Lord, it is provided that if any of the brethren of the same Brotherhood shall hap to fall in poverty, sickness, or bedrid, that then he or they so being shall weekly have out of their boxes and treasure 20*d.* to sustain their poor lives, and at their decease to be honestly brought to be buried with *dirige* and mass of requiem; and every brother to offer which offering is for the same opportunity to auge[1] their Brotherhood. And where now of late certain presumptuous and malicious persons of the same Brotherhood, intending to break the good order beforesaid and to exclude and put out your said bedeman from the said Brotherhood, so that your said beseecher cannot have nor enjoy the custom of the said Brotherhood according to the effect of the books and rolls of the same. Wherefore, to the intent that right, equity, and good order

[1] Increase.

may be had and from henceforth used in the said Brotherhood, it may therefore please your Grace of your benign charity to grant your most gracious letters of commission to be directed to certain indifferent persons, strangers dwelling and inhabited in London, to call before them the Wardens of the said Brotherhood accordingly to make answer to the premises. And further the same commissioners to settle such order therein as your said bedeman may be taken and admitted a brother and to enjoy all the customs and privileges of the same; or else the said Wardens to restore unto your said bedeman all such sums of money as they have received for his admission and yearly payment by him made for the same Brotherhood, with his reasonable costs and charges. This, gracious Lord, in the honour of God; and he shall be your daily bedeman during his life.

Leadam, p. 29.

BURGES v. LACY, BEFORE 1541 (?)

This case throws some light on the position of a domestic chaplain in the sixteenth century.

To the King our Sovereign Lord

In most humble wise sheweth and complaineth unto your Grace your daily orator Sir William Burges, priest. That where he hath continued in service with one Mistress Luce Lacy of the said City[1] by the space of one whole year, according to his promise and covenant, and now at his year's end would lawfully depart for his most profit, so it is, most gracious Lord, that the said Mistress Luce wrongfully and untruly surmiseth that your said orator should grant to serve her another year, which is untrue and but matter feigned of malice, as your said orator can and will evidently prove and justify by sufficient records and proofs; and over this, gracious Lord, the same Mistress Luce, of her royal power without cause or matter of right, wrongfully withholdeth and keepeth from your said orator all his quarter's wages, 13s. 4d., and his gown, the price thereof is 23s. 4d., and his letters of his orders, contrary to right and good conscience. Please it therefore, your noble Grace, the premises tenderly to consider, and that your said orator is but lately come to the City, and have small acquaintance and very few friends, and also is of none power to sue for his right and remedy by the course of the law, of your most godly and blessed disposition and at the reverence of God and in the way of charity to command the said Mistress Luce personally to appear before your Grace there to answer to the premises, and further to be ordered in the same as by your Grace

<hr>

[1] Of London.

T. D.   20

shall be thought most according with right, law, equity, justice, and good conscience; and your said orator shall daily pray to God for your prosperity and state long to endure....

The answer of Luce Lacy to the bill of complaint of Sir William Burges, priest.

The said Luce saith that the said bill of complaint is untrue, uncertain, and unsufficient to be answered unto, and the matter therein contained determinable by course of the common law, whereof she prayeth allowance. Notwithstanding, for the further declaration of the truth, the said Luce saith that for a truth the said Sir William was in service and retained with the said Luce for 2 years, and the said Sir William promised, covenanted, and granted to serve the said Luce by the space of 2 years, and not for one year in manner and form as is in the said bill specified. And as touching the said wages and gown, the said Luce saith that she is and at all time hath been ready to deliver it to the said Sir William so that the said Sir William will do his service according to the covenant made with the said Luce. Without that[1] that anything effectual in the said bill contained is true otherwise than is specified in this present answer. All which matters the said Luce is ready to prove as this Court will award, and prayeth to be dismissed out of the same with her reasonable costs for her wrongful [vexation] and trouble in that behalf.   *Leadam, p. 59.*

(3) Extracts

1. WILLIAM LAMBARDE, 1591

See p. 285 above.

In that the Court of Requests handleth causes that desireth moderation of the rigour which the common law denounceth, it doth plainly participate with the nature of the Chancery; but in that the bills here be exhibited to the Majesty of the King only and to none other, and in that it hath continually been served with a Clerk that was ever therewithal one of the clerks of the King's Privy Seal, it seemeth to communicate with the Star Chamber itself, and to derive the authority immediately from the royal person as that doth....

...It is out of all doubt...that as our Kings have used personally to receive complaints of criminal condition, and have adjudged thereof of themselves or by their Council of Estate, so have they also from time to time taken knowledge of civil suits especially offered by the poorer sort of subjects or by their own Household men, and have for the most part recommended the

---

[1] See note on p. 274 above.

same to the care of some of their said Council assisted with the advice of men learned both in the civil and common laws, so as some one temporal lord or bishop, two doctors, and two common lawyers have been many times known to have sitten here together....

Now albeit there can no other beginning therefore be conceived than together with the very regality and kingdom itself, yet forasmuch as they of this Court have not always had their standing place of resort, but have, until the age next before this, remained and removed with the King wheresoever he went, travelling between the Prince and petitioners by direction from the mouth of the King, I have in this, as in the Star Chamber, also taken the first apparent settling and manifest continuance thereof for the very spring and original itself.

And I have lately seen that from the eighth year of King H. 7, ever since which time this Court hath rested in the place called the White-hall, the books of the acts of entries there have been orderly digested and kept[1], in which you may read the handling of the causes, not only of poor men and the King's servants, but also of sundry abbots, knights, esquires, and other rich and wealthy complainants. Howbeit I do well remember that within these 40 years the bills of complaints presented there did ordinarily carry the one or the other of these two suggestions, namely, that the plaintiff was a very poor man, not able to sue at the common law, or the King's servants ordinarily attendant upon his person or in his Household. But because enlargement of jurisdiction is not proper to [this] Court alone but common to it with all the rest, I will not now stand to object it, but hasten to an end.

The Masters of the Requests are neither called by writ nor appointed by commission nor created by patent, but only have letters patent for their fees and salary; and do take the same oath which the Councillors do conceive.

The Clerkship of this Court hath, as I said, beyond all memory been committed to a clerk of the Privy Seal....

The attorneys were in my first knowledge of them but two only, and now are three, whose places are at the disposition of the Clerk.

The usual process is by privy seal...attachment, and writ of rebellion if the contumacy of the defendant do so deserve; in the rest of the proceedings the course is not much different from the order of the Chancery. Lambarde, *Archeion* (1635), p. 224.

---

[1] It is true that the records of the Court begin in 1493, but it was not established in the White Hall until c. 1516 (see pp. 299–300 above).

2. SIR JULIUS CAESAR, *c.* 1597

Sir Julius Caesar (1558–1636) was Judge of the Admiralty and afterwards Master of the Rolls. In 1591 he was appointed Master of Requests, and hence his interest in the history of the Court.

The following quotations are from a volume among the Lansdowne MSS. (No. 125) partly in manuscript and partly printed, the latter published in 1597 under the title *The Ancient State, Authority, and Proceedings of the Court of Requests.* Extracts from the part in manuscript have been printed in Leadam, *Select Cases in the Court of Requests.* The first passage quoted is in Sir Julius Caesar's own hand, and the second also is probably by him.

Reasons to prove that the Court of Whitehall or Requests is a member and parcel of the King's most honourable Council attendant on his person

1. The Masters of Requests, judges of this Court, are sworn of the King's P[rivy] or S[ecret] Council, as appeareth by the oath. . . which myself and my predecessors in this place have taken.

2. The bills here be directed to the King himself.

3. The appearances here are before the King and his Council.

4. The process here is sealed with the S[eal] proper to the King's Council.

5. The judges here always called in the acts of this Court the King's Council, or the King's honourable Council, or the King's most honourable Council; sometimes with this addition—in his Court of Requests or Whitehall.

6. The Register or Clerk here hath always been a clerk of the P[rivy] S[eal] and of the Council. . . .

. . . 8. No court (under the highest Court of Parliament) can re-examine a cause decreed in Chancery, or discharge a prisoner committed from thence, saving only the King's Council; but this Court hath done it. . . .

9. No court (under the highest Court of Parliament) hath accustomed to cause noblemen to attend on it *de die in diem*, and not to depart without license. . . saving only the King's Council; but this Court hath always accustomed the same.

10. This Court is one of the King's Courts. . . and standeth only by prescription of the King's Council, as appeareth by the acts of this Court and the common law, it having neither commission under the Great Seal or Act of Parliament to establish it otherwise; but the King's Council prescribeth only for itself, *ergo*

. . . 12. Some judges of this Court have from time to time till 1 Eliz. sat, *alternis vicibus*, as judges in the Star Chamber, where none may sit as judges but such as be of the King's most honourable Council, saving only the two Justices named in the Statute of 3 H. 7, cap. 1 et 21 H. 8, cap. 20. The former is proved by the records of both Courts, the Star Chamber and Requests.

13. The judges of this Court (now commonly since 4 E. 6 called Masters of Requests) were always numbered and provided for in the books of the King's Household as the King's Council, without any distinction or difference of more Councils than one, as may appear by the Black Book of the said Household, and by the titles given unto them who then had the care to take and answer the requests and supplications made unto the King....

...15. No man's hand but a Councillor's can command the King's P[rivy] S[eal], as appeareth by the ancient oath of the Clerks of the P[rivy] S[eal]. But every of the judges of this Court his hand commandeth the said P[rivy] S[eal]; ergo

16. That Council, which since 33 H. 8 hath been called commonly the King's P[rivy] C[ouncil], was always heretofore called the King's C[ouncil] without any other title, or else entitled the King's honourable or most honourable C[ouncil] with this further title sometimes—daily attendant on his person— as appeareth by the statutes imprinted; but the King's C[ouncil] in Whitehall hath all those titles, as appeareth by the records of that Court *tempore* H. 7, H. 8, E. 6, M. 1, *et* Eliz.; *ergo*

Leadam, *Select Cases in the Court of Requests* 1497–1569 (Selden Society, vol. XII, 1898), p. xxx.

Moreover if the Court of White Hall be no lawful Court

1. Why hath it continued ever since 9 H. 7 without interruption?

2. Why have the Judges of the Common Pleas, when they were serjeants and sworn to maintain the course of law, took men's money for drawing bills to be preferred into this Court?

3. Why have all the learned Judges of the Common Law in their serjeanty and time of practice persuaded their clients this hundred and ten years past to commence causes in that Court?

4. Why have the subjects of England thus long been deluded to spend their money in an unlawful Court?

5. Why have the Judges of the Common Pleas recommended suitors to the Court of Requests, namely, to procure injunctions, and in the mean time stayed the proceedings at the common law in that Court?

6. Why have the noblemen and the Judges of the one Bench and the other endured the censure and paid that which hath been decreed against them in the Court of Whitehall?

7. Why have the Kings and Queens reigning, in their proclamations or adjournments of terms respectively, named the
Court of Requests or Whitehall one of the Courts?

8. Why hath the wisdom of the whole land in Parliament
assembled, in *anno* 32 H. 8 (cap. 9) and in *anno* 5 Eliz. (cap. 9),
called the Court of Whitehall one of the King's Courts?

Surely if Time in all other things justly esteemed the daughter
of Truth; if the learned Judges of former times who have left
unto us that learning which we now have, if we have any; if the
common reputation of the world which in causes of this nature
hath bred this principle receivable for the common good—*com-
munis error facit jus*; if the noblest and wisest of this state, if five
Kings and Queens of England successively, if all the three states
of England correspondently, and, which is more, if the four Judges
of the Common Pleas in the time of their serjeanty for a long time
respectively have pleaded causes in the said Court and allowed
the Court of Whitehall for a lawful Court, I wonder what hath
moved them being Judges openly to protest and maintain in
public places that the Judges of the Court of Whitehall have no
authority to sit nor to commit any man to prison, and that the
same is no lawful Court, thereby to give advantage to the malign-
ants over-curiously to scan the authority of this Court, which may
prove a dangerous precedent against the proceedings and jurisdiction of other Courts....   Leadam, p. xxxv.

Cases quoted in Sir Julius Caesar's printed work, *The Ancient State,
Authority, and Proceedings of the Court of Requests* (1597), shew (1) that the
proceedings of the Court ran in the name of the Council, and that the Court,
like the Council, could delegate the business of inquiry into a particular
case[1]; (2) that the Court, like the Council, took recognisances[2]; (3) that the
Court of Requests at the end of the reign of Henry VIII still regarded both
the Star Chamber and itself as part of the King's Council[3]; (4) that the
Court sometimes refused to proceed in a case where the parties were 'men
of wealth.'[4]

[1] *Reade* v. *Hesketh* (1512), p. 49.
[2] *Addington* v. *Wake* (*c.* 1530), p. 82.
[3] ...'The King's most honourable Council of White hall, having a respect to a
former order and decree made by the King's most honourable Council in the Star
Chamber at Westminster'... (38 H. VIII), p. 99; cf. also p. 100, where the Court
is described in the same year as 'the King's honourable Council attendant upon
his person, and commonly sitting in the King's Majesty's Court of White-hall in
Westminster.'
[4] *Kingston* v. *Sampford* (1553), p. 111. Cf. pp. 117 and 119. It often happened,
however, that such men came into the Court under a legal fiction.

3. ANONYMOUS, *c.* 1600

From an apologist of the Court of Requests in British Museum, Additional MSS. 25248, fol. 57, quoted in Leadam, p. xliii.

By reason of the premises, and like both proceedings and speeches oftentimes within the space of 10 years last past used in the Court of Common Pleas in the open hearing of all comers thither, the Court of Whitehall hath received a general and public disgrace amongst the vulgar sort, and the Judges sitting there only upon her Majesty's express word and commandment (as their predecessors have ever done since 9 H. 7, as appeareth by the acts of that Court, relying much upon the judgment and censure of such four reverend Judges as the Court of Common Pleas doth afford), are fearful to sit any longer as judges in Whitehall, where

Their sittings are not warranted.

Their decrees cannot be executed.

Their authorities are contemned.

Their prisoners are discharged by *habeas corpus*.

Their suitors' proceedings are stayed by prohibitions.

Their orders scorned and publicly slandered.

Themselves unmeasurably toiled without profit, yea to their great hindrance, and, which is most of all, subject in the censure of four grave Judges to most severe punishment as mad busybodies that sit in places of judgment without warrant of law.

Leadam, p. xliii.

4. SIR EDWARD COKE, *c.* 1628

Coke, who was hostile to the Court of Requests, here states the case against its jurisdiction, and abstracts the leading case of Stepney *v.* Flood.

The Court of Requests

...It shall be fit in this place to treat of the jurisdiction of the Court of Requests, wherein the Lord Privy Seal at his pleasure and the Masters of Requests do assemble and sit. And the original institution hereof was, that such petitions as were exhibited to the King and delivered to the Masters of the Requests should be perused by them, and the party directed by them to take his remedy, according to their case, either at the common law or in the Court of Chancery. And thereupon they were called *Magistri a libellis supplicum*; and in this respect this meeting and consultation was called the Court of Requests, as the Court of Audience[1] and Faculties are called Courts albeit they hold no plea of controversy. Those which in former times would have this Court to be a

---

[1] See p. 359 below.

court of judicature took their aim from a court in France.... But others, taking this jurisdiction to be too narrow, contend to have it extend to all causes in equity equal with the Chancery and their decrees to be absolute and uncontrollable. But neither of these are warranted by law, as shall evidently appear.

In the reign of H. 8 the Masters of Requests thought (as they intended) to strengthen their jurisdiction by commission to hear and determine causes in equity. But those commissions being not warranted by law (for no court of equity can be raised by commission) soon vanished, for that it had neither Act of Parliament nor prescription time out of mind of man to establish it.

Mich. 40 & 41 Eliz. In the Court of Common Pleas, upon a bill exhibited in the Court of Requests against Flood, for default of answer an attachment was awarded against Flood under the privy seal to Stepney, then Sheriff of Carnarvon, who by force of the said writ attached Flood, and would not let him go until he had entered into an obligation to the Sheriff to appear before his Majesty's Council in the Court of Requests; upon which obligation the Sheriff brought an action of debt for default of appearance, and all this matter appeared in pleading. And it was adjudged upon solemn argument that this which was called a Court of Requests or the White Hall was no court that had power of judicature, but all the proceedings thereupon were *coram non judice*, and the arrest of Flood was false imprisonment....

The punishment of perjury in the Court of Whitehall by the Statutes of [32] H. 8, cap. 9[1] and 5 Eliz., cap. 9[2] doth not give it any jurisdiction of judicature, no more than the statutes that give against a gaoler an action for an escape, or punisheth a gaoler of his own wrong for extortion, an officer of his own wrong shall be punished by the statutes in that case provided, and yet the statutes thereby make them no lawful officers, for it is one thing to punish and another to give authority. So it was justice in the Parliaments to punish perjury in the Whitehall although the Court were holden by usurpation, and so before it appeareth to be by the judgment in Stepney's case.... And as gold or silver may as current money pass, even with the proper artificer, though it hath too much allay, until he hath tried it with the touchstone,

---

[1] 32 H. 8, c. 9, prohibits unlawful maintenance 'in any action...in any of the King's Courts of Chancery, the Star Chamber, the White Hall, or elsewhere.'

[2] 5 Eliz. c. 9, recites 32 H. 8, c. 9, § 3, and imposes a penalty for suborning witnesses to commit perjury in any of the Courts mentioned in that Act or in other Courts now enumerated.

even so this nominative[1] court may pass with the learned as justifiable in respect of the outside by vulgar allowance, until he advisedly looketh into the roots of it and try it by the rule of law; as (to say the truth) I myself did.. . .

. . . And although the law be such as we have set down, yet in respect of the continuance that it hath had by permission, and of the number of decrees therein had, it were worthy of the wisdom of a Parliament, both for the establishment of things for the time past and for some certain provision with reasonable limitations (if so it shall be thought convenient to that High Court) for the time to come.. . .

Coke, *Fourth Institute* (edition of 1669), ch. 9.

---

[1] 'Appointed by nomination,' but perhaps used here in the sense of 'so-called.'

Council Courts

Besides the Star Chamber and the Court of Requests, there were other subordinate councils localised in particular parts of the country and exercising Star Chamber jurisdiction there. The organisation and procedure of these were modelled on the Council, and they were controlled by the Council, which could withdraw cases from their jurisdiction and deal with them itself. Of these localised councils the most important were the Council of the North, the Council of Wales and the Marches, and the Council of the West. Their history illustrates the remarkable development of government, both central and local, which characterises the Tudor period.

§ 1. The Council of the North[1]

The project for the establishment of a Council in the North grew in the first instance out of the anarchy of the Scottish Border. In the face of hostile Scotland the defence of the Border had been in the Middle Ages a military problem of the first importance, and the medieval kings had naturally attempted to deal with it on feudal lines. They had built the great Border castles,—such as Norham, Berwick, and Carlisle, and had maintained on the frontier military lords like the Percies, who were strong enough to establish an efficient defensive, or even to pursue the invaders and to take the offensive against them in their own country. In 1309 the permanent office of Warden of the Marches came into existence[2], and the holders of it soon acquired the custody of the castles, and entire responsibility for the organisation of the defence of the Border. Their commission in its final form, that of 1399, gave them authority to call out armed forces, to hold Warden Courts[3], to punish breaches of the truce with Scotland in accordance with the ancient Laws of the Marches, and to confer with the Scottish Warden concerning wrongs inflicted by raiders from either side. The three March shires were Northumberland, Cumberland, and Westmorland; and although for a time the Wardenship of the whole March was concentrated in the hands of the Percies, the East, West, and Middle Marches were sometimes under separate control[4].

[1] For the detailed history of this Council see Miss R. R. Reid, *The King's Council in the North*, published just as the present volume was going to press. It traces the first establishment of a Council in the North to Richard III in 1484, and regards the Tudors as copyists rather than originators.

[2] On the origin and early history of this office see *E.H.R.* xxxii, 479–96.

[3] These were in full activity in Henry VIII's reign. See *State Papers*, iv, 611; and 23 Henr. VIII, c. 16 (1532), which prohibited the sale of horses into Scotland, and provided that offences against the Act should be tried by 'the Warden and Wardens of the East, West, and Middle Marches...in their Warden's Courts.' See also 43 Eliz. c. 13, § 5 (p. 331 below).

[4] 'And seeing I stand charged as your Grace's Warden for redress of attemptates, as well done by sea as by land, upon the East and Middle Marches against Scotland, like as the Lord Dacre doth upon your Highness's West Marches...' (*Northumberland to Henry VIII, State Papers*, iv, 627).

In the Middle Ages the Border had been a scene of perpetual anarchy. When England and Scotland were at war, the great lords of the Border had to face military operations conducted upon a large scale[1]; and even when the two countries were nominally at peace, plundering raids continued to keep the farther north in a state of backwardness and barbarism. 'Poverty is the best protection against pillage,' and it was not worth while to develop civilisation in districts exposed to perpetual invasion. In the Tudor period, however, the chronic war with Scotland began to draw to an end, as one result of the Reformation was the separation of Scotland from France and its attachment to the religious group to which England belonged, and thus the fundamental cause of the anarchy of the Border ceased to operate. But it was not the case that anarchy itself ceased—only that the efforts to put it down had now a better chance of success. Open war between the two countries ceased with the peace of 1550, and from that time onwards special efforts were made to keep the Border quiet. Fortifications were repaired; watch and ward was more systematically kept; the passes were staked to render the country more accessible. The Border administration passed from the great lords of the north into the hands of skilled and experienced royal officials acting under instructions from the centre of affairs; and with the officials came the principles of business. The records of the Border afford strong testimony to the general efficiency of government, especially during the reign of Elizabeth.

After the union of England and Scotland in 1603 the office of Lord Warden of the Scottish Marches was abolished, and the Border passed under the ordinary law. But anarchy, like Charles II, took an unconscionable time in dying. Generations of disorder had created habits which it took long to eradicate; the men from the Border were looked upon with suspicion in the orderly places and especially in the towns[2], and this feeling lingered long. Eventually, however, the moss-troopers of the seventeenth century became the mere sheepstealers of the eighteenth, who were dealt with by the ordinary process of law; and the Border ceased to present a special problem for English statesmanship.

For the Tudors the problem of the anarchy of the Border was associated with the wider question of the anarchy of the North. There the feudal structure of society was vigorous and tenacious of life, and the Tudor centralised government found itself confronted by feudal franchises and feudal ideas. In Yorkshire even as late as the reign of Elizabeth it could be

---

[1] Cf. the speech which Shakespeare puts into the mouth of Henry V:

'For you shall read that my great-grandfather
Never went with his forces into France,
But that the Scot on his unfurnished kingdom
Came pouring, like the tide into a breach,
With ample and brim fulness of his force....'

Henry V, i, ii.

[2] In 1564 the Merchant Adventurers of Newcastle passed a bye-law forbidding anyone to take as an apprentice a native of Tynedale and Redesdale, because they 'commit frequent thefts and felonies,' and no good can proceed 'from such lewd and wicked progenitors.'

said[1], 'The Sheriff has small force, the liberties are so many and so great,' and 'throughout Northumberland they know no prince but a Percy.' Thus the conditions which in the rest of England had been successfully dealt with by the Star Chamber still survived in the intractable North, and there a localised Council with Star Chamber powers would find plenty of work to do.

Henry VIII's reorganisation of the North began in connexion with the defence of the Border. In 1522, when the Duke of Albany was known to be preparing an invasion in force, the King designed 'to send some nobleman to Yorkshire as his Lieutenant, to set the country north of the Trent in readiness.'[2] In 1525 Henry Fitzroy, Duke of Richmond, the King's natural son, then six years of age, was appointed Lieutenant-General north of the Trent and Warden of the Scottish Marches, to govern with the advice of a council described as the 'Duke of Richmond's Council,'[3] but also as the 'Council of the North.'[4] The child-duke resided in the north from 1525 to 1532, but in 1530 a 'King's Council in the North Parts' was separated from the Duke's Household Council[5] and the Bishop of Durham was appointed President. This Council acted in close association with the Lord Warden of the Marches, under the title of the Council of the North[6] Although the references in the correspondence after 1533 are rather ambiguous, it is probable that this co-operation continued until the outbreak of the Pilgrimage of Grace in 1536[7].

The idea of converting the Council of 1530 into a permanent institution may have occurred to Cromwell before the insurrection supplied a new and urgent cause for it. In a letter of 8 April, 1535[8], Maunsell calls his attention to one of the standing difficulties of government in the North which was unconnected with the problem of the defence of the Border,— 'It is time to see reformation, for commissions often do little good in these parts by reason of their affinities and confederacies'; and in June a memorandum by Cromwell himself refers to 'the establishment of a Council in the North.'[9] After the suppression of the rising, an inquiry into its causes and the adoption of special measures for the settlement of the country became of pressing importance, and a scheme was prepared in Council 'for the perfect establishment of the North Parts.'[10] This provided for the sending down of the Duke of Norfolk as the King's Lieutenant, and joined with him 'a Council of personages of honour, worship, and learning.'[11] Meanwhile, the

---

[1] By Lord Hunsdon, Warden of the East Marches and Governor of Berwick under Elizabeth (quoted in Pollard, *Polit. Hist.* p. 278).

[2] *L. and P.* vol. iii, pt i, no. 2075.

[3] *Ib.* vol. iv, pt ii, nos. 2402, 3477, 3552, 3610; pt iii, no. 5430.

[4] See the letters to Wolsey of 29 October and 22 November, 1525, from 'the Council of the North' (*ib.* vol. iv, pt i, nos. 1727 and 1779).

[5] Reid, pp. 113, 114.

[6] *L. and P.* vi, nos. 155, 174, 217; *State Papers, Henry VIII*, iv, 636.

[7] Lapsley, p. 259. On the part played in the rising by the Council of the North, see Reid, p. 139.   [8] *L. and P.* viii, no. 515.

[9] *Ib.* viii, no. 892; on this memorandum see Reid, p. 120.

[10] *Ib.* xi, no. 1410.

[11] 'A Council such as the Duke of Richmond had' (*ib.* xi, no. 1363). For the instructions given to the Duke, see *ib.* vol. xii, pt i, no. 98.

plan for a permanent Council was maturing[1], and in a letter to the Duke of Norfolk, written 12 June, 1537, the King announced his intentions with regard to it: 'We do purpose shortly to revoke you and to establish a standing Council there, for the conservation of those countries in quiet, and the administration of common justice.'[2] The Lord President was to be Cuthbert Tunstall, Bishop of Durham, and six other Councillors were appointed, one of whom was Robert Holgate, Bishop of Llandaff, himself to be Lord President later on when Archbishop of York. Their commission [p. 318][3] was issued in July, 1537. By this they received authority over all offences which disturbed the peace and tranquillity of the King's subjects in the counties of York, Northumberland, Westmorland, and Durham, and the cities of York, Kingston-upon-Hull, and Newcastle-upon-Tyne, and also over real and personal actions in cases where either party was too poor to proceed at common law. The King's Commission was supplemented by Instructions [p. 320][4]. These assign a dominant position to the President of the Council, giving him 'a voice negative'; they establish a distinction between a small body of paid Councillors in constant attendance and a larger body of honorary Councillors required to be present at the 'four general sittings'; they authorise the use of recognisances and the infliction of Star Chamber punishments; and they follow the tradition of the Court of Requests in requiring special consideration for poor men, whether suitors to the Court or not, and in establishing an expeditious procedure and a strict limitation of the fees to be charged for the processes of the Court. They also provide for the reference of difficult cases on points of law to the Judges at Westminster, and on questions of fact to the King's Council attendant upon his person.

By the end of 1538 the new Council was in full activity[5], in Durham as well as in the March shires; and its authority received indirect statutory confirmation by the Subsidy Act of 1540 [p. 328] and the Tillage Act of 1571 [p. 329].

The Council of the North thus constituted in 1537 as a permanent organisation proved itself during the Tudor period a most efficient instrument of the central government, but the terms of the preamble of a statute of 1601 [p. 329] suggest that even by the end of the period the work of establishing order in those turbulent counties was still incomplete.

The Council of the North was abolished in 1641 by the Act which put an end to the Star Chamber and the High Commission Court.

---

[1] *L. and P.* xii, pt. ii, nos. 100, 102.   [2] *State Papers*, i, 554.

[3] The greater part of the Latin text is quoted by Coke in his *Fourth Institute*, and is printed below.

[4] The earliest extant are those of 1545, and they establish a precedent which was followed throughout the Tudor period. The instructions issued by James I in 1603 follow the same form, although there are differences in detail; these are printed in Prothero, p. 363.

[5] See a letter from the Council of the North to the King, dated 8 December, 1538, describing their activities (*State Papers, Henry VIII*, v, 142)

(1) Coke on the Commission of 1537

Sir Edward Coke's account of the establishment of the Council of the North assigns the earliest commission to 1540. On the *Institutes* see p. 289 above.

The President and Council in the North

This Council is neither warranted by Act of Parliament nor by prescription, but raised by King H. 8 by his commission, upon these occasions and in the manner hereafter expressed. After the suppression of monasteries of the yearly value of two hundred pound or under, which was by Act of Parliament 4 Febr. *Anno* 27 H. 8, in the beginning of 28 H. 8 there was a great insurrection...in Lincolnshire, pretending it to be for the cause of religion....As soon as they were appeased, a great rebellion for the same pretence of 40,000 of that county, of whom Sir Robert Aske was leader....Soon after, a great commotion for the same pretence was raised in Lancashire by men of that county, and in Cumberland, Westmorland, and Northumberland....After this ...a great multitude did rise and assaulted Carlisle Castle.... Soon after Sir Francis Bigod with a great number rose...in Yorkshire....And after this the Lord Darcy...and others began a new rebellion about Hull in Yorkshire...And all these rebellions fell out between the beginning of 28 H. 8 and 30 H. 8.

The King, intending the suppression of the great monasteries, which in effect he brought to pass in *anno* 31 H. 8, for preventing of future dangers and keeping those northern counties in quiet, in *anno* 31 of his reign raised a President and Council there, and gave them besides two several powers and authorities under one Great Seal, the one of Oyer and Terminer, De quibuscunque congregationibus et conventiculis illicitis, coadunationibus, confederationibus, Lollardiis, misprisionibus, falsis allegantiis, transgressionibus, riotis, routis, retentionibus, contemptibus, falsitatibus, manutenentiis, oppressionibus, violentiis, extortionibus, et aliis malefactis, offensis, et injuriis quibuscunque, per quae pax et tranquillitas subditorum nostrorum in Com. Eborum, Northumberland, Westmorland, Durham, et Com. Civitatis Eborum, Kingston super Hull, et Newcastle super Tinam gravetur, etc., secundum legem et consuetudinem regni nostri Angliae, vel aliter secundum sanas discretiones vestras audiend. et terminand. The other authority was, Necnon quascunque actiones reales seu de libero tenemento, et personales causasque debitorum et demandorum quorumcunque in Com. praedictis, quando ambae partes vel altera pars sic paupertate gravata fuer. quod commode jus suum secundum legem regni nostri aliter prosequi non possit, similiter secundum leges et consuetudines regni nostri Angliae vel aliter secundum sanas discretiones vestras audiend. et terminand.

But these authorities were granted to the end that Commissioners by mediation might quiet controversies when one of the parties or both were poor, who are ever most clamorous. And all the authority they had was expressed in the patents or commission under the great seal, without any reference to instructions, or any instructions at all. But afterwards, for that the said commission was against law, and to the end that their authority should not be known, they procured the first institution to be *ex diametro* altered, *viz.* that their commission should not give them any express authority at all, but wholly did refer their authority to certain instructions[1] which they kept themselves in private, and were not enrolled in any court whereunto the subject might have resort. *Sed misera servitus est ubi jus est vagum aut incognitum.* And thereupon King James, being informed hereof by the Judges of the Common Pleas (who had granted prohibitions to the President and Council) gave order that their instructions should be enrolled[2], to the end that the subject might take advice of learned counsel what course he might take to enjoy the benefit of the laws of the realm, his best birthright.

And it appeareth in the Subsidy in *Anno* 32 H. 8, cap. 50[3] that H. 8 raised not only this President and Council but a President and Council also having like authority in the Western Parts, pretending it to be for their ease to receive justice at their own doors, but they of Cornwall, Devon, etc., desirous to live under the immediate government of the King and the common law, opposed it, *et sic Commissio illa cito evanuit*; which Commission under the Great Seal we have seen. See in the statute of 13 Eliz.[4] where the President and Council of York is mentioned, and no man doubteth but that there is a President and Council *de facto*, but what jurisdiction they have is the question....

And in respect of some continuance it hath had and many decrees made, it were worthy of the wisdom of a Parliament for some establishment to be had therein.

Coke, *Fourth Institute* (edn. of 1669), c. 49.

---

[1] See the Instructions of 1545, printed on p. 320 below.
[2] See the Instructions of 1603 printed in Prothero, p. 363.
[3] See p. 328 below.
[4] See p. 329 below.

(2) Instructions for the Council of the North, 1545

Instructions given by the King's Highness to...the Archbishop of York[1] and such other as shall be named hereafter, whom his Majesty hath appointed to be of his Council resident in the North parts....

His Majesty, much desiring the quietness and good governance of the people there, and for speedy and indifferent administration of justice to be had between party and party, intendeth to continue his right honourable Council called the King's Council in the North Parts. And his Highness, knowing the approved truth, wisdom, and experience of the said Archbishop of York, with his assured discretion and dexterity in executing of justice, hath first appointed him to be President of the said Council so established, and by these presents do give unto him the name and title of Lord President of the said Council; and with the said name, power and authority to call all such others as shall be named of the said Council, at this time or hereafter, together, at all such seasons as he shall think the same expedient, and otherwise by his letters, when they shall be absent, to appoint them and every of them to do such things for the advancement of justice and for the repression and punishment of malefactors as, by the advice of such part of the said Council as then shall be present with him, he shall think meet for the furtherance of his Grace's affairs and the due administration of justice between his Highness's subjects. And further, his Majesty by these presents giveth unto the said Lord President, in all Councils where things shall be debated at length for the bringing out of the most perfect sentence—which his Majesty's pleasure is shall be observed in all cases where the same shall be such as may abide advisement and consultation—a voice negative, to the intent nothing shall pass but his express commandment, consent, and order. And his Highness also willeth and commandeth that all and every of the said Councillors to be hereafter named shall exhibit to the said Lord President as much honour, obedience, and reverent behaviour in all things (kneeling only excepted) as they would exhibit unto his own Person if he were there present amongst them; and in like sort receive and execute all his precepts and commandments to be addressed unto them or any of them, for any matter touching his Majesty or any process or thing to be done or served in his Grace's name.

And to the intent the said President, being thus established

---

[1] Robert Holgate.

as head and director of such Council as his Highness hath erected and established there for the purposes abovesaid, may be furnished with such assistants and members as be of wisdom, experience, gravity, and truth, meet to have the name of his Grace's Councillors, his Majesty upon good advisement and deliberation hath elected and chosen these persons whose names ensue hereafter to be his Councillors joined in the said Council in the North Parts with the said President, that is to say... the Earls of Westmorland and Shrewsbury[1];... William, Lord Dacre of the North; William, Lord Eure; Thomas, Lord Wharton; John Hynde[2], serjeant-at-law; Edmund Molyneux[3], serjeant-at-law;... Sir Marmaduke Constable the elder, Sir Henry Savile, knights; Sir Robert Bowes[4], knight; William Babthorpe, knight; Mr Thomas Magnus, clerk[5]; Robert Challoner, Thomas Gargrave[6], Richard Norton, and John Uvedale, esquires; the which John Uvedale his Highness doth also appoint to be both Secretary to the said Council and to keep his Grace's signet where he is with the said President and Council and not in his absence,—wherewith nevertheless he shall seal nothing but by express warrant of the said Lord President, or of two other of the Council by the consent of the said President—and also to be sworn a Master of the Chancery for taking of recognisance in such cases as by the said President and such of the said Council as shall be from time to time present with him shall be thought convenient, the case so requiring....

...His Majesty ordereth that... the Earl of Westmorland, the Lord Dacre, the Lord Eure, the Lord Wharton, John Hynde, Edmund Molyneux, Sir Marmaduke Constable, Sir Henry Savile, Mr Thomas Magnus, and Richard Norton, shall give their attendance at their own pleasure, that is to say, go and come when their will is, unless they shall be otherwise by the said President appointed, saving only at four general sittings, where every of the said Council shall be present unless they have some just necessary impediment to the contrary. And because it shall be convenient that a number shall be continually abiding with the said President, to whom he may commit the charge and hearing of such matters as shall be exhibited unto him for the more expedition of the same, by

---

[1] The Earl of Cumberland was added 11 December, 1546.
[2] Judge of the Common Pleas, 1545–50; knighted, 1545.
[3] Knighted, 1547; Judge of the Common Pleas, 1550.
[4] Warden of the East and Middle Marches, 1550; Master of the Rolls, 1552.
[5] Archdeacon of the East Riding, 1504.
[6] Knighted, 1549; Speaker of the House of Commons, 1559.

these presents his Highness doth also order that William Babthorpe, Robert Challoner, Thomas Gargrave, and John Uvedale
shall give their continual attendance upon the said President, or at
the least two of them, so as none of this number appointed to give
his continual attendance shall in any wise depart at any time from
the said President without his special licence, and the same not
to extend above six weeks at one season. And for better intreatment of the said President and all the said Council of both sorts
when they or any of them should be present in the said Council,
his Highness doth give a yearly stipend or salary of £300...to
the said President towards the furniture of the diets of himself
and the rest of the said Councillors, with such number of servants
as shall be hereafter allowed to every of them, that is to say, every
of the said Council himself to sit with the President at his table,
or at a place in his house to be by him prepared conveniently for
him after his degree and haviour[1]: and the said Sir Marmaduke
Constable to have sitting in the said Lord President's hall or fed
in some convenient place in his house, four servants; Sir Robert
Bowes to have sitting in the said Lord President's hall, four servants; Thomas Gargrave to have sitting in the said hall, three
servants; and Mr Magnus and every esquire of the said Council
to have sitting in the said hall, three servants, at all times when
they shall resort thither; provided always that, when the said
President and Council remain and keep their sitting in any city
or town where any of the said Council dwelleth and keep his
house, then the same Councillor or Councillors there dwelling to
keep their said servants in their own houses on their own proper
costs and charges. And further his Majesty, of his mere goodness
and great benignity, for the better intreatment of such of the said
Council as either be not able without further help for their
charges of their horse-meat and lodging when they shall thus
attend in Council to serve his Highness, or as not being detained
there about his Grace's affairs might with their learning and
policies better themselves in other places, doth by these presents
limit unto such of the said Council as shall be named hereafter
certain particular fees after the rate ensuing: that is to say, to Sir
Marmaduke Constable in respect of his attendance, towards his
horse-meat and other charges, £20 yearly; to Sir Robert Bowes
for the like, yearly 100 marks; to William Babthorpe for the like,
£50 yearly; to Robert Challoner for the like, £50 yearly; to
Thomas Gargrave for the like, £50 yearly; to Richard Norton
for the like, £40; and to John Uvedale for the like, £20 yearly....

[1] Estate, wealth, substance.

And to furnish the said President and Council in all things with authority sufficient and ready to execute justice as well in causes criminal as in matters of controversy between party and party, his Majesty hath commanded two commissions to be made out under his Great Seal of England by virtue whereof they shall have full power and authority in either case to proceed as the matter occurrent shall require. And for the more speedy expedition to be used in all cases of justice, his Majesty's pleasure is that the said President and Council shall cause every complainant and defendant that shall have to do before them to put their whole matter in their bill of complaint and answer, without replication[1], rejoinder, or other delay to be had or used therein, which order the said President and Council shall manifest to all such as shall be counsellors in any matter to be intreated and defined before them, charging all and every the said counsellors, upon such penalty as their wisdoms shall think convenient, to observe duly this order as they will eschew the danger of the same: no attorney to take for his fee at one sitting above 12d. nor any counsellor above 20d. To the which President and Council the King's Majesty by these presents doth give full power and authority, as well to punish such persons as in anything shall neglect or contemn their commandments as all other that shall speak any seditious words, invent rumours, or commit any such offences, not being treason, whereof any inconvenience might grow, by pillory, cutting their ears, wearing of papers, or otherwise at their discretions; and to poor suitors having no money, at their discretions to appoint counsel and other requisites without paying of any money for the same. And likewise his Highness giveth full power and authority to the said President, and Council being with him, to cess fines of all persons that shall be convict of any riots, how many soever they be in number, unless the matter of such riot shall be thought unto them of such importance as the same shall be meet to be signified unto his Majesty, and punished in such sort, by the order of his Council attendant upon his person, as the same may be noted for an example to others. And semblably, his Grace giveth full power and authority unto them by their discretions to award costs and damages, as well to the plaintiff as to the defendants, and execution of their decrees, all which decrees the said Secretary shall be bounden, incontinently upon the promulgation of every of the same, to write or cause to be written fair in a book, which book shall remain in the hands and custody of the said President. And to the intent it may appear to

---

[1] See p. 255 note 7 above.

all people there what fees shall be taken of them for all manner of process and writings that shall be used by this Council, like as his Majesty straitly chargeth the said President and Council upon their allegiance to suffer no more to be taken for anything the nature whereof shall be expressed hereafter than shall be taxed upon the same, so his Highness will, and by these presents appointeth, that there shall be a table affixed in every place where the said President and Council shall sit at any sessions, and a like table to hang openly, that all men may see it, in the office where the said Secretary shall commonly expedite the said writings, what shall be paid for every of the same: that is to say, for every recognisance wherein one person and sureties are bound for him, 12d.; for cancelling of one like recognisance, 12d.; for entering of one decree, 6d.; for the copy of the same decree, if it be asked, 6d.; for every letter, commission, attachment, or other precepts sent to any person, 4d.; for every dismission[1] before the said Commissioners, if it be asked, 4d.; for the copies of bills and answers, to have for every 10 lines reasonably written, 1d.; for every *subpoena*, 4d.; for letters of appearance under the signet, 4d.; for every leaf of paper written in copy, so that the same contain 20 lines, 2d.; for examination of every witness, 4d. And his Grace's pleasure is that there shall be no examiner of witness nor writer of either bills, answers, copies, or other process in the said Court but by the special licence of the said President and some of the Council, so that the said President may ever have a voice negative in the same. And for the more certain and brief determination of all matters that shall chance in those parts, his Majesty by these presents ordaineth that his said Council shall, by the space of one whole month in the year at least, remain at York, by the space [of] one other month at Newcastle, by the space of one other month at Kingston-upon-Hull, and by the space of one other month at Durham, within the limits whereof the inhabitants there shall be called and to none other place. And they shall in every of the said places keep one gaol delivery before their departure from thence. His Grace nevertheless referreth it to their discretion to take such other place or places for the said four months or four general sittings as they shall think most convenient for the time, if by death or any other occasion they shall think the towns appointed or any of them not meet for them; so that they keep the full term of one month in every place where they shall sit, if they can in any wise conveniently so do.

[1] Discharge.

And forasmuch as the King's Majesty, calling to his remembrance how that the great number of his tenants in this realm have been heretofore retained, either by wages, livery, badge, or cognisance, with divers persons of the countries where the same do inhabit, by reason whereof when his Majesty should have had service of them they were rather at commandment of other men than, according to their duties of allegiance, of his Highness of whom they had their livings; his Majesty's express pleasure and high commandment first is, that none of his said Council shall by any livery, wages, badge, token, or cognisance, retain or entertain any of his Grace's tenants in such sort as whereby he should account himself bounden to do unto him or under him any other than as his Highness's officers, if he be so in any manner of service.

And further, his Majesty's like pleasure and commandment is, that the said President and Council shall in any of their principal sittings give special notice and charge that none other nobleman, gentleman, or other person presume to retain any of his Grace's said tenants in such wise as is aforesaid and as hath been accustomed; charging all the said tenants, upon pain of forfeiture of their holdings and incurring of his Majesty's further displeasure and indignation, in no wise to agree to any such retainder with any other man, but wholly to depend upon his Highness, and upon such as his Majesty shall appoint to be his officers, rulers, and directors over them.

And semblably, his Grace's express pleasure and command ment is, that in every such sitting, and in all other places where the said President and Council shall have any notable assembly before them, they shall give strait charge and commandment to the people to conform themselves in all things to the observation of such laws, ordinances, and determinations as be made, passed, and agreed upon by his Grace's Parliament and Clergy, and specially the laws touching the abolishing of usurped and pretended power of the Bishop of Rome, whose abuses they shall so beat into their heads by continual inculcation, as they may smell the same, and perceive that they declare it with their hearts, and not with their tongues only for a form. And likewise they shall declare the order and determination taken and agreed upon for the abrogation of such vain holy days as be appointed only by the Bishops of Rome to make the world blind, and to persuade the same that they might also make saints at their pleasure, do give occasion by idleness of the increase of many vices and inconveniences. Which two points his Majesty doth most heartily require and straitly command the said President and Council to set forth with dexterity; and to punish extremely, for example, all contemptuous offenders in the same.. . .

Furthermore, the said President and Council shall from time to time make diligent inquisition who hath taken and enclosed commons, called intakes; who be extreme in taking of gressoms[1] and onering of rents[2]; and so call the parties that have so used themselves evil herein before them; and...they shall take such order for the redress of the enormities used in the same as the poor people be not oppressed, but that they may live after their sorts and qualities.

And if it shall chance that the said President and Council shall be variant in opinion, either in law or for any order to be taken upon any fact, that like as if the case be not of very great importance, that part wherein shall be the greater number of the Councillors appointed to give continual attendance shall determine, or else, if they be of like number, that part whereunto the President shall consent and lean, who in all causes as is aforesaid shall ever have a voice negative[3]; so, being the case of great importance, if the question be of the law, the said President and Council shall signify the case to the Judges at Westminster, who shall with diligence advertise them again of their opinions in it. And if it be an order to be taken upon the fact, the said President and Council shall in that case advertise the King's Majesty, or his Council attendant upon his person, upon the same; whereupon they shall have knowledge how to use themselves in that behalf. And the said President and Council shall specially take regard that in cases between party and party, where the question and complaint shall be of any spoil, extortion, or oppression, that the party grieved may have due and undelayed restitution, or for want of ability thereunto the offenders to be punished to the example of others, as well in things that may hereafter be complained of as of such as be passed heretofore at any time for the which agreement is not already made. And if it happen that any man, of what degree soever he be, shall, upon such a ground and cause as the law will allow for good and reasonable, and shall so appear unto the said President and Council, demand surety of peace or justice against any great lord of the country, the said President shall in that case grant the petition of the poorest man

---

[1] A 'gressom' or 'gersum' is a premium or fine paid to a feudal superior on entering upon a holding (*Oxford Dictionary*).

[2] *I.e.* raising of rents so as to be onerous or burdensome.

[3] In 1538 this was amended so as to give the decision on points of law to the majority of lawyers on the Council (Reid, p. 246).

against the richest and greatest lord, whether he be of his Council or no, as he would grant the same, being lawfully asked, of men of the meanest sort, degree, and haviour.

And forasmuch as it may chance the said Lord President to be sometime diseased, that he shall not be able to travail for the direction of such matters as shall then occur, or to be called to the Parliament, or otherwise to be employed in the King's Grace's affairs or about necessary business for good reformation within his rule; to the intent the said Council may be ever full, and that there may be at all times in the same a personage to direct all things in such sort, order, and form as the said President shall do by virtue of these instructions, his Majesty's pleasure is, that when the said Lord President shall be in any wise so diseased or absent as is aforesaid that he cannot supply his room, he shall name one of the number of such Councillors as be appointed to give continual attendance to supply his room for that season, to whom, for so long time as the said Lord President shall be diseased that he cannot execute his office or otherwise to be absent as is aforesaid, his Highness giveth the name of Vice-President, which name nevertheless he shall no longer have than the said President shall be recovered, there present, or returned home again. So his Majesty's pleasure is, that for the time only that any of the said Council shall occupy the room and place of a Vice-President by assignment of the said Lord President as is aforesaid, all the rest of the Council shall in all things use him in like sort and with like reverence as they be bounden by these instructions to use the Lord President himself; whereunto his Grace doubteth not every of them will conform themselves accordingly.

Furthermore, his Majesty by these presents giveth full power and authority to the said President and Council that when the condition of any recognisance taken before them shall be fulfilled, they shall at their discretions in open court cause the same to be cancelled for the discharge of the parties; provided ever, that no recognisance be in any wise cancelled but before the President, or a Vice-President in time of his disease and sickness or absence, and three others of the Council at least sitting in court with him.

And whereas in an article before written it is contained that every of the said Council shall be present at every of the said four general sittings; forasmuch as the King's Majesty doth consider that it should be much tedious and chargeable to divers of the Lords and some others of the said Council to come to every of the said sittings, their habitations being far off, his Highness is contented that those Councillors which be not bounden to continual attendance shall be only present at the sitting or sittings that shall be near unto their dwelling-places, unless they shall be commanded by the President to attend upon him at the other sittings that be further off from them, in which case they shall obey his commandment therein, all excuses set apart, as appertaineth. And where in another article it is also provided that no person shall retain any of the King's tenants by any livery, wages, badge, or cognisance, his Grace doth intimate to the said President and Council that the meaning of his Grace is that no man shall retain any such his Grace's tenants as is aforesaid, unless he shall keep the same continually in household with him and give unto them meat, drink, wages, and lodging; in which case his Majesty is contented that his tenants may be retained, so as the same be not such persons as have any office or certain authority amongst their neighbours.

State Papers, Henry VIII, v, 402.

(3) Subsidy Act of 1540

The Bill for the Subsidy

The King's most loving subjects in this present Parliament assembled, lovingly calling to their remembrance the innumerable benefits and goodness which they always have found in the King's most royal Majesty, their natural and most dread Sovereign Lord, reigning over them the space of 31 years full and more, during the which they have wealthily lived and prosperously continued under his Majesty, well defended, governed, and maintained from and against all manner of enemies, to their no little surety, wealth, quiet, and rest.... Considering also the exceeding great costs, charges, and expenses that his Highness hath sustained in and about the repression of the great late rebellion in Lincolnshire and the north parts of this realm; what yearly costs and charges also his Majesty is at, and of long time hath been, for and about the stablishing of three Presidents and discreet several Councils, as well in the Marches of Wales and the shires thereunto adjoining as in the North and West parties of this realm, By reason whereof his true subjects, poor and rich, without tract of time[1] or any great charges or expenses, have undelayed justice daily administered unto them....

32 Henr. VIII, c. 50: Statutes of the Realm, iii, 812.

---

[1] Without delay.

(4) Tillage Act of 1571

An Act for the Increase of Tillage, etc.

For the better increase of tillage and for maintenance and increase of the navy and mariners of this realm, Be it enacted, That. . . it shall be lawful to all and every person and persons being subjects of the Queen's Majesty, her heirs and successors, and inhabiting within her Highness's realms and dominions [*to export corn to friendly countries from certain ports*] at all such times as the several prices thereof shall be so reasonable and moderate in the several counties where any such transportation shall be intended as that no prohibition shall be made, . . . by the Queen's Majesty . . . by proclamation to be made in the shire town or in any port towns of the county, or else by some order of the Lord President and Council in the North, or the Lord President and Council in Wales, within their several jurisdictions, or of the Justices of Assizes at their sessions in other shires out of the jurisdiction of the said two Presidents and Councils, or by the more part of the Justices of the Peace of the county at their Quarter Sessions. . . .

13 Eliz. c. 13: *Statutes of the Realm*, iv, 547.

(5) Blackmail Act, 1601

An Act for the more peaceable Government of the parts of Cumberland, Northumberland, Westmorland, and the Bishopric of Durham

Forasmuch as now of late years very many of her Majesty's subjects dwelling and inhabiting within the counties of Cumberland, Northumberland, Westmorland, and the Bishopric of Durham have been taken, some forth of their own houses and some in travelling by the highway or otherwise, and carried out of the same counties or to some other places within some of the said several counties as prisoners, and kept barbarously and cruelly until they have been redeemed by great ransoms; And where now of late time there have been many incursions, raids, robberies, and burning and spoiling of towns, villages, and houses within the said counties, that divers and sundry of her Majesty's loving subjects within the said counties, and the inhabitants of divers towns there, have been inforced to pay a certain rate of money, corn, cattle, or other consideration, commonly there called by the name of Black mail[1], unto divers and sundry inhabiting upon or near the Borders being men of name, and friended and allied with divers in those parts who are commonly known to be

---

[1] 'Mail' is a rent or tribute; cf. 'silver mail,' rent paid in money.

great robbers and spoil-takers[1] within the said counties, to the
end thereby to be by them freed, protected, and kept in safety
from the danger of such as do usually rob and steal in those parts;
By reason whereof many of the inhabitants thereabouts, being her
Majesty's tenants or other good subjects, are much impoverished,
and theft and robbery much increased, and the maintainers thereof
greatly encouraged, and the service of those borders and frontiers
much weakened and decayed, and divers towns thereabouts much
dispeopled and laid waste, and her Majesty's own revenue greatly
diminished, which heinous and outrageous misdemeanors there
cannot so well by the ordinary officers of her Majesty in those
parts be speedily prevented or suppressed without further provision of law: For remedy whereof be it enacted.... That whosoever shall at any time hereafter, without good and lawful warrant
or authority, take any of her Majesty's subjects against his or
their will or wills and carry them out of the same counties, or to
any other place within any of the said counties, or detain, force,
or imprison him or them as prisoners, or against his or their
wills to ransom them[2] or to make a prey or spoil of his or their
person or goods upon deadly feud or otherwise, or whosoever
shall be privy, consenting, aiding, or assisting unto any such
taking, detaining, carrying away, or procure the taking, detaining,
or carrying away of any such person or persons prisoners as aforesaid, or whosoever shall take, receive, or carry, to the use of himself or wittingly to the use of any other, any money, corn, cattle,
or other consideration, commonly called Black mail, for the protecting or defending of him or them or his or their lands, tenements, goods, or chattels from such thefts, spoils, and robberies as
is aforesaid, or whosoever shall give any such money, corn, cattle,
or other consideration called Black mail for such protection as is
aforesaid, or shall wilfully and of malice burn or cause to be
burned, or aid, procure, or consent to the burning of, any barn or
stack of corn or grain within any the said counties or places
aforesaid, and shall be of the said several offences or of any of
them indicted and lawfully convicted, or shall stand mute[3], or
shall challenge peremptorily above the number of 20[4], before the
Justices of Assizes, Justices of Gaol Delivery, Justices of Oyer
and Terminer, or Justices of Peace within any of the said counties

---

[1] Cf. the description in *Waverley* of the relations between Fergus MacIvor, the
'man of name,' and the robber, Donald Bean Lean.

[2] *I.e.* to hold them to ransom.   [3] *I.e.* refuse to plead.

[4] A prisoner had the right to challenge a certain number of jurors 'peremptorily,'
i.e. without showing cause.

at some of their general sessions within some of the said counties to be holden, shall be reputed, adjudged, and taken to be as felons, and shall suffer pains of death without any benefit of clergy, sanctuary, or abjuration[1], and shall forfeit as in case of felony.

* * * * * *

V. Provided always, That this Act nor anything therein contained shall not extend to abridge or impeach the jurisdiction or authority of any the Lords Wardens of any the Marches of England for and anenst[2] Scotland; Anything in this present Act to the contrary notwithstanding.

43 Eliz. c. 13: Statutes of the Realm, iv, 979.

§ 2. THE COUNCIL OF WALES[3]

The origin of the Council of the Marches in Wales may be assigned to the reign of Edward IV. From the time of the first Prince of Wales there had been a Prince's Council to administer his estates within the Principality, and Edward IV only developed an earlier institution. His son was born in November, 1470, and was created Prince of Wales, 26 June, 1471; and by letters patent of 8 July a Council of fifteen was established to administer for him the Principality of Wales, the Duchy of Cornwall, and the County of Chester, until he should be fourteen years of age. In February, 1473, a Council of twenty-five was appointed with wider powers. The Prince's Council received by commission from the Crown large judicial and military powers not only in Wales but also in the Marches, with a view to the repression of disorder, and thus both Wales and the Marches were brought under one control.

As most of the records of the Council of the Marches down to the reign of Henry VIII have disappeared, its earlier history is obscure, but it is probable that it did not become a permanent institution until the beginning of the sixteenth century. Henry VII appointed a Prince's Council for his eldest son, Arthur, and after his death in 1502 this became 'the Council in the Marches of Wales.' Certain statutory powers were conferred upon this body in 1534 by 26 Henr. VIII, c. 6 [p. 333], and in 1543 the jurisdiction of the Council 'in manner and form as hath heretofore been used and accustomed' was confirmed by 34 & 35 Henr. VIII, c. 26 [p. 335]. Thus the authority of the Council of Wales, although it originated in a royal commission, came to rest upon a statutory foundation.

As in the case of the Council of the North, the Council's commission was supplemented by instructions. These were first issued in 1574, and from time to time they were reissued with alterations and additions[4]. Those of 1574 provide for a Lord President and 20 Councillors, two of these being appointed to continual attendance. The quorum was to be two, of whom the

---

[1] See p. 15 above.   [2] Over against.

[3] For the detailed history of this Council see Miss C. A. J. Skeel, *The Council in the Marches of Wales*; also the supplementary article in *English Historical Review*, xxx, 19.

[4] The Instructions of 1617 are printed in Prothero, p. 378.

Lord President or the Vice-President must be one, and the Council was to have jurisdiction over 'all manner of complaints and petitions' in matters civil or criminal, 'exhibited or put unto them by any poor persons that shall manifestly appear not to be able to sue or defend after the course of the common law, or by any person like to be oppressed by maintenance, riches, strength, power, degree, or affinity of the parties adversaries.' They were also empowered to hear and determine all manner of 'extortions, maintenance, embraceries, oppressions, conspiracies, escapes, corruptions, falsehoods, and all other evil doings, defaults and misdemeanours of all sheriffs, justices of peace, mayors, bailiffs, stewards, lieutenants' and other officials, and to punish them with fine and imprisonment; and similarly to punish jurors who gave wrong verdicts[1].

The area of the Council's jurisdiction included not only Wales and the Marcher Lordships, but also the four English counties of Salop, Worcester, Hereford, and Gloucester[2]; but the main object of the institution of the Council was to suppress the privileges of the Marcher Lords, who claimed royal rights on their own estates, holding their own courts, and waging private war at their pleasure. The King's writ did not run upon these lordships, and as far as the administration of justice was concerned Wales was 'a congeries of petty states in which no extradition treaties existed'[3]; it was therefore of vital importance to the Tudor policy of centralisation that Council government should be applied to the Marches, as it was being applied to the similar problems of the Scottish Border by the Council of the North.

The procedure of the Council of Wales followed that of the King's Council, and its relation, both to the Council and to the Star Chamber, was intimate, although it was clearly subordinate to both. The instructions under which it acted were drawn up by the Privy Council, and the Council could control its proceedings, either withdrawing cases into its own jurisdiction[4], or remitting them to the Council of Wales for decision[5]. In the same way the Star Chamber could claim to supersede the Welsh Council and call cases to London, and this was frequently done where persons of quality were concerned. But both Courts existed for the same purpose, used the same legal forms, and inflicted similar punishments; and they were both successful in repressing disorder and making justice, especially upon great offenders, speedy and comparatively cheap. A writer of 1594[6] refers to it as 'the very place of refuge for the poor oppressed of this country of Wales to fly unto'; 'the best cheap Court in England for fees, and there is great speed made in trial of all causes'; and 'so necessary a Court for the quiet government of that country as without the same Wales would be turned into her former chaos of troubles.'

After the end of the sixteenth century the Council of Wales declined in

---

[1] See Skeel, pp. 89–96.

[2] Ludlow was the centre of the Council's authority and there its records were kept, but meetings were often summoned at Bewdley and Shrewsbury; and sessions were also held from time to time at Hereford, Worcester, Gloucester, Tewkesbury, Hartlebury, Bridgworth, Oswestry, and Wrexham.

[3] Skeel, p. 16.　　　　[4] See Dasent, x, 432.　　　　[5] See Dasent, xi, 67.

[6] George Owen's unpublished *Dialogue on the Government of Wales*, quoted in Skeel, p. 282.

importance. As early as 1561 or 1562 the City of Bristol, although in the English border county of Gloucester, obtained exemption from its jurisdiction, and in 1569 Chester established its independence of the Council on the ground that it was a County Palatine. In 1604, however, the much wider question was raised whether the jurisdiction of the Council extended over the four English border counties, and here an agitation against it was set up and its processes systematically ignored. The Act of 1641 which abolished the Star Chamber also put an end to the criminal jurisdiction of the 'Court holden before the President and Council in the Marches of Wales,' although as a civil court it lasted until the war broke out, and was revived at the Restoration, to be finally abolished by statute[1] as unnecessary at the Revolution.

(1) Act of 1534

An Act that murders and felonies done or committed within any Lordship Marcher in Wales shall be enquired of at the Sessions holden within the Shire grounds next adjoining, with many good orders for ministration of Justice there to be had

Forasmuch as the people of Wales and Marches of the same, not dreading the good and wholesome laws and statutes of this realm, have of long time continued and persevered in perpetration and commission of divers and manifold thefts, murders, rebellions, wilful burning of houses, and other scelerous deeds and abominable malefacts, to the high displeasure of God, inquietation of the King's well-disposed subjects, and disturbance of the public weal; which malefacts and scelerous deeds be so rooted and fixed in the same people, that they be not like to cease unless some sharp correction and punishment for redress and amputation of the premises be provided according to the demerits of the offenders; Be it therefore enacted. . . That all and singular person and persons dwelling or resiant within Wales or in the Lordships Marches of the same, from time to time and at all times hereafter, upon such monition or warning given for the Court to be kept in Wales or in any of the Lordships Marches aforesaid, as before this time hath been used, shall personally repair, resort, and appear before the Justice, Steward, Lieutenant, or other officer, at all and every Sessions, Court, and Courts, . . . And then and there shall give his and their personal attendance to do, execute, and accomplish all and every thing and things which to him or them shall affeir[2] and appertain, upon pain of such fines, forfeitures, and amerciaments as shall be affeered[3], assessed, and taxed by the Justice, Steward, or other officer, to the King's use if it be within any of the King's Lordships Marchers, And

---

[1] 1 Will. & Mary c. 27.   [2] Belong.   [3] Assessed.

if it be within any other Lordships Marches then to the use of
the Lord of the said Lordship Marcher for the time being....

II. And forasmuch as the officers in the Lordships Marchers
in Wales have oft and sundry times heretofore unlawfully exacted
the King's subjects within such Lordships where they have rule
or authority by many and sundry ways and means, and also committed them to strait duress and imprisonment for small and light
feigned causes, and extorciously compelled them thereby to pay
unto them fines for their redemptions, contrary to the law, Therefore be it further enacted, that if any Steward, Lieutenant, or any
other officer of any Lordship Marcher do feign, procure, or
imagine any untrue surmise against any person or persons that
shall so give their personal attendance before them at such Court
or Courts, and upon the same untrue surmise commit them to
any duress or imprisonment contrary to the law, or contrary to
the true and laudable custom of that Lordship, that then upon
suit made unto the King's Commissioners or Council of Marches
...the same Commissioners or Council shall have full power and
authority to send for such Steward, Lieutenant, or officer, and also
for the person or persons so imprisoned; And if the same person
or persons so imprisoned can evidently prove before the said
Council...that his imprisonment was upon any feigned surmise,
without cause reasonable or lawful, that then the same Commissioners shall have full power and authority to assess the said
officer to pay to the said person or persons wrongfully imprisoned
6s. 8d. for every day of their imprisonment, or more by the
discretions of the said Commissioners according to the hurts and
behaviour of the person or persons imprisoned; And that the same
Commissioners shall set further fine upon the said officer to be
paid to the King's use as by their discretions shall be thought
convenient; And in case the same officer do refuse to appear before
the same Commissioners incontinent after any commandment to
them directed and delivered after any such complaint made to the
same Commissioners, that then the same Commissioners shall
have full power and authority [*to fine the officer and to imprison him
if he refuse to pay*]....

     *   *   *   *   *   *

26 Henr. VIII, c. 6: *Statutes of the Realm*, iii, 500.

(2) Act of 1543

An Act for Certain Ordinances in the King's Majesty's Dominion and Principality of Wales

*   *   *   *   *   *

III. Item, That there shall be and remain a President and Council in the said Dominion and Principality of Wales and the Marches of the same, with all officers, clerks, and incidents to the same, in manner and form as hath heretofore been used and accustomed; which President and Council shall have power and authority to hear and determine by their wisdoms and discretions such causes and matters as be or hereafter shall be assigned to them by the King's Majesty, as heretofore hath been accustomed and used.. . .

*   *   *   *   *   *

34 & 35 Henr. VIII, c. 26: *Statutes of the Realm*, iii, 926.

§ 3. THE COUNCIL OF THE WEST

Little is known of the Council of the West. It may have been set up, presumably by commission, as a result of the Western Insurrection of 1537, and it is referred to in the preamble of the Subsidy Act of 1540[1], where one of the reasons for the subsidy is stated to be the 'yearly costs and charges' incurred by the King 'for and about the stablishing of three Presidents and discreet several Councils, as well in the Marches of Wales and the shires thereunto adjoining as in the North and West parties of this realm.' In consequence of local opposition, however, it soon disappeared[2].

[1] 32 Henr. VIII, c. 50 (see p. 328 above). Some text-books make the erroneous statement that the Council of the West was set up by this statute, and is therefore of a different origin to the Councils of Wales and the North.

[2] 'But they of Cornwall, Devon, etc., desirous to live under the immediate government of the King and the common law, opposed it, *et sic Commissio illa cito evanuit*' (Coke, *Fourth Institute*; see p. 319 above).

Financial Courts

The application of Tudor principles of business to the management of the King's affairs, led to the creation by statute in the reign of Henry VIII of four financial Courts with combined judicial and administrative authority. These Courts were under the direct control of the Council

§ 1. COURT OF AUGMENTATIONS

The Court of Augmentations was set up by statute in 1536 [see below] to deal with the confiscated estates of the lesser monasteries. So great a transfer of real property required special machinery, and the Act established an office for the purpose of handling the augmentations of the royal revenue due to this and future dissolutions. An Act of 1540 [p. 339] expressly assigned to the Court the control of monastic liberties and franchises; and this was confirmed by an Act of 1542 [p. 340].

Henry VIII dissolved the statutory Court and then re-erected it by letters patent, but this course failed to satisfy the legal conscience of the time, and the preamble of an Act of 1553[1] refers to 'divers ambiguities' 'risen and grown among such as be learned in the laws of the realm, whether the... said late Courts erected by authority of Parliament...might by the order of the law be dissolved, extinguished, and repealed by letters patents, considering that the commencement of them were first had and made by authority of Parliament.' The Act therefore declares Henry VIII's letters patent to be valid, and empowers his successor during his life to dissolve, unite, or change any of the said Courts and to erect new Courts by letters patent. As Edward VI did not use this power, a similar authority was conferred on Queen Mary by another Act of 1553[2]. The episode illustrates the importance that was now being assigned to statutory authority.

(1) Act for the Court of Augmentations, 1536

The extracts from the statute here given will serve to shew the structural design of a typical Tudor financial court.

An Act establishing the Court of Augmentations

Forasmuch as in this present Parliament....It is enacted, ordained, and established [*here follows a recital of the Act for the Dissolution of the Lesser Monasteries*, 27 Henr. VIII, c. 28]: For the more surety and establishment whereof, and to the intent that the King's Majesty, his heirs and successors, shall be yearly

---

[1] 7 Edw. VI, c. 2.   [2] 1 Mar. st. ii, c. 10.

as well truly and justly answered, contented, and paid of the rents, ferms, issues, revenues, and profits rising, coming, and growing of the said manors, lands, tenements, and other hereditaments before specified, as of the goods, chattels, plate, stuff of household, debts, money, stock, store, and other whatsoever profit and commodity given, granted, or appointed to the King's Majesty by the same, in such court, place, form, manner, and condition as hereafter shall be limited, declared, and appointed; Be it enacted...in manner and form as hereafter followeth in articles, that is to say: First, the King our said Sovereign Lord, by authority aforesaid, ordaineth, maketh, establisheth, and erecteth a certain court commonly to be called the Court of the Augmentations of the Revenues of the King's Crown; which Court by authority aforesaid continually shall be a court of record, and shall have one great seal and one privy seal to be engraved and made after such form, fashion, and manner as shall be appointed by the King's Highness, and shall remain and be ordered as hereafter shall be declared.

II. Also be it enacted by authority aforesaid that there shall be one certain person, to be named and assigned by the King's Highness, which shall be Chancellor of the said Court...and shall have the keeping of the said great seal and privy seal to be assigned for the said Court. Also that there shall be one person to be named by the King's Highness, which shall be called the King's Treasurer of the Court...and shall be the second officer of the same Court.

III. Also it is ordained by authority aforesaid, that there shall be one person learned in the laws of the land to be named by the King's Highness, which shall be called the King's Attorney of the said Court, and shall be the third officer of the same Court. Also that there shall be one person to be named by the King's Highness, which shall be called the King's Solicitor of the same Court, and shall be the fourth officer of the Court. Also that there shall be ten particular auditors to be named by the King's Highness, which shall be called Auditors of the Revenues of the said Augmentations. Also there shall be 17 particular receivers to be named by the King's Highness, which shall be called Receivers of the said Revenues. Also that there shall be one person to be named by the King's Highness, which shall be called Clerk of the said Court; and one other person which shall be Usher of the same Court; and one other person which shall be called Messenger of the same Court; which Usher and Messenger shall be named by the King's Highness; and every of them shall have such yearly fees, rewards, and profits as the Usher and Messenger of the Duchy[1] Chamber of Westminster have and perceive[2].

* * * * * *

V. Also be it enacted by authority aforesaid, that all the said monasteries, priories, and other religious houses which be dissolved and come or shall come to the King's Highness by the Act aforesaid, and all the manors, meses[3], lands, tenements, rents, services, tithes, pensions, portions, advowsons, patronages, and all hereditaments appertaining or belonging to any the said monasteries, priories, or other religious houses, shall be in the order, survey, and governance of the said Court and of the officers and ministers thereof; and all the ferms[4], issues, revenues, and profits coming and growing of the premises or any part thereof, shall be taken and received to the King's use by the ministers and officers of the same Court in manner and form as hereafter shall be declared: Except always and reserved such and as many of the same monasteries, priories, and houses, with all their hereditaments, possessions, goods, and chattels, which the King's Majesty by his letters patents under his great seal shall declare and limit to continue and be in their essential estate and to persevere[5] in the body and corporation as they were before the making of the said Act.

VI. Also be it enacted by authority aforesaid that all those manors, lands, tenements, and hereditaments which the King's Highness hath purchased, and now remain in his Grace's hands, or in the hands or possession of any person or persons to his use, and which hereafter his Highness shall purchase, shall be and remain in the order, survey, and governance of the said Court in form as is above rehearsed.

[VII. All 'gifts, grants, releases, confirmations, leases, letters patents, and other writings' are to be under the great seal of the Court, the Chancellor and other officers taking 'for the ensealing and writing of every patent such fee or fees as is taken by the Chancellor or other officer or officers of the King's Duchy of Lancaster in like case.' The Clerk of the Court is to 'enrol and register in a great book in parchment' all such gifts and grants made under the great seal of the Court, and also to enter in a book the appearance of every person summoned before the Chancellor, and all 'acts, decrees, and orders' made by the Court, taking such fees as are allowed to the Clerk of the Duchy of Lancaster.]

* * * * * *

---

[1] *I.e.* the Duchy of Lancaster: see p. 351 below.
[2] See note on p. 34 above.   [3] Messuages.
[4] See note on p. 39 above.
[5] In the sense of 'continue' or 'remain.'

XI. Also that the said Chancellor for the time being shall have full power and authority to award, under the privy seal appointed to the said Court, in the King's name, such process and precepts with reasonable pains to be therein limited as be now commonly used in the Court of the King's Duchy Chamber of Lancaster being at Westminster, against every person or persons, whatsoever they be, for and concerning the interest, right, and title of the King's Majesty, his heirs and successors, of, in, or to any of the premises limited to the survey and governance of the said Court, or of or for any rent, account, receipt, or services in any wise touching or concerning the same premises or any part of them for and on the behalf of our said Sovereign Lord the King, or of or for any debt rising or growing by occasion of the same.

* * * * * *

[There are 24 sections in all, but §§ 12–24 are concerned only with details.]

27 Henr. VIII, c. 27: *Statutes of the Realm*, iii, 569.

(2) Act of 1540

The Liberties to be used

I. Where divers and sundry sites, circuits, and precincts of late monasteries, abbacies, priories, nunneries, colleges, hospitals, and other ecclesiastical and religious houses and places, and divers honours, castles, manors, messuages, lands, tenements, liberties, privileges, franchises, and other hereditaments, by divers and sundry statutes heretofore made, be assigned, limited, and appointed to the order, rule, survey, and governance of the... Court of Augmentations;... by the which statutes it is not fully, plainly, nor expressly declared or rehearsed how...the liberties, privileges, and franchises which the late owners of the said sites [etc.] ...should be ordered, used, exercised, and put in execution; Be it therefore enacted...that all and singular the same liberties, franchises, privileges, and temporal jurisdictions which the said late owners have used and exercised lawfully...shall be by virtue of this present Act revived, and...shall be in the rule, order, survey, and governance of the King's said Court of Augmentations....

* * * * * *

32 Henr. VIII, c. 20: *Statutes of the Realm*, iii, 770.

(3) Act of 1542

The Bill for the establishment of the Court of Surveyors

*   *   *   *   *   *

XXXIV. And where the King's Highness of late [*by* 27 *H. VIII, c.* 27]...hath erected a certain Court called the Court of the Augmentations of the Revenues of his Crown, and by the same made the same a Court of Record...and where also [*by* 32 *H. VIII, c.* 20]...it was enacted...that certain liberties, franchises, jurisdictions, and preeminences...should be revived and be in the order, rule, and survey of the same Court....Be it now ...enacted...that the same Act concerning the establishment of the said Court of Augmentations...and also the said Act for reviving of Liberties, shall from henceforth for ever stand and abide in their full strength, effect, and virtue, after and according to the true intent and meaning of the same several Acts aforesaid.

*   *   *   *   *   *

33 Henr. VIII, c. 39: *Statutes of the Realm,* iii, 885.

The Act establishing the Court of Augmentations may be regarded as typical of this kind of legislation, and the other three financial Courts can be dealt with more briefly.

§ 2. COURT OF FIRST FRUITS AND TENTHS

The Court of First Fruits and Tenths was created by statute in 1540[1], 'to the intent that the King's Majesty...shall be the better served in obtaining' his dues. Like the Augmentations it was to be a Court of Record, presided over by a Chancellor who kept the seal of the Court, and having upon its staff a Treasurer, a King's Attorney, Auditors, a Clerk, a Messenger, and an Usher. The First Fruits and Tenths, 'and all the revenues and profits thereof which now be or hereafter shall grow or be by any manner of means' were to be 'from henceforth in the order, survey, and governance of the said Court and the ministers of the same,' who were authorised to summon persons to appear in court under penalties, and to issue legal process against the King's debtors for the ecclesiastical dues with which the Court was concerned.

§ 3. COURT OF WARDS AND LIVERIES

In 1540 Henry VIII created by statute[2] a Court for the control of the King's wards and the administration of their lands. The preamble of the Act refers to the 'great rents, revenues, and profits which to his Highness hath or shall grow, as well by reason of such persons as have been or hereafter shall be in ward to his Highness, as also by mean of idiots and fools natural, now remaining or being, or that hereafter shall remain or be, in his Grace's custody, and also for licences to marry made and to be made to women

[1] 32 Henr. VIII, c 45.   [2] 32 Henr. VIII, c. 46.

being his Grace's widows, and fines made by them for marrying without his Highness's licence.' In order that these dues may be better secured to the Crown, the Act establishes a Court of Record, to be called the Court of the King's Wards, presided over by a Master of the Wards who was to have the custody of the seal of the Court. There were also to be appointed a King's Attorney of the Court of Wards, a Receiver-General, two Auditors, two Clerks, a Messenger, and an Usher. With some differences of detail, the Court is organised on the same lines as the Court of Augmentations and the Court of First Fruits and Tenths. In 1542 the business of liveries of seisin was transferred to the Court by statute[1], the office of Master of the Liveries being annexed to that of the Master of the Wards, and the name of the Court was changed to 'the King's Court of his Wards and Liveries.' It continued until the abolition of the feudal incidents in the reign of Charles II[2].

§ 4. Court of Surveyors

The King's Surveyors were charged with the administration of the royal castles and manors, and in 1542[3] Henry VIII consolidated their authority by establishing a statutory Court to control his 'honours, castles, lordships, manors, lands, tenements, and other hereditaments.' This was to be a Court of Record, and was to bear the title of the 'Court of the General Surveyors of the King's Lands.' Its seal was to be in the custody of the Surveyor first named in the King's letters patent. The Treasurer of the King's Chamber was always to be Treasurer of the new Court; and there was a King's Attorney, a Master of the Woods, Auditors, Receivers, a Clerk, a Messenger, and an Usher. The Court was dissolved by letters patent before the end of the reign[4].

[1] 33 Henr. VIII, c. 22.
[3] By 33 Henr. VIII, c. 39.
[2] By 12 Car. II, c. 24.
[4] See 7 Edw. VI, c. 2, § 1.

Ancient Courts

The ancient courts did not undergo any fundamental changes during the Tudor period. Their constitution was fixed by their antiquity, and they did not readily adapt themselves to new conditions—a fact which helps to explain the need for flexible institutions like the courts which derived from the jurisdiction of the Council.

§ 1. The Courts of Common Law

The tenure of the Judges during the Tudor period was in theory precarious but in practice secure. The staff of the King's Bench and of the Common Pleas each consisted of a Lord Chief Justice and three ordinary Judges, and that of the Exchequer of a Lord Chief Baron and three ordinary Barons[1]. As a rule these held office *durante bene placito*, although the Chief Baron of the Exchequer held on a permanent tenure, and cases occur of special appointments *quamdiu se bene gesserint*. But it made little difference whether the Judges held 'during pleasure' or 'during good behaviour,' for although they might be liable to dismissal, in the practice of the Tudor period they were not dismissed.

It was in this period that the Barons of the Exchequer acquired equal dignity with the Judges of the other two Courts. Hitherto they had been appointed from among the departmental officers of the Exchequer, whereas the Judges of the King's Bench and the Common Pleas were selected from the serjeants-at-law[2]. The Exchequer Barons did not go on circuit, and the value of the rings presented to them by a new serjeant was considerably less than that of those given to the judges[3]. In 1579, however, the increase in the volume of litigation due to the development of commerce[4], called for a larger staff of judges, and this was obtained by utilising the services of the Exchequer Barons for all judicial purposes. This could be more easily effected as the distinction between civil cases and revenue cases was in process of disappearing. Thus, on the appointment of Robert Shute as second Baron of the Exchequer in 1579, his patent provided that he should be 'of the same order, rank, estimation, dignity, and preeminence to all intents and purposes as any puisne judge of either of the two other Courts.'[5] From this time onward the Exchequer Barons were always chosen, like the Judges, from among the serjeants-at-law, and went on circuit as Judges of Assize.

[1] Foss, v, 405.
[2] Bartholomew Westby, appointed second Baron, and William Bolling, appointed third Baron in 1501, were members of the Middle Temple after they became Barons; if they had been serjeants they would have been members of Serjeants' Inn (Foss, v, 11). [3] Foss, v, 409.
[4] *Ib*. Harrison offers a different explanation—'that the number of lawyers and attorneys hath so exceedingly increased, that some shifts must needs be found and matters sought out whereby they may be set on work' (*Description of England*, pt. i. p. 102). [5] Foss, v, 410.

A large increase also takes place in this period in the official salaries of the Judges, although the Exchequer Barons were still paid less than their colleagues. The scale of 1578 is printed on p. 209 and p. 210 above.

During the Tudor period the system of appeals from the three Courts was reorganised by statute. An Act of 1357[1] had laid the foundation of a court of appeal by providing that in case of any complaint of error made in a process in the Exchequer, the Chancellor and Treasurer should cause to come before them 'in any Chamber of Council nigh the Exchequer' the record of the process complained of, and 'taking the Justices and other sage persons such as to them seemeth meet to be taken,' they were, after hearing what the Barons of the Exchequer had to say in support of their judgments, to 'examine the business' and if necessary to amend the record, returning the amended roll into the Exchequer in order that the judgment of the Court might be executed there. In this appeal court the Chancellor and the Treasurer were the judges, and the Justices and others only came before them as assessors; and the Court was not a 'Court of Record' having rolls of its own, but its amended judgments were placed upon the rolls of the Exchequer[2]. The place selected for the meetings of the Court—'a Chamber of Council nigh the Exchequer'—was convenient because the Exchequer Barons and their records had not far to come; and by the commonest of transitions the name of its meeting-place was applied to the Court, which came to be called the Exchequer Chamber.

In 1585 Elizabeth by statute [below] established a Court for hearing appeals from the King's Bench when Parliament was not sitting, upon the same lines as the earlier Court for hearing appeals from the Exchequer; and this also was called Exchequer Chamber. The resemblance between the old Court and the new was made still closer by an Act of 1589 [p. 345]; and from this time forward appeals from the Exchequer were heard by the Judges of the King's Bench and Common Pleas, and appeals from the King's Bench were heard by the Judges of the Common Pleas and Exchequer; and both Courts were called Exchequer Chamber. Appeals from the Common Pleas, by very ancient usage, went to the Court of King's Bench.

'Exchequer Chamber' is also used in a third sense. If a case of special importance arose it was usual, without any statutory authority, to focus upon it all the available legal wisdom by causing it to be heard before all the Judges of all the three Courts, sometimes reinforced by the Lord Chancellor. This Court was a court of debate only, and gave advice but not decisions. Judgment was always given in the Court below, from which the case came.

(1) Act of 1585
An Act for Redress of erroneous Judgments in the Court commonly called the King's Bench

Forasmuch as erroneous judgments given in the Court called the King's Bench are only to be reformed by the High Court of Parliament, which Court of Parliament is not in these days so often holden as in ancient time it hath been, neither yet in respect of greater affairs of this realm such erroneous judg-

---

[1] 31 Edw. III, st. i, c. 12 recited on p. 345 below.   [2] Baldwin, p. 234.

ments can be well considered of and determined during the time of the Parliament, whereby the subjects of this realm are greatly hindered and delayed of justice in such cases; Be it therefore enacted by the authority of this present Parliament, That where any judgment shall at any time hereafter be given in the said Court of the King's Bench in any suit or action of debt, detinue[1], covenant, account, action upon the case, ejection, ferm[2], or trespass, first commenced or to be first commenced there, other than such only where the Queen's Majesty shall be party, the party, plaintiff or defendant, against whom any such judgment shall be given, may at his election sue forth out of the Court of Chancery a special writ of error, to be devised in the said Court of Chancery, directed to the Chief Justice of the said Court of the King's Bench for the time being, commanding him to cause the said record and all things concerning the said judgment to be brought before the Justices of the Common Bench and the Barons of the Exchequer into the Exchequer Chamber, there to be examined by the said Justices of the Common Bench and Barons aforesaid; which said Justices of the Common Bench and such Barons of the Exchequer as are of the degree of the coif[3], or six of them at the least, by virtue of this present Act shall thereupon have full power and authority to examine all such errors as shall be assigned or found in or upon any such judgment, and thereupon to reverse or affirm the said judgment as the law shall require, other than for errors to be assigned or found for or concerning the jurisdiction of the said Court of King's Bench, or for any want of form in any writ, return, plaint, bill, declaration, or other pleading, process, verdict, or proceeding whatsoever; And that after that the said judgment shall be affirmed or reversed, the said record and all things concerning the same shall be removed and brought back into the said Court of the King's Bench, that such further proceeding may be thereupon as well for execution or otherwise as shall appertain.

II. And be it further enacted, That such reversal or affirmation of any such former judgment shall not be so final but that the party who findeth him grieved therewith shall and may sue in the High Court of Parliament for the further and due examination of the said judgment in such sort as is now used upon erroneous judgments in the said Court of King's Bench.

27 Eliz. c. 8: *Statutes of the Realm*, iv, 714.

[1] An action for the recovery of a personal chattel wrongfully detained.
[2] Rent.
[3] *I.e.* serjeants-at-law; a special feature of whose distinctive dress was a white coif of silk. For an account of this corporation see Holdsworth, ii, 407–14.

(2) Act of 1589

*An Act against Discontinuances of Writs of Error in the Court
of Exchequer and King's Bench*

Whereas by an estatute made in the one and thirtieth year of the reign of King Edward the Third[1] it is enacted, That upon complaint concerning error made in the Exchequer touching the King or other persons, the Lord Chancellor and Lord Treasurer shall do to come before them in any Chamber of Council nigh the Exchequer the record and process of the Exchequer, and taking to them such Justices and other sage persons as to them shall be thought meet, shall hear and determine such errors; as by the said estatute more at large appeareth; And whereas those two, being great officers of the realm, are employed, not only in their several offices and places of justice elsewhere but also for the other weighty affairs of the realm in Council attendant on the Queen's Majesty's person, and otherwise they be many times upon sudden warning called away, in such wise as they both many times and sometimes neither of them can be present in the Exchequer at the day of adjournment in such suit of error; and then by not coming of them at the day of adjournment every such writ of error depending is by the laws of the realm discontinued, and the party cannot proceed but must begin his suit of new, to the great loss of the party and hindrance of justice; For remedy whereof, Be it ordained and enacted...That the not coming of the Lord Chancellor and Lord Treasurer or of either of them at the day of adjournment in any such suit of error depending by virtue of the said former estatute shall not be any discontinuance of any such writ of error; but if both the Chief Justices of either Bench, or any one of the said great officers the Lord Chancellor or Lord Treasurer, shall come to the Exchequer Chamber and there be present at the day of adjournment in such suit of error, it shall be no discontinuance, but the suit shall proceed in law to all intents and purposes as if both the Lord Chancellor and Lord Treasurer had come and been present at the day and place of adjournment: Provided always, That no judgment shall be given in such suit or writ of error unless both the Lord Chancellor and Lord Treasurer shall be present thereat.

II. ...[*After reciting* 27 *Eliz. c.* 8, *the Act proceeds*] Forasmuch as it doth many times fall out that the full number of the said Justices of the Common Bench and Barons of the Exchequer

[1] 31 Edw. III, st. i, c. 12.

so authorised by the said Statute, sometimes for want of health, sometimes through other weighty services and earnest occasions, cannot be present at the days and times of the returns and continuances of the same writs of error; And by reason of their absence and not coming the said writs of error are discontinued, justice delayed, and the parties put to begin new suit, to their great charges and prejudice; For remedy thereof be it also enacted...That from henceforth, if the full number of Justices and Barons authorised by the said Act come not at the day or time of return or continuance of any such writ of error, that it shall be lawful for any three of the said Justices and Barons, at every of the said days and times, to receive writs of error, to award process thereupon, to make and prefix[1] days from time to time of and for the continuance of all such writs of error as shall be there returned certified or depending; and the same shall be to these respects as good and available as if all the Justices and Barons authorised by the same Act were present.... Provided, nevertheless, That no judgment shall be given in any such suit or error unless it be by such full number of the said Justices and Barons as are in that behalf authorised and appointed by the said Act.

III. Provided also, and be it nevertheless enacted...That the party, plaintiff or defendant, against whom any such judgment hath been heretofore or hereafter shall be given in the said Court of King's Bench, may at his election sue in the High Court of Parliament for the reversal of any such judgment, as heretofore hath been usual or accustomed; Anything in this Statute or in the said former Act to the contrary thereof notwithstanding.

31 Eliz. c. 1: *Statutes of the Realm*, iv, 799.

§ 2. COURT OF ADMIRALTY

Until the reign of Henry VIII the Court of the Lord High Admiral[2] was not a strong Court, as its operations were constantly interfered with by the Council[3]; and its procedure in criminal cases was ineffective because it was based upon the Civil Law[4]. The growth of a vigorous maritime jurisdiction dates from the Act of 1536 [p. 347], which assimilated the procedure of the Court to that of the Courts of Common Law, and so laid the foundations of modern Admiralty law.

The Court was presided over by an expert judge[5], who was appointed

[1] Fix beforehand.
[2] For the earlier history of the Court see the Introduction to R. G. Marsden, *Select Pleas in the Court of Admiralty* (Selden Society); see also Holdsworth, i, 313–37.
[3] Baldwin, p. 274. [4] For the reasons given on p. 347.
[5] The most distinguished of the Admiralty Judges in this period was Sir Julius Caesar, who held office from 1584 until the end of Elizabeth's reign. He was afterwards Chancellor of the Exchequer and Master of the Rolls.

by the Lord High Admiral on the authority of the letters patent by which he held his office.

The traditional criminal jurisdiction of the Court was in respect of crimes upon the sea and 'in great ships, being and hovering in the main stream of great rivers, only beneath the bridges of the same rivers nigh to the sea.'[1] It could be exercised over the King's subjects; over the crew of an English ship, whether subjects or not; and over anyone in cases of piracy at common law[2]. As the 'substantial persons' appointed under the Act of 1536 were always Judges of the Courts of Common Law, the criminal jurisdiction of the Admiralty came to be exercised under their supervision and in accordance with the principles of the common law. In this connexion a curious point arose. The coast between high and low water mark was subject to the jurisdiction of the Courts of Common Law when the tide was out, and to the jurisdiction of the Court of Admiralty when the tide was in[3].

The civil jurisdiction of the Court covered all mercantile and shipping cases, and included contracts made abroad, negligent navigation, collision, and salvage. The Court was also concerned with the collection and adjudication upon the Admiralty droits in respect of property found upon the sea or stranded upon the shore, and in time of war it exercised a prize jurisdiction.

From the Court of Admiralty an appeal lay to the King in Chancery. These appeals were heard by special commissioners (*judices delegati*) appointed *ad hoc*. The decisions of these 'delegates' were not at first final, and it was possible to protract a suit by successive appeals. A useful reform was therefore effected when an Act of 1563[4] provided that every 'judgment and sentence definitive' pronounced 'in any civil and marine cause upon appeal lawfully to be made therein to the Queen's Majesty in her Highness's Court of Chancery by such Commissioners or Delegates as shall be nominated and appointed by her Majesty' 'shall be final, and no further appeal to be had or made.'

Act of 1536

An Act for punishment of Pirates and Robbers of the Sea

Where traitors, pirates, thieves, robbers, murderers, and confederators upon the sea many times escape unpunished because the trial of their offences hath heretofore been ordered, judged, and determined before the Admiral, or his lieutenant or commissary, after the course of the civil laws, the nature whereof is that before any judgment of death can be given against the offenders, either they must plainly confess their offences (which they will never do without torture or pains), or else their offences be so plainly and directly proved by witness indifferent, such as saw their offences committed, which cannot be gotten but by chance at few times because such offenders commit their offences upon the sea, and at many times murder and kill such persons being in

---

[1] 15 Rich. II, c. 3.   [2] Holdsworth, i, 318.
[3] Stephen, ii, 26.   [4] 5 Eliz. c. 5.

the ship or boat where they commit their offences which should witness against them in that behalf, and also such as should bear witness be commonly mariners and shipmen, which because of their often voyages and passages in the seas, depart without long tarrying and protraction of time, to the great costs and charges as well of the King's Highness as such as would pursue such offenders; For reformation whereof be it enacted...That all treasons, felonies, robberies, murders, and confederacies, hereafter to be committed in or upon the sea, or in any other haven, river, creek, or place where the Admiral or Admirals have or pretend to have power, authority, or jurisdiction, shall be enquired, tried, heard, determined, and judged in such shires and places in the realm as shall be limited by the King's commission or commissions to be directed for the same, in like form and condition as if any such offence or offences had been committed or done in or upon the land; And such commissions shall be had under the King's great seal directed to the Admiral or Admirals or to his or their lieutenant, deputy, or deputies, and to 3 or 4 such other substantial persons as shall be named or appointed by the Lord Chancellor of England for the time being from time to time and as often as need shall require, to hear and determine such offences after the common course of the laws of this land, used for treasons, felonies, robberies, murders, and confederacies of the same done and committed upon the land within this realm.

II. And be it enacted...that such persons to whom such commission or commissions shall be directed, or 4 of them at the least, shall have full power and authority to enquire of such offences and every of them by the oaths of twelve good and lawful inhabitants[1] in the shire limited in their commission, in such like manner and form as if such offences had been committed upon the land, within the same shire....And that the trial of such offence or offences, if it be denied by the offender or offenders, shall be had by 12 lawful men[2] inhabited in the shire limited within such commission....

* * * * * *

28 Henr. VIII, c. 15: *Statutes of the Realm*, iii, 671.

§ 3. Court of the Constable and Marshal[3]

The Court of the Constable and Marshal originally represented the military jurisdiction of the Crown over the feudal array in time of war, and these great officers were empowered 'during the actual wars to hold

[1] *I.e.* by a grand jury.   [2] *I.e.* by a petty jury.
[3] See Holdsworth, i, 337, and Barnard, p. 144.

court for the determinations of all offences committed against the laws of war, and for the decision of all civil causes arising in the army concerning the rights of prisoners and booties taken.'[1] The Court also decided disputes arising out of questions of precedence and the right to bear heraldic coat armour, and superintended tournaments and duels.

During the Wars of the Roses, the special military powers of the Court, which had only been exercised hitherto in France during the English invasions, were employed to give a show of justice to the military executions which followed the victories on either side. Such applications of martial law to cases which might have been decided by the verdict of a jury under the ordinary law of treason were, however, peculiar to times of disorder, and in the Tudor period the Court on the whole reverted to its earlier function as an arbiter in disputes of honour; although attempts were made from time to time to apply its jurisdiction to cases of apprehended civil commotion. These were in the long run met and defeated by the Courts of Common Law.

After the execution of the Duke of Buckingham in 1521, the Lord High Constableship was not maintained as a permanent office, although temporary Constables were appointed for coronations, or to superintend a trial by combat, and the Court therefore came to be known as the Earl Marshal's Court.

---

[1] Carte, *History of England*, ii, 269, from Anstis, quoted in Stubbs, i, 354 *n.*

Franchise Courts

The special franchises had at one time been very numerous in England. The Hundred Rolls of Edward I, which constitute a kind of Domesday of special jurisdictions, shew that in every shire nobles had criminal courts of their own, with the right to inflict capital punishment[1], and the number of lesser jurisdictions without this right was very large. These franchises were all highly valued because the fines levied in the courts were a source of profit to the lords who owned them, and it was only gradually that they were annexed to the county jurisdictions in which they were situated. A few of the special franchises survived into the Tudor period, and of these the most important were the Palatinates of Lancaster, Chester, and Durham, and the Stannary Courts of Cornwall and Devon.

§ 1. The Palatine Courts

The Palatine jurisdictions did not survive without a reason, for in the Middle Ages each had constituted a special case of government. The Duchy of Lancaster was exposed to the disorders of the Scottish and Welsh borders, and was liable to coast raids from the plundering Scandinavians who held the Isle of Man; the Earldom of Chester was the seat of the war against Wales and also commanded the navigation to Ireland; and the Bishopric of Durham faced the anarchy of the Scottish Border and was the pivot of its defence. The only effective way of dealing with an area so peculiarly placed was to grant it out to some great lord to govern, so Lancaster and Chester became palatine earldoms; while Durham, although it had a different origin in an ecclesiastical immunity and not in a secular franchise[2], enjoyed the same kind of independence under its Prince Bishop that Lancaster and Chester did under their Palatine Earls.

Thus the Counties Palatine 'were in effect great fiefs, answering in most essentials to the county or duchy of medieval France,' and 'they constitute...a striking exception to all generalizations about English feudalism.'[3] For instance, Durham was 'a tiny feudal England surviving into the Tudor period'[4]; and it illustrates the danger which England had escaped. The Counties Palatine might easily have become separate kingdoms, but for the fact that Lancaster and Chester passed to the Crown and so the King became Count Palatine, while the regalities of Durham were wielded by a celibate ecclesiastic who could not found a family and who was chosen by an election in which the Crown had considerable influence.

In the Tudor period each of the Palatinates possessed a complete apparatus of independent Courts. In the Duchy of Lancaster there was a Court of Common Pleas; a Chancery Court presided over by a Vice-Chancellor; and Justices of Assize, Oyer and Terminer, and Gaol Delivery. There was also

---

[1] In Bedfordshire it is recorded of eight local lords, *habet furcas*—'he has a gallows'; and in Berkshire there were 35.
[2] Lapsley, p. 25.   [3] *Ib.* p. 1.   [4] *Ib.* p. 2.

a Court of Duchy Chamber [below], presided over by the Chancellor of the Duchy, which sat at Westminster to hear appeals from the Chancery Court of the Duchy. At Chester the Justice of Chester held a Court for Pleas of the Crown and Common Pleas; and the Chamberlain of Chester exercised a Chancery and Exchequer jurisdiction in his Court. In Durham the Bishop possessed all the attributes of royalty, and the judicial and administrative arrangements of the Bishopric were those of the kingdom in miniature. There was a central Court of Pleas, and a body of Justices holding from the Bishop their commissions of Assize, Oyer and Terminer, and Gaol Delivery. The Bishop had a Council, which possessed an original jurisdiction and also acted as a court of appeal from the Justices and the Court of Pleas. There was also a Court of Chancery, with an exchequer as well as an equitable jurisdiction[1].

In the history of the Counties Palatine the Tudor period occupies a most important place, for it saw the end of their independence, and their partial absorption into the general judicial system of the country. In 1536 Henry VIII reclaimed by statute [p. 352] 'certain liberties and franchises heretofore taken from the Crown,' and thus although the separate Courts remained, they passed under the royal control. As far as Lancaster and Chester were concerned the Act of 1536 made little difference. As they had already passed to the Crown, the transfer of the ultimate judicial authority from Henry VIII as Count Palatine to Henry VIII as King of England was a matter of small importance. But in Durham the palatine lord and the King were physically distinct as well as distinct in law, so the transfer here is a constitutional landmark. A further change was effected when the Council of the North was erected, and began to compete with the courts of the Bishopric. Eventually it 'drained all life out of the palatine judiciary by practically assuming the entire administration of justice in the northern counties.'[2]

The separate courts in Chester were abolished by an Act of 1830[3]. In Lancaster and Durham the Courts of Pleas were merged in the High Court by the Judicature Act of 1873[4], but the Chancery Courts survive. A re-arrangement of appeals by an Act of 1890[5] had the effect of abolishing the Duchy Chamber of Lancaster, and the Chancellor of the Duchy, who used to preside there, is now a political officer only and has no longer any judicial functions.

(1) The Duchy Chamber of Lancaster

The Court of the Duchy Chamber of Lancaster at Westminster

...It is called *Comitatus Palatinus*, a County Palatine, not *a Comite*, in respect of the dignity of an earl, but *a Comitatu* and *a Palatio Regis*, because the owner thereof, be he duke or earl, etc., hath in that county *jura regalia* as fully as the King had in his

---

[1] For further information about the Palatine Courts, see Holdsworth, i, 50–55, and Lapsley, *passim*.

[2] Lapsley, p. 259.   [3] 11 Geo. IV, 1 Will. IV, c. 70.

[4] 36, 37 Vict. c. 66.   [5] 53, 54 Vict. c. 23.

palace, from whence all justice, honours, dignities, franchises, and privileges, as from the fountain, at the first flowed.... The power and authority of those that had county palatines was king-like, for they might pardon treasons, murders, felonies, and outlawries thereupon. They might also make Justices of Eyre, Justices of Assize, of Gaol Delivery, and of the Peace. And all original and judicial writs, and all manner of indictment of treasons and felony, and the process thereupon, were made in the name of the persons having such county palatine. And in every writ and indictment within any county palatine, it was supposed to be *contra pacem* of him that had the county palatine...(pp. 204–5).

...The proceeding in this Court of the Duchy Chamber at Westminster is as in a Court of Chancery for lands, etc., within the survey of that Court, by English bill, etc., and decree; but this Chancery Court is not a mixed Court as the Chancery of England is, partly of the common law and partly of equity.... The process is by privy seal, attachment, etc., as in the Chancery. The officers of this Court be the Chancellor, the Attorney, the Receiver-General, Clerk of the Court, the Auditors, Surveyors, the Messenger. There is an Attorney of the Duchy in Chancery and another in the Exchequer. There be four learned in the law Assistants, and of counsel with the Court...(p. 206).

...The seal of the Duchy of Lancaster remains with the Chancellor at Westminster. And the seal of the County Palatine remains always in a chest in the County Palatine under the safe custody of the keeper thereof. All grants and leases of lands, tenements, offices, etc., in the County Palatine of Lancaster shall pass under that seal and no other; and all grants and leases of lands, tenements, offices, etc., out of the County Palatine and within the survey of the Duchy, shall pass under the seal of the Duchy and no other; otherwise such grants and leases shall be void... (p. 210).

Coke, Fourth Institute (edn. of 1669), c. 36.

(2) Act of 1536

An Act for recontinuing of certain Liberties and Franchises heretofore taken from the Crown

Where divers of the most ancient prerogatives and authorities of justice appertaining to the imperial Crown of this realm have been severed and taken from the same by sundry gifts of the King's most noble progenitors, kings of this realm, to the great diminution and detriment of the royal estate of the same and to the hindrance and great delay of justice; For reformation whereof be it enacted...that no person or persons, of what estate or degree soever they be of, from the first day of July which shall be in the year of our Lord God 1536, shall have any power or authority to pardon or remit any treasons, murders, manslaughters, or...felonies...or any outlawries for any such offences afore rehearsed, committed, perpetrated, done, or divulged, or hereafter to be committed, done, or divulged, by or against any person or persons in any parts of this realm, Wales, or the marches of the same; but that the King's Highness, his heirs and successors kings of this realm, shall have the whole and sole power and authority thereof united and knit to the imperial Crown of this realm, as of good right and equity it appertaineth, any grants, usages, prescription, Act or Acts of Parliament, or any other thing to the contrary thereof notwithstanding.

II. And be it also enacted...that no person or persons, of what estate, degree, or condition soever they be, from the said first day of July shall have any power or authority to make any Justices of Eyre, Justices of Assize, Justices of Peace, or Justices of Gaol Delivery, but that all such officers and ministers shall be made by letters patents under the King's great seal in the name and by authority of the King's Highness, his heirs kings of this realm, in all shires, counties, counties palatine, and other places of this realm, Wales, and marches of the same or in any other his dominions, at their pleasure and wills, in such manner and form as Justices of Eyre, Justices of Assize, Justices of Peace, and Justices of Gaol Delivery be commonly made in every shire of this realm; any grants, usages, prescriptions, allowances, Act or Acts of Parliament, or any other thing or things to the contrary thereof notwithstanding.

III. And be it further enacted...that all original writs and judicial writs, and all manner of indictments of treason, felony, or trespass, and all manner of process to be made upon the same in every county palatine and other liberty within this realm of England, Wales, and marches of the same, shall from the said first day of July be made only in the name of our said Sovereign Lord the King, and his heirs kings of England, And that every person or persons having such county palatine or any other such liberty to make such originals, judicials[1], or other process of justice, shall make the teste[2] in the said original writs and judicial

---

[1] Writs in civil actions are either 'original' or 'judicial.' An original writ issues out of Chancery before the suit is begun and is the foundation of it. A judicial writ issues out of the Court where the original is returned, after the suit is begun by original writ (Jacob, under 'writ').

[2] The 'teste' was the final clause in a royal writ naming the person who authorises the affixing of the King's Seal (Oxford Dictionary).

in the name of the same person or persons that have such county palatine or liberty. And that in every writ and indictment that shall be made within any such county palatine or liberty, after the said first day of July next coming, whereby it shall be supposed anything to be done against the King's peace, shall be made and supposed to be done only against the King's peace, his heirs and successors, and not against the peace of any other person or persons, whatsoever they be; any Act of Parliament, grant, custom, usage, or allowance in eyre[1] before this time had, granted, or used to the contrary notwithstanding.

IV. Provided alway that Justices of Assize, Justices of Gaol Delivery, and Justices of Peace to be made and assigned by the King's Highness within the County Palatine of Lancaster, shall be made and ordained by commission under the King's usual seal of Lancaster, in manner and form as hath been accustomed; anything in this Act to the contrary thereof notwithstanding.

* * * * * *

XIX. Provided alway and be it enacted, that Cuthbert now Bishop of Durham, and his successors Bishops of Durham, and their temporal Chancellor of the County Palatine of Durham for the time being, and every of them, shall from henceforth be Justices of Peace within the said County Palatine of Durham, and shall exercise and use all manner things within the same County Palatine that appertaineth or belongeth to any Justice of Peace within any county of this realm of England to do, exercise, and use, by virtue and authority that they be Justice of Peace, in as ample and large manner as any other Justices of Peace in any county within this realm have or might do, exercise, or use; any thing or things in this Act contained to the contrary notwithstanding. * * * * * *

27 Henr. VIII, c. 24: *Statutes of the Realm*, iii, 555.

§ 2. The Stannary Courts

The Stannary Courts were a special franchise founded on an ancient privilege granted to the workers of the stannaries or tin-mining districts of Devon and Cornwall to sue and be sued, except in cases of land, life, and limb, only before the Vice-Warden of the Stannaries. This privilege, granted because the working of precious metals was a royal prerogative, was confirmed in comprehensive terms by Edward I in a charter of 1305. The Courts were held by the Stewards of the Stannaries, but from them an appeal lay to the Court of the Vice-Warden, then to the Lord Warden, and finally to the Council of the Prince of Wales as Duke of Cornwall.

[1] Justices in Eyre had ceased to function in the course of the 14th century, but ancient 'allowances' could still be pleaded in the 16th.

In the Tudor period there occurs the leading case of Trewynard, first in the Court of Chancery (1562) [below] and afterwards in the Star Chamber (1564) [p. 356], by which it was decided that a writ of error from the Stannary Court to the ordinary courts of law did not lie.

The Court of the Lord Warden was merged in the Court of Appeal created by the Judicature Act of 1873; but the Court of the Vice-Warden was not abolished until 1896[1].

Trewynard's Case, 1562 and 1564

The Court of the Stannaries in Cornwall and Devon

...The jurisdiction of this Court is guided by special laws, by customs, and by prescription time out of mind...(p. 229).

[In the Court of Chancery, 14 November, 1562]

...Where the 14 day of October last past the matter in question touching the allowing or disallowing of writs of error, as well between the parties aforesaid, as also for and concerning all other writs of error touching all causes determinable in the Stannary Court in Cornwall, was by the order of the Lord Keeper of the Great Seal of England committed to the hearing and examination of Sir William Cordell[2], knight, Master of the Rolls, and Sir James Dyer[3], knight, Chief Justice of the Common Pleas, and Justice Weston[4], to the intent upon the due consideration of the cause they should make report unto the said Lord Keeper of their opinions and proceedings therein, as in their judgments should seem most agreeable to justice and equity; who having accordingly travailed diligently for the understanding of the truth of the premises, upon the deliberate hearing and examining of the cause in the presence of the counsel learned of both sides, and upon the perusing and consideration of the ancient prescriptions, customs, liberties, and charters exhibited by the said parties concerning the premises, have this day made their report unto the said Lord Keeper as followeth, that is to say: That forasmuch as the said plaintiff could not nor did not shew forth any record or precedent whereby any judgments or executions heretofore passed in any of the said Stannary Courts have been reversed by writ of error in any of the Queen's Majesty's Courts of her Bench or Common Pleas, and for that it appeareth unto them that divers and sundry inconveniencies were likely to ensue by allowing of such writs of error, and upon other causes and considerations them especially moving; they in their opinions think it not meet

---

[1] 59, 60 Vict. c. 45.   [2] Master of the Rolls, 1557–81.
[3] Appointed Chief Justice of the Common Pleas, 1559.
[4] Richard Weston, Judge of the Common Pleas, 1559–72.

nor convenient that any writs of error should pass or be suffered in such case to reverse any of the said judgments or executions. Upon which report made, it is this day ordered by the said Lord Keeper of the Great Seal...that from henceforth no writ or writs of error or false judgment be hereafter sued in any of the said Courts of the King's Bench or Common Pleas to reverse any judgment or judgments in any of the said Courts of Stannaries heretofore given or hereafter to be given, until upon further consideration of the ancient grants and liberties of the said Courts of Stannaries, or upon some other sufficient cause or matter, it shall be otherwise ordered and determined by this Court of the Chancery...(p. 229).

[In the Star Chamber, 29 November, 1564]

...The said complainant hath complained as well in the Court of Chancery by bill, and in the King's Bench by writ of error, as also in this Court...and was out of the said several Courts by order discharged and dismissed, referring the proceeding upon the said judgment to the order of the said Stannary Court, according to divers ordinances by divers ancient charters, customs, and liberties belonging to the Stannary ratified by Act of Parliament[1]....And where also it doth further appear that by the laws and ordinances of the said Stannary, if any such cause of complaint be ministered the same is to be redressed by appellation in several degrees, *viz.*, first to the Steward of the Stannary Court where the matter lieth, then to the Under-Warden of the Stannaries, and from him to the Lord Warden of the same Stannaries; and for default of justice at his hands to the Prince's[2] Privy Council, and not examinable either here in this Court or in any other Court...(p. 230). Coke, *Fourth Institute* (edn. of 1669), c. 45.

---

[1] On the supposed ratification of Edward I's charter of 1305 by an Act of 50 Edw. III, see Coke, iv, c. 45, p. 232.

[2] *I.e.* The Prince of Wales, as Duke of Cornwall.

Ecclesiastical Courts[1]

The medieval Church exercised jurisdiction over marriage and kinship, the law of inheritance, family relations, education, and a number of other matters which were closely bound up with the civilisation of the country, and yet were not at that time regarded as falling within the sphere of the State. These were the proper business of the Ecclesiastical Courts, which administered the canon law just as the royal courts administered the common law, and possessed authority to enforce that law by means of definite punishments.

Judicial authority was exercised by the archdeacon in his archdeaconry, by the bishop in his diocese, and by the archbishop in his province; and there were also courts of special ecclesiastical jurisdiction called 'peculiars' belonging to various bodies—the Crown, the archbishops, bishops, deans and chapters, exempt monasteries, and even to individual prebendaries, rectors, and vicars[2]. The secular parallel is the franchise court.

The ecclesiastical courts administered the canon law of Rome[3], and this law was penally enforced by them upon both clergy and laity. They punished not only heresy, blasphemy, neglect of church services, contempt of the clergy, neglect by the clergy of their clerical duties, all of which might be regarded as strictly ecclesiastical offences, but also perjury, defamation, witchcraft, drunkenness, and breaches of faith—a range of activity which made them formidable to the laity. They were also concerned with adultery, incontinence, and all crimes arising out of sexual relations which were not punishable at common law. Some selected cases are printed on pp. 362–367 below.

The principal sanction at the command of the courts was excommunication, but this was no mere empty cursing with bell, book, and candle. The lesser excommunication deprived the excommunicated of all the offices of the Church, while the greater cut him off from the society of Christian men; but both involved serious civil incapacities. 'An excommunicated person could not sue, nor give evidence, nor receive a legacy. Moreover, if he refused to submit to penance, the ecclesiastical court signified his contumacy to the King in his Chancery, whereupon a writ was issued *de excommunicato capiendo*[4], and upon this the party might be imprisoned till he submitted.'[5]

The ecclesiastical courts were abolished in 1641 along with the Star Chamber and the High Commission Court, and revived at the Restoration, but without the 'oath *ex officio*,' which was the foundation of their procedure. Thus, as far as the laity were concerned, they lost all practical power.

[1] See especially the Appendix contributed by Bishop Stubbs to the *Report of the Ecclesiastical Courts Commission* of 1883 (Historical Appendix i in vol. i, pp. 21–51).

[2] About 300 peculiars survived until the early part of Queen Victoria's reign (Stephen, ii, 400).

[3] See F. W. Maitland, *Roman Canon Law in the Church of England.*

[4] For a copy of this writ see Holdsworth, i, 433.   [5] Stephen, ii, 412.

§ 1. The Archdeacon's Court

In theory the Archdeacon was the deputy of the Bishop, and his authority was only an emanation from the Bishop's authority, but early in the twelfth century the archdeacons acquired a customary jurisdiction of their own. Thus the powers of the Archdeacon's Court varied in different dioceses, being determined either by the custom of each particular diocese, or by a special arrangement between the Bishop and his archdeacons.

The judicial authority of the Archdeacon was exercised by him in his Court—usually in person but sometimes through an official—over ecclesiastical causes generally[1], but he had other functions which were not judicial. He had special charge of the fabric and furniture of the churches in his archdeaconry, and he exercised the right of visitation there in the intervals between the regular visitations of the Bishop.

§ 2. Court of the Bishop

The Consistory Court of the Bishop heard appeals from the courts of the archdeacons within the diocese, but proceedings could also be originated there. The judge was not the Bishop himself, but the Chancellor—an official appointed by him to act as his representative for judicial purposes. It was the case, however, that the authority of the Bishop was not exhausted by the appointment of a Chancellor to hear cases in the Consistory Court; he could also appoint commissaries to hear cases in special districts, and from their decisions an appeal would lie to the Bishop himself. This distinction between the organised and formal jurisdiction of the Bishop, and his unorganised and informal jurisdiction, may be compared to the distinction between the ordinary law courts and the Council Table.

§ 3. Courts of the Archbishop

The Archbishop of Canterbury had four provincial Courts.

(a) The Consistory Court of the Archbishop, held at the church of St Mary-le-Bow[2], was more usually called the 'Court of Arches.' It was presided over by the 'official principal,' who represented the Archbishop in the same way as the Chancellor represented the Bishop, or the Chief Justice of the King's Bench represented the King. The Court heard appeals from the diocesan Consistory Courts, but it also gradually established a claim to be a court of first instance also, although this jurisdiction was strictly limited by the Act of Citations[3]. Like the King's Bench, the Court of Arches stands for organised and formal authority only.

---

[1] See Chaucer's account of the Archdeacon in the *Friar's Tale*, beginning
'Whilom there was dwelling in my countré
An erchedeken, a man of high degree,'
where a list is given in rhyming couplets of the offences on which he 'boldly did execution.'

[2] *I.e.* St Mary of the Arches (*de Arcubus*) so called because the church was built on arches or 'bows,' being upon marshy ground.

[3] See p. 16 above.

(*b*) Just as the King, after the separation of the courts of law, retained power to decide cases himself in Council, so the judicial virtue of the Archbishop was not exhausted by the appointment of an 'official principal' to hold public sittings in the Court of Arches. He had also a 'Court of Audience,' which was his personal as contrasted with his official Court, and may perhaps be regarded as 'the ecclesiastical counterpart of the King's Court of Requests.'[1] Originally its jurisdiction, which was concurrent with that of the Court of Arches, was exercised by the Archbishop himself, and the auditors followed his person; but in process of time the Court of Audience also became officialised. It ceased to be peripatetic, and was no longer held at the Archbishop's palace at Canterbury when he was there, but obtained a fixed seat at the Consistory Court of St Paul's, where it was presided over by a professional judge. As the practice of the Court followed that of the Court of Arches, and it admitted the same body of proctors and advocates, it was eventually absorbed by the simple method of uniting the two judgeships in the same person. The date of this amalgamation is uncertain, but there was no separate Court of Audience after the Restoration.

(*c*) The Archbishop's Court of Peculiars was held at Bow Church to decide cases arising in thirteen London parishes that were exempt from the diocesan jurisdiction of the Bishop of London. The judge of this Court was originally called the Dean of Arches, and he was a subordinate of the 'official principal' who presided in the Court of Arches; but eventually the two offices were combined in the same person, and the Dean of Arches came to preside in the Court of Arches. Thus the title of the office and the name of the Court have a different pedigree, although they both derive ultimately from the Church of St Mary-le-Bow. The Archbishop of Canterbury had also other peculiars under commissaries in the dioceses of Rochester, Chichester, Winchester, Lincoln, and Norwich; besides certain peculiars in Essex under the jurisdiction of the Dean of Bocking.

(*d*) The Prerogative Court of Canterbury exercised the testamentary jurisdiction of the Archbishop. It was presided over by a professional judge who sat originally in the Archbishop's palace at Canterbury; but owing to a great increase in the volume of business, the Court was moved, about the time of the Reformation, to London, and sat at Doctors' Commons[2].

The Archbishop of York's Chancery Court corresponded to the Court of Arches; he also had a Court of Audience and a Prerogative Court.

§ 4. HIGH COURT OF DELEGATES

The Act for the Submission of the Clergy [p. 22] provided a new court of appeal for ecclesiastical causes, known as the High Court of Delegates[3]. Persons who failed to obtain justice in the provincial courts of the archbishops or in the exempt peculiar jurisdictions could appeal to the King in Chancery, who might issue a commission under the great seal to such persons as he might select to hear each case, 'like as in case of appeal from

---

[1] Leadam, *Star Chamber*, i, p. lxxxv.
[2] It is to be found there in the pages of *David Copperfield*.
[3] A full account of this Court is given in Holdsworth, i, 373.

the Admiral Court.'[1] Under Henry VIII's statute the decision of the Delegates was to be final, but the Elizabethan lawyers decided that the Crown could issue a commission of review to re-hear the case.

This system of appointing a commission *ad hoc* to hear each appeal was, for various reasons, unsatisfactory, and in 1832 the jurisdiction of the Court of Delegates was transferred by statute[2] to the Crown in Council. It is now exercised by the Judicial Committee of the Privy Council created in 1833[3].

§ 5. COURT OF HIGH COMMISSION[4]

The first general Commission for ecclesiastical affairs was issued about 1535 to Thomas Cromwell, appointing him the King's Vicegerent and investing him with full authority in the sphere of the Church. This was, however, exceptional in character, and the earliest Commission to adopt the form which was followed later was that of 1549. The Commissioners were empowered to inquire concerning heresies and heretics, to examine witnesses upon oath, and to punish by imprisonment all persons who opposed the Book of Common Prayer. There appears in this patent of 1549[5] a provision characteristic of all subsequent Commissions which enabled the Commissioners to subdivide their operations and so to be efficient locally in more places than one at the same time. It may be regarded as the ecclesiastical counterpart of the device for maintaining the local efficiency of the Courts of Common Law by means of the circuits of the Judges of Assize. There were to be 25 Commissioners, eleven of whom—seven bishops, two other ecclesiastics, and two ministers of state—were to be 'of the quorum,' and out of the 25 any three had power to act provided that one of the three was 'of the quorum.' The patent of 1549 was reissued in 1551, but the number of Commissioners was now increased from 25 to 31. The Marian Commission of 1557 named no quorum and authorised any three of the Commissioners to act; it also empowered them to fine as well as to imprison, and directed them to use the *ex officio* oath [p. 373], by which the accused swore beforehand to answer truly any questions that might be asked of him before he learned the nature of the charge against him.

The first Elizabethan Commission, that of 1559 [p. 367], follows closely that of 1557, but it restores the quorum, fixing it at seven—two bishops, one minister of state, and four lawyers. The number of Commissioners was nineteen, and any six of these could act, provided that one was of the quorum. The Commission also recites the clause of the Act of Supremacy which authorised the appointment by letters patent of Commissioners in causes ecclesiastical[6], and so claimed a statutory authority which the earlier Commissions had not possessed[7]. The subsequent Commissions of 1562, 1572,

[1] See p. 24 above. [2] 2 & 3 Will. IV, c. 92. [3] By 3 & 4 Will. IV, c. 41.
[4] See R. G. Usher, *The Rise and Fall of the High Commission.*
[5] It is impossible to say whether this appeared earlier, as many of the records of the High Commission, including the patents of Henry VIII's reign, have disappeared. [6] See p. 133 above.
[7] It is often said that the High Commission Court was 'created' by the Act of Supremacy, but the researches of Mr R. G. Usher prove the existence of earlier commissions of a similar kind which possessed full authority, although it was derived from the Royal Supremacy and not from any statute.

1576, and 1601[1] differ from each other in various ways, but they are all drafted on the same general lines. The most important difference is in the number of the Commissioners. These rise from 19 in 1559 to 27 in 1562, to 70 in 1572, to 73 in 1576, declining to 54 in 1601; and in all these later Commissions the number empowered to act is only three.

The term 'High Commission' begins to appear about 1570, and after 1580 it is regularly employed. This corresponds with the transformation of an ecclesiastical commission into a regular court. The work of the Commissioners[2] was at first visitatorial—the removal of clergy whose sympathies were with the old worship, the watching of Catholics, and the suppression of the followers of Cartwright. Administrative duties soon followed—the tendering of the oath of supremacy to the clergy, the collection of fines levied by the churchwardens under the Act of Uniformity, and the punishment of offences against the Thirty-nine Articles. The Commissioners also concerned themselves with the censorship of the press, and superintended the carrying out of the Star Chamber Decrees. A strict supervision and control over them were exercised by the Privy Council, and when offenders came before them there was as yet no definite procedure[3]. But about 1565 the Council began to refer some of the petitions which were coming before it in increasing numbers to the Ecclesiastical Commissioners, and as litigants soon found that they could themselves apply direct to the Commissioners, there was a great multiplication of what were practically suits between party and party. This led inevitably to the introduction of judicial forms into the method of handling cases. Articles, depositions, and examinations replaced casual conversations; professional lawyers appeared before the Commission; procedure gradually hardened; and 'insensibly the Commissioners drifted into the formalities of a Court.'[4] The process has been roughly assigned to 1570–80, and by 1592, if not earlier, it may be regarded as complete. This involved a relaxation in practice of the control of the Privy Council, and a lighter emphasis upon the visitatorial functions which had been the original business of the Commission. The watching of Jesuits and recusants passed to special commissions appointed for that purpose; after 1590 the churchwardens' fines were collected by the Exchequer; much of the work of dealing with Nonconformists devolved upon the Bishops; and the Commissioners, now the 'High Commission Court,' concerned themselves more and more with the suitors who were brought to them in increasing numbers by the slow procedure of the Ecclesiastical Courts in cases of appeal. Until 1660 appeals to the Court of Delegates were mainly in cases of slander, and on testamentary questions which came from the

---

[1] Extracts from these Commissions are printed in Prothero, pp. 232–41.

[2] Owing to the deficiency of records for Elizabeth's reign, it is not possible to quote illustrative cases, but a number of seventeenth century cases, illustrating the action of the Court in dealing with erroneous opinions, are printed in *Reports of Cases in the Courts of Star Chamber and High Commission*, ed. S. R. Gardiner (Camden Society, 1886).

[3] 'The Commissioners sat down before the culprit and questioned him as searchingly as their combined ingenuity could suggest. He replied as best he could, and the debate soon degenerated into a series of recriminations and insults' (Usher, p. 56). [4] Usher, p. 76.

Prerogative Court. Appeals on matters of doctrine and discipline nearly always went to the High Commission Court, until it was abolished.

Like the Court of Requests, the High Commission Court was exposed to frequent attacks from the Courts of Common Law. As soon as the High Commission became a regular Court, it appeared as a rival jurisdiction which tempted litigants away from the ordinary courts; and as the salaries of the judges were largely supplemented from the fees paid by the suitors, the question was one in which they were personally interested. The principal points of attack were the right of the Court to fine[1] and imprison, and the legality of the *ex officio* oath. Fine and imprisonment were not, strictly speaking, ecclesiastical penalties, and their use by the Commission therefore depended upon the terms of their patent; while the *ex officio* procedure was so different from that of the common law as to appear illegal to the common lawyers. There was also the further question of the demarcation of frontiers between the ecclesiastical and common law jurisdictions, and here their ancient right of issuing writs of prohibition to the ecclesiastical courts forbidding them to proceed further in a case on the ground that it concerned temporal matters, placed the common law judges in a strong position.

In Cawdrey's case[2] in 1591 [p. 372], the judges supported in general terms the authority of the High Commission Court. Cawdrey, a Suffolk clergyman, was suspended by the Bishop of London for refusing the oath *ex officio*, and was then deprived by the Commission for resisting the Bishop's authority. He sued his successor in the living for trespass in the Court of Queen's Bench, and the jury found that the defendant was not guilty, provided that the High Commission had legal authority to deprive Cawdrey of his benefice. On the point of law the judges decided 'that the King or Queen of England for the time being may make such an ecclesiastical commission ... by the ancient prerogative and law of England,' and thus recognised the Commission as a legal ecclesiastical Court. But this decision of the Tudor period did not prevent in the Stuart period a general attack, led by Coke, upon both the procedure and the authority of the Court[3]. The authority of the High Commission was supported by the Crown, and Coke's onslaught was unsuccessful; but the Court, which had become increasingly unpopular, was abolished in 1641 by the Act which destroyed the Star Chamber. It was revived for a short time, in a different form, to aid James II in his attempt to Catholicise the Church of England.

(1) Cases in the Ecclesiastical Courts

The cases from which the following selections are made were extracted from the Act Books (1475–1640) of the Commissary Court of London, the Consistory Court of London, and the Archidiaconal Courts of London, Colchester, and Essex by Archdeacon W. H. Hale, and are printed in *Criminal Precedents* (1847). They include adultery, assaults on priests, blasphemy, breaches of faith, misbehaviour in

[1] As in the case of the Star Chamber, the larger fines inflicted by the Court of High Commission were reconsidered on an appointed 'day of mitigation,' and were usually either reduced, or remitted altogether (Usher, p. 324).

[2] Stephen, ii, 416.

[3] *Fourth Institute*, cap. 74. Coke's criticism of the High Commission is fully discussed in Usher, pp. 180–235; but Coke's view has more to be said for it than is allowed here.

church, clerical misconduct, contempt of the clergy, conventicles, defamation, drunkenness, heresy, incontinence, recusancy, sacrilege, simony, failure to observe Sundays and Holy Days, usury, witchcraft, and a variety of other offences. They also include testamentary causes, and such minor ecclesiastical offences as omitting to go to confession before marriage, or taking turf from the churchyard.

(1) *Heresy*
[Archdeaconry of Essex, 13 December, 1587]
Contra Augustinum Draper, de Leigh

Comparuit, et dominus objecit, that the common report is that he doth not acknowledge the immortality of the soul, and by his own speeches he hath affirmed the same. Dominus ei injunxit, that he shall have conference with Mr Bernan, Mr Negus, and Mr Dent sundry times in meeting in Leigh church, whereby he may be fully persuaded of the immortality of the soul; and to certify under their hands of his full persuasion of the immortality of the soul...(p. 193).

(2) *Neglecting services*
[Archdeaconry of Essex, 14 July, 1572]
Contra Robertum Browne, de Leyton

Detectus[1] xii° die Julii, 1572. Quo die comparuit dictus Browne, ac objecto ei articulo per dominum archidiaconum, *viz.* for that he had in his house certain that did dance in the service time; quod fatetur, and said that it was a wedding day, and that he could not rule the youth. Unde dominus ex causis eum moventibus, propter paupertatem dimisit eum, et injunxit eum ut non habeatur hujusmodi culpam iterum; quod in se assumpsit (p. 153).

[Archdeaconry of Essex, 15 April, 1584]
Contra Ricardum Yawlinge, de Woodham Mortimer

Detected for being absent from his parish church vi weeks, and saith that he will not come to church unless there be a sermon preached; for he saith that public service read in the church is no service unless there be a sermon....Further that he is not so well edified by reading as by preaching. Dominus monuit ad recipiendam citra proximum et agnoscat culpam in ecclesia (p.180).

[Archdeaconry of Essex, 7 November, 1586]
Contra Matheum Fisher, de Romford

Detected for playing at stool ball in service time, and gave cruel words to the churchwardens for demanding xiid. of him for his absence...[2 Dec. *To pay* 12d. *to the use of the poor*] (p. 188).

[1] 'Detectus' is not 'detected,' but 'accused' or 'presented.'

(3) *Contempt of the clergy*
[Commissary's Court of London, 1493]
Omnium Sanctorum in Muro

Dominus Johannes Roow ibidem rector dixit die dominica ultima in domo Wellys, in presencia parochianorum haec verba sequencia in Anglicis, *viz.* I will not learn of my Lord of London nor none of his officers, for I am as well learned as the best of them all, et vilipendit ordinarium... (p. 34).

[Commissary's Court of London, 1502]
Clementis in Eastcheap

Willielmus Sevill aquebajulus[1] ibidem notatur officio quod vilipendit et adnichilavit ac diffamavit dominum Thomam Ward, sic maliciose dicendo, Go forth, fool, and set a cock's comb on thy crown, sacerdotalem ordinem nequiter contempnendo. Citatur xi die Junii in domo sua infra eandem parochiam ad comparendum, xiii die ejusdem; quo die comparuit et dimittitur, quia concordati sunt, etc. (p. 76).

(4) *Clerical misbehaviour*
[Commissary's Court of London, 1496. The chaplain assaults the curate, who then proceeds to assault the chaplain.]

Mildredis Pultre

Dominus Simon Grene capellanus ibidem notatur officio quod injecit violentas manus in dominum Johannem White curatum ibidem, et eum ad summum altare predictae ecclesiae violenter percussit....

Dominus Johannes White notatur officio quod violenter percussit dominum Simonem capellanum ecclesiae predictae... (pp. 54, 55).

(5) *Drunkenness*
[Commissary's Court of London, 1493]

Dominus Thomas Stokes est pessimi regiminis sedendo in tabernis et potando horis inconsuetis, et violenter percussit dominum Robertum Godderd presbiterum in domo cujusdam Johannis Cooke in Silver Street, et projecit quandam ollam ad caput dicti domini Roberti, et fregit ollam (p. 43).

[Archdeaconry of Essex, 26 April, 1585]
Contra Ricardum Atkis, curatum de Romford

Detected for that he was so drunk the 21st of March last, being Sunday, that he could neither examine the youth in the

---

[1] *Lit.* water-bearer; but it is a common name for the parish clerk, one of whose duties was to asperge the congregation with holy water.

Catechism nor say Evening Prayer; but would have said one lesson twice...Dominus excommunicavit eum (p. 186).

[Archdeaconry of Essex, 22 October, 1600]

Thomam Peryn, de Rayleigh

Detected for a common drunkard and a railer and chider, to the grief of the godly and great danger of his soul...(p. 223).

(6) *Witchcraft*

This case illustrates the procedure of the Court, and also the nature of the penance inflicted.

[Commissary's Court of London, 1492]

Fama publica referente, nostro est detectum officio quod quidam Ricardus Laukiston, de parochia Sanctae Mariae Magdalenae in Veteri Piscaria, et Margareta Geffrey vidua, nuper de parochia Sancti Bartholomei Parvi, de et super certis articulis crimen heresiae tangentibus et sorseriae; *viz.* quod idem Ricardus ...protulit ista verba vel eis consimilia predictae Margaretae in Anglicis, 'Thou art a poor widow, and it were alms to help thee to a marriage, and if thou wilt do any cost in spending any money, thou shalt have a man worth a thousand pounds.' Tunc respondebat predicta Margareta vidua, 'How may that be?' Tunc dixit Laukiston, 'My wife knoweth a cunning man, that by his cunning can cause a woman to have any man that she hath favour to, and that shall be upon warrantise, for she hath put it in execution aforetime; and this shall cost money.' Tunc dixit predicta Margareta, 'I have no goods save ii mazers[1] for to find me, my mother, and my children, and if they were sold and I fail of my purpose, I, my mother, and my children were undone.' Tunc dixit dictus Ricardus Laukiston, 'Deliver me the mazers and I will warrant thine intent shall be fulfilled.' Tunc predicta Margareta deliberavit sibi ii murras ad valorem v marcarum et x*s.* in pecuniis. Super quibus dicti Ricardus et Margareta coram nobis Ricardo Blodiwell, legum doctore, in judicio comparuerunt, et jurati, tactis sacrosanctis evangeliis, de fideliter respondendo predictis articulis; et eorum cuilibet fatebantur haec omnia esse vera, prout hic suprascribuntur. Tunc judex, tactis evangeliis, de penitentia utrique parti injungenda perimplendo, injunxit penitentiam predictis Ricardo et Margaretae; *viz.* quod predictus Ricardus restituat seu restitui faciat predictas ii murras, vel eorum valorem, dictae Margaretae, sub pena excommunicationis majoris, infra viii dies; quam tulit judex nunc pro tunc et tunc pro nunc; residuam

---

[1] Drinking-cups.

partem penitentiae judex sibi reservavit usque in crastinum diei Andreae tunc proximum sequentem, et judex injunxit dictae Margaretae publicam penitentiam, *viz.* tribus dominicis, nudis pedibus, capite flammiola[1] nodata, cooperta kirtela, manu sua dextra deferentem candelam precii unius denarii, crucem processionaliter precedat (p. 32).

(7) *Miscellaneous*
[Archdeaconry of Colchester, 14 December, 1542]
Fordham
Symon Patryke notatur quod nunquam ibat ad lectum in charitate per spatium xx^{ti} annorum...(p. 120).

[Archdeaconry of Essex, 5 December, 1566]
Contra Thomam Arter, de Baddow Magna
Because he will give but obolum pauperibus. Comparuit dictus Arter, et objecto articulo, he saith that he is not of the wealth that men taketh him to be. Unde dominus assignavit eum solvere obolum every week, et sic dimisit (p. 149).

[Archdeaconry of Essex, 5 December, 1566]
Contra Johannem Trussell, de Purleigh
Because he will not be churchwarden according to the Archdeacon's judgment, facta fide ac facta preconisatione, dominus excommunicavit eum (p. 150).

[Archdeaconry of Essex, 19 April, 1575]
Officium Domini contra Laurencium Boyden [de Fobbing]
Detectum, that he writeth scoffing and uncomely rhymes in the church. Comparuit Johannes Boyden, pater dicti Laurentii, et assumpsit in se ad puniendum suum filium verberibus in ecclesia predicta coram gardianis[2] et parochianis die dominica proxima (p. 157).

[Archdeaconry of Essex, 12 September, 1576]
Contra Willielmum Rooke, de West Ham
Detectum, that he pulled away a man's hat and threw it from him, and would not suffer him to sit in his seat in the time of divine service, but molested him; whereby all the whole parish was disquieted in the service time, and the minister was compelled to stay his service, through his rudeness which he sundry times hath and doth use in the church in service time. Comparuit

---

[1] A veil.   [2] Churchwardens.

et fassus est that upon a certain Sunday happening in summer last he, this respondent, in the time of divine service coming into the parish church of West Ham and entering in his pew in which he was placed by the churchwardens, and from time his ancestors have there been placed, he by chance did throw down the hat of Mr Shipman, which hung as he entered into the pew, and not otherwise; in which pew the same Mr Shipman wilfully and stubbornly entereth and entered, being not there placed by the churchwardens. Et tunc dominus acceptavit confessionem et quod non constat de probacione, etc. Dominus eum dimisit donec et quousque (p. 164).

[Archdeaconry of Essex, 1584]

Contra Nicholaum Lynch, de Theydon Bois

...He shall openly before the congregation penitently confess that he is heartily sorry for offending Almighty God; and that he hath abused the congregation in procuring the banns openly to be asked in the church between him and Joan Roberts, and not proceeding in the marriage (p. 181).

(2) Ecclesiastical Commission of 1559

I. Elizabeth by the grace of God, etc., to the Reverend Father in God Matthew Parker, nominated[1] Bishop of Canterbury, and Edmund Grindal, nominated[2] Bishop of London, and to our right trusted and right well-beloved Councillors, Francis Knowles our Vice-Chamberlain and Ambrose Cave, knights, and to... Anthony Cooke and Thomas Smith[3], knights, William Bill our Almoner, Walter Haddon and Thomas Sackford, Masters of our Requests, Rowland Hill and William Chester, knights, Randall Cholmely and John Southcote, serjeants-at-the-law, William May, doctor of law, Francis Cave, Richard Goodrich, and Gilbert Gerard, esquires, Robert Weston and [Thomas] Huick, doctors of law, greeting.

II. Where at our Parliament holden at Westminster the 25th day of January...there was two Acts and Statutes made and established [*viz. the Acts of Uniformity and Supremacy*]...and whereas divers seditious and slanderous persons do not cease daily to invent and set forth false rumours, tales, and seditious slanders,

[1] The royal letters for Parker's election to the Archbishopric were issued 18 July. He was not elected until 1 August or ordered to be consecrated until 9 September, whereas the date of the Commission is 19 July.

[2] Grindal was elected 26 July and consecrated 21 December.

[3] The author of *De Republica Anglorum*.

not only against us and the said good laws and statutes, but also have set forth divers seditious books within this our realm of England, meaning thereby to move and procure strife, division, and dissension amongst our loving and obedient subjects, much to the disquieting of us and our people.

III. Wherefore we, earnestly minding to have the same Acts before mentioned to be duly put in execution, and such persons as shall hereafter offend in anything contrary to the tenor and effect of the said several Statutes to be condignly punished; and having especial trust and confidence in your wisdoms and discretions, have authorised, assigned, and appointed you to be our Commissioners, and by these presents do give our full power and authority to you, or six of you, whereof you the said Matthew Parker, Edmund Grindal, Thomas Smith, Walter Haddon, Thomas Sackford, Richard Goodrich, and Gilbert Gerard to be one, from time to time hereafter during our pleasure to enquire, as well by the oaths of twelve good and lawful men as also by witnesses and other ways and means ye can devise, for all offences, misdoers, and misdemeanours done and committed, and hereafter to be committed or done, contrary to the tenor of the said several Acts and Statutes and either of them; and also of all and singular heretical opinions, seditious books, contempts, conspiracies, false rumours, tales, seditious misbehaviours, slanderous words or showings, published, invented, or set forth by any person or persons against us, or contrary or against...the quiet government and rule of our people and subjects, in any county, city, borough, or other place or places within this our realm of England, and of all and every the coadjutors, counsellors, comforters, procurers, and abettors of every such offender.

IV. And further, we do give power and authority to you or six of you, whereof the said Matthew Parker [etc.]...to be one, from time to time hereafter during our pleasure, as well to hear and determine all the premises as also to enquire, hear, and determine all and singular enormities, disturbances, and misbehaviour done and committed, or hereafter to be done and committed,...in any church or chapel, or against any divine service or the minister or ministers of the same, contrary to the law[s] and statutes of this realm; and also to enquire of, search out, and to order, correct, and reform all such persons as hereafter shall or will obstinately absent themselves from church and such divine service as by the laws and statutes of this realm is appointed to be had and used.

V. And also we do give and grant full power and authority unto you and six of you, whereof you the said Matthew Parker [etc.]...to be one, from time to time and at all times during our pleasure to visit, reform, redress, order, correct, and amend, in all places within this our realm of England, all such errors, heresies, crimes, abuses, offences, contempts, and enormities, spiritual and ecclesiastical, whatsoever[1], which by any spiritual or ecclesiastical power, authority, or jurisdiction can or may lawfully be reformed, ordered, redressed, corrected, restrained, or amended, to the pleasure of Almighty God, the increase of virtue, and the conservation of the peace and unity of this our realm, and according to the authority and power limited, given, and appointed by any laws or statutes of this realm.

VI. And also that you and six of you, whereof the said Matthew Parker [etc.]...to be one, shall likewise have full power and authority from time to time to enquire and search out [all masterless] men, quarrellers, vagrant and suspect persons within our City of London and ten miles compass about the same City, and of all assaults and affrays done and committed within the same City and compass aforesaid[2].

VII. And also we give full power and authority unto you and six of you, as before, summarily to hear and finally to determine, according to your discretions and by the laws of this realm, all causes and complaints of all them which in respect of religion, or for lawful matrimony contracted and allowed by the same, were injuriously deprived, defrauded, or spoiled of their lands, goods, possessions, rights, dignities, livings, offices, spiritual or temporal; and them so deprived, as before, to restore into their said livings and to put them in possession, amoving the usurpers in convenient speed, as it shall seem to your discretions good, by your letters missive or otherwise; all frustatory appellations clearly rejected.

VIII. And further, we do give unto you and six of you, whereof you the said Matthew Parker [etc.]...to be one, by virtue hereof full power and authority, not only to hear and determine the same and all other offences and matters before mentioned and rehearsed, but also all other notorious and manifest advoutries[3], fornications, and ecclesiastical crimes and offences within this our realm, according to your wisdoms, consciences, and discretions; willing and commanding you or six of you, whereof you the said Matthew Parker [etc.]...to be one, from

---

[1] Printed as 'wheresoever.'

[2] The inclusion of this clause in the Commission runs counter to Coke's argument that it was intended to be strictly limited by the terms of the Act of Supremacy.

[3] Adulteries.

time to time hereafter to use and devise all such politic ways and means for the trial and searching out of all the premises as by you or six of you, as aforesaid, shall be thought most expedient and necessary; and upon due proof had, and the offence or offences before specified, or any of them, sufficiently proved against any person or persons as by you or six of you, by confession of the party or by lawful witnesses or by any due mean, before you or six of you, whereof the said Matthew Parker [etc.]...to be one, that then you or six of you, as aforesaid, shall have full power and authority to award such punishment to every offender by fine, imprisonment, or otherwise, by all or any of the ways aforesaid, and to take such order for the redress of the same as to your wisdoms and discretions [shall be thought meet and convenient][1].

IX. [And further we do give full power and authority unto you] or six of you, whereof the said Matthew Parker [etc.]...to be one, to call before you or six of you, as aforesaid, from time to time all and every offender or offenders, and such as by you or six of you, as aforesaid, shall seem to be suspect persons in any of the premises; and also all such witnesses as you or six of you, as aforesaid, shall think [meet] to be called before you or six of you, as aforesaid; and them and every of them to examine upon their corporal oath, for the better trial and opening of the premises or any part thereof.

X. And if you or six of you, as aforesaid, shall find any person or persons obstinate or disobedient, either in their appearance before you or six of you, as aforesaid, at your calling and commandment, or else not accomplishing or not obeying your order, decrees, and commandments in anything touching the premises or any part thereof; that then you or six of you, as aforesaid, shall have full power and authority to commit the same person or persons so offending to ward, there to remain until he or they shall be by you or six of you, as aforesaid, enlarged and delivered.

XI. And further we do give unto you and six of you, whereof the said Matthew Parker [etc.]...to be one, full power and authority by these presents to take and receive by your discretions of every offender or suspect person to be convented or brought before you, a recognisance or recognisances, obligation or obligations, to our use, in such sum or sums of money as to you or six of you, as aforesaid, shall seem convenient, as well for their personal appearance before you or six of you, as aforesaid, as also for

---

[1] In order to make sense of this and the next clause it is necessary to adopt the emendations suggested in Prothero, p. 230.

the performance and accomplishment of your orders and decrees, in case you or six of you, as aforesaid, shall see it so convenient.

XII. And further, our will and pleasure is that you shall appoint our trusty and well-beloved John Skinner to be your Register of all your acts, decrees, and proceedings by virtue of this Commission, and in his default one other sufficient person, and that you or six of you, as aforesaid, shall give such allowance to the said Register for his pains and his clerks, to be levied of the fines and other profits that shall rise by force of this Commission and your doings in the premises, as to your discretions shall be thought meet.

XIII. And further, our will and pleasure is that you or six of you, as aforesaid, shall name and appoint one other sufficient person to gather up and receive all such sums of money as shall be assessed and taxed by you or six of you, as aforesaid, for any fine or fines upon any person or persons for their offences; and that you or six of you, as aforesaid, by bill or bills signed with your hands, shall and may assign and appoint, as well to the said person for his pains in recovering the said sums as also to your messengers and attendants upon you for their travail, pains, and charges to be sustained for or about the premises or any part thereof, such sums of money for their rewards as by you or six of you, as aforesaid, shall be thought expedient: willing and commanding you or six of you, as aforesaid, after the time of this our Commission expired, to certify into our Court of Exchequer as well the name of the said receiver as also a note of such fines as shall be set or taxed before you; to the intent that upon the determination of the account of the said receiver we be answered of that that to us shall justly appertain: willing and commanding also our auditors and other officers, upon the sight of the said bills signed with the hand of you or six of you, as aforesaid, to make unto the said receiver due allowances according to the said bills upon his accounts.

XIV. Wherefore we will and command you our Commissioners with diligence to execute the premises with effect; any of our laws, statutes, proclamations, or other grants, privileges, or ordinances which be or may seem to be contrary to the premises notwithstanding.

XV. And more, we will and command all and singular justices of the peace, mayors, sheriffs, bailiffs, constables, and other our officers, ministers, and faithful subjects to be aiding, helping, and assisting, and at your commandment in the due execution hereof, as they tender our pleasure and [will] answer to the contrary at their utmost perils.

XVI. And we will and grant that this our letters patents shall be a sufficient warrant and discharge for you and every of you against us, our heirs and successors, and all and every other person or persons, whatsoever they be, of and for or concerning the premises or any parcel thereof, or for the execution of this our Commission or any part thereof. Witness the Queen at Westminster, the 19th day of July in the first year of her reign over England, etc.

PER IPSAM REGINAM.

Cardwell, *Documentary Annals*, i, 223 (printed from Tanner MSS. 1. 5)[1].

(3) Cawdrey's Case, 1591

Part of the judgment as reported by Sir Edward Coke.

...It was resolved, That the said Act of the first year of the said late Queen concerning Ecclesiastical Jurisdiction was not a statute introductory of a new law, but declaratory of the old; which appeareth as well by the title of the said Act, viz., 'An Act restoring to the Crown the ancient Jurisdiction over the state Ecclesiastical and Spiritual, etc.,' as also by the body of the Act in divers parts thereof. For that Act doth not annex any jurisdiction to the Crown but that which in truth was, or of right ought to be, by the ancient laws of the realm parcel of the King's jurisdiction and united to his imperial Crown, and which lawfully had been or might be exercised within the realm; the end of which jurisdiction and of all the proceeding thereupon was, that all things might be done in causes ecclesiastical to the pleasure of Almighty God, the increase of virtue, and the conservation of the peace and unity of this realm, as by divers parts of the said Act appeareth. And therefore as by that Act no pretended jurisdiction exercised within this realm, being either ungodly or repugnant to the prerogative or the ancient law of the Crown of this realm, was or could be restored to the same Crown, according to the ancient right and law of the same, so that if that Act of the first year of the late Queen had never been made, it was resolved by all the Judges that the King or Queen of England for the time being may make such an Ecclesiastical Commission as is before mentioned, by the ancient prerogative and law of England. And therefore by the ancient laws of this realm this kingdom of England is an absolute empire and monarchy consisting of one head, which is the King, and of a body politic compact and compounded

---

[1] See also Prothero, p. 227, printed from the Patent Rolls, 1 Eliz. pt 9.

of many and almost infinite several and yet well agreeing members; all which the Law divideth into two general parts, that is to say, the Clergy and the Laity, both of them, next and immediately under God, subject and obedient unto the head. Also the kingly head of this politic body is instituted and furnished with plenary and entire power, prerogative, and jurisdiction to render justice and right to every part and member of this body, of what estate, degree, or calling soever, in all causes ecclesiastical or temporal, otherwise he should not be a head of the whole body. And as in temporal causes the King by the mouth of the Judges in his Courts of Justice doth judge and determine the same by the temporal laws of England, so in causes ecclesiastical and spiritual, as namely blasphemy, apostasy from Christianity, heresies, schisms, ordering admissions, institutions of clerks, celebration of divine service, rights of matrimony, divorces, general bastardy, subtraction and right of tithes, oblations, obventions, dilapidations, reparation of churches, probate of testaments, administrations and accounts upon the same, simony, incests, fornications, adulteries, solicitation of chastity, pensions, procurations, appeals in ecclesiastical causes, commutation of penance, and others (the conusance whereof belong not to the Common Laws of England) the same are to be determined and decided by ecclesiastical judges, according to the King's Ecclesiastical Laws of this realm....

Coke, *Fifth Report* (pp. 344–5 in edition of 1658).

(4) Lord Burghley's criticism of the Commission, 1584

Lord Burghley's objection is to the tendering of complex articles to be answered upon oath; it is therefore directed to the use of the oath *ex officio* on which the procedure of the Commission was founded.

Lord Burghley to Archbishop Whitgift, 1 *July,* 1584

...But now, my good Lord, by chance I have come to the sight of an instrument of twenty-four articles of great length and curiosity, found in a Romish style, to examine all manner of ministers in this time without distinction of persons, which articles are entitled, *Apud Lambeth, May* 1584, *to be executed ex officio mero, etc....* I sent for the Register, who brought me the articles, which I have read, and find so curiously penned, so full of branches and circumstances, that I think the inquisitors of Spain use not so many questions to comprehend and trap their preys. I know your canonists can defend these with all their particles, but surely, under your Grace's correction, this judicial and canonical sifting of poor ministers is not to edify or reform. And in charity I think they ought not to answer to all these nice points, except they were very notorious offenders in Papistry or heresy. Now, my good Lord, bear with my scribbling. I write with the testimony of a good conscience. I desire the peace of the Church. I desire concord and unity in the exercise of our religion. I fear no sensual and wilful recusants. But I conclude that, according to my simple judgment, this kind of proceeding is too much favouring of the Romish Inquisition, and is rather a device to seek for offenders than to reform any. This is not the charitable instruction that I thought was intended... This is not a charitable way to send them to answer to your common Register upon so many articles at one instant, without any commodity of instruction by your Register, whose office is only to receive their answers. By which the parties are first subject to condemnation before they be taught their error. It may be, as I said, the canonists may maintain this proceeding by rules of their laws; but though *omnia licent* yet *omnia non expediunt.*

Strype, Life of Whitgift (1718), bk. iii, appendix, p. 63.

Archbishop Whitgift to Lord Burghley, 3 *July*, 1584

My singular good Lord,... Touching the twenty-four articles which your Lordship seemeth so much to mislike... I cannot but greatly marvel at your Lordship's vehement speeches against them (I hope without cause), seeing it is the ordinary course in other courts likewise: as in the Star Chamber, the Court of the Marches, and other places. And (without offence be it spoken) I think these articles to be more tolerable, and better agreeing with the rule of justice and charity, and less captious than those in other courts.... And therefore I see no cause why our judicial and canonical proceedings in this point should be misliked....

Strype, Life of Whitgift, bk. iii, appendix, p. 65.

The Law of Treason

At common law the crime of Treason was vague and ill-defined. The principle on which it rested was that of allegiance, which was due to the Sovereign from every subject over the age of fourteen, and any act that was held by the judges to be a breach of allegiance was liable to be treated as though it constituted the crime of treason. Thus in 1305 bringing a charge in the courts of the King of France seems to have been regarded as treason to the King of England, although the crime is not specifically mentioned[1]. Under Edward II the Despensers were accused of treason for 'accroaching royal power'[2]; and in 1348 Sir John Gerberge was indicted for accroaching royal power, because he had assaulted one of the King's subjects on the highway, and had detained him until he paid £90, although as he refused to plead, he 'was not convicted as in case of treason, but was put to penance.'[3] In 1349 killing a King's messenger was accounted treason.

The vagueness of the offence at common law led the Commons to complain of the arbitrary decisions of the Courts, and in 1351 they presented a petition praying 'that whereas the King's Justices in various counties adjudge persons indicted before them to be traitors for sundry matters not known to the Commons to be treason, it would please the King, by his Council and the great and wise men of the law, to declare what are treasons in this present Parliament.'[4] On this petition was founded the Statute of Treasons of 1352[5], which is the starting-point for the history of a systematic law of treason. The Statute recognised, among other offences, three main treasons, (1) compassing or imagining the King's death, (2) levying war against the King, and (3) adhering to the King's enemies. It also contains a proviso: 'And because that many other like cases of treason may happen in time to come, which a man cannot think nor declare at this present time, it is accorded, That if any other case supposed treason which is not above specified doth happen before any Justices, the Justices shall tarry without any going to judgment of the treason till the cause be shewed and declared before the King and his Parliament, whether it ought to be judged treason or other felony'; which Sir J. F. Stephen reads 'as enacting that Parliament in its judicial capacity may, upon the conviction of any person for any political offence, hold that it amounts to high treason though not specified in the Act.'[6]

The Statute of Treasons was passed at a time when the sovereign was firmly seated on the throne by a title which no one disputed, and in these circumstances it was natural that it should aim at nothing more than the security of the King's throne and person. Except in so far as the offences are covered by the proviso, the Act says nothing about compassing the King's imprison-

[1] Stephen, ii, 245.   [2] *Ib.* ii, 246.   [3] *Ib.*
[4] The motive of this petition was not humanitarian. It was an attempt to limit in the interest of the nobility the number of offences which involved perpetual forfeiture of lands to the Crown (*History*, vi, 107).
[5] 25 Edw. III, st. 5, c. 2.   [6] ii, 250.

ment[1] or his deposition, or interference with the exercise of his functions; nor does it punish conspiracy to levy war[2] or conspiracy to compass the King's death, notwithstanding the fact that in the case of treason above all other crimes a conspiracy to commit it must be made penal, because if the conspiracy succeeds it is impossible to punish it. The result of this incompleteness of the law was that in times of political disorder new treasons were temporarily developed to meet the needs of threatened governments, although the Statute of 1352 remained 'the normal measure of treason,'[3] to be applied again when ordinary conditions were restored. These new treasons were developed in two ways, (1) by means of judicial constructions of the Statute of 1352, and (2) by means of exceptional legislation, afterwards repealed.

§ 1. CONSTRUCTIVE TREASONS

Although the Statute of 1352 defined treason, it was possible to extend the definition by means of judicial constructions, and the ingenuity of the judges was successfully applied to this end. In the reign of Henry VI it was laid down that the Statute of 1352 was only declaratory, and not an exhaustive list of treasons[4], and therefore to rescue a traitor out of prison continued to be treason at common law. It was also held that various acts not enumerated in the Statute of 1352 as treasons, might nevertheless be overt acts proving the traitorous imagination of compassing the King's death, and might therefore bring the offender under the Statute[5].

The Tudor period is a period of attainder and statutory treason, rather than of treason by judicial construction, but two cases may be referred to, one at the beginning of the period and the other at the end. If the tradition concerning the trial of Sir William Stanley in 1495 may be relied upon, in the form in which it found its way into Bacon's *History of Henry VII*, the charge against him was for words spoken which disclosed a traitorous imagination—that in discourse with Sir Robert Clifford he had said that if he were

---

[1] In this connexion a sentence is often quoted from Sir Michael Foster, a judge whose legal writings belong to the middle of the 18th century: 'experience hath shewn that between the prisons and the graves of princes the distance is very small' (Stephen, ii, 267). It is interesting to find that James II had said the same thing in 1689: 'I can no longer remain here but as a cipher, or be a prisoner to the Prince of Orange, and you know there is but a small distance between the prisons and graves of kings' (*Balcarres MS. Memoirs*; quoted in C. S. Terry, *Dundee*, p. 242).

[2] It has been pointed out that in the 14th century conspiracy to levy war was scarcely regarded as a crime, provided that the war was properly declared (Holdsworth, iii, 251).

[3] Maitland, p. 228.

[4] Miss I. D. Thornley, in *History*, vi, 106–8, gives reasons for thinking that this was the correct view.

[5] Maitland quotes, although without vouching for its truth, the story of Walter Walker, who was declared guilty of treason under Edward IV because he tried to soothe a child by telling him that if he would be quiet he would make him heir to the Crown (p. 228). Witchcraft, sorcery, or enchantment, although not made felony until 33 Henr. VIII, c. 8, and until then punishable as heresy by burning, was in some circumstances held to be constructive treason.

sure Perkin Warbeck were King Edward's son, he would not bear arms against him. 'This case seems somewhat a hard case,' says Bacon[1], 'both in respect of the conditional and in respect of the other words. But for the conditional, it seemeth the judges of that time...thought it was a dangerous thing to admit Ifs and Ands to qualify words of treason; whereby every man might express his malice and blanch his danger.... And as for the positive words, That he would not bear arms against King Edward's son; though the words seem calm, yet it was a plain and direct over-ruling of the King's title, either by the line of Lancaster or by Act of Parliament.' The other case is that of the Earl of Essex in 1601 [p. 448], in the course of which the judges advised the peers who sat to try the case that every rebellion was an overt act proving the traitorous imagination of compassing the King's death[2].

The phrase 'levying war against the King' has also received various fictitious interpretations The Statute of 1352, passed at a time when private war was a common occurrence, insists that the levying must be 'against the King.' 'No amount of violence, however great...will make an attack by one subject on another high treason. On the other hand, any amount of violence, however insignificant, directed against the King, will be high treason, and as soon as violence has any political object, it is impossible to say that it is not directed against the King, in the sense of being armed opposition to the lawful exercise of his power.'[3] As soon as order was firmly established by the Tudors, private war died down into mere riot, and the question arose, where did rioting end and levying war begin. The test of treason came to be the generality of the object[4].

Sir Edward Coke on Treason

...A compassing or conspiracy to levy war is no treason, for there must be a levying of war *in facto*. But if many conspire to levy war, and some of them do levy the same according to the conspiracy, this is high treason in all, for in treason all be principals, and war is levied.

If any levy war to expulse strangers, to deliver men out of prisons, to remove councillors, or against any statute, or to any other end, pretending reformation of their own heads, without warrant, this is levying of war against the King, because they take upon them royal authority....There is a diversity between levying of war and committing of a great riot, a rout, or an unlawful

---

[1] vi, 151.

[2] See also Coke's opinion; p. 378 below.
After the Revolution of 1688 the fictitious interpretations of the crime of compassing were carried still further; as in Lord Preston's case in 1691, when the act of taking a boat at Surrey Stairs in Middlesex in order to go on board a ship in Kent for the purpose of conveying military and naval information to Louis XIV was held to be an overt act proving the traitorous imagination of compassing the death of William and Mary (Stephen, ii, 267). It was held by the later legal writers that levying war against the King directly might be itself an overt act proving the compassing of his death (*ib*. ii, 266).

[3] Stephen, ii, 269.   [4] See Coke, p. 378 below.

assembly. For example, as if three or four or more do rise to burn or pull down an enclosure in Dale which the lord of the manor of Dale hath made there in that particular place, this or the like is a riot, a rout, or an unlawful assembly, and no treason. But if they had risen of purpose to alter religion established within the realm, or laws, or to go from town to town generally and to cast down enclosures, this is a levying of war (though there be no great number of the conspirators) within the purview of this statute, because the pretence is public and general and not private in particular ... (p. 9).

...If divers do conspire the death of the King, and the manner how, and thereupon provide weapons, powder, poison, assay harness, send letters, etc., or the like, for the execution of the conspiracy, also some preparation by some overt act to depose the King, or take the King by force and strong hand and to imprison him until he hath yielded to certain demands, this is a sufficient overt act to prove the compassing and imagination of the death of the King; for this upon the matter is to make the King a subject, and to despoil him of his kingly office of royal government... (p. 12).

If a subject conspire with a foreign prince beyond the seas to invade the realm by open hostility, and prepare for the same by some overt act, this is a sufficient overt act for the death of the King... (p. 14).

Divers later Acts of Parliament have ordained that compassing by bare words or sayings should be high treason; but all they are either repealed or expired. And it is commonly said that bare words may make an heretic, but not a traitor, without an overt act. And the wisdom of the makers of this law[1] would not make words only to be treason, seeing such variety amongst the witnesses are about the same, as few of them agree together. But if the same be set down in writing by the delinquent himself, this is a sufficient overt act within this statute... (p. 14).

Coke, *Third Institute* (edn. of 1669), cap. 1

§ 2. STATUTORY TREASONS

Before 1485 the offence of treason had from time to time been extended by statute. For instance, an Act of 1381[2], passed after the Peasants' Revolt, made it treason to begin a riot; and by an Act of 1429[3] extorting money by threats to burn houses was made treason[4]. During the Tudor period, however, there was an extraordinary development of statutory treasons under the influence of two main causes—the necessity of maintaining the ecclesiastical

---

[1] The Statute of 1352.   [2] 5 Rich. II, c. 6.
[3] 8 Henr. VI, c. 6.   [4] For other instances see Holdsworth, ii, 373.

Supremacy, and the necessity of protecting an uncertain succession to the throne. These statutory treasons fall into three groups: (1) general treasons; (2) treasons connected with the Supremacy; and (3) a group of Succession Acts. The two last groups belong mainly to the reign of Henry VIII.

A characteristic of Henry VIII's legislation on the subject of treason is that it abandons any logical legal principle, and converts treason into a crime which has no character except heinousness. This appears in an Act of 1531 [p. 381] to provide that poisoning any person should be deemed high treason, and the offender 'committed to execution of death by boiling.' The Acts connected with the Supremacy and the succession shew the same disregard of legal principle. They have no logical connexion with the Statute of 1352. The subject need not compass the King's death or levy war against him to incur the penalties of treason. He is a traitor if he fails to follow the King in matters of religious belief, or in the changes he makes from time to time in the status of his different wives. There is here, however, something more than mere caprice. The question at issue between King and Pope was really a question of sovereignty, and as Stephen remarks[1], 'questions of sovereignty can be determined only by force.' In this war, if the weapons on the one side were interdict and excommunication, those on the other were statutory treasons. The Succession Acts also were justified to that generation by the experience of the Wars of the Roses, and the enormous evils which attended a disputed succession.

The first of Henry VIII's Acts connected with the Supremacy was the Treasons Act of 1534 [p. 388], passed in the same year as the Act of Supremacy and the year after the marriage with Anne Boleyn. This made it treason (1) 'maliciously to wish, will, or desire by words[2] or writing,' or by any craft to 'imagine, invent, practise, or attempt any bodily harm' to the King, Queen, or their heirs apparent; (2) to deprive them of their dignity, title, name, or of their royal estates; (3) slanderously or maliciously to publish and pronounce, by express writing or words, that the King our Sovereign Lord is an heretic, schismatic, tyrant, infidel, or usurper; (4) rebelliously to detain or keep any of the King's ships, ammunition, or artillery. An Act of 1536[3], for 'extinguishing the authority of the Bishop of Rome,' made it high treason on the part of any clerical or lay official to refuse an oath imposed by the Act to renounce all jurisdiction of the See of Rome, and to support the King's Supremacy. By an Act of 1539[4] persons going beyond sea to escape penalties provided in the King's proclamations concerning religion were to be deemed guilty of high treason. Finally, an Act of 1543[5] made it high treason to imagine to deprive the King, Queen, Prince, or the heirs of the King's body, or any to whom the Crown is or shall be limited, of any of their titles, styles, names, degrees, royal estate, or regal power annexed to the Crown of England.

[1] ii, 258.
[2] It has been said that treason by words was invented by Henry VIII, but see E.H.R. xxxii, 556, where Miss I. D. Thornley shews that in the 15th century words could constitute high treason at common law. Cf. also the same writer in Royal Historical Society's Transactions, 3rd series, xi, 107.
[3] 28 Henr. VIII, c. 10.   [4] 31 Henr. VIII, c. 8.
[5] 35 Henr. VIII, c. 3.

Henry VIII's statutes concerning the succession are four in number—three resettling the order of succession, and one invalidating the marriage with Anne of Cleves. The First Succession Act [p. 382] passed in 1534, which annulled the marriage with Catharine of Aragon and confirmed that with Anne Boleyn, entailing the Crown upon children by her, made it high treason 'by writing[1], print, deed, or act' to 'procure or do or cause to be procured or done any thing or things to the prejudice, slander, disturbance, or derogation' of the Boleyn marriage. The Second Succession Act [p. 389], passed in 1536, soon after the King's marriage with Jane Seymour, declared the two previous marriages null and void, and entailed the Crown first on her male children; next on male children by any future wife; and lastly on the female children of Jane Seymour or of any future wife. Failing these, the King is empowered to devise the Crown by will or letters patent. But the Act also creates three new treasons: (1) To speak, write, or act against the Seymour marriage; (2) by 'words, writing, imprinting, or any other exterior act, directly or indirectly,' to 'accept or take, judge or believe' that the Aragon and Boleyn marriages were either of them lawful; (3) to refuse to take an oath to answer questions concerning the Act, or, having taken the oath to refuse to answer. The Act to annul the marriage with Anne of Cleves [p. 395], passed in 1540, made it high treason 'by writing or imprinting, or by any other exterior act, word, or deed, directly or indirectly,' to 'accept or take, judge or believe' this marriage to be lawful. Finally, the Third Succession Act [p. 397], passed in 1543, placed the Princesses Mary and Elizabeth into the entail next after the lawful issue, male or female, of the King and Prince Edward, subject to such conditions as the King might appoint by will; and failing these heirs, he could devise the Crown by will as before. But the Act also made it high treason to do anything to interrupt the succession as laid down in the Act, and imposed a new form of oath under the penalties of treason.

As soon as Henry VIII died, his legislation with regard to treason was repealed, and in 1547 the First Treasons Act of Edward VI [p. 401] provided that nothing should be held to be treason except offences against the Statute of 1352, and offences created by the Act of 1547 itself. In 1549[2] riots of a certain degree of importance were made treason; and in 1552 the Second Treasons Act of Edward VI [p. 405] revived Henry VIII's legislation, and made it treason to affirm that the King was an 'heretic, schismatic, tyrant, infidel, or usurper' by 'writing, printing, painting, carving, or graving,' or by words on a third offence.

On the accession of Mary her First Treasons Act [p. 406], passed in 1553, once more brought back the law of treason to the Statute of 1352; but it was not long before the Spanish marriage established a necessity for fresh legislation, and the Second Treasons Act [p. 408], of 1555, made it treason to shew by writing any treasonable intent against the King Consort, or by words on a second offence. In the same session an Act against traitorous words [p. 407] was also passed.

[1] This is the first Act of Parliament to state that writings might constitute treason; but they were held to do so in the fifteenth century, so the principle was not as novel as has been sometimes supposed (*Royal Histor. Soc. Trans.* xi, 111).

[2] By 3 & 4 Edw. VI, c. 5, §§ 2 and 4.

The First Treasons Act of Elizabeth [p. 411], passed in 1559, re-enacted Mary's Second Treasons Act, and made it apply to her successor. Elizabeth's Second Treasons Act [p. 413], is, however, much more important, because, unlike the capricious treasons of Henry VIII, it is a logical development of the Statute of 1352, and supplies some of its defects. It made it high treason to compass the death or bodily harm of the Queen, or to deprive her of her imperial Crown, and to declare such compassing in writing or words. Thus, in effect, it adds to the old offence of compassing the King's death the newer crimes of compassing or conspiring to compass his bodily harm or deposition. A temporary Act of 1572 [p. 417], also made it treason to detain the Queen's castles, ships, or artillery. A special statute of 1585 [p. 417] dealt with attempted assassination of the Queen in the interests of any pretended successor, and made provision for 'the pursuing and taking revenge of any person' on whose behalf 'any such wicked act or attempt should be made.' Thus it legalises in advance the otherwise treasonable offence of levying war against Elizabeth's heir. This statute comes into importance in connexion with the trial of Mary Queen of Scots [p. 443].

(1) Act against Poisoners, 1531

An Act for poisoning

The King's Royal Majesty calling to his most blessed re-membrance that the making of good and wholesome laws and due execution of the same against the offenders thereof is the only cause that good obedience and order hath been preserved in this realm, and his Highness having most tender zeal to the same, among other things considering that man's life above all things is chiefly to be favoured, and voluntary murders most highly to be detested and abhorred, and specially of all kinds of murders poisoning, which in this realm hitherto, our Lord be thanked, hath been most rare and seldom committed or practised; and now in the time of this present Parliament...one Richard Roose...of his most wicked and damnable disposition did cast a certain venom or poison into a vessel replenished with yeast or barm standing in the kitchen of the Reverend Father in God John, Bishop of Rochester,...with which yeast or barm and other things con-venient porridge or gruel was forthwith made for his family... whereby not only the number of 17 persons of his said family which did eat of that porridge were mortally infected and poisoned, and one of them...thereof is deceased, but also certain poor people which resorted to the said Bishop's place and were there charitably fed with the remain of the said porridge and other victuals were in like wise infected, and one poor woman of them ...is also thereof now deceased: Our said Sovereign Lord the

King of his blessed disposition inwardly abhorring all such abominable offences because that in manner no person can live in surety out of danger of death by that mean if practice thereof should not be eschewed, hath ordained and enacted by authority of this present Parliament that the said poisoning be adjudged and deemed as high treason, And... that the said Richard Roose shall be therefor boiled to death without having any advantage of his clergy[1]. And that from henceforth every wilful murder of any person or persons by any whatsoever person or persons hereafter to be committed and done by mean or way of poisoning shall be reputed, deemed, and judged in the law to be high treason; And that all and every person or persons which hereafter shall be lawfully indicted or appealed, and attainted or condemned by order of the law of such treason for any manner poisoning of any person shall not be admitted to the benefit of his or their clergy, but shall be immediately after such attainder or condemnation committed to execution of death by boiling for the same....

*   *   *   *   *   *

22 Henr. VIII, c. 9: Statutes of the Realm, iii, 326.

(2) First Succession Act, 1534

An Act for the establishment of the King's succession

In their most humble wise shew unto your Majesty your most humble and obedient subjects, the Lords spiritual and temporal and the Commons in this present Parliament assembled, that since it is the natural inclination of every man gladly and willingly to provide for the surety of both his title and succession, although it touch his only private cause; We therefore, most rightful and dreadful Sovereign Lord, reckon ourselves much more bounden to beseech and instant[2] your Highness, although we doubt not of your princely heart and wisdom, mixed with a natural affection to the same, to foresee and provide for the perfect surety of both you and of your most lawful succession and heirs, upon which dependeth all our joy and wealth[3], in whom also is united and knit the only mere[4] true inheritance and title of this realm without any contradiction: Wherefore we your said most humble and obedient subjects in this present Parliament

---

[1] The sentence was carried out shortly after at Smithfield.
[2] In use at the time as a verb, in the sense of to urge or importune any one.
[3] See note on p. 33 above.
[4] The word is here used in the sense of pure or unmixed.

assembled, calling to our remembrance the great divisions which
in times past hath been in this realm by reason of several titles
pretended to the imperial Crown of the same, which some times
and for the most part ensued by occasion of ambiguity and doubts
then not so perfectly declared but that men might upon froward
intents expound them to every man's sinister appetite and affection after their sense, contrary to the right legality of the succession and posterity of the lawful kings and emperors[1] of this
realm, whereof hath ensued great effusion and destruction of
man's blood, as well of a great number of the nobles as of other
the subjects and specially inheritors in the same[2]; And the greatest occasion thereof hath been because no perfect and substantial
provision by law hath been made within this realm of itself when
doubts and questions have been moved and proponed[3] of the certainty and legality of the succession and posterity of the Crown;
By reason whereof the Bishop of Rome and See Apostolic,
contrary to the great and inviolable grants of jurisdictions given
by God immediately to emperors, kings, and princes in succession
to their heirs, hath presumed in times past to invest who should
please them to inherit in other men's kingdoms and dominions,
which thing we your most humble subjects both spiritual and
temporal do most abhor and detest; And sometimes other foreign
princes and potentates of sundry degrees, minding rather dissension and discord to continue in the realm to the utter desolation
thereof than charity, equity, or unity, have many times supported
wrong titles, whereby they might the more easily and facilely aspire
to the superiority of the same; The continuance and sufferance
whereof deeply considered and pondered, were too dangerous
and perilous to be suffered any longer within this realm, and
too much contrary to the unity, peace, and tranquillity of the
same, being greatly reproachable and dishonourable to the whole
realm:

In consideration whereof your said most humble and obedient
subjects the nobles and commons of this realm, calling further to
their remembrance that the good unity, peace, and wealth of this
realm and the succession of the subjects of the same most specially
and principally above all worldly things consisteth and resteth in
the certainty and surety of the procreation and posterity of your
Highness, in whose most royal person at this present time is no
manner of doubt nor question, do therefore most humbly beseech

---

[1] See note on p. 41 above.
[2] A reference to the experience of the Wars of the Roses.
[3] Propounded.

your Highness, that it may please your Majesty that it may be enacted...that the marriage heretofore solemnised between your Highness and the Lady Katherine, being before lawful wife to Prince Arthur your elder brother, which by him was carnally known, as doth duly appear by sufficient proof in a lawful process had and made before Thomas, by the sufferance of God now Archbishop of Canterbury and Metropolitan and Primate of all this realm[1], shall be by authority of this present Parliament definitively, clearly, and absolutely declared, deemed, and adjudged to be against the laws of Almighty God, and also accepted, reputed, and taken of no value nor effect but utterly void and adnichiled[2], and the separation thereof made by the said Archbishop shall be good and effectual to all intents and purposes, any license, dispensation, or any other act or acts going afore or ensuing the same to the contrary thereof in any wise notwithstanding; And that every such license, dispensation, act or acts, thing or things, heretofore had, made, done, or to be done, to the contrary thereof shall be void and of none effect; and that the said Lady Katherine shall be from henceforth called and reputed only Dowager to Prince Arthur and not Queen of this realm. And that the lawful matrimony had and solemnised between your Highness and your most dear and entirely beloved wife Queen Anne shall be established, and taken for undoubtful, true, sincere, and perfect ever hereafter, according to the just judgment of the said Thomas, Archbishop of Canterbury, Metropolitan and Primate of all this realm[3], whose grounds of judgment have been confirmed as well by the whole clergy of this realm in both the Convocations[4], and by both the Universities thereof[5], as by the Universities of Bologna, Padua, Paris, Orleans, Toulouse, Angers, and divers others[6], And also by the private writings of many right excellent well-learned men; which grounds so confirmed and judgment of the said Archbishop ensuing the same[1], together with your marriage solemnised between your Highness and your

---

[1] Cranmer had pronounced the marriage with Catharine of Aragon invalid in his archiepiscopal court at Dunstable, 23 May, 1533.

[2] Annulled.

[3] Cranmer had pronounced the marriage with Anne Boleyn to be valid, after a secret inquiry held at Lambeth, 28 May, 1533.

[4] Both Houses of Convocation had pronounced against Henry's marriage with his deceased brother's wife in 1533, Bishop Fisher resisting in the Upper House (28 March) and a minority of seven in the Lower (2 April).

[5] Oxford and Cambridge, after some manipulation, had pronounced in 1530 against the validity of a marriage with a deceased brother's wife.

[6] The opinions of foreign universities had been obtained in 1530.

said lawful wife Queen Anne[1], We your said subjects, both spiritual and temporal, do purely, plainly, constantly, and firmly accept, approve, and ratify for good, and consonant to the laws of Almighty God, without error or default, most humbly beseeching your Majesty that it may be so established for ever by your most gracious and royal assent.

*　　*　　*　　*　　*　　*

IV. And also be it enacted by authority aforesaid that all the issue had and procreate, or after to be had and procreate, between your Highness and your said most dearly and entirely beloved wife Queen Anne, shall be your lawful children, and be inheritable and inherit, according to the course of inheritance and laws of this realm, the imperial Crown of the same, with all dignities, honours, preeminences, prerogatives, authorities, and jurisdictions to the same annexed or belonging, in as large and ample manner as your Highness to this present time hath the same as King of this realm, the inheritance thereof to be and remain to your said children and right heirs in manner and form as hereafter shall be declared: That is to say, first the said imperial Crown and other the premises shall be to your Majesty and to your heirs of your body lawfully begotten, that is to say to the first son of your body between your Highness and your said lawful wife Queen Anne begotten, and to the heirs of the body of the same first son lawfully begotten; And for default of such heirs, then to the second son of your body and of the body of the said Queen Anne begotten, and to the heirs of the body of the said second son lawfully begotten; and so to every son of your body and of the body of the said Queen Anne begotten, and to the heirs of the body of every such son begotten, according to the course of inheritance in that behalf. And if it shall happen your said dear and entirely beloved wife Queen Anne to decease without issue male of the body of your Highness to be gotten (which God defend) then the same imperial Crown and all other the premises to be to your Majesty as is aforesaid, and to the son and heir male of your body lawfully begotten and to the heirs of the body of the same son and heir male lawfully begotten; And for default of such issue then to your second son of your body lawfully begotten and to the heirs of the body of the same second son lawfully begotten; And so from son and heir male to son and heir male, and to the heirs of the several bodies of every such son and heir male to be gotten, according to the course of inheritance in

---

[1] Anne Boleyn had been secretly married to the King on or about 25 January, 1533; and on Whitsunday, June 1, 1533, she had been crowned Queen.

like manner and form as is above said; And for default of such
sons of your body begotten, and the heirs of the several bodies of
every such sons lawfully begotten, that then the said imperial
Crown and other the premises shall be to the issue female between
your Majesty and your said most dear and entirely beloved wife
Queen Anne begotten, That is to say: first to the eldest issue
female, which is the Lady Elizabeth, now princess, and to the
heirs of her body lawfully begotten, and for default of such issue
then to the second issue female and to the heirs of her body lawfully begotten; And so from issue female to issue female and to
their heirs of their bodies one after another by course of inheritance according to their ages, as the Crown of England hath been
accustomed and ought to go in cases when there be heirs females
to the same: And for default of such issue then the said imperial
Crown and all other the premises shall be in the right heirs of
your Highness for ever.

V. And be it further enacted by authority aforesaid that, on
this side the first day of May next coming, proclamations shall be
made in all shires within this realm of the tenor and contents of
this Act; And if any person or persons, of what estate, dignity, or
condition soever they be, subject or resiant[1] within this realm or
elsewhere within any the King's dominions, after the said first
day of May by writing or imprinting or by any exterior act or
deed maliciously procure or do, or cause to be procured or done,
any thing or things to the peril of your most royal person, or
maliciously give occasion by writing, print, deed, or act whereby
your Highness might be disturbed or interrupted of the Crown
of this realm, or by writing, print, deed, or act procure or do, or
cause to be procured or done, any thing or things to the prejudice,
slander, disturbance, or derogation of the said lawful matrimony
solemnised between your Majesty and the said Queen Anne, or
to the peril, slander, or disherison of any the issues and heirs of
your Highness being limited by this Act to inherit and to be inheritable to the Crown of this realm in such form as is aforesaid,
whereby any such issues or heirs of your Highness might be
destroyed, disturbed, or interrupted in body or title of inheritance
to the Crown of this realm as to them is limited in this Act in
form above rehearsed, that then every such person and persons, of
what estate, degree, or condition they be of, subject or resiant
within this realm, and their aiders, counsellors, maintainers, and
abettors, and every of them, for every such offence shall be adjudged high traitors, and every such offence shall be adjudged

1 Resident.

high treason, and the offender and their aiders, counsellors, maintainers, and abettors, and every of them, being lawfully convict of such offence by presentment, verdict, confession, or process according to the laws and customs of this realm, shall suffer pains of death as in cases of high treason. And that also every such offender, being convict as is aforesaid, shall lose and forfeit to your Highness and to your heirs, kings of this realm, all such manors, lands, tenements, rents, annuities, and hereditaments which they had in possession as owners or were sole seised of[1] by or in any right, title, or means, or any other person or persons had to their use, of any estate of inheritance at the day of such treasons and offences by them committed and done; And shall also lose and forfeit to your Highness and to your said heirs as well all manner such estates of freehold and interests for years of lands and rents as all their goods, chattels, and debts which they had at the time of conviction or attainder of any such offence: Saving always to every person and persons and bodies politic, to their heirs, assigns, and successors, and every of them, other than such persons as shall be so convict and their heirs and successors and all other claiming to their uses, all such right, title, use, interest, possession, condition, rents, fees, offices, annuities, and commons which they or any of them shall happen to have in, to, or upon any such manors, lands, tenements, rents, annuities, or hereditaments that shall so happen to be lost and forfeit by reason of attainder for any the treasons and offences above rehearsed at any time before the said treasons and offences committed.

VI. And be it further enacted by authority aforesaid, that if any person or persons, after the said first day of May, by any words without writing, or any exterior deed or act, maliciously and obstinately publish, divulge, or utter any thing or things to the peril of your Highness, or to the slander or prejudice of the said matrimony solemnised between your Highness and the said Queen Anne, or to the slander or disherison of the issue and heirs of your body begotten and to be gotten of the said Queen Anne or any other your lawful heirs which shall be inheritable to the Crown of this realm as is afore limited by this Act, that then every such offence shall be taken and adjudged for misprision of treason[2]; And that every person and persons, of what estate, degree, or condition soever they be, subject or resiant within this realm or in any the King's dominions, so doing and offending

---

[1] 'To be seised of' = to be the legal possessor (of freehold land).

[2] *I.e.* 'concealment of treason'; but misprisions are created by this statute which do not involve concealment.

and being thereof lawfully convict by presentment, verdict, process, or confession, shall suffer imprisonment of their bodies at the King's will, and shall lose as well all their goods, chattels, and debts as all such interests and estates of freehold or for years which any such offenders shall have of or in any lands, rents, or hereditaments whatsoever at the time of conviction and attainder of such offence.

*   *   *   *   *   *

25 Henr. VIII, c. 22: Statutes of the Realm, iii, 471

(3) Treasons Act of Henry VIII, 1534

An Act whereby divers offences be made high treason, and taking away all Sanctuaries for all manner of high treasons

Forasmuch as it is most necessary, both for common policy and duty of subjects, above all things to prohibit, provide, restrain, and extinct all manner of shameful slanders, perils, or imminent danger or dangers which might grow, happen, or arise to their Sovereign Lord the King, the Queen, or their heirs, which when they be heard, seen, or understood cannot be but odible[1] and also abhorred of all those sorts that be true and loving subjects, if in any point they may, do, or shall touch the King, his Queen, their heirs or successors, upon which dependeth the whole unity and universal weal of this realm, without providing wherefor too great a scope of unreasonable liberty should be given to all cankered and traitorous hearts, willers and workers of the same; And also the King's loving subjects should not declare unto their Sovereign Lord now being, which unto them hath been and is most entirely both beloved and esteemed, their undoubted sincerity and truth; Be it therefore enacted... that if any person or persons, after the first day of February next coming, do maliciously wish, will, or desire by words or writing, or by crafty images invent, practise, or attempt any bodily harm to be done or committed to the King's most royal person, the Queen's, or their heirs apparent, or to deprive them or any of them of the dignity, title, or name of their royal estates[2], or slanderously and maliciously publish and pronounce, by express writing or words, that the King our Sovereign Lord should be heretic, schismatic, tyrant, infidel, or usurper of the Crown, or rebelliously do detain, keep, or withhold from our said Sovereign Lord, his heirs or successors, any of his or their castles, fortresses, fortalices, or holds, within this realm or in any other the King's dominions or marches,

---

[1] Hateful.   [2] *I.e.* their royal rank or dignity.

or rebelliously detain, keep, or withhold from the King's said Highness, his heirs or successors, any of his or their ships, ordnance, artillery, or other munitions or fortifications of war, and do not humbly render and give up to our said Sovereign Lord, his heirs or successors, or to such persons as shall be deputed by them, such castles, fortresses, fortalices, holds, ships, ordnance, artillery, and other munitions and fortifications of war rebelliously kept or detained, within 6 days next after they shall be commanded by our said Sovereign Lord, his heirs or successors, by open proclamation under the great seal, that then every such person and persons so offending in any the premises after the said first day of February, their aiders, counsellors, consenters, and abettors, being thereof lawfully convict according to the laws and customs of this realm, shall be adjudged traitors; and that every such offence in any the premises that shall be committed or done after the said first day of February, shall be reputed, accepted, and adjudged high treason, And the offenders therein, and their aiders, consenters, counsellors, and abettors, being lawfully convict of any such offence as is aforesaid, shall have and suffer such pains of death and other penalties as is limited and accustomed in cases of high treason.

II. And to the intent that all treasons should be the more dread, hated, and detested to be done by any person or persons, and also because it is a great boldness and an occasion to ill-disposed persons to adventure and embrace their malicious intents and enterprises, which all true subjects ought to study to eschew; Be it therefore enacted by the authority aforesaid that none offender in any kinds of high treasons, whatsoever they be, their aiders, consenters, counsellors, nor abettors, shall be admitted to have the benefit or privilege of any manner of sanctuary; considering that matters of treasons toucheth so nigh both the surety of the King our Sovereign Lord's person and his heirs and successors.

*   *   *   *   *   *

26 Henr. VIII, c. 13: *Statutes of the Realm*, iii. 508.

(4) Second Succession Act, 1536

An Act for the establishment of the succession of the Imperial Crown of this Realm

[I recites and repeals 25 Henr. VIII, c. 22 (the First Succession Act, and 26 Henr. VIII, c. 2 (Act for an oath of succession).

*   *   *   *   *   *

V. And over this, most gracious Sovereign Lord, forasmuch as it hath pleased your most royal Majesty, notwithstanding the great and intolerable perils and occasions which your Highness hath suffered and sustained, as well by occasion of your first unlawful marriage solemnised between your Highness and the Lady Katherine, late Princess Dowager, as by occasion of the said unlawful marriage between your Highness and the said late Queen Anne, at the most humble petition and intercession of us your nobles of this realm, for the ardent love and fervent affection which your Highness beareth to the conservation of the peace and unity of the same and for the good and quiet governance thereof, of your most excellent goodness to enter into marriage again, and have chosen and taken a right noble, virtuous, and excellent Lady, Queen Jane, to your true and lawful wife, and have lawfully celebrated and solemnised marriage with her according to the laws of Holy Church, who for her convenient years, excellent beauty, and pureness of flesh and blood is apt (God willing) to conceive issue by your Highness, which marriage is so pure and sincere, without spot, doubt, or impediment, that the issue procreated under the same, when it shall please Almighty God to send it, cannot be lawfully, truly, nor justly interrupted or disturbed of the right and title in the succession of your Crown; It may therefore now please your most gracious Majesty, at the most humble petition and intercession of us your Nobles and Commons in this present Parliament assembled, as well for the clear extinguishment of all ambiguities and doubts as for a pure and perfect unity of us your most humble and obedient subjects and of all our posterities, that it may be enacted:

[That the marriage with the Lady Katherine is void, 'any licence, dispensation, or any other act or acts going before or ensuing the same or to the contrary thereof in any wise notwithstanding'; and the issue of the marriage is illegitimate.]

[VI. The marriage with the 'late Queen Anne' 'shall be taken, reputed, deemed, and adjudged to be of no force, strength, virtue, nor effect'; and the issue of the marriage shall be deemed to be illegitimate.]

* * * * * *

[VIII entails the Crown, first, on male heirs by the marriage with Queen Jane; next, on male heirs 'by any other lawful wife'; next, on female heirs by Queen Jane; and lastly on female heirs by any future wife.]

IX. And forasmuch as it standeth at this present time in the only pleasure and will of Almighty God whether your Majesty shall have heirs begotten and procreated between your Highness and your said most dear and entirely beloved wife Queen Jane, or else any lawful heirs and issues hereafter of your own body begotten by any other lawful wife, and if such heirs should fail (as God defend) and no provision made in your life who should rule

and govern this realm for lack of such heirs, that then this realm
after your transitory life shall be destitute of a Governor, or else
percase[1] encumbered with such a person that would covet to
aspire to the same whom the subjects of this realm shall not find
in their hearts to love, dread, and obediently serve as their
Sovereign Lord; And if your Grace, afore it may be certainly
known whether ye shall have heirs or no, should suddenly name
and declare any person or persons to succeed after your decease
and for lack of heirs of your body lawfully begotten into the royal
estate of the imperial Crown of this realm, then it is to be doubted
that such person that should be so named might happen to take
great heart and courage and by presumption fall to inobedience
and rebellion; By occasion of which premises great division and
dissension may be and is very likely to arise and spring in this
realm, to the great peril and destruction of us your most humble
and obedient subjects and of all our posterities, if remedy for the
same should not be provided: For reformation and remedy
whereof, we your most bounden and loving subjects, most obediently knowledging that your Majesty most victoriously, prudently, politicly, and indifferently hath maintained, defended,
governed, and ruled this realm in good peace, rest, quietness, and
obedience during all the time of your most gracious reign, which we
most heartily desire might continue for ever, putting all our whole
trust and confidence in your Highness and nothing doubting but
your Majesty, if ye should fail of heirs of your body lawfully begotten (which God defend), for the hearty love and fervent affection that ye bear to this realm, and for avoiding all the occasions
of division afore rehearsed, so earnestly mindeth the wealth[2] of
the same that ye can best and most prudently provide such a
Governor for us and this your realm as shall and will succeed and
follow in the just and right tract of all your proceedings, and
maintain, keep, and defend the same, and all the laws and ordinances established in your gracious time for the wealth of this
realm, which all we desire, whereby we your most loving and
obedient subjects and our heirs and successors shall and may live,
as near as may be, in as good peace, unity, and obedience after
your decease as we have lived in the time of your most gracious
reign; Do therefore most humbly beseech your Highness that it
may be enacted, for avoiding of all ambiguities, doubts, divisions,
and occasions in that behalf, by your most royal Majesty, by the
assent of us the Lords spiritual and temporal and the Commons
in this your present Parliament assembled and by authority of

---

[1] Peradventure, perhaps.　　　　　　[2] See note on p. 33 above.

the same, That your Highness shall have full and plenar[1] power
and authority to give, dispose, appoint, assign, declare, and limit,
by your letters patents under your great seal or else by your last
Will made in writing and signed with your most gracious hand, at
your only pleasure from time to time hereafter, the imperial Crown
of this realm and all other the premises thereunto belonging, to
be, remain, succeed, and come after your decease, and for lack
of lawful heirs of your body to be procreated and begotten as is
afore limited by this Act, to such person or persons in possession
and remainder as shall please your Highness, and according to
such estate and after such manner, form, fashion, order, and condition, as shall be expressed, declared, named, and limited in your
said letters patents or by your said last Will. And we your most
humble and obedient subjects do faithfully promise to your
Majesty, by one common assent, that after your decease and for
lack of heirs of your body lawfully begotten as is afore rehearsed,
we our heirs and successors shall accept and take, love, dread,
serve, and allonly[2] obey such person and persons, males or females,
as your Majesty shall give your said imperial Crown unto by
authority of this Act, and to none other, and wholly to stick to
them, as true and faithful subjects ought to do to their regal
rulers, governors, and supreme heads.

X. And for sure corroboration thereof, be it further enacted by
authority aforesaid that such person and persons as to whom it
shall please your Majesty to dispose, limit, and assign your said
Crown and other the premises thereto appertaining by your
letters patents or by your last Will as is aforesaid, shall have and
enjoy the same, after your decease and for lack of heirs of your
body lawfully begotten, according to such estate and after such
manner, form, fashion, order, and condition, as shall be thereof
expressed, mentioned, and contained in your said letters patents
or in your said last Will, in as large and ample manner as if such
person and persons had been your lawful heirs to the imperial
Crown of this realm, and as if the same Crown of this realm had
been given and limited to them plainly and particularly by special
names and sufficient terms and words by the full and immediate
authority of this your most High Court of Parliament.

XI. And it is further enacted by authority aforesaid, that if
any of your heirs or children hereafter do usurp the one of them
upon the other in the Crown of this realm, or claim or challenge
your said imperial Crown in any other form or degree of descent or
succession than is afore limited by this Act, or if any person or

---

[1] Complete, entire.   [2] See note on p. 396 below.

persons to whom it shall please your Highness of your most
excellent goodness by authority of this Act to give and dispose
your said Crown and dignity of this realm, or the heirs of any of
them, do at any time hereafter demand, challenge, or claim
your said Crown...otherwise or in any other course, form,
degree, or condition than the same shall be given, disposed, and
limited unto them by your Highness by virtue and authority of
this Act; or if any such person or persons to whom your Majesty
shall hereafter give or dispose your said Crown by authority of
this Act, or any of their heirs, do interrupt or let any of the heirs
of your Majesty that is or shall be begotten, born, and procreated
under your lawful, pure, sincere, and undoubted marriage now
had and solemnised between your Highness and your said most
dear and entirely beloved wife Queen Jane, or any other your
lawful heirs hereafter to be begotten of your body by any other
lawful marriage, peaceably and quietly to keep, have, and enjoy
the said imperial Crown and other the premises by course of inheritance according to the limitation thereof expressed and declared by this Act, that then all and singular the offenders in any
of the premises contrary to this Act, and all their abettors, maintainers, fautors[1], counsellors, and aiders therein shall be deemed
and adjudged high traitors to the realm; And that every such
offence shall be accepted, reputed, and taken to be high treason,
and the offenders therein, their aiders, maintainers, fautors, counsellors, abettors, and every of them, for every such offence shall
suffer such judgment and pains of death, losses, and forfeitures of
lands, goods, and privileges of sanctuary as in any cases of high
treason; And over that, as well your said heirs and children, as
every such person and persons to whom your Highness shall
limit your said Crown in form as is aforesaid, and every of their
heirs, for every such offence above specified by them or any of
them to be committed, shall lose and forfeit as well all such right,
title, and interest that they may claim or challenge in or to the
Crown of this realm, as heirs by descent, or by reason of any gift
or act that shall be done by your Highness for his or their advancement by authority of this Act, or otherwise by any manner
of means or pretence, whatsoever it be.

XII. And be it further enacted by authority aforesaid, that
if any person or persons, of what estate, dignity, degree, or condition soever they be, at any time hereafter, by words, writing,
imprinting, or by any exterior act or deed, maliciously or willingly
procure or do, or cause to be procured and done, directly or in-

[1] See note on p. 45 above.

directly, any thing or things to the peril of your most royal person, or to the peril of the person of any of your heirs or successors having the royal estate of the Crown of this realm, or maliciously or willingly give occasion by words, writing, print, deed, or act whereby your Highness or any your said heirs or successors having the royal estate of the Crown of this realm might be disturbed or interrupted of the Crown of this realm; or by words, writing, print, deed, or act, procure or do, or cause to be procured or done, any thing or things to or for the interruption, repeal, or adnullation of this Act or of anything therein contained, or of anything that shall be done by your Highness in the limitation and disposition of your Crown by authority of the same; or by words, writing, print, deed, or act, procure or cause to be procured or done any thing or things to the prejudice, slander, disturbance, or derogation of the said lawful matrimony solemnised between your Majesty and the said Queen Jane or any other your lawful wife or wives hereafter by your Highness to be taken, or to the peril, slander, or disherison of any of the issues and heirs of your Highness being limited by this Act to inherit and to be inheritable to the Crown of this realm in such form as is aforesaid, or to the interruption or disherison of any such person or persons to whom your Highness shall assign and dispose your said imperial Crown by authority of this Act, as is afore remembered, whereby any such issues or heirs of your Highness or such other person or persons might be destroyed, disturbed, or interrupted, in fame, body, or title, of the inheritance to the Crown of this realm as to them is limited in this Act in form above rehearsed, or as to them shall be limited and assigned by your Highness by virtue and authority of this Act; or if any person or persons, by words, writing, imprinting, or any other exterior act, directly or indirectly, accept or take, judge or believe, any of the marriages had and solemnised between the King's Highness and the said Lady Katherine, or between the King's Highness and the said late Queen Anne, to be good, lawful, or of any effect; or by words, writing, printing, or any other exterior act, directly or indirectly, slander, interrupt, impeach, gainsay, or impugn the lawful judgments and sentences of the said most Reverend Father in God, Thomas, Archbishop of Canterbury and Primate of all England, for and concerning the divorces and separations of the said unlawful marriages or any of them; or by words, writing, print, or any other exterior act, directly or indirectly, take, accept, name, or call, by any pretence, any of the children born and procreated under any of the said unlawful marriages to be legitimate and lawful children of your Majesty; or if any person or persons craftily imagine, invent, or attempt, by colour of any pretence, to deprive the King's Highness, the Queen, or the heirs of their bodies begotten, or any other the heirs of the King's body lawfully begotten, or any person or persons to whom the King's Highness shall dispose, give, and limit the Crown of this realm by authority of this Act, of any of their titles, styles, names, degrees, or royal estates[1] or regal power; or if any person or persons at any time hereafter, being required or commanded by the King's Highness or by such person or persons as shall be authorised by his Grace or his lawful heirs to make or take an oath to answer such questions and interrogatories as shall be objected[2] to them, upon any clause, article, sentence, or word contained in this Act, do contemptuously or utterly refuse to make or take such oath, or without frustatory delay do not make or take the same oath, or after the making or taking such oath do contemptuously refuse directly to answer to such questions and interrogatories as shall be objected concerning the same or any part thereof; that then every such person and persons, of what estate, degree, or condition soever he or they be, and their aiders, counsellors, maintainers, and abettors, and every of them, for every such offence afore declared shall be adjudged high traitors, And that every such offence afore specified shall be adjudged high treason....

[XIII. Offenders are not to have the privileges of Sanctuary.]

[XIV. Upon the King's demise, issue male under 18 or female unmarried under 16 shall be under the guardianship of their mother and a Council, or of a Council only, as the King's Will shall direct; and persons who 'by writing, printing, or exterior deed or act, directly or indirectly, procure or do, or cause to be procured or done, any thing or things to the let or disturbance of the same' shall be guilty of high treason.]

[XV. All subjects are to be sworn to the performance of the Act in a form of oath recited in the statute.]

* * * * *

28 Henr. VIII, c. 7: *Statutes of the Realm*, iii, 655.

(5) Act dissolving the Cleves Marriage, 1540

The dissolution of the pretensed marriage with the Lady Anne of Cleves

The Lords spiritual and temporal and the Commons in this present Parliament assembled, calling to their remembrance the manifold detestable conflicts intestine, battles, mortalities of

---

[1] See note on p. 388 above.

[2] *I.e.* offered in discourse or argument.

people, and disherisons which heretofore have sprongen and
growen in this realm by occasion of diversities of titles to the
Crown of the same, which most chiefly grew and insurged by
doubts of marriages and of the incertainty of the succession of
the same; Considering also that, thanks be to God, all manner
titles be now conjoined, consolidate, united, and vested allonly[1]
in the King's most royal person, so that his Majesty is and standeth presently[2] a just and undoubted, pure and perfect King of
this realm, against whom none impediment or objection can or
may be by any manner of means alleged, And that it appertaineth
to the office and policy of all civil bodies of realms and countries,
most chiefly next to their duties to God, to foresee and provide
for the surety and certainty of the succession of their Kings and
chief governors, forasmuch as upon the certainty thereof dependeth their whole common wealth[3], rest, peace, and tranquillity;
And lately understanding that great ambiguities, doubts, and
questions have been moved in the marriage solemnised between
the King's Majesty and the Lady Anne of Cleves, whereby great
troubles and inconveniences might hereafter spring and grow in
this realm to the imminent danger of the destruction of the subjects thereof if remedy should not speedily be provided for the
same: The temporal Lords and Commons have therefore made
their most humble intercession and petition to the King's most
royal Majesty, That it may please his Highness of his accustomable goodness to commit the state of his said marriage, with all
the circumstances and dependances thereof, unto the prelates and
clergy of this realm to be searched, examined, defined, and determined by them according to the truth, justice, and equity, in such
wise as should stand with God's pleasure, the King's honour, and
the wealth and tranquillity of this realm [*then follows the decision
of the synod of the clergy of Canterbury and York against the validity
of the marriage, and the Lady Anne's assent thereto*]. In consideration whereof the said Lords spiritual and temporal and the Commons in this present Parliament assembled most humbly beseech
the King's most royal Majesty that it may be assented, declared,
and enacted by authority of this present Parliament, as well for
the surety and certainty of his Highness's posterity and succession
as for the wealth, quietness, rest, and tranquillity of this realm,
that the marriage between his Highness and the said Lady Anne
of Cleves is clearly void and of no force, value, nor effect; And

[1] An emphatic form of 'only.'
[2] At the present time.
[3] See note on p. 33 above.

that his Majesty is at his liberty and pleasure to contract matrimony and marry with any other women not prohibited by the Law of God to marry with his Highness....

II. And be it also enacted by the authority abovesaid, that if any person or persons, of what estate, degree, dignity, or condition soever he or they be, after the first day of September next coming, by writing or imprinting, or by any other exterior act, word, or deed, directly or indirectly, accept or take, judge or believe the said pretensed marriage had between his Majesty and the said Lady Anne of Cleves to be good, lawful, or of any effect, Or by words, writing, printing, deed, or act, procure or do, or cause to be procured or done, any thing or things to or for the interruption, repeal, or annullation of this Act, or of anything therein contained, That then every such person and persons, of what estate, degree, or condition soever he or they be, and their aiders, counsellors, maintainers, and abettors, and every of them, for every such offence before specified shall be adjudged high traitors, and every such offence shall be adjudged high treason....

[III. Pardon of all acts done for dissolving the said marriage.]
32 Henr. VIII, c. 25: *Statutes of the Realm*, iii, 781.

(6) Third Succession Act, 1543

An Act concerning the establishment of the King's Majesty's Succession in the Imperial Crown of the Realm

[*After reciting* 28 *Henr. VIII, c.* 7 (*the Second Succession Act*) *the statute continues*] Since the making of which Act, the King's Majesty hath only issue of his body lawfully begotten betwixt his Highness and his said late wife Queen Jane, the noble and excellent prince Prince Edward, whom Almighty God long preserve; and also his Majesty hath now of late...taken to his wife the most virtuous and gracious Lady Katherine, now Queen of England, late wife of John Neville, knight, Lord Latymer, deceased, by whom as yet his Majesty hath none issue, but may have full well when it shall please God; And forasmuch as our said most dread Sovereign Lord the King, upon good and just grounds and causes, intendeth by God's grace to make a voyage royal in his Majesty's most royal person into the realm of France against his ancient enemy the French King[1], his Highness most prudently and wisely considering and calling to his remembrance how this realm standeth at this present time in the case of

---

[1] Henry declared war on France on June 22, and on July 14 he crossed the Channel to Calais.

succession...recognising and knowledging also that it is the only pleasure and will of Almighty God how long his Highness or his said entirely beloved son Prince Edward shall live, and whether the said Prince shall have heirs of his body lawfully begotten or not, or whether his Highness shall have heirs begotten and procreated between his Majesty and his said most dear and entirely beloved wife Queen Katherine that now is, or any lawful heirs and issues hereafter of his own body begotten by any other his lawful wife; And albeit that the King's most excellent Majesty, for default of such heirs as be inheritable by the said Act, might, by the authority of the said Act, give and dispose the said imperial Crown and other the premises by his letters patents under his great seal, or by his last Will in writing signed with his most gracious hand, to any person or persons of such estate therein as should please his Highness to limit and appoint, yet to the intent that his Majesty's disposition and mind therein should be openly declared and manifestly known and notified, as well to the Lords spiritual and temporal as to all other his loving and obedient subjects of this his realm, to the intent that their assent and consent might appear to concur with thus far as followeth of his Majesty's declaration in this behalf; His Majesty therefore thinketh convenient afore his departure beyond the seas that it be enacted...that in case it shall happen to the King's Majesty and the said excellent Prince his yet only son...and heir apparent to decease without heir of either of their bodies lawfully begotten (as God defend), so that there be no such heir male or female of any of their two bodies to have and inherit the said imperial Crown and other his dominions according and in such manner and form as in the foresaid Act and now in this is declared, That then the said imperial Crown and all other the premises shall be to the Lady Mary the King's Highness's daughter and to the heirs of the body of the same Lady Mary lawfully begotten, with such conditions as by his Highness shall be limited by his letters patents under his great seal, or by his Majesty's last Will in writing signed with his gracious hand; and for default of such issue the said imperial Crown and other the premises shall be to the Lady Elizabeth the King's second daughter and to the heirs of the body of the said Lady Elizabeth lawfully begotten, with such conditions, [etc.]...

[II. On breach of these conditions by the Lady Mary, the Crown shall come to the Lady Elizabeth and her heirs 'in such like manner and form as though the said Lady Mary were then dead without any heir of her body begotten.']

[III. On breach of the conditions by the Lady Elizabeth, the Crown shall come 'to such person and persons and of such estate and estates as the King's Highness by his letters patents sealed under his great seal, or by his last Will in writing signed with his Majesty's hand, shall limit and appoint.']

[IV. Provided that if on breach of the conditions by the Lady Mary the Lady Elizabeth be then dead without heirs, the Crown shall come 'to such person and persons,' etc. . . . *as above*.]

[V. If no condition be limited by letters patent or Will, then the estate of the Ladies Mary and Elizabeth in the Crown shall be absolute.]

VI. And forasmuch as it standeth in the only pleasure and will of Almighty God whether the King's Majesty shall have any heirs begotten and procreated between his Highness and his said most entirely beloved wife Queen Katherine or by any other his lawful wife, or whether the said Prince Edward shall have issue of his body lawfully begotten, or whether the Lady Mary and Lady Elizabeth or any of them shall have any issue of any of their several bodies lawfully begotten, and if such heirs should fail (which God defend) and no provision made in the King's life who should rule and govern this realm for lack of such heirs as in this present Act is afore mentioned, that then this realm after the King's transitory life and for lack of such heirs should be destitute of a lawful Governor to order, rule, and govern the same; Be it therefore enacted by the authority of this present Parliament, that the King's Highness shall have full power and authority to give, dispose, appoint, assign, declare, and limit, by his gracious letters patents under his great seal, or else by his Highness's last Will made in writing and signed with his most gracious hand, at his only pleasure from time to time hereafter, the imperial Crown of this realm and all other the premises to be, remain, succeed, and come, after his decease and for lack of lawful heirs...to such person or persons in remainder or reversion as shall please his Highness, and according to such estate and after such manner and form, fashion, order, or condition as shall be expressed, declared, named, and limited in his Highness's letters patents or by his last Will in writing signed with his most gracious hand as is aforesaid; anything contained in this present Act or in the said former Act to the contrary thereof in any wise notwithstanding.

[VII imposes a new form of oath in place of the two oaths hitherto required, one under 28 Henr. VIII, c. 7 (the Second Succession Act) and the other under 28 Henr. VIII, c. 10 (the Act against the authority of the See of Rome). The new oath repudiates the Papal authority, declares allegiance to the King and his successors as determined by the Act, and affirms the Royal Supremacy.]

[VIII indicates the persons, spiritual and temporal, who are required to take the oath.]

IX. And it is also enacted by the authority aforesaid, that if any person or persons limited or commanded by the authority of this Act to make and take the said oath, or commanded by any other person or persons authorised by the King's Highness's commission under his great seal to make the said oath, obstinately refuse that to do, that then every such offence and contempt shall be high treason. . . .

X. And be it further enacted by authority aforesaid, that if any person or persons, of what estate, degree, dignity, or condition soever they be, at any time hereafter by words, writing, imprinting, or by any exterior act or deed, maliciously or willingly procure or do, or cause to be procured or done, directly or indirectly, any thing or things to or for the interruption, repeal, or adnullation of this Act, or of any thing therein contained, or of anything that shall be done by the King's Highness in the limitation and disposition of his Majesty's Crown and other the premises by authority of the same, or to the peril, slander, or disinherison of any of the issues and heirs of the King's Majesty being limited by this Act to inherit and to be inheritable to the Crown of this realm in such form as is aforesaid, or to the interruption or disherison of any person or persons to whom the imperial Crown of this realm and other the premises is assigned, limited, and appointed by this Act, or shall be by the King's Majesty's letters patents under his Highness's great seal or by his last Will in writing signed with his most gracious hand limited and disposed by authority of this Act as is aforesaid, whereby any such issues or heirs of the King's Majesty or such other person or persons might be destroyed, disturbed, or interrupted in body or title of the inheritance of the Crown of this realm as to them is limited in this Act in form above rehearsed, or as to them shall be limited and assigned by the King's Highness by virtue and authority of this Act, that then every such person and persons, of what estate, degree, or condition soever he or they be, and their aiders, counsellors, maintainers, and abettors, and every of them, for every such offence afore declared shall be adjudged high traitors, and that every such offence afore specified shall be adjudged high treason. . . .

*   *   *   *   *   *

35 Henr. VIII, c. 1: *Statutes of the Realm*, iii, 955.

(7) First Treasons Act of Edward VI, 1547

An Act for the Repeal of certain Statutes concerning Treasons,
Felonies, etc.

Nothing being more godly, more sure, more to be wished
and desired, betwixt a Prince the Supreme Head and Ruler and
the subjects whose governor and head he is, than on the Prince's
part great clemency and indulgency, and rather too much forgiveness and remission of his royal power and just punishment
than exact severity and justice to be shewed, and on the subjects'
behalf that they should obey rather for love, and for the necessity
and love of a king and prince, than for fear of his strait and severe
laws; yet such times at some time cometh in the commonwealth
that it is necessary and expedient for the repressing of the insolency and unruliness of men and for the foreseeing and providing of remedies against rebellion, insurrection, or such mischiefs as God, sometime with us displeased, for our punishment
doth inflict and lay upon us, or the Devil at God's permission, to
assay[1] the good and God's elect, doth sow and set amongst us,
the which Almighty God with his help and man's policy hath
always been content and pleased to have stayed[2] that sharper
laws as a harder bridle should be made to stay those men and
facts[3] that might else be occasion, cause, and authors of further
inconvenience; The which thing caused the Prince of most
famous memory King Henry the Eighth...to make and enact
certain laws and statutes which might seem and appear to men of
exterior realms and many of the King's Majesty's subjects very
strait, sore, extreme, and terrible, although they were then when
they were made not without great consideration and policy moved
and established, and for the time to the avoidance of further inconvenience very expedient and necessary; But, as in tempest or
winter one course[4] and garment is convenient, in calm or warm
weather a more liberal race or lighter garment both may and ought
to be followed and used, so we have seen divers strait and sore
laws made in one Parliament, the time so requiring, in a more
calm and quiet reign of another Prince by like authority and
Parliament repealed and taken away; the which most high
clemency and royal example of his Majesty's most noble progenitors, the King's Highness, of his tender and godly nature

---

[1] Test.
[2] In the sense of hinder or prevent.
[3] In the common 16th and 17th century sense of crimes or evil deeds.
[4] Race.

most given to mercy and love of his subjects, willing to follow, and perceiving the hearty and sincere love that his most loving subjects, both the Lords and Commons, doth bear unto his Highness now in this his Majesty's tender age, willing also to gratify the same therefore, and minding further to provoke his said subjects with great indulgency and clemency shewed on his Highness's behalf to more love and kindness towards his Majesty (if it may be) and upon trust that they will not abuse the same, but rather be encouraged thereby more faithfully and with more diligence (if it may be) and care for his Majesty to serve his Highness now in this his tender age, is contented and pleased that the severity of certain laws here following be mitigated and remitted: Be it therefore ordained and enacted....That from henceforth none act, deed, or offence being by Act of Parliament or Statute made treason or petit treason¹ by words, writing, ciphering², deeds, or otherwise whatsoever, shall be taken, had, deemed, or adjudged to be high treason or petit treason but only such as be treason or petit treason in or by [25 *Edw. III, st. 5, c.* 2] and such offences as hereafter shall by this present Act be expressed and declared to be treason or petit treason, and none other; Nor that any pains of death, penalty, or forfeiture in any wise ensue or be to any of the offenders for the doing or committing any treason or petit treason, other than such as be in the said Estatute made in the said 25th year of the reign of the said King Edward the Third or by this present Estatute ordained or provided; Any Act or Acts of Parliament, Statute or Statutes, had or made at any time heretofore, or after the said 25th year of the reign of the said late King Edward the Third, or any other declaration or matter to the contrary in any wise notwithstanding.

[II repeals 'all Acts of Parliament and Estatutes touching, mentioning, or in any wise concerning religion or opinions,' namely, 5 Rich. II, st. 2, c. 5; 2 Henr. V, st. 1, c. 7; 25 Henr. VIII, c. 14; 31 Henr. VIII, c. 14 (the Statute of Six Articles); 34 & 35 Henr. VIII, c. 1; and 35 Henr. VIII, c. 5.]

[III repeals all new felonies created by statute since 23 April, 1547.]

[IV repeals 31 Henr. VIII, c. 8 and 34 & 35 Henr. VIII, c. 23, giving statutory authority to royal proclamations.]

V. And be it enacted by the authority aforesaid, that if any person or persons at any time after the first day of March next

¹ 25 Edw. III, st. 5, c. 2, defined petit treason as 'when a servant slayeth his master, or a wife her husband, or when a man secular or religious slayeth his prelate to whom he oweth faith and obedience.' It continued to exist as a separate offence until 1828 (Stephen, iii, 35).

² *I.e.* by writing in cipher.

coming, by open preaching, express words or sayings, do affirm or set forth that the King, his heirs or successors, kings of this realm for the time being, is not or ought not to be Supreme Head in earth of the Church of England and Ireland or of any of them immediately under God, or that the Bishop of Rome or any other person or persons other than the King of England for the time being is or ought to be by the laws of God Supreme Head of the same Churches or of any of them, or that the King, his heirs or successors kings of this realm, is not or ought not to be King of England, France, and Ireland, or of any of them, Or, after the said first day of March, do compass or imagine by open preaching, express words or sayings, to depose or deprive the King, his heirs or successors kings of this realm, from his or their royal estate or titles to or of the realms aforesaid, or do openly publish or say by express words or sayings that any other person or persons other than the King, his heirs or successors kings of this realm, of right ought to be kings of the realms aforesaid or of any of them, or to have and enjoy the same or any of them; That then every such offender, being thereof duly convicted or attainted by the laws of this realm, their aiders, comforters, abettors, procurers, and counsellors,...shall [*suffer forfeiture of goods and imprisonment during the King's pleasure for the first offence: forfeiture of lands and imprisonment for life for the second: and the penalties of high treason for the third*].

VI. And be it further enacted by the authority aforesaid, that if any person or persons, at any time after the said first day of March next coming, by writing, printing, overt deed or act, affirm or set forth [*that the King is not or...*] that the Bishop of Rome or any other person or persons other than the King of England for the time being is or ought to be by the laws of God or otherwise the Supreme Head in earth of the same Church or any of them, or do, after the said first day of March, compass or imagine, by writing, printing, overt deed or act, to depose or deprive the King, his heirs or successors kings of this realm, from his or their royal estate or titles of the King of England, France, and Ireland, or of any of them, or by writing, printing, overt deed or act, do affirm that any other person or persons other than the King, his heirs and successors, is or of right ought to be King of the realms of England, France, or Ireland or to have and enjoy the same or any of them, That then every such offence and offences shall be deemed and adjudged high treason, and the offender and offenders, their aiders, comforters, abettors, procurers, and counsellors therein, convicted or attainted according to the laws and statutes of this

realm, shall be deemed and adjudged high traitors, and shall suffer
pains of death and lose and forfeit all their goods and chattels,
lands and tenements, to the King as in cases of high treason.

    *   *   *   *   *   *

VIII. And be it further enacted by the authority aforesaid,
that if any of the heirs of the King our said Sovereign Lord that
now is, or any person or persons to whom the Crown and dignity
of this realm is limited and appointed by [35 *Henr. VIII, c.* 1 . . .]
or the heirs of any of them, do at any time hereafter usurp the one
of them upon the other in the Crown of this realm, or demand,
challenge, or claim the same otherwise or in any other form or
degree of descent or succession, or in any other course, form,
degree, or condition but only in such manner and form as is
declared by the said Estatute, Or if any of the said heirs or persons aforesaid do interrupt or let the King's Highness that now is
peaceably and quietly to keep, have, and enjoy the said imperial
Crown, That then all and singular the offenders, their aiders,
comforters, abettors, procurers, and counsellors therein, shall be
deemed and adjudged high traitors, and shall suffer and incur
the pains of death, losses, and forfeitures as is aforesaid in cases of
high treason.

    *   *   *   *   *   *

XX. Provided also and be it declared and enacted by the
authority abovesaid, that concealment or keeping secret any high
treason shall be from henceforth adjudged, deemed, and taken
misprision of treason[1], and the offenders therein shall forfeit and
suffer as in cases of misprision of treason, as heretofore hath been
used; anything abovementioned to the contrary notwithstanding.

    *   *   *   *   *   *

XXII. Provided always and be it enacted by the authority
aforesaid, that no person or persons, after the first day of February
next coming, shall be indicted, arraigned, condemned, or convicted for any offence of treason, petit treason, misprision of
treason, or for any words before specified to be spoken after the
said first day of February, for which the same offender, speaker,
offenders, or speakers, shall in any wise suffer any pains of death,
imprisonment, loss or forfeiture of his goods, chattels, lands, or
tenements, unless the same offender, speaker, offenders, or
speakers be accused by two sufficient and lawful witnesses, or
shall willingly without violence confess the same.

    1 Edw. VI, c. 12: *Statutes of the Realm,* iv, 18

---

[1] See note on p. 149 above.

(8) Second Treasons Act of Edward VI, 1552

An Act for the punishment of divers Treasons

Forasmuch as it is most necessary for common policy and duty of subjects above all things to prohibit, restrain, and extinct all manner of shameful slanders which might grow, happen, or arise to their Sovereign Lord the King's Majesty, which when they be heard, seen, or understood cannot be but odible[1] and also abhorred of all those sorts that be true and loving subjects, if in any point they may, do, or shall touch his Majesty, upon whom dependeth the whole unity and universal weal of this realm; Without providing wherefor too great a scope of unreasonable liberty should be given to all cankered and traitorous hearts, and the King's loving subjects should not declare unto their Sovereign Lord now being, which unto them hath been and is most entirely both beloved and esteemed, their undoubted sincerity and truth: Be it therefore enacted...that if any person or persons, after the first day of June next coming, by open preaching, express words or sayings, do expressly, directly, and advisedly set forth and affirm that the King that now is is an heretic, schismatic, tyrant, infidel, or usurper of the Crown, or that any his heirs or successors to whom the Crown of this realm is limited [*by 35 Henr. VIII, c. 1...*] being in lawful possession of the Crown, is an heretic [etc....], That then every such offender, being thereof duly convicted or attainted by the laws of this realm, their abettors, procurers, and counsellors, and all and every their aiders and comforters, knowing the said offences or any of them to be done [*shall suffer forfeiture of goods and imprisonment during the King's pleasure for the first offence: forfeiture of profits of lands and spiritual promotions for life, and of all goods, and perpetual imprisonment for the second offence: and the penalties of high treason with forfeiture of lands and goods for the third offence*].

II. And be it further enacted by the authority aforesaid, that if any person or persons, at any time after the said first day of June next coming, by writing, printing, painting, carving, or graving, do directly, expressly, and advisedly publish, set forth, and affirm that the King that now is, or any his heirs or successors limited as is beforesaid, is an heretic [etc....], that then every such offence and offences shall be deemed and adjudged high treason, and the offender and offenders, their abettors, procurers, and counsellors, and all and every their aiders and comforters, knowing the said offences or any of them to be done, being thereof

[1] Hateful.

convicted or attainted according to the laws and statutes of this realm, shall be deemed and adjudged high traitors, and shall suffer pains of death, and lose and forfeit all their goods and chattels, lands and tenements, to the King as in cases of high treason.

[III. Detaining the King's ships and fortresses is declared high treason[1].]

* * * * * *

IX. Provided always and be it enacted by the authority aforesaid, that no person or persons, after the first day of June next coming, shall be indicted, arraigned, condemned, convicted, or attainted for any of the treasons or offences aforesaid, or for any other treasons that now be or hereafter shall be, which shall hereafter be perpetrated, committed, or done, unless the same offender or offenders be thereof accused by two lawful accusers, which said accusers at the time of the arraignment of the party accused, if they be then living, shall be brought in person before the party so accused, and avow and maintain that that they have to say against the said party to prove him guilty of the treasons or offences contained in the bill of indictment laid against the party arraigned; unless the said party arraigned shall willingly without violence confess the same.

* * * * * *

5 & 6 Edw. VI, c. 11: *Statutes of the Realm*, iv, 144.

(9) First Treasons Act of Mary, 1553

An Act repealing certain Treasons, Felonies, and Praemunire

Forasmuch as the state of every King, Ruler, and Governor of any realm, dominion, or commonalty standeth and consisteth more assured by the love and favour of the subject toward their Sovereign Ruler and Governor than in the dread and fear of laws made with rigorous pains and extreme punishment for not obeying of their Sovereign Ruler and Governor; And laws also justly made for the preservation of the common weal, without extreme punishment or great penalty, are more often for the most part obeyed and kept than laws and statutes made with great and extreme punishments, and in especial such laws and statutes so made, whereby not only the ignorant and rude, unlearned people, but also learned and expert people minding honesty, are often and many times trapped and snared, yea, many times for words only, without other fact or deed done or perpetrated: The Queen's most excellent Majesty, calling to remembrance that many, as well honourable and noble persons as other of good reputation

---

[1] Cf. Henry VIII's Treasons Act of 1534 (p. 388 above) and Elizabeth's Act of 1572 (p. 417 below).

within this her Grace's realm of England, have of late, for words only without other opinion, fact, or deed, suffered shameful death not accustomed to nobles; Her Highness therefore, of her accustomed clemency and mercy, minding to avoid and put away the occasion and cause of like chances hereafter to ensue, trusting her loving subjects will, for her clemency to them shewed, love, serve, and obey her Grace the more heartily and faithfully than for dread or fear of pains of body, is contented and pleased that the severity of suchlike extreme dangerous and painful laws shall be abolished, adnulled, and made frustrate and void: Be it therefore ordained and enacted [*that no act or offence shall be treason, petty treason, or misprision of treason but such as are so declared by 25 Edw. III, st. 5, c. 2*].

* * * * *

1 Mary, st. 1, c. 1: *Statutes of the Realm*, iv, 198.

(10) Act against Traitorous Words, 1555

An Act for the punishment of Traitorous Words against the Queen's Majesty

Forasmuch as now of late divers naughty, seditious, malicious, and heretical persons, not having the fear of God before their eyes, but in a devilish sort, contrary to the duty of their allegiance, have congregated themselves together in conventicles[1] in divers and sundry profane places within the City of London, esteeming themselves to be in the true faith where indeed they are in errors and heresies and out of the true trade[2] of Christ's Catholic Religion, and in the same places at several times using their fantastical and schismatical services lately taken away and abolished by authority of Parliament, have of their most malicious and cankered stomachs prayed against the Queen's Majesty that God would turn her heart from idolatry to the true faith or else to shorten her days or take her quickly out of the way: Which prayer was never heard nor read to have been used by any good Christian man against any Prince though he were a pagan and infidel, and much less against any Christian Prince, and especially so virtuous a Princess as our Sovereign Lady that now is is known to be, whose faith is and always hath been most true and Catholic, and consonant and agreeing with Christ's Catholic Church throughout the world dispersed: For reformation whereof, Be it enacted by the authority of this present Parliament, that every

---

[1] In the sense of a meeting for the exercise of religion otherwise than as sanctioned by law. This special sense of the word begins with Henry VIII (*Oxford Dictionary*).

[2] *I.e.* way or path.

such person and persons which, since the beginning of this present Parliament, have by express words and sayings prayed, required, or desired as is aforesaid, or hereafter shall pray by express words or sayings that God should shorten her days or take her out of the way (whose life Almighty God long preserve), or any such like malicious prayer amounting to the same effect, their procurers and abettors therein, shall be taken, reputed, and judged traitors, and every such praying, requiring, or desiring shall be judged, taken, and reputed high treason, and the offenders therein, their procurers and abettors, being thereof lawfully convict according to the laws of this realm, shall have, suffer, and forfeit as in cases of high treason.

[II. Persons repenting of such offences committed, 'during this session of this present Parliament,' and upon arraignment submitting themselves to the Queen's mercy, may be adjudged 'such corporal punishment other than death' as the judges before whom they are tried may appoint.]

1 & 2 Philip & Mary, c. 9: *Statutes of the Realm*, iv, 254.

(11) Second Treasons Act of Mary, 1555

An Act whereby certain Offences be made Treasons: and also for the Government of the King's and Queen's Majesties' Issue

Forasmuch as the great mercy and clemency heretofore declared by the Queen's Highness, in releasing the penal laws made by her progenitors, hath given occasion to many cankered and traitorous hearts to imagine, practise, and attempt things stirring the people to disobedience and rebellion against her Highness, common policy and duty of subjects require that some law be eftsoons[1] established to restrain the malice of such wicked and evil doers, whereby they may be prohibited to blow abroad such shameful slanders and lies as they daily invent and imagine of her Highness and of the King's Majesty her most lawful husband, which when they be heard cannot be but odible[2] and detested of all good men, considering they touch their Majesties, upon whom dependeth the whole unity and universal wealth[3] of this realm: In consideration whereof be it ordained and enacted . . . That if any person or persons, after the first day of February next to come, during the marriage between the King and the Queen's Majesties, do compass or imagine to deprive the King's Majesty that now is from the having and enjoying jointly together with the Queen's Highness the style, honour, and kingly name of the realms and dominions unto our said Sovereign Lady the

---

[1] A second time.   [2] Hateful.
[3] See note on p. 33 above.

Queen's Highness appertaining, or to destroy the King that now
is during the said matrimony, or to destroy the Queen's Majesty
that now is, or the heirs of her body begotten being kings or
queens of this realm, or to levy war . . . against the King . . . or Queen
. . . or . . . her . . . heirs, or to depose the Queen . . . or the heirs of her
body . . . from the imperial Crown . . . And the same compasses or
imaginations, or any of them, maliciously, advisedly, and directly
shall or do utter by open preaching, express words or sayings; Or if
any person or persons after the said first day of February, by
preaching, express words or sayings, shall maliciously, advisedly,
and directly say, publish, declare, maintain, or hold opinion that the
King's Majesty that now is, during the said matrimony, ought not
to have or enjoy jointly together with the Queen's Majesty the style,
honour, and kingly name of this realm, Or that any person or
persons, being neither the King or the Queen's Majesty that now
are, during the said matrimony between them, ought to have or
enjoy the style, honour, and kingly name of this realm, or that
the Queen's Majesty that now is during her life is not or of right
ought not to be Queen of this realm, or after her death that the
heirs of her Highness's body being kings or queens of this realm
of right ought not to be kings or queens of this realm or to have
and enjoy the same, Or that any person or persons other than the
Queen's Majesty that now is, during her life, ought to be Queen
of this realm, or after her death other than the heirs of her body
being kings or queens of this realm, as long as any of her said
heirs of her body begotten shall be in life, of right ought to have
and enjoy the imperial Crown of this realm; That then every such
offender, being thereof duly convicted or attainted by the laws of
this realm, their abettors, procurers, and counsellors, and all and
every their comforters, knowing the said offences or any of them
be done, and being thereof convicted or attainted as is abovesaid,
for his or their such offence shall forfeit and lose to the Queen's
Highness, her heirs and successors, all his and their goods and
chattels and the whole issues and profits of his and their lands,
tenements, and other hereditaments for term of the life of every
such offender or offenders, and also shall have and suffer during
his or their lives perpetual imprisonment.

[II. Ecclesiastics offending shall be deprived of benefices and promotions; and all persons offending a second time shall be guilty of high
treason.]

III. And be it further enacted by the said authority, That if
any person or persons, at any time after the said first day of

February next to come, during the said marriage, compass or imagine the death of the King's Majesty that now is and the same maliciously, advisedly, and directly shall utter and attempt by any writing, printing, overt deed or act; Or if any person or persons, at any time after the said first day of February next coming, shall maliciously, advisedly, and directly, by writing, printing, overt deed or act, [*deny the title of the King or Queen or their issue, shall be guilty of high treason*].

[IV provides for the care of the realm and the King's and Queen's issue during minority under the guardianship of the King.]

V. And be it further enacted by the authority aforesaid, That if any person or persons, during the time that our said Sovereign Lord the King that now is shall and ought to have the order, rule, education, and government of such issue or issues, being king or queen of this realm, according to the order and provision aforesaid, maliciously, advisedly, and directly, by writing, printing, overt deed or act, do compass, attempt, and go about to destroy the person of our said Sovereign Lord, or to deprive or remove his said Highness from the order, rule, education, and government of the same issue or issues, being king or queen of this realm, contrary to the tenor, intent, and true meaning of this present Act, That then every such person or persons so offending, their procurers and abettors, being thereof lawfully convict or attainted by the laws of this realm, shall be deemed and adjudged high traitors, and that all and every such offence and offences shall be deemed and adjudged high treason....

VI. And be it further enacted by the authority aforesaid, That all trials hereafter to be had, awarded, or made for any treason shall be had and used only according to the due order and course of the common laws of this realm, and not otherwise.

      *   *   *   *   *   *

XI. Provided always and be it enacted by the authority aforesaid, That upon the arraignment of any person which hereafter shall fortune to be arraigned for any treason mentioned in this Act, All and every such person and persons, or two of them at the least, as shall hereafter write, declare, confess, or depose any thing or things against the person to be arraigned, shall, if they be then living and within the realm, be brought forth in person before the party arraigned, if he require the same, and object and say openly in his hearing what they or any of them can against

him for or concerning any the treasons contained in the indictment whereupon the party shall be so arraigned, unless the party
arraigned for any such treason shall willingly confess the same at
the time of his or their arraignment.

*   *   *   *   *   *

1 & 2 Philip & Mary, c. 10: Statutes of the Realm, iv, 255.

(12) First Treasons Act of Elizabeth, 1559

An Act whereby certain Offences be made Treason

[*Whereas* 1 *& 2 Philip & Mary, c.* 10 *extends only to the*] late
Queen Mary and the heirs of her body, therefore if any such
like offences as be mentioned and contained within the said
Statute should hereafter happen to be committed against our said
Sovereign Lady that now is, there were no due remedy or condign
punishment provided for the same: In consideration whereof and
to the intent that the malice of wicked and evil doers may the
better be restrained by the extending of the effect and benefit of
the matters contained in the said Estatute to our most dear
Sovereign Lady that now is, and for the more surety and preservation of her Highness's royal estate; Be it enacted. . . That if
any person or persons, after the first day of May next to come, do
maliciously, advisedly, and directly compass or imagine to deprive
the Queen's Majesty that now is, or the heirs of her body to be
begotten, being kings or queens of this realm, from the style,
honour, and kingly name of the imperial Crown of this realm, or
from any other the realms and dominions unto our said Sovereign
Lady appertaining and belonging, or to destroy the Queen's
Majesty that now is or any the heirs of her body being kings or
queens of this realm, or to levy war within this realm or within
any the marches or dominions to the same belonging against the
Queen's Majesty that now is or any the heirs of her body being
kings or queens of this realm, or to depose the Queen's Majesty
that now is or any the heirs of her body being kings or queens
of this realm from the imperial Crown of the realms and dominions
aforesaid; and the same compasses or imaginations or any of them
maliciously, advisedly, and directly shall or do utter by open
preaching, express words or sayings; or if any person or persons,
after the said first day of May next coming, shall maliciously,
advisedly, and directly say, publish, maintain, declare, or hold
opinion that the Queen's Majesty that now is during her life is
not or ought not to be Queen of this realm, or after her death

that the heirs of her Highness's body being kings or queens of this realm of right ought not to be kings or queens of this realm, or that any other person or persons other than the Queen's Highness that now is during her life ought to be king or queen of this realm or any other the realms or dominions aforesaid, or after her death other than the heirs of her body being kings or queens of this realm, as long as any of her said heirs of her body begotten shall be in life, of right ought to have and enjoy the imperial Crown of this realm or any the realms and dominions aforesaid; that then every such offender being thereof duly convicted or attainted by the laws of this realm, their abettors, procurers, and counsellors, and all and every their comforters, knowing the said offences or any of them to be done, and being thereof duly convicted or attainted as is abovesaid for his or their such offence, shall forfeit and lose to the Queen's Highness, her heirs and successors, all his and their goods and chattels, and the whole issues and profits of his and their lands, tenements, and hereditaments, for term of the life of every such offender or offenders, and also shall have and suffer during his and their lives perpetual imprisonment.

*   *   *   *   *   *

[III declares second offences to be treason.]

IV. And be it further enacted by the authority aforesaid, That if any person or persons, at any time after the said first day of May next to come, by any writing, printing, overt deed or act, maliciously, advisedly, and directly do affirm that the Queen's Majesty that now is ought not to have and enjoy the style, honour, and kingly name of this realm, Or that any person or persons other than the Queen's Majesty that now is ought to have or enjoy the style, honour, and kingly name of this realm, or that the Queen's Majesty that now is during her life is not or ought not to be Queen of this realm; or after her death that the heirs of her Highness's body being kings or queens of this realm of right ought not to have and enjoy the imperial Crown of this realm; or that any person or persons other than the Queen's Majesty that now is during her life, or after her death other than the heirs of her body begotten being kings or queens of this realm as long as any of her said heirs of her body shall be in life, of right ought to have and enjoy the imperial Crown of this realm; that then every such offence and offences shall be adjudged high treason....

*   *   *   *   *   *

X. Provided always and be it enacted by the authority aforesaid, That no person or persons shall be hereafter indicted or arraigned for any offence or offences made treason or misprision of treason by this Act, unless the same offence and offences of treason and misprision of treason aforesaid be proved by the testimony, deposition, and oath of two lawful and sufficient witnesses at the time of his and their indictment; which said witnesses also at the time of the arraignment of the party so indicted (if they be then living) shall be brought forth in person before the party so arraigned face to face, and there shall avow and openly declare all they can say against the said party so indicted, unless the said party so indicted shall willingly without violence confess the same.

1 Eliz. c. 5: *Statutes of the Realm*, iv, 365.

(13) Second Treasons Act of Elizabeth, 1571

An Act whereby certain Offences be made Treason

Forasmuch as it is of some doubted whether the laws and statutes of this realm remaining at this present in force are vailable[1] and sufficient enough for the surety and preservation of the Queen's most royal person, in whom consisteth all the happiness and comfort of the whole state and subjects of the realm, which thing all faithful, loving, and dutiful subjects ought and will with all careful study and zeal consider, foresee, and provide for; by the neglecting and passing over whereof with winking eyes there might happen to grow the subversion and ruin of the quiet and most happy state and present government of this realm (which God defend): Therefore at the humble suit and petition of the Lords and Commons in this present Parliament assembled, Be it enacted, declared, and established by authority of the same Parliament, That if any person or persons whatsoever, at any time after the last day of June next coming, during the natural life of our most gracious Sovereign Lady Queen Elizabeth (whom Almighty God preserve and bless with long and prosperous reign over this realm), shall, within the realm or without, compass, imagine, invent, devise, or intend the death or destruction, or any bodily harm tending to death, destruction, maim, or wounding of the royal person of the same our Sovereign Lady Queen Elizabeth; or to deprive or depose her of or from the style, honour, or kingly name of the imperial Crown of this realm or of any other realm or dominion to her Majesty belonging; or to levy war against her Majesty within this realm or without; or

[1] Effective.

to move or to stir any foreigners or strangers with force to invade
this realm or the realm of Ireland or any other her Majesty's
dominions being under her Majesty's obeisance[1]; and such compasses, imaginations, inventions, devices, or intentions or any of
them shall maliciously, advisedly, and expressly utter or declare
by any printing, writing, ciphering[2], speech, words, or sayings;
or if any person or persons whatsoever, after the said last day of
June, shall maliciously, advisedly, and directly publish, declare,
hold opinion, affirm, or say by any speech, express words or
sayings, that our said Sovereign Lady Queen Elizabeth during her
life is not or ought not to be Queen of this realm of England and
also of the realms of France and Ireland; or that any other person
or persons ought of right to be King or Queen of the said realms
of England and Ireland or of any other her Majesty's dominions
being under her Majesty's obeisance, during her Majesty's life;
or shall by writing, printing, preaching, speech, express words
or sayings, maliciously, advisedly, and directly publish, set forth,
and affirm that the Queen our said Sovereign Lady Queen
Elizabeth is an heretic, schismatic, tyrant, infidel, or an usurper
of the Crown of the said realms or any of them, That then all and
every such said offence or offences shall be taken, deemed, and
declared, by the authority of this Act and Parliament, to be high
treason; and that as well the principal offender or offenders therein
as all and every the abettors, counsellors, and procurers to the
same offence or offences, and all and every aiders and comforters
of the same offender or offenders, knowing the same offence or
offences to be done and committed in any place within this realm
or without, being thereof lawfully and duly indicted, convicted,
and attainted, according to the usual order and course of the
common laws of this realm, or according to [35 Henr. VIII, c. 2[3]...]
as the case shall require, shall be deemed, declared, and adjudged traitors to the Queen and the realm, and shall suffer pains of
death and also forfeit unto the Queen's Majesty, her heirs and successors, all and singular lands, tenements, and hereditaments, goods,
and chattels, as in cases of high treason by the laws and statutes
of this realm at this day of right ought to be forfeited and lost.

II. And be it also enacted by the authority aforesaid, That
all and every person and persons, of what degree, condition,
place, nation, or estate soever they be, which shall, after the end
of thirty days next after the last day of this present session of this

---

[1] Authority, obedience.　　　　[2] I.e. by writing in cipher.
[3] An Act providing that the trial of treasons committed without the realm
should be in the King's Bench or before a special Commission.

Parliament, at any time in the life of our Sovereign Lady Queen Elizabeth in any wise claim, pretend, utter, declare, affirm, or publish themselves or any of them, or any other than our said Sovereign Lady Elizabeth the Queen's Majesty that now is, to have right or title to have or enjoy the Crown of England during or in the life of our said Sovereign Lady; Or shall usurp the same Crown or the royal style, title, or dignity of the Crown or realm of England during or in the life of our said Sovereign Lady, or shall hold and affirm that our said Sovereign Lady hath not right to hold and enjoy the said Crown and realm, style, title, or dignity, or shall not, after any demand on our said Sovereign Lady's part to be made, effectually acknowledge our said Sovereign Lady to be in right true and lawful Queen of this realm, they and every of them so offending shall be utterly disabled, during their natural lives only, to have or enjoy the Crown or realm of England, or the style, title, or dignity thereof, at any time in succession, inheritance, or otherwise after the decease of our said Sovereign Lady as if such person were naturally dead; Any law, custom, pretence, or matter whatsoever to the contrary notwithstanding.

III. And be it further enacted, That if any person shall, during the Queen's Majesty's life, in any wise hold, affirm, or maintain any right, title, interest, or possibility in succession or inheritance in or to the Crown of England, after our said Sovereign Lady the Queen, to be rightfully in or lawfully due or belonging unto any such claimer, pretender, usurper, utterer, declarer, affirmer, publisher, or not-acknowledger, so that our said Sovereign Lady the Queen shall, by proclamation to be published through the realm, or else in the more part of those shires of this realm, as well on the south side as the north side of Trent, and also in the Dominion of Wales, in which shires no war or rebellion then shall be, set forth, notify, or declare such claiming, pretence, uttering, declaration, affirming, publishing, usurpation, or not-acknowledging, then every person which after such proclamation shall during the Queen's Majesty's life maintain, hold, or affirm any right in succession, inheritance, or possibility in or to the Crown or realm of England or the rights thereof to be in or to any such claimer, pretender, utterer, declarer, affirmer, usurper, publisher, or not-acknowledger, shall be a high traitor and suffer and forfeit as in cases of high treason is accustomed.

IV. And be it further enacted, That if any person shall in any wise hold and affirm or maintain that the common laws of this realm not altered by Parliament ought not to direct the right of the Crown of England, or that our said Sovereign Lady Elizabeth

the Queen's Majesty that now is, with and by the authority
of the Parliament of England, is not able to make laws and
statutes of sufficient force and validity to limit and bind the
Crown of this realm and the descent, limitation, inheritance, and
government thereof, or that this present Statute, or any part
thereof, or any other statute to be made by the authority of the
Parliament of England with the royal assent of our said Sovereign
Lady the Queen for limiting of the Crown, or any statute for
recognising the right of the said Crown and realm to be justly
and lawfully in the most royal person of our said Sovereign Lady
the Queen, is not, are not, or shall not, or ought not to be for ever
of good and sufficient force and validity to bind, limit, restrain,
and govern all persons, their rights and titles, that in any wise
may or might claim any interest or possibility in or to the Crown
of England in possession, remainder, inheritance, succession, or
otherwise howsoever, and all other persons whatsoever, every
such person so holding, affirming, or maintaining during the life
of the Queen's Majesty shall be judged a high traitor and suffer
and forfeit as in cases of high treason is accustomed; And every
person so holding, affirming, or maintaining after the decease of
our said Sovereign Lady shall forfeit all his goods and chattels.

V. And for the avoiding of contentious and seditious spread-
ing abroad of titles to the succession of the Crown of this realm,
to the disturbing of the common quiet of the realm; Be it enacted
by the authority aforesaid, That whosoever shall hereafter, during
the life of our said Sovereign Lady, by any book or work, printed
or written, directly and expressly declare and affirm, at any time
before the same be by Act of Parliament of this realm established
and affirmed, that any one particular person, whosoever it be, is
or ought to be the right heir and successor to the Queen's Majesty
that now is (whom God long preserve) except the same be the
natural issue of her Majesty's body, or shall wilfully set up in
open place, publish, or spread any books or scrolls to that effect,
or shall print, bind, or put to sale, or utter, or cause to be printed,
bound, or put to sale, or uttered, any such book or writing wittingly,
that he or they, their abettors and counsellors, and every of them,
shall for the first offence suffer imprisonment of one whole year
and forfeit half his goods, whereof the one moiety to the Queen's
Majesty, the other moiety to him or them that will sue for the
same by bill, action of debt, plaint, information, or otherwise in
any of the Queen's Majesty's Courts, wherein no essoin[1] or protection shall be allowed; And if any shall eftsoons[2] offend therein,

---

[1] Excuse.   [2] A second time.

then they and every of them, their abettors and counsellors, shall incur the pains and forfeitures which in the Statutes of Provisions or Praemunire[1] are appointed and limited.

*   *   *   *   *   *

[IX, as in previous statutes, requires proof of the offences mentioned in the Act by two witnesses in the presence of the party arraigned.]

[X. The aiders and comforters of offenders affirming that the Queen is 'an heretic, schismatic, tyrant, infidel, or usurper of the Crown' incur, for the first offence, the penalties of praemunire, and for the second offence, the penalties of high treason.]

XI. Provided always and be it enacted by the authority aforesaid, That the giving of charitable alms, in money, meat, drink, apparel, or bedding, for the sustentation of the body or health of any person or persons that shall commit any the offences made treason or praemunire by this Act during the time that the same offender shall be in prison, shall not in any wise be deemed or taken to be any offence; Anything in this Act contained to the contrary thereof notwithstanding.

13 Eliz. c. 1: *Statutes of the Realm*, iv, 526.

A statute of the following year[2] declared it felony without benefit of clergy to 'compass, imagine, conspire, practise, or devise, by any ways or means with force, or by any craft, device, or sleight, maliciously and rebelliously to take or to detain or keep from our said Sovereign Lady the Queen any of her castles, towers, fortresses, or holds, or maliciously and rebelliously to raze, burn, or destroy any castle, bulwark, or fort, or any part of them, having any munition or ordnance of the Queen's Majesty's therein, or appointed to be guarded with any soldiers for defence thereof'; as also to express 'the same compasses, imaginations, practices, conspiracies, or devices' by 'words, speech, act, deed, or writing.' Further, it was made high treason 'with force maliciously and rebelliously' to 'detain, keep, or withhold from the Queen's Majesty any of her castles, towers, fortresses, or holds...or... any of her ships, ordnance, artillery, or other munitions or fortifications of wars...' or to burn any of the Queen's ships or to bar any haven. The Act was limited to the Queen's life.

(14) Act for the Surety of the Queen's Person, 1585

An Act for Provision to be made for the Surety of the Queen's Majesty's most Royal Person, and the continuance of the Realm in Peace

Forasmuch as the good felicity and comfort of the whole estate of this realm consisteth (only next under God) in the surety and preservation of the Queen's most excellent Majesty; And for that it hath manifestly appeared that sundry wicked plots and

---

[1] See notes on p. 18 above.   [2] 14 Eliz. c. 1 (1572).

means have of late been devised and laid, as well in foreign parts beyond the seas as also within this realm, to the great endangering of her Highness's most royal person and to the utter ruin of the whole common weal, if by God's merciful providence the same had not been revealed: Therefore for preventing of such great perils as might hereafter otherwise grow by the like detestable and devilish practices.... Be it enacted and ordained, If at any time after the end of this present session of Parliament any open invasion or rebellion shall be had or made into or within any of her Majesty's realms or dominions, or any act attempted tending to the hurt of her Majesty's most royal person, by or for any person that shall or may pretend any title to the Crown of this realm after her Majesty's decease; or if anything shall be compassed or imagined tending to the hurt of her Majesty's royal person by any person or with the privity of any person that shall or may pretend title to the Crown of this realm, That then by her Majesty's commission under her great seal the Lords and others of her Highness's Privy Council and such other Lords of Parliament to be named by her Majesty as with the said Privy Council shall make up the number of 24 at the least, having with them for their assistance in that behalf such of the Judges of the Courts of Record[1] at Westminster as her Highness shall for that purpose assign and appoint, or the more part of the same Council, Lords, and Judges, shall by virtue of this Act have authority to examine all and every the offences aforesaid and all circumstances thereof, and thereupon to give sentence or judgment as upon good proof the matter shall appear unto them: And that after such sentence or judgment given and declaration thereof made and published by her Majesty's proclamation under the great seal of England, all persons against whom such sentence or judgment shall be so given and published shall be excluded and disabled for ever to have or claim, or to pretend to have or claim, the Crown of this realm or of any her Majesty's dominions; Any former law or statute whatsoever to the contrary in any wise notwithstanding: And that thereupon all her Highness's subjects shall and may lawfully, by virtue of this Act and her Majesty's direction in that behalf, by all forcible and possible means pursue to death every of such wicked person by whom or by whose means, assent, or privity any such invasion or rebellion shall be in form aforesaid denounced to have been made, or such wicked act attempted, or

---

[1] A court of record is 'a court whose proceedings are formally enrolled and valid as evidence of fact, being also a court of the Sovereign, and having authority to fine or imprison' (*Oxford Dictionary*).

other thing compassed or imagined against her Majesty's person, and all their aiders, comforters, and abettors: And if any such detestable act shall be executed against her Highness's most royal person whereby her Majesty's life shall be taken away (which God of his great mercy forbid), That then every such person by or for whom any such act shall be executed, and their issues being any wise assenting or privy to the same, shall by virtue of this Act be excluded and disabled for ever to have or claim, or to pretend to have or claim, the said Crown of this realm or of any other her Highness's dominions; Any former law or statute whatsoever to the contrary in any wise notwithstanding: And that all the subjects of this realm and all other her Majesty's dominions shall and may lawfully, by virtue of this Act, by all forcible and possible means pursue to death every such wicked person by whom or by whose means any such detestable fact shall be, in form hereafter expressed, denounced to have been committed, and also their issues being any way assenting or privy to the same, and all their aiders, comforters, and abettors in that behalf.

II. And to the end that the intention of this law may be effectually executed, if her Majesty's life shall be taken away by any violent or unnatural means (which God defend): Be it further enacted by the authority aforesaid, That the Lords and others which shall be of her Majesty's Privy Council at the time of such her decease, or the more part of the same Council, joining unto them for their better assistance five other Earls and seven other Lords of Parliament at the least (foreseeing that none of the said Earls, Lords, or Council be known to be persons that may make any title to the Crown), those persons which were Chief Justices of every Bench, Master of the Rolls, and Chief Baron of the Exchequer at the time of her Majesty's death, or in default of the said Justices, Master of the Rolls, and Chief Baron, some other of those which were Justices of some of the Courts of Record at Westminster at the time of her Highness's decease to supply their places, or any 24 or more of them, whereof eight to be Lords of Parliament not being of the Privy Council, shall to the uttermost of their power and skill examine the cause and manner of such her Majesty's death, and what persons shall be any way guilty thereof, and all circumstances concerning the same, according to the true meaning of this Act; and thereupon shall by open proclamation publish the same, and without any delay by all forcible and possible means prosecute to death all such as shall be found to be offenders therein and all their aiders and abettors; And for the doing thereof, and for the withstanding and suppressing of all such power and force as shall any way be levied or stirred in disturbance of the due execution of this law, shall by virtue of this Act have power and authority not only to raise and use such forces as shall in that behalf be needful and convenient, but also to use all other means and things possible and necessary for the maintenance of the same forces and prosecution of the said offenders; And if any such power and force shall be levied or stirred in disturbance of the due execution of this law by any person that shall or may pretend any title to the Crown of this realm, whereby this law in all things may not be fully executed according to the effect and true meaning of the same, that then every such person shall by virtue of this Act be therefor excluded and disabled for ever to have or claim, or to pretend to have or claim, the Crown of this realm or of any other her Highness's dominions; Any former law or statute whatsoever to the contrary notwithstanding.

III. And be it further enacted by the authority aforesaid, That all and every the subjects of all her Majesty's realms and dominions shall, to the uttermost of their power, aid and assist the said Council and all other the Lords and other persons to be adjoined unto them for assistance as is aforesaid in all things to be done and executed according to the effect and intention of this law: And that no subject of this realm shall in any wise be impeached in body, lands, or goods at any time hereafter for any thing to be done or executed according to the tenor of this law; Any law or statute heretofore made to the contrary in any wise notwithstanding.

IV. And whereas of late many of her Majesty's good and faithful subjects have, in the name of God and with the testimony of good consciences, by one uniform manner of writing under their hands and seals and by their several oaths voluntarily taken, joined themselves together in one Bond and Association[1] to withstand and revenge to the uttermost all such malicious actions and attempts against her Majesty's most royal person: Now for the full explaining of all such ambiguities and questions as otherwise might happen to grow by reason of any sinister or wrong construction or interpretation to be made or inferred of or upon the

---

[1] After the murder of William the Silent, 10 July, 1584, and the discovery of further designs against the Queen, a voluntary association of Englishmen of all ranks was formed 'to withstand and revenge to the uttermost all such malicious actions and attempts against her Majesty's most royal person' (Pollard, *Hist.* p. 386). This is now legalised by the Act. The Bond of Association is printed in *State Trials*, i, 1162.

words or meaning thereof, Be it declared and enacted by the authority of this present Parliament, That the same Association and every article and sentence therein contained, as well concerning the disallowing, excluding, or disabling of any person that may or shall pretend any title to come to the Crown of this realm, and also for the pursuing and taking revenge of any person for any such wicked act or attempt as is mentioned in the same Association, shall and ought to be in all things expounded and adjudged according to the true intent and meaning of this Act, and not otherwise nor against any other person or persons.

27 Eliz. c. 1: Statutes of the Realm, iv, 704.

§ 3. PROCEDURE IN TRIALS FOR TREASON

In a trial for treason the prisoner was placed at a peculiar disadvantage by the recognised procedure of the Courts. (1) By an ancient rule of law persons accused of treason or felony were denied the assistance of counsel on matters of fact. This was defended by two arguments, both equally fallacious. It was maintained (*a*) that the judge is the prisoner's counsel in matters of fact; and (*b*) that in order to obtain a conviction, the proof must be so plain that no counsel could contend against it [p. 430]. This might be true in simple cases, but as soon as the smallest complication was introduced, the prisoner was helpless without skilled legal advice. It is true that he was allowed to cross-examine the witnesses, but cross-examination is a high art, and the success of it depends, not upon random speculation, but upon previous knowledge of what the witness is called in order to prove. Of such knowledge the prisoner was deprived by the very fact of his imprisonment. His best protection against perjured or prejudiced testimony was skilled legal advice and the free access to him of his legal adviser, and of this he was deprived, not by any caprice of an unjust judge but by the established practice of the Courts. (2) The prisoner was denied a copy of the indictment; he was not always furnished with a list of the jury in order that he might have an opportunity of considering beforehand how he should exercise his right of challenge; and he was not provided with copies of the depositions, or even with a list of the witnesses whom the Crown proposed to call. (3) The witnesses for the Crown were put upon their oath, but in cases of treason and felony the prisoner's witnesses, at any rate in the later part of the Tudor period, were not allowed to be sworn; and yet on that account their testimony was considered to be of inferior value. (4) While the Crown had power by legal process to compel the attendance of witnesses for the prosecution, the prisoner had no such legal power to compel the attendance of witnesses for the defence. (5) The confessions of accomplices were admitted without corroboration, and 'were regarded a specially cogent evidence.'[1] (6) There were no definite rules of evidence; the witnesses were allowed to make speeches full of irrelevant matter, and leading questions and hearsay evidence were freely admitted.

Thus, in the trial of the Duke of Buckingham, in 1521, the indictment

<hr />

[1] Stephen, i, 350.

was founded upon the depositions of Gilbert, his chancellor, Delacourt, his confessor, and the discharged surveyor, Charles Knyvet[1], and he was not allowed to cross-examine them, or to test their accuracy or good faith Nothing was open to him but a bare denial of the charges made against him. In the case of the Duke of Norfolk, in 1572 [p. 440], part of the evidence was obtained from servants imprisoned and threatened with torture, and admissions were obtained from the Duke himself in examination before the Council. At his trial he was not allowed counsel, or a copy of the indictment. The witnesses against him were not produced in open Court, but their evidence was read over and commented upon by the Crown lawyers, and the prisoner was left to meet it as best he could on the spur of the moment.

The reasons for thus restricting the defence are indicated by Sir J. F. Stephen[2]. 'In judging of the trials of the period in question we must remember that there was no standing army, and no organised police on which the government could rely; that the maintenance of the public peace depended mainly on the life of the sovereign for the time being, and that the question between one ruler and another was a question on which the most momentous issues, religious, political, and social, depended. In such a state of things it was not unnatural to act on a different view as to the presumptions to be made as to guilt or innocence from that which guides our own proceedings.'

During the Tudor period certain changes were made by statute in the law affecting procedure in trials for treason. Henry VIII legislated against the accused, (1) by depriving persons convicted of treason of benefit of clergy and sanctuary[3]; (2) by making a lunatic punishable for treason, and providing a special kind of trial for his benefit[4]; (3) by taking power for the Crown in cases of treason to issue a special Commission of Oyer and Terminer to try the case in any county the King might select—that is to say, where he had the best chance of obtaining a conviction. The same statute[5] also deprives the accused of his right to challenge jurors except for want of freehold. On the other hand the legislation of Edward VI told in favour of the accused. The First Treasons Act [p. 401] contains a provision of the utmost importance to him, requiring two 'sufficient and lawful witnesses,' in place of the one positive witness required by the common law. This was confirmed by the Second Treasons Act of the reign [p. 405], which required further that the witnesses should be personally confronted with the accused.

Besides proceedings taken in the ordinary courts of law, there were three other ways in which traitors could be dealt with: (1) by impeachment before the House of Lords at the suit of the Commons; (2) by attainder;

---

[1] This witness appears in the scene in the Council Chamber in Shakespeare's *Henry VIII*, where the King examines him. The only attempt to throw doubt upon his evidence is made by Queen Catharine:

> 'If I know you well,
> You were the Duke's surveyor, and lost your office
> On the complaint of the tenants; take good heed
> You charge not in your spleen a noble person,
> And spoil your nobler soul.'—Act I, sc. ii.

[2] i, 354.

[3] 23 Henr. VIII, c. 1, 26 Henr. VIII, c. 13, and 28 Henr. VIII, c. 15; see pp. 14–16 above.   [4] By 33 Henr. VIII, c. 20.

[5] 33 Henr. VIII, c. 23.

and (3) by trial before the Court of the Lord High Steward. No case of impeachment occurs during the Tudor period, as from the case of Lord Stanley in 1459 down to that of Sir Giles Mompesson in 1621 this form of parliamentary procedure was dormant. The other two methods require special notice.

§ 4. ATTAINDER[1]

The conditions of royal insecurity which prevailed during the Wars of the Roses called for prompt dealing with living traitors and the effective punishment through forfeiture of those who had fallen in battle. The result of this was that the legislative power of Parliament tended to displace its judicial power, and Acts of Attainder superseded impeachment and indictment, both of which caused delay in dealing with the living and failed altogether to touch the dead. These statutes recited in the preamble the charges against the offender, and then proceeded to declare his guilt. They possessed two technical advantages, both important in times of civil insecurity: (1) they dealt with traitors who had escaped and refused to stand their trial; and (2) procedure by statute cured any legal informalities in the proceedings against those who elected to be tried.

In the Tudor period an Act of Attainder was rarely a substitute for a legal trial; it usually confirmed a judgment already given by a Court, and made detailed provision for the confiscation of the traitor's property and estates. Elizabeth Barton, the Nun of Kent, and her accomplices, were condemned by Act of Attainder in 1534, after a proposed trial had broken down because the offence had been by words only, and treason by words was not then recognised[2]. The Countess of Salisbury, however, was attainted in 1539, without trial; and Cromwell, who had advised this unusual proceeding, was himself condemned unheard by Parliament in the following year. In the case of Queen Catherine Howard also [p. 425] there seems to have been no public or formal trial.

(1) Attainder of the Duke of Buckingham, 1523

This is the usual form of Attainder, in which the Act confirms the result of a previous trial—in this case before the Lord High Steward, in recognition of the Duke's right to be tried by his peers.

The Act of Attainder of Edward, late Duke of Buckingham

Forasmuch as Edward, late Duke of Buckingham, late of Thornbury in the county of Gloucester, the 24th day of April in the fourth year of the reign of our Sovereign Lord the King that now is and divers times after, imagined and compassed traitorously and unnaturally the destruction of the most royal person of our said Sovereign Lord and subversion of this his realm, and

[1] See L. W. Vernon Harcourt, *Trial of Peers*, pp. 388–90.
[2] It was included in the Treasons Act of 1534, probably as a result of this experience.

then traitorously committed and did divers and many treasons against our said Sovereign Lord the King, contrary to his allegiance, in the counties of Gloucester and Somerset, the City of London, the counties of Kent and Surrey, Of the which treasons and offences the said late Duke...was severally indicted. And afterward for and upon the same treasons the 13th day of May the 13th year of the reign of our said Sovereign Lord the King at Westminster in the county of Middlesex before Thomas, Duke of Norfolk, for that time only being Great Steward of England by the King's letters patents, by verdict of his peers and by judgment of the said Steward against the said late Duke then and there given after the due order of the law and custom of England, was attainted[1] of high treason, as by records thereof more plainly appeareth. Wherefore be it ordained, enacted, and established by the King our Sovereign Lord, with the assent of the Lords spiritual and temporal and the Commons in this present Parliament assembled and by the authority of the same, That the said late Duke for the offences above rehearsed stand and be convicted, adjudged, and attainted[1] of high treason, and forfeit to the King our Sovereign Lord and his heirs for ever all honours[2], castles, manors, lordships, hundreds[3], franchises, liberties, privileges, advowsons, nominations, knight's fees, lands, tenements, rents, services, reversions, remainders, portions, annuities, pensions, rights, possessions, and other hereditaments whatsoever, in England, Ireland, Wales, Calais, and Marches of the same, or elsewhere, whereof the said late Duke or any other person or persons to his use were seised or possessed in fee simple, fee tail, or for time of any other man's life or lives, or any estate of inheritance or otherwise the said 24th day of April or any time since, or in the which the said late Duke or any other person or persons seised to his use had then or any time since lawful cause of entry within England, Ireland, Wales, Calais, and Marches of the same, or elsewhere; And over that, the said Edward to forfeit unto our said Sovereign Lord all goods and chattels, as well real as personal, whatsoever whereof the said Edward was possessed to his own use, or any other person or persons was possessed to the use of the same late Duke, the said 13th day of May, or whereof the

1 To 'attaint' is simply to convict, and might be applied to the decision of any criminal Court; it was only sometimes that it was used in the special sense of condemnation by an Act of Attainder.

2 Used here in the special feudal sense of a seignory of several manors held under one lord paramount.

3 Hundred-courts; the term here being another variant for franchises and liberties.

said late Duke had lawful cause of seisure[1] to his own proper use the said 13th day of May; And also to forfeit unto our said Sovereign Lord all debts which were owing by any person or persons unto the said late Duke or unto any other person or persons to the use of the said late Duke the said 13th day of May.

* * * * * *

14 & 15 Henr. VIII, c. 20: *Statutes of the Realm*, iii, 246.

(2) Attainder of Queen Catherine Howard, 1542

The accomplices were attainted after legal trial, but Queen Catherine Howard herself had only been examined by the Privy Council. The Act is notable for the new treasons created by §§ 8 and 9; and also as the first statute to which the royal assent was given by commission—in this case to spare the feelings of Henry VIII.

The Bill of Attainder of Mistress Katherine Howard, late Queen of England, and divers other persons her complices

In their most humble wise beseechen your most royal Majesty the Lords spiritual and temporal and all other your most loving and obedient subjects the Commons of this your most High Court of Parliament assembled; That where, besides any man's expectation, such chance hath happened, by Mistress Katherine Howard which your Highness took to your wife, both to your Majesty chiefly and so consequently to us all that the like we think hath scarce been seen, the likelihoods and appearances being so far contrary to that which by evident and due proof is now found true; First, that it will please your Majesty to take it in such part as thereby arise not to us all a greater inconvenience, which is the trouble of your heart and unquietness of your mind, for that should be a shortening of that which we all should repent and most desire the contrary; Secondly, that it would please your Majesty to pardon all your loving subjects which since these matters came to their knowledge have detested and abhorred her for this fact both in word, manner, and deed, and of words uttered by them of her and her adherents not maintainable in your laws, considering that they did and do it only for the great zeal and love that they bear to your Majesty and the abomination of the detestable fact; Thirdly, that since it pleased your Majesty upon those likely outward appearances to take the said Mistress Katherine Howard to your wife and Queen of your most excellent goodness and for a godly purpose, and also most liberally to endue her with great possessions for the maintenance of the same, thinking and taking her at that time to be chaste and of pure, clean, and honest living, the contrary whereof is now duly proved,

[1] Possession (seisin).

both by her own confession and others also.... It may therefore please your Highness of your most excellent and accustomable goodness, and for the entire love, favour, and hearty affection that your Majesty hath always heretofore borne and yet beareth to the common wealth of this your realm of England, and for the conservation of your most excellent Highness and posterity, and of the good peace, unity, and rest of us your most bounden and obedient subjects, to grant and assent at the most humble desire and petition of your loving and obedient subjects the Lords spiritual and temporal and the Commons in this present Parliament assembled, That this their lawful indictments and attainders of such as have lately suffered may be approved by the authority of this present Parliament: And that it may be enacted that the said Queen Katherine and Jane Lady Rochford, for their said abominable and detestable treasons by them and every of them most abominably and traitorously committed and done against your Majesty and this your realm, shall be by the authority of this present Parliament convicted and attainted of high treason; and that the same Queen Katherine and Jane Lady Rochford, and either of them, shall have and suffer pains of death, loss of goods, chattels, debts, ferms[1], and all other things as in cases of high treason by the laws of this your realm hath been accustomed, granted, and given to the Crown: And also that the said Queen Katherine, Jane Lady Rochford, Thomas Culpepper, and Francis Dereham[2], and every of them, shall lose and forfeit to your Highness and to your heirs all such right, title, interest, use, and possession which they or any of them had the 25th day of August in the 33rd year of your reign, or any time since, of, in, or to all such their honours[3], manors, meses[4], lands, tenements, rents, reversions, remainders, uses, possessions, offices, rights, conditions, and all other their hereditaments, of what names, natures, or qualities soever they be; and that all such rights, title, interest, use, and possession which they or any of them had or of right ought to have the said 25th day of August, or any time since, of, in, or to the same honours, castles, manors, meses, lands, tenements, rents, reversions, remainders, uses, possessions, offices, rights, commodities, and hereditaments, by the authority aforesaid shall be deemed vested, and judged to be in the actual

---

[1] See note on p. 39 above.

[2] Dereham and Culpepper were said to have been the Queen's lovers, and Lady Rochford the channel of communication between them.

[3] See note on p. 424 above.

[4] Messuages.

and real possession of your Majesty, without any office[1] or inquisition thereof hereafter to be taken or found according to the common laws of this your realm.

* * * * * *

[VIII provides that an unchaste woman marrying the King is thereby guilty of high treason.]

[IX. Any person concealing such unchastity is guilty of misprision of treason.]

* * * * * *

33 Henr. VIII, c. 21; *Statutes of the Realm*, iii, 857.

§ 5. Court of the Lord Steward

The Court of the Lord High Steward[2] was the Court which, in the case of treason or felony by a peer, recognised his right to be tried by his peers. This right was originally a right to be tried in Parliament, where the Lord High Steward was to call upon the offender to answer for his crimes before the whole body of the Lords. At the beginning of the Tudor period, however, this general privilege of the whole body to try individual members of it came to be delegated to the Lord High Steward and a small body of peers, who could act when Parliament was not sitting. Before this time peers who were tried when Parliament was not sitting were tried in the Court of the Constable and Marshal, but this jurisdiction was subject to the definite limitation that it only applied in the case of war within the realm, and thus the Court of the Steward was in the hands of the Tudor sovereigns a far more useful and convenient means of striking at great nobles who conspired against the throne.

The first Tudor case was that of the Earl of Warwick in 1499. He was charged with having conspired to depose Henry VII and to place Perkin Warbeck on the throne; and as the jurisdiction of the Constable's Court did not apply to the case, the King appointed the Earl of Oxford Lord High Steward[3], with authority to summon such peers as he chose to act as 'Lords Triers.' The Earl pleaded guilty, and was forthwith condemned and afterwards executed. For such a departure there must be a precedent, and this was found in the trial of the Earl of Cambridge and Lord Scrope in 1415[4] for conspiring against the life of Henry V when he was at Southampton, preparing for his French campaign. A commission was issued to the Earl Marshal and others to inquire by the oath of a jury at Southampton into all treasons and felonies committed in the county, and the two peers, together with a commoner, Sir Thomas Grey, were indicted. The Earl of Cambridge pleaded guilty, but Lord Scrope claimed to be tried by his peers, and for this purpose the Duke of Clarence, who was at the time holding the office of Lord High Steward of England, was commissioned to summon peers and to

[1] See note on p. 105 above

[2] See Harcourt, ch. xii; and L. O. Pike, *Constitutional History of the House of Lords*, ch. xi.

[3] His commission is printed in Harcourt, p. 460.

[4] For a discussion of the still earlier forged precedent of 1400, see Harcourt, pp. 416–29.

hold a Court. The procedure was similar to that adopted in the trial of the Earl of Warwick, and afterwards described by Coke [see below] as the regular procedure of the Court.

From the reign of Henry VII the Court of the Lord High Steward became a recognised institution for the trial of peers when Parliament was not sitting. The number of peers selected by the Steward to serve as Lords Triers was always small[1]; and as the Lord High Steward was appointed *pro hac vice* by the Crown, it was easy for the Crown, if Parliament was not sitting—and in the days of infrequent Parliaments and short sessions this would be the rule—to pack the Court and secure a conviction. When Parliament was sitting the accused would have a better chance, as any Lord of Parliament who chose to do so might attend. The system of a selection of peers was abolished by an Act of William III's reign[2], which placed the jurisdiction in trials for treason in the whole body of the peers, whether Parliament was sitting or not.

The spiritual peers did not claim to be tried by their peers, nor were they summoned to serve as Lords Triers. The first point was finally established when Archbishop Cranmer in 1553 was convicted of treason by the verdict of a jury and made no claim of peerage; and the second was governed by the principle that the spiritual lords cannot take part in judgments affecting life or limb, except by sending a single procurator to represent them. In the case of the Duke of Buckingham, the Prior of St John of Jerusalem was summoned and sat among the nineteen Lords Triers, and gave a vote against the Duke, but after 1521 no spiritual lord appears to have been summoned.

Coke on the Court of the Steward, c. 1628

The application to a particular case of the procedure here described can be seen in the trial of the Earl of Essex [p. 448].

And forasmuch as the proceeding against a noble peer of the realm, being a Lord of Parliament, in some points agrees and in other points differeth from the proceeding against a subject under the degree of nobility, it shall be necessary to shew wherein they agree and wherein they differ.

1. The noble peer of the realm must be indicted before Commissioners of Oyer and Terminer or in the King's Bench if the treason... be committed in that county where the King's Bench sits... And this is common to both degrees, to be indicted by jurors[3] of that county where the offence was committed.

2. When he is indicted, then the King by his Commission under the Great Seal constitutes some peer of the realm to be *hac vice* Steward of England.... This Commission reciteth the

---

[1] *E.g.* in the Earl of Warwick's case in 1499 there were 22 peers present; in the Duke of Buckingham's case in 1521, there were 19; in the case of the Earl of Essex in 1601, there were 25.

[2] Will. III, stat. 7, c. 3, § 11.   [3] *I.e.* by the grand jury.

indictment generally as it is found; and power given to the Lord
Steward to receive the indictment, etc., and to proceed *secundum
legem et consuetudinem Angliae*. And a commandment is given
thereby to the peers of the realm to be attendant and obedient
to him, and a commandment to the Lieutenant of the Tower to
bring the prisoner before him.

3. A *certiorari* is awarded out of the Chancery to remove the
indictment itself before the Steward of England....

4. The Steward directs his precept under his seal to the
Commissioners[1], etc., to certify the indictment such a day and
place.

5. Another writ goeth out of the Chancery directed to the
Lieutenant of the Tower to bring the body of the prisoner before
the Steward at such a day and place as he shall appoint.

6. The Lord Steward maketh a precept under his seal to the
Lieutenant of the Tower, etc., and therein expresseth a day and
place when he shall bring the prisoner before him.

7. The Steward maketh another precept under his seal to a
Serjeant-at-Arms to summon *tot et tales dominos, magnates et
proceres hujus regni Angliae praedicti* R., *comitis* E., *pares, per quos
rei veritas melius sciri poterit, quod ipsi personaliter compareant coram
praedicto Seneschallo apud Westm. tali die et hora, ad faciend. ea
quae ex parte Domini Regis forent facienda, etc.* Wherein four things
are to be observed. First, that all these precepts most commonly
bear date all in one day. Secondly, that no number of peers are
named in the precept, and yet there must be twelve or above.
Thirdly, that the precept is awarded for the return of the peers
before any arraignment, or plea pleaded by the prisoner. Fourthly,
that in this case the Lords are not *de vicineto*, and therefore the
sitting and trial may be in any county of England. And herein
are great differences between a case of a peer of the realm and of
one under the degree of nobility.

8. At the day, the Steward with six serjeants-at-arms before
him takes his place under a cloth of estate, and then the Clerk of
the Crown delivereth unto him his Commission, who re-delivereth
the same unto him. And the Clerk of the Crown causeth a serjeant-at-arms to make three *O yes*, and commandment is given in
the name of the Lord High Steward of England to keep silence;
and then is the Commission read. And then the Usher delivereth
to the Steward a white rod, who re-delivereth the same to him again,
who holdeth it before the Steward. Then another *O yes* is made,
and commandment given in the name of the High Steward of

---

[1] *I.e.* to the Commissioners of Oyer and Terminer.

England to all Justices and Commissioners to certify all indictments and records, etc.; which being delivered into Court, the
Clerk of the Crown readeth the return. Another *O yes* is made
that the Lieutenant of the Tower, etc., return his writ and precept
and do bring the prisoner to the bar; which being done, the Clerk
reads the return. Another *O yes* is made, that the Serjeant-at-
Arms return his precept with the names of the barons and peers
by him summoned, and the return of that is also read. Another
O yes is made, that all earls, barons, and peers which by the commandment of the High Steward be summoned answer to their
names, and then they take their places and sit down, and their
names are recorded; and the entry of the record is that they
appear *ad faciendum ea quae ex parte Domini Regis eis injungentur.*
And when they be all in their places and the prisoner at the bar,
the High Steward declares to the prisoner the cause of their
assembly, and persuades him to answer without fear, that he shall
be heard with patience, and that justice should be done. Then the
Clerk of the Crown reads the indictment, and proceeds to the
arraignment of the prisoner; and if he plead Not Guilty, the
entry is, *et de hoc de bono et malo ponit se super pares suos, etc.*
Then the High Steward giveth a charge to the peers, exhorting
them to try the prisoner indifferently according to their evidence.

9. The peers are not sworn, but are charged *super fidelitatibus
et ligeantiis Domino Regi debitis*; for so the record speaketh.

10. Then the King's learned counsel give evidence, and produce their proofs for the King against the prisoner.

11. But the prisoner when he pleadeth Not Guilty, whereby
he denieth the fact, he needs have no advice of counsel to that
plea. But if he hath any matter of law to plead...he shall have
counsel assigned him to plead the same, or any other matter in
law....And after the plea of Not Guilty the prisoner can have
no counsel learned assigned to him to answer the King's counsel
learned nor to defend him. And the reason thereof is, not because
it concerneth matter of fact, for *ex facto jus oritur*; but the true
reasons of the law in this case are, First, that the testimonies and
the proofs of the offence ought to be so clear and manifest as
there can be no defence of it; Secondly, the Court ought to be
instead of counsel for the prisoner, to see that nothing be urged
against him contrary to law and right—nay, any learned man
that is present may inform the Court for the benefit of the prisoner
of anything that may make the proceedings erroneous. And
herein there is no diversity between the peer and another
subject....

12. There be always either all or some of the Judges ever attendant upon the High Steward, and sit at the feet of the peers, or about a table in the midst, or in some other convenient place.

13. After all the evidence given for the King, and the prisoner's answers, and proofs at large and with patience heard, then is the prisoner withdrawn from the bar to some private place under the custody of the Lieutenant, etc. And after that he is withdrawn, the Lords that are triers of the prisoner go to some place to consider of their evidence; and if upon debate thereof they shall doubt of any matter, and thereupon send to the High Steward to have conference with the Judges or with the High Steward, they ought to have no conference either with the Judges or the High Steward but openly in court and in the presence and hearing of the prisoner[1]....

14. A nobleman cannot waive his trial by his peers and put himself upon the trial of the country, that is, of twelve freeholders; for the Statute of Magna Charta is that he must be tried *per pares*....

15. The peers ought to continue together (as juries in case of other subjects ought to do) until they be agreed of their verdict, and when they are agreed, they all come again into the court and take their places; and then the Lord High Steward publicly in open court, beginning with the puisne[2] Lord, who in the case of the Lord Dacre[3] was the Lord Mordaunt, said unto him, My Lord Mordaunt, is William, Lord Dacre, guilty of the treasons whereof he hath been indicted or arraigned, or of any of them? And the Lord, standing up, said, Not Guilty; and so upward of all the other Lords *seriatim*, who all gave the same verdict....

16. The peers give their verdict in the absence of the prisoner, and then is the prisoner brought to the bar again; and then doth the Lord Steward acquaint the prisoner with the verdict of his peers, and give judgment accordingly, either of condemnation or acquittal. But it is not so in the case of another subject; for there the verdict is given in his presence....

...20. No peer of the realm or any other subject shall be convicted by verdict but the said offences must be found by above four-and-twenty[4], viz., by twelve or above at his indictment, or

---

[1] But see the procedure in the case of the Earl of Essex, p. 450 below.

[2] Junior.

[3] Lord Dacre was tried in 1541 before the Lord High Steward for murder arising out of a poaching affray. He pleaded guilty and was convicted and executed. The case was afterwards always regarded by the lawyers as an important precedent.

[4] In the case of a commoner, both by a grand jury and a petty jury.

by twelve peers or above if he be noble, and by twelve and not above if he be under the degree of nobility.

...25. And when the service is performed, then is an *O yes* made for the dissolving of the Commission; and then is the white rod which hath been borne and holden before the Steward by him taken in both his hands and broken over his head.

Lastly, the indictments, together with the record of the arraignment, trial, and judgment, shall be delivered into the King's Bench, there to be kept and inrolled....

Coke, *Third Institute*, cap. ii (edn. of 1669), pp. 27–31.

§ 6. PUNISHMENT OF TREASON

The effects of a conviction for treason, besides the actual execution by being hanged, drawn, and quartered, are thus described by Coke[1]: 'Implied in this judgment is, first, the forfeiture of all his manors, lands, tenements, and hereditaments, in fee simple or fee tail, of whomsoever they be holden; secondly, his wife to lose her dower; thirdly, he shall lose his children, for they become base and ignoble; fourthly, he shall lose his posterity, for his blood is stained and corrupted, and they cannot inherit to him or any other ancestor; fifthly, all his goods and chattels, etc   And reason is that his body, lands, goods, posterity, etc., should be torn, pulled asunder, and destroyed, that intended to tear and destroy the majesty of government. And all these several punishments are found for treason in Holy Scripture.'

Under pre-Tudor law forfeiture for treason or felony[2] did not extend to estates tail except for the term of the offender's life, although Acts of Attainder had usually contained a special forfeiture clause which included estates tail; but by the Succession Act of 1534 and by the Treasons Act of the same year lands of any estate of inheritance were to be forfeited for treason (although not for felony), as also lands held to the use of the person attainted, which were not subject to forfeiture at common law. Until the Dissolution of the Monasteries the estates of an abbey whose abbot was convicted of treason were treated like estates tail, and were only forfeited during the lifetime of the offender; but by the Dissolution Acts it was made clear[3] that the possessions of monasteries whose heads were attainted of treason came to the Crown. This last forfeiture was surrendered and the older law restored by Edward VI's Second Treasons Act, which saved the rights of all persons other than the traitors and their heirs, and said nothing about their successors. Forfeiture for treason or felony was abolished altogether by an Act of 1870[4].

---

[1] *Third Institute* (edn. of 1669), p. 211.

[2] On this question see Miss I. D. Thornley, "The Treason Legislation of Henry VIII" (*Royal Historical Society's Transactions*, 3rd series, xi, 116).

[3] In the first Act of Dissolution by excluding from the saving clause the 'offenders in any treasons, their heirs and successors,' and therefore the successor of an attainted abbot (*ib.* xi, 118).

[4] 33 & 34 Vict. c. 23, § 1.

§ 7. TRIALS FOR TREASON[1]

The extracts printed below from certain famous trials for treason are directed to particular constitutional points. The trials of More and Fisher are those of commoners, for Fisher had ceased to be Bishop of Rochester and therefore a Lord of Parliament, and in any case, as a spiritual lord only, he could not have claimed peerage rights. The trials of the Duke of Norfolk and the Earl of Essex are before the Court of the Lord High Steward. The trial of Mary Queen of Scots is in every way a special case.

(1) Trial of Sir Thomas More, 1535

More was indicted of high treason in Westminster Hall, 1 July, 1535, before a special Commission of Oyer and Terminer, consisting of ten peers and ten judges, presided over by Audley, the Lord Chancellor. He was charged with having infringed the Treasons Act of 1534 by traitorously imagining and attempting to deprive the King of his title as Supreme Head of the Church. First, he had refused to answer directly when examined by Cromwell and others of the Council, saying, 'I will not meddle with any such matters, for I am fully determined to serve God, and to think upon his passion, and my passage out of this world.' Secondly, he had said in a letter to Bishop Fisher, and also in the course of his examination in the Tower, 'The Act is like a two-edged sword; if I speak against it I shall cause the death of my body, and if I assent to it I shall purchase the death of my soul.' Thirdly, in a conversation with Rich, the Solicitor-General, he had said that if a statute made the King Supreme Head of the Church the subject cannot be bound by it[2].

The extracts printed below are from the account of the trial given in the *Life* written by his great-grandson, Cresacre More[3], about 1631, and largely based on the earlier *Life* by his son-in-law, William Roper. They shew that imprisonment had not broken his spirit or cast a shadow upon the brightness of his wit. 'This man,' says Holinshed[4], 'was both learned and wise, and given much to a certain pleasure in merry taunts and jesting in most of his communication, which manner he forgat not at the very hour of his death.' There is nothing more graceful than his farewell to his judges[5]; and his composure on the scaffold has few precedents[6]. 'No such culprit as More had stood at any European bar for a thousand years; the condemnation of Socrates is the only parallel in history.'[7]

After that the King had endeavoured by all means possible to get Sir Thomas's consent unto his laws, knowing that his example

---

[1] Other trials are abstracted from the *State Trials* and discussed in J. W. Willis-Bund, *Trials for Treason*, vol. i, 1327–1660.

[2] Stephen, i, 322.

[3] See also the account in Cobbett and Howell (i, 386) which adds a few details. Cresacre More was a strong Catholic, and his style resembles that of Foxe's *Book o, Martyrs* with the standpoint reversed; his account should be taken with the same reservations.

[4] iii, 793.   [5] See p. 439 below.   [6] *Ib.*

[7] Sir James Mackintosh; quoted in Dixon, i, 296.

would move many, being so eminent for wisdom and rare virtues, and could by no means obtain his desire, he commanded him to be called to his arraignment at the King's Bench bar, having been a prisoner in the Tower somewhat more than a twelve-month,...He went thither leaning on his staff, because he had been much weakened by his imprisonment, his countenance cheerful and constant...where the King's Attorney reading a long and odious indictment, containing all the crimes that could be laid against any notorious malefactor[1]—so long, as Sir Thomas professed, he could not remember a third part of that which was objected against him....Presently after this indictment was read, the Lord Chancellor and the Duke of Norfolk spoke to this effect unto him: 'You see now how grievously you have offended his Majesty. Yet he is so merciful, that if you will lay away your obstinacy and change your opinion, we hope you may obtain pardon of his Highness.' Whereto the stout champion of Christ replied, 'Most noble Lords, I have great cause to thank your honours for this your courtesy; but I beseech Almighty God that I may continue in the mind I am in through his grace unto death....'

After this he was suffered to say what he could in his own defence, and then he began in this sort: 'When I think how long my accusation is, and what heinous matters are laid to my charge, I am stroken with fear lest my memory and wit both, which are decayed together with the health of my body, through an impediment contracted by my long imprisonment, so as I shall not be able to answer these things on the sudden as I ought and otherwise could.' After this there was brought him a chair, in which when he was sate he began again thus:

'There are four principal heads, if I be not deceived of this indictment, every of which I purpose, God willing, to answer in order. To the first that is objected against me, to wit, that I have been an enemy of a stubbornness of mind to the King's second marriage, I confess that I always told the King my opinion therein as my conscience dictated unto me, which I neither ever would nor ought to have concealed; for which I am so far from thinking myself guilty of high treason, as that, of the contrary, I being demanded my opinion by so great a prince in a matter of such importance, whereupon the quietness of a kingdom dependeth, I should have basely flattered him against mine own conscience,

---

[1] Stephen (i, 322) points out that the abstract of the indictment only fills a folio page, so it could not have been very long; nor does this description of it appear to be justified by its contents, so far as we know them.

and not uttered the truth as I thought, then I should worthily have been accounted a most wicked subject and a perfidious traitor to God. If herein I had offended the King, if it can be an offence to tell one's mind plainly when our prince asketh us, I suppose I have been already punished enough for this fault with most grievous afflictions, with the loss of all my goods, and committed to perpetual imprisonment, having been shut up already almost these fifteen months.'

'My second accusation is, that I have transgressed the statute in the last Parliament, that is to say, being a prisoner, and twice examined by the Lords of the Council, I would not disclose unto them my opinion, out of a malignant, perfidious, obstinate, and traitorous mind, whether the King were Supreme Head of the Church or no, but answered them that this law belonged not to me, whether it were just or unjust, because I did not enjoy any benefice from the Church; yet I then protested that I never had said or done anything against it, neither can any one word or action of mine be produced to make me culpable—yea, this I confess was then my speech unto their honours, that I hereafter would think of nothing else but of the bitter passion of our blessed Saviour and of my passage out of this miserable world. I wish no harm to any, and if this will not keep me alive, I desire not to live; by all which I know that I could not transgress any law or incur any crime of treason, for neither this statute nor any law in the world can punish any man for holding his peace; for they can only punish either words or deeds, God only being judge of our secret thoughts.'

Of which words, because they were urgent indeed, the King's Attorney interrupted him and said: 'Although we have not one word or deed of yours to object against you, yet we have your silence, which is an evident sign of a malicious mind, because no dutiful subject being lawfully asked this question will refuse to answer....'

'I now come to the third capital matter of my indictment, whereby I am accused that I maliciously attempted, traitorously endeavoured, and perfidiously practised against this statute, as the words thereof affirm, because I wrote eight sundry packets of letters, whilst I was in the Tower, unto Bishop Fisher, by which I exhorted him to break the same law and induced him to the like obstinacy. I would have these letters produced and read against me, which may either free me or convince me of a lie. But because you say the Bishop burnt them all, I will here tell the truth of the whole matter. Some were only of private matters, as about our old friendship and acquaintance; one of them was in answer to his, whereby he desired of me to know how I had answered in my examinations to this oath of supremacy, touching which this only I wrote unto him again,—that I had already settled my conscience, let him settle his to his own good liking, —and no other answer I gave him, God is my witness, as God shall, I hope, save this my soul; and this I trust is no breach of your laws.'

'The last objected crime is, that being examined in the Tower I did say that this law was like a two-edged sword, for in consenting thereto I should endanger my soul, in refusing it I should lose my life; which answer, because Bishop Fisher made the like, it is evidently gathered, as you say, that we both conspired together. Whereto I reply that my answer there was but conditional, if there be danger in both either to allow or disallow this statute; and therefore, like a two-edged sword, it seemeth a hard thing that it should be offered to me, that never have hitherto contradicted it either in word or deed. These were my words. What the Bishop answered I know not. If his answer were like mine, it proceeded not from any conspiracy of ours but from the likeness of our wits and learning. To conclude, I unfeignedly avouch that I never spake word against this law to any living man, although perhaps the King's Majesty hath been told the contrary.'

To this full answer the Attorney did not reply any more, but the word *malice* was in the mouth of all the Court, yet could no man produce either word or deed to prove it; yet for all this clearing of himself, for a last proof to the jury that Sir Thomas was guilty, Mr Rich was called forth to give evidence unto them upon his oath, which he did forthwith, affirming that which we have spoken of before in their communication in the Tower[1],

[1] 'After all these examinations came Mr Rich,...then newly made the King's Solicitor, Sir Richard Southwell, and one Mr Palmer, Mr Secretary's man, sent by the King to take away all his books; and while Sir Richard and Mr Palmer were busy in trussing up the books, Mr Rich, pretending to talk friendly with Sir Thomas, said thus unto him (as it proved after, of set purpose), "Forasmuch as it is well known, Mr More, that you are a man both wise and well learned in the laws of this realm and in all other studies, I pray you, Sir, let me be so bold as of good will to put unto you this case: admit there were an Act of Parliament made, that all the realm should take me for king, would not you, Mr More, take me for king?" "Yes, Sir," said Sir Thomas, "that I would." "I put the case further," said Mr Rich, "that there were an Act of Parliament that all the realm should take me for pope, would not you then take me for pope?" "For answer," said Sir Thomas, "to your first case, the Parliament may well, Mr Rich, meddle with the state of temporal princes; but to make answer to your other case, suppose the Parliament should make a law that God should not be God, would you then, Mr Rich, say so?" "No, Sir," said he,

against whom, now sworn and forsworn, Sir Thomas began in this wise to speak, 'If I were a man, my Lords, that did not regard an oath, I needed not at this time in this place, as is well known unto everyone, to stand as an accused person. And if this oath, Mr Rich, which you have taken be true, then I pray that I never see God in the face; which I would not say, were it otherwise, to gain the whole world.'

Then did he recite their whole communication in the Tower according as it was, truly and sincerely, adding this: 'In good faith, Mr Rich, I am more sorry for your perjury than for mine own peril; and know you, that neither I nor any man else to my knowledge ever took you to be a man of such credit as either I or any other would vouchsafe to communicate with you in any matter of importance....'

Mr Rich, seeing himself so evidently to be disproved, and his credit so foully defaced, caused Sir Richard Southwell and Mr Palmer, who in the time of their communication were in the same chamber with them, to be there sworn what words passed between them. Whereupon Mr Palmer upon his deposition said that he was so busy in the trussing up Sir Thomas's books in a sack, that he took no heed to their talk. Sir Richard Southwell also said likewise that because he was appointed only to look to the conveying of these books he gave no ear unto them. And after all this Sir Thomas alleged many other reasons in his own defence, to the utter discredit of Mr Rich's foresaid evidence, and for proof of the clearness of his own conscience.

But for all that ever he could do or say, the jury of twelve men.... These, I say, going together and staying scarce one quarter of an hour (for they knew what the King would have done in that case) returned with their verdict, Guilty.

Wherefore the Lord Chancellor, as chief Judge in that matter, began presently[1] to proceed to judgment; which Sir Thomas perceiving said unto him, 'My Lord, when I was towards the law the manner in such cases was to ask the prisoner before sentence whether he could give any reason why judgment should not proceed against him.' Upon which words the Lord Chancellor,

"that I would not, for no Parliament can make such a law." "No more," reported he that Sir Thomas should say (but indeed he made no such inference, as he avouched after to Mr Rich's face) "could the Parliament make the King Supreme Head of the Church"; and upon this only report of Mr Rich Sir Thomas was shortly after indicted of high treason upon the new Statute of Supremacy. At this time Mr Lieutenant reported after to Sir Thomas that Mr Rich had so vile a smell about him that he could scarce endure him, which Sir Thomas also felt' (More, p. 252).

[1] Immediately.

staying his sentence, wherein he had already partly proceeded, asked Sir Thomas what he was able to say to the contrary, who forthwith made answer in this sort.. . .

Then follows a speech by Sir Thomas More, which soon resolved itself into an argument with the Lord Chancellor.

Now when Sir Thomas had taken as many exceptions as he thought meet for the avoiding[1] of this indictment, and alleging many more substantial reasons than can be here set down, the Lord Chancellor having bethought himself, and being loath now to have the whole burden of this condemnation to lie upon himself, asked openly there the advice of my Lord Chief Justice of England, Sir John Fitzjames, whether this indictment were sufficient or no, who wisely answered thus: 'My Lords all, by St Gillian,' for that was ever his oath, 'I must needs confess that if the Act of Parliament be not unlawful, then the indictment is not in my conscience insufficient.' An answer like that of the Scribes and Pharisees to Pilate: 'If this man were not a malefactor we would never have delivered him unto you.' And so with *ifs* and *ans* he added to the matter a slender evasion. Upon whose words my Lord Chancellor spoke, even as Caiaphas spoke to the Jewish Council: *Quid adhuc desideramus testimonium, reus est mortis.* And so presently he pronounced this sentence [*the usual sentence in cases of treason*].. . .

The sentence yet was, by the King's pardon, changed afterwards only into beheading, because he had borne the greatest office of the realm; of which mercy of the King's word being brought to Sir Thomas, he answered merrily, 'God forbid the King should use any more such mercy unto any of my friends, and God bless all my posterity from such pardons.'

When Sir Thomas had now fully perceived that he was called to martyrdom, having received sentence of death, with a bold and constant countenance he spoke in this manner: 'Well, seeing I am condemned, God knows how justly. I will freely speak for the disburdening of my conscience what I think of this law. When I perceived that the King's pleasure was to sift out from whence the Pope's authority was derived, I confess I studied seven years together to find out the truth thereof; and I could not read in any one doctor's writings which the Church alloweth any one saying that avouched that a layman was or could ever be Head of the Church.'

To this my Lord Chancellor again: 'Would you be accounted

---

[1] Refuting.

more wise and of more sincere conscience than all the bishops, learned doctors, nobility, and commons of this realm?' To which Sir Thomas replied: 'I am able to produce against one bishop which you can bring forth of your side, one hundred holy and Catholic bishops for my opinion; and against one realm the consent of all Christendom for more than a thousand years.' The Duke of Norfolk hearing this said, 'Now, Sir Thomas, you shew your obstinate and malicious mind.' To whom Sir Thomas said, 'Noble Sir, not any malice or obstinacy causeth me to say this, but the just necessity of the cause constraineth me for the discharge of my conscience, and I call God to witness no other than this hath moved me thereunto.'

After this the judges courteously offered him their favourable audience if he had anything to allege in his own defence; who answered most mildly and charitably, 'More have I not to say, my Lords, but that like as the blessed apostle St Paul, as we read in the Acts of the Apostles, was present and consenting to the death of the protomartyr St Stephen, keeping their clothes that stoned him to death, and yet they be now both twain holy saints in heaven, and there shall continue friends together for ever; so I verily trust, and shall therefore most heartily pray, that though your Lordships have been on earth my judges to condemnation yet we may hereafter meet in heaven merrily together to our everlasting salvation; and God preserve you all, especially my Sovereign Lord the King, and grant him faithful counsellors....'

Being now brought to the scaffold whereon he was to be beheaded, it seemed to him so weak that it was ready to fall; wherefore he said merrily to Mr Lieutenant, 'I pray you, Sir, see me safe up, and for my coming down let me shift for myself.' When he began to speak a little to the people, which were in great troops there to hear and see him, he was interrupted by the Sheriff; wherefore briefly he desired all the people to pray for him, and to bear witness with him that he there died in and for the faith of the Holy Catholic Church, a faithful servant both of God and the King. Having spoken but this, he kneeled down and pronounced with great devotion the *Miserere* psalm, which being ended, he cheerfully rose up, and the executioner asking him forgiveness, he kissed him.... Then, laying his head upon the block, he bade the executioner stay until he had removed his beard aside, saying, 'That had never committed treason.' So with great alacrity and spiritual joy he received the fatal axe....

More, *Life of More* (ed. J. Hunter, 1828), pp. 255–73 and 286.

A fortnight before the trial of Sir Thomas More, Bishop Fisher had been brought to trial in Westminster Hall. The case against him was technically stronger than that against More, but the evidence had been obtained by a trick. On 7 May, 1535, he was visited by Cromwell and others of the Council in the Tower. They read to him the Act of Supremacy, which had been passed in the preceding November, and elicited from him the statement that he could not recognise the King as Supreme Head of the Church. They then read to him the new Treasons Act, of which he had hitherto been ignorant, by which it was made high treason to deprive the King of his title, name, or dignity, and pointed out that his previous admission had now brought him within its terms. This admission, made in ignorance of its consequences by a prisoner cut off by his imprisonment from the means of knowing, was the only evidence against him at his trial. The charge in the indictment was that he did '7 May, 27 Henry VIII, openly declare in English, "The King our Sovereign Lord is not Supreme Head in earth of the Church of England."'

After the jury's verdict of guilty, he was sentenced to the usual punishment of treason, but as in the case of More this was commuted to beheading; and he suffered on Tower Hill, 22 June, 1535. More's execution, at the same place, was on 6 July. It is possible that the traditions of the two trials have become somewhat confused.

(2) Trial of the Duke of Norfolk, 1572

The Duke of Norfolk was brought to trial 16 January, 1572, before the Earl of Shrewsbury as Lord High Steward, and 26 Lords Triers. He was indicted for having compassed and imagined the death and deposition of the Queen, the overt act being that he had endeavoured to marry Mary Queen of Scots, well knowing that she claimed the Crown as against Elizabeth; and the indictment also charged him at great length with participation in other treasonable undertakings.

The evidence that Norfolk was implicated in the Ridolfi Plot is very strong; but his trial exhibits the efficiency of Tudor justice as a system for condemning the guilty rather than protecting the innocent. The extracts printed below are selected to illustrate this.

... After the reading of the indictment, the Clerk of the Crown said to the Duke: 'How sayest thou, Thomas, Duke of Norfolk, art thou guilty of these treasons whereof thou art indicted in manner and form as thou art thereof indicted, Yea or No?'

Thereupon the Duke began, and said to this effect: May it please your Grace, and you the rest of my Lords here; the hearing of this indictment giveth me occasion to enter into the making of a suit which I meant not to have done before my coming hither. I beseech you, if the law will permit it, that I may have counsel allowed me for the answering of this indictment.

The Lord Chief Justice answered, That in case of high treason he cannot have counsel allowed; and that he was to answer to his own fact only, which himself best knew, and might without counsel sufficiently answer.

Duke. That you may understand I speak it not without some ground, these be the causes that move me to make this suit. I was told before I came here that I was indicted upon the Statute of the 25th of Edw. III. I have had very short warning to provide to answer so great a matter; I have not had 14 hours in all, both day and night, and now I neither hear the same statute alleged, and yet I am put at once to the whole herd of laws, not knowing which particularity to answer unto. The indictment containeth sundry points and matters to touch me by circumstance, and so to draw me into matter of treason, which are not treasons themselves; therefore with reverence and humble submission I am led to think I may have counsel. And this I shew that you may think I move not this suit without any ground. I am hardly handled; I have had short warning and no books—neither Book of Statutes nor so much as the Breviate of Statutes. I am brought to fight without a weapon; yet I remember one case in law—I think it is in the first year of King Henry VII. It is the case of one Humphrey Stafford, which was indicted of high treason and had counsel allowed him. If the precedent in his case be such as it may extend to me, I require it at your hands that I may have it allowed; I shew you my ground why I crave it; I refer me to your opinions therein.

Then Sir James Dyer, Lord Chief Justice of the Common Pleas, said: My Lord, that case of Humphrey Stafford *in primo* of Henry VII was about pleading of sanctuary, for that he was taken out of sanctuary at Culneham, which belonged to the Abbot of Abingdon, so the question was whether he should be allowed sanctuary in that case, and with that form of pleading, which was matter of law; in which case he had counsel, and not upon the point or fact of high treason, but only for the allowance of sanctuary, and whether it might be allowed being claimed by prescription and without shewing any former allowances in Eyre, and such like matters. But all our books do forbid allowing of counsel in the point of treason, but only it is to be answered Guilty or Not Guilty.

Duke. Humphrey Stafford's case was high treason, and he had counsel. . . . If the law do not allow me counsel, I must submit me to your opinions. . . . I am now to make another suit to you, my Lords the Judges; I beseech you tell me if my indictment be perfect and sufficient in law, and whether in whole or in the parts, and in which parts, that I may know to what I should answer.

Lord Chief Justice Catlin. For the sufficiency of your indictment, it hath been well debated and considered by us all; and we
have all with one assent resolved, and so do certify you, that if the
causes in the indictment expressed be true in fact, the indictment
is wholly and in every part sufficient.

Duke. Be all the points treasons?

L.C.J. Catlin. All be treasons, if the truth of the case be so
in fact.

Duke. I will tell you what moveth me to ask you this. I have
heard of the case of the Lord Scrope; it was in the time of Henry
IV (the Judges said Henry V), he confessed the indictment and
yet traversed that the points thereof were no treasons.

L.C.J. Catlin. My Lord, he had his judgments for treason
upon that indictment, and was executed.... (ff. 965–7.)

    *   *   *   *   *   *

Duke. ...Go directly to the indictment; it is no praise nor
glory for you to overlay[1] me. I am unlearned, unable to speak,
and worst of all to speak for myself. I have neither good utterance,
as the world well knoweth, nor good understanding. For God's
sake, do not overlay me with superfluous matter.... (f. 969.)

    *   *   *   *   *   *

A great part of the trial consisted of arguments exchanged between the prisoner
and the four counsel who were conducting the case for the Crown. Many depositions
were also read, and explanations given at great length. The effect of the Duke's
speeches was thus summed up by the Solicitor-General.

Solic. This your answer is in all no more than a bare denying, and
so be all your speeches, all upon your own credit only.... (f. 1018.)

    *   *   *   *   *   *

Duke. I shall hardly come, after so smooth a tale as Mr
Attorney of the Wards can tell; yet one good proof I have to my
comfort, that they [*i.e.* the witnesses against him] be as please
your Lordships to weigh them. If you would not have dealt thus
untruly with me, I would not have taken exception against them,
though I chiefly challenge none but Barker, in whom you may
see what fear may do; besides that they have confessed themselves
traitors, and so men of no conscience or credit. It is well known
that Barker's stomach[2] is nothing; he hath been known well
enough. Fear hath done much in him. The Bishop of Ross is
also a fearful man. As touching Barker and the Bishop of Ross,
Bracton hath a saying that witnesses must be freemen and not
traitors, neither outlawed nor attainted.

Catlin. None of them be outlawed, attainted, or indicted.

---

    [1] Overpower.   [2] Courage.

Duke. I mean not that they were indicted, but they be in as ill case, for they have confessed themselves traitors....(f. 1026.)

*   *   *   *   *   *

Duke. You say my indictment is only upon the Statute of 25 Edw. III. That statute standeth upon three points; compassing the death of the Prince's person, levying of war against the Prince, and aiding of the Prince's enemies; and all these must be proved overt-fact. If by any way, by any overt-fact, you can prove that I have directly touched the Prince's person, or done any of the said things that the Statute extendeth to, I will yield myself guilty. If anything be doubtful, the Statute referreth it to the judgment of the Parliament[1].

Catlin. Usage is the best expounder of the law, that is, the common use how the Statute hath been taken and expounded; and the same Statute is but the declaration of the common law.

Duke. The preamble of the Statute is to bring the laws of treason to a certainty, that men may certainly know what is treason.

Attorney-General. You complained of your close keeping, that you had no books to provide for your answer. It seemeth you have had books and counsel. You allege books, statutes, and Bracton. I am sure the study of such books is not your profession.

Duke. I have been in trouble these two years. Think you that in all this time I have not had cause to look for myself?....(f. 1027.)

*   *   *   *   *   *

State Trials, i, 957–1042.

(3) Trial of Mary Queen of Scots, 1586

Mary Queen of Scots was brought to trial in Fotheringay Castle, 14 and 15 October, 1586, before a Special Commission[2] consisting of John Whitgift, Archbishop of Canterbury, Sir Thomas Bromley, Lord Chancellor, Lord Burghley, Lord Treasurer, and 43 others, namely: 29 peers, 9 Privy Councillors who were commoners, and 5 Judges. The Commissioners were authorised 'to examine all and singular matters compassed and imagined tending to the hurt of our royal person, as well by the aforesaid Mary as by any other person or persons...with the privity of the same Mary,'[3] and to give judgment according to the tenor of the Act of 1585 for the Security of the Queen's Person [p. 417]. The proceedings were exceptional in character, for Mary had lately been a reigning sovereign, and in any case she was not one of Elizabeth's subjects; but the terms of the Act pointed at her unmistakeably, and they gave sufficient authority under the law of England to bring her to trial.

Of her complicity in the Babington conspiracy there is little doubt, but from a modern point of view her trial is open to criticism upon three grounds: (1) at that part of the trial when witnesses were examined in public, the prisoner was neither

---

[1] On this proviso see p. 375 above.
[2] The commission is printed in Prothero, p. 140.   [3] *State Trials*, i, 1168.

present in person or represented by counsel; (2) the Court allowed her case to be prejudiced by going at length into her dealings with Spain, which were not relevant to the issue they were empowered to try—whether she had conspired against Elizabeth's life; and (3) when copies of her letters were produced in Court no attempt was made formally to prove that they were correct copies, or that the letters had been actually sent; but in formalities of this kind Tudor procedure was always defective. The human interest of the trial lies in the remarkable skill with which Mary met and parried the thrusts of her antagonists; but this failed to save her. After long hesitation on the part of Elizabeth, she was executed in the great hall of Fotheringay Castle, 8 February, 1587.

The trial is closely parodied by Spenser in the ninth canto of the fifth book of the *Faery Queene*, where the false Duessa is tried before Queen Mercilla, who, following the part which the real Elizabeth elected to play, deferred the execution 'till strong constraint did her thereto enforce,' and 'even then ruing her wiful fall,' at last pronounced her doom 'with more than needful natural remorse' (x. 4).

The most part of these Commissioners came the 11th of October to Fotheringay Castle.... The next day the Commissioners sent to her Sir Walter Mildmay, Paulet, and Edward Barker, a public notary, who delivered into her hands Queen Elizabeth's letter, which when she had read she, with a countenance composed to royal dignity and with a mind untroubled, said... As for this letter, it seemeth strange to me that the Queen should command me as a subject to appear personally in judgment. I am an absolute queen, and will do nothing which may prejudice either mine own royal majesty, or other princes of my place and rank, or my son.... The laws and statutes of England are to me most unknown; I am destitute of counsellors, and who shall be my peers I am utterly ignorant. My papers and notes are taken from me, and no man dareth step forth to be my advocate. I am clear from all crime against the Queen; I have excited no man against her; and I am not to be charged but by mine own word or writing, which cannot be produced against me. Yet can I not deny but I have commended myself and my cause to foreign princes. (ff. 1168–9.)

The next day...in the afternoon came unto her certain selected persons from amongst the Commissioners, with men learned in the Civil and Canon Law. But the Lord Chancellor and the Lord Treasurer declared their authority by patent, and shewed that neither her imprisonment nor her prerogative of royal majesty could exempt her from answering in this kingdom, with fair words advising her to hear what matters were to be objected against her; otherwise they threatened that by authority of law they both could and would proceed against her though she were absent. She answered that she was no subject, and rather would she die a thousand deaths than acknowledge herself a subject, considering that by such an acknowledgment she should both prejudice the height of regal majesty[1], and withal confess herself to be bound by all the laws of England, even in matter of religion; nevertheless, she was ready to answer to all things in a free and full Parliament, for that she knew not whether this meeting and assembly were appointed against her, being already condemned by fore-judgings, to give some show and colour of a just and legal proceeding. She warned them therefore to look to their consciences, and to remember that the theatre of the whole world is much wider than the kingdom of England.... (ff. 1169–70.)

...Within few hours after, they delivered unto her...the chief points of their Commission and the names of the Commissioners, that she might see that they were to proceed according to equity and right, and not by any cunning point of law and extraordinary course. She took no exceptions against the Commissioners, but most sharply excepted against the late law upon which the authority of their Commission wholly depended; as that it was unjust, devised of purpose against her, that it was without example, and such whereunto she would never subject herself.... (f. 1170.)

...Then she required to have her protestation shewed and allowed which she had formerly made. It was answered that it never had been nor now was to be allowed, for that it was prejudicial to the Crown of England. She asked by what authority they would proceed. It was answered, by authority of their Commission and by the common law of England.

But, said she, ye make laws at your pleasure whereunto I have no reason to submit myself, considering that the English in times past refused to submit themselves to the Law Salique of France; and if they would proceed by the common law of England they should produce precedents and cases, forasmuch as that law consisteth much of cases and custom....

From hence she fell into other speeches....Thus while she wandered far in these digressions, they called her back again, and prayed her to speak plainly whether she would answer before the Commissioners. She replied, That the authority of their delegation was founded upon a late law made to entrap her; that she could not away with the Queen's laws, which she had good reason to suspect; that she was still full of good courage, and would not offend against her progenitors the Kings of Scots by acknowledging herself a subject to the Crown of England, for

[1] To a Tudor sovereign, nurtured in the doctrine of a royal caste, this argument would make a strong appeal.

this were nothing else but to profess them openly to have been rebels and traitors. Yet she refused not to answer, so as she might not be reduced to the rank of a subject; but she had rather perish utterly than to answer as a criminal person.

Whereunto Hatton, Vice-Chamberlain to Queen Elizabeth, answered: You are accused (but not condemned) to have conspired the destruction of our Lady and Queen anointed. You say you are a queen; be it so. But in such a crime the royal dignity is not exempted from answering, neither by the Civil nor Canon Law, nor by the Law of Nations, nor of Nature. For if such kind of offences might be committed without punishment, all justice would stagger, yea, fall to the ground. If you be innocent, you wrong your reputation in avoiding a trial.... Wherefore lay aside the bootless privilege of royal dignity, which now can be of no use unto you; appear in judgment and shew your innocency, lest by avoiding trial you draw upon yourself suspicion, and lay upon your reputation an eternal blot and aspersion.

I refuse not (said she) to answer in a full Parliament before the Estates of the Realm lawfully assembled, so as I may be declared the next to the succession; yea, before the Queen and Council, so as my protestation may be admitted, and I may be acknowledged the next of kin to the Queen. To the judgment of mine adversaries, amongst whom I know all defence of mine innocency will be barred, flatly, I will not submit myself.

The Lord Chancellor asked her whether she would answer if her protestation were admitted. I will never (said she) submit myself to the late law mentioned in the Commission.

Hereupon the Lord Treasurer answered, We notwithstanding will proceed to-morrow in the cause, though you be absent and continue *contumax*.

Search (said she) your consciences; look to your honour; God reward you and yours for your judgment against me.

On the morrow, which was the 14th of the month, she sent for certain of the Commissioners and prayed them that her protestation might be admitted and allowed. The Lord Treasurer asked her whether she would appear to her trial if her protestation were only received and put in writing, without allowance. She yielded at length, yet with much ado and with an ill-will, lest she should seem (as she said) to derogate from her predecessors or successors; but was very desirous to purge herself of the crime objected against her, being persuaded by Hatton's reasons, which she had weighed with advisement.

Soon after the Commissioners which were present assembled

themselves in the Presence Chamber.... When she was come and had settled herself in her seat, after silence proclaimed, Bromley, Lord Chancellor, turning to her, spake briefly to this effect....

...She, rising up,...protested that she was no subject of the Queen's, but had been and was a free and absolute queen, and not to be constrained to appear before Commissioners or any other judge whatsoever for any cause whatsoever, save before God alone, the highest Judge, lest she should prejudice her own royal majesty, the King of Scots her son, her successors, or other absolute princes. But that she now appeared personally, to the end to refute the crimes objected against her....

Then, after the Commission was openly read, which was grounded upon the Act already often mentioned, she stoutly opposed her protestation against the said Act as enacted directly and purposely against her, and herein she appealed to their consciences.

When answer was made by the Lord Treasurer, that every person in this kingdom was bound even by the latest laws, and that she ought not to speak against the laws....

Gawdy[1] now opened the law from point to point, affirming that she had offended against the same; and hereupon he made an historical discourse of Babington's conspiracy, and concluded, That she knew of it, approved it, assented unto it, promised her assistance, and shewed the way and means.

She answered with stout courage, That she knew not Babington, that she never received any letters from him nor wrote any to him.... She required that her own subscription under her hand might be produced.... Then were read the copies of letters between her and Babington, wherein the whole conspiracy was set down. (ff. 1170–4.)

* * * * * *

[She said] that it was an easy matter to counterfeit the ciphers and characters of others;... That she feared also lest this were done now by Walsingham to bring her to her death, who, as she heard, had practised against her life and her son's.... And withal she shed plenty of tears.... (f. 1182.)

* * * * * *

[She said], Letters may be directed to others than those to whom they are written, and many things have been often inserted which she never dictated. If her papers had not been taken away, and she had her secretary, she could better confute the things objected against her.... (f. 1186.)

* * * * * *

[1] Sir Thomas Gawdy, Justice of the Queen's Bench, one of the Commissioners.

These things being done, the assembly was prorogued to the 25th of October at the Star Chamber at Westminster...and after Naw and Curle had by oath, *viva voce*, voluntarily, without hope of reward, before them avowedly affirmed and confirmed all and every the letters and copies of letters before produced to be most true, sentence[1] was pronounced against the Queen of Scots.... (ff. 1188–9.)

* * * * * *

State Trials, i, 1161–1228.

(4) Trial of the Earl of Essex, 1601

The following extracts shew the nature of the procedure in the Court of the Lord High Steward. Cf. Sir Edward Coke's description on p. 428 above.

A spacious Court was made in Westminster Hall, where the Lord Treasurer Buckhurst sat as High Steward of England under a canopy of state; where sat also about the table the earls, barons, and judges of the land, according to their degrees. The Judges were these: the Lord Chief Justice Popham, and the Lord Chief Justice Anderson. The Lord Chief Baron, Sir William Periam. Justices Gawdy, Fenner, Walmesley, Warburton, Kingsmill, and Mr Baron Clarke.

These sat all in the Court next the bar, before the High Steward. Seven serjeants-at-arms came in with maces before the High Steward and laid them down before him in the Court. The King-at-Arms stood on the one side of the High Steward by his chair of estate, and one of her Majesty's gentlemen ushers with his white rod in his hand on the other side. The Clerk of the Crown and his assistant sat before him to read the common indictments and examinations. The Captain of the Guard (Sir Walter Ralegh) and forty of the Queen's Guard were there to attend the service. Then the Serjeant-at-Arms made three *O yes*, and proclamation, That the Lord High Steward of England commanded silence, and to hear the Commission read, upon pain of imprisonment. Then the Clerk of the Crown read the Commission, whereunto the Earl of Essex was very attentive. Another proclamation was made, That the Lord High Steward of England commanded all Justices to whom any writs had been directed for this service, to bring them in and certify the same. Another proclamation was made by a serjeant-at-arms, That the Lieuten-

---

[1] Mary was not sentenced by the Commission to death as a traitor; but the Commissioners reported that the Babington conspiracy had been 'with the privity of the said Mary'; and that she had compassed and imagined 'divers matters tending to the hurt, death, and destruction of the royal person of our Sovereign Lady the Queen,' contrary to the Act for the Surety of the Queen's Person.

ant of the Tower of London should return his precept, and bring forth his prisoners, Robert, Earl of Essex, and Henry, Earl of Southampton.

Then the Lord High Constable of the Tower, the Lieutenant of the Tower, and the gentleman-porter who carried the axe before the prisoners, came first in, and the prisoners followed and made their appearance at the bar, the gentleman-porter with the axe standing before them, with the axe's edge from them; and so the Lieutenant delivered his precept into the Court. The two Earls which were prisoners kissed one another's hands and embraced each other. Another proclamation was made, That the Serjeant-at-Arms to the Queen's Majesty do return his precept of the names of all the peers of Robert, Earl of Essex, and Henry, Earl of Southampton, the which he delivered into the Court accordingly. Another proclamation was made, That all earls, viscounts, and barons of the realm of England which were peers of Robert, Earl of Essex, and Henry, Earl of Southampton, and summoned to appear this day, do make answer to their names, upon pain and peril that will fall thereon.

Then the Lords were called, and answered and appeared as followeth [*Twenty-five Lords answered to their names*]....

Then the Earl of Essex desired to know of my Lord Chief Justice whether he might challenge any of the peers or no; whereunto the Lord Chief Justice answered, No.... Whereupon the Earl bade them go on. When the Lord Grey was called, the Earl of Essex laughed upon the Earl of Southampton, and jogged him by his sleeve.

Then they were called to hold up their hands at the bar, which they did. And then the Clerk of the Crown read the indictments. That being done, they were bid to hold up their hands again, which they did, and another indictment was read, whereunto the Earl of Essex was attentive. After which the Clerk of the Crown asked them whether they were Guilty or Not Guilty: they pleaded Not Guilty, and for their trials they put themselves upon God and their peers. They spake this severally. Then my Lord High Steward in a few words gave the peers a charge, requiring them to have a due regard of their consciences.

Then Serjeant Yelverton opened the evidence.... Good my Lord, I beseech your Grace, and you, my Lords, that are the peers, to understand that if any man do but intend the death of the King it is death by the law; for he is the head of the Commonwealth, and all his subjects as members ought to obey and stand with him.... (ff. 1333–6.)

Attorney-General (Sir Edward Coke). May it please your Grace, the Lords Chief Judges, which are the fathers of the law, do know that the thought of treason to the Prince by the law is death, and he that is guilty of rebellion is guilty of an intent (by the laws of the land) to seek the destruction of the Prince, and so adjudged treason.... He that raiseth power and strength in a settled government, the law will not suffer it, but it is construed as in cases of high treason; he that doth usurp upon it, the law doth intend that he hath purposed the destruction of the Prince; he that doth assemble power, if the King doth command him upon his allegiance to dissolve his company and he continue it, without any question it is high treason; he that doth levy forces to take any town in the Prince's dominions, it is so likewise. But my Lord of Essex hath levied power to take the Tower of London and to surprise the Queen's own Court; then this must needs be higher than the highest, and he that doth fortify himself against the Prince's power must needs be within the compass of treason.... (f. 1337.)

The examinations of the witnesses were then read, and a series of altercations took place between the prisoners, who by the regular rule of law in cases of high treason were not allowed counsel, and the lawyers who represented the Crown.

... Then proclamation was made, 'Lieutenant of the Tower, withdraw your prisoners from the bar.' They being removed, the lords and peers went together into a private place made of purpose behind the canopy and chair of estate. Then the two Chief Judges and the Lord Chief Baron were sent for in to them to deliver their opinions in law, which they did upon two points: the one 'That in case where a subject attempteth to put himself into such strength as the King shall not be able to resist him, and to force and compel the King to govern otherwise than according to his royal authority and direction, it is manifest rebellion.' The other: 'That in every rebellion the law intendeth as a consequent the compassing the death and deprivation of the King, as foreseeing that the rebel will never suffer that King to live or reign who might punish or take revenge of his treason or rebellion.'

After half an hour they came all out again, and each man took his place; which being done, the Serjeant-at-Arms began at the puisne lord and called Thomas, Lord Howard, who stood up bare-headed.

Lord Steward. My Lord Thomas Howard, whether is Robert, Earl of Essex, guilty of this treason whereupon he hath been indicted, as you take it upon your honour, or no? ... Whereupon the Lord Thomas Howard made answer, bending his body and, laying his left hand upon his right side, said, 'Guilty, my Lord, of high treason.' After which manner all the peers found him guilty, from the puisne to the highest, and so delivered in like sort upon their honours. Being called over anew, they found Henry, Earl of Southampton, guilty of high treason also.

Then the Serjeant-at-Arms commanded the Lieutenant of the Tower to bring his prisoners to the bar again. Then the Clerk of the Crown, speaking first to the Earl of Essex, said, 'Robert, Earl of Essex, you have been arraigned and indicted of high treason; you have pleaded Not Guilty, and for your trial you have put yourself upon God and your peers; the peers here (who have heard the evidence and your answer in your defence) have found you Guilty; now what can you say for yourself why you should not have judgment of death?...' (ff. 1355–6.)

...Then the Lord High Steward, after a few exhortations to the Earls to prepare themselves for God, told them, seeing the law had found them guilty, it followed of course that he must proceed to judgment.

The Earl of Essex replied very cheerfully and said: 'Yea, my Lord, with a very good will I pray you go on.'

Then the Lord High Steward gave judgment as followeth: 'You must go to the place from whence you came, and there remain during her Majesty's pleasure; from thence to be drawn on a hurdle through London streets and so to the place of execution, where you shall be hanged, bowelled, and quartered, your head and quarters to be disposed of at her Majesty's pleasure; and so God have mercy on your souls....' (f. 1357.)

Then the Serjeant-at-Arms stood up with the mace on his shoulder, and after proclamation was made said thus: 'All peers that were summoned to be here this day may now take their ease; and all other persons attending here this service may depart in her Majesty's peace, for my Lord High Steward is pleased to dissolve this Commission....'

The Earl of Southampton obtained a reprieve, but the Earl of Essex was ordered for execution....(f. 1358.)

State Trials, i, 1333–60.

Local Government[1]

The Tudor kings, who possessed 'a genius for gaining and holding power,'[2] used their power not only to destroy but to build; and their reorganisation of the English system of local government is a monument to their constructive genius. In the feudal period the government of localities had been liable to interference from the great lords; but after the Wars of the Roses 'there was never a time when a faction of the nobility, relying upon their own retainers, could meet a King on equal terms,'[2] and their place in relation to local government was taken by the Tudor centralised administration. This involved a general reconstruction of the system of local administration, which now took over new duties and discharged them under more efficient central control.

The functionary who now came to occupy the most dignified position in the local hierarchy—the Lord Lieutenant of the county—was a Tudor creation. Under Henry VIII special commissions were issued from time to time to Lieutenants of the King to organise and equip military contingents in particular localities. Under Edward VI, to meet the danger of Catholic risings in 1550 and 1551, these were appointed for nearly every county; and in the reign of Mary they received Parliamentary sanction[3]. They became a permanent institution, and gradually took over the military duties hitherto discharged by the sheriffs; but they were also charged with the conservation of the peace, and were authorised to command the assistance of the local justices[4]. The Lord Lieutenant was usually also *Custos Rotulorum*—the official keeper of the records of the shire [p. 459]; and in this capacity he appointed the Clerk of the Peace [p. 460].

The key to the Tudor reconstruction of local government is, however, to be found in the ancient office of Justice of the Peace. The weakness of all organisations for maintaining order in the localities by acting from the centre is that they are deficient in local knowledge—an essential condition of success; and yet it was upon the efficiency of the provision for maintaining order in the localities that the every-day happiness of the English people depended. The Tudor sovereigns might have established a bureaucracy of experts under the new office of Lord Lieutenant, or revivified the declining power of the ancient office of the sheriff; they preferred to utilise the existing organisation of a local magistracy, and to provide themselves with local knowledge by employing local men. 'The justices of the peace,' says Sir Thomas Smith [p. 455], 'be those in whom at this time for the repressing of robbers, thieves, and vagabonds, of privy complots and conspiracies, of riots and violences, and all other misdemeanours in the Commonwealth, the Prince putteth his special trust,...and generally...for the good government of the shire the Prince putteth his trust in them.' And to those

---

[1] See C. A. Beard, *The Office of the Justice of the Peace*; R. Gneist, *History of the English Constitution*, vol. ii, ch. 36; Miss E. Trotter, *The Country Parish*.
[2] Macy, p. 201.   [3] 4 & 5 P. & M. c. 3.
[4] A Commission of Lieutenancy of 27 Eliz. is printed in Prothero, p. 154.

who were faithful over a few things jurisdiction over many things was given. It is a special characteristic of Tudor legislation, in so far as it affects local government, that it is perpetually imposing new duties upon the Justices of the Peace. In this way they acquired an excellent political training. 'Nothing could so well have prepared the country gentry and the burgesses of the great towns for the share they were to take in the Parliaments of the coming age.'[1]

As a matter of pedigree, the Justices of the Peace derive from the *Conservatores pacis* who were first appointed under a proclamation issued in 1195 by Archbishop Hubert, Richard I's Justiciar; but the final establishment of the office as a permanent institution dates from a statute of 1360[2], which in every county 'assigned for the keeping of the peace one lord and with him three or four of the most worthy in the county, with some learned in the law,' and authorised them not only to arrest and imprison offenders but also 'to hear and determine at the King's suit all manner of felonies and trespasses done in the same county.' This statute is the foundation of the jurisdiction of the Courts of Quarter-Sessions for counties, and it is from this time, according to Lambarde [p. 457] 'that they were both commonly reputed and called Justices.'

The Justices of the Peace were appointed by the Lord Chancellor, and the Commission under which they acted was issued out of the Chancery, but suggestions as to fit and proper persons to be appointed were made from time to time to the Chancellor by the Council, by local magnates, and by the judges of assize; while in Wales the selections were practically made by the Council of the Marches[3]. By a statute of Henry VI[4] a property qualification of £20 a year in land was required from Justices of the Peace [p. 457], but the Chancellor was authorised to appoint 'discreet persons learned in the law,' even if they were not so qualified. There were no regular wages attached to the office, but certain small allowances[5] were made out of the fines, especially 4*s.* a day during attendance at Quarter Sessions, and the 5*s.* a day assigned to them by Elizabeth's Statute of Labour of 1563[6] while they were sitting in execution of the Act.

§ 1. THE COMMISSION OF THE PEACE

In the Tudor period the Commission under which the Justices of the Peace acted was entirely recast. As new duties were placed upon the Justices, it had become increasingly unintelligible, partly through clerical errors which had grown out of the constant copying and re-copying of the words of the Commission, but much more because it was overloaded with quotations from Acts of Parliament and references to obsolete statutes. This led in 1590 to the important revision by Sir Christopher Wray referred to by Lambarde [p. 457]. The terms of the Commission as revised [p. 461] indicate clearly the double capacity of the Justices of the Peace as administrators and judges, and grant them wide powers, including jurisdiction over nearly

---

[1] Prothero, p. cxiv.
[2] 34 Edw. III, c. 1.
[3] Beard, p. 140.
[4] 18 Henr. VI, c. 11.
[5] The rewards of a Justice of the Peace are set out in Lambarde, *Eirenarcha*, Book iii, ch. 4.
[6] 5 Eliz. c. 4, § 31.

every crime except treason. The form adopted in 1590 was not altered for nearly three centuries and until 1875 the magistrates sitting in Quarter Sessions were expressly authorised by their Commission to punish 'enchantments, sorceries, and arts magic,' and the medieval offences of 'forestalling, regrating, and engrossing,' as well as felonies, poisonings, trespasses, and extortions, 'and all other crimes and offences of which such justices can or ought lawfully to enquire.'

Both the old Commission and the new provide for the important institution of the 'Quorum' [p. 455]. In order to furnish a sufficient representation on the Commission of the Peace for each county of persons learned in the law, the document was so worded as to authorise A, B, C, D, E, and F, or any two of them, to hear and determine, *quorum*—of whom—certain justices specially mentioned by name, or one of them, must be present, *e.g.* A, D, or F, all lawyers, and these specially named justices are described as 'of the Quorum.' Thus there was secured for the body of the justices the skilled legal advice which is provided under the modern system by the appointment of a professional clerk to the magistrates. For some time there was rivalry between the landowners and the lawyers—between the rest of the justices and the Quorum; but as the custom grew up among the landowners of declining to claim the allowances to which a Justice of the Peace was entitled, the lawyers ceased to display any eagerness to serve on the Commission, and in course of time the Quorum came to consist of senior justices who had had experience. Thus in the 17th century for a country justice to be 'of the Quorum' was a testimonial to his weight and standing in the county[1]. Later on, when the professional clerk appeared upon the scene, the Quorum disappeared in practice, although it continued according to the letter of the law, for it became usual to include the great majority of the justices in the Quorum, omitting from it a few names only in order to maintain the custom; and now even the omission of these has ceased, and the whole body of commissioned justices may be regarded as 'of the Quorum.'

The Sessions [p. 459] of the Justices of the Peace were of three kinds: (1) Discretionary Sessions, (2) Quarter Sessions, and (3) Petty Sessions.

Discretionary Sessions might be held at any time on a writ from any two justices, one of whom must be of the Quorum, addressed to the sheriff of the county, requiring him to summon at a specified day and place 24 jurors from each hundred and 24 from the whole body of the county, and from these a grand jury of presentment of twelve men at least was sworn in. This jury returned indictments or made presentments to the Court, and the trial of these was before a petty jury as in the ordinary courts of law.

Quarter Sessions, which was a Court of Record, must be held four times a year on days prescribed by statute[2], in the week after Easter, the Translation of St Thomas the Martyr[3], the Feast of St Michael[4], and the Epiphany. To these days the investigation of certain offences was assigned by statute, but the justices were not limited to these offences, and could deal with any other

---

[1] Sir Roger de Coverley occupied this coveted position, and at Spring Garden he thought himself 'obliged as a member of the Quorum to animadvert upon the morals of the place' (*Spectator*, No. 383).
[2] 2 Henr. V, st. 1, c. 4.   [3] July 7.   [4] Sept. 29.

kind of business in Quarter Sessions by the same procedure as in the sessions that were discretionary. Oaths of loyalty to the government, such as the oaths of allegiance and supremacy, were also directed to be taken in Quarter Sessions. Its appellate jurisdiction, now an important part of its functions, did not develop until the 17th century.

Special or Petty Sessions were held frequently in particular localities at the discretion of any two justices, one being of the Quorum; and at these various offences could be heard and determined by the verdict of a jury of the hundred. Further, any individual justice resident in a parish discharged particular duties, such as binding apprentices, giving order for the relief of the impotent poor, and granting licences to beg.

In the reign of Henry VIII the system of Justices of the Peace was extended to Wales by statute[1]. They were to be appointed by the Lord Chancellor, to have the same powers as English justices, and to proceed in the same way.

The oath required of a Justice of the Peace on admission to his office is printed on p. 458 below.

(1) Extracts

1. SIR THOMAS SMITH, 1565

Sir Thomas Smith's treatise, *De Republica Anglorum*, was completed in 1565, and was first published in 1583.

...The Justices of Peace be men elected out of the nobility, higher and lower, that is the dukes, marquises, barons, knights, esquires, and gentlemen, and of such as be learned in the laws, such and in such number as the Prince shall think meet, and in whom for wisdom and discretion he putteth his trust, inhabitants within the county; saving that some of the high nobility and chief magistrates for honour's sake are put in all or in the most of the Commissions of all the shires of England. These have no time of their rule limited but by Commission from the Prince alterable at pleasure.

At the first they were but 4, after 8, now they come commonly to 30 or 40 in every shire, either by increase of riches, learning, or activity in policy and government. So many more being found which have either will or power or both, are not too many to handle the affairs of the common wealth in this behalf. Of these in the same Commission be certain named which be called of the *Quorum*, in whom is especial trust reposed, that where the Commission is given to 40 or 30, and so at the last it cometh to 4 or 3, it is necessary for the performance of many affairs to have likewise divers of the *Quorum*. The words of the Commission be such, *Quorum vos* A.B., C.D., E.F. *unum esse volumus.*

The Justices of the Peace be those in whom at this time for

---

[1] 27 Henr. VIII, c. 5; see also 34 & 35 Henr. VIII, c. 26, §§ 21–25.

the repressing of robbers, thieves, and vagabonds, of privy complots and conspiracies, of riots and violences, and all other misdemeanours in the common wealth the Prince putteth his special
trust. Each of them hath authority upon complaint to him made
of any theft, robbery, manslaughter, murder, violence, complots,
riots, unlawful games, or any such disturbance of the peace and
quiet of the realm, to commit the persons whom he supposeth
offenders to the prison. . . till he and his fellows do meet. A few
lines signed with his hand is enough for that purpose: these do
meet four times in the year, that is, in each quarter once, to enquire of all the misdemeanours aforesaid. . . .

. . . The Justices of the Peace do meet also at other times by
commandment of the Prince upon suspicion of war, to take order
for the safety of the shire, sometimes to take musters of harness
and able men, and sometimes to take order for the excessive
wages of servants and labourers, for excess of apparel, for unlawful games, for conventicles and evil orders in alehouses and
taverns, for punishment of idle and vagabond persons, and
generally, as I have said, for the good government of the shire
the Prince putteth his confidence in them. And commonly every
year, or each second year in the beginning of summer or afterwards
(for in the warm time the people for the most part be more unruly,
even in the calm time of peace) the Prince with his Council
chooseth out certain articles out of penal laws already made for
to repress the pride and evil rule of the popular and sendeth them
down to the Justices, willing them to look upon those points, and
after they have met together and consulted among themselves
how to order that matter most wisely and circumspectly, whereby
the people might be kept in good order and obedience after the
law, they divide themselves by three or four, and so each in his
quarter taketh order for the execution of the said articles. And
then within certain space they meet again and certify the Prince
or his Privy Council how they do find the shire in rule and order
touching those points and all other disorders. There was never
in any common wealth devised a more wise, a more dulce and
gentle, nor a more certain way to rule the people, whereby they
are kept always as it were in a bridle of good order, and sooner
looked unto that they should not offend, than punished when they
have offended. . . .

Sir Thomas Smith, De Republica Anglorum (ed. L. Alston, 1906),
Book ii, ch. 19.

2. WILLIAM LAMBARDE, 1581

Eirenarcha, by William Lambarde, the historian of Kent, was for a long time the standard authority on the office of Justice of the Peace. It was 'gathered' in 1579, and first published in 1581. The extracts are from the edition of 1610.

...And it is plain (in mine opinion) that the general power of determining felonies was first given unto the Wardens of the Peace (as to themselves) by the Statute 34 E. III, cap. 1. After which time also it is very true that they were both commonly reputed and called Justices...(p. 23).

...Now although this portion of twenty pounds by year be not at this day in account answerable to the charge and countenance of a fit Justice of the Peace, yet who knoweth not that at the making of this law it was far otherwise; and therefore I do not doubt but as the rate of all things is greatly grown since that time, so also there is good care taken that none be now placed in the Commission whose livings be not answerable to the same proportion...(p. 31).

...And in this plight...stood the Commission of the Peace till it was even now of late; notwithstanding that it was both surcharged with vain recital and often repetitions of some of these statutes that were a good while before repealed, and also foully blemished with sundry other corruptions that had crept into it, partly by the miswriting of clerks and partly by the untoward huddling of things together which were at strife the one with the other of them. Which imperfections being made known to the late Reverend Judge Sir Christopher Wray (then Lord Chief Justice of the King's Bench), he communicated the same with the other Judges and Barons of the Coif[1], so as by a general conference had amongst them, the Commission was carefully refined in the Michaelmas Term, 1590, and being then also presented to the Lord Chancellor as a meet pattern of a Commission of the Peace to be uniformly put in ure[2] throughout the realm, he forthwith both accordingly accepted thereof and commanded the same to be sealed and sent abroad...(p. 43).

For these of the Quorum were wont (and that not without just cause) to be chosen specially for their knowledge in the laws of the land....For, albeit that a discreet person (not conversant in the study of the laws) may sufficiently follow sundry particular directions concerning this service of the peace, yet when the proceeding must be by way of presentment upon the evidence of witnesses and oaths of jurors, and by the order of hearing and

[1] See note on p. 344 above.   [2] See note on p. 23 above.

determining, according to the strait rule and course of the law, it must be confessed that learning in the laws is so necessary a light as without the which all the labour is but groping in the dark, the end whereof must needs be error and dangerous falling...(p. 48).

And here, lest these Justices should rather ground their judgments upon the number of voices than upon the weight of reasons, this latter clause[1] is shut up with a provision and restraint that in all cases of ambiguity and doubt they shall spare to proceed to judgment, and shall expect the presence either of some one of the Judges of the King's Bench or the Common Pleas, or at the least of one of the Justices of Assize in that county which be their more near and ready oracle. And yet...is not their judgment void if they list to proceed without such advice, but it standeth good and effectual until it shall be reversed by a writ of error...(p. 49).

Such as do occupy judicial places ought to take heed what they do, knowing (as Jehoshaphat said) that they exercise not the judgments of men only but of God himself, whose power as they do participate so he also is present on the Bench with them: And therefore it hath been always the policy of Christian laws to appoint meet forms of religious attestations (or oaths) for such officers to take and conceive, meaning thereby not only to set God continually before their eyes (whom by such oath they take to witness of their promise and call for revenge of their falsehood) but also threaten them (as it were) with temporal pains provided against corrupt dealings, and withal to strengthen their minds and arm their courages against the force of human affections, which otherwise might allure and draw them out of the way... (p. 51).

The Oath of the Office

Ye shall swear that as Justices of the Peace in the county of Kent, in all articles in the King's Commission to you directed, ye shall do equal right to the poor and to the rich after your cunning, wit, and power, and after the laws and customs of the realm and statutes thereof made; and ye shall not be of counsel of any quarrel hanging before you; and that ye hold your Sessions after the form of statutes thereof made; and the issues, fines, and amercements that shall happen to be made, and all forfeitures which shall fall before you, ye shall cause to be entered without any concealment or embezzling and truly send them to the King's Exchequer. Ye shall not let[2] for gift or other cause, but well and

---

[1] In the Commission as re-drawn in 1590.   [2] Delay.

truly you shall do your office of Justice of the Peace in that behalf; and that you take nothing for your office of Justice of the
Peace to be done, but of the King, and fees accustomed, and costs
limited by the statute; and ye shall not direct nor cause to be
directed any warrant (by you to be made) to the parties, but ye
shall direct them to the bailiffs of the said county or other the
King's officers or ministers, or other indifferent persons, to do
execution thereof. *So help you God and by the contents of this Book*. . .
(p. 53).

Justices of the Peace had also to take the Oath of Supremacy imposed by 1 Eliz.
c. 1.

. . . The common. . . manner is, to call the officers and county
together for this service [*of a Sessions*] by a precept to the Sheriff.
. . . This precept may be made. . . by any two Justices of the
Peace, so that the one of them be of the Quorum, for two such
may hold a Session of the Peace, as it doth plainly appear by the
Commission. . . . The place of holding them is arbitrable and at
the pleasure of the Justices themselves, so that it be meet for
access. And although the precept do appoint the Sessions to be
holden in some one town by name, yet may the Justices keep it
in any other town, and all the presentments shall be good that
shall be taken where they hold it; but then again no amerciament
can be set upon any man for his default of appearance there, because he had no warning of it. So if two such Justices make a
precept for a Session to be holden in one town, and two other
Justices make another precept for another Session to be holden at
another town (or in another part of the same town) the same day,
then the presentments taken before either of them shall be good.
And then also it seemeth that he which serveth at the one Session
(as a juror or officer) shall be excused for his default at the other,
because as they both be the King's Courts and of equal authority
so he cannot present himself in them both at once. . . (pp. 381–4).

Amongst the officers the *Custos Rotulorum* hath worthily the
first place, both for that he is always a Justice of the Quorum in the
Commission, and amongst them of the Quorum a man (for the
most part) especially picked out either for wisdom, countenance,
or credit; and yet in this behalf he beareth the person of an
officer, and ought to attend by himself or his deputy. . . . This
man (as his very name bewrayeth) hath the custody of the rolls
or records of the Sessions of the Peace. . . . And now as this man
is (by name and office) keeper of the Records of the Peace, so
would it not a little amend the service if he were (in deed also)
careful for the due preservation of them, and would not loosely

leave them (as commonly it is found) to the only custody of the Clerk of the Peace, without having any register of their number and sorts, and without appointing any convenient place certain for the more ready search and safe bestowing of them; whereby it falleth out very often that after the death of such a Clerk these records are hardly recovered and that piecemeal from his widow, servants, or executors, who at their pleasure may embezzle, misuse, or conceal what they will;...And this office of the *Custos Rotulorum* was of ancient time given by the discretion of the Lord Chancellor...(pp. 387, 390, 391).

The Clerk of the Peace oweth his attendance at the Sessions also, for...he readeth the indictments and serveth the Court, he enrolleth the acts of the Sessions, and draweth the process. He must record the proclamations of rate for servants' wages, and enroll the discharge of apprentices, 5 Eliz. c. 4. He keepeth the register-book of licences given to badgers[1] and laders of corn, 5 Eliz. c. 12, and of those that are licensed to shoot in guns, 2 Edw. VI, c. 14. Presentments for not coming to church, and the certificate of the oath of allegiance are to be recorded by him, 3 Jac. I, c. 4. And he is bound (under the pain of 40s.) to certify unto the King's Bench transcripts of indictments, outlawries, attainders, and convictions had before the Justices of the Peace within the time limited by the Statute 34 Henr. VIII, c. 14....The nomination and appointment of him hath long time belonged to the *Custos Rotulorum*, and he is to enjoy his office as long as the *Custos Rotulorum* keepeth his place...(pp. 393–5).

The general Sessions of the Peace be those which are provided for the general execution of the authority of the Justices of Peace....These be moreover called the Quarter Sessions, because they be holden quarterly or four times in the year; and the Statute 4 Henr. VII, c. 12, termed them principal Sessions, for that in them chiefly the power of Justices of the Peace doth shine and shew itself, in which respect 27 Eliz. c. 19 and some other statutes do give them the name of open Sessions...(pp. 592, 593).

The special Sessions of the Peace do vary from the general in this chiefly, that they be holden at other times, when it shall please the Justices themselves or any two of them (the one being of the Quorum) to appoint them....They be also (for the most part) summoned for some special business and not directed to the general service of the Commission; And yet there is no doubt but that all the articles within the Commission of the Peace are

---

[1] Itinerant dealers or hawkers.

both inquirable and determinable at any special Session of the Peace...(p. 623). Lambarde, *Eirenarcha* (ed. of 1610).

(2) The Commission after 1590

See p. 453 above. For the Commission as it was before 1590 see Prothero, p. 144.

...Sciatis quod assignavimus vos, conjunctim et divisim et quemlibet vestrum, Justiciarios nostros, ad pacem nostram in comitatu nostro Kanciae conservandam: Ac ad omnia ordinationes et statuta pro bono pacis nostrae, ac pro conservatione ejusdem, et pro quieto regimine et gubernatione populi nostri edita, in omnibus et singulis suis articulis, in dicto comitatu nostro, tam infra libertates quam extra, juxta vim, formam, et effectum eorundem, custodiendum et custodiri faciendum. Et ad omnes contra formam ordinationum vel statutorum illorum, aut eorum alicujus in comitatu praedicto delinquentes, castigandum et puniendum, prout secundum formam ordinationum et statutorum illorum fuerit faciendum; et ad omnes illos qui alicui vel aliquibus de populo nostro de corporibus suis, vel de incendio domorum suarum minas fecerint, ad sufficientem securitatem de pace vel bono gestu suo erga nos et populum nostrum inveniendam coram vobis seu aliquo vestrum venire faciendum, et (si hujusmodi securitatem invenire recusaverint) tunc eos in prisonis (quousque hujusmodi securitatem invenerint) salvo custodiri faciendum.

Assignavimus etiam vos et quoslibet duos vel plures vestrum (quorum aliquem nostrum A, B, C, D, E, F, etc., unum esse volumus) Justiciarios nostros, ad inquirendum per sacramentum proborum et legalium hominum de comitatu praedicto (per quos rei veritas melius sciri poterit) de omnibus et omnimodis feloniis, veneficiis, incantationibus, sortilegiis, arte magica, transgressionibus, forstallariis, regratariis, ingrossariis, et extortionibus quibuscunque; ac de omnibus et singulis aliis malefactis et offensis (de quibus Justiciarii pacis nostrae legitime inquirere possunt aut debent) per quoscunque et qualitercunque in comitatu praedicto factis sive perpetratis, vel quae imposterum[1] ibidem fieri vel attemptari contigerit; ac etiam de omnibus illis qui in comitatu praedicto in conventiculis contra pacem nostram in perturbationem populi nostri, seu vi armata ierunt vel equitaverunt, seu imposterum ire vel equitare praesumpserint; ac etiam de omnibus hiis qui ibidem ad gentem nostram mayhemandam[2] vel interficiendam in insidiis jacuerunt vel imposterum

---

[1] Hereafter.

[2] 'Mayhem' signifies a maim, wound, or bodily hurt by which a man is deprived of the use of any member which is or might be of use to him in defence (Jacob).

jacere praesumpserint; ac etiam de hostellariis et iis omnibus et singulis personis qui in abusu ponderum vel mensurarum sive in venditione victualium contra formam ordinationum vel statutorum vel eorum alicujus inde pro communi utilitate regni nostri Angliae et populi nostri ejusdem editorum deliquerunt vel attemptaverunt seu imposterum delinquere vel attemptare praesumpserint in comitatu praedicto; ac etiam de quibuscunque vicecomitibus[1], ballivis[2], seneschallis[3], constabulariis, custodibus gaolarum, et aliis officiariis qui in executione officiorum suorum (circa praemissa seu eorum aliqua) indebite se habuerunt aut imposterum indebite se habere praesumpserint, aut tepidi, remissi, vel negligentes fuerunt aut imposterum fore contigerit in comitatu praedicto; et de omnibus et singulis articulis et circumstantiis et aliis rebus quibuscunque, per quoscunque et qualitercunque in comitatu praedicto factis sive perpetratis vel quae imposterum ibidem fieri vel attemptari contigerit, qualitercunque praemissorum vel eorum alicujus concernentibus plenius veritatem.

Et ad indictamenta quaecunque sic coram vobis seu aliquibus vestrum capta sive capienda, aut coram aliis nuper Justiciariis pacis in comitatu praedicto facta sive capta (et nondum terminata) inspiciendum, ac ad processus inde versus omnes et singulos sic indictatos, vel quos coram vobis imposterum indictari contigerit (quousque capiantur, reddant se, vel utlagentur) faciendum et continuandum.

Et ad omnia et singula felonias, veneficia, incantationes, sortilegia, artes magicas, transgressiones, forstallarias, regratarias, ingrossarias, extortiones, conventicula, indictamenta praedicta, ceteraque omnia et singula praemissa, secundum leges et statuta regni nostri Angliae (prout in hujusmodi casu fieri consuevit aut debuit) audiendum et terminandum; et ad eosdem delinquentes et quemlibet eorum pro delictis quis per fines, redemptiones, amerciamenta, forisfacturas[4], ac alio modo (prout secundum legem et consuetudinem regni nostri Angliae aut formam ordinationum vel statutorum praedictorum fieri consuevit aut debuit) castigandum et puniendum.

Proviso semper, quod si casus difficultatis super determinatione aliquorum praemissorum coram vobis vel aliquibus duobus vel pluribus vestrum evenire contigerit, tunc ad judicium inde reddendum (nisi in praesentia unius Justiciariorum nostrorum de uno vel de altero Banco aut unius Justiciariorum nostrorum

---

[1] Sheriffs.   [2] Bailiffs.
[3] Stewards.   [4] Forfeitures.

ad Assisas in comitatu praedicto capiendas assignatorum) coram vobis vel aliquibus duobus vel pluribus vestrum minime procedatur.

Et ideo vobis et cuilibet vestrum mandamus, quod circa custodiam pacis, ordinationum, statutorum, et omnium et singulorum caeterorum praemissorum diligenter intendatis; et ad certos dies et loca quae vos vel aliqui hujusmodi duo vel plures vestrum (ut praedictum est) ad hoc provideritis super praemissis faciatis inquisitiones, et praemissa omnia et singula audiatis et terminetis, ac ea faciatis et expleatis in forma praedicta facturi inde quod ad justitiam pertinet secundum legem et consuetudinem regni nostri Angliae; salvis nobis amerciamentis et aliis ad nos inde spectantibus.

Mandamus enim tenore praesentium vicecomiti nostro Kanciae quod ad certos dies et loca (quae vos vel aliqui hujusmodi duo vel plures vestrum, ut praedictum est, ei, ut praedictum est, scire feceritis) venire faciat coram vobis vel hujusmodi duobus vel pluribus vestrum (ut dictum est) tot et tales probos et legales homines de balliva sua (tam infra libertates quam extra) per quos rei veritas in praemissis melius sciri poterit et inquiri.

Assignavimus denique te praefatum Edw. Hoby, militem, Custodem Rotulorum pacis nostrae in dicto comitatu nostro; ac propterea tu ad dies et loca praedicta brevia, praecepta, processus, et indictamenta praedicta coram te et dictis sociis tuis venire facias, ut ea inspiciantur et debito fine terminentur sicut praedictum est....

Lambarde, *Eirenarcha* (ed. of 1610), p. 35.

§ 2. JUDICIAL FUNCTIONS OF THE JUSTICES OF THE PEACE

The social conditions of the 15th century, which interfered with the proper administration of justice in all departments, had affected the local magistracy; and one of the earlier measures of Henry VII, an Act of 1489 [p. 465], was directed against the negligence and corruption of the Justices of the Peace. An important feature of this statute was the public proclamation of the duties of the Justices, and of the remedies open to aggrieved persons if they should fail to discharge them properly. This may be regarded as an attempt to stimulate them by the public opinion of the localities; but steps were also taken to subject them to the control of the central administration, thus applying in this department the fundamental Tudor principle that independent local authorities could not be tolerated. By an Act of 1542[1] the Judges of Assize were authorised to hear and determine negligence or other misdemeanours of the Justices of the Peace; and another Act of the following year[2] made this central review of the acts of the Justices more efficient by requiring the Clerk of the Peace of every county to send into the King's

---

[1] 33 Henr. VIII, c. 10, § 7.   [2] 34 & 35 Henr. VIII, c. 14.

Bench a transcript of every indictment and conviction for murder, robbery, felony, or other offence, made before the Justices of the Peace. Cases of maladministration by the Justices could also be taken to the Council, the Star Chamber, or the Chancery; and by writ of *certiorari* causes could be removed from the Justices to the higher courts. On the other hand the Justices, thus controlled and supervised, were empowered to control and supervise others. An Act of 1495[1] against extortions by the Sheriffs authorised the Justices to convict and punish them and their subordinates; and Quarter Sessions appointed and supervised the Constables of the Hundreds, who had formerly been elected in the Hundred Court.

To a magistracy efficiently controlled the Tudor sovereigns were prepared to entrust large powers, and during this period, by what Lambarde calls 'stacks of statutes,'[2] the duties of the office were extended in every direction. In the judicial sphere the two most important extensions were preliminary investigation and summary jurisdiction.

The duty of preliminary investigation had formerly been undertaken by the Sheriff, but he was deprived of it by statute in 1461[3], and his place was taken by the Justices of the Peace. A single Justice already had power to commit, and an Act of 1483[4] authorised him to take bail of an accused person. In 1487 Henry VII reorganised by statute [below] the system of bail, and in 1555 an Act of Mary's reign [p. 468] provided that before bail was granted the Justices should take an examination of the prisoner and an information of the circumstances of the crime, and forward them to the Judges of Assize, and empowered the Justices to bind over the prosecutor and witnesses to appear at the Assizes and give evidence.

In the Tudor period the foundations of the summary jurisdiction of the Justices of the Peace were also laid. In the preceding period the dominant theory had been that the proper tribunal for the trial of all criminal cases was a judge and a jury, and where the Justices had received judicial powers it had been for the most part in their open Sessions, where they sat with a jury. But as soon as their functions were enlarged, and a number of small cases began to arise under the more elaborate Tudor legislation, experience proved that Quarter Sessions was too cumbrous a machine for the purpose. Thus the statutes which imposed new duties on the Justices authorised two Justices in Petty Sessions to inflict minor penalties and to dispose finally of minor cases. This is the beginning of the development of summary jurisdiction by statute, which after the Revolution of 1688 was widely extended.

(1) Bail Act of 1487

An Act that Justices of Peace may take bail

Where [*by* 1 *Rich. III. c.* 3 . . .] it was . . . enacted . . . that every Justice of the Peace, in every shire, city, or town, should have authority and power by his or their discretion to let prisoners and persons arrested for light suspicion of felony in bail or mainprize[5]; by colour whereof afterward divers persons such as were

[1] 11 Henr. VII, c. 15.   [2] *Eirenarcha*, p. 34.   [3] 1 Edw. IV, c. 2.
[4] 1 Rich. III, c. 3.   [5] See note on p. 10 above.

not mainpernable[1] were ofttimes let to bail and mainprize by
Justices of the Peace against the due form of the law, whereby
many murderers and felons escaped, to the great displeasure of
the King and annoyance of his liege people: Wherefore the King
our Sovereign Lord considering it, by the advice, [etc.]...ordain-
eth, establisheth, and enacteth that the Justices of the Peace in
every shire, city, and town, or two of them at the least whereof
one to be of the Quorum, have authority and power to let any
such prisoners or persons mainpernable by the law that be imprisoned within their several counties, city, or town, to bail or
mainprize unto their next general Sessions or unto the next
general Gaol Delivery of the same gaols in every shire, city, or
town...; and that the said Justices of the Peace, or one of them,
so taking any such bail or mainprize do certify the same at the
next general Sessions of the Peace or at the next general Gaol
Deliverance...next following after any such bail or mainprize
so taken; upon pain to forfeit unto the King for every default
thereupon recorded £10. And over that, to be enacted...that
every sheriff, bailiff of franchise, and every other person having
authority or power of keeping of gaols or of prisoners for felony,
in like manner and form do certify the names of every such
prisoner in their keeping and of every prisoner unto them committed for any such cause, at the next general Gaol Delivery in
any county or franchise where any such gaol or gaols be or hereafter shall be, there to be calendared[2] before the Justices of the
deliverance of the same gaol, whereby they may, as well for the
King as for the party, proceed to make deliverance of such prisoners according to the law; upon pain to forfeit unto the King, for
every default thereof recorded, 100s. And that the foresaid Act[3]
giving authority and power in the premises to any one Justice of
the Peace by himself, be in that behalf utterly void and of none
effect by the said authority of this present Parliament.

3 Henr. VII, c. 4: *Statutes of the Realm,* ii, 512.

(2) Justices Act of 1489

*An Act for Justices of Peace for the due execution of their
Commissions*

The King our Sovereign Lord considereth that by the negligence and misdemeaning, favour, and other inordinate causes of
the Justice of Peace in every shire of this his realm, the laws and
ordinances made for the politic weal, peace, and good rule of the

[1] Capable of being mainprized.   [2] Registered.   [3] *I.e.* 1 Rich. III, c. 3.

same, and for perfect security and restful living of his subjects of the same, be not duly executed according to the tenor and effect that they were made and ordained for; wherefore his subjects be grievously hurt and out of surety of their bodies and goods, to his great displeasure; for to him is nothing more joyous than to know his subjects to live peaceably under his laws and to increase in wealth and prosperity, and to avoid such enormities and injuries, so that his said subjects may live more restful under his peace and laws to their increase: He will that it be ordained and enacted by the authority of this present Parliament, that every Justice of the Peace within every shire of this his said realm, within the shire where he is Justice of Peace, do cause openly and solemnly to be proclaimed yearly 4 times in a year in four principal Sessions the tenor of this proclamation to this bill annexed; and that every Justice of Peace being present at any of the said Sessions, if they cause not the said proclamation to be made in form abovesaid, shall forfeit to our said Sovereign Lord at every time 20*s.*

The Proclamation

Henricus Dei gratia, etc. The King our Sovereign Lord considereth how daily within this realm his coin is traitorously counterfeited, murders, robberies, felonies, be grievously committed and done, and also unlawful retainers, idleness, unlawful plays, extortions, misdemeanings of sheriffs, escheators[1], and many other enormities and unlawful demeanings daily groweth and increaseth within this his realm, to the great displeasure of God, hurt and impoverishing of his subjects, and to the subversion of the policy and good governance of this his realm; For by these said enormities and mischiefs his peace is broken, his subjects inquieted and impoverished, the husbandry of this land decayed, whereby the Church of England is upholden, the service of God continued, every man thereby hath sustenance, every inheritor his rent for his land: For repressing and avoiding of the said mischiefs sufficient laws and ordinances be made by authority of many and divers Parliaments holden within this realm, to the great cost of the King, his Lords and Commons of the same, And lacketh nothing but that the said laws be not put in due execution, which laws ought to be put in due execution by the Justice of Peace in every shire of this realm, to whom his Grace hath put and given full authority so to do since the beginning of his reign; And now it is come to his knowledge that his subjects be little

---

[1] An officer appointed to certify into the Exchequer escheats arising in his district.

eased of the said mischiefs by the said Justices, but by many of
them rather hurt than helped, And if his subjects complain to
these Justices of Peace of any wrongs done to them they have
thereby no remedy, And the said mischiefs do increase and not
subdued; And his Grace considereth that a great part of the
wealth and prosperity of this land standeth in that, that his subjects may live in surety under his peace in their bodies and goods,
And that the husbandry of this land may increase and be upholden, which must be had by due execution of the said laws and
ordinances, chargeth and commandeth all the Justices of the
Peace of this his shire to endeavour them to execute the tenor of
their Commission the said laws and ordinances ordained for sub-
duing of the premises, as they will stand in the love and favour of
his Grace, and in avoiding the pains that be ordained if they do
the contrary: And over that, he chargeth and commandeth that
every man, what degree or condition that he be of, that let[1] them
in word or deed to execute their said authorities in any manner
form abovesaid, that they shew it to his Grace; and if they do it
not and it come to his knowledge by other than by them, they shall
not be in his favour but taken as men out of credence and be put
out of Commission for ever. And over this, he chargeth and commandeth all manner of men, as well the poor as the rich, which be
to him all one in due ministration of justice[2], that is hurt or grieved
in anything that the said Justice of Peace may hear or determine
or execute in any wise, that he so grieved make his complaint to
the Justice of the Peace that next dwelleth unto him, or to any of
his fellows, and desire a remedy; And if he then have no remedy,
if it be nigh such time as his Justices of Assizes come into that
shire, that then he so grieved shew his complaint to the same
Justices, and if he then have no remedy, or if the complaint be
made long after the coming of the Justices of Assizes, then he so
grieved come to the King's Highness or to his Chancellor for the
time being and shew his grief; and his said Highness then shall
send for the said Justices to know the cause why his said subjects
be not eased and his laws executed, whereupon if he find any of
them in default of executing of his laws in these premises according to this his high commandment, he shall do him so offending
to be put out of the Commission, and further to be punished
according to his demerits. And over that, his said Highness shall
not let[3] for any favour, affection, cost, charge, nor none other

[1] Hinder.
[2] This is the modern doctrine of equality before the law.
[3] Omit.

cause, but that he shall see his laws to have plain and due execution, and his subjects to live in surety of their lands, bodies, and
goods, according to his said laws, and the said mischiefs to be
avoided, that his said subjects may increase in wealth and prosperity to the pleasure of God.

4 Henr. VII, c. 12: *Statutes of the Realm,* ii, 536

(3) Bail Act of 1555

An Act appointing an Order to Justices of Peace for the Bailment of Prisoners

[*Recites 3 Henr. VII, c. 3*]...Since the making of which
Estatute one Justice of Peace, in the name of himself and one
other of the Justices his companion, not making the said Justice
party nor privy unto the case wherefor the prisoner should be
bailed, hath oftentimes by sinister labour and means set at large
the greatest and notablest offenders, such as be not replevisable[1]
by the laws of this realm, and yet the rather to hide their affections
in that behalf, have signified the cause of their apprehension to
be but only for suspicion of felony....For reformation whereof
be it enacted...That [*none shall be bailed for offences declared not
bailable by the Statute of Westminster, I, 3 Edw. I, c. 15*]...And
furthermore that any person or persons arrested for manslaughter
or felony or suspicion of manslaughter or felony, being bailable
by the law, shall not...be let to bail...by any Justices of Peace
if it be not in open Sessions, except it be by two Justices of
Peace at the least whereof one to be of the Quorum, and the same
Justices to be present together at the time of the said bailment or
mainprize; which bailment or mainprize they shall certify in
writing signed or subscribed with their own hands at the next
general Gaol Delivery....And that the said Justices, or one of
them being of the Quorum, when any such prisoner is brought
before them for any manslaughter or felony, before any bailment
or mainprize, shall take the examination of the said prisoner, and
information of them that bring him, of the fact and circumstances
thereof, and the same, or as much thereof as shall be material to
prove the felony, shall put in writing before they make the same
bailment, which said examination together with the said bailment
the said Justices shall certify at the next general Gaol Delivery to
be held within the limits of their Commission: And that every
Coroner, upon any inquisition before him found, whereby any
person or persons shall be indicted for murder or manslaughter,

---

[1] Bailable.

or as accessory or accessories to the same before the murder or manslaughter committed, shall put in writing the effect of the evidence given to the jury before him being material; and as well the said Justices as the said Coroner shall have authority by this Act to bind all such by recognisance or obligation as do declare anything material to prove the said murder or manslaughter, offences or felonies, or to be accessory or accessories to the same as is aforesaid, to appear at the next general Gaol Delivery to be holden within the county, city, or town corporate where the trial thereof shall be, then and there to give evidence against the party so indicted at the time of his trial; and shall certify as well the same evidence as such bond and bonds in writing as he shall take, together with the inquisition or indictment before him taken and found, at or before the time of his said trial thereof to be had or made; And likewise the said Justices shall certify all and every such bond taken before them in like manner as before is said of bailments and examination: And in case any Justice of Peace or Quorum, or Coroner, shall...offend in anything contrary to the true intent and meaning of this present Act, that then the Justices of Gaol Delivery...upon due proof thereof by examination before them, shall for every such offence set such fine on every of the same Justices of Peace and Coroner as the same Justices of Gaol Delivery shall think meet....

      *   *   *   *   *   *

1 & 2 Philip & Mary, c. 13: *Statutes of the Realm*, iv, 259

§ 3. Vagabonds, Beggars, and Poor Relief

The earliest legislation concerning beggars is an Act of 1349[1] forbidding under pain of imprisonment the giving of alms to anyone who is able to labour. By an Act of 1383[2] the Justices of Assize, Justices of the Peace, and Sheriffs of counties were empowered to bind over vagabonds to be of good behaviour, or, in default of sureties, to commit them to the assizes. The principles afterwards adopted by the Tudor legislators do not make their first appearance until 1388, when it was provided that beggars 'impotent to serve' might be required 'to draw them...to the towns where they were born'[3]; and travelling beggars must carry letters testimonial, and shall be sworn to 'hold their right way towards their country, except they have letters patents under the King's great seal to do otherwise.'[4] These provisions contain the germs of later legislation, including the law of settlement.

The Tudor statutes against vagabondage are numerous, but only some of them develop new principles and are therefore historically important. The earliest of them, passed in 1495 [p. 473], only provides for the punishment of vagabonds and their return to their own districts, and it throws no

[1] 23 Edw. III, c. 7.   [2] 7 Rich. II, c. 5.   [3] 12 Rich. II, c. 7.   [4] 12 Rich. II, c. 8.

responsibility for this upon the Justices of the Peace. Their services are first requisitioned by the Act of 1501[1], which closely follows the Act of 1495, but empowers the Lord Chancellor and the Judges to punish such officers as are negligent in executing the statute, and authorises the Justices of the Peace in Quarter Sessions to make 'a due and a diligent and a secret search' for offenders against the Act.

In the important Statute of 1531 [p. 475] novel principles appear, and a characteristically didactic preamble introduces a remarkable achievement of constructive legislation. The burden of administration is thrown mainly upon the Justices of the Peace. The distinction is clearly laid down between 'aged, poor, and impotent persons,' who, under certain restrictions, are to be allowed to solicit alms, and those 'whole and mighty in body and able to labour,' who are to suffer punishment. Out of this early recognition of a duty towards the impotent poor the whole system of poor relief was destined to grow; and the business instincts of the Tudor officials were already exhibited in the Act in the provision made for the registration of all impotent persons officially licensed to beg.

The Act of 1536 [p. 479] in some respects strengthened the law against vagabonds and beggars, but it is mainly concerned with the application of a new principle—the legal responsibility of each parish for the relief of its own poor. This takes the form of an authorised and systematic collection of alms, whereby the impotent poor might be relieved, and sturdy and 'valiant' beggars set to work. It has been said that the need for the Tudor Poor Law was created by the Dissolution of the Monasteries and the consequent cessation of monastic alms and doles. It should therefore be observed that this first step towards the establishment of a Poor Law was taken in the year of the dissolution of the smaller monasteries; that it precedes the Act of Dissolution upon the Statute Book; and that when it was passed the future of monasticism was sufficiently uncertain for the collection of alms by mendicant friars and the continuation of monastic doles to be made the subject of special provisions in the Poor Law Act. The Dissolution no doubt made a Poor Law more necessary, but they do not stand to each other in the simple relation of cause and effect.

The reign of Edward VI saw temporary legislation of a most savage character directed against rogues and vagabonds. An Act of 1547[2] provided that on conviction before two Justices of the Peace they might be branded 'in the breast' and reduced to slavery for the space of two years; on a conviction of escape there was a second branding 'on the forehead or the ball of the cheek,' and the slavery became perpetual; and on conviction of a second escape the slave suffered death as a felon. That part of the Act which relates to the impotent poor provides for their relief on the lines of the Act of 1536, relying still upon voluntary alms, to be collected on every Sunday and Holy Day, and requiring that 'after the reading of the Gospel of the day,' the curate of every parish should 'make, according to such talent as God hath given him, a godly and brief exhortation to his parishioners moving and exciting them to remember the poor people and the duty of Christian charity in relieving of them which be their brethren in Christ, born in the same parish, and needing their help.' The Act of 1547 was, however, re-

[1] 19 Henr. VII, c. 12.   [2] 1 Edw. VI, c. 3.

pealed in 1550[1], and the Act of 1531, with a few minor amendments, was revived to replace it. Notwithstanding the Act of 1572[2] referred to below [p. 472], which repealed the Acts of 1531 and 1550 and stated the law afresh, the principles of 1531 and 1550 continue to govern the action of authority in relation to vagabondage until Elizabeth's Act of 1598 [p. 484] codified and superseded all previous statutes. An Act of 1576 [p. 481] had already empowered Quarter Sessions to build Houses of Correction where both the needy poor and those who went abroad begging might be set to work, and the Act of 1598 further develops this policy; makes additional detailed provision for the whipping and expulsion from the parish of sturdy rogues and vagabonds, of whom a comprehensive definition is given; and provides special treatment for such rogues as should be deemed dangerous.

Meanwhile the relief of the poor was coming to be treated as a separate problem. An Act of 1552[3], 'for the provision and relief of the poor,' passed 'to the intent that valiant beggars, idle and loitering persons, may be avoided, and the impotent, feeble, and lame provided for, which are poor in very deed,' although it confirms the Acts of 1531 and 1550 as to vagabonds, is mainly directed to the increase of the charitable fund out of which the poor are to be relieved. Two Collectors of Alms are to be chosen from the inhabitants of every town or parish yearly 'in Whitsun week,' 'which Collectors, the Sunday next after their election...when the people is at the church and hath heard God's holy word, shall gently ask and demand of every man and woman what they of their charity will be contented to give weekly towards the relief of the poor.' The contributions so promised were to be entered in a register containing the names of the inhabitants and of the impotent poor of the parish for whom provision had to be made; and the Collectors were to make a weekly distribution of alms to the poor so registered. A novel provision brings the Bishop to bear upon recalcitrant householders. 'And be it further enacted,...that if any person or persons being able to further this charitable work do obstinately and frowardly refuse to give towards the help of the poor, or do wilfully discourage other from so charitable a deed, the parson, vicar, or curate, and churchwardens of the parish where he dwelleth shall gently exhort him or them towards the relief of the poor; and if he or they will not so be persuaded, then upon the certificate of the parson, vicar, or curate of the parish to the Bishop of the diocese the same Bishop shall send for him or them to induce and persuade him or them by charitable ways and means, and so according to his discretion to take order for the reformation thereof.' This Act was amended in some minor points by an Act of 1555[4].

Elizabeth's Act of 1563[5] makes a new departure of considerable importance in the history of the Poor Law, as it applies for the first time the principle of compulsion to the collection of funds for poor relief. Persons sent for by the Bishop and of 'froward and wilful mind' declining to be moved by his exhortations, were to be bound over by him in recognisances to appear before the Justices of the Peace at their next general Sessions, and might be committed to prison by him if they refused to be so bound. When he appeared at the Sessions, the Justices 'shall charitably and gently persuade

---

[1] By 3 & 4 Edw. VI, c. 16.   [2] 14 Eliz. c. 5.   [3] 5 & 6 Edw. VI, c. 2.
[4] 2 & 3 P. & M. c. 5.   [5] 5 Eliz. c. 3.

and move the said obstinate persons to extend his or their charity towards the relief of the poor of the parish where he or she inhabiteth and dwelleth'; and if they were no more successful than the Bishop had been, they were empowered by the Act 'to cess, tax, and limit upon every such obstinate person so refusing, according to their good discretions, what sum the said obstinate person shall pay weekly towards the relief of the poor' of his parish, and in default to commit him to prison until payment should be made. This statute also takes the first step in the direction of requiring the rich parishes to help the poorer, which was afterwards to lead to the development of the system of rates in aid. In towns 'within which be divers parishes,' if the Mayor 'shall understand...that the parishioners of any one of the said parishes...have no poverty among them, or be able sufficiently to relieve the poverty of the parish where they...dwell and also to...succour poverty elsewhere further,' he shall 'with the assent of two of the most honest and substantial inhabitants of every such wealthy parish' 'persuade the parishioners of the wealthier parish charitably to contribute somewhat' to the weekly relief of the poorer parishes within the town.

An Act of 1572[1] repealed the Acts of 1531 and 1550 [pp. 470, 471] against vagabonds and beggars, and also the Act of 1563 for the relief of the poor, and substituted fresh legislation, once more dealing with the two problems in combination. On the ground that 'all the parts of this realm of England and Wales be presently with rogues, vagabonds, and sturdy beggars exceedingly pestered, by means whereof daily happeneth in the same realm horrible murders, thefts, and other great outrages, to the high displeasure of Almighty God and to the great annoy of the common weal,' the law against vagabonds and beggars is made more severe, but no new principle is introduced. In dealing with the relief of the poor also the methods of 1563 are, in general, followed, with the additional provision that the Justices of the Peace in Quarter Sessions shall appoint yearly at Easter 'overseers' of the poor, as well as the collectors of alms referred to in the statute of 1563. The provision of work for the poor was also developed by the Act of 1576 [p. 481].

The English Poor Law reached the final stage of its development in Elizabeth's famous Act of 1601[2], which, notwithstanding later changes, determined the main features of the national policy in relation to the poor until the reforms which followed the Poor Law Commission of 1834. But the principles of 1601 are all contained in the earlier Act of 1598 [p. 488], and this is therefore historically the more important[3]. The financial difficulties of poor relief are now solved by the institution of the poor rate, which was destined to become and still remains the basis of all local taxation. In this new organisation the Justices of the Peace, both in the locality where they reside and also in Quarter Sessions, play a most important part. Two Justices appoint yearly in Easter week four householders to be overseers of the poor and supervise their proceedings; levy poor rate by distress; and assent to the binding of poor children as apprentices. Quarter Sessions is empowered to make order for the erection of 'convenient houses of dwelling' for the impotent poor; to hear appeals against the poor rate; and to rate other parishes in aid of those unable to support their own poor.

---

[1] 14 Eliz. c. 5.   [2] 43 Eliz. c. 2.
[3] The modifications which the Act of 1601 made in that of 1598 may be studied in Prothero, pp. 96–100, 103–5.

The Act of 1598 was amended and confirmed by the Act of 1601, which was to be in force until the end of the next Parliament, but it was prolonged by subsequent Acts, and finally made permanent by an Act of 1640[1]. Its main features have been summarised thus: 'Poor relief is recognised in principle as a public concern. It is to be administered by individual parishes through overseers, who are to be appointed and constantly controlled by the justices. The burden of relief is distributed by taxation. In the first instance, however, the nearest of kin are made responsible for the maintenance of their relations; and in case a single parish is overburdened, the neighbouring parishes may be called upon to contribute proportionately. The persons to be relieved are divided into three classes: children, able-bodied, and infirm. The kind of assistance consists, in the case of children, in apprenticing them till their twenty-first or twenty-fourth year; in the case of the able-bodied, by setting them to work (which they must perform, under penalty for refusal); in the case of the infirm, in maintaining them, with power to place them in poor houses.'[2]

(1) Beggars Act of 1495

An Act against vagabonds and beggars

Forasmuch as the King's Grace most entirely desireth amongst all earthly things the prosperity and restfulness of this his land and his subjects of the same to live quietly and surefully to the pleasure of God and according to his laws, willing and always of his pity intending to reduce them thereunto by softer means than by such extreme rigour therefor purveyed in [*st.* 7, *Rich. II, c.* 5...], considering also the great charges that should grow to his subjects for bringing of vagabonds to the gaols according to the same Statute and the long abiding of them therein, whereby by likelihood many of them should lose their lives, In modering[3] of the said Estatute his Highness will by the authority of this present Parliament it be ordained and enacted, That where such misdoers should be by examination committed to the common gaol there to remain as is aforesaid, that the sheriff, mayors, bailiffs, high constables, and petty constables...within 3 days after this Act proclaimed, make due search, and take or cause to be taken all such vagabonds, idle and suspect persons, living suspiciously, and them so taken to set in stocks, there to remain by the space of 3 days and 3 nights and there to have none other sustenance but bread and water; and after the said 3 days and 3 nights to be had out and set at large and then to be commanded to avoid[4] the town; And if eftsoons[5] he be taken in such default in the same town or township, then he to be set in the like wise

---

[1] 16 Car. I, c. 4, § 31.   [2] Aschrott, p. 7.   [3] Moderating.
[4] Depart from.   [5] A second time.

in stocks by the space of 6 days with like diet as is before rehearsed; and if any person or persons give any other meat or
drink to the said misdoers being in stocks in form aforesaid, or
the same prisoners favour in their misdoing, that then they forfeit
for every time so doing 12*d.*

II. And also it is ordained by the said authority that all manner
of beggars not able to work...go, rest, and abide in his hundred
where he last dwelled, or there where he is best known or born,
there to remain or abide without begging out of the said hundred,
upon pain to be punished as is beforesaid. And that no man be
excused by that he is a clerk of one University or of other, without
he shew the letters of the Chancellor of the University from whence
he saith he cometh, nor none other calling himself a soldier, shipman, or travelling-man, without he bring a letter from his captain
or from the town where he landed, and that he then to be commanded to go the straight highway into his country.

*   *   *   *   *   *

V. And furthermore it is ordained and enacted...that none
apprentice nor servant of husbandry, labourer nor servant
artificer, play at the tables[1]...but only for meat and drink, nor
at the tennis, closh[2], dice, cards, bowls, nor any other unlawful
game in no wise out of Christmas, and in Christmas to play only
in the dwelling-house of his master or where the master of any of
the said servants is present, upon pain of imprisonment by the
space of a day in the stocks openly; And that the householder
where...any...unlawful game afore rehearsed shall be used
otherwise than is afore rehearsed, and that lawfully be presented
before Justices of Peace...or by examination had afore the said
Justices of Peace, that process be made upon the same as upon
indictment of trespass against the King's peace, and that the said
misdoer be admitted to no fine under the sum of 6*s.* 8*d.* And that
it be lawful to 2 of the Justices of the Peace, whereof one shall be
of the Quorum, within their authority to reject and put away
common ale-selling in towns and places where they shall think
convenient, and take surety of the keepers of ale-houses of their
good behaving by the discretion of the said Justices, and in the
same to be advised and agreed at the time of their Sessions.

*   *   *   *   *   *

11 Henr. VII, c. 2: *Statutes of the Realm,* ii, 569.

[1] Backgammon.
[2] A game played with a ball or bowl which was driven through a hoop with
a spade-shaped instrument (*Oxford Dictionary*).

(2) Beggars Act of 1531

An Act concerning punishment of Beggars and Vagabonds

Where in all places throughout this realm of England vagabonds and beggars have of long time increased and daily do increase in great and excessive numbers, by the occasion of idleness, mother and root of all vices, whereby hath insurged and sprung and daily insurgeth and springeth continual thefts, murders, and other heinous offences and great enormities, to the high displeasure of God, the inquietation and damage of the King's people, and to the marvellous disturbance of the common weal of this realm. And whereas many and sundry good laws, strait statutes and ordinances, have been before this time devised and made[1], as well by the King our Sovereign Lord as also by divers his most noble progenitors, kings of England, for the most necessary and due reformation of the premises, yet that, notwithstanding, the said numbers of vagabonds and beggars be not seen in any party to be minished, but rather daily augmented and increased into great routs[2] and companies, as evidently and manifestly it doth and may appear; Be it therefore enacted...That the Justices of the Peace...shall from time to time, as often as need shall require, by their discretions divide themselves within the said shires [etc....] and so being divided shall make diligent search and enquiry of all aged, poor, and impotent persons which live or of necessity be compelled to live by alms of the charity of the people that be or shall be hereafter abiding...within the limits of their division, and after and upon such search made the said Justices of Peace...shall have power and authority by their discretions to enable to beg, within such...limits as they shall appoint, such of the said impotent persons which they shall find and think most convenient within the limits of their division to live of the charity and alms of the people, and to give in commandment to every such aged and impotent beggar (by them enabled) that none of them shall beg without the limits to them so appointed, and shall also register and write the names of every such impotent beggar (by them appointed) in a bill or roll indented[3], the one part thereof to remain with themselves and the other part by them to be certified before the Justices of Peace at

---

[1] This is rather an exaggeration. The earlier Acts were those of 1349, 1383, 1388, and 1495.

[2] In law an assembly of three or more persons proceeding to commit an unlawful act; but applied to any disorderly gathering; see also note on p. 292 above.

[3] See note on p. 497 below.

the next Sessions after such search had...there to remain under the keeping of the Custos Rotulorum; And that the said Justices of Peace...shall make and deliver to every such impotent person by them enabled to beg, a letter containing the name of such impotent person and witnessing that he is authorised to beg and the limits within which he is appointed to beg, the same letter to be sealed with such...seals as shall be engraved with the name of the limit wherein such impotent person shall be appointed to beg in, and to be subscribed with the name of one of the said Justices. ...And if any such impotent person so authorised to beg do beg in any other place than within such limits that he shall be assigned unto, that then the Justices of Peace...shall by their discretions punish all such persons by imprisonment in the stocks by the space of 2 days and 2 nights, giving them but only bread and water, and after that cause every such impotent person to be sworn to return again without delay to the [*limits*...] where they be authorised to beg in.

II. And be it enacted, That no such impotent person (as is abovesaid)...shall beg within any part of this realm except he be authorised by writing under seal as is abovesaid. And if any such impotent person...be vagrant and go a-begging having no such letter under seal as is above specified, that then the constables and all other inhabitants within such town or parish where such person shall beg shall cause every such beggar to be taken and brought to the next Justice of Peace or High Constable of the Hundred; and thereupon the said Justice of Peace or High Constable shall command the said constables and other inhabitants of the town or parish which shall bring before him any such beggar that they shall strip him naked from the middle upward and cause him to be whipped within the town where he was taken, or within some other town where the same Justice or High Constable shall appoint...; And if not, then to command such beggar to be set in the stocks in the same town or parish where he was taken by the space of 3 days and 3 nights, there to have only bread and water; and thereupon the said Justice or High Constable afore whom such beggar shall be brought shall limit to him a place to beg in, and give to him a letter under seal in form above remembered, and swear him to depart and repair thither immediately after his punishment to him executed.

III. And be it further enacted...That if any person or persons being whole and mighty in body and able to labour,...or if any man or woman being whole and mighty in body and able to labour having no land, master, nor using any lawful merchand-

ise, craft, or mystery, whereby he might get his living...be
vagrant and can give none reckoning how he doth lawfully get
his living, that then it shall be lawful to the constables and all
other the King's officers, ministers, and subjects of every town,
parish, and hamlet to arrest the said vagabonds and idle persons
and them to bring to any of the Justices of Peace of the same
shire or liberty...and that every such Justice of Peace...shall
cause every such idle person so to him brought to be had to the
next market town or other place where the said Justices of Peace
...shall think most convenient,...and there to be tied to the end
of a cart naked and be beaten with whips throughout the same
market town or other place till his body be bloody by reason of
such whipping; and after such punishment and whipping had,
the person so punished...shall be enjoined upon his oath to
return forthwith without delay in the next and straight way to the
place where he was born, or where he last dwelled before the
same punishment by the space of 3 years, and there put himself
to labour like as a true man oweth to do; and after that done,
every such person so punished and ordered shall have a letter[1]
sealed with the seal of the hundred, rape[2], wapentake[3], city,
borough, town, liberty, or franchise wherein he shall be punished,
witnessing that he hath been punished according to this Estatute,
and containing the day and place of his punishment, and the place
whereunto he is limited to go, and by what time he is limited to
come thither, within which time he may lawfully beg by the way,
shewing the same letter, and otherwise not; And if he do not
accomplish the order to him appointed by the said letter, then to
be eftsoons[4] taken and whipped, and so as often as any default
shall be found in him contrary to the order of this Estatute, in
every place to be taken and whipped till he be repaired where he
was born or where he last dwelled by the space of three year, and
there put his body to labour for his living or otherwise truly get
his living without begging as long as he is able so to do; And if
the person so whipped be an idle person and no common beggar,
then after such whipping he shall be kept in the stocks till he hath
found surety to go to service or else to labour after the discretion of
the said Justice of Peace...afore whom any such idle person being
no common beggar shall be brought,...or else to be ordered
and sworn to repair to the place where he was born or where

---

[1] See p. 494 below.

[2] The administrative districts of Sussex, each including several hundreds.

[3] The administrative divisions, corresponding to hundreds elsewhere, of the
counties of York, Lincoln, and Nottingham.   [4] A second time.

he last dwelled by the space of three years, and to have like letter
and such further punishment if he eftsoons offend this Estatute
as is above appointed to and for the common, strong, and able
beggars, and so from time to time to be ordered and punished till
he put his body to labour or otherwise get his living truly according to the law: And that the Justices of the Peace of every
shire. . . shall have power and authority within the limits of their
Commissions to enquire of all mayors, bailiffs, constables, and
other officers and persons that shall be negligent in executing of
this Act: And if the constables and inhabitants within any town
or parish. . . be negligent. . . that then the township or parish. . .
shall lose and forfeit for every such impotent beggar. . . 3s. 4d.,
and for every strong beggar,. . . 6s. 8d.. . . And that all Justices
of Peace. . . shall have full power and authority as well to hear
and determine every such default by presentment as by such bill
of information, and upon every presentment afore them and upon
every such bill of information to make process by distress against
the inhabitants of every such town and parish.. . .

IV. And be it enacted. . . That scholars of the Universities
of Oxford and Cambridge that go about begging, not being
authorised under the seal of the said Universities by the Commissary, Chancellor, or Vice-Chancellor of the same, and all and
singular shipmen pretending losses of their ships and goods of
the sea going about the country begging without sufficient
authority witnessing the same, shall be punished and ordered in
manner and form as is above rehearsed of strong beggars; and
that all proctors[1] and pardoners[2] going about in any country or
countries without sufficient authority, and all other idle persons
going about in any countries or abiding in any city, borough, or
town, some of them using divers and subtile crafty and unlawful
games and plays, and some of them feigning themselves to have

---

[1] Persons who went about the country collecting alms for lepers and the inhabitants of 'spital-houses.' They were in very low repute.

[2] The itinerant hawkers of pardons and relics. Cf. Chaucer (*Prologue*, l. 696 ff.),
who gives a list of the relics the pardoner had for sale: a piece of the Virgin's veil;
a fragment of the sail 'that St Peter had when that he went upon the sea, till Jesu
Christ him hent.'

> He had a cross of laten, full of stones,
> And in a glass he haddé pigge's bones;
> And with these relikes, when that he fond
> A pooré parson dwelling upon lond,
> Upon a day he gat him more moneie
> Than that the parson gat in monthes tweie;
> And thus with fainèd flattery and japes
> He made the parson and the people his apes.

knowledge in physic, physnamy[1], palmistry, or other crafty sciences, whereby they bear the people in hand[2] that they can tell their destinies, deceases, and fortunes, and such other like fantastical imaginations, to the great deceit of the King's subjects, shall upon examination had before two Justices of Peace, whereof the one shall be of the Quorum, if he by provable witness be found guilty of any such deceits, be punished by whipping at two days together after the manner above rehearsed: And if he eftsoons offend in the said offence or any like offence, then to be scourged two days and the third day to be put upon the pillory from 9 of the clock till 11 before noon of the same day, and to have one of his ears cut off; and if he offend the third time, to have like punishment with whipping, standing on the pillory, and to have his other ear cut off; and that Justices of Peace have like authority in every liberty and franchise within their shires where they be Justices of Peace for the execution of this Act in every part thereof as they shall have without the liberty or franchise.

*   *   *   *   *   *

22 Henr. VIII, c. 12: Statutes of the Realm, iii, 328.

(3) Beggars Act of 1536

An Act for punishment of sturdy vagabonds and beggars

[*After referring to* 22 *Henr. VIII, c.* 12, § 3...] And forasmuch as it was not provided in the said Act how and in what wise the said poor people and sturdy vagabonds should be ordered at their repair and at their coming into their countries, nor how the inhabitants of every hundred should be charged for the relief of the same poor people, nor yet for the setting and keeping in work and labour of the aforesaid valiant vagabonds at their said repair into every hundred of this realm, It is therefore now ordained and established and enacted...That all the governors and ministers of...cities, shires, towns, hundreds, wapentakes, lathes[3], rapes, ridings, tithings, hamlets, and parishes, as well within liberties as without, shall not only succour, find, and keep all and every of the same poor people by way of voluntary and charitable alms...in such wise as none of them of very necessity shall be compelled to wander idly and go openly in begging to ask alms in any of the same cities, shires, towns, and parishes; but also to cause and to compel all and every the said sturdy vagabonds and valiant beggars to be set and kept to continual labour, in such

---

[1] Physiognomy.   [2] Delude.
[3] The administrative districts of Kent, each including several hundreds.

wise as by their said labours they and every of them may get their own livings with the continual labour of their own hands....

*   *   *   *   *   *

IV. Item, It is ordained and enacted...that all and every the mayors, governors, and head officers of every city, borough, and town corporate and the churchwardens or two others of every parish of this realm shall in good and charitable wise take such discreet and convenient order, by gathering and procuring of such charitable and voluntary alms of the good Christian people within the same with boxes every Sunday, Holy Day, and other Festival Day or otherwise among themselves, in such good and discreet wise as the poor, impotent, lame, feeble, sick, and diseased people, being not able to work, may be provided, holpen, and relieved, so that in no wise they nor none of them be suffered to go openly in begging; And that such as be lusty or having their limbs strong enough to labour may be daily kept in continual labour, whereby every one of them may get their own substance and living with their own hands....

*   *   *   *   *   *

IX. Item, It is enacted...that every preacher, parson, vicar, curate of this realm, as well in all and every their sermons, collations[1], biddings of the beads, as in time of all confessions, and at the making of the wills or testaments of any persons, at all times of the year shall exhort, move, stir, and provoke people to be liberal, and bountifully to extend their good and charitable alms and contributions from time to time for and toward the comfort and relief of the said poor, impotent, decrepit, indigent, and needy people, as for the setting and keeping to continual work and labour of the foresaid rufflers[2], sturdy vagabonds, and valiant beggars in every city, ward, town, hundred, and parish, of this realm, as well within liberties as without.

*   *   *   *   *   *

XIII. And for the avoiding of all such inconveniences and infections as oftentime have and daily do chance amongst the people by common and open doles, and that most commonly unto such doles many persons do resort which have no need of the same, It is therefore enacted...that no manner of person or persons shall make or cause to be made any such common or open dole, or shall give any ready money in alms, otherwise than to the common boxes and common gatherings...to and for the putting in...due execution...this present Act; upon pain to leese[3] and forfeit ten times the value of all such ready money as shall be

---

[1] Homilies.   [2] Swaggering vagabonds.   [3] Lose.

given in alms contrary to the tenor and purport of the same; And
that every person or persons of this realm, bodies politic, corporate, and others that be bound or charged yearly, monthly, or
weekly to give or to distribute any ready money, bread, victual,
or other sustentation to poor people in any place within this
realm, shall...give and distribute the same money or the value
of all such bread, victual, or sustentation unto such common
boxes, to the intent the same may be employed towards the relieving of the said poor, needy, sick, sore, and indigent persons,
and also toward the setting in work of the said sturdy and idle
vagabonds and valiant beggars....

*   *   *   *   *   *

[XXV–XXVIII contain provisos in favour, among others, of (1)
'noblemen and other keeping houses,' who might give in alms 'the fragments or broken meat or drink' from their households; (2) mendicant friars
collecting alms; (3) 'Abbots, priors, or other person or persons of the clergy,
or other that by any means be bound to give yearly, weekly, or daily alms
in money, victual, lodging, clothing, or other thing, in any monasteries,
almshouses, hospitals, or other foundations or brotherhoods, by any good
authority or ancient custom, or of daily charity by keeping of poor men,
established for that purpose.']

27 Henr. VIII, c. 25: *Statutes of the Realm*, iii, 558.

(4) Poor Relief Act of 1576

*An Act for the setting of the Poor on Work, and for the avoiding
of Idleness*

[I. Two Justices of the Peace, 'whereof one to be of the Quorum,'
are empowered to make orders for the punishment of the reputed parents of
illegitimate children, and for the maintenance of the children by the parents.
Persons not obeying such orders to be committed to the common gaol.]

II. Also concerning rogues, inasmuch as by [14 *Eliz. c. 5*...]
they are to be conveyed to the gaol or prison by the constable...
at the charges of the parish where such rogue is apprehended, For
avoiding of great travail and charges rising thereby many are
suffered to pass and winked at; Be it ordained and enacted...
That from henceforth every such rogue apprehended shall be
conveyed by the constable...of the parish where such apprehension shall be, but to the constable[1]...of the next township or
parish in the next hundred, and so from one hundred to another
by the constables...of every such township or parish which shall
be next in every such hundred, and so from one hundred to
another...to the gaol or prison appointed....

*   *   *   *   *   *

[1] On the functions of the parish constable see p. 509 below.

IV. Also to the intent youth may be accustomed and brought up in labour and work, and then not like to grow to be idle rogues, and to the intent also that such as be already grown up in idleness, and so rogues at this present, may not have any just excuse in saying that they cannot get any service or work and then without any favour or toleration worthy to be executed, and that other poor and needy persons being willing to work may be set on work: Be it ordained and enacted. . . That in every city and town corporate within this realm a competent store and stock of wool, hemp, flax, iron, or other stuff[1] by the appointment and order of the Mayor, Bailiffs, Justices, or other head officers having rule in the said cities or towns corporate (of themselves and all others the inhabitants within their several authorities to be taxed, levied, and gathered) shall be provided: And that likewise in every other market town or other place within every county of this realm (where to the Justices of Peace or greater part of them in their general Sessions yearly next after Easter within every limit shall be thought most meet and convenient) a like competent store and stock of wool, hemp, flax, iron, or other stuff, as the country is most meet for, by appointment and order of the said Justices of Peace or the greater part of them in their said general Sessions (of all the inhabitants within their several authorities to be taxed, levied, and gathered) shall be provided, the said stores and stocks in such cities and towns corporate to be committed to the hands and custody of such persons as shall by the Mayor [*etc., as above* . . .] be appointed, and in other towns and places to such persons as to the said Justices of Peace or the greater part of them in their said general Sessions of the Peace in their several counties shall be by them appointed: Which said persons so appointed as aforesaid shall have power and authority (by the advice of them who do appoint them) to dispose, order, and give rules for the division and manner of working of the said stocks and stores, who shall from henceforth be called the Collectors and Governors of the Poor, to the intent every such poor and needy person, old or young, able to do any work, standing in necessity of relief, shall not for want of work go abroad either begging or committing pilferings or other misdemeanours, living in idleness; which Collectors and Governors of the Poor from time to time (as cause requireth) shall and may of the same stock and store deliver to such poor and needy person a competent portion to be wrought into yarn or other matter within such time and in such sort as in their discretions shall be from time to time limited and

[1] Materials.

prefixed, and the same afterwards being wrought, to be from time to time delivered to the said Collectors and Governors of the Poor, for which they shall make payment to them which work the same according to the desert of the work, and of new deliver more to be wrought; and so from time to time to deliver stuff unwrought and receive the same again wrought as often as cause shall require; Which hemp, wool, flax, or other stuff wrought from time to time shall be sold by the said Collectors and Governors of the Poor either at some market or other place, and at such time as they shall think meet, and with the money coming of the sale to buy more stuff in such wise as the stocks or store shall not be decayed in value; And if hereafter any such person able to do any such work shall refuse to work, or shall go abroad begging or live idly, or taking such work shall spoil or embezzle the same in such wise that after monition given the Minister and Churchwardens of the parish and Collectors and Governors of the Poor, or the more part of them, shall think the same person not meet to have any more work delivered out of the same store and stock, that then upon certificate thereof made under their hands and brought by one of the said Collectors and Governors of the Poor to the hands of such person or persons as shall in that county have the oversight and government of one of the Houses of Correction hereafter mentioned in this Act, in convenient apparel meet for such a body to wear, he, she, or they from such town, place, or parish shall be received into such House of Correction, there to be straitly kept, as well in diet as in work, and also punished from time to time as to the said persons having the oversight and government of the said House of Correction shall be appointed, as hereafter in this Act is declared; All which stocks and stores shall be provided and delivered to the hands of the said Collectors and Governors of the Poor before the first day of November next coming, and at all times hereafter as occasion shall serve; and that every person refusing to pay or not paying such sum of money towards the said stocks and stores as upon them or any of them shall be by order aforesaid taxed, and at such time as by the same order shall be appointed, shall for every default forfeit double so much as he or they shall be so taxed unto.

V. And moreover be it ordained and enacted. . . That within every county of this realm, one, two, or more abiding-houses or places convenient in some market town or corporate town or other place or places, by purchase, lease, building, or otherwise, by the appointment and order of the Justices of Peace or the more part of them in their said general Sessions (of the inhabitants

within their several authorities to be taxed, levied, and gathered)
shall be provided, and called the House or Houses of Correction,
and also stock and store and implements to be in like sort also
provided for setting on work and punishing not only of those
which by the Collectors and Governors of the Poor for causes
aforesaid to the said Houses of Correction shall be brought, but
also of such as be or shall be inhabiting in no parish, or be or
shall be taken as rogues, or once punished as rogues, and by
reason of the uncertainty of their birth or of their dwelling by
the space of three years, or for any other cause, ought to be abiding
and kept within the same county;...and that every person refusing to pay or not paying such sum of money towards the
making, obtaining, and furnishing of the said Houses of Correction, and buying of stocks and stores, and for the relief and sustentation of such persons as shall be appointed to the said Houses
of Correction, [as] upon them or any of them shall be by order
aforesaid taxed, and at such time as by the same order shall be
appointed, shall for every default forfeit double so much as he or
they shall be so taxed unto.

   VI. And be it also further enacted...That the said Justices
of Peace or the more part of them in their said general Sessions
in every county shall and may appoint from time to time persons
which shall be overseers of every such House of Correction,
which said persons shall be called the Censors and Wardens of
the Houses of Correction, and shall have the rule, government,
and order of such Houses of Correction, according to such orders
as by the said Justices of Peace or the more part of them in their
general Sessions in every county shall be prescribed; And shall
also by like authority appoint others for the gathering of such
money as shall be taxed upon any person or persons within their
several jurisdictions towards the maintenance of the said Houses
of Correction, which shall be called the Collectors for the Houses
of Correction; And if any person or persons refuse to be Collector
and Governor of the Poor, or Censor and Warden or Collector
of or for any the Houses of Correction, that every person so refusing shall forfeit and lose the sum of five pounds.

   *   *   *   *   *   *
              18 Eliz. c. 3: *Statutes of the Realm*, iv, 610.

(5) Beggars Act of 1598

An Act for punishment of Rogues, Vagabonds, and Sturdy Beggars

   For the suppressing of rogues, vagabonds, and sturdy
beggars, Be it enacted...[*that former Acts for the punishment of*

rogues, etc., be repealed and that]...from time to time it shall and may be lawful to and for the Justices of Peace of any county or city in this realm or the dominions of Wales, assembled at any Quarter Sessions of the Peace within the same county, city, borough, or town corporate, or the more part of them, to set down order to erect and to cause to be erected one or more Houses of Correction within their several counties or cities; for the doing and performing whereof, and for the providing of stocks of money and all other things necessary for the same, and for raising and governing of the same, and for correction and punishment of offenders thither to be committed, such orders as the same Justices or the more part of them shall from time to time take, reform, or set down in any their said Quarter Sessions in that behalf shall be of force and be duly performed and put in execution.

II. And be it also further enacted...That all persons calling themselves scholars going about begging[1], all seafaring men pretending losses of their ships or goods on the sea going about the country begging, all idle persons going about in any country either begging or using any subtile craft or unlawful games and plays, or feigning themselves to have knowledge in physiognomy, palmistry, or other like crafty science, or pretending that they can tell destinies, fortunes, or such other like fantastical imaginations; all persons that be or utter themselves to be proctors, procurors, patent gatherers, or collectors for gaols, prisons, or hospitals[2]; all fencers, bearwards, common players of interludes, and minstrels wandering abroad (other than players of interludes belonging to any baron of this realm, or any other honourable personage of greater degree, to be authorised to play under the hand and seal of arms of such baron or personage); all jugglers, tinkers, pedlars, and petty chapmen wandering abroad; all wandering persons and common labourers being persons able in body, using loitering and refusing to work for such reasonable wages as is taxed[3] or commonly given in such parts where such persons do or shall happen to dwell or abide, not having living otherwise to maintain themselves; all persons delivered out of gaols that beg for their fees or otherwise do travel begging; all such persons as shall wander abroad begging pretending losses by fire or otherwise; all such persons not being felons wandering and pretending

---

[1] Cf. p. 478 above.
[2] See note on p. 478 above. On the various kinds of vagrants who frequented the English roads, see Jusserand, ch. i.
[3] Prescribed, ordained.

themselves to be Egyptians, or wandering in the habit, form, or attire of counterfeit Egyptians; shall be taken, adjudged, and deemed rogues, vagabonds, and sturdy beggars, and shall sustain such pain and punishment as by this Act is in that behalf appointed.

III. And be it enacted...That every person which is by this present Act declared to be a rogue, vagabond, or sturdy beggar, which shall be...taken begging, vagrant, wandering, or misordering themselves in any part of this realm or the dominion of Wales, shall upon their apprehension by the appointment of any Justice of the Peace, constable, headborough, or tithing-man of the same county, hundred, parish, or tithing where such person shall be taken, the tithing-man or headborough being assisted therein with the advice of the minister and one other of that parish, be stripped naked from the middle upwards and shall be openly whipped until his or her body be bloody, and shall be forthwith sent from parish to parish by the officers of every the same the next straight way to the parish where he was born, if the same may be known by the party's confession or otherwise; and if the same be not known, then to the parish where he or she last dwelt before the same punishment by the space of one whole year, there to put him or her self to labour as a true subject ought to do; or not being known where he or she was born or last dwelt, then to the parish through which he or she last passed without punishment; After which whipping the same person shall have a testimonial[1] subscribed with the hand and sealed with the seal of the same Justice of the Peace, constable, headborough, or tithing-man, and of the minister of the same parish, or any two of them, testifying that the same person hath been punished according to this Act, and mentioning the day and place of his or her punishment, and the place whereunto such person is limited to go, and by what time the said person is limited to pass thither at his peril. And if the said person through his or her default do not accomplish the order appointed by the said testimonial, then to be eftsoons[2] taken and whipped, and so as often as any default shall be found in him or her contrary to the form of this Statute, in every place to be whipped till such person be repaired to the place limited; The substance of which testimonial shall be registered by the minister of the parish in a book to be provided for that purpose, upon pain to forfeit 5s. for every default thereof; And the party so whipped and not known where he or she was born

---

[1] For specimens of such a 'testimonial' see p. 494 below.
[2] A second time.

or last dwelt by the space of a year, shall by the officers of the said village where he or she so last passed through without punishment, be conveyed to the House of Correction of the limit wherein the said village standeth, or to the common gaol of that county or place, there to remain and be employed in work until he or she shall be placed in some service, and so to continue by the space of one whole year, or not being able of body until he or she shall be placed to remain in some almshouse in the same county or place.

IV. Provided always and be it enacted, If any of the said rogues shall appear to be dangerous to the inferior sort of people where they shall be taken, or otherwise be such as will not be reformed of their roguish kind of life by the former provisions of this Act, That in every such case it shall and may be lawful to the said Justices of the limits where any such rogue shall be taken, or any two of them whereof one to be of the Quorum, to commit that rogue to the House of Correction, or otherwise to the gaol of that county, there to remain until their next Quarter Sessions to be holden in that county, and then such of the same rogues so committed as by the Justices of the Peace then and there present or the most part of them shall be thought fit not to be delivered, shall and may lawfully by the same Justices or the most part of them be banished out of this realm and all other the dominions thereof, and at the charges of that country[1] shall be conveyed unto such parts beyond the seas as shall be at any time hereafter for that purpose assigned by the Privy Council unto her Majesty, her heirs or successors, or by any six or more of them whereof the Lord Chancellor or Lord Keeper of the Great Seal or the Lord Treasurer for the time being to be one, or otherwise be judged perpetually to the galleys of this realm, as by the same Justices or the most part of them it shall be thought fit and expedient; And if any such rogue so banished as aforesaid shall return again into any part of this realm or dominion of Wales without lawful licence or warrant so to do, that in every such case such offence shall be felony, and the party offending therein suffer death as in case of felony; The said felony to be heard and determined in that county of this realm or Wales in which the offender shall be apprehended. * * * * * *

XII. And be it also further enacted... That any two or more Justices of the Peace within all the said several shires, cities, boroughs, or towns corporate, whereof one to be of the Quorum, shall have full power by authority of this present Act to hear and

---

[1] In the sense of 'district.'

determine all causes that shall grow or come in question by reason of this Act.

*   *   *   *   *   *

XIV. Provided always nevertheless, That every seafaring-man suffering shipwreck, not having wherewith to relieve himself in his travels homewards, but having a testimonial under the hand of some one Justice of the Peace of or near the place where he landed, setting down therein the place and time where and when he landed, and the place of the party's dwelling or birth unto which he is to pass, and a convenient time therein to be limited for his passage, shall and may, without incurring the danger and penalty of this Act, in the usual ways directly to the place unto which he is directed to pass, and within the time in such his testimonial limited for his passage, ask and receive such relief as shall be necessary in and for his passage.

XV. Provided also, That this Statute nor anything therein contained shall [not] extend to any children under the age of seven years....

*   *   *   *   *   *

39 Eliz. c. 4: *Statutes of the Realm*, iv, 899.

(6) Poor Relief Act of 1598

An Act for the Relief of the Poor

Be it enacted by the authority of this present Parliament, That the Churchwardens of every parish, and four substantial householders there...who shall be nominated yearly in Easter week, under the hand and seal of two or more Justices of the Peace in the same county, whereof one to be of the Quorum, dwelling in or near the same parish, shall be called Overseers of the Poor of the same parish; and they or the greater part of them shall take order from time to time by and with the consent of two or more such Justices of Peace for setting to work of the children of all such whose parents shall not by the said persons be thought able to keep and maintain their children[1], And also all such persons married or unmarried as having no means to maintain them use no ordinary and daily trade of life to get their living by; and also to raise weekly or otherwise (by taxation of every inhabitant and every occupier of lands in the said parish in such competent sum and sums of money as they shall think fit) a convenient stock of flax, hemp, wool, thread, iron, and other necessary ware and stuff to set the poor on work, and also com-

---

[1] This principle, in so far as it applied to illegitimate children, had been recognised in the Act of 1576; see p. 481 above.

petent sums of money for and towards the necessary relief of the
lame, impotent, old, blind, and such other among them being
poor and not able to work, and also for the putting out of such
children to be apprentices, to be gathered out of the same parish
according to the ability of the said parish; and to do and execute
all other things, as well for disposing of the said stock as otherwise
concerning the premises, as to them shall seem convenient:
Which said Churchwardens, and Overseers so to be nominated,
or such of them as shall not be let[1] by sickness or other just
excuse to be allowed by such two Justices of Peace or more, shall
meet together at the least once every month in the church of the
said parish, upon the Sunday in the afternoon after divine service,
there to consider of some good course to be taken and of some
meet orders to be set down in the premises; and shall within four
days after the end of their year, and after other overseers nominated as aforesaid, make and yield up to such two Justices of Peace
a true and perfect account of all sums of money by them received,
or rated and cessed and not received, and also of such stock as
shall be in their hands or in the hands of any of the poor to work,
and of all other things concerning their said office, and such sum
or sums of money as shall be in their hands shall pay and deliver
over to the said Churchwardens and Overseers newly nominated
and appointed as aforesaid: upon pain that every one of them
absenting themselves without lawful cause as aforesaid from such
monthly meeting for the purpose aforesaid, or being negligent in
their office or in the execution of the orders aforesaid being made
by and with the assent of the said Justices of Peace, to forfeit for
every such default twenty shillings.

II. And be it also enacted, That if the said Justices of Peace
do perceive that the inhabitants of any parish are not able to levy
among themselves sufficient sums of money for the purposes
aforesaid, That then the said Justices shall and may tax, rate, and
assess as aforesaid any other of other parishes[2], or out of any
parish within the hundred where the said parish is, to pay such
sum and sums of money to the Churchwardens and Overseers of
the said poor parish for the said purposes as the said Justices
shall think fit, according to the intent of this law; And if the said
hundred shall not be thought to the said Justices able and fit to
relieve the said several parishes not able to provide for themselves
as aforesaid, then the Justices of Peace at their general Quarter

---

[1] Prevented.

[2] The principle of requiring rich parishes to help the poorer ones had been
recognised in the Act of 1563; see p. 472 above.

Sessions, or the greater number of them, shall rate and assess as aforesaid, . . . other parishes. . . as in their discretion shall seem fit.

III. And that it shall be lawful for the said Churchwardens and Overseers or any of them, by warrant from any such two Justices of Peace, to levy as well the said sums of money of every one that shall refuse to contribute according as they shall be assessed, by distress and sale of the offender's goods, as the sums of money or stock which shall be behind upon any account to be made as aforesaid, rendering to the party the overplus; and in defect of such distress, it shall be lawful for any such two Justices of the Peace to commit him to prison, there to remain without bail or mainprize till payment of the said sum or stock; And the said Justices of Peace or any one of them to send to the House of Correction such as shall not employ themselves to work being appointed thereunto as aforesaid; And also any two such Justices of Peace to commit to prison every one of the said Churchwardens and Overseers which shall refuse to account, there to remain without bail or mainprize till he have made a true account and satisfied and paid so much as upon the said account shall be remaining in his hands.

IV. And be it further enacted, That it shall be lawful for the said Churchwardens and Overseers or the greater part of them, by the assent of any two Justices of the Peace, to bind any such children as aforesaid to be apprentices where they shall see convenient, till such man-child shall come to the age of four and twenty years, and such woman-child to the age of one and twenty years; the same to be as effectual to all purposes as if such child were of full age and by indenture of covenant bound him or herself.

V. And to the intent that necessary places of habitation may more conveniently be provided for such poor impotent people, Be it enacted by the authority aforesaid, That it shall and may be lawful for the said Churchwardens and Overseers or the greater part of them, by the leave of the lord or lords of the manor whereof any waste or common within their parish is or shall be parcel. . . to erect, build, and set up in fit and convenient places of habitation in such waste or common, at the general charges of the parish or otherwise of the hundred or county as aforesaid, to be taxed, rated, and gathered in manner before expressed, convenient Houses of Dwelling for the said impotent poor; And also to place inmates or more families than one in one cottage or house. . . .

VI. Provided always, That if any person or persons shall find themselves grieved with any cess or tax or other act done by the

said Churchwardens and other persons or by the said Justices of
Peace, that then it shall be lawful for the Justices of Peace at their
general Quarter Sessions, or the greater number of them, to take
such order therein as to them shall be thought convenient, and
the same to conclude and bind all the said parties.

VII. And be it further enacted, That the parents or children
of every poor, old, blind, lame, and impotent person, or other
poor person not able to work, being of sufficient ability, shall at
their own charges relieve and maintain every such poor person
in that manner and according to that rate as by the Justices of
Peace of that county where such sufficient persons dwell, or the
greater number of them, at their general Quarter Sessions shall
be assessed; upon pain that every one of them to forfeit 20s. for
every month which they shall fail therein.

VIII. And be it further hereby enacted, That the Mayors,
Bailiffs, or other head officers of every corporate town within
this realm being Justice or Justices of Peace, shall have the same
authority by virtue of this Act within the limits and precincts of
their corporations, as well out of Sessions as at their Sessions, as
is herein limited, prescribed, and appointed to any of the Justices
of Peace in the county for all the uses and purposes in this Act prescribed, and no other Justice of Peace to enter or meddle there.

IX. And be it also enacted, That if it shall happen any parish
to extend itself into more counties than one, or part to lie within
the liberties of any city or town corporate and part without, That
then as well the Justices of Peace of every county as also the head
officers of such city or town corporate shall deal and intermeddle
only in so much of the said parish as lieth within their liberty, and
not any further.

X. And be it further enacted by the authority aforesaid,
That...no person or persons whatsoever shall go wandering
abroad and beg in any place whatsoever, by licence or without[1],
upon pain to be esteemed, taken, and punished as a rogue: Provided always, That this present Act shall not extend to any poor
people which shall ask relief of victuals only in the same parish
where such poor people do dwell, so the same be in such time
only and according to such order and direction as shall be made and
appointed by the Churchwardens and Overseers of the Poor of the
same parish according to the true intent and meaning of this Act.

[XI. All penalties and forfeitures to be applied to the use of the poor of
the parish.]

[1] The system of begging by licence appears first in the Act of 1531 (see p. 475
above); the fully developed Poor Law now prohibits begging altogether.

XII. And forasmuch as all begging is forbidden by this present Act; Be it further enacted by the authority aforesaid, That the Justices of Peace of every county or place corporate, or the more part of them, in their general Sessions to be holden next after the end of this session of Parliament, or in default thereof at the Quarter Sessions to be holden about the Feast of Easter next, shall rate every parish to such a weekly sum of money as they shall think convenient, so as no parish be rated above the sum of 6*d*. nor under the sum of an halfpenny weekly to be paid, and so as the total sum of such taxation of the parishes in every county amount not above the rate of twopence for every parish in the said county; which sums so taxed shall be yearly assessed by the agreement of the parishioners within themselves, or in default thereof by the Churchwardens and Constables of the same parish or the more part of them, or in default of their agreement by the order of such Justice or Justices of Peace as shall dwell in the same parish or (if none be there dwelling) in the parts next adjoining; And if any person shall refuse or neglect to pay any such portion of money so taxed, it shall be lawful for the said Churchwardens and Constables, or in their default for the Justices of the Peace, to levy the same by distress and sale of the goods of the party so refusing or neglecting, rendering to the party the overplus, and in default of such distress it shall be lawful to any Justice of that limit to commit such persons to prison, there to abide without bail or mainprize till he have paid the same.

XIII. And be it also enacted, That the said Justices of the Peace at their general Quarter Sessions to be holden at the time of such taxation, shall set down what competent sum of money shall be sent quarterly out of every county or place corporate for the relief of the poor prisoners of the King's Bench and Marshalsea, and also of such hospitals and almshouses as shall be in the said county, and what sums of money shall be sent to every one of the said hospitals and almshouses, so as there be sent out of every county yearly twenty shillings at the least to the prisoners of the King's Bench and Marshalsea; which sums, rateably to be assessed upon every parish, the Churchwardens of every parish shall truly collect and pay over to the High Constable[1] in whose division such parish shall be situate. . .and every such Constable at every such Quarter Sessions in such county shall pay over the

---

[1] The High Constable of the Hundred had been originally appointed under the Statute of Winchester (13 Edw. I, st. 2, c. 6) to make the view of arms twice a year, but he came to be generally responsible for the peace of the hundred. The office was abolished in practice by 32 & 33 Vict. c. 47.

same to two such Justices of Peace, or to one of them, as shall be by the more part of the Justices of Peace of the county elected to be Treasurers of the said collection; which Treasurers in every county so chosen shall continue but for the space of one whole year, and then give up their charge with a due account of their receipts and disbursements at their meeting in the Quarter Sessions to be holden after the Feast of Easter in every year to such others as shall from year to year in form aforesaid successively be elected; which said Treasurers or one of them shall pay over the same to the Lord Chief Justice of England and Knight Marshal for the time being, equally to be divided to the use aforesaid, taking their acquittances for the same, or in default of the said Chief Justice to the next ancientest Justice of the King's Bench as aforesaid: And if any Churchwarden or High Constable or his executors or administrators shall fail to make payment in form above specified, then every Churchwarden, his executors or administrators, so offending shall forfeit for every time the sum of ten shillings; and every High Constable, his executors or administrators, shall forfeit for every time the sum of twenty shillings; the same forfeitures, together with the sums behind, to be levied by the said Treasurer and Treasurers by way of distress and sale of the goods as aforesaid in form aforesaid, and by them to be employed towards the charitable uses comprised in this Act.

XIV. And be it further enacted, That all the surplusage of money which shall be remaining in the said stock of any county shall by discretion of the more part of the Justices of Peace in their Quarter Sessions be ordered, distributed, and bestowed for the relief of the poor hospitals of that county, and of those that shall sustain losses by fire, water, the sea, or other casualties, and to such other charitable purposes for the relief of the poor as to the more part of the said Justices of Peace shall seem convenient.

XV. And be it further enacted, That if any Treasurer shall wilfully refuse to take upon him the said office of Treasurership, or refuse to distribute and give relief according to such form as shall be appointed by the more part of the said Justices of Peace, That then it shall be lawful for the Justices of Peace in their Quarter Sessions, or in their default for the Justices of Assize at the Assizes to be holden in the same county, to fine the same Treasurer by their discretion; the same fine to be levied by sale of his goods, and to be prosecuted by any two of the said Justices of Peace whom they shall authorise.

XVI. Provided always nevertheless, That every soldier being discharged of his service or otherwise lawfully licensed to pass into his country, and not having wherewith to relieve himself in his travel homewards, and every seafaring man landing from sea not having wherewith to relieve himself in his travel homewards, having a testimonial under the hand of some one Justice of Peace of or near the place where he was landed or was discharged, setting down therein the place and time where and when he landed or was discharged, and the place of the party's dwelling-place or birth unto which he is to pass, and a convenient time to be limited therein for his passage, shall and may, without incurring the danger or penalty of this Act, in the usual ways directly to the place unto which he is directed to pass and within the time in such his testimonial limited for his passage, ask and receive such relief as shall be necessary in and for his passage; This Act or anything therein contained to the contrary notwithstanding.

XVII. Provided always, That this Act shall endure no longer than to the end of the next Session of Parliament[1].

39 Eliz. c. 3: Statutes of the Realm, iv, 896.

(7) Testimonials for a Sturdy Rogue

1. 1598

The form of this 'testimonial,' in use under the Act of 1598, was probably that originally adopted under the Act of 1531.

A.B., a sturdy rogue, of tall stature, red-haired and bearded, about the age of 30 years and having a wart near under his right eye, born (as he confesseth) at East Tilbury in Essex, was taken begging at Shorne in this county of Kent the 10 of March, 1598, and was then there lawfully whipped therefor, and he is appointed to go to East Tilbury aforesaid the direct way by Gravesend, over the River of Thames; for which he is allowed one whole day and no more, at his peril. Subscribed and sealed the day and year aforesaid.

By us { C.D. *Minister*[2] / E.F. *Borsholder*[3] / G.H. *Parishioner* } of Shorne aforesaid.

Lambarde, The Duties of Constables (ed. of 1610), p. 46.

2. 1604

John at Stile, a sturdy vagrant beggar, of low personage, red-haired, and having the nail of his right thumb cloven, was the sixth day of April in the second year of the reign of our Sovereign

---

[1] But see p. 473 above.   [2] See p. 486 above.
[3] The Kentish equivalent of a petty constable.

Lord King James openly whipped at Dale in the said county [*of Kent*] for a wandering rogue according to the law; and is assigned to pass forthwith from parish to parish by the officers thereof the next straight way to Sale in the county of Middlesex, where (as he confesseth) he was born [*or dwelled last by one whole year, etc.,* if the case be such] and he is limited to be at Sale aforesaid within ten days now next ensuing, at his peril.

Lambarde, *Eirenarcha*, p. 205

§ 4. ROADS AND BRIDGES

Until the Tudor period little attention was paid by Parliament to the maintenance of roads and bridges. The medieval obligation of keeping them in repair attached to particular persons or corporations owning property, and in some cases guilds or monasteries undertook the repair of particular roads, bridges, and sea walls. The only remedy against neglect was the cumbrous one of presentment by the grand jury at the Assizes or an indictment by private persons. But a government so concerned with commercial development as that of the Tudors could not afford to neglect the arteries of commerce, and an Act of 1531 [below] empowered the Justices of the Peace to inquire into broken bridges[1], and where no person or corporation could be made responsible, to tax the inhabitants of the town or parish for the repair of bridges situated within its limits, and the inhabitants of the whole shire for the repair of bridges outside those limits. They were also to appoint collectors of these taxes, and surveyors to inspect the bridges and spend upon them the moneys so collected. Another Act, of 1555 [p. 498], provided for the repair of highways, as in the case of the Poor Law taking the parish as the responsible unit, and empowering the Justices of the Peace to inquire into all failures to carry out the law, and to inflict in Quarter Sessions fines for default. The Act also established a new elective parochial office—that of Surveyor of Highways, whose duty it was to keep the roads in repair, and who was authorised for that purpose to levy services in kind—either cart-service or manual labour—upon every householder, cottager, and labourer in the parish. An Act of 1563 [p. 499] empowered Quarter Sessions to inquire into and punish any surveyors who might be guilty of neglect of duty. The liability to service in kind afterwards became a money rate, assessed upon the basis of the poor rate.

(1) Statute of Bridges, 1531

An Act concerning the amendment of Bridges in Highways

Be it enacted...That the Justices of the Peace in every shire of this realm, franchise, city, or borough, or 4 of them at the least, whereof one to be of the Quorum, shall have power and authority to enquire, hear, and determine in the King's general Sessions of Peace of all manner of anoysances[2] of bridges broken in the highways to the damage of the King's liege people; and to

---

[1] As the bridges were often made of wood, they required constant supervision and repair. [2] Nuisances.

make such process and pains upon every presentment afore them for the reformation of the same, against such as ought to be charged for the making or amending of such bridges, as the King's Justices of his Bench use commonly to do, or as it shall seem by their discretion to be necessary and convenient for the speedy amendment of such bridges.

II. And where in many parts of this realm it cannot be known and proved what hundred, riding, wapentake, city, borough, town, or parish, nor what person certain or body politic ought of right to make such bridges decayed, by reason whereof such decayed bridges, for lack of knowledge of such as ought to make them, for the most part lie long without any amendment, to the great annoyance of the King's subjects; For the remedy thereof be it enacted...that in every such case the said bridges if they be without city or town corporate shall be made by the inhabitants of the shire or riding within the which the said bridge decayed shall happen to be: And if it be within any city or town corporate then by the inhabitants of every such city or town corporate wherein such bridges shall happen to be....

III. And be it farther enacted, That in every such case where it cannot be known and proved what persons, lands, tenements, and bodies politic ought to make and repair such bridges, that for speedy reformation and amending of such bridges the Justices of Peace within the shires or ridings wherein such decayed bridges be out of cities and towns corporate, and if it be within cities or towns corporate then the Justices of Peace within every such city or town corporate, or four of the said Justices at the least, whereof one to be of the Quorum, shall have power and authority within the limits of their several commissions and authorities to call before them the constables of every town and parish being within the shire, riding, city, or town corporate, as well within liberty[1] as without, wherein such bridges or any parcel thereof shall happen to be, or else 2 of the most honest inhabitants within every such town or parish in the said shire, riding, city, or town corporate, by the discretion of the said Justices of Peace or 4 of them at the least, whereof one to be of the Quorum; And at and upon the appearance of such constables or inhabitants the said Justices of Peace or 4 of them, whereof one to be of the Quorum, with the assent of the said constables or inhabitants shall have power and authority to tax and set[2] every inhabitant in any such city, town, or parish within the limits of their commissions and authorities

[1] Before 1850 a 'liberty' was any district exempt from the jurisdiction of the sheriff of the county and having a separate commission of the peace.   [2] Assess.

to such reasonable aid and sum of money as they shall think by their discretions convenient and sufficient for the repairing, re-edifying, and amendment of such bridges; And after such taxation made, the said Justices shall cause the names and sums of every particular person so by them taxed to be written in a roll indented[1], and shall also have power and authority to make two Collectors of every Hundred for collection of all such sums of money by them set and taxed; which Collectors, receiving the one part of the said roll indented under the seals of the said Justices, shall have power and authority to collect and receive all the particular sums of money therein contained, and to distrain every such inhabitant as shall be taxed and refuse payment thereof in his lands, goods, and chattels, and to sell such distress and of the sale thereof retain and perceive[2] all the money taxed, and the residue (if the distress be better) to deliver to the owner thereof; And that the same Justices or 4 of them within the limits of their commissions and authorities shall also have power and authority to name and appoint 2 Surveyors which shall see every such decayed bridge repaired and amended from time to time, as often as need shall require, to whose hands the said Collectors shall pay the said sums of money taxed and by them received; And that the Collectors and Surveyors and every of them and their executors and administrators, and the executors and administrators of them and every of them, from time to time shall make a true declaration and account to the Justices of Peace. . . or to 4 of the same Justices, whereof one to be of the Quorum, of the receipts, payments, and expenses of the said sums of money: And if they or any of them refuse that to do, that then the same Justices of Peace or 4 of them from time to time by their discretions shall have power and authority to make process against the said Collectors and Surveyors and every of them their executors and administrators, and the executors and administrators of every of them, by attachments under their seals returnable at the general Sessions of the Peace, and if they appear, then to compel them to account as is aforesaid, or else if they or any of them refuse that to do, then to commit such of them as shall refuse to ward, there to remain without bail or mainprize till the same declaration and account be truly made.

* * * * * *

22 Henr. VIII, c. 5: *Statutes of the Realm*, iii, 321.

---

[1] *I.e.* a roll drawn up in duplicate with the two halves separated by a zigzag or wavy line, so that when cut they would exactly fit.
[2] Receive (of rents or dues).

(2) First Statute of Highways, 1555

An Act for the amending of Highways

For amending of highways, being now both very noisome and tedious to travel in and dangerous to all passengers and carriages; Be it enacted... That the constables and churchwardens of every parish within this realm shall yearly, upon the Tuesday or Wednesday in Easter week, call together a number of the parochians and shall then elect and choose two honest persons of the parish to be surveyors and orderers for one year of the works for amendment of the highways in their parish leading to any market town, the which persons shall have authority by virtue hereof to order and direct the persons and carriages that shall be appointed for those works by their discretions; And the said persons so named shall take upon them the execution of their said offices upon pain of every of them making default to forfeit 20*s*. And the said constables and churchwardens shall then also name and appoint four days for the amending of the said ways before the Feast of the Nativity of St John Baptist then next following; And shall openly in the church the next Sunday after Easter give knowledge of the same four days, and upon the said days the parochians shall endeavour themselves to the amending of the said ways, and shall be chargeable thereunto as followeth; that is to say, Every person for every ploughland[1] in tillage or pasture that he or she shall occupy in the same parish, and every other person keeping there a draught[2] or plough, shall find and send at every day and place to be appointed for the amending of the ways in that parish as is aforesaid, one wain or cart furnished after the custom of the country, with oxen, horses, or other cattle, and all other necessaries meet to carry things convenient for that purpose, and also two able men with the same, upon pain of every draught making default 10*s*.; and every other householder, and also every cottager and labourer of that parish able to labour and being no hired servant by the year, shall by themselves or one sufficient labourer for every of them upon every of the said four days work and travail in the amendment of the said highways, upon pain of every person making default to lose for every day 12*d*.; And if the carriages of the parish or any of them shall not be thought needful by the supervisors to be occupied upon any of the said days, that then every such person that should have

---

[1] A unit of assessment in the northern and eastern counties corresponding to the hide in the south and west (*Oxford Dictionary*).

[2] Team.

sent any such carriage, shall send to the said work for every carriage so spared two able men there to labour for that day, upon pain to lose for every man not so sent to the said work 12*d*. And every person and carriage abovesaid shall have and bring with them such shovels, spades, picks, mattocks, and other tools and instruments as they do make their own ditches and fences withal, and such as be necessary for their said work: And all the said persons and carriages shall do and keep their work, as they shall be appointed by the said supervisors or one of them, eight hours of every of the said days, unless they shall be otherways licensed by the said supervisors or one of them.

II. And Be it enacted...That the Steward and Stewards of every Leet or Law-day[1] shall therein have full power and authority to enquire by the oaths of the suitors of all and every the offences that shall be committed within the Leet or Law-day against every point and article of this Estatute, and to assess such reasonable fines and amerciaments for the same as shall be thought meet by the said Steward: And in default of such enquiry or presentment, the Justices of Peace of every place or county shall have authority to enquire of the same offences which shall be committed within the limits of their Commission at every their Quarter Sessions, and to assess such fines therefor as they or two of them, whereof one to be of the Quorum, shall think meet....

* * * * * *

2 & 3 Philip & Mary, c. 8: *Statutes of the Realm*, iv, 284.

(3) Second Statute of Highways, 1563

An Act for the continuing of a Statute made Anno 2 & 3
P. & M. for the amending of Highways

[I. 2 & 3 P. & M. c. 8, originally passed for seven years, is now continued for another twenty.]

[II. Supervisors of highways are empowered to take rubbish from quarries and to dig for gravel to amend highways without permission of the owners.] * * * * * *

[VI. The period of four days in the year assigned to the amending of highways in the earlier Act is increased to six.]

VII. And be it further enacted...That from henceforth all and every such supervisor or supervisors for the time being, within one month next after default or offence made, done, or committed by any person or persons contrary to the provision, purport, and true meaning of [2 & 3 *P. & M. c.* 8...] or...

---

[1] The day of meeting of the court leet, and therefore used of the court itself.

of this present Act, shall present every such default or offence to the next Justice of Peace for the time being, upon pain to forfeit for every such default and offence in such sort not by them presented, forty shillings; And that every such Justice of Peace to whom any such default or offences shall be presented as is aforesaid, shall certify the same presentment so to him made at the next general Sessions within the said county then next after to be holden, upon pain to forfeit for not certifying of every such presentment of every such default or offence as is aforesaid, five pounds: And that the Justices of Peace of every county where the said defaults or offences shall be committed shall immediately[1] have authority to enquire of any such default or offence committed within the limits of their Commission at every their Quarter Sessions, and to assess such fines for the same as they or two of them, whereof the one to be of the Quorum, shall think meet.

VIII. And be it further enacted...That every Justice of Peace shall have authority by this Statute upon his own proper knowledge in the open general Sessions to make presentment of any highway not well and sufficiently repaired and amended, or of any other default or offence committed or done within the county and limits of his Commission contrary to the provision and intent of this Statute or [2 & 3 P. & M. c. 8...]; And that every such presentment made by any such Justice of Peace upon his own knowledge as is aforesaid, shall be as good and of the same force, strength, and effect in the law as if the same had been presented, found, and adjudged by the oath of twelve men: And that for every such default so presented as is aforesaid, the Justices of the Peace of the said county shall immediately[1] at the said general Sessions have authority to assess such fines as to them or two of them, whereof the one to be of the Quorum, shall be thought meet....

                    5 Eliz. c. 13: *Statutes of the Realm*, iv, 441.

§ 5. LICENSING OF ALE-HOUSES

The Justices of the Peace were empowered by the Act of 1495 against vagabonds and beggars [p. 473] 'to reject and put away common ale-selling' at their discretion, and to take surety of the keepers of ale-houses. But the important statute of the period is that of 1552 [p. 501], which laid the foundation of the modern licensing law.

            [1] Directly, without any intermediary.

Licensing Act, 1552
An Act for Keepers of Ale-houses to be bound by Recognisances

Forasmuch as intolerable hurts and troubles to the common wealth of this realm doth daily grow and increase through such abuses and disorders as are had and used in common ale-houses and other houses called tippling-houses[1]; It is therefore enacted...That the Justices of Peace within every shire, city, borough, town corporate, franchise, or liberty within this realm, or two of them at the least, whereof one of them to be of the Quorum, shall have full power and authority, by virtue of this Act, within every shire [etc....] where they be Justices of Peace to remove, discharge, and put away common selling of ale and beer in the said common ale-houses and tippling-houses in such town or towns and places where they shall think meet and convenient; And that none...shall be admitted or suffered to keep any common ale-house or tippling-house but such as shall be thereunto admitted and allowed in the open Sessions of the Peace, or else by two Justices of the Peace, whereof the one to be of the Quorum: And that the said Justices...shall take bond and surety from time to time by recognisance of such as shall be admitted and allowed hereafter to keep any common ale-house or tippling-house, as well for and against the using of unlawful games as also for the using and maintenance of good order and rule to be had and used within the same, as by their discretion shall be thought necessary and convenient...And the said Justices shall certify the same recognisance at the next Quarter Sessions of the Peace to be holden within the same shire [etc....] where such ale-house or tippling-house shall be; the same recognisance there to remain of record before the Justices of Peace of that shire [etc....]; upon pain of forfeiture to the King for every such recognisance taken and not certified, £3. 6. 8.

* * * * * *

IV. Provided alway, That in such towns and places where any fair or fairs shall be kept, that for the time only of the same fair or fairs it shall be lawful for every person and persons to use common selling of ale or beer in booths or other places there for the relief of the King's subjects that shall repair to the same, in such like manner and sort as hath been used or done in times past; This Act or anything therein contained to the contrary notwithstanding.   5 & 6 Edw. VI, c. 25: *Statutes of the Realm*, iv, 157.

[1] 'Tippler' was a technical term for a retailer of ale, and a 'tippling-house' was a place where ale was sold. Excessive drinking is not implied.

§ 6. Regulation of Labour and Wages

By Elizabeth's Statute of Labour of 1563 [below] the Justices of the Peace were empowered to fix the rate of wages once a year; to bind apprentices either to crafts or husbandry; to assign labour where it was required; and to adjudicate in labour disputes.

Statute of Labour[1], 1563

The complicated provisions of this Statute fall mainly within the sphere of Economic History. The extracts here given concern only the duties which it throws upon the Justices of the Peace.

Although there remain and stand in force presently[2] a great number of Acts and Statutes concerning the retaining, departing, wages, and orders of apprentices, servants, and labourers, as well in husbandry as in divers other arts, mysteries, and occupations, yet partly for the imperfection and contrariety that is found and do appear in sundry of the said laws, and for the variety and number of them, and chiefly for that the wages and allowances limited and rated in many of the said Statutes are in divers places too small and not answerable to this time, respecting the advancement of prices of all things belonging to the said servants and labourers, the said laws cannot conveniently without the great grief and burden of the poor labourer and hired man be put in good and due execution: And as the said several Acts and Statutes were at the time of the making of them thought to be very good and beneficial for the common wealth of this realm, as divers of them yet are, So if the substance of as many of the said laws as are meet to be continued shall be digested and reduced into one sole Law and Statute, and in the same an uniform order prescribed and limited concerning the wages and other orders for apprentices, servants, and labourers, there is good hope that it will come to pass that the same Law, being duly executed, should banish idleness, advance husbandry, and yield unto the hired person both in the time of scarcity and in the time of plenty a convenient proportion of wages: Be it therefore enacted....

*   *   *   *   *   *

[III. Persons unmarried, not having 40s. by the year nor being otherwise employed, shall be compellable to serve as yearly servants in the crafts in which they were brought up.]

IV. And be it further enacted, That no person which shall retain any servant shall put away his or her said servant, and that

---

[1] Often called the Statute of Apprentices, but the Act covers much wider ground than this title suggests.

[2] At the present time.

no person retained according to this Statute shall depart from his master, mistress, or dame before the end of his or her term... unless it be for some reasonable and sufficient cause or matter to be allowed before two Justices of Peace, or one at the least, within the said county, or before the Mayor or other chief officer of the city, borough, or town corporate wherein the said master, mistress, or dame inhabiteth, to whom any of the parties grieved shall complain; which said Justices or Justice, Mayor or chief officer, shall have and take upon them or him the hearing and ordering of the matter between the said master, mistress, or dame, and servant according to the equity of the cause: And that no such master, mistress, or dame shall put away any such servant at the end of his term, or that any such servant shall depart from his said master, mistress, or dame at the end of his term, without one quarter warning given before the end of his said term, either by the said master, mistress, or dame, or servant the one to the other....

[V. All persons between the ages of 12 and 60, not being otherwise employed, are declared compellable to be yearly servants in husbandry.]

VI. And be it further enacted...That if any person after he hath retained any servant shall put away the same servant before the end of his term, unless it be for some reasonable and sufficient cause to be allowed as is aforesaid, or if any such master, mistress, or dame shall put away any such servant at the end of his term without one quarter's warning given before the said end as is above remembered, that then every such master, mistress, or dame so offending, unless he or they be able to prove by two sufficient witnesses such reasonable and sufficient cause of putting away of their servant or servants during their term, or a quarter's warning given afore the end of the said term as is aforesaid, before the Justices of Oyer and Terminer, Justices of Assize, Justices of the Peace in the Quarter Sessions [*or in a city, borough, or corporate town before the Mayor and two Aldermen, or 'two other discreet Burgesses'*...]...shall forfeit the sum of 40s.; And if any servant [*unduly departs from service or refuses to serve, he shall be imprisoned until he undertakes to complete his service*...].

*   *   *   *   *   *

XI. And for the declaration and limitation what wages servants, labourers, and artificers, either by the year or day or otherwise, shall have and receive; Be it enacted...That the Justices of Peace...shall yearly at every general Sessions first to be holden and kept after Easter...assemble themselves together, and they so assembled calling unto them such grave and discreet

persons of the said county or of the said city or town corporate
as they shall think meet, and conferring together respecting the
plenty or scarcity of the time and other circumstances necessary
to be considered, shall have authority. . . to limit, rate, and appoint
the wages. . . of. . . artificers, handicraftsmen, husbandmen, or any
other labourer, servant, or workman. . . and shall. . . certify the
same engrossed in parchment, with the considerations and causes
thereof, under their hands and seals into the Queen's most honourable Court of Chancery, whereupon it shall be lawful to the Lord
Chancellor of England, . . . upon declaration thereof to the Queen's
Majesty, her heirs or successors, or to the Lords and others of the
Privy Council for the time being attendant on their persons, to
cause to be printed and sent down. . . into every county to the
Sheriff and Justices of Peace there. . . ten or twelve proclamations
or more, containing in every of them the several rates appointed
by the said Justices, . . . with commandment by the said proclamations to all persons in the name of the Queen's Majesty. . . straitly
to observe the same, and to all Justices, Sheriffs, and other officers
to see the same duly and severely observed. . . And if the said. . .
Justices. . . shall at their said general Sessions. . . upon their assembly and conference together think it convenient to retain and
keep for the year then to come the rates and proportion of wages
that they certified the year before, or to change or reform them or
some part of them, then they shall. . . yearly certify into the said
Court of Chancery their resolutions and determinations therein,
to the intent that proclamations may accordingly be renewed and
sent down; And if it shall happen that there be no need of any
reformation or alteration of the rates of the said wages, but that
the former shall be thought meet to be continued, then the proclamations for the year past shall remain in force until new proclamations upon new rates concerning the said wages shall be
sent down. . . .

[XII. Penalty on any Justices, etc., absent from the Sessions for rating
wages, 'and not visited with any such sickness as he could not travel thither
without peril and danger of his life, or not having any other lawful and good
excuse,' £10.]

[XIII. Penalty on giving higher wages than are so rated, ten days imprisonment and £5; on receiving, twenty-one days imprisonment.]

* * * * * *

XV. Provided always and be it enacted, . . . That in the time
of hay or corn harvest, the Justices of Peace and every of them, and
also the constable or other head officer of every township, upon
request and for the avoiding of the loss of any corn, grain, or

hay, shall and may cause all such artificers and persons as be meet to labour...to serve by the day for the mowing, reaping, shearing, getting, or inning of corn, grain, and hay, according to the skill and quality of the person; and that none of the said persons shall refuse so to do, upon pain to suffer imprisonment in the stocks by the space of two days and one night....

* * * * * *

XVII. And be it further enacted...That two Justices of Peace, the Mayor...of any city, borough, or town corporate and two Aldermen...shall and may by virtue hereof appoint any such woman as is of the age of twelve years and under the age of forty years and unmarried and forth of service as they shall think meet to serve, to be retained or serve by the year or by the week or day, for such wages and in such reasonable sort and manner as they shall think meet: And if any such woman shall refuse so to serve, then it shall be lawful for the said Justices of Peace, Mayor, or head officers to commit such woman to ward until she shall be bounden to serve as aforesaid.

* * * * * *

XXVIII. And be it further enacted, That if any person shall be required by any householder having and using half a plough-land at the least in tillage to be an apprentice and to serve in husbandry or in any other kind of art, mystery, or science before expressed, and shall refuse so to do; that then upon the complaint of such housekeeper made to one Justice of Peace of the county wherein the said refusal is or shall be made, or [*in a city or town corporate to the Mayor...*] they shall have full power and authority by virtue hereof to send for the same person so refusing; And if the said Justice or the said Mayor...shall think the said person meet and convenient to serve as an apprentice in that art, labour, science, or mystery wherein he shall be so then required to serve, That then the said Justice or the said Mayor...shall have power and authority by virtue hereof, if the said person refuse to be bound as an apprentice, to commit him unto ward, there to remain until he be contented and will be bounden to serve as an apprentice should serve, according to the true intent and meaning of this present Act: And if any such master shall misuse or evil intreat his apprentice, or that the said apprentice shall have any just cause to complain, or the apprentice do not his duty to his master, then the said master or prentice being grieved and having just cause to complain shall repair unto one Justice of Peace within the said county or to the Mayor...of the city, town corporate, market town, or other place where the said master dwelleth, who shall by his wisdom and discretion take such order and direction between the said master and his apprentice as the equity of the cause shall require; And if for want of good conformity in the said master, the said Justice of Peace or... Mayor... cannot compound and agree the matter between him and his apprentice, then the said Justice or... Mayor... shall take bond of the said master to appear at the next Sessions then to be holden in the said county or... town,... and upon his appearance and hearing of the matter before the said Justices or the said Mayor,... if it be thought meet unto them to discharge the said apprentice of his apprenticehood, that then the said Justices or four of them at the least, whereof one to be of the Quorum, or the said Mayor... with the consent of three other of his brethren or men of best reputation within the said... town,... shall have power by authority hereof in writing under their hands and seals to pronounce and declare that they have discharged the said apprentice of his apprenticehood, and the cause thereof, and the said writing so being made and enrolled by the Clerk of the Peace or Town Clerk amongst the records that he keepeth, shall be a sufficient discharge for the said apprentice against his master, his executors and administrators...; And if the default shall be found to be in the apprentice, then the said Justices or... Mayor... with the assistants aforesaid, shall cause such due correction and punishment to be ministered unto him as by their wisdom and discretions shall be thought meet.

*   *   *   *   *   *

5 Eliz. c. 4: Statutes of the Realm, iv, 414.

§ 7. Miscellaneous Police Duties

In addition to the more important functions connected with the administration of justice, vagabonds and beggars, the poor law, the regulation of labour and wages, the maintenance of roads and bridges, and the licensing of ale-houses, the Justices of the Peace were charged by the Tudor statutes with a vast number of minor duties which may be brought together under the vague term of Police.

For instance, the Justices were to order the arrest of persons engaged in unlawful hunting by day or night in 'divers forests, parks, and warrens,' especially in the counties of Kent, Surrey, and Sussex, 'some with painted faces, some with visors, and otherwise disguised, to the intent they should not be known,'[1] and on confession to bind them over to appear at the Sessions for trespass; and they also dealt with the stealing of partridges and the eggs of hawks and swans[2]. They enforced the sumptuary laws[3]; fined and imprisoned persons who wrote, sang, or spoke any 'phantastical

---

[1] 1 Henr. VII, c. 7.   [2] 11 Henr. VII, c. 17.
[3] 1 Henr. VIII, c. 14; 6 Henr. VIII, c. 1.

or false prophecy' with the purpose of making rebellions[1], or spread abroad 'false, seditious, and slanderous news'[2]; and determined offences concerning musters for the defence of the realm[3]. They were also to hear and determine cases of the breaking of fences and robbing of orchards[4]. After the Reformation the Justices came to be concerned with a number of offences of an ecclesiastical or quasi-ecclesiastical character, such as wilful perjury[5], unlawful usury[6], upholding the authority of the Bishop of Rome[7], attending services other than those prescribed by the Act of Uniformity[8], and offences against the recusancy laws of Elizabeth[9].

These are illustrations of duties laid upon the Justices of the Peace by statute, but they were also relied upon by the Privy Council for the discharge of a variety of other functions. In 1538 a circular letter[10] was sent to them, enjoining them, among other things, to search out 'cankered parsons, vicars, and curates, who do not substantially declare our Injunctions, but mumble them confusely'[11]; and a circular letter of 1541 expressed the King's desire 'that privy maintainers of that papistical faction be tried out as the most cankerous and venomous worms in the commonwealth, enemies to God and traitors.'[12] In 1582 the Sheriffs and Justices of the Peace were instructed to supply the Council with information concerning recusants who had been indicted or bound over, in order that the Council lists of Jesuits, priests, and recusants might be properly kept up[13]. They were also required by the Council to arrest priests going about disguised, and to examine at the coasts persons entering or leaving the realm[14].

In their policy of regulating prices the Council depended upon the Justices, both for the necessary local information and for carrying out the work of restriction; and instructions were sent to them from time to time to regulate grain, search the granaries, and supply the markets in time of scarcity at 'reasonable and convenient' prices. Any persons who refused to obey the instructions of the Council in this matter were to be bound over by the Justices to appear in London to answer for their contempt[15].

The Council not only supplemented the statutes by orders to the Justices stimulating them to greater activity and instructing them how to proceed, but imposed upon them special police duties of a miscellaneous kind. Thus, they were ordered to apprehend prisoners escaped from the Marshalsea; to make special inquiries into important murder cases; to arrest and punish pirates and assist in the search for their booty; to keep order at fairs and wakes; to relieve discharged soldiers[16]; and to examine embezzlers and report to the Council[17]. In times of plague they 'did the work of a health committee.'[18]

[1] 3 & 4 Edw. VI, c. 15. [2] 1 & 2 P. & M. c. 3.
[3] 4 & 5 P. & M. c. 3. [4] 43 Eliz. c. 7. [5] 5 Eliz. c. 9.
[6] 13 Eliz. c. 8. [7] 28 Henr. VIII, c. 10.
[8] 5 & 6 Edw. VI, c. 1. [9] See pp. 141–163 above.
[10] L. and P. vol. xiii, pt 2, No. 1171. [11] Indistinctly.
[12] L. and P. vol. xvi, No. 945. [13] Beard, p. 127. [14] Ib. p. 130.
[15] Ib. p. 132. [16] See p. 509 below. [17] Beard, pp. 135–6.
[18] Ib. p. 134. Much information about the practical working of the system of local government, and the way in which the Justices of the Peace discharged their functions, will be found in West Riding Sessions Rolls, 1598–1602, ed. J. Lister (Yorkshire Archaeological Society, Record Series, vol. iii, 1888).

§ 8. The Ecclesiastical Parish

Although the parish was selected by the Tudor sovereigns as the unit of local civil administration, it still retained its ancient ecclesiastical character. This accounts for the existence of other parish officials and a different kind of parish rate.

The principal parochial personage was the parson, and to his ecclesiastical office Tudor legislation added certain duties of an administrative and police character. The provision for the relief of the poor which began with the Act of 1536 depended largely for financial support upon the statutory exhortations of the vicar of the parish. He was required to be present at whippings in his parish, and to sign the 'testimonial' returning the sturdy rogue so whipped to the place where he was born[1]. He superintended the public confessions sometimes required of offenders by Quarter Sessions, and the penances imposed by the ecclesiastical courts. Failing the action of the churchwardens, he was responsible for prosecuting recusants who refused to attend their parish church[2]. For a short time also he was charged with the registration of the character of domestic servants.

The churchwardens were the legal guardians of all property belonging to the church; and from early times they had been charged with the duty of presenting to the ecclesiastical authorities notorious crimes touching the church, clergy, or parishioners. But on the civil side also the office had become important by the institution of church rates. Every parish had a regular income derived from property—the rents of houses and lands bequeathed to the church, or the profits of a different kind of endowment, such as a parish flock of sheep[3]. This income from endowments, supplemented by pew-rents, and fees for graves within the church, was assigned to the maintenance of the church buildings and other expenses for which the churchwardens were responsible, such as the church plate, surplices, books, and a dress for the beadle[4]. It was often the case, however, that the parish revenue was insufficient to meet the church expenses, and it was necessary to supply the deficiency by means of a rate. This was originally voluntary, but in process of time it became compulsory by ancient custom, although a trace of its voluntary origin is to be found in the fact that it was imposed by a parish meeting, named, like the Star Chamber, from the place where it met, and called the 'vestry.' This consisted in theory of all the parishioners, but in many places a 'select vestry'[5] of 12 or 24 parishioners, holding office for life and filling vacancies by co-optation, had come to represent the parish and to manage its affairs. In the 15th century the exaction of the church rate had become one of the principal duties of the churchwardens, who summoned the vestry on Easter Tuesday to impose the rate, and collected the rate after its imposition, presenting to the ecclesiastical courts those who refused to pay. At this meeting both the churchwardens were elected; it was not until much later that one of them came to be appointed by the incumbent, and the distinction was made between the 'vicar's warden' and the 'people's warden.'

Upon these officials, already important, the Tudor statutes imposed

---

[1] See p. 494 above.   [2] Trotter, p. 43.   [3] Ib. p. 27.
[4] Ib. p. 24.   [5] Ib. p. 18.

fresh duties. They were associated in the administration of the new Poor Law as *ex officio* overseers of the poor. The Act of 1555[1] for the amending of highways imposed on them the duty of summoning a parish meeting on the Tuesday in Easter week to elect surveyors of the highways for the year. By an Act of 1566[2] the churchwardens and six other parishioners were to assess a rate for the destruction of vermin, and were to appoint 'two honest and substantial persons' of the parish to be 'distributors of the provision for the destruction of noyful fowls and vermin,' who were to offer rewards for the heads and eggs of certain birds and the heads of certain beasts[3], 'all which said heads and eggs shall be...in the presence of the said churchwardens...burned, consumed, or cut in sunder.' The churchwardens were also concerned with prosecuting for non-attendance at church and receiving the fines paid by the delinquents to the use of the poor of the parish[4]; and with the breaking of fasts, attendance at conventicles, drunkenness, the game laws, vagrancy, and weights and measures. The churchwardens were also responsible for collecting the sums which the Justices of the Peace in Quarter Sessions were authorised by statute to assess upon each parish within their jurisdiction for the relief of poor prisoners in the county gaol[5], the King's Bench, and the Marshalsea[6]; for hospitals and almshouses within the county[7]; and for the relief of maimed soldiers[8].

The lower ecclesiastical officers in the parish were the parish clerk, the sexton, and the beadle. The clerk, as his name implies, was originally a young assistant cleric who rang the bell, led the responses in church, and took part in parochial work. In course of time he completely lost his clerical character, but became an increasingly active member of the parochial administration, being appointed by the parish and paid out of the parish funds; and eventually he came to enjoy a freehold tenure. In country villages his office was sometimes combined with that of the sexton, who was responsible for the cleaning and warming of the church, and received special fees for the digging of graves. The beadle summoned the parishioners to the parish meeting, impounded stray cattle, and drove dogs out of church[9]; but his 'chief work was of a punitive nature.'[10]

The petty constable was not in any sense an ecclesiastical officer and not always a parish officer, but he played an important part in the system of local government. He was elected and sworn in the Court Leet, and held office by ancient custom under the common law, his duty being to assist the High Constable of the Hundred[11]; and he represented the township rather than the parish. As some large parishes might include several townships, this limited the area of his jurisdiction, but in country places there would be only one constable to each parish. It was his duty to prevent

---

[1] See p. 498 above.　　　　　　[2] 8 Eliz. c. 15.
[3] Crows, hawks, weasels, etc.　　[4] See p. 139 above.
[5] 14 Eliz. c. 5, § 38.　　　　　　[6] 39 Eliz. c. 3, § 13.
[7] *Ib.*　　　　　　　　　　　　　[8] 43 Eliz. c. 3; see p. 507 above.
[9] The following suggestive items occur in the churchwardens' books for Barton-on-Humber: 'For whipping dogs out of church, 2s.; to Brocklebank for waking sleepers, 2s.; to pacify Sharp's wife, 1s.' (W. Andrews, *Bygone Lincolnshire*, i, 123).
[10] Trotter, p. 7.　　　　　　　　[11] See note on p. 492 above.

breaches of the peace, profane swearing, unlawful games, Sabbath-breaking, and eating of flesh on fast-days; and to deal in the first instance with rogues and vagabonds, wandering players, and breaches of trade regulations. He conducted whippings under the instructions of the local Justice of the Peace, and carried out other sentences inflicted in Petty or Quarter Sessions. He had also to carry out the instructions of the Coroners and the Judges of Assize. In some cases he collected rates in the township for which he was responsible, and the Tudor statutes expressly associated him with the church-wardens in the administration of the Poor Law and of Elizabeth's Statute of Labour. He acted with the Surveyor of Highways, and summoned those liable for service to work upon the roads; he also organised the service of watch and ward, and raised the hue and cry The office was unpaid, but it was not usually held by the same person for more than a year[1].

[1] An account of the office of petty constable, with illustrations from the history of Yorkshire, will be found in Trotter, ch. 5. These illustrations are from the 17th century.

Parliament

Sir Thomas Smith begins his discussion of Parliament with an assertion of its authority. 'The most high and absolute power of the realm of England consisteth in the Parliament.' Whatever is done in Parliament, 'that is the Prince's and whole realm's deed: whereupon justly no man can complain, but must accommodate himself to find it good and obey it.'[1] Here he appears to claim for Parliament the legislative omnipotence which it enjoys to-day; but at the end of the same section he calls it 'the highest and most authentical *court* of England,'[2] and we now know that during the 16th century, as in the Middle Ages, Parliament was conceived as a judicial tribunal rather than as a legislative assembly[3]. The Middle Ages knew nothing of a separation of functions in the constitutional sphere, and all the courts, of which the High Court of Parliament was the greatest, pursued activities which today would be regarded as legislative. In the Tudor period this was specially the case with the Council Courts. The work of the Council itself was legislative as well as administrative and judicial, and we find the Star Chamber making decrees as well as punishing the breach of them. It is true that the chief business of a Tudor Parliament had come to be what we should call legislation, but the change in its position was not perceived by Tudor statesmen, who continued to think and speak of it in the old way as a Court. In 1589 the Speaker reminded the Commons 'that every member of this House is a Judge of this Court, being the highest Court of all other courts, and the Great Council also of this realm,' and urged upon them a sobriety of demeanour such as became the office of a judge[4]. In 1591 Lambarde called it 'our chief and highest court,'[5] and wrote of the making of new law there almost as if it were 'the decision of a new case,' or 'the reversal of an error of a preceding Parliament.'[6] Even Sir Thomas Smith, although he claims for Parliament absolute power, uses 'absolute' in the legal sense of 'not subject to appeal,'[7] and is not really ascribing to Parliament anything so modern as legislative omnipotence. This judicial character of Parliament made it natural for the House of Commons in Seymour's case in 1549 [p. 513] to demand evidence before passing a bill of attainder; it explains why in Fitzherbert's case in 1593 the House claimed to be a 'court of record'[8]; and it accounts for the form of procedure by a suit and witnesses in modern legislation by private bill[9]. It was not until the Civil War of the 17th century that Parliament ceased to be conceived as a Court. First the Long Parliament and then the Parliaments of the Interregnum developed legislative activity over a far wider

---

[1] p. 48.   [2] p. 58.

[3] On this see C. H. McIlwain, *The High Court of Parliament and its Supremacy*, and A. F. Pollard, *The Evolution of Parliament*. The House of Lords, in one of its aspects, is still a Court.

[4] McIlwain, p. 122; the passage is printed on p. 548 below.   [5] *Archeion*, p. 275.

[6] McIlwain, p. 124; the passage from Lambarde is quoted on p. 123.

[7] *Ib.* p. 129.   [8] D'Ewes, p. 502.

[9] The differentiation between public and private acts first appears in 16th century statutes (Pollard, *Parliament*, p. 145).

field, and therefore the current view concerning Parliament insensibly changed; it came to be no longer regarded as a Court but as a legislative assembly. And from practical experience of the omnipotence of Parliament there grew a novel theory of the sovereignty of Parliament[1]. Hitherto it had been regarded as a judicial body interpreting a fundamental law, and legislation was only the occasional provision of new rules to meet altered circumstances. It was not until the 17th century that Parliament began to *make* laws—that it found itself free to range over the whole province of national affairs, and to issue decrees of unlimited authority which must be obeyed at his peril by every subject.

The great position which Parliament came to occupy in the 17th century was due in part to the Tudor sovereigns and especially to Henry VIII. For the purposes of his crusade against the feudal franchises and the immunities of the Church he had special need of Parliament, and he therefore exalted Parliament in the body politic. It was summoned more frequently, sat for a longer time, and there was a remarkable increase in the privileges and prestige of the Lower House. It is conceivable that the Tudors, if they had chosen to do so, might have dispensed with Parliaments, legislating by ordinances of the King-in-Council and levying taxes by royal writ instead of Parliamentary grant. They did none of these things because they were not despots in the ordinary sense of the term. They had only small military means of enforcing their commands, for there was no standing army of mercenaries; the monarchy depended upon the active co-operation of the governing classes and the willing acquiescence of the common people, and not upon any force which could be exercised by a few yeomen of the royal guard. The Tudor sovereigns all possessed a strong sense of legality. Bacon says of Henry VII, 'he was a great observer of formality in all his proceedings,' although he adds, 'which notwithstanding was no impediment to the working of his will.'[2] A modern biographer says much the same thing of Henry VIII: 'strictly speaking he was not an unconstitutional sovereign; all his doings were clothed with the form of legality.'[3] He worked the constitutional machine to his own ends, but he did not tamper with the machine itself. He achieved his objects rather by 'the extraordinary degree of personal weight that he was able to throw into the government of the realm,'[4] than by any alteration in the forms under which the realm was governed. No Tudor sovereign ever quarrelled with the common law, or attempted to deprive a man of his freehold as Ahab deprived Naboth of his vineyard[5]. In the same way, in relation to Parliament the attitude of the Tudors is not despotic. It is, as a rule, the first business of a despot to silence the assembly—'or else he purgeth it,' as Cromwell was to do by the aid of soldiers in the next century. The Tudors, on the other hand, foster the assembly, and during the period of their rule Parliament is growing into a new sense of its own dignity, and is training the statesmen whose sons were to take the lead in the great conflict of the next generation. The English sovereigns of the 16th century were the careful nursing-fathers to a representative assembly which was destined to become in the 17th century capable of competing with the Crown upon equal terms.

---

[1] McIlwain, p. 93. [2] vi, 21. [3] *D.N.B.* xxvi, 93.
[4] *Ib.* [5] Cf. Hearn, p. 37.

Seymour's Case, 1549

[2 March, 1549]...The Master of the Rolls, Serjeant Molyneux, Serjeant Hales, and the King's Solicitor, sent from the Lords to know the pleasure of the House, if it be resolved there to pass upon the attainder of the Admiral in such order as was passed in the Higher House: Whereupon...It is resolved, That the evidence shall be heard orderly, as it was before the Lords; and also to require that the Lords which affirm that evidence may come hither and declare it *viva voce*....

Commons' Journals, i, 9.

§ 1. COMPOSITION OF PARLIAMENT

It has been said that the Wars of the Roses caused a great decline in the numbers of the House of Lords. In the 14th century the numbers shew wide variations because writs of summons were issued, not as a matter of hereditary right, but at the discretion of the Crown. Peers might be summoned for one Parliament only, or during the term of their lives without summons to their heirs. Thus under Edward II the number of earls and barons summoned varied from 44 to 99; and under Edward III from 16 to 75[1]. In the 15th century the numbers were smaller and the fluctuations not so great; the number called to the Parliament of 1454—the last Parliament before the Civil Wars—being 53. To the last Parliament of Edward IV 45 lay lords were summoned, but in the first Parliament of Henry VII there were only 29. The decline in numbers is evident, but it was not a permanent decline. Some of the missing lords are attainted, others suspended from Parliament, others again represented by minors. In later Parliaments the minors grow up, the suspended peerages revive, and even some of the attainders are reversed. Further, during the Tudor period additions to the peerage—although at no time large additions—were made by the Crown. Under Henry VII there were about 5 new creations; in the first 30 years of Henry VIII about 20 more[2]. By the end of the reign of Elizabeth there were some 60 temporal peers qualified to sit[3], but if the Tudor period is taken as a whole, the number fluctuates in the neighbourhood of 50[4]. Thus it was not the case that the Civil Wars wiped out whole families and reduced the peerage to a state of numerical weakness. The enfeeblement of the baronage was of a different kind. It was financially exhausted, deprived of its private armed forces, and in some important cases represented only by minors, who could neither attend Parliament nor lead troops to victory in the field.

Henry VII did nothing to interfere with the issue of writs of summons from the Chancery to the traditional persons in the traditional way, and his example was followed by Henry VIII. Thus, as far as the direct action of the Crown was concerned, there was no change in the composition of the Upper House. But a momentous change was accomplished with the

---

[1] Details will be found in Pike, pp. 96–99. [2] Pike, p. 349.
[3] *Ib.* p. 355. [4] Maitland, p. 238.

sanction of Parliament itself, for the Dissolution of the Monasteries involved a diminution in the number of the spiritual peers and an alteration in the proportion which they bore to the peers temporal. To the Parliaments of Henry VII were summoned 2 archbishops, 19 bishops, and 28 mitred abbots. Henry VIII added three more mitred abbots, but these 31 all disappeared at the Dissolution, and came to be represented by the holders of five new bishoprics founded out of the monastic spoils. Thus whereas Henry VII's House of Lords had contained 49 spiritual to 29 temporal peers, after the Dissolution Henry VIII's House only contained 26 spiritual peers, while the temporal peerage was never less than 36 and often nearer 50. Thus the balance of power was changed, and laymen came to be in a majority in the Upper House.

The decline in the numbers of the House of Lords did not of itself involve any decline in the strength of the House against the Crown, for this depended, not on how many persons sat there but on what those persons represented. Before the Civil Wars the lay peers stood for vast estates, military power, and feudal independence, and the spiritual peers were either great independent prelates or the representatives of wealthy and powerful corporations. In the Tudor period these elements of power were in process of being dissolved, and the importance of a lay peer was coming to depend upon his holding a great office of state under the Crown, while the bishops were no longer independent princes, but nominees and employees of the Crown.

In addition to the lay and spiritual peers, writs of summons to the Upper House were sent to the judges and the law officers of the Crown[1] and to the sworn members of the King's Council, but although the lawyers in particular discharged important functions in the House in connexion with the preparation of legislation[2], they and the other official members of the Council were present as assistants only, and had no vote. An important change of the Tudor period is that the privy councillors, although they continued to receive their writs of summons to the House of Lords, were beginning to find seats in the House of Commons, thus preferring to appear in Parliament 'as elected representatives instead of as crown nominees.'[3]

The composition of the House of Commons was not greatly changed, although the numbers steadily increased. Henry VIII's first House consisted of 298 members—74 for the counties and 224 for the cities and boroughs. By an Act of 1536[4] Wales was incorporated into the parliamentary constitution of England, each of its 12 counties and its 11 boroughs sending one member, while the county of Monmouth and the borough of Monmouth sent two members each—a total increase of 27. Another Act, of 1543[5], incorporated the County Palatine of Chester[6], giving two members to the county and two to the city of Chester—thus bringing the increase up to 31. The right of the Crown to issue writs to new boroughs accounts for five more under Henry VIII, 48 under Edward VI, 21 under Mary,

[1] *I.e.* the Attorney and Solicitor-General and the King's Serjeants. The Masters in Chancery were also summoned, but they acted rather as messengers than advisers. For a full discussion of these 'writs of assistance,' see *E.H.R.* xxxvi, 356.
[2] See Pollard, *Parliament*, pp. 292–5.   [3] *Ib.* p. 296.
[4] 27 Henr. VIII, c. 26.   [5] 34 & 35 Henr. VIII, c. 13.
[6] The Palatinate of Durham was not incorporated until after the Restoration.

and 60 under Elizabeth[1]. In the first Parliament of Elizabeth's reign there actually sat 398 members, returned by 212 constituencies, and of these 398 only about 90 represented English and Welsh counties, the remainder being borough members[2]. On the accession of James I the total numbers of the House of Commons had reached 467; but the increase in numbers throughout the Tudor period is mainly accounted for by an increase in borough representation.

It is by no means clear that this multiplication of boroughs was invariably intended to influence Parliament by packing it with members likely to support the Crown. In the 16th century representation was beginning to be coveted by the localities[3], and the Crown, in creating new boroughs, may very well have been responding to pressure from below. Most of the boroughs created by Elizabeth, however, fall into the category of rotten boroughs. In 1559 three new boroughs sent members to Parliament, two of which were small villages[4], and the same policy was pursued in 1562 in order to secure the Queen's ascendancy in her second Parliament[5]. Between 1588 and 1603 the additions were numerous, and most of the new boroughs came to be controlled either by the Crown or by the neighbouring landowners[6].

An analysis of the composition of Elizabeth's first Parliament[7] shews that the officials and courtiers only numbered 75, or 21 per cent. of the House of Commons; but the official element was more important than these figures suggest by reason of the standing and experience of its representatives.

§ 2. Sessions of Parliament

At the beginning of the Tudor period the sessions of Parliament were infrequent, and there were long intervals between them. 'Continuous parliamentary government was neither expected nor desired'[8]; for attendance at Parliament was irksome to the members, and the payment of their representatives' wages was burdensome to the constituencies. 'The medieval Parliament was an affair of weeks; it seldom had more than one session, and members rarely sought re-election.'[9] The first Parliament to hold sittings on modern lines was the 'Reformation Parliament' of 1529, with its eight sessions extending over seven years. This was the first opportunity for the establishment of a Parliamentary tradition and the acquisition of corporate experience; and from this time onward members were often re-elected. But important as this constitutional experiment is, it stands alone in the 16th century. The striking fact about the sessions of Parliament taken over the whole period is that they were so short and were separated by such long intervals. Thus in the 38 years of his reign Henry VIII held only nine Parliaments. Even the sessions of the 'Reformation Parliament' were short; and from 22 December, 1515, to 15 April, 1523, there was an interval of seven years without any Parliament at all[10]. Edward VI in his

[1] Maitland, p. 239.
[2] E.H.R. xxiii, 643.
[3] See Pollard, Parliament, pp. 158, 163.
[4] E.H.R. xxiii, 678.
[5] Porritt, i, 375.
[6] Ib.
[7] E.H.R. xxiii, 681.
[8] Fisher, Polit. Hist. p. 165.
[9] Pollard, Parliament, p. 161.
[10] Maitland, p. 249.

reign of 6½ years called two Parliaments, and the first of these extended over 4½ years—from 4 November, 1547, to 15 April, 1552—but of its five sessions the longest lasted for less than three months. Mary held five Parliaments in five years, but the duration of the shortest was less than a month and of the longest less than two. Elizabeth in 44½ years held ten Parliaments, one of them lasting for nearly 11 years—from 8 May, 1572, to 19 April, 1583—but there were only three sessions, in 1572, 1576, and 1581. The other nine Parliaments were all short, with the exception of the Queen's second Parliament, which lasted four years—from 11 January, 1563, to 2 January, 1567. Between the Parliaments there were long intervals—one of three years, three of four years, and one of 4½ years. The shortest session was 35 days and the longest 145; while the whole parliamentary time of Elizabeth's reign was only about 35 months out of 44½ years.

This infrequency of Parliaments made it impossible, under Tudor conditions, that the members should establish any control over the executive government. When the business of the realm could be carried on for years at a time by the Privy Council, without Parliament meeting at all, the executive remained, in practice as well as in theory, responsible to the sovereign who was there, and not to a Parliament which was not there. Parliamentary government in the modern sense is impossible until the age of long Parliaments.

Another result of infrequent Parliaments and short sessions was that it was almost impossible in any particular Parliament to build up anything of the nature of an organised opposition. In modern Parliaments the opposition, quite as much as the government, is in the habit of acting together, but this habit can only be acquired and maintained where Parliament meets often and sits for a long time. When a Tudor Parliament met, three-quarters of the members were new members[1], and therefore for the most part unknown to each other, as the difficulties of travelling shut every man up into his shire; it was not often that recognised leaders and a grouping of members under them could be inherited by one Parliament from another; and there were never the modern facilities for the constant study of personal equations. The preparation of bills was in the hands of the Privy Councillors and the legal experts, and the ordinary member did not possess, and there was no time for him to acquire, sufficient knowledge of affairs to enable him to resist the government, or even to criticise it effectively. And before Parliament could throw up great leaders, and the rank and file could learn the habit of acting together, a prorogation or a dissolution would intervene. It is remarkable that under conditions so generally unfavourable, so much effective discussion and criticism should have proceeded from Tudor Parliaments, and that their methods should have so steadily ripened to the maturity reached in the latter part of the reign of Elizabeth.

[1] *E.g.* In Mary's second Parliament the percentage of new members was 76; in her third, 70; in her fourth, 73½; in her fifth, 81; and in Elizabeth's first Parliament, 75 (*E.H.R.* xxiii, 645).

§ 3. FRANCHISE AND QUALIFICATIONS

The franchise for counties was determined by the statute of 1430[1], which had restricted it to persons resident in the county having freehold to the value of 40s. per annum at the least. By a statute of 1445[2] the county representatives to be chosen by the 40s. freeholders were to be 'notable knights of the same counties for the which they shall be chosen, or otherwise such notable esquires, gentlemen of birth of the same counties as shall be able to be knights; and no man to be such knight which standeth in the degree of a yeoman and under.' This involved a property qualification, as no one was eligible for knighthood who did not possess land of the annual value of £20. The electors also were to be resident within the shire[3].

The franchise for boroughs had probably once been in the hands of all who could call themselves burgesses—that is to say, of all the free inhabitants of the borough who paid the proper dues and were enrolled at the court leet. But the tendency of local custom seems to have been uniformly towards the restriction of the franchise; and by the end of the 15th century select bodies of burgesses under various names had appropriated in many places the exclusive right of exercising the parliamentary franchise. Further, in the numerous cases in which the Tudor sovereigns conferred representation upon new boroughs by charter, it was vested in a small body. 'The only general principle that can be laid down is this,' says Maitland[4], 'that the later the charter the more oligarchic is the constitution of the borough.' Thus the popular basis of the Tudor Parliaments is not to be found in the boroughs, but rather in the 40s. freeholders of the counties; and the knights of the shire elected by them, although in number less than a quarter of the House, supply the most vigorous and independent part of it, as the borough representatives were often under the influence of the local territorial magnates.

The Tudor period witnessed two changes of considerable importance in connexion with the election of members of Parliament. (1) The old restrictions requiring both the knights of the shire and the burgesses of the towns to be 'dwelling and resident' within the constituencies which they represented, gradually fell into disuse, and it is clear from a debate in the Parliament of 1571 that they had by that time become inoperative[5]. (2) From the end of the reign of Henry VIII members of Parliament ceased to claim wages of their constituents. They had hitherto been entitled to payment at the rate of 4s. a day for a county member and 2s. a day for a borough member, and this rate makes its last appearance in a statute in 1544[6], when it was adopted for the Welsh constituencies which were being incorporated into the English Parliamentary system; but wages had by that time already begun to disappear in English constituencies. For instance, although Lincoln was paying its members in 1535, it ceased to do so very soon after[7]. After the discontinuance of compulsory payments, many boroughs continued to make voluntary payments to their members.

---

[1] 8 Henr. VI, c. 7.   [2] 23 Henr. VI, c. 14.
[3] 1 Henr. V, c. 1.   [4] p. 175.
[5] D'Ewes, p. 168.   [6] 35 Henr. VIII, c. 11.
[7] Porritt, i, 257.

and Andrew Marvell was receiving them from his constituents at Hull as late as the time of Charles II's Pension Parliament.

The disuse of the restrictions about residence and the discontinuance of the payment of wages deprived the constituencies of their control over their representatives, and they could no longer insist upon their regular attendance in the House. Another result was a tendency for the old distinction between the county and borough members to disappear. At one time the counties were represented by landowners and the boroughs by tradesmen or craftsmen, and the distinction was therefore sharply drawn. The county representation remained unaffected, but as soon as the boroughs began to elect non-residents, the merchant or tradesman was to a considerable extent displaced by the courtier and the lawyer; and by the end of the century only a few of the borough constituencies were represented by members of the old type.

§ 4. Influence of the Crown on Parliament

The medieval tradition provided for the personal presence of the King in Parliament, and 'down to the middle of the 17th century no one visualized and no artist depicted Parliament without the King enthroned in the midst thereof.'[1] The appearance of Henry VIII there was therefore strictly in accordance with precedent, and was not a sinister attempt to interfere with its proceedings.

The Crown also possessed the right of summons, prorogation, and dissolution, and its assent was necessary to legislation. 'It is in me and my power,' said Elizabeth in 1593, 'to call Parliaments; it is in my power to end and determine the same; it is in my power to assent or dissent to anything done in Parliaments'[2] [p. 572]. How important these rights were to the Crown appears from the constitutional position in which Charles I found himself after he had agreed that the Long Parliament should not be dissolved without its own consent.

During the Tudor period the Crown still controlled the composition of the House of Lords. A peer could be compelled to attend; the royal licence was necessary for the appointment of proxies; and hereditary right was not so far established as to compel the issue of a writ of summons to any peer whose presence was not desired[3].

(a) Interference in Elections

In connexion with the House of Commons the question arises, how far Tudor Parliaments were packed.

[1] Pollard, *Parliament*, p. 261. 'The minority of Edward VI, followed by the reigns of two Queens, contributed as much towards the Sovereign's absence from Parliament as the reign of Queen Anne, followed by those of two Germans, did to a similar absence from the Privy Council' (p. 261 *n.*).

[2] It has been said that in the Parliament of 1597–8 Queen Elizabeth assented to 24 bills, but vetoed 48, and this has been quoted to prove the power of the Crown in legislation; but Mr J. E. Neale gives reasons for the view that in this session the royal assent was refused to 12 bills only (*E.H.R.* xxxiv, 586 and xxxvi, 480).

[3] Pollard, *Parliament*, p. 273.

There is no doubt that the Crown from time to time interested itself in elections. Henry VIII occasionally wrote letters to constituencies inviting them to elect persons recommended by him, and although the burgesses of Colchester on one occasion refused to comply with the request[1], they felt it necessary to embellish their letter of refusal with expressions of loyal devotion But there is no reason for thinking that the Reformation Parliament of 1529 was packed[2]; although at the elections of 1536 and 1539 Cromwell attempted something of the nature of systematic interference [p. 521] in order to secure a majority in favour of his own policy[3]. It was the packed Parliament of 1539 that turned upon the packer, and passed an Act of Attainder against him without opposition.

In the reign of Edward VI letters of recommendation were sent out in certain cases by the Privy Council [p. 522]; although the case of the county of Kent in 1547 [p. 522] makes it clear that the Council's recommendation was a request and not a command. In 1553, however, interference with particular constituencies was supplemented by a circular letter to the sheriffs [p. 522], urging the choice of 'men of knowledge and experience' to serve in Parliament, and declaring the King's pleasure that if the Privy Council in particular cases should recommend 'men of learning and wisdom' their directions should be carried out. In the reign of Mary also the influence of the Crown was exercised by general instructions to the sheriffs concerning the class of persons to be chosen. In 1555 she commanded the choice of men of 'the wise, grave, and Catholic sort' [p. 523].

In the case of Elizabeth's first Parliament, that of 1559, which overthrew the church settlement of Mary and made the final repudiation of the Papal jurisdiction, there was no government interference in the elections that was not covered by the precedents of the two previous reigns; the suggestion that it was an assembly of government nominees is entirely without foundation[4]. In 1571 the Queen attempted to control the composition of Parliament by bringing to bear upon the constituencies the great personages influential in the localities[5]. Letters went out from the Privy Council 'to the Lords and others throughout the realm' [p. 524], relating to the election; of these the letter to Archbishop Parker and Lord Cobham concerning the elections in the county of Kent printed below [p. 523] may serve as a specimen. In 1586 the Council obtained from the Lord Chancellor a writ for a new election for the county of Norfolk [p. 524], one of

---

[1] Merewether and Stephens, p. 1093.

[2] The famous letter from Ralph Sadleir to Cromwell (see p. 520 below), which Brewer (ii, 466) quotes in support of the opposite view, affords slender ground for such a conclusion (Pollard, *Henry VIII*, p. 254).

[3] Pollard, *Henry VIII*, p. 260; see also p. 317 on Cromwell's interference with the bye-elections of 1534.

[4] See the careful discussion of this question in *E.H.R.* xxiii, 455, 643.

[5] These local territorial influences were often very important in determining elections, although they did not always tell in favour of the Crown. In the debate of 19 April, 1571, on the bill requiring burgesses to be resident in the constituency, it was objected that if it passed, 'lords' letters shall from henceforth bear all the sway' (D'Ewes, p. 168); and it was urged 'that there might be the penalty of forty pound upon every borough that should make such election at the nomination of any nobleman' (p. 171).

the reasons for annulling the first election being that the sheriff had ignored directions proceeding from the Crown, although they thought it necessary to explain that 'her Majesty hath no meaning to impeach any way their free election.' General instructions to the sheriffs were also issued by the Council in 1597 [p. 525]; and a special recommendation to a constituency appears on the minutes of the Council in 1601 [p. 526].

Subject to the qualifications made above, it is true to say that the Tudors did not pack their Parliaments. They make recommendations in certain cases, which would be received with great respect; they issue advice to the sheriffs in general terms; but they do not interfere in any serious or systematic way with the electors' freedom of choice. Nor do they bribe; for although the first case of bribery on record occurs in 1571 [p. 526], it is the candidate and not the Crown that does the bribing. The harmony between the Tudors and their Parliaments is due to a genuine community of interest between the Crown and the people, in the ecclesiastical as well as in the secular sphere; there is no need to create it artificially by interfering on any great scale with the composition of the House of Commons.

(1) Elections of 1529

Ralph Sadleir to [Thomas Cromwell], 1 November, 1529

This letter has been quoted to prove that the King determined elections and issued instructions to members for their behaviour in the House; but it scarcely supports this conclusion. Cromwell had been in Wolsey's service and was now offering himself to the King, so it was not unnatural that he should take the King's instructions. Further, the King's intervention was so far from being decisive that the result of the election at Oxford was regarded as uncertain, and Cromwell did not, as a matter of fact, sit for a town in the diocese of Winchester but for the borough of Taunton (Pollard, *Henry VIII*, p. 255).

A little before the receipt of your letter, I spoke with Mr Gage at the Court, and, as you commanded, moved him to speak to the Duke of Norfolk for the burgess's room of the Parliament on your behalf, which he did. The Duke said he had spoken with the King, who was well contented that you should be a burgess, if you would follow the Duke's instructions. The Duke wishes to speak with you to-morrow.... Will speak with Mr Rush to-night and know whether you shall be burgess of Oxford or not. If you are not elected there, I will desire Mr Paulet to name you as burgess for one of my Lord's[1] towns of his Bishopric of Winchester. It would be well for you to speak with the Duke of Norfolk as soon as possible to-morrow, to know the King's pleasure how you shall order yourself in the Parliament House....

Letters and Papers, Foreign and Domestic, Henry VIII, iv, Appendix, No. 238.

[1] Wolsey's.

(2) Elections of 1536

1. *John Hobbys, Sheriff of Canterbury, to Cromwell,*
12 *May,* 1536

[Abstract]

Held 'the county' at Canterbury on the 11 May by virtue
of the King's writ of summons to Parliament. There were over
80 persons present, who unanimously chose two burgesses, viz.
John Starkey, chamberlain and alderman of the city, and Chr.
Levyns, common clerk of the same. After the election the mayor
shewed him a letter directed to himself and the writer by Cromwell and my Lord Chancellor, desiring that John Briggs and
Robert Darknall 'should fulfil the said rooms.' Regrets that he
was not made aware of the King's pleasure in time.

Letters and Papers, Foreign and Domestic, Henry VIII, x,
No. 852.

2. *Cromwell to the Magistrates of Canterbury,* 18 *May,* 1536

...Forasmuch as the King's pleasure and commandment is
that Robert Derknall and John Bryges should be elect and chosen
citizen or burgesses for that city, by reason whereof my Lord
Chancellor and I by our letters written unto you advertised you
thereof, and ye, the same little or nothing regarding but rather
contemning, have chosen other at your own wills and minds,
contrary to the King's pleasure and commandment in that behalf,
Whereat the King's Highness doth not a little marvel; Wherefore,
in avoiding of further displeasure that might thereby ensue, I
require you on the King's behalf that notwithstanding the said
election ye proceed to a new, and elect those other, according to
the tenor of the former letters to you directed for that purpose,
without failing so to do, as the King's trust and expectation is in
you and as ye intend to avoid his Highness's displeasure at your
peril. And if any person will obstinately gainsay the same, I require you to advertise me thereof, that I may order him as the
King's pleasure shall be in that case to command....

R. B. Merriman, *Life and Letters of Thomas Cromwell,* ii, 13.

3. *John Alcock, Mayor, and the Corporation of Canterbury to
Cromwell,* 20 *May,* 1536

[Abstract]

Received his letter this 20th of May, signifying the King's
command that Rob. Darknall and John Bryges should be burgesses for the city of Canterbury. Ordered the commonalty to

assemble in the Court Hall, where 97 citizens and others appeared, and, according to the King's pleasure, 'freely, with one voice, and without any contradiction,' elected the aforesaid.

Letters and Papers, Foreign and Domestic, Henry VIII, x, No. 929.

(3) Elections of 1547

[28 September, 1547]

To the Sheriff of Kent that where the Lords wrote to him afore to the end to make his friends for the election of Sir John Baker to be knight of the shire, understanding that he did abuse towards those of the shire their request into a commandment, their Lordships advertise him that as they meant not nor mean to deprive the shire by any their commandment of their liberty of election whom they should think meet, so nevertheless if they would in satisfaction of their Lordships' request grant their voices to Mr Baker they would take it thankfully.

A like letter written to the Lord Warden of the Cinque Ports with this addition, that being informed he should abuse their request to menace them of the shire of Kent, as they would not believe it, so they advised him to use things in such sort as the shire might have the free election....

Dasent, *Acts of the Privy Council*, ii, 518–9

(4) Bye-elections of 1552

[At Greenwich, 10 January, 1552]

...A letter to the Mayor and burgesses of Reading to elect a new burgess of Parliament instead of John Seymour, by them chosen in the place of William Grey, late deceased....

Dasent, *Acts of the Privy Council*, iii, 457

[At Greenwich, 19 January, 1552]

...A letter to the Sheriff of Essex and Hertfordshire to elect a new knight of that shire, in lieu of Sir Henry Parker deceased, at the next county day, and to use the matter in such sort as Mr Sadleir may be elected and returned, for that he seemeth most fittest of any other person thereabouts....   Dasent, iii, 459.

(5) Elections of 1553

The King's Letter to the Sheriffs for Parliament Men, 1553

Trusty and well-beloved, We greet you well. Forasmuch as we have, for divers good considerations, caused a summonition for a Parliament to be made, as we doubt not but ye understand the same by our writs sent in that behalf unto you; we have thought it meet...that in the election of such persons as shall

be sent to the Parliament... there be good regard had that choice
be made of men of gravity and knowledge in their own countries
and towns, fit, for their understanding and qualities, to be in such
a great Council. And therefore... we do... at this present will and
command you, that ye shall give notice as well to the freeholders of
your county as to the citizens and burgesses of any city or borough
which shall have any of our writs by your direction... that our
pleasure and commandment is, that they shall choose and appoint
(as nigh as they possibly may) men of knowledge and experience.
... And yet nevertheless our pleasure is, that where our Privy
Council or any of them within their jurisdictions in our behalf
shall recommend men of learning and wisdom, in such case their
directions be regarded and followed, as tending to the same which
we desire,—that is, to have this assembly to be of the most
chiefest men in our realm for advice and good counsel.

Strype, *Ecclesiastical Memorials* (edn. of 1721), ii, 394.

(6) Elections of 1555
The Queen to the Sheriffs

Trusty and well-beloved, We greet you well.... These shall
be to will and command you that, for withstanding such malice
as the Devil worketh by his ministers for the maintenance of
heresies and seditions, ye now on our behalf admonish such our
good loving subjects as by order of our writs should within that
county choose knights, citizens, and burgesses to repair from
thence to this our Parliament, to be of their inhabitants, as the old
laws require, and of the wise, grave, and Catholic sort, such as
indeed mean the true honour of God, with the prosperity of the
commonwealth. The advancement whereof We and our dear
husband the King do chiefly profess and intend, without alteration of any particular man's possessions, as, among other false
rumours, is spread abroad to hinder our godly purpose....

Strype, *Ecclesiastical Memorials* (edn. of 1721), iii, 155.

(7) Elections of 1571
The Lords of the Council to Archbishop Parker and Lord Cobham[1], 17 February, 1571

... Where the Queen's Majesty hath determined for divers
necessary great causes concerning the state of the realm to have
a Parliament holden at Westminster this next April;... upon
some deliberation had by her Majesty with us... her Majesty
hath called to her remembrance (which also we think to be true)

[1] Lord Warden of the Cinque Ports.

that though the greater number of knights, citizens, and burgesses for the more part are duly and orderly chosen, yet in many places such consideration is not usually had herein as reason would, that is, to choose persons able to give good information and advice for the places for which they are nominated, and to treat and consult discreetly upon such matters as are to be propounded to them in their assemblies. But contrariwise that many in late Parliaments (as her Majesty thinketh) have been named, some for private respects and favour upon their own suits, some to enjoy some immunities from arrests upon actions during the time of the Parliaments, and some other to set forth private causes by sinister labour and frivolous talks and arguments, to the prolongation of time without just cause, and without regard to the public benefit and weal of the realm; and therefore her Majesty, being very desirous to have redress herein, hath charged us to devise some speedy good ways for reformation hereof at this time, so as all the persons to be assembled in this next Parliament for the cities, shires, and boroughs, may be found (as near as may be) discreet, wise, and well-disposed, according as the intention of their choosing ought to be. And therefore, as we have thought meet to give knowledge hereof to such as we think both for their wisdoms, dispositions, and authorities in sundry counties in the realm can and will take care hereof, so have we for this purpose made special choice of your Lordships, requiring you in her Majesty's name to consider well of these premises, and to confer with the Sheriff of that shire of Kent by all such good means as you shall think meet, and with such special men of livelihood and worship of the same county as have interest herein, and in like manner with the head officers of cities and boroughs, so as by your good advice and direction the persons to be chosen may be well qualified with knowledge, discretion, and modesty, and meet for those places....

Correspondence of Matthew Parker (Parker Society, 1853), p. 379.

[At Westminster, 17 February, 1571]
Letters to the Lords and others throughout the realm to have good regard for the election and choice of the chiefest within every county to be present at this next Parliament....

Dasent, viii, 15.

(8) Elections of 1586
[8 October, 1586]
...A letter to the Lord Chancellor signifying to his Lordship that whereas their Lordships have received letters out of Norfolk

from the Deputy Lieutenants there concerning the election of the knights of that shire for the present Parliament, whereby it appeareth that the Sheriff of that county hath proceeded to that election unorderly, not regarding also such letters as were sent from their Lordships by her Majesty's special appointment in that behalf; whereupon they pray his Lordship, if he shall so think good, to grant a new writ forth that they may proceed to a new election....

A letter to Henry Hugon, Sheriff of the county of Norfolk, signifying that their Lordships, understanding of the disorder committed in the late election of the knights of that shire, have procured a new writ, whereby he is to proceed to a new election which may be free and not solicited; howbeit their Lordships do find it strange that they would suffer themselves to be laboured to choose one for knight of the shire whom they had for his misdemeanours thought unfit to be of the Commission of the Peace, and though her Majesty hath no meaning to impeach any way their free election, yet she thinketh some regard should have been had to such letters as were sent from hence by her directions....

Dasent, xiv, 241–2.

(9) Elections of 1597

[22 August, 1597]

Another minute of letters to the High Sheriffs of all the several counties of the realm. Whereas the Queen's Majesty hath upon great considerations...determined to hold her Parliament at Westminster....Her Majesty meaning to have this her intended Parliament to be served with men of understanding and knowledge for the particular estate of the places whereunto they ought to be chosen, and of discretion also requisite in consultation for causes concerning the public weal of the realm, hath commanded us of her Privy Council to admonish you to whom her Majesty's writs of summons are now directed to have good regard how this her Majesty's good meaning may be observed and fulfilled. And to that intent, though we doubt not much but the principal persons of that county will have good regard to make choice without partiality or affection, as sometimes hath been used, of men meet for all good respects to serve as knights for that shire, yet in the choice of burgesses for borough towns we doubt (except better regard be had herein than commonly hath been) there will be many unmeet men and unacquainted with the state of the boroughs named thereto, and therefore we require you that shall have the direction of the writs to any boroughs in that county to inform them by your letter (or otherwise) of the contents of this her Majesty's good meaning for the choice of persons meet for the service of the said boroughs in this intended Parliament, which if it shall otherwise appear to be evil supplied, we shall have occasion to enquire and find out by whose default the same hath happened.... Dasent, xxvii, 361.

(10) Elections of 1601
[7 October, 1601]

A letter to Mr Ralph Sheldon, esquire. Whereas we understand that some difference is like to grow amongst you of that shire about the election of the knights for the Parliament, and that the name of Sir Thomas Leighton being in question for one of the said places it is doubted there will be some opposition made out of faction to cross him therein. As we shall not need to say anything in the favour of the gentleman, because his quality and merit sundry ways by special services towards her Majesty and the State and the good account which deservedly her Majesty holdeth of him do sufficiently recommend him, so it is not our meaning in any sort to restrain or hinder the liberty of a free election which ought to be amongst you, but because it is suspected that some undue proceeding may be used against him, especially out of animosity of religion, which would greatly displease her Majesty if she should be acquainted therewith, we thought good to admonish you which are of judgment to have regard not to do yourself the wrong to be transported with any such passion, for that as any favour which should be conferred on the gentleman whom she doth so well esteem would be very agreeable unto her Majesty, so she would be very sensible of any evil measure which by undue practices should be offered him.... Dasent, xxxii, 251

(11) First Case of Bribery, 1571
[10 May, 1571]. ...Forasmuch as Thomas Long, gentleman, returned one of the burgesses for the borough of Westbury in the county of Wilts for this present Parliament, being a very simple man and of small capacity to serve in that place, did this day in open court confess that he did give to Anthony Garland, Mayor of the said town of Westbury, and unto one Watts of the same town, the sum of four pound for that place and room of burgessship; It was ordered by this House that the said Anthony Garland and the said Watts shall forthwith repay unto the said Thomas

Long the same sum of four pound, and also that a fine of twenty pound be assessed upon the said corporation or inhabitants of the said town of Westbury, for the Queen's Majesty's use, for their said lewd and slanderous attempt....

...On Friday the 11th day of May it was ordered that a pursuivant be sent with letters from this House unto Anthony Garland, Mayor of the town of Westbury in the county of Wilts, and Watts of the same town, for their personal appearance forthwith to be made in this House; and also to bring with them all such bonds as Thomas Long, gentleman, lately returned one of the burgesses for the same town, standeth bound in unto them or either of them, or unto any other to their use. And also to answer unto such matters as at their coming shall be objected against them by this House.

D'Ewes, *Journal* (edn. of 1693), p. 182.

(b) Choice of a Speaker

As in the Tudor period the Speaker was the agent of the Crown in the Commons, who managed the government business there in somewhat the same way as the Lord Chancellor, who was avowedly the King's servant, managed it in the Lords, it was of vital importance that his appointment should be controlled by the Crown. The nomination was therefore always made by the Crown[1] [below] through one of the royal officials in the House. Thus, in the Parliament of 1559 the nomination was made by the Treasurer of the Household [p. 528]; in 1597 by Sir William Knollys, the Comptroller [p. 528]; and in 1601 by the same officer[2]. The form of an election was, however, always carefully preserved, as the extracts printed below clearly suggest; and in 1566 objection was taken in the House to the election of Onslow as Speaker, although without success[3], on the ground that he was a serjeant-at-law and his duty was therefore to the Upper House[4].

The Speaker was paid by the Crown, his 'accustomed fee and reward' for the session being £100 paid out of the Exchequer on a Privy Council warrant[5].

Procedure at the election of a Speaker

It is true the Commons are to choose their Speaker; but, seeing that after their choice the King may refuse him, for avoiding of expense of time and contestation the use is (as in the *conge d'élire* of a Bishop) that the King doth name a discreet and learned

---

[1] See Porritt, i, 432, 433. Henry VII obtained the election of Empson in 1491 and of Dudley in 1504, and these were the two most unpopular men in England (Busch, i, 300).

[2] D'Ewes, p. 621; in the Parliament of 1566 also the Speaker was proposed by the Comptroller of the Household (*ib.* p. 121).

[3] On a division Onslow was elected by 82 votes to 60 (D'Ewes, p. 121).

[4] Pollard, *Parliament*, p. 272 *n.*   [5] Dasent, iv, 39 (8 May, 1552).

man whom the Commons elect; but without their election no Speaker can be appointed for them, because he is their mouth, and trusted by them, and so necessary as the House of Commons cannot sit without him.... Coke, *Institutes* (edn. of 1669), iv, 8.

[25 January, 1559]. . . Whereupon the knights, citizens, and burgesses departing to their own House, did there take their several places, and most remaining silent, or speaking very submissively, Mr Treasurer of the Queen's House, standing up uncovered, did first put the House in remembrance of the Lord Keeper's late speech, and of his declaration of her Majesty's pleasure that they should choose a Speaker[1], and therefore in humble obedience to her Majesty's said pleasure, seeing others remain silent, he thought it his duty to take that occasion to commend to their choice Sir Thomas Gargrave, knight, one of the honourable Council in the North Parts, a worthy member of the House and learned in the laws of this realm; By which commendations of his of the aforesaid worthy member of the House to their consideration he said he did not intend to debar any other there present from uttering their free opinions and nominating any other whom they thought to be more fitting, and therefore desired them to make known their opinions, who thereupon did with one consent and voice allow and approve of Mr Treasurer's nomination, and elected the said Sir Thomas Gargrave to be the Prolocutor or Speaker of the said House.... D'Ewes, *Journal* (edn. of 1693), p. 40

[24 October, 1597]...The...Lord Keeper...delivered unto the said Commons the causes of her Majesty's calling of this Parliament; and so in the end willed them...to make choice of their Speaker...which done, the said Commons presently repaired unto their own House, and there being assembled and sitting some space of time very silent, at last...Sir William Knollys, one of her Highness's most honourable Privy Council and Comptroller of her Majesty's Household, stood up and spake to the effect following:—Necessity constraineth me to break off this silence and to give others cause for speech...I will... deliver my opinion unto you who is most fit for this place, being a member of this House, and those good abilities which I know to be in him (here he made a little pause and the House hawked and spat, and after silence made he proceeded) unto this place of dignity and calling in my opinion (here he

---

[1] A commission from the Crown to choose a Speaker, dated 16 January, 1581, is printed in D'Ewes, p. 280.

stayed a little) Mr Serjeant Yelverton (looking upon him) is the fittest man to be preferred (after which words Mr Yelverton blushed and put off his hat, and after sat bare-headed), for I am assured that he is, yea, and I dare avow it, I know him to be a man wise and learned, secret and circumspect, religious and faithful, no way disable but every way able to supply this place. Wherefore in my judgment I deem him, though I will not say best worthy amongst us, yet sufficient enough to supply this place; and herein if any man think I err, I wish him to deliver his mind as freely as I have done; if not, that we all join together in giving general consent and approbation to this motion. So that the whole House cried, 'Aye, Aye, Aye, let him be.'...

D'Ewes, *Journal*, pp. 548-9.

(c) *Influence of the Crown upon legislation*

In a House of Commons where no parties yet existed, the Crown had all the advantages of organisation and initiative, and it also had a monopoly of official experience. Although the attorney-general, the solicitor-general, and the King's serjeants-at-law received writs of summons to the House of Lords, in the Tudor period they began to covet election to the House of Commons, and as the constituencies appreciated the distinction of having great personages to represent them, the privy councillors mustered strongly in the House of Commons[1], where their official experience was used to pilot, explain, and defend government measures.

The judges also had definite functions to perform in connexion with the making of laws. As late as Henry VII's reign 'the main principles of his legislation were formulated by the judges in common session before submission' to Parliament[2]; and under Henry VIII 'it was the custom of the Lords in Parliament to secure copies of bills introduced in the House of Commons and take the opinion of the judges upon them before they were sent up from the Lower House.'[3] Further, the legal members of the Council had much to do with the moulding of legislation. They advised on both the principles and the drafting of bills; and in all probability they influenced the decision of the Crown whether to give the royal assent[4].

It was open to the Crown to add provisos to bills when giving the royal assent, and these were never discussed in Parliament at all[5]. Moreover, the administration of statutes after they were passed came within the discretion of the Crown, which enjoyed in practice a dispensing power[6].

It has been pointed out that Parliament itself gave the Crown by statute 'a wide legislative discretion' outside Parliament[7]. In 1504 and again in 1523 the King was empowered to repeal statutes by letters patent; in 1495 a benevolence was legalised after the event, and the King was empowered to collect arrears as if it had been a tax; and in 1534 Henry VIII

---

[1] Pollard, *Parliament*, pp. 292, 296.   [2] *Ib.* p. 34.   [3] *Ib.*
[4] *Ib.* p. 294.   [5] *Ib.* pp. 130, 274.
[6] For illustrations see *ib.* p. 275.   [7] *Ib.* p. 265.

was empowered to repeal all Acts passed since 1529 concerning exports or imports. Further he was authorised to devise the Crown by will; and his proclamations received by statute the force of law.

The Statute of Proclamations [p. 532] has been described as marking 'the highest point of legal authority ever reached by the Crown.'[1] It was passed in the 'tractable Parliament'[2] of 1539, where the royal influence was at its strongest, and the preamble makes a remarkable reference to the mystery of royal power which might have come from James I himself. It asserts that divers froward persons have broken proclamations in the past 'not considering what a King by his royal power may do,' and seeks to restore their prestige, hitherto impaired 'for lack of a direct statute.' The enacting clauses provide that, subject to certain limitations, proclamations may be set forth by the King and Council by authority of the Act which 'shall be obeyed, observed, and kept as though they were made by Act of Parliament.' It is, however, easy to exaggerate the importance of this statute. The King already had the power to issue proclamations in the wide spaces left uncovered by statute or common law, and the preamble of the Act recognises this by implication. The passing of the Act in 1539 did not confer this power, nor did its repeal in 1547 take it away. Elizabeth issued proclamations as freely as her father had done[3], although she could quote no statutory authority.

It has been pointed out[4] that in practice the persons chiefly affected by this legislation were the offenders against proclamations to be made 'for and concerning any kind of heresies against Christian religion'—a class untouched by the Act of Supremacy, which imposed no penalties. This was one of the purposes for which the Act was deliberately designed. 'The Supreme Head of the Church was not to be subject to parliamentary conditions in the exercise of his Supremacy; and the ecclesiastical sovereign was to be the Crown in Council and not the Crown in Parliament.' Another important feature of the Statute of Proclamations is that it created, for the purpose of punishing breaches of proclamations issued under its authority, a statutory tribunal analogous to that created by the Act of 1487 'pro camera stellata.' Certain great officers are mentioned, the two Chief Judges and the Chief Baron of the Exchequer are included, and in addition to the Archbishop of Canterbury there are to be two Bishops 'being of the King's Council.' The quorum is to be half the total number at the least[5], and it was required that, out of six enumerated great officers and the two Chief Justices, two should be among those who constituted it. It is possible that the object of this arrangement was to relieve the Privy Council of a mass of business with which it could not adequately cope[6].

Although the Tudor sovereigns were influential in Parliament, it was

[1] Dicey, *Constitution*, p. 48.   [2] Merriman, ii, 199.
[3] For illustrations see Maitland, p. 256.   [4] Pollard, *Parliament*, pp. 267–8.
[5] Owing to the difficulty of getting Councillors to attend, the quorum was in 1543 reduced to nine (34 & 35 Henr. VIII, c. 23).
[6] See Mr E. R. Adair, in *E.H.R.* xxxii, 34–46. The writer appears to depreciate rather too much the importance of the Act. He takes the view that it was not concerned with the legality of proclamations at all, but only with the relief of the congestion of Council business (p. 43).

not the case that Parliament was servile. The first draft of the Statute of Proclamations itself, after passing a third reading in the House of Lords, was re-moulded by the two Chief Justices, the Master of the Rolls, the King's Attorney, and the Solicitor-General, before it received a final assent and was carried to the House of Commons. There the government proposal was rejected altogether, and a new bill was substituted for it which passed, after amendment by the Lords[1]. Mary's bill of 1554 for reviving the Statute of Six Articles, after passing the Commons, was rejected on a third reading in the Lords; and a companion bill to restore the statutes against the Lollards was read twice in the Lords and then abandoned[2]. Elizabeth's Acts of Supremacy and Uniformity were opposed by all the spiritual lords, and the Act of Uniformity was only carried by 21 temporal against 18 temporal and spiritual votes[3].

The Commons upon occasion shewed the same independence. In 1534 they declined to make spoken words treason[4], and rejected various government measures[5]; and the Act of 1547 for the dissolution of the chantries was only saved at the last moment by concessions on the part of the government[6] [p. 535]. Of Elizabeth's Parliaments Naunton writes[7], 'I find not that they were at any time given to any violent or pertinacious dispute, elections being made of grave and discreet persons, not factious and ambitious of fame, such as came not to the House with a malevolent spirit of contention, but...rather to comply than contest with her Majesty'; and Peter Wentworth's complaint in 1576 [p. 537] of 'rumours' and 'messages' suggests that the influence of the Queen in Parliament was potent. The House 'out of a reverent regard of her Majesty's honour' stopped him 'before he had fully finished his speech,' and after examination ordered his imprisonment in the Tower; but there is no sign of servility in the record of the proceedings, and the cases collected below under Privilege of Parliament [p. 550] shew that the House could and did stand up to the Queen. Indeed the speech of the Lord Keeper at the dissolution of the Parliament of 1571 [p. 536] points to the existence of critics in the Commons who were no respecters of persons. On the other hand, the passing of the Statute of Six Articles in 1539 was due to the vigorous personal intervention of Henry VIII, who came to the Upper House, argued with the opponents of the bill, and 'confounded them all with God's learning.'[8] In estimating the forces on the side of the Crown in Tudor times, we must not omit the part played by the effective personalities who occupied the throne. They held a great position in the eyes of their subjects; they wielded powers which enabled them to ruin individuals; and they were able to draw upon that reserve force of vigorous character which has sometimes played a great

[1] *E.H.R.* xxxii, 35. [2] Pollard, *Polit. Hist.* p. 119.
[3] Pollard, *Parliament*, p. 76.
[4] See the detailed account in *Transactions of the Royal Historical Society*, 3rd series, xi, 122–3.
[5] So also in 1545. 'The bill of books, albeit it was at the beginning earnestly set forward, is finally dashed in the Common House, as are divers others' (Secretary Petre, quoted in Pollard, *Parliament*, p. 336).
[6] Pollard, *Polit. Hist.* p. 19.
[7] *Fragmenta Regalia* (edn. of 1641), p. 9. [8] Fisher, p. 435.

part in human affairs[1]. Nor must the advantage which organisation gave
to the Crown be forgotten. This is illustrated by the proceedings over the
bill of 1533 in restraint of appeals to Rome. The members were not prepared for so open an attack upon the Papacy, and the burgesses of the towns,
in particular, feared that the breach with the Emperor to which the Divorce
Question was leading, especially if followed by a papal interdict, would
have a disastrous effect upon the Flanders trade. The Commons were
interviewed, wires were pulled, and by various devices the opposition was
broken up; nevertheless the business of getting the bill through occupied
nearly three weeks[2].

(1) Statute of Proclamations, 1539

An Act that Proclamations made by the King shall be obeyed

Forasmuch as the King's most royal Majesty for divers
considerations by the advice of his Council hath heretofore set
forth divers and sundry his Grace's proclamations, as well for
and concerning divers and sundry articles of Christ's Religion,
as for an unity and concord to be had amongst the loving and
obedient subjects of this his realm and other his dominions, And
also concerning the advancement of his common wealth and good
quiet of his people, which nevertheless divers and many froward,
wilful, and obstinate persons have wilfully contemned and broken,
not considering what a King by his royal power may do, and for
lack of a direct statute and law to coarct[3] offenders to obey the
said proclamations, which being still suffered should not only en-
courage offenders to the disobedience of the precepts and laws of
Almighty God, but also sin too much to the great dishonour of the
King's most royal Majesty, who may full ill bear it, and also
give too great heart and boldness to all malefactors and offenders;
considering also that sudden causes and occasions fortune many
times which do require speedy remedies, and that by abiding for
a Parliament in the mean time might happen great prejudice to
ensue to the realm; and weighing also that his Majesty (which
by the kingly and regal power given him by God may do many

---

[1] We need not accept Spelman's picturesque account of the passing of the Act for
the Dissolution of the Lesser Monasteries. 'When the bill had stuck long in the Lower
House and could get no passage, [the King] commanded the Commons to attend him
in the forenoon in his gallery, where he let them wait till late in the afternoon; and
then coming out of his chamber, walking a turn or two amongst them, and looking
angrily on them, first on the one side, then on the other, at last "I hear," (saith he),
"that my bill will not pass; but I will have it pass, or I will have some of your heads";
and without other rhetoric or persuasion returned to his chamber. Enough was said;
the bill passed; and all was given him as he desired' (*History of Sacrilege*, 1632; edn.
of 1853, p. 206).

[2] Friedmann, i, 195.   [3] Constrain.

things in such cases) should not be driven to extend the liberty and supremacy of his regal power and dignity by wilfulness of froward subjects; It is therefore thought in manner more than necessary that the King's Highness of this realm for the time being, with the advice of his honourable Council, should make and set forth proclamations for the good and politic order and governance of this his realm of England, Wales, and other his dominions from time to time for the defence of his regal dignity and the advancement of his common wealth and good quiet of his people, as the cases of necessity shall require, and that an ordinary law should be provided, by the assent of his Majesty and Parliament, for the due punishment, correction, and reformation of such offences and disobediences; Be it therefore enacted...that always the King for the time being, with the advice of his honourable Council, whose names hereafter followeth, or with the advice of the more part of them, may set forth at all times by authority of this Act his proclamations, under such penalties and pains and of such sort as to his Highness and his said honourable Council or the more part of them shall see[m] necessary and requisite; And that those same shall be obeyed, observed, and kept as though they were made by Act of Parliament for the time in them limited, unless the King's Highness dispense with them or any of them under his great seal.

II. Provided always that the words, meaning, and intent of this Act be not understood, interpretate, construed, or extended, that by virtue of it any of the King's liege people...should have any of his or their inheritances, lawful possessions, offices, liberties, privileges, franchises, goods, or chattels taken from them...nor by virtue of the said Act suffer any pains of death, other than shall be hereafter in this Act declared, nor that by any proclamation to be made by virtue of this Act, any acts, common laws, standing at this present time in strength and force, nor yet any lawful or laudable customs of this realm...shall be infringed, broken, or subverted; and specially all those Acts standing this hour in force which have been made in the King's Highness's time; but that every such person...shall stand and be in the same state and condition, to every respect and purpose, as if this Act or proviso had never been had or made....Except...such persons which shall offend any proclamation to be made by the King's Highness, his heirs or successors, for and concerning any kind of heresies against Christian religion.

* * * * * *

IV. And be it further enacted...that if any person or persons...which at any time hereafter do wilfully offend and break

or obstinately not observe and keep any such proclamation...
that then all and every such offender or offenders, being thereof
...convicted by confession or lawful witness and proofs before
the Archbishop of Canterbury metropolitan, the Chancellor of
England, the Lord Treasurer of England, the President of the
King's most honourable Council, the Lord Privy Seal, the Great
Chamberlain of England, Lord Admiral, Lord Steward, or Grand
Master, Lord Chamberlain of the King's most honourable
Household, two other Bishops being of the King's Council such
as his Grace shall appoint for the same, the Secretary, the
Treasurer and Controller of the King's most honourable House-
hold, the Master of the Horse, the two Chief Judges and the
Master of the Rolls for the time being, the Chancellor of the
Augmentations, the Chancellor of the Duchy, the Chief Baron of
the Exchequer, the two General Surveyors[1], the Chancellor of
the Exchequer, the Under Treasurer of the same, the Treasurer
of the King's Chamber for the time being, in the Star Chamber at
Westminster or elsewhere, or at the least before the half of the
number afore rehearsed, of which number the Lord Chancellor,
the Lord Treasurer, the Lord President of the King's most
honourable Council, the Lord Privy Seal, the Chamberlain of
England, the Lord Admiral, the two Chief Judges for the time
being, or two of them, shall be two, shall lose and pay such penalties
forfeitures of sums of money... And also suffer such imprisonments of his body as shall be expressed, mentioned, and declared
in any such proclamation....

V. And be it further enacted...that the Lord Chancellor,
the Lord Privy Seal, and either of them, with the assent of six of
the forenamed, shall have power and authority by their discretions, upon every information to be given to them or to either of
them touching the premises, to cause process to be made against
all and singular such offenders by writs under the King's great
seal or under his Grace's privy seal in form following, that is to
say; first by proclamation under a pain or a penalty by the discretion of the aforesaid Councillors appointed for the awarding
of process, and if he appear not to the same without a lawful excuse, then the said Councillors to award out another proclamation
upon allegiance of the same offender, for the due examination,
trial, and conviction of every such person and persons as shall
offend contrary to this Act, for the due execution to be had of
and for the same in manner and form as is above remembered;
Except it be within the liberty of the County Palatine of the Duchy

[1] See p. 341 above.

of Lancaster; And in case it so be, then to pass by the Chancellor of the King's Duchy of Lancaster under the seal of the said Duchy, with the assent of six at the least of the aforenamed Councillors.

[VI. Offenders who 'obstinately, willingly, or contemptuously avoid and depart out of' the realm, in order to escape the necessity of answering for offences against the Act, are to suffer death as traitors and to forfeit their lands and goods.]

* * * * * *

VIII. And be it further enacted, that if it shall happen our said Sovereign Lord the King to decease (whose life God long preserve) before such time as that person which shall be his next heir or successor to the imperial Crown of this realm shall accomplish and come to the age of eighteen years, that then all and singular proclamations which shall be in any wise made and set forth into any part of this realm or other the King's dominions by virtue of this Act, within the foresaid years of the said next heir or successor, shall be set forth in the successor's name then being King, and shall import or bear underwritten the full names of such of the King's honourable Council then being as shall be the devisers or setters-forth of the same, which shall be in this case the whole number afore rehearsed, or at the least the more part of them, or else the proclamations to be void and of none effect.

* * * * * *

31 Henr. VIII, c. 8: *Statutes of the Realm*, iii, 726.

(2) Passing of the Chantries Act

[At Westminster, 6 May, 1548]

Whereas in the last Parliament...among other articles contained in the Act for Colleges and Chantry Lands etc., to be given unto his Highness, it was also inserted that the lands pertaining to all guilds and brotherhoods within this realm should pass unto his Majesty by way of like gift, at which time divers then being of the Lower House did not only reason and argue against that article made for the guildable lands, but also incensed many others to hold with them, amongst the which none were stiffer nor more busily went about to impugn the said article than the burgesses for...Lynn...and...Coventry....
In respect of which their allegations and great labour made herein unto the House, such of his Highness's Council as were of the same House there present thought it very likely and apparent that not only that article for the guildable lands should

be dashed[1], but also that the whole body of the Act might either sustain peril or hindrance, being already ingrossed and the time of the Parliament prorogation hard at hand, unless by some good policy the principal speakers against the passing of that article might be stayed; whereupon they did participate[2] this matter with the Lord Protector's Grace and others of the Lords of his Highness's Council, who, pondering on the one part how the guildable lands throughout this realm amounted to no small yearly value, which by the article aforesaid were to be accrued to his Majesty's possessions of the Crown, and on the other part, weighing in a multitude of free voices what moment the labour of a few setters on had been of heretofore in like cases, thought it better to stay and content them of Lynn and Coventry by granting to them to have and enjoy their guild lands, etc., as they did before, than through their means, on whose importune labour and suggestion the great part of the Lower House rested, to have the article defaced, and so his Majesty to forgo the whole guild lands throughout the realm; and for these respects, and also for avoiding of the proviso which the said burgesses would have had added for the guilds to this article, which might have ministered occasion to others to have laboured for the like, they resolved that certain of his Highness's Councillors being of the Lower House should persuade with the said burgesses of Lynn and Coventry to desist from further speaking or labouring against the said article, upon promise to them that if they meddled no further against it, his Majesty, once having the guildable lands granted unto him by the Act as it was penned unto him, should make them over a new grant of the lands pertaining then unto their guilds, etc., to be had and used to them as afore. Which thing the said Councillors did execute as was devised, and thereby stayed the speakers against it, so as the Act passed with the clause for guildable lands accordingly....

Dasent, *Acts of the Privy Council*, ii, 193–5.

(3) Parliament of 1571

The Lord Keeper's Speech at the Dissolution of the Queen's Third Parliament, 29 May, 1571

Mr Speaker,...her Majesty hath commanded me to say unto you that, like as the greatest number of them of the Lower House have in the proceedings of this session shewed themselves

---

[1] In the 16th and 17th centuries this was the regular term for the rejection of a clause or bill; cf. p. 531, note 5, above.   [2] Share.

modest, discreet, and dutiful, as becomes good and loving subjects, and meet for the places that they be called unto, so there be
certain of them, although not many in number, who in the proceedings of this session have shewed themselves audacious, arrogant, and presumptuous, calling her Majesty's grants and prerogatives also in question, contrary to their duty and place that
they be called unto, and contrary to the express admonition given
in her Majesty's name in the beginning of this Parliament[1];
which it might very well have become them to have more regard
unto. But her Majesty saith, that seeing they will thus wilfully
forget themselves they are otherwise to be remembered; and like
as her Majesty allows and much commends the former sort for
the respects aforesaid, so doth her Highness utterly disallow and
condemn the second sort for their audacious, arrogant, and presumptuous folly, thus by superfluous speech spending much
time in meddling with matters neither pertaining to them nor
within the capacity of their understanding.

D'Ewes, Journal, p. 151.

(4) Case of Peter Wentworth, 1576

Peter Wentworth, who is described by Strype as 'a man of hot temper, and
impatient for the new discipline,' had written this speech two or three years before
it was delivered[2].

[8 February, 1576]...Peter Wentworth, esquire, one of the
burgesses for the borough of Tregoney in the county of Cornwall, was, for unreverent and undutiful words uttered by him in
this House of our Sovereign Lady the Queen's Majesty, sequestered, that the House might proceed to conference and consideration of his said speech...viz.:—

"Mr Speaker, I find written in a little volume these words in
effect: Sweet is the name of liberty, but the thing itself a value
beyond all inestimable treasure. So much the more it behoveth
us to take care lest we, contenting ourselves with the sweetness
of the name, lose and forego the thing, being of the greatest value
that can come unto this noble realm. The inestimable treasure is
the use of it in this House....

"...Sometime it happeneth that a good man will in this
place (for argument sake) prefer an evil cause, both for that he
would have a doubtful truth to be opened and manifested, and
also the evil prevented; so that to this point I conclude, that in
this House, which is termed a place of free speech, there is nothing
so necessary for the preservation of the Prince and State as free

---

[1] See p. 563 below.   [2] *D.N.B.* lx, 262.

speech, and without, it is a scorn and mockery to call it a Parliament House, for in truth it is none, but a very school of flattery and dissimulation, and so a fit place to serve the Devil and his angels in, and not to glorify God and benefit the Commonwealth....

"...Amongst other, Mr Speaker, two things do great hurt in this place, of the which I do mean to speak. The one is a rumour which runneth about the House, and this it is, 'Take heed what you do; the Queen's Majesty liketh not such a matter; whosoever preferreth it, she will be offended with him': or the contrary, 'Her Majesty liketh of such a matter; whosoever speaketh against it, she will be much offended with him.' The other: sometimes a message is brought into the House, either of commanding or inhibiting, very injurious to the freedom of speech and consultation. I would to God, Mr Speaker, that these two were buried in hell, I mean rumours and messages, for wicked undoubtedly they are; the reason is, the Devil was the first author of them, from whom proceedeth nothing but wickedness....

"...Now the other was a message Mr Speaker brought the last Sessions into the House, that we should not deal in any matters of religion, but first to receive from the Bishops. Surely this was a doleful message, for it was as much as to say, Sirs, ye shall not deal in God's causes, no, ye shall in no wise seek to advance his glory.... Truly I assure you, Mr Speaker, there were divers of this House that said with grievous hearts immediately upon the message, that God of his justice could not prosper the Session;... God... was the last Session shut out of doors. But what fell out of it, forsooth? His great indignation was therefore poured upon this House, for he did put into the Queen's Majesty's heart to refuse good and wholesome laws for her own preservation, the which caused many faithful hearts for grief to burst out with sorrowful tears, and moved all Papists, traitors to God and her Majesty,... in their sleeves to laugh all the whole Parliament House to scorn.... So certain it is, Mr Speaker, that none is without fault, no, not our noble Queen, since then her Majesty hath committed great fault, yea, dangerous faults to herself....

"...It is a dangerous thing in a Prince unkindly to abuse his or her nobility and people, and it is a dangerous thing in a Prince to oppose or bend herself against her nobility and people.... And how could any Prince more unkindly intreat, abuse, oppose herself against her nobility and people than her Majesty did the last Parliament?...And will not this her Majesty's handling, think you, Mr Speaker, make cold dealing in any of her Majesty's subjects toward her again? I fear it will...And I beseech... God to endue her Majesty with his wisdom, whereby she may discern faithful advice from traitorous, sugared speeches, and to send her Majesty a melting, yielding heart unto sound counsel, that will may not stand for a reason; and then her Majesty will stand when her enemies are fallen, for no estate can stand where the Prince will not be governed by advice. And I doubt not but that some of her Majesty's Council have dealt plainly and faithfully with her Majesty herein;...And I do surely think, before God I speak it, that the Bishops were the cause of that doleful message, and I will shew you what moveth me so to think: I was, amongst others, the last Parliament, sent unto the Bishop of Canterbury for the Articles of Religion that then passed this House. He asked us why we did put out of the book the articles for the Homilies, Consecrating of Bishops, and such like? 'Surely, sir,' said I, 'because we were so occupied in other matters that we had no time to examine them how they agreed with the word of God.' 'What?' said he, 'surely you mistook the matter; you will refer yourselves wholly to us therein?' 'No, by the faith I bear to God,' said I, 'we will pass nothing before we understand what it is; for that were but to make you Popes.' 'Make you Popes who list,' said I, 'for we will make you none.' And sure, Mr Speaker, the speech seemed to me to be a Pope-like speech, and I fear lest our Bishops do attribute this of the Pope's canons to themselves, *Papa non potest errare....*"

*   *   *   *   *   *

Upon this speech the House, out of a reverent regard of her Majesty's honour, stopped his further proceeding before he had fully finished his speech. The message he meant and intended was that which was sent by her Majesty to the House of Commons in the said fourteenth year of her reign upon Wednesday the 28th day of May by Sir Francis Knollys, knight, Treasurer of her Majesty's Household, inhibiting them for a certain time to treat or deal in the matter touching the Scottish Queen...(pp. 236–41).

[9 February, 1576]...This day Mr Treasurer, in the name of all the committees[1] yesterday appointed for the examination of Peter Wentworth, burgess for Tregoney, declared that all the said committees did meet yesterday in the afternoon in the Star Chamber...and there examining the said Peter Wentworth touching the violent and wicked words yesterday pronounced by

_____
[1] *I.e.* members of the committee.

him in this House touching the Queen's Majesty, made a collection of the same words; which words so collected the said Peter Wentworth did acknowledge and confess. And then did the said Mr Treasurer read unto the House the said note of collection, which being read, he declared further that the said Peter Wentworth, being examined what he could say for the extenuating of his said fault and offence, could neither say anything at all to that purpose, neither yet did charge any other person as author of the said speech, but did take all the burden thereof unto himself; and so the said Mr Treasurer thereupon moved for his punishment and imprisonment in the Tower as the House should think good and consider of; whereupon, after sundry disputations and speeches, it was ordered upon the question that the said Peter Wentworth should be committed close prisoner to the Tower for his said offence, there to remain until such time as this House should have further consideration of him. And thereupon immediately the said Peter Wentworth, being brought to the Bar by the Serjeant, received his said judgment accordingly by the mouth of Mr Speaker in form above recited; and so Mr Lieutenant of the Tower was presently charged with the custody of the said Peter Wentworth. But the said Peter Wentworth was shortly by the Queen's special favour restored again to his liberty and place in the House...(p. 244).

[12 March, 1576]...Mr Captain of the Guard did...shortly declare and make report unto the House that whereas a member of the same had [on 8 February]...uttered in a prepared speech divers offensive matters touching her Majesty, and had for the same been sent prisoner to the Tower by the House, yet that her Majesty was now graciously pleased to remit her just-occasioned displeasure for the said offence, and to refer the enlargement of the party to the House, which was most thankfully accepted by the same upon the said report...(p. 259).

...Mr Peter Wentworth was brought by the Serjeant-at-Arms that attended the House to the Bar within the same, and after some declaration made unto him by Mr Speaker, in the name of the whole House, both of his own great fault and offence and also of her Majesty's great and bountiful mercy shewed unto him, and after his humble submission upon his knees acknowledging his fault and craving her Majesty's pardon and favour, he was received again into the House and restored to his place, to the great contentment of all that were present...(p. 260).

D'Ewes, *Journal*, pp. 236–44, 259–60.

§ 5. PARLIAMENTARY PROCEDURE

In the Tudor period a great part of the procedure of Parliament had already taken the shape which it still retains. Parliament was opened by the sovereign in state [p. 542]. In the House of Lords the first business of the session was the constitution of proxies [p. 545]. A Lord of Parliament might, with the King's licence, appoint a procurator or proxy to act for him, and so obtain exemption from the burdensome duty of attending in person; and this practice was not discontinued until 1868[1]. In the reign of Elizabeth it was directed by a resolution of the House of Commons in 1571 that 'the litany shall be read every day as in the last Parliament, and also a prayer said by Mr Speaker, as he shall think fittest for this time'[2]; and towards the close of the reign a chaplain was appointed to read prayers, who was remunerated by a collection among the members [pp. 546, 547]. The House also took control of the attendance of its members[3], and the resolution of 1571 required them to be present at prayers at half-past eight, 'and that each then making default shall forfeit for every time fourpence to the poor man's box.' Any member desiring leave of absence 'for his great business and affairs' was required to obtain license from the Speaker [p. 546]; and in 1585, on the motion of the Recorder of London, certain legal members who were busy pleading in the Courts were recalled to their service in the House by the Serjeant-at-Arms, among them the Recorder himself [p. 546].

Sir Thomas Smith's account of the procedure of Parliament [p. 547] shews that all bills were read three times before they were passed[4]. After 1572 bills were usually referred to a committee after the second reading, in place of the earlier practice, still sometimes followed under Elizabeth, of committing them after a first reading[5]. As yet, however, there were no committees of the whole House. The members who were to serve were named, and thus formed a select committee[6]. Until 1593 divisions were rare and there was no settled procedure, but in that year the Speaker gave a formal explanation from the chair of the way in which a division should be taken [p. 547], although tellers were not regularly appointed until the reign of Charles II[7]. The first conference between the two Houses of which there is any record in the Journals took place in 1554[8].

In the House of Commons the rules for preserving the decencies of debate bear a close resemblance to those of the present day. Members must address the Speaker; it is out of order 'to name him whom ye do confute but by circumlocution'; no one may speak more than once in the course of a debate [pp. 547, 548]. 'Reviling or nipping words' must not be used

[1] The question of proxies is discussed in Pike, pp. 243–5. [2] Porritt, i, 129.
[3] The right of the Speaker and the House to license the absence of members was recognised in 1515 by 6 Henr. VIII, c. 16, which forbade their departure before the end of the session without such licence; but until 1558 ordinary leave of absence was granted by the Crown (Pollard, *Parliament*, p. 161).
[4] In 1515 there is a reference in the *Lords' Journals* to a seventh (i, 55) and an eighth reading (i, 56); and as late as 1563 a case occurs of a bill being read a fourth time in the House of Commons (D'Ewes, p. 90), but this had now become exceptional.
[5] Porritt, i, 530. [6] *Ib.* p. 531. [7] *Ib* p. 536. [8] *Ib.* p. 557.

[p. 548]; interruptions are discouraged [pp. 548, 549]; whispering, and the wearing of spurs are a breach of the good order of the House [p. 549].

The meeting-place of the Lords was the royal palace of Westminster, in the Chamber of Parliament or White Chamber[1], and thither the Commons also came when they appeared *in pleno parliamento*. But 'their private confabulations were their own concern,'[2] and for these they met outside the Palace, first in the Refectory and then in the Chapter House of the Abbey. About 1550[3], however, there was assigned to them the upper part of St Stephen's Chapel, and thus the two Houses were united within the Palace.

(1) The Opening of Parliament, 1563

On Tuesday the 12th day of January [1563]...about eleven of the clock in the forenoon, the Queen's Majesty took her horse at the Hall door and proceeded in manner as followeth:

First, all gentlemen, two and two, then esquires, knights, and bannerets, and lords being no barons or under age.

Then the trumpeters sounding.

Then the Queen's Serjeant, Mr Carus, in his surcoat, hood, and mantle unlined of scarlet.

Then Mr Gerard, the Queen's Attorney, and Mr Russell, Solicitor.

Then Anthony Browne, Justice of the Common Pleas, and Mr Weston of the King's Bench[4].

Then the Barons of the Exchequer.

Then Mr Corbet and Mr Whiddon, two Justices of the King's Bench.

Then Sir Thomas Saunders, Chief Baron of the Exchequer, and Sir James Dyer, Chief Justice of the Common Pleas.

Then Sir William Cordell, Master of the Rolls, in his gown, and Sir Robert Catlin, Chief Justice of the King's Bench; and these Justices and Barons of the Exchequer in their scarlet mantles, hood, and surcoat edged with miniver, the mantle shorter than the surcoat by a foot.

Then Knights Councillors in their gowns....

Then Sir William Cecil, Chief Secretary, and Sir Edward Rogers, Comptroller[5].

Then William Howard, bearing the Queen's cloak and hat.

Then Barons, in all 40 but there in number 30[6]...their

---

[1] Porritt, i, 424.   [2] Pollard, *Parliament*, p. 333.

[3] For a discussion of the date see *E.H.R.* xxxvi, 225.

[4] Richard Weston was a Judge of the Common Pleas. The mistake in the text spoils the symmetry of the procession.   [5] Of the Household.

[6] The *Lords' Journals* for 15 January, 1563, three days later, record the attendance of 39 barons. There also attended 1 duke, 2 marquises, 13 earls, and 3 viscounts—58 temporal peers in all. The number of bishops attending on April 3 was 24, so 22 was not a full attendance for so important a ceremonial occasion.

mantles, hoods, and surcoat furred, and two rows of miniver on their right shoulder.

Then proceeded the Bishops, all that were there present were but 22[1]...their robes of scarlet lined, and a hood down their back of miniver.

Then the Viscounts, their robes as the Barons, but that they had two rows and an half of miniver, as the Viscount of Bindon absent, Viscount Montague and Viscount Hereford present.

Then the Earls, but 19 present...their robes of scarlet with three rows of miniver.

Then the Marquis of Winchester, but now as Lord Treasurer, and the Marquis of Northampton; the Duke of Norfolk went as Earl Marshal.

Then the Lord Keeper's Serjeant and Seal, and after Sir Nicholas Bacon, Lord Keeper of the Great Seal, in his gown.

Here Clarencieux and Norroy.

Then the Queen's Serjeant-at-Arms, and after, Garter.

Then the Duke of Norfolk with the gilt rod as Marshal, the Lord Treasurer with the Cap of Estate, and the Earl of Worcester with the Sword.

Then the Queen's Majesty on horseback, a little behind the Lord Chamberlain and Vice-Chamberlain; her Grace apparelled in her mantle, opened before, furred with ermines, and her kirtle of crimson velvet, close before, and close sleeves, but the bands turned up with ermines, and a hood hanging low round about her neck of ermines. Over all a rich collar, set with stones and other jewels, and on her head a rich caul[2]. And the next after her the Lord Robert Dudley[3], Master of the Horse, leading the spare horse. And after all other ladies, two and two, in their ordinary apparel. Beside the Queen went her footmen, and along on either side of her went the Pensioners with their axes; after the ladies followed the Captain of the Guard, Sir William St Loe, and after him the Guard.

In which order her Majesty proceeded to the north door of the Church of Westminster, where the Dean there and the Dean of the Chapel[4] met her, and the whole Chapel in copes; and St Edward's staff with the inlet in the top[5] was delivered unto her, her arm for the bearing thereof assisted by the Baron of Hunsdon; the Canopy borne over her by Charles Howard, esquire [and 5

---

[1] See note 6 on previous page.   [2] A close-fitting cap worn by women.
[3] Created Earl of Leicester in 1564.   [4] The Chapel Royal.
[5] This sceptre was surmounted by the cross and orb, and the orb contained a fragment of the true cross.

knights]; her Grace's train borne up and assisted, for the weight thereof from her arms, by the Lord Robert Dudley, Master of the Horse, and Sir Francis Knollys, Vice-Chamberlain; and so orderly proceeded to the traverse[1] beside the Table of Administration, although other Princes have used to be placed in the Choir till the Offering, but not now because there was neither Communion nor Offering. And so she being placed, all the Lords sat down on forms besides the traverse, the spiritualty on the north side and the temporalty on the south side; the Sword and the Cap of Estate laid down on the Table. Then the choir sung the English Procession; which ended, Mr Nowell, Dean of Paul's, began his sermon, and first made his prayer orderly for the Queen's Majesty and the Universal Church, and especially for that honourable Assembly of Three Estates there present, that they might make such laws as should be to God's glory and the good of the realm.

The sermon being ended and a psalm sung, her Majesty and the rest orderly on foot proceeded out of the south door, where she delivered the Dean the sceptre, and so proceeded into the Parliament Chamber, where the Queen stayed awhile in her Privy Chamber till all the Lords and others were placed, and then her Highness came forth and went and sat her down in her Royal Place and Chair of Estate (the Sword and Cap of Maintenance borne before her) and when she stood up her mantle was assisted and borne up from her arms by the Lord Robert Dudley, Master of the Horse, and Sir Francis Knollys, Vice-Chamberlain.

The Lord Keeper sat alone upon the uppermost Sack until the Queen was sat, and then went and stood without the rail, on the right hand the Cloth of Estate; and the Lord Treasurer, holding the Cap of Estate, on the right hand before the Queen, Garter standing by him, and on the left hand standing the Earl of Worcester with the Sword, and by him the Lord Chamberlain.

The Duke of Norfolk began the first form and the Viscount Montague (for that the Viscount Bindon was not there) ended it.

The Lord Clinton, the Lord Admiral, began the form behind that of the Barons, and the Lord St John of Bletsoe ended it.

The Archbishop of Canterbury began the Bishops' form, and the Bishop of Gloucester ended the same.

On the Woolsack on the right hand and north side sat Sir Robert Catlin and Sir James Dyer, Chief Justices, Sir William Petre, Anthony Browne, Corbet, Weston, and Mr Gerard the Queen's Attorney.

[1] Used of a small compartment cut off by a curtain or screen. See illustrative quotations in the *Oxford Dictionary*.

On the Sack on the left hand and south side sat Sir William Cordell Master of the Rolls, Sir Edward Saunders Chief Baron, Justice Whiddon, Serjeant Carus, and Mr Russell the Queen's Solicitor, and at their backs sat Sir Richard Rede, Dr Yale, and Dr Vaughan.

On the other Sack sat Dr Huicke[1], Spilman Clerk of the Parliament, and Mr Martin Clerk of the Crown; and behind them kneeled Mr Smith, Allen, Dyeter, Nicasius, Cliffe, and Parmiter.

At the side hand of the Queen sat on the ground three or four Ladies and no more; and at the back of the rail, behind the Cloth of Estate, kneeled the Earls of Oxford and Rutland, under age, the Earl of Desmond, the Lord Roos, the Lord Herbert of Cardiff, and divers other noblemen's sons and heirs....

... The Queen's Majesty, being set (as aforesaid) under the Cloth of Estate, the House of Commons had notice thereof; and thereupon the Knights, Citizens, and Burgesses of the same repaired to the Upper House, and being, as many as conveniently could, let in, she commanded Sir Nicholas Bacon, the Lord Keeper, to open the cause of calling and assembling this Parliament.... D'Ewes, *Journal*, p. 58.

(2) Proxies in the House of Lords, 1563

This day [11 January, 1563] although the Parliament began not, nor any peers sat in the Upper House,...were divers proxies returned from many of the Lords both spiritual and temporal, who in their absence did constitute others to give their voices for them.

Nota, That the Duke of Norfolk was constituted the sole or joint proctor of four several peers, and Francis, Earl of Bedford, was nominated the sole or joint proctor of seven several lords, whereof one was Thomas, Archbishop of York, and another of them was William, Bishop of Exeter; By which it doth appear, not only that a spiritual lord did constitute a temporal (which at this day[2] is altogether forborne, as also for a temporal lord to constitute a spiritual, which was but rarely used during this Queen's reign) but likewise that any peer of the Upper House, by the ancient and undoubted usages and custom of the same, is capable of as many proxies as shall be sent unto him.

D'Ewes, *Journal*, p. 58.

[1] Robert Huicke was one of the Queen's physicians, and afterwards her chief physician.
[2] D'Ewes died in 1650, but his *Journal* was not published until 1682.

(3) The Chaplain of the House of Commons, 1597

See also p. 547 below.

[1 December, 1597]...Sir Robert Wroth and Mr Southerton are nominated to make collection of the members of this House, both for the Minister his pains in saying prayers in this House, and for the poor....

...Sir Henry Knyvet, one of the burgesses for the borough of Malmesbury in the county of Wilts, is for his necessary businesses licensed by Mr Speaker to depart into the country, leaving with Mr Fulk Onslow, Clerk of this House, ten shillings for the poor and three shillings and fourpence towards the recompense of the Minister that said prayers in the House, which he received accordingly....

D'Ewes, *Journal*, p. 566.

(4) Attendance at the House of Commons, 1572–1601

This is a typical entry.

[30 May, 1572]...Martin Cole, one of the burgesses for the borough of Sudbury in the county of Suffolk, was for his great business and affairs licensed to be absent for eight days.

D'Ewes, *Journal*, p. 220.

[11 February, 1585]...Upon a motion made by Mr Recorder that those of this House towards the Law, being the most part of them at the bars in her Majesty's Courts attending their clients' causes and neglecting the service of this House, be called by the Serjeant to repair unto this House presently[1] and to give their attendance in the service of the same, It was ordered [*accordingly...*].

...Upon a motion made by Sir William Herbert that Mr Recorder of London, who erst made a motion to this House, That those of the Law [*etc....*] being now since their coming in gone out of the House himself, and, as he was informed, was presently pleading at the Common Pleas bar, to the great abuse of this whole House, might be forthwith sent for by the Serjeant....It was ordered [*accordingly...*]. D'Ewes, *Journal*, p. 347

[1 December, 1601]...Mr Wiseman moved the House to remember two things: one, that it had been an ancient custom in Parliament sometimes to call the House, which as yet was not done; the other, that whereas heretofore collection had been used for the poor, those which went out of town would ask leave of the Speaker and pay their money.

[1] Immediately.

Sir Edward Hobby said... May it please you, it hath been a most laudable custom that some contribution or collection should be made amongst us *in pios usus*, and I do humbly pray we do not forget our Parliamental charity. Every knight paid 10*s.*, every burgess 5*s.*....

Mr Fettiplace said, It is true, Mr Speaker, I was collector the last year. There was paid out of the money collected, to the Minister, £10, to the Serjeant, £30, to Sir John Leveson for the redemption of Mr Foxe his son that made the Book of Martyrs, £30; there was money given to prisons, that is the two Counters, Ludgate and Newgate in London, in Southwark two, and Westminster one. How old the custom is I know not; but how good it is I know....

D'Ewes, *Journal*, p. 661.

(5) Divisions in the House of Commons, 1593

[20 March, 1593]... Mr Speaker said, The order of the House is, that the Aye being for the bill must go out, and the No against the bill doth always sit. The reason is that the inventor that will have a new law is to go out and bring it in; and they that are for the law in possession must keep the House, for they sit to continue it.

D'Ewes, *Journal*, p. 505.

(6) Procedure of the House of Commons

All bills be thrice in three divers days read and disputed upon, before they come to the question. In the disputing is a marvellous good order used in the Lower House. He that standeth up bareheaded is understanded that he will speak to the bill. If more stand up, who that first is judged to arise is first heard; though the one do praise the law, the other dissuade it, yet there is no altercation. For every man speaketh as to the Speaker, not as one to another, for that is against the order of the House. It is also taken against the order to name him whom ye do confute but by circumlocution, as 'He that speaketh with the bill,' or ' He that spake against the bill and gave this and this reason.' And so with perpetual oration, not with altercation, he goeth through till he do make an end. He that once hath spoken in a bill, though he be confuted straight, that day may not reply; no, though he would change his opinion. So that to one bill in one day one may not in that House speak twice, for else one or two with altercation would spend all the time. The next day he may, but then also but once.

No reviling or nipping words must be used[1]. For then all the House will cry, 'It is against the order': and if any speak unreverently or seditiously against the Prince or the Privy Council, I have seen them not only interrupted but it hath been moved after to the House and they have sent them to the Tower. So that in such a multitude, and in such diversity of minds and opinions, there is the greatest modesty and temperance of speech that can be used. Nevertheless, with much doulce and gentle terms they make their reasons as violent and as vehement the one against the other as they may ordinarily, except it be for urgent causes and hasting of time.

Sir Thomas Smith, *De Republica Anglorum* (edn. of 1906), Bk. ii, ch. 2.

[2 December, 1584]...This bill had been much argued upon before it was committed; and it seems some arguments being not liked, divers of the House had endeavoured by coughing and spitting to shorten them. Whereupon Sir Francis Hastings made a motion...that...it were now to be wished that in respect of the gravity and honour of this House, when any member thereof shall speak unto a bill the residue would forbear to interrupt or trouble him by unnecessary coughing, spitting, or the like.

D'Ewes, *Journal*, p. 335

[18 February, 1589]...Mr Speaker, noting the great disorder in this House by some that standing up and offering to speak, sometimes three or four together, and persisting still without offering to give place one of them to another, knowing well nevertheless which of themselves did first stand up and so by the order of this House ought to be first heard, but yet expecting by acclamation of the residue of the House, growing for the most part to a great confused noise and sound of senseless words, do stand still continuing their offer to speak first, and do also many times in their motions and arguments utter very sharp and bitter speeches, sometimes rather particularly offensive than necessarily with such great vehemency delivered—putteth them in remembrance that every member of this House is a Judge of this Court, being the highest Court of all other courts, and the Great Council also of this realm, and so moveth them in regard thereof

---

[1] That this rule was not always observed appears from Mr Wentworth's attack upon Sir Humphrey Gilbert in a debate of 20 April, 1571. 'He proved his speech (without naming him) to be an injury to the House; he noted his disposition to flatter and fawn on the Prince, comparing him to the chameleon, which can change himself into all colours saving white; even so (said he) this reporter can change himself to all fashions but honesty' (D'Ewes, *Journal*, p. 175).

that as in all other courts, being each of them inferior to this High Court, such confused courses, either of contention, acclamations, or reciprocal bitter and sharp speeches, terms, or words are not any way either used or permitted amongst the judges of the said inferior courts or the counsellors admitted in the same courts, so they would hereafter forbear to attempt the like disorders, as the honour and gravity of this House justly requireth....

D'Ewes, *Journal*, p. 434.

[7 March, 1593]...Now stood up two or three to have spoken, striving who might speak first. Then the Speaker propounds it as an order in the House in such a case, for him to ask the parties that would speak on which side they would speak—whether with him that spake next before, or against him; and the party that speaketh against the last speaker is to be heard first. And so it was ruled. Where it may seem that the Speaker did give admonishment sitting in the House as a member thereof, and not sitting in his Chair as Speaker, which he never doth at any Committee, although it be of the whole House.

D'Ewes, *Journal*, p. 493.

[27 October, 1597]...The House being set, and before Mr Speaker went up to her Majesty in the Upper House, Mr Chancellor of the Exchequer moved and admonished that none of this House should after this present day enter into the same House with their spurs on, for offending of others; and withal that none do come into this House before they have paid the Serjeant's fees of this House due unto him according to the accustomed usage of this House in that case.

D'Ewes, *Journal*, p. 550.

[3 March, 1593]...Mr Speaker perceiving some men to whisper together, said that it was not the manner of the House that any should whisper and talk secretly, for here only public speeches are to be used... D'Ewes, *Journal*, p. 487.

[9 November, 1601]...Then Serjeant [Heyle] stood up and made a motion saying: 'Mr Speaker, I marvel much that the House will stand upon granting of a subsidy, or the time of payment, when all we have is her Majesty's, and she may lawfully at her pleasure take it from us....' At which all the House hemmed and laughed and talked. 'Well,' quoth Serjeant Heyle, 'all your hemming shall not put me out of countenance.' So Mr Speaker stood up and said: 'It is a great disorder that this should be used, for it is the ancient use of every man to be silent when anyone speaketh, and he that is speaking should be suffered to deliver his mind without interruption.' So the said Serjeant proceeded, and when he had spoken a little while the House hemmed again, and so he sat down....

D'Ewes, Journal, p. 633.

§ 6. Privilege of Parliament

It is remarkable that in the Tudor period—the period of despotic government—there should have been steady progress in the development and definition of the privilege of Parliament. The explanation is to be found not in the strength of Parliament but in its weakness. It was the Tudor policy to rule by means of Parliament because the Tudor sovereigns were not afraid of Parliament. They were too strong to be threatened by their assemblies, and they could scarcely be expected to look a century ahead, and see to what height the claims of an assembly might grow. Thus they were ready to do what they could to promote the efficiency of Parliament, and this led them to look with favour upon the growth of Parliamentary privilege.

(a) *The Speaker's claim of Privilege*

At the beginning of every Parliament, the Speaker claimed freedom of access to the sovereign, freedom of speech, freedom from arrest, and the right to have the most favourable construction placed upon his proceedings on behalf of the House. His earlier claim had been for access for himself alone, as representing the House, and this continued to be the case as late as 1515[1]; but in later Tudor practice this became a demand for freedom of access for the whole House [p. 551]. The extract from the proceedings of 1593 printed below [p. 552] suggests that the privilege was sometimes in danger of abuse[2]. The right of access of the peers rests upon a different foundation. It has been held that as the peers are hereditary Councillors of the Crown, the right is enjoyed by each individual peer[3].

In the Middle Ages freedom of speech was claimed by the Speaker for himself alone as Prolocutor of the House, and it applied only to the joint meetings of Lords and Commons in the Parliament Chamber, where he and no other member of the Commons had the right of speaking[4]. The entirely different claim of freedom of speech for each individual member of the Lower House taking part in its deliberations first appears in the Parliament of 1542 [p. 551]. The form in which it was claimed at the beginning of Elizabeth's reign [p. 551], and Sir Thomas Smith's treatment of it in his *De Republica Anglorum* [p. 554] appear below.

'The discussions in the English Parliament,' wrote Henry VIII to the Pope, 'are free and unrestricted; the Crown has no power to limit their debates or to control the votes of the members. They determine everything for themselves, as the interests of the commonwealth require.'[5] But this principle was not always applied in practice, and Queen Elizabeth's answers to the Speaker's claim in 1593 [p. 552] and again in 1601 [p. 553] shew that she regarded the privilege as having definite limitations.

---

[1] Prothero, p. lxxxvii.   [2] Cf. also the answer of 1559 (p. 552 below).
[3] For a discussion of this question see Pike, p. 252.
[4] Pollard, *Parliament*, p. 126.   [5] Quoted in Redlich, i, 35.

(1) Petition for Privilege and the royal answer, 1542

[20 January, 1542]...Hodie Communes presentabant Regie Majestati *Thomam Moyle*, singulorum suffragiis electum Prolocutorem suum....Supplicavit Regie Majestati 'Ut in dicendis sententiis quivis libere et impune eloqui posset quid animi haberet et quid consilii.' Itaque, finiens orationem, nomine Communium petiit, 'Accedendi veniam ad Regiam Personam in causis magis perplexis et gravioribus quam ut ipsi inter se definire sufficerent.'

Cui quidem orationi Regia Majestas, maxima cum humanitate, sic respondit per Cancellarium....'Honestam dicendi libertatem non negare Regiam Majestatem, tum etiam accessum permittere ad suam personam, quoties usus postulaverit; ita tamen ut perplexas hujusmodi causas non per universam multitudinem sed per pauculos aliquot cordatiores viros, ejus Majestati significare satagerent....'

Lords' Journals, i, 167.

(2) Petition for Privilege and the royal answer, 1559

[28 January, 1559]...And lastly [Sir Thomas Gargrave] came, according to the usual form, first, to desire liberty of access for the House of Commons to the Queen's Majesty's presence upon all urgent and necessary occasions. Secondly, that if in anything himself should mistake or misreport or overslip that which should be committed unto him to declare, that it might without prejudice to the House be better declared, and that his unwilling miscarriage therein might be pardoned. Thirdly, that they might have liberty and freedom of speech in whatsoever they treated of or had occasion to propound and debate in the House. The fourth and last, that all the members of the House, with their servants and necessary attendants, might be exempted from all manner of arrests and suits during the continuance of the Parliament, and the usual space both before the beginning and after the ending thereof, as in former times hath always been accustomed.

To which speech of the said Speaker...the Lord Keeper... replied:

...For the third and last you have divided into four petitions: The first, for your access to the Queen's Highness and her nobles for your reports and conference. The second, that you be borne with in anything if you should in any of your reports be mistaken or overslipped, and that without prejudice to the House it be better declared. The third, liberty of speech, for well debating of matters propounded. The fourth and last, that all the members of the House and their servants may have the same freedom from all manner of suits as beforetime they used to have.

To these petitions the Queen's Majesty hath commanded me to say unto you, that her Highness is right well contented to grant them unto you as largely as amply and as liberally as ever they were granted by any her noble progenitors; and to confirm the same with as great an authority. Marry, with these conditions and cautions: first, that your access be void of importunity, and for matters needful, and in time convenient. For the second, that your diligence and carefulness be such, Mr Speaker, that the defaults in that part be as rare as may be; whereof her Majesty doubteth little. For the third, which is liberty of speech, therewith her Highness is right well contented, but so as they be neither unmindful or uncareful of their duties, reverence, and obedience to their Sovereign. For the last, great heed would be taken that no evil-disposed person seek of purpose that privilege for the only defrauding of his creditors and for the maintenance of injuries and wrongs. These admonitions being well remembered, her Majesty thinketh all the said liberties and privileges well granted.... *D'Ewes, Journal*, p. 16.

(3) Answer to the Petition for Privilege, 1593

The more famous version of the Lord Keeper's speech given in D'Ewes (p. 460), which includes the phrase 'your privilege is Aye and No,' does not rest on good authority (see *E.H.R.* xxxi, 128).

[22 February, 1593]...I...will therefore descend to your last part, wherein I noted three petitions for your company and a fourth for yourself. Her gracious Majesty is well pleased to grant them so far as they be grantable. She sayeth there be two things in a man most behoveful if they be well used, and most deadly if they be ill used: wit and tongue, they are those; they be most happy possessions and needful helps, and all as they be placed. Having therefore especial care that that may never hurt you which she by her grant doth yield you, she wills you take good heed in what sort she permits it. She would be sorry that folly past should by new redouble the faults, and chargeth you, Mr Speaker, if any shall deliver to you any bill that passeth the reach of a subject's brain to mention, that same you receive not but with purpose to shew it where it best becometh you. Next, if any speech undecent or matter unfit for that place be used, remember them of this lesson: Your petitions...must be ruled, and that thus her Majesty granteth you liberal but not licentious speech, liberty therefore but with due limitation. For even as there can be no good consultation where all freedom of advice is barred, so will there be no good conclusion where every man may speak what he listeth, without fit observation of persons, matters, times, places, and other needful circumstances. It shall be meet therefore that each man of you contain his speech within the bounds of loyalty and good discretion, being assured that as the contrary is punishable in all men, so most of all in them that take upon them to be counsellors and procurators of the common-wealth. For liberty of speech her Majesty commandeth me to tell you that to say yea or no to bills, God forbid that any man should be restrained or afraid to answer according to his best liking, with some short declaration of his reason therein, and therein to have a free voice, which is the very true liberty of the House; not, as some suppose, to speak there of all causes as him listeth, and to frame a form of religion or a state of government as to their idle brains shall seem meetest. She saith no king fit for his state will suffer such absurdities, and though she hopeth no man here longeth so much for his ruin as that he mindeth to make such a peril to his own safety, yet that you may better follow what she wisheth, she makes of her goodness you the partakers of her intent and meaning. Access to her Majesty's most sacred presence her Highness is likewise pleased to vouchsafe, so that the same be desired only in matters of the greatest exigency and weight, and with due respect of times, that her Majesty's more important cogitations be not interpelled[1] thereby. Neither is the mind of her gracious Majesty to deny you those other good privileges of the Court of Parliament which the Commons of the realm heretofore have usually enjoyed, howbeit with this caution, that the pro-tection of your House be not worn by any man for a cloak to defraud others of their debts and duties....

Harleian MS. 6265; printed by Mr J. E. Neale in *English Historical Review*, xxxi, 136.

(4) Answer to the Petition for Privilege, 1601

[30 October, 1601]...Touching your other requests for freedom of speech, her Majesty willingly consenteth thereto, with this caution, that the time be not spent in idle and vain matter, painting the same out with froth and volubility of words, whereby the speakers may seem to gain some reputed credit by embolden-ing themselves to contradiction, and by troubling the House of

[1] Interrupted.

purpose with long and vain orations to hinder the proceeding in matters of greater and more weighty importance. . . .

D'Ewes, *Journal*, p. 601

(5) Sir Thomas Smith on the claim of Privilege, 1565

. . . The knights of the shire and burgesses of the Parliament . . . are willed to choose an able and discreet man to be as it were the mouth of them all, and to speak for and in the name of them, and to present him so chosen by them to the Prince: which done, they coming all with him to a bar which is at the nether end of the Upper House, there he first praiseth the Prince, then maketh his excuse of unability and prayeth the Prince that he would command the Commons to choose another. The Chancellor in the Prince's name doth so much declare him able as he did declare himself unable, and thanketh the Commons for choosing so wise, discreet, and eloquent a man, and willeth them to go and consult of laws for the common wealth. Then the Speaker maketh certain requests to the Prince in the name of the Commons: First, that his Majesty would be content that they may use and enjoy all their liberties and privileges that the Common House was wont to enjoy. Secondly, that they might frankly and freely say their minds in disputing of such matters as may come in question, and that without offence to his Majesty. Thirdly, that if any should chance of that Lower House to offend, or not to do or say as should become him, or if any should offend any of them being called to that his Highness's Court, that they themselves might (according to the ancient custom) have the punishment of them. And fourthly, that if there came any doubt whereupon they shall desire to have the advice or conference with his Majesty or with any of the Lords, that they might do it: All which he promiseth in the Commons' names that they shall not abuse, but have such regard as most faithful, true, and loving subjects ought to have to their Prince. . . .

Sir Thomas Smith, *De Republica Anglorum* (edn. of 1906), Bk. ii, ch. 2.

(b) *The Privilege of Freedom of Speech*

The privilege of freedom of speech is essential to the independence of Parliament and to its authority over legislation. 'No man can make a doubt,' said the Commons in 1667[1], 'but whatever is once enacted is lawful; but nothing can come into an Act of Parliament but it must first be affirmed or propounded by somebody; so that if the Act can wrong nobody, no more can the first propounding. The members must be as free as the Houses; an Act of Parliament cannot disturb the State; therefore the debate that tends to it

[1] *Lords' Journals*, xii, 166.

cannot; for it must be propounded and debated before it can be enacted.' This passage supplies the key to the meaning of freedom of speech as it was understood in the 16th and 17th centuries. Now it means freedom to say anything that can be expressed in parliamentary terms; to bring criticism to bear upon the government without being called in question for it except by Parliament itself. Then it meant freedom to initiate discussion upon any subject; and it was their choice of subjects that brought members of the House of Commons into collision with the Tudor kings.

The view of the Crown was that the Commons were summoned 'merely to vote such sums as were asked of them, to formulate or to approve legislation or topics of legislation submitted to them, and to give an opinion on matters of policy if, and only if, they were asked for one.'[1] Elizabeth, in particular, warned the Commons off three great departments of affairs, religion, foreign policy, and trade, which there was some justification for regarding as outside their proper province; and she also refused to allow them to discuss the important question of the succession to the throne.

Early in the reign of Henry VIII there occurred what has sometimes been regarded as a striking assertion of the claim to freedom of speech. In 1512 Richard Strode, a member of the House of Commons, was imprisoned by the Stannary Court of Devon 'in a dungeon and a deep pit underground in the castle of Lidford,' 'one of the most annoyous, contagious, and detestablest place[s] within this realm,' because he had proposed 'certain bills' in Parliament for the regulation of tin-mining. He was delivered by a writ of privilege out of the Exchequer, and an Act [p. 558] was passed declaring his condemnation void, and enacting that legal proceedings taken in any court against members of Parliament 'for any bill, speaking, reasoning, or declaring of any matter or matters concerning the Parliament to be communed and treated of' should be 'void and of none effect.' The words of the Act do not bear the interpretation which has been put upon them, and the importance of the episode has been greatly exaggerated. The Act was drawn to meet the particular case of interference by legal proceedings in a court, and there is no attempt to assert freedom of speech against the Crown.

The question of the succession came up in 1559, but the Queen put the Commons off with polite evasions. 'The dangers which you fear,' she said in her wise way, 'are neither so certain nor of such nature but you may repose yourselves upon the Providence of God and the good provisions of the State. Wits curious in casting things to come are often hurtful, for that the affairs of this world are subject to so many accidents that seldom doth that happen which the wisdom of men doth seem to foresee.'[2] In the session of 1563 a petition from the Commons was sent to the Queen, praying her to choose a successor[3], but in her speech on the prorogation of Parliament [p. 559] she gave them small encouragement. When they returned to the subject in 1566 there was a passage of arms with the Queen. After serious debate in the Lower House [p. 560], a joint petition was presented to her by 30 Lords and 30 Commoners on behalf of the two Houses[4], and received an answer [p. 561] which failed to satisfy the Commons [p. 561];

---

[1] Anson, i, 158.   [2] Hayward, p. 33.
[3] D'Ewes, p. 81. See also Mr J. E. Neale in *E.H.R.* xxxvi, 497, on the whole question.
[4] See D'Ewes, p. 104. The petition is printed on p. 105.

and when they pursued the subject, she sent 'her express inhibition' to proceed. Paul Wentworth, Peter Wentworth's brother, raised the question of privilege, and a long debate ensued [p. 561], followed by another expression of the Queen's displeasure [p. 562]. In the end, however, she revoked 'her two former commandments requiring the House no further to proceed at this time in the matter,' which was 'taken of all the House most joyfully' [p. 562]. The Commons were content with having made their point, and they did not pursue the subject; but the Queen, in her speech at the dissolution of Parliament, did not fail to express her resentment[1] [p. 562]. 'Those two great businesses,' observes D'Ewes[2], 'of her Majesty's marriage and declaring a successor, coming into agitation at this time[3]. . . . Mr Paul Wentworth and others used so great liberty of speech as (I conceive) was never used in any Parliament or session of Parliament before or since.'

At the opening of the Parliament of 1571 the Queen, replying through the Lord Keeper to the Speaker's petition of privilege [p. 563], referred to her 'experience of late of some disorder,' and warned the Commons 'to meddle with no matters of state[4] but such as should be propounded unto them.' This admonition was so far effective that at the end of the session of 1576 the Queen, through the Lord Keeper, paid the Parliament a special compliment, and her observations upon the subject of her marriage shew a change of tone [p. 563]. This change of tone was maintained in the Parliament of 1586; and her answer to the Houses [p. 564] when they attempted to put pressure upon her to order the execution of the next heiress to the throne, Mary Queen of Scots, was conciliatory in tone, although it postponed a definite decision. But the Queen still held to her view that the succession was in the first instance a matter for herself alone, and when in 1593 Peter Wentworth and others raised the question in the House of Commons, they were suspended from Parliament, and committed to prison[5] by order of the Council [p. 564].

In resisting Parliamentary intrusion into the sphere of religion, the Queen was asserting her ecclesiastical supremacy, and she frequently warned the Commons off the forbidden ground.

In the Parliament of 1571 a bill 'for reformation of the Book of Common Prayer' was brought into the House of Commons by Mr Strickland [p. 565], and the House, before proceeding with it, agreed to apply for the Queen's permission; but Mr Strickland was at once suspended from Parliament by the Privy Council, and summoned to appear before it. His cause was taken up in the name of 'the liberty of the House,' and it was urged that he should be heard at its Bar. It was argued on behalf of the government that 'he was in no sort stayed for any word or speech by him in that place offered,

---

[1] Elizabeth had a low opinion of the Parliament of 1566. She told the Lords that 'she was not surprised at the Commons, for they had small experience and acted like boys' (quoted in Redlich, i, 36 n.).   [2] p. 122.

[3] The note is inserted at the beginning of the second session, under date 2 October, 1566.

[4] I.e. matters of royal estate, such as the Queen's marriage, as here referred to, or causes ecclesiastical, as on p. 565 below.

[5] There is reason for thinking that Peter Wentworth remained in prison until his death in 1596 (D.N.B. lx, 263).

but for the exhibiting of a bill into the House against the prerogative of the Queen, which was not to be tolerated.' This drew from Yelverton an eloquent speech [p. 566] in defence of the right of the Commons to initiate discussion upon any subject, and on the following day Mr Strickland was restored to his place in the House. A few days later, after a conference with the Lords 'touching articles of religion,' the Commons were informed that this was not a matter for Parliament, but for the Bishops acting 'by direction of her Highness's regal authority of Supremacy of the Church of England.' A year later the Queen ordered that 'from henceforth no bills concerning religion shall be preferred or received into this House unless the same should be first considered and liked by the clergy'; and she sent for and impounded two bills 'touching rites and ceremonies' [p. 568].

In 1581 Paul Wentworth moved for 'a public fast and daily preaching,' and after a debate, followed by a division, this was carried by 115 votes to 100 [p. 568]. The Queen expressed her displeasure at 'such an innovation as the same fast' being made 'without her...privity and pleasure first known,' and the House made the humble submission which she required of it; in accepting the submission she explained that she did not object to fasting and prayer but to the method of its institution, 'which was to intrude upon her authority ecclesiastical.'

In the Parliament of 1587 Mr Cope introduced a bill for repealing all existing laws 'touching ecclesiastical government,' together with a book containing a new form of common prayer; but after the first debate the Queen intervened, and commanded the Speaker to deliver up both the bill and the book. Peter Wentworth attempted to raise the question of freedom of speech by means of a series of questions which he handed to the Speaker [p. 571], but he was at once sent to the Tower, and his questions were not moved in the House. On the following day Mr Cope, and other supporters of the bill and the book, joined him there. Again, in 1593, when Mr Morice, the Attorney of the Court of Wards, brought in two bills for the reform of the ecclesiastical courts [p. 572], he suffered the same fate. On this occasion the Queen sent a message to the House [p. 572] 'that no bill touching the said matters of state or reformation in causes ecclesiastical be exhibited,' and commanded the Speaker upon his allegiance, 'if any such bill be exhibited, not to read it.' In 1597 the prohibition was withdrawn for a special purpose [p. 573]; and in 1601 a bill for amending the Statute of Pluralities [p. 573] was read a second time and committed, although the doubt was expressed in debate that this course would incur the Queen's displeasure.

Matters of trade had long been regarded as belonging to the sphere of prerogative, and in the debate on monopolies in 1601 [p. 573] Bacon, speaking out of the fulness of his legal knowledge, claimed for the Crown extensive powers, and advised the House to proceed by petition. But the grievance was so seriously felt that Parliament would be content with nothing less than a statute, and the Queen was obliged to surrender as if she had been James I or Charles I; although the difference between her and her successors is illustrated nowhere better than in the grace and skill with which the surrender was made [p. 577].

It has been pointed out[1] that in the later Parliaments of Elizabeth a new spirit appears. The power of Henry VIII had depended partly upon national timidity—the recollection of the Wars of the Roses; fear of attack from France or Scotland; later, fear of the Emperor; and the earlier greatness of Elizabeth herself had been to a certain extent grounded upon fear of Spain. But with the defeat of the Spanish Armada in 1588 a new buoyancy and self-confidence inspire the English mind, and 'we might almost say that from the Armada the glory of Elizabeth begins to wane.' Her most trusted counsellors died before her—Walsingham in 1590 and Burghley in 1598. The new men were younger, less cautious, more ambitious, perhaps less purely patriotic, and there was not among them the old unquestioning submission to the Queen. The increase of wealth was strengthening the political classes, while Puritanism 'developed independence of character among the younger generation, already stirred up by the struggle with Spain.'[2] After 1588 the House of Commons begins to grumble when applied to for subsidies, and in 1593 the subsidy bills only passed after a debate which lasted the unprecedented time of eleven days[3]. In 1593 also the Queen complains of 'irreverence' shewn to privy councillors [p. 578]. At the opening of the Parliament of 1601 there were signs of a declining popularity [p. 578]. In the course of the session Robert Cecil compared the Commons to a grammar-school, and complained of 'levity and disorder' [p. 575]. 'Leaders of opposition...stand forward, the genuine precursors of the leaders of the Long Parliament;...Parliamentary oratory has become a power. The language held in debate...sounds like a tocsin.'[4]

(1) Strode's Act, 1512

Pro Ricardo Strode

Lamentably complaineth and sheweth unto your most discreet wisdoms in this present Parliament assembled Richard Strode, gentleman, of the county of Devonshire, one of the burgesses of this honourable House for the borough of Plympton....That where the said Richard condescended and agreed with other of this House to put forth certain bills in this present Parliament against certain persons named tinners in the county aforesaid for the reformation of the perishing, hurting, and destroying of divers ports, havens, and creeks, and other bills for the common weal of the said county, the which here in this High Court of Parliament should and ought to be commended and treated of; And for by cause the said Richard is a tinner, for the causes and matters afore rehearsed one John Fursse, tinner, Under-Steward of the Stannary in the said county, in and at four courts of the said Stannary at divers places and times before him severally holden in the said county, he and other hath condemned the said Richard in the sum of £160, that is to wit, at every court £40....
[and] the said Richard was taken and imprisoned in a dungeon

---

[1] Redlich, i, 36.   [2] Traill, iii, 420.   [3] D'Ewes, p. 507.   [4] Goldwin Smith, i, 398.

and a deep pit underground in the Castle of Lidford...and there and elsewhere remained by the space of three weeks and more, unto such time he was delivered by a writ of privilege out of the King's Exchequer at Westminster, for that he was one of the collectors in the said county for the first of the two quindecims granted at and in this present Parliament; the which prison is one of the most annoyous, contagious, and detestablest place[s] within this realm, so that by reason of the same imprisonment he was put in great jeopardy and peril of his life.
... Wherefore the premises by your great wisdoms tenderly considered, the said Richard humbly prayeth that it may be ordained, established, and enacted...that the said condemnation...to be utterly void against the said Richard, and of none effect.

II. And over that, be it enacted...that suits, accusements, condemnations, executions, fines, amerciaments, punishments, corrections, grievances, charges, and impositions, put or had, or hereafter to be put or had, unto or upon the said Richard, and to every other of the person or persons afore specified that now be of this present Parliament or that of any Parliament hereafter shall be, for any bill, speaking, reasoning, or declaring of any matter or matters concerning the Parliament to be communed and treated of, be utterly void and of none effect. And over that, be it enacted...that if the said Richard Strode or any of all the said other person or persons hereafter be vexed, troubled, or otherwise charged for any causes as is aforesaid, that then he or they...to have action upon the case against every such person...so vexing or troubling any, contrary to this ordinance and provision, in the which action the party grieved shall recover treble damages and costs....

4 Henr. VIII, c. 8: *Statutes of the Realm*, iii, 53.

(2) The Queen's Marriage and the Succession to the Throne

Queen's Answer to the Speaker at the Prorogation, 10 April, 1563[1]

Since there can be no duer debt than Prince's words, which I would observe, therefore I answer to the same; thus it is. The two petitions which you made unto me do contain two things, my marriage, and succession after me. For the first, if I had let slip too much time, or if my strength had been decayed, you might the better have spoke therein; or if any think I never meant to try that life, they be deceived; but if I may hereafter bend my mind thereunto, the rather for fulfilling your request, I shall be therewith very well content.

[1] A fuller version is in D'Ewes, p. 107, wrongly assigned to 1566. See *E.H.R.* xxxvi, 502 *n*.

For the second, the greatness thereof maketh me to say and pray that I may linger here in this vale of misery for your comfort, wherein I have witness of my study and travail for your surety; And I cannot with *Nunc Dimittis* end my life, without I see some foundation of your surety after my gravestone.

D'Ewes, *Journal*, p. 75.

Proceedings in Parliament, 1566

On Friday the 18th day of October [1566]...a motion was made...for the reviving of the suit touching the declaration of a successor, in case her Majesty should die without issue of her own body, which suit had been first moved by the House and their petition preferred therein in the first session of this Parliament.... And thereupon divers propositions and reasonings ensued, this great business being once moved, although it should seem in the conclusion thereof that the greater part of the House were resolved to recontinue the said suit and to know her Highness's answer; although Sir Ralph Sadler,...one of her Privy Council, had declared and affirmed unto the House that he had heard the Queen say, in the presence of divers of the nobility, that for the wealth[1] of the realm her Highness was minded to marry....

On Saturday, the 19th day of October,...Mr Secretary Cecil and Sir Francis Knollys, her Majesty's Vice-Chamberlain, declared unto the House that the Queen's Majesty was, by God's special providence, moved to marriage, and that she mindeth for the wealth of her Commons to prosecute the same.

Sir Ambrose Cave, Chancellor of the Duchy, and Sir Edward Rogers, Comptroller of her Majesty's Household, affirmed the same, and thereupon persuaded and advised the House to see the sequel of that before they made further suit touching the declaration of a successor.

But against this opinion divers lawyers of the House...did argue very boldly and judiciously, and so prevailed with the greatest part of the House as that it was resolved, contrary to the foregoing motion of those of her Majesty's Privy Council, to recontinue their suit touching the declaration of a successor and to get the Queen's answer. And to that end it was ordered, that all the Privy Council being members of this House, with 44 others... should meet to-morrow to consult and advise in what manner they might move the Lords of the Upper House to join with them in this matter.... D'Ewes, *Journal*, p. 124.

On Wednesday the 6th day of November [1566]...Sir

---

[1] See note on p. 33 above.

Edward Rogers, knight, Comptroller of her Highness's Household, and Sir William Cecil, knight, her Majesty's Principal Secretary, read in writing notes of the Queen's Majesty's saying before the Lords and committees of this House; tending that her Grace had signified to both Houses by words of a Prince that she by God's grace would marry, and would have it therefore believed; and touching limitation for succession, the perils be so great to her person, and whereof she hath felt part in her sister's time, that time will not yet suffer to treat of it....

D'Ewes, *Journal*, p. 127.

On Friday the 8th day of November [1566]...Mr Lambert began a learned oration for iteration of the suit to the Queen's Majesty for limitation of succession, and thereupon strongly reasoned for both parts: whence it appeareth plainly, that though her Majesty satisfied the Lords by her former answer on Tuesday the 5th of this instant November preceding (the effect of which was that she was desirous to incline her mind to marriage, but could not declare a successor in respect of the great danger thereof) yet those of the House of Commons rested not contented therewith, but only resting upon her Majesty's promise touching her marriage, they still discoursed of and resolved to press further that other part of their former suit touching the declaration of a successor; as appeareth by this foregoing motion of Mr Lambert and by the sequel afterwards....

On Saturday the 9th day of November...Sir Francis Knollys, knight, her Majesty's Vice-Chamberlain, declared the Queen's Majesty's express commands to this House that they should no further proceed in their suit, but to satisfy themselves with her Highness's promise of marriage. After whom Mr Secretary Cecil and Mr Comptroller severally rehearsed the like matter. So that by this it may be gathered that her Majesty, understanding of Mr Lambert's motion made yesterday, and fearing that the House should fall afresh upon the discussion of this business, did now send her express inhibition to prevent it by these forenamed honourable personages....

On Monday the 11th day of November...Paul Wentworth[1], a burgess of the House, desired to know whether the Queen's command and inhibition that they should no longer dispute of the matter of succession (sent yesterday to the House) were not against the liberties and privileges of the said House? And thereupon arose divers arguments, which continued from 9 of the

---

[1] The younger brother of Peter Wentworth.

clock in the morning till 2 of the clock in the afternoon. But then, because the time was far spent, all further debate and reasoning was deferred until the next morning....

On Tuesday the 12th day of November, Mr Speaker being sent for to attend upon the Queen's Majesty at the Court about 9 of the clock, sent word to the House where he was, requiring the House to have patience; and at his coming after 10 of the clock began to shew that he had received a special command from her Highness to this House, notwithstanding her first commandment, that there should not be further talk of that matter in the House (touching the declaration of a successor in case that her Majesty should die without issue) and if any person thought himself not satisfied but had further reasons, let him come before the Privy Council and there shew them....

On Monday the 25th day of November...Mr Speaker, coming from the Queen's Majesty, declared her Highness's pleasure to be that for her good will to the House she did revoke her two former commandments requiring the House no further to proceed at this time in the matter. Which revocation was taken of all the House most joyfully, with most hearty prayer and thanks for the same.

D'Ewes, *Journal*, pp. 128–30.

Queen's Speech at the Dissolution of Parliament, 2 *January*, 1567

...I have in this assembly found much dissimulation, where I always professed plainness, that I marvel thereat; yea, two faces under one hood, and the body rotten, being covered with two visors, succession and liberty, which they determined must be either presently granted, denied, or deferred....

...But do you think that either I am unmindful of your surety by succession, wherein is all my care, considering I know myself to be mortal? No, I warrant you: Or that I went about to break your liberties? No, it was never in my meaning, but to stay you before you fell into the ditch. For all things have their time. And although perhaps you may have after me one better learned or wiser, yet I assure you none more careful over you; And therefore henceforth, whether I live to see the like assembly or no, or whoever it be, yet beware however you prove your Prince's patience as you have now done mine. And now to conclude, all this notwithstanding (not meaning to make a Lent of Christmas) the most part of you may assure yourselves that you depart in your Prince's grace.

D'Ewes, *Journal*, p. 116.

Queen's Answer, through the Lord Keeper, to the Speaker's claim of privilege, 4 April, 1571

...For his petitions, he said,...the fourth [*i.e.* 'that in the House all men might have free speech'] was such that her Majesty, having experience of late of some disorder, and certain offences which though they were not punished yet were they offences still and so must be accounted, therefore said they should do well to meddle with no matters of state but such as should be propounded unto them, and to occupy themselves in other matters concerning the common wealth.   D'Ewes, *Journal*, p. 141.

Lord Keeper's speech at the end of the Session of 1576

[14 March, 1576]...I am to affirm unto you from her Majesty that she taketh your proceedings in the Parliament, both in the midst and also in the ending, so graciously and in so thankful part that if both parts and nature did concur in me abundantly to make me eloquent (as neither of them do) yet I am sure I were not able to set forth this point according to her Highness's desire or to the worthiness of it. And for the more manifest declaration of this, and of the great good liking her Majesty hath conceived of you that be of this Parliament, her Highness meaneth not to determine the same, but to prorogue it until the next winter....

...She conceiveth the abundance of your inward affection, grounded upon her good governance of you, to be so great, that it doth not only content you to have her Majesty reign and govern over you, but also you do desire that some proceeding from her Majesty's body might by a perpetual succession reign over your posterity also: a matter greatly to move her Majesty (she saith) to incline to this your suit. Besides her Highness is not unmindful of all the benefits that will grow to the realm by such marriage, neither doth she forget any perils that are like to grow for want thereof. All which matters considered, her Majesty willed me to say, that albeit of her own natural disposition she is not disposed or inclined to marriage, neither could she ever marry were she a private person, yet for your sakes and the benefit of the realm she is contented to dispose and incline herself to the satisfaction of your humble petition so that all things convenient may concur that be meet for such a marriage; whereof there be very many, —some touching the state of her most royal person, some touching the person of him whom God shall join, some touching the state of the whole realm: these things concurring and considered, her Majesty hath assented (as is before remembered). And thus much touching this matter.   D'Ewes, *Journal*, p. 233.

Lord Chancellor's Report to the Lords of the Queen's Answer to a Petition, 24 November, 1586

The fuller version of this speech now accessible shews that it was much more conciliatory in tone than the more famous rendering printed by D'Ewes (p. 380): 'If. . . I should say unto you that I mean not to grant your petition, by my faith I should say unto you more than perhaps I mean; and if I should say unto you that I mean to grant your petition, I should then tell you more than is fit for you to know. And thus I must deliver you an answer answerless. . .' (see *E.H.R.* xxxv, 112).

Afterwards, the five and twentieth day of November, the Lord Chancellor declared to the whole House that on Thursday, the four and twentieth of November, the Lords last before named, and the Speaker of the Lower House, with certain of the same House, had access to her Majesty at Richmond, And that he the said Lord Chancellor for the Lords of the Higher House, and the Speaker for the Commons, did declare unto her Highness their answer as is aforesaid, And did further in most humble and instant manner beseech and move her Highness that she would be pleased, for the preservation and safety not only of her most royal person but of the whole estate of the realm, to grant and take order that effectual proceeding might be speedily had according to their said petition. And that thereupon her Majesty in most princely and gracious manner did thankfully accept those their consultations and labours, protesting nevertheless that it was an exceeding grief unto her to perceive that by their advices, prayers, and desires there did fall out this sorrowful accident, that only her injurer's bane must be her life's surety, And that her earnest desire was rather to have found by their consultations some other means for her own safety joined with their assurance, and that therefore touching their petition, the matter being of so great weight and importance, her Highness thought good to take yet some further deliberation before she would make direct answer unto them, willing them for the time to content themselves and to take it in good part.

Harleian MS. 158, f. 160: printed by Mr J. E. Neale in *E.H.R.* xxxv, 112.

Proceedings in Parliament, 1593

[24 February, 1593]. . . This day Mr Peter Wentworth and Sir Henry Bromley delivered a petition unto the Lord Keeper, therein desiring the Lords of the Upper House to be suppliants with them of the Lower House unto her Majesty for entailing the succession of the Crown, whereof a bill was readily drawn by them. Her Majesty was highly displeased therewith after she knew thereof, as a matter contrary to her former strait commandment; and charged the Council to call the parties before them. Sir Thomas Heneage presently sent for them, and after speeches had with them, commanded them to forbear the Parliament and not to go out from their several lodgings. The day after being Sunday,... though the House sat not, yet they were called before the Lord Treasurer, the Lord Buckhurst, and Sir Thomas Heneage. The Lords intreated them favourably and with good speeches; but so highly was her Majesty offended that they must needs commit them, and so they told them. Whereupon Mr Peter Wentworth was sent prisoner unto the Tower; Sir Henry Bromley and one Mr Richard Stevens, to whom Sir Henry Bromley had imparted the matter, were sent to the Fleet, as also Mr Welch...(p. 470).

[10 March, 1593]...Mr Wroth...desired that we might be humble and earnest suitors to her Majesty, that she would be pleased to set at liberty those members of the House that were restrained. To this was answered by all the Privy Councillors, that her Majesty had committed them for causes best known to herself, and for us to press her Majesty with this suit, we should but hinder them whose good we seek. And it is not to be doubted but her Majesty of her gracious disposition will shortly of herself yield to them that which we would ask for them, and it will like her better to have it left unto herself than sought by us... (p. 497).

D'Ewes, *Journal*, pp. 470, 497.

(3) Ecclesiastical affairs in Parliament

Mr Strickland's Bill, 1571

[14 April, 1571]...The bill for reformation of the Book of Common Prayer was read the first time, after which (the bill being preferred by Mr Strickland) ensued divers long arguments.... After which arguments, it was upon the question agreed, That a petition should be made by this House unto the Queen's Majesty for her licence and privity to proceed in this bill before it be any further dealt in....

The Parliament was then by the consent of the House, for that it was Easter Eve, adjourned until Thursday next...during which said time of Easter Mr Strickland...was called before the Lords of the Privy Council and required to attend upon them, and to make stay from coming to the House in the mean season.

D'Ewes, *Journal*, pp. 166, 167, 168.

[20 April, 1571]... Mr Carleton, with a very good zeal and orderly show of obedience, made signification how that a member of the House was detained from them (meaning Mr Strickland), by whose commandment or for what cause he knew not. But forasmuch as he was not now a private person, but to supply the room, person, and place of a multitude, specially chosen and therefor sent, he thought that neither in regard of the country, which was not to be wronged, nor for the liberty of the House, which was not to be infringed, we should permit him to be detained from us. But whatsoever the intendment of this offence might be, that he should be sent for to the Bar of that House, there to be heard and there to answer.

Mr Treasurer in some case gave advertisement to be wary in our proceedings, and neither to venture further than our assured warrant might stretch, nor to hazard our good opinion with her Majesty on any doubtful cause. Withal he wished us not to think worse than there was cause. For the man (quoth he) that is meant, is neither detained nor misused, but on considerations is required to expect the Queen's pleasure upon certain special points; wherein (he said) he durst to assure that the man should neither have cause to dislike or complain, since so much favour was meant unto him as he reasonably could wish. He further said, that he was in no sort stayed for any word or speech by him in that place offered, but for the exhibiting of a bill into the House against the prerogative of the Queen, which was not to be tolerated. Nevertheless, the construction of him was rather to have erred in his zeal and bill offered, than maliciously to have meant anything contrary to the dignity royal....

...Mr Yelverton said he was to be sent for, arguing in this sort. First, he said, the precedent was perilous, and though in this happy time of lenity, among so good and honourable personages, under so gracious a Prince, nothing of extremity or injury was to be feared, yet the times might be altered, and what now is permitted hereafter might be construed as of duty, and enforced even on this ground of the present permission. He further said, that all matters not treason, or too much to the derogation of the imperial Crown, were tolerable there, where all things came to be considered of, and where there was such fulness of power as even the right of the Crown was to be determined, and by warrant whereof we had so resolved. That to say the Parliament had no power to determine of the Crown was high treason. He remembered how that men are not there for themselves but for their countries. He shewed it was fit for princes to have their prerogatives; but yet the same to be straitened within reasonable limits. The Prince, he shewed, could not of herself make laws; neither might she by the same reason break laws....

Mr Fleetwood...resolved that the only and whole help of the House for ease of their grief in this case, was to be humble suitors to her Majesty, and neither send for him nor demand him of right.

During which speech the Council whispered together, and thereupon the Speaker moved that the House should make stay of any further consultation thereupon....

D'Ewes, Journal, pp. 175–6.

...The above-mentioned Mr Strickland did this forenoon [21 April, 1571], upon an advertisement (as it should seem) from her Majesty's Council, repair again to the said House soon after it was set. And coming just upon the time when the foregoing bill for coming to church and receiving the communion was in the referring to committees, the said House did, in witness of their joy for the restitution of one of their said members awhile from them restrained, presently nominate him one of the said committees....

D'Ewes, Journal, p. 176.

Proceedings concerning Articles of Religion, 1571

[1 May, 1571]...Mr Serjeant Barham and Mr Attorney-General did desire from the Lords that a convenient number be sent presently unto their Lordships from this House for answer touching Articles for Religion. Whereupon my Lord Deputy of Ireland, Mr Treasurer, and divers others were sent for that purpose....And afterwards returned answer from the Lords that the Queen's Majesty, having been made privy to the said Articles, liketh very well of them and mindeth to publish them, and have them executed by the Bishops by direction of her Highness's regal authority of Supremacy of the Church of England, and not to have the same dealt in by Parliament.

D'Ewes, Journal, p. 180.

...Notwithstanding which message...the House of Commons still proceeded....

Ib. p. 185.

The Impounding of Bills, 1572

[22 May, 1572]... Upon declaration made unto this House by Mr Speaker from the Queen's Majesty that her Highness's pleasure is that from henceforth no bills concerning religion shall be preferred or received into this House, unless the same should be first considered and liked by the Clergy; And further, that her Majesty's pleasure is to see the two last bills read in this House touching rites and ceremonies: It is ordered by the House that the same bills shall be delivered unto her Majesty by all the Privy Council that are of this House, Mr Heneage, and Mr Doctor Wilson, Master of the Requests, or by any four of them....

[23 May, 1572]... Mr Treasurer reported to the House the delivery of the two bills of rites and ceremonies to her Majesty, together with the humble request of this House most humbly to beseech her Highness not to conceive ill opinion of this House, if it so were that her Majesty should not like well of the said bills or of the parties that preferred them. And declared further, that her Majesty seemed utterly to mislike of the first bill, and of him that brought the same into the House; and that her Highness's express will and pleasure was, that no preacher or minister should be impeached or indicted, or otherwise molested or troubled, as the preamble of the said bill did purport: adding these comfortable words farther, that her Majesty as Defender of the Faith will aid and maintain all good Protestants to the discouraging of all Papists[1].

D'Ewes, *Journal*, pp. 213-4.

The Question of Fasting, 1581

[21 January, 1581]... Mr Paul Wentworth made a motion for a public fast and daily preaching; the fast to be appointed upon some one certain day, but the preaching to be every morning at seven of the clock before the House did sit; that so they beginning their proceeding with the service and worship of God, He might the better bless them in all their consultations and actions....

...The House being divided, and many arguments being spent, *pro* and *con*, at length the said matter in question was put to voices, and the better side had the greater number, for there were 115 voices for it and but 100 against it; and so it was ordered, that as many of the House of Commons as convenient could should on the Sunday seven-night after, being the 29th day

[1] This is a curious perversion of the original meaning of the title 'Defender of the Faith.'

of this instant January, assemble and meet together in the Temple Church, there to hear preaching and join in prayer together, with humiliation and fasting, for the assistance of God's Spirit in all their consultations during this Parliament, and for the preservation of the Queen's Majesty and her realms; and that the preachers who should perform the work and service of that day might be appointed by such of her Majesty's Council as were of the House, to the intent that they may be discreet persons and keep convenient proportion of time, without intermeddling with matter of innovation or unquietness...(p. 282).

[24 January, 1581]...Mr Speaker declared himself for his own part to be very sorry for the error that happened here in this House upon Saturday last in resolving to have a public fast, and sheweth her Majesty's great misliking of the proceeding of this House therein, declaring it to fall out in such sort as he before did fear it would do, and advising the House to a submission in that behalf...(p. 283).

Mr Vice-Chamberlain declaring a message from her Majesty to this whole House, by her Highness's commandment shewed unto them her great admiration of[1] the rashness of this House in committing such an apparent contempt against her Majesty's express commandment, very lately before delivered unto the whole House by the Lord Chancellor in her Highness's name, as to attempt and put in execution such an innovation as the same fast without her Majesty's privity, and pleasure first known;...but ...declared,...to the great joy and comfort of this whole House, that her Majesty nevertheless, of her inestimable and princely good love and disposition, and of her Highness's most gracious clemency, construeth the said offence and contempt to be rash, unadvised, and an inconsiderate error of this House, proceeding of zeal and not of the wilful and malicious intent of this House or of any member of the same, imputing the cause thereof partly to her own lenity towards a brother of that man which now made this motion (Mr Wentworth), who in the last session was by this House for just causes reprehended and committed, but by her Majesty graciously pardoned and restored again[2]....And so persuading this House to employ the time about the necessary service of the Queen's Majesty and of the commonwealth, with due and grave regard to the ancient orders of this House, concludeth, that he thinketh it very meet that this whole House, or some one of this House by warrant of the House in the name of the said House, do make most humble submission unto her

[1] Astonishment at. [2] See p. 540 above.

Majesty, acknowledging the said offence and contempt, and in most humble and dutiful wise to pray remission of the same at her Highness's hands, with full purpose hereafter to forbear committing of the like offence....

[*After some debate*]...Then Mr Speaker asked the question whether Mr Vice-Chamberlain should carry the submission of the House to her Majesty, and it was agreed by consent of the whole House...(p. 284).

[25 January, 1581]....Mr Vice-Chamberlain brought answer from her Majesty of her most gracious acceptation of the submission, and of her Majesty's admonition and confidence of their discreet proceeding; with one special note, that they do not misreport the cause of her misliking, which was not for that they desired fasting and prayer, but for the manner in presuming to indict a form of public fast without order and without her privity, which was to intrude upon her authority ecclesiastical...(p. 285).

D'Ewes, Journal, pp. 282-5.

Mr Cope's Bill and Book, 1587

On Monday the 27th day of February [1587]...Mr Cope ...offered to the House a bill and a book written—the bill containing a petition that it might be enacted that all laws now in force touching ecclesiastical government should be void, and that it might be enacted that that book of common prayer now offered, and none other, might be received into the Church to be used; the book contained the form of prayer and administration of sacraments, with divers rites and ceremonies to be used in the Church—and desired that the book might be read. Whereupon Mr Speaker in effect used this speech: For that her Majesty before this time had commanded the House not to meddle with this matter...he desired that it would please them to spare the reading of it. Notwithstanding, the House desired the reading of it. Whereupon Mr Speaker willed the Clerk to read it. And the Clerk being ready to read it, Mr Dalton made a motion against the reading of it, saying that it was not meet to be read... and thought that this dealing would bring her Majesty's indignation against the House, thus to enterprise the dealing with those things which her Majesty especially had taken into her own charge and direction....And so the time being passed the House brake up, and the petition nor book read.

This done, her Majesty sent to Mr Speaker as well for this petition and book as for that other petition and book for the like effect that was delivered the last session of Parliament; which Mr Speaker sent to her Majesty...(p. 410).

On Wednesday the 1st day of March Mr Wentworth delivered unto Mr Speaker certain articles which contained questions touching the liberties of the House:...Whether this Council be not a place for any member of the same here assembled, freely and without controlment of any person or danger of laws, by bill or speech to utter any of the griefs of this commonwealth whatsoever touching the service of God, the safety of the Prince and this noble realm? Whether that great honour may be done unto God and benefit and service unto the Prince and State without free speech in this Council which may be done with it? Whether there be any Council which can make, add to, or diminish from the laws of the realm but only this Council of Parliament? Whether it be not against the orders of this Council to make any secret or matter of weight which is here in hand known to the Prince or any other concerning the high service of God, Prince, or State, without the consent of the House? Whether the Speaker or any other may interrupt any member of this Council in his speech used in this House, tending to any of the fore-named high services? Whether the Speaker may rise when he will, any matter being propounded, without consent of the House or not? Whether the Speaker may over-rule the House in any matter or cause there in question, or whether he is to be ruled or over-ruled in any matter or not? Whether the Prince and State can continue, stand, and be maintained without this Council of Parliament, not altering the government of the State?...(pp. 410–11).

These questions [the Speaker] pocketed up and shewed Sir Thomas Heneage, who so handled the matter that Mr Wentworth went to the Tower, and the questions not at all moved... (p. 411).

[4 March, 1587]...Sir John Higham made a motion to this House, for that divers good and necessary members thereof were taken from them[1], that it would please them to be humble petitioners to her Majesty for the restitution of them again to the House. To which speeches Mr Vice-Chamberlain answered, That if the gentlemen were committed for matter within the compass of the privilege of this House, then there might be a petition, but if not, then we should give occasion of her Majesty's farther displeasure, and therefore advised to stay until they heard more, which could not be long; and further he said touching the book

---

[1] Mr Cope and three others had been sent to the Tower on March 2 (D'Ewes, p. 411).

and the petition, her Majesty had for divers good causes best known to herself thought fit to suppress the same without any further examination thereof; and yet conceived it very unfit for her Majesty to give any account of her doings.... Mr Vice-Chamberlain did answer with this supposition only, that they might perhaps be committed for somewhat that concerned not the business or privilege of this House. But whatsoever he pretended, it is most probable they were committed for intermeddling with matters touching the Church, which her Majesty had so often inhibited, and which had caused so much disputation and so many meetings between the two Houses the last Parliament...(p. 412).

D'Ewes, *Journal*, pp. 410–2.

Mr Morice's Bills, 1593

[27 February, 1593]... Mr Morice, Attorney of the Court of Wards, moveth the House touching the hard courses of the bishops and ordinaries and other ecclesiastical judges in their courts, used towards sundry learned and godly ministers and preachers of this realm by way of inquisition... compelling them upon their own oaths to accuse themselves... and offereth unto Mr Speaker two bills, the one concerning the said inquisitions, subscriptions, and offering of oaths, and the other concerning the imprisonments upon their refusal to the said oaths...(p. 474).

[28 February, 1593]... Mr Speaker stood up and said, That he had a message to deliver from her Majesty to the said House. ...The message delivered me from her Majesty consisteth in three things: First, the end for which the Parliament was called; secondly, the speech which the Lord Keeper used from her Majesty; thirdly, what her pleasure and commandment now is. For the first, it is in me and my power (I speak now in her Majesty's person) to call Parliaments; it is in my power to end and determine the same; it is in my power to assent or dissent to anything done in Parliaments.... Her Majesty's pleasure being then delivered unto us by the Lord Keeper, it was not meant we should meddle with matters of state or causes ecclesiastical, for so her Majesty termed them. She wondered that any could be of so high commandment to attempt (I use her own words) a thing so expressly contrary to that which she had forbidden; wherefore with this she was highly offended. And because the words then spoken by my Lord Keeper are not now perhaps well remembered, or some be now here that were not then present, her Majesty's present charge and express commandment is that no bill touching the said matters of state or reformation in causes ecclesiastical be exhibited. And upon my allegiance I am commanded, if any such bill be exhibited, not to read it...(p. 478).

D'Ewes, *Journal*, pp. 474–8.

Queen's Permission to proceed in Ecclesiastical Reformation, 1597

[16 November, 1597]...*Nota*, That although her Majesty had formerly been exceeding unwilling and opposite to all manner of innovations in ecclesiastical government, yet understanding at this Parliament of divers gross and great abuses therein, she had on Monday the 14th day of this instant November foregoing not only given leave and liberty to the House of Commons to treat thereof, but also had encouraged them to proceed in the reformation thereof by a message brought unto the said House....

D'Ewes, *Journal*, p. 557.

Bill to amend the Act against Pluralities, 1601

[16 November, 1601]...The bill for redressing certain inconveniences in the statute of 21 Henr. VIII, c. 13, entitled An Act against Pluralities [*etc.*]...was read the second time and disputed whether it should be committed...Mr Serjeant Harris said, We seem to defend the privileges and customs of the House, but if we proceed to determine of this bill, Mr Speaker, we shall not only infringe a custom which we have ever observed, viz., to meddle with no matter that toucheth her Majesty's prerogative, but also procure her great displeasure....It was ordered by the more voices that it should be committed....

D'Ewes, *Journal*, pp. 639–41.

(4) Trade Questions in Parliament

The Debate on Monopolies, 1601

[20 November, 1601]...Mr Francis Bacon said...I confess the bill as it is is in few words, but yet ponderous and weighty. For the prerogative royal of the Prince, for my own part I ever allowed of it, and it is such as I hope shall never be discussed. The Queen, as she is our Sovereign, hath both an enlarging and restraining power. For by her prerogative she may first set at liberty things restrained by statute law or otherwise; and secondly by her prerogative she may restrain things which be at liberty. For the first, she may grant *non obstante* contrary to the penal laws, which truly according to my own conscience (and so struck himself on the breast) are as hateful to the subject as monopolies. For the second, if any man out of his own wit, industry, or endeavour finds out anything beneficial for the commonwealth, or brings in any new invention which every subject of this kingdom may use; yet in regard of his pains and travail therein her Majesty perhaps is pleased to grant him a privilege to use the same only by himself or his deputies for a certain time. This is one kind of monopoly. Sometimes there is a glut of things when they be in excessive quantity, as perhaps of corn, and her Majesty gives licence of transportation to one man; this is another kind of monopoly. Sometimes there is a scarcity or a small quantity, and the like is granted also. These and divers of this nature have been in trial both at the Common Pleas upon actions of trespass, where if the Judges do find the privilege good and beneficial to the commonwealth they then will allow it, otherwise disallow it; and also I know that her Majesty herself hath given commandment to her Attorney-General to bring divers of them since the last Parliament to trial in the Exchequer, since which time at least fifteen or sixteen to my knowledge have been repealed, some by her Majesty's own express commandment upon complaint made unto her by petition and some by *quo warranto* in the Exchequer. But, Mr Speaker, said he (pointing to the bill) this is no stranger in this place but a stranger in this vestment; the use hath been ever to humble ourselves unto her Majesty, and by petition desire to have our grievances remedied, especially when the remedy toucheth her so nigh in point of prerogative... (p. 644).

[20 November, 1601]...Dr Bennet said...In respect of a grievance out of the city for which I come, I think myself bound to speak that now which I had not intended to speak before—I mean, a monopoly of salt. It is an old proverb, *Sal sapit omnia*; fire and water are not more necessary. But for other monopolies, of cards (at which word Sir Walter Raleigh blushed), dice, starch, and the like, they are (because monopolies) I must confess very hurtful, though not all alike hurtful. I know there is a great difference in them, and I think if the abuses in this monopoly of salt were particularised this would walk in the fore rank...(p. 645).

[20 November, 1601]...Mr Francis Moore said...We have a law for the true and faithful currying of leather; there is a patent sets all at liberty, notwithstanding the statute. And to what purpose is it to do anything by Act of Parliament, when the Queen will undo the same by her prerogative?...(p. 645).

Mr Martin said, I do speak for a town that grieves and pines, for a country that groaneth and languisheth under the burden of monstrous and unconscionable substitutes to the monopolitans of starch, tin, fish, cloth, oil, vinegar, salt, and I know not what, nay, what not? The principalest commodities both of my town and country are ingrossed into the hand of those bloodsuckers of the commonwealth...(p. 645).

[21 November, 1601]...Sir Robert Wroth said...There have been divers patents granted since the last Parliament; these are now in being[1], viz. the patents for currants, iron, powder, cards, ox-shin bones, train oil, transportation of leather, lists of cloth, ashes, aniseeds, vinegar, sea-coals, steel, *aqua vitae*, brushes, pots, saltpetre, lead, accidences, oil, calamine stone[2], oil of blubber, fumathoes or dried pilchards in the smoke, and divers others.

Upon the reading of the patents aforesaid, Mr Hakewill, of Lincoln's Inn, stood up and asked thus: Is not bread there? Bread, quoth one. Bread, quoth another....This voice seems strange, quoth a third. No, quoth Mr Hakewill, if order be not taken for these, bread will be there before the next Parliament... (p. 648).

[24 November, 1601]...Upon some loud confusion in the House touching some private murmur of monopolies, Mr Secretary Cecil said...I have been (though unworthy) a member of this House in six or seven Parliaments, yet never did I see the House in so great confusion. I believe there never was in any Parliament a more tender point handled than the liberty of the subject, that when any is discussing this point he should be cried and coughed down. This is more fit for a grammar-school than a Court of Parliament. I have been a Councillor of State this twelve years, yet did I never know it subject to construction of levity and disorder. Much more ought we to be regardful in so great and grave an assembly. Why, we have had speeches upon speeches, without either order or discretion. One would have us proceed by bill and see if the Queen would have denied it; another, that the patents should be brought here before us and cancelled—and this were bravely done. Others would have us to proceed by way of petition, which course doubtless is best; but for the first, and especially for the second, it is so ridiculous that I think we should have as bad success as the Devil himself would have wished in so good a cause. Why, if idle courses had been followed, we should have gone forsooth to the Queen with a petition to have repealed a patent of monopoly of tobacco pipes...and I know

---

[1] For a list of monopolies laid before Parliament see D'Ewes, p. 650.
[2] 'Calamine stone' was an ore of zinc.

not how many conceits; but I wish every man to rest satisfied till the committees have brought in their resolutions...(p. 651).

[25 November, 1601]...Mr Speaker (after a silence, and every man marvelling why the Speaker stood up) spake to this effect: It pleased her Majesty to command me to attend upon her yesterday in the afternoon, from whom I am to deliver unto you all her Majesty's most gracious message....She said that partly by intimation of her Council, and partly by divers petitions that have been delivered unto her both going to the Chapel and also to walk abroad, she understood that divers patents which she had granted were grievous to her subjects, and that the substitutes of the patentees had used great oppressions. But she said she never assented to grant anything which was *malum in se*; and if in the abuse of her grant there be anything evil...she herself would take present order of reformation....Further order should be taken presently and not *in futuro*...and that some should be presently repealed, some suspended, and none put in execution but such as should first have a trial according to the law for the good of the people[1]...(p. 651).

Mr Francis Moore said, I must confess, Mr Speaker, I moved the House both the last Parliament and this touching this point, but I never meant...to set limits and bounds to the prerogative royal. But now, seeing it hath pleased her Majesty of herself, out of the abundance of her princely goodness, to set at liberty her subjects from the thraldom of those monopolies from which there was no town, city, or country free, I would be bold in one motion to offer two considerations to this House: The first, that Mr Speaker might go unto her Majesty to yield her most humble and hearty thanks and withal to shew the joy of her subjects for their delivery and their thankfulness unto her for the same; The other, that where divers speeches have been made extravagantly in this House, which doubtless have been told her Majesty and perhaps all ill-conceived of by her, I would therefore that Mr Speaker not only should satisfy her Majesty by way of apology therein but also humbly crave pardon for the same...(p. 653).

...So it was put to the question and concluded, That thanks should be returned by the Speaker, and some twelve were named to go with him as a convenient number, and entreaty made to the Privy Council to obtain liberty to be admitted...(p. 654).

[1] The Queen's surrender was not abject. 'There is no reason,' said Cecil, 'that all should be revoked, for the Queen means not to be swept out of her prerogative' (D'Ewes, p. 653).

The Queen's speech to a Deputation of the Commons,
30 November, 1601

[30 November, 1601]...In the afternoon, about three of
the clock, some seven score[1] of the House met at the great chamber before the Council Chamber in Whitehall. At length the
Queen came into the Council Chamber, where, sitting under the
Cloth of State at the upper end, the Speaker with all the company came in, and after three low reverences made [*he delivered
his speech*]...And after three low reverences made, he with the
rest kneeled down, and her Majesty began thus to answer herself,
viz.....(p. 658).

...Mr Speaker, you give me thanks, but I doubt me I have
more cause to thank you all than you me; And I charge you to
thank them of the House of Commons from me, for had I not
received a knowledge from you, I might have fallen into the lap
of an error only for lack of true information. Since I was Queen
yet did I never put my pen to any grant but that upon pretext
and semblance made unto me that it was both good and beneficial
to the subjects in general, though a private profit to some of my
ancient servants who had deserved well. But the contrary being
found by experience, I am exceeding beholden to such subjects
as would move the same at first. And I am not so simple to suppose
but that there be some of the Lower House whom these grievances
never touched; and for them I think they speak out of zeal for
their countries, and not out of spleen or malevolent affection as
being parties grieved; and I take it exceeding grateful from
them, because it gives us to know that no respects or interests
had moved them other than the minds they bear to suffer no
diminution of our honour and our subjects' love unto us. The zeal
of which affection tending to ease my people and knit their
hearts unto me, I embrace with a princely care; for above all
earthly treasure I esteem my people's love, more than which I
desire not to merit....I have ever used to set the last Judgment
Day before mine eyes, and so to rule as I shall be judged to answer
before a Higher Judge. To whose judgment seat I do appeal, that
never thought was cherished in my heart that tended not to my
people's good....And though you have had and may have many
Princes more mighty and wise sitting in this seat, yet you never
had or shall have any that will be more careful and loving....
And so I commit you all to your best fortunes and further counsels. And I pray you, Mr Comptroller, Mr Secretary, and you of

[1] The large number was the Queen's own suggestion (D'Ewes, p. 657).

T. D.   37

my Council, that before these gentlemen depart into their countries you bring them all to kiss my hand...(p. 659).

D'Ewes, Journal, pp. 644–60.

(5) Change of tone in later Parliaments

The Lord Keeper's Answer to the Speaker, 10 *April*, 1593

[10 April, 1593]...The Lord Keeper received instructions from the Queen, and afterwards replied unto the Speaker...That her Majesty did most graciously accept of these services and devotions of this Parliament, commending them that they had employed the time so well and spent it in so necessary affairs, save only that in some things they had spent more time than needed. But she perceived that some men did it more for their satisfaction than the necessity of the thing deserved. She misliketh also that such irreverence was shewed towards privy councillors, who were not to be accounted as common knights and burgesses of the House that are counsellors but during the Parliament, whereas the other are standing counsellors, and for their wisdom and great service are called to the Council of the State....

D'Ewes, Journal, p. 466.

The Queen's last Parliament, 1601

[30 October, 1601]...After which...room being made, the Queen came through the Commons to go to the Great Chamber, who graciously offering her hand to the Speaker he kissed it, but not one word she spake unto him; and as she went through the Commons very few said 'God save your Majesty,' as they were wont in all great assemblies; and so she returned back again to Whitehall by water.

D'Ewes, Journal, p. 602.

(c) The Privilege of Freedom from Arrest

Freedom from arrest in civil actions[1] was a privilege belonging to both Houses.

In the case of the Lords[2], by very ancient custom the person of a peer was 'for ever sacred and inviolable'[3] from arrest for debt or any claim arising out of property, it being an assumption in law that there would always be sufficient goods on his barony available for distraint in satisfaction of any debt. The privilege was, however, enforced in the Tudor period on wider grounds. In 1572, in the case of Lord Cromwell [p. 583], a peer arrested for contempt of an injunction of the Court of Chancery was

---

[1] The privilege did not usually extend to criminal process, as it was not allowed in cases of treason, felony, or breach of the peace.

[2] See Pike, pp. 259–60. [3] May, p. 106.

liberated by the Lords on the ground that the arrest was 'contrary to the ancient privilege and immunity time out of memory unto the Lords of Parliament and Peers of this realm in such case used and allowed.' The privilege was enjoyed by spiritual as well as temporal peers, although 'the prelates seem to have had it as prelates and not necessarily as peers.'[1] Freedom from arrest lost much of its value when arrest on mesne process, *i.e.* before judgment was given, was abolished in 1838. As arrest was one of the stages in the process of outlawry, the privilege also protected the person of a peer from outlawry in a civil action[2].

The privilege of the Commons is equally ancient[3]; but it only covered the period when Parliament was sitting, and 'a reasonable time' before and after the assembling of the House. In 1587, in Martin's case [p. 587] the House declined to 'limit a time certain,' but held that an arrest 20 days before the reassembling of a prorogued Parliament was within the period of privilege, although they refused to punish the breach of privilege committed, in consideration of the ignorance of the offender as to what constituted 'a reasonable time.'[4]

The important feature in the development of this privilege in the Tudor period is that it is now for the first time enforced by order of the House itself. Hitherto remedy for a violation of privilege had been obtained in one of two ways: (1) When a member was imprisoned on a final judgment of a court of law, the Commons, in order to save the right of the plaintiff to bring his action again when the 'time of privilege' had expired, were accustomed to obtain a special statute authorising the Lord Chancellor to issue a writ for his release; (2) when he was imprisoned on mesne process only, he was released by a writ of privilege, also issued out of Chancery. But in 1543 there occurred the important leading case of George Ferrers [p. 580], when the imprisoned member was released by the direct action of the House, and the officials who had resisted his liberation on this authority were punished for contempt. The King's speech approving the action of the Commons, shews how ready he was to look with favour upon the development of a privilege which made Parliament more important in the eyes of the community without interfering with the authority of the Crown. The precedent of 1543 was not at once followed up, and the practice of releasing members by writ of privilege still continued; but in 1593, in Fitzherbert's case [p. 588] a member was brought up from prison by the Serjeant-at-Arms to appear before the House; and from the end of the century the right of the House to enforce its privilege by independent action may be regarded as established. In Fitzherbert's case it was further held that a member was not protected by privilege who had been outlawed at the suit of the Crown.

The privilege of freedom from arrest is associated with certain sub-

[1] Pike, p. 259.   [2] *Ib.* p. 260.
[3] In Atwyll's case, in 1477, the Commons affirmed that it had existed 'whereof time that man's mind is not the contrary' (May, p. 101).
[4] The duration of the privilege of freedom from arrest has never been defined by Parliament, but it has been generally held to extend in the case of the Commons to 40 days after each prorogation and 40 days before the reassembling of Parliament (May, p. 107).

sidiary forms of privilege. (1) The freedom of members' servants from arrest was a natural corollary to the freedom of their masters in days when a retinue was indispensable for travelling. For the House of Lords, leading cases are those of James Digges [p. 585] and Robert Finnies [p. 585] in 1584 and William Hogan [p. 589] in 1601; in these the House acted independently through the Gentleman Usher of the Black Rod. In the case of Finnies the privilege was refused. For the House of Commons, the leading case is that of Edward Smalley in 1576 [p. 584], when the privilege was enforced, as in Ferrers's case, by the direct action of the House through the Serjeant-at-Arms[1]. It afterwards turned out that Smalley had fraudulently procured his own arrest in order to avoid paying a debt; and this illustrates the danger of abuse which led to the omission of members' servants from the Act of 1770 to confirm the privilege of members themselves[2]. (2) The protection of members from being impleaded in civil suits was claimed on the ground that a member absent on the service of Parliament could not properly defend his rights in a court of law. It therefore became customary to issue a writ of *supersedeas* to the judge, staying civil process during the time of privilege[3] [p. 587]. (3) Exemption from serving on a jury was well established in the Tudor period, and was applied in 1597 in Sir John Tracy's case [p. 588] by sending the Serjeant-at-Arms to summon the member to his duty in the House. (4) Exemption from being summoned as a witness in a court of law was in process of formation, but had not been completely acquired. It was established against the inferior courts of law, and Anthony Kyrle's case [p. 586] in 1585 and a case of 1597 [p. 589] shew that it was successfully asserted against the Star Chamber; but the Court of Chancery resisted the claim to privilege in the case of Richard Cook [p. 586] in 1585, and again in William Bowyer's case [p. 589] in 1597.

(1) Ferrers's Case, 1543

In the Lent season, whilst the Parliament yet continued, one George Ferrers, gentleman, servant to the King, being elected a burgess for the town of Plymouth in the county of Devonshire, in going to the Parliament House was arrested in London by a process out of the King's Bench at the suit of one White for the sum of 200 marks or thereabouts, wherein he was late afore condemned as a surety for the debt of one Weldon of Salisbury; which arrest being signified to Sir Thomas Moyle, knight, then Speaker of the Parliament, and to the knights and burgesses there, order was taken that the Serjeant of the Parliament, called St John, should forthwith repair to the Counter in Bread Street

---

[1] In Thomas Wickham's case, in 1571 (see p. 583), liberation had been effected by a writ of privilege.

[2] 10 Geo. III, c. 50; see May, p. 105.

[3] Early in the reign of James I a letter from the Speaker was substituted for the writ (May, p. 109).

(whither the said Ferrers was carried) and there demand delivery of the prisoner.

The Serjeant (as he had in charge) went to the Counter, and declared to the clerks there what he had in commandment. But they and other officers of the City were so far from obeying the said commandment as after many stout words they forcibly resisted the said Serjeant, whereof ensued a fray within the Counter gates between the said Ferrers and the said officers, not without hurt of either part; so that the said Serjeant was driven to defend himself with his mace of arms, and had the crown thereof broken by bearing off a stroke, and his man stricken down. During this brawl the Sheriffs of London...came thither, to whom the Serjeant complained of this injury, and required of them the delivery of the said burgess, as afore. But they, bearing with[1] their officers, made little account either of his complaint or of his message, rejecting the same contemptuously with much proud language, so as the Serjeant was forced to return without the prisoner....

The Serjeant, thus hardly intreated, made return to the Parliament House, and finding the Speaker and all the burgesses set in their places, declared unto them the whole case as it fell, who took the same in so ill part that they all together (of whom there were not a few as well of the King's Council as also of his Privy Chamber) would sit no longer without their burgess, but rose up wholly and repaired to the Upper House, where the whole case was declared by the mouth of the Speaker before Sir Thomas Audley, knight, then Lord Chancellor of England, and all the Lords and Judges there assembled, who, judging the contempt to be very great, referred the punishment thereof to the order of the Common House. They returning to their places again, upon new debate of the case, took order that their Serjeant should eftsoons[2] repair to the Sheriff of London, and require delivery of the said burgess without any writ or warrant had for the same, but only as afore.

And yet the Lord Chancellor offered there to grant a writ, which they of the Common House refused, being in a clear opinion that all commandments and other acts of proceeding from the Nether House were to be done and executed by their Serjeant without writ, only by show of his mace, which was his warrant. But before the Serjeant's return into London, the Sheriffs, having intelligence how heinously the matter was taken, became

[1] Probably in the sense of upholding.
[2] A second time.

somewhat more mild, so as upon the said second demand they delivered the prisoner without any denial. But the Serjeant, having then further in commandment from those of the Nether House, charged the said Sheriffs to appear personally on the morrow by eight of the clock before the Speaker in the Nether House, and to bring thither the clerks of the Counter and such officers as were parties to the said affray, and in like manner to take into his custody the said White, which wittingly procured the said arrest in contempt of the privilege of the Parliament.

Which commandment being done by the said Serjeant accordingly, on the morrow... the said Sheriffs and the same White were committed to the Tower of London, and the said clerk (which was the occasion of the affray) to a place there called 'Little Ease,' and the officer of London which did the arrest... with four other officers to Newgate, where they remained from the 28th until the 30th of March, and then they were delivered, not without humble suit made by the Mayor of London and other their friends....

...The King then being advertised of all this proceeding, called immediately before him the Lord Chancellor of England and his Judges, with the Speaker of the Parliament and other of the gravest persons of the Nether House, to whom he declared his opinion to this effect. First commending their wisdoms in maintaining the privileges of their House (which he would not have to be infringed in any point), he alleged that he, being head of the Parliament and attending in his own person upon the business thereof, ought in reason to have privilege for him and all his servants attending there upon him. So that if the said Ferrers had been no burgess, but only his servant, yet in respect thereof he was to have the privilege as well as any other. 'For I understand,' quoth he, 'that you not only for your own persons but also for your necessary servants, even to your cooks and horsekeepers, enjoy the said privilege....And further we be informed by our Judges that we at no time stand so highly in our estate royal as in the time of Parliament, wherein we as head and you as members are conjoined and knit together into one body politic, so as whatsoever offence or injury (during that time) is offered to the meanest member of the House is to be judged as done against our person and the whole Court of Parliament. Which prerogative of the Court is so great...as all acts and processes coming out of any other inferior courts must for the time cease and give place to the highest....And this may be a good example to other to learn good manners, and not to attempt anything against the privilege of this Court, but to take their time better.. . .

Holinshed, Chronicles (4to edn. 1808), iii, 824.

(2) Wickham's Case, 1571

[3 May, 1571].. . It was ordered that Sir Nicholas Poyntz, knight, one of the knights from the county of Gloucester, shall have a writ of privilege for his servant, Thomas Wickham, being attached in the City of London upon two actions of trespass, the one at the suit of Christopher Temple, goldsmith, and the other at the suit of Fr. Acton, grocer. D'Ewes, Journal, p. 181.

(3) Lord Cromwell's Case, 1572

[30 June, 1572].. . Whereas upon complaint and declaration made to the said Lords spiritual and temporal by Henry, Lord Cromwell, a Lord of the Parliament, that in a case between one James Tavernor against the said Lord Cromwell depending in the Court of Chancery, for not obeying to an injunction given in the said Court of Chancery, in the absence of the Lord Keeper of the Great Seal, at the suit of the said Tavernor the person of the said Lord Cromwell was by the Sheriff of the county of Norfolk attached, by virtue of a writ of attachment proceeding out of the said Court of Chancery, contrary to the ancient privilege and immunity time out of memory unto the Lords of Parliament and Peers of this realm in such case used and allowed, as on behalf of the said Lord Cromwell was declared and affirmed, wherein the said Lord Cromwell as a Lord of Parliament prayed remedy.

Forasmuch as, upon deliberate examination of this case in the said Parliament Chamber in the presence of the Judges and other of the Queen's Majesty's learned counsel there attendant in Parliament, and upon declaration of the opinions of the said Judges and learned counsel, there hath been no matter directly produced or declared whereby it did appear or seem to the said Lords of Parliament there assembled that by the common law or custom of the realm, or by any statute law, or by any precedent of the said Court of Chancery, it is warranted that the person of any Lord having place and voice in Parliament in the like case in the said Court of Chancery before this time hath been attached, so as the awarding of the said attachment at the suit of the said Tavernor against the said Lord Cromwell for anything as yet declared to the said Lords, appeareth to be derogatory and prejudicial to the ancient privilege claimed to belong to the Lords of this realm.

Therefore it is...ordered by consent of all the said Lords in Parliament there assembled, that the person of the said Lord Cromwell be from henceforth discharged of and from the said attachment....

D'Ewes, *Journal*, p. 203.

(4) Smalley's Case, 1576

[20 February, 1576]...Upon the question, and also upon the division of the House, it was ordered that Edward Smalley, yeoman, servant unto Arthur Hall, esquire, one of the burgesses for Grantham, shall have privilege....(p. 249).

[22 February, 1576]...Report was made by Mr Attorney of the Duchy...that the committees found no precedent for setting at large by the mace any person in arrest, but only by writ, and that by divers precedents of records perused by the said committees it appeareth that every knight, citizen, and burgess of this House which doth require privilege, hath used in that case to take a corporal oath before the Lord Chancellor or Lord Keeper...that the party for whom such writ is prayed came up with him and was his servant at the time of the arrest made; and that Mr Hall was thereupon moved by this House that he should repair to the Lord Keeper and make oath in form aforesaid, and then to proceed to the taking of a warrant for a writ of privilege for his said servant according to the said report of the said former precedents...(p. 249).

[27 February, 1576]...After sundry reasons and arguments, it was resolved that Edward Smalley, servant unto Arthur Hall, esquire, shall be brought hither to-morrow by the Serjeant, and set at liberty by warrant of the mace, and not by writ...(p. 250).

[28 February, 1576]...Edward Smalley...being this day brought to the Bar in the House by the Serjeant of this House and accompanied with two serjeants of London, was presently delivered from his imprisonment and execution according to the former judgment of this House, and the said serjeants of London discharged of their said prisoner; and immediately after that, the said serjeants of London were sequestered out of this House, and the said Edward Smalley was committed to the charge of the Serjeant of this House. And thereupon the said Edward Smalley was sequestered till this House should be resolved upon some former motions, whether the said Edward Smalley did procure himself to be arrested upon the said execution in the abusing and contempt of this House or not...(p. 251).

[7 March, 1576]...Upon the question, it was ordered that Mr Hall be sequestered the House while the matter touching the supposed contempt done to this House be argued and debated. Edward Smalley, upon the question, was adjudged guilty of contempt, and abusing of this House by fraudulent practice of procuring himself to be arrested upon the execution of his own assent, and intention to be discharged as well of his imprisonment as of the said execution.... Upon another question it was adjudged by the House that the said Smalley be for his misdemeanour and contempt committed to the prison of the Tower ...(p. 254).

[10 March, 1576]...Edward Smalley...appearing in this House this day at the Bar, it was pronounced unto him by Mr Speaker, in the name and by the appointment and order of this House, for execution of the former judgment of this House awarded against him, That he the said Edward Smalley shall be forthwith committed prisoner from this House to the Tower of London, and there remain for one whole month next ensuing from this present day, and further after the same month expired, until such time as good and sufficient assurance shall be had and made for payment of £100 [to his creditor]...and also forty shillings for the Serjeant's fees...(p. 258).

D'Ewes, *Journal*, pp. 249–58.

(5) Digges's Case, 1584

[1 December, 1584]...Whereas James Digges, one of the ordinary gentlemen of my Lord's Grace of Canterbury, was committed to the Fleet upon a *reddit se* in the Exchequer since the beginning of this present Parliament; the Lords, at the motion of the Lord Archbishop of Canterbury, claiming the ancient privilege of this High Court, gave commandment to the Gentleman Usher that the said James should be brought before them. And this day the said Lords having openly heard both Sir Roger Manwood, then Lord Chief Baron of the Exchequer, and the same James Digges, they ordered that the said Digges, by virtue of the privilege of this Court, should be enlarged and set at liberty....

D'Ewes, *Journal*, p. 314.

(6) Case of Robert Finnies, 1584

[7 December, 1584]...Whereas the Lord Viscount Bindon moved the Lords for the privilege of the House for Robert Finnies, alleging that he was his servant, the Lords gave commandment to the Gentleman Usher to go to the Counter in Wood Street, where the said Robert Finnies then lay upon an execution, and to bring him and the parties that arrested him before them. And this day the said Lords, after the hearing of the cause, thought it not convenient that the said Robert Finnies should enjoy the privilege of this House, as well because he claimed not the privilege when he was first arrested nor in the Counter when he was charged with the execution, as also for that he was not a menial servant nor yet ordinary attendant upon the said Viscount....

D'Ewes, *Journal*, p. 315.

(7) Richard Cook's Case, 1585

[10 February, 1585]...Upon a motion this day made touching the opinion of this House for privilege in a case of *subpoena* out of the Chancery served upon Richard Cook, esquire, a member of this House...It was ordered, That Mr Recorder of London, Mr Sands, and Mr Cromwell, attended on by the Serjeant of this House, shall presently repair in the name of the whole House into the body of the Court of Chancery, and there to signify unto the Lord Chancellor and the Master of the Rolls that by the ancient liberties of this House the members of the same are privileged from being served with *subpoenas*....

[11 February, 1585]...Mr Recorder of London, Mr Cromwell, and Mr Sands being returned from the Chancery, did declare unto the House that they have been in Chancery within the Court and there were very gently and courteously heard in the delivery of the message and charge of this House committed unto them; and were answered by the Lord Chancellor, that he thought this House had no such liberty of privilege for *subpoenas* as they pretended, neither would he allow of any precedents of this House committed unto them formerly used in that behalf, unless this House could also prove the same to have been likewise thereupon allowed and ratified also by the precedents in the said Court of Chancery....

D'Ewes, *Journal*, p. 347.

(8) Kyrle's Case, 1585

[11 February, 1585]...Mr Anthony Kyrle was brought to the Bar by the Serjeant of this House, and charged by Mr Speaker in the name of this whole House with a contempt to this House, for that he had served Alban Stepneth, esquire, being a member of this House,...with a *subpoena* out of the Star

Chamber in the Parliament time, and within the Palace of Westminster, as the said Mr Stepneth was coming to this House to give his attendance there, and further afterwards procured an attachment out of the said Court against him....It was at last resolved by this House, That the said Mr Kyrle had committed a great contempt to this whole House and the liberties and privileges of the same...And thereupon ordered and adjudged by this House, That the said Anthony Kyrle shall for his said contempt be committed prisoner to the Serjeant's ward and custody, there to remain during the pleasure of this House, and shall also satisfy and pay unto the said Mr Stepneth...his costs and charges....   D'Ewes, *Journal*, p. 348.

(9) Martin's Case, 1587

[11 March, 1587]...This day the committees made report of the privilege of Mr Martin, a member of this House, arrested upon mesne process by White above 20 days before the beginning of this Parliament holden by prorogation,...and in respect that the House was divided about it in opinion, Mr Speaker, with the consent of the House, the sooner to grow to some certainty of the judgment of the House in this cause, moved these questions to the House, viz.

First, Whether they would limit a time certain or a reasonable time to any member of the House for his privilege?

The House answered, A convenient time.

Secondly, Whether Mr Martin was arrested within this reasonable time?

The House answered, Yea.

Thirdly, If White should be punished for arresting Martin?

The House answered, No, because the arrest was 20 days before the beginning of the Parliament, and unknown to him that would be taken for reasonable time....

D'Ewes, *Journal*, p. 414.

(10) Procedure by writ of Supersedeas, 1589

[21 February, 1589]...Upon a motion made by Mr Harris, that divers members of this House having writs of *nisi prius* brought against them to be tried at the assizes in sundry places of this realm to be holden and kept in the circuits of this present vacation, and that writs of *supersedeas* might be awarded in those cases in respect of the privilege of this House due and appertaining to the members of the same; It is agreed, that those of this House which shall have occasion to require such benefit of privilege in that behalf may repair unto Mr Speaker to declare unto him the state of their cases, and that he upon his discretion (if the cases shall so require) may direct the warrant of this House to the Lord Chancellor of England for the awarding of such writs of *supersedeas* accordingly....

D'Ewes, *Journal*, p. 436.

(11) Fitzherbert's Case, 1593

[7 March, 1593]...Sir Edward Hobby, moving the cause of Mr Fitzherbert his bringing up unto this House by a writ of *habeas corpus cum causa* from the Lord Keeper, sheweth, That he hath moved the Lord Keeper touching the said writ, and that his Lordship thinketh best, in regard of the ancient liberties and privileges of this House, that a Serjeant-at-Arms be sent by order of this House for the said Mr Fitzherbert at his own charge, by reason whereof he may be brought hither to this House without peril of further being arrested by the way, and the state of this cause to be considered of and examined when he shall be come hither: Which was thereupon well liked and allowed by this House.

D'Ewes, *Journal*, p. 490.

[5 April, 1593]...The business so much before agitated touching Mr Fitzherbert received this day the final resolution of the House...which said case was singly this. Thomas Fitzherbert's being elected a burgess of the Parliament, two hours after his election and before the return of the writ to the Sheriff with the indenture of his election, the said Sheriff arresteth him upon a *capias utlagatum* in an outlawry after judgment at the Queen's suit...Upon all which matters there grew two questions: First, whether the said Mr Fitzherbert were a member of the House; And secondly, admitting he were, yet whether he ought to have privilege....The judgment of the House was, That Thomas Fitzherbert was by his election a member thereof, yet that he ought not to have privilege in three respects. First, because he was taken in execution before the return of the indenture of his election; Secondly, because he had been outlawed at the Queen's suit and was now taken in execution for her Majesty's debt; Thirdly and lastly, in regard that he was so taken by the sheriff neither *sedente Parliamento*, nor *eundo*, nor *redeundo*.

D'Ewes, *Journal*, p. 518.

(12) Tracy's Case, 1597

[22 November, 1597]...Sir Edward Hobby moved the House for privilege for Sir John Tracy, being a member of this

House and now presently at the Common Pleas to be put on a jury. Whereupon the Serjeant of this House was presently sent with the mace to call the said Sir John Tracy to his attendance in this House, which was thereupon so done accordingly, and the said Sir John then returned to this House.

D'Ewes, *Journal*, p. 560.

(13) Subpoenas from the Chancery and Star Chamber, 1597

[28 November, 1597]... Mr William Bowyer shewed, that being a member of this House he was this day served with a *subpoena* to appear in the Chancery by one James Biddell, and so moved for privilege;...

Mr Combes and Mr Henry Powle, being likewise members of this House, do shew, that they were this day served with a *subpoena ad testificandum* in the Star Chamber by one Anne, the wife of one Thomas Wye, gentleman; and so in like manner moving for privilege, the Serjeant of this House was thereupon charged by this House to bring in the said James Biddell and the said Anne, the wife of the said Thomas, to appear in this House and answer the said contempt.... D'Ewes, *Journal*, p. 564.

(14) Hogan's Case, 1601

[16 November, 1601]... A motion was made again by some of the Lords touching William Hogan, prisoner in the Fleet, that he might be sent for out of the same prison.... Upon which motion it was debated by what course the said Hogan should be brought out of the Fleet, being then in execution, whether by warrant to be directed from the Lords to the Lord Keeper, requiring him to grant forth a writ in her Majesty's name for the bringing of the said Hogan from thence, or by immediate direction and order from the House to the Gentleman Usher or Serjeant-at-Arms, without any such writ. Which being put to the question by the Lord Keeper, it was resolved and ordered by the general consent of the House that it should be done by immediate direction and order from the House.... And accordingly ordered, that the said William Hogan should be sent for and brought before the Lords by the Gentleman Usher....

D'Ewes, *Journal*, p. 604.

(d) *The right of either House to commit to prison*

What made it possible for the House of Commons to vindicate its privileges was the power to commit to prison. As the Court of King's

Bench can punish contempt of court, so either House of the High Court of Parliament can punish breaches of privilege.

By very ancient usage the House of Lords can summon persons before it by simple order of the House, and as the highest court of record in the kingdom, it can fine, sentence to imprisonment for a fixed time, and take security for good behaviour; and the acts of the House in this capacity are not controllable by the courts of law[1].

The right of the Commons to commit does not now extend so far. In Fitzherbert's case in 1593[2] and again in 1604 the Commons claimed to be a court of record[3], and therefore to fine, and to imprison for a fixed time; but since the middle of the 17th century the claim has been abandoned. The Commons do not now fine, and they do not imprison beyond the end of the session; but the right to commit for this limited time is sufficient to protect the other privileges.

The right to commit to prison could be used for other purposes besides the protection of privilege. It was employed in the Tudor period to punish members of the House itself. In 1581 Arthur Hall [p. 592], a member of the House, was imprisoned for six months, fined 500 marks, and expelled the House, for slandering the House and 'sundry particular members' of it; and in 1584 Dr Parry [p. 593] was committed and eventually expelled the House in connexion with a violent speech which he delivered on the bill against Jesuits and seminary priests. Further, in 1581 the House fined all persons absent during the whole session without sufficient excuse [p. 593].

The powers of the House were also used against non-members in 1571 [below], 1576 [p. 591], and 1584, [p. 591], to secure the privacy of debate and to prevent the intrusion of strangers; in 1576 [p. 591] to punish assault; in 1581 [p. 592] to deal with 'disordered serving-men'; and in 1586 [p. 594] to punish an attack upon the justice of the House. In connexion with the secrecy of debate, the Speaker's admonition to the whole House in 1589 [p. 591] that speeches delivered by members should not be 'used as table-talk' is worthy of consideration.

(1) Privacy of Debate, 1571–89

On Thursday the 5th day of April [1571] Thomas Clark and Anthony Bull, of the Inner Temple, London, gentlemen, were by this House committed to the Serjeant's ward...for that they presumed to enter into this House and were no members of the same, as themselves at the Bar confessed.

D'Ewes, *Journal*, p. 156.

---

[1] 'If the matter is to rest upon precedent...there seems nothing (decency and discretion excepted) to prevent their repeating the sentences of James I's reign, whipping, branding, hard labour for life. Nay, they might order the Usher of the Black Rod to take a man from their bar and hang him up in the lobby' (Hallam, iii, 286).

[2] 'It was in the end resolved by this House, that this House, being a court of record, would take no notice of any matter of fact at all in the said case, but only of matter of record' (D'Ewes, p. 502).

[3] May, p. 89.

[13 February, 1576]... Charles Johnson, of the Inner Temple, gentleman, being examined at the Bar for coming into this House this present day (the House sitting) confessing himself to be no member of this House, is ordered that Mr Wilson Master of the Requests, Mr Recorder of London, and Mr Cromwell to examine him (wherein he feigned to excuse himself by ignorance); he was committed to the Serjeant's ward till further order should be taken by this House.... *D'Ewes, Journal*, p. 248.

[28 November, 1584]...One being no member of this House, being found to have sit here this present day by the space of two hours, during the whole time of the speeches delivered by Mr Chancellor and Mr Vice-Chamberlain...did upon examination confess his name to be Richard Robinson, and that he was by occupation a skinner....Whereupon himself having been stripped to his shirt and his pockets all searched, the custody and further examination of him was by this House referred to Mr Recorder of London, Mr Topcliffe, Mr Beale, and another....

[30 November, 1584]...[*This Committee's report having been read by the Clerk of the Parliament*]...the said Robinson was brought to the Bar and was there censured by the House...to suffer imprisonment in the Serjeant's ward until Saturday next, and then having swore to keep secret what he had heard, to be released.... *D'Ewes, Journal*, p. 334.

[15 February, 1589]...Sir Edward Hobby moved (he said) upon good cause, that Mr Speaker do give admonition unto this whole House that speeches used in this House by the members of the same be not any of them made or used as table-talk, or in any wise delivered in notes of writing to any person or persons whatsoever not being members of this House, as of late (is thought) hath been done in this present session: And thereupon, by consent of this House, admonition was given by Mr Speaker in that behalf accordingly, shewing unto them that they are the Common Council of the Realm.... *D'Ewes, Journal*, p. 432.

(2) Punishment of Assault, 1576

[29 February, 1576]...Walter Williams, being brought to the Bar, confessed that he did strike Mr Bainbrigge, and that he offered to strike at him with his dagger: Whereupon it was ordered that he remain in the Serjeant's ward till the order of this House be further known.... *D'Ewes, Journal*, p. 251.

(3) Repression of Disorder, 1581

[1 February, 1581]...It is ordered, that Mr Speaker, in the name of this House, do require the Warden of the Fleet, being a member of this House, that he do cause from henceforth two of his servants to attend at the stair-head near unto the outer door of this House, and to lay hands upon two or three of such disordered serving-men or pages as shall happen to use such lewd disorder and outrage as hath been accustomed to be exercised there this Parliament time, to the end they may thereupon be brought into this House and receive such punishment as to this House shall seem meet.

D'Ewes, *Journal*, p. 290.

(4) Case of Arthur Hall, 1581

[14 February, 1581]...Where it was informed unto this House...that Arthur Hall, of Grantham in the county of Lincoln, esquire, had, since the last session of this Parliament made, ...published a book, dedicated unto Sir Henry Knyvett, knight, a good member of this House, without his privity, liking, or allowance, in part tending greatly to the slander and reproach, not only of Sir Robert Bell, knight, deceased, late Speaker of this Parliament, and of sundry particular members of this House, but also of the proceedings of this House in the same last session of Parliament in a cause that concerned the said Arthur Hall and one Smalley, his man[1]; and that there was also contained a long discourse tending to the diminishment of the ancient authority of this House. And that thereupon by order of this House the said Arthur Hall was sent for by the Serjeant of this House to appear ...which he did accordingly. Whereupon being called to the Bar and charged by the Speaker with the information given against him, he confessed the making and setting forth thereof. Whereupon the said Arthur Hall being sequestered, the House did presently appoint divers committees[2] to take a more particular examination of the said cause, and of all such as had been doers therein...(p. 296).

...It was...resolved and ordered, that he should remain in the ...prison of the Tower by the space of six months, and so much longer as until himself should willingly make a particular revocation or retractation under his hand in writing of the said errors and slanders contained in the said book, to the satisfaction of this House, or of such order as this House shall take for the same, during the continuance of this present session of Parliament.

[1] See p. 584 above.   [2] See note on p. 539 above.

And. . .it was also. . .resolved and ordered, that a fine should be assessed by this House to the Queen's Majesty's use upon the said Arthur Hall for his said offence. . .and. . .that the same fine should be 500 marks. . . . It was likewise resolved and ordered, that the said Arthur Hall should presently be removed, severed, and cut off from being any longer a member of this House during the continuance of this present Parliament, and that the Speaker by authority from this House should direct a warrant from this House to the Clerk of the Crown Office in the Chancery for awarding of the Queen's Majesty's writ to the Sheriff of the said county of Lincoln for a new burgess to be returned into this present Parliament for the said borough of Grantham, in the lieu and stead of the said Arthur Hall so as before disabled any longer to be a member of this House. . .(p. 298).

D'Ewes, *Journal*, pp. 296–8.

(5) Fining of Absentees, 1581

[18 March, 1581]. . .It is ordered and resolved by this House upon the question, That every knight for the shire that hath been absent this whole session of Parliament without excuse allowed by this House, shall have by order and appointment of this House £20 for a fine set and assessed upon him to her Majesty's use for such his default, and for and upon every citizen, burgess, and baron[1] for the like default, £10. . . .   D'Ewes, *Journal*, p. 309.

(6) Case of Dr Parry, 1584

[17 December, 1584]. . .The bill against Jesuits, seminary priests, and such like disobedient subjects. . .passed the House with little or no argument, except it were from one Doctor Parry, who in very violent terms spake directly against the whole bill, affirming it to savour of treasons, to be full of blood, danger, despair, and terror or dread to the English subjects of this realm, our brethren, uncles, and kinsfolks, and also full of confiscations . . .Whereupon Dr Parry, by order of this House, was appointed to be sequestered into the outer room of this House into the Serjeant's custody. . . .And afterwards being brought to the Bar and there kneeling upon his knee, he was told by Mr Speaker, in the name of the whole House, that if he thought good the House was contented to hear him what reasons he could yield for himself in maintenance of his said speeches against the aforesaid bill. . . . Whereupon. . .he answered. . .that as before when he spake to the bill. . .he then concealed his said reasons from this House, so

[1] Of the Cinque Ports.

he would now conceal the same still. Whereupon being sequestered again, it was resolved, That for that he did speak to the bill and gave his negative voice so directly and undutifully, and in contempt of this House would not shew his reasons for the same, being merely against the ancient orders and usage of this High Court... That he should be committed to the Serjeant's ward till the matter shall be further considered of by this House, the day being then very far spent....

[18 December, 1584]... Mr Vice-Chamberlain also declared unto this House, that her Majesty having been made privy unto the misbehaviour of Mr Doctor Parry yesterday shewed in this House, and of the order of this House taken therein with him for the same, her Highness doth not only deem him to have given just cause of offence unto this House in the same his misdemeanour, but also doth very well allow of the grave discretion of this House in forbearing for the time to use any sharp course of correction against him for his said offence, in respect that he had said he reserved his reasons to be imparted to her Majesty only; which as he had discovered unto some of the Lords of the Council by her Highness's appointment, and that partly to the satisfaction of her Majesty, so her Highness did think that upon his humble submission unto this House, with a dutiful acknowledgment of his fault, this House would the rather dispense with him therein. Which done, Mr Doctor Parry was called to the Bar... And then kneeling upon his knee in very humble manner, affirmed directly that he had very undutifully misbehaved himself, and had rashly and unadvisedly uttered those speeches he used, and was with all his heart very sorry for it.... Whereupon, being sequestered again out of the House, it was, after some arguments and speeches had, resolved, That upon his said acknowledgment of his fault and his humble submission, he should be received into this House again as a member of the same and take his place as before, so that he would afterwards use himself in good sort as he ought to do[1]....

D'Ewes, *Journal*, pp. 340-2.

(7) Case of John Bland, 1586

[13 March, 1586]... Upon report made unto this House by Mr Speaker, that one John Bland, a currier of London, had given out to some honourable persons... that the curriers could have no

---

[1] On 18 February, 1585, as Dr Parry was now a prisoner in the Tower on a charge of high treason, he was expelled the House, and a new writ was issued for his constituency of Queenborough (D'Ewes, p. 352).

justice in this House... it was thereupon resolved, That Sir William
Moore, Mr Cromwell, and Mr Utrecht should presently examine
the said Bland, being now without the door of this House, who
did then go forth for that purpose accordingly; and returning
back into the said House from the examination of the said John
Bland... it was afterwards resolved... that in respect he was a
poor man and had a great charge of children, he should, if he
would acknowledge his fault and submit himself to the satisfaction of this House, be then delivered, paying his fees, and that he
should pay to the Serjeant therein for his fee twenty shillings,
and taking the oath of supremacy....

D'Ewes, Journal, p. 366.

(e) The right to determine questions connected with membership of the House of Commons

The right of the House of Commons to determine questions connected
with membership of the House was asserted for the first time in the Tudor
period. It was applied in two ways: to determine contested elections, and
to decide the qualifications of members.

In earlier times the sheriffs, in making their election returns, had been
liable to interference, either from the Crown, or from great lords anxious
to influence the elections by procuring false returns. The position was,
however, regularised by the Act of 1406[1], which prescribed the time and
manner of the election of knights of the shire, and prevented the falsification
of the returns by requiring them to be made into Chancery, authenticated
by the seals of the electors. Questions arising out of the returns so made
were at first decided by the Lords, who, in virtue of an opinion of the Judges
delivered in 1453, claimed to be 'the supreme arbiters with regard to
privilege of Parliament'[2]; but in the Tudor period the right was claimed
by the Commons. Committees were appointed in 1581 and again in 1584
to examine the returns[3]; and this supplied a precedent for their action in
1586 in the important case of the County of Norfolk [p. 596]. There had
been an election for the county, and when the return was made into Chancery
the discovery of some irregularity led to a second writ being issued by the
Chancellor. The matter was referred to in the House, and the Queen thereupon directed the Speaker to express her displeasure to the House, as the
returns belonged 'to the charge and office of the Lord Chancellor,' whom
she had instructed to confer with the Judges and to take such action as
justice might require. The Commons, nevertheless, appointed a committee,
which reported in favour of the first return [p. 597]. When the next
Parliament met in 1593, the duty of examining the returns was entrusted
to the standing committee of privileges, first appointed in 1589 but now
enlarged so as to include all the Privy Councillors in the House and 30
other members.

[1] 7 Henr. IV, c. 15.　　　　　[2] Pike, p. 249.
[3] Prothero, p. xci.

Doubtful points connected with the qualification of members were no longer referred to the Lords and the Judges, but were decided as they arose by the House of Commons itself. In 1550, in Russell's case [below], the Commons held that the eldest son of an earl could sit in the House. In 1553, in the case of Alexander Nowell [below], a committee of the House reported that a spiritual person having a seat in Convocation could not also sit in the Commons. In the same year the House called for the charter of the borough of Maidstone, and excluded its representatives until their right to sit was determined[1]. In 1566 the House disqualified a lunatic by applying for a writ for a new election.

(1) Russell's Case, 1550

[21 January, 1550]... It is ordered, That Sir Francis Russell, son and heir-apparent of the now Earl of Bedford, shall abide in this House in the state he was before....

Commons' Journals, i, 15.

(2) Nowell's Case, 1553

[13 October, 1553]... It is declared by the Commissioners[2] that Alex. Nowell, being Prebendary in Westminster, and thereby having voice in the Convocation House, cannot be a member of this House; and so agreed by the House, and the Queen's writ to be directed for another burgess in that place.

Commons' Journals, i, 27

(3) Case of the County of Norfolk, 1586

[3 November, 1586]... Mr Speaker shewed unto the House, that he received commandment from my Lord Chancellor from her Majesty to signify unto them, that her Highness was sorry this House was troubled the last sitting thereof with the matter touching the choosing and returning of the knights for the county of Norfolk: a thing in truth impertinent[3] for this House to deal withal, and only belonging to the charge and office of the Lord Chancellor, from whence the writs for the same elections issued out and are thither returnable again. And also that her Majesty had appointed the said Lord Chancellor to confer therein with the Judges; and so thereupon examining the said returns, and the Sheriff touching the matter and circumstances of his proceedings

---

[1] Pollard, *Parliament*, p. 326.

[2] *I.e.* the Committee of six members of the House, which had been appointed on October 12 to look into the question. Mr Nowell had been elected for the borough of Looe in Cornwall. In 1560 he was appointed Dean of St Paul's.

[3] Irrelevant.

in the said elections, to set down such course for making the true return as to justice and right shall therein appertain...(p. 393).

[11 November, 1586]...Mr Cromwell, one of the committees for the examination of writs and the returns for the knights of the county of Norfolk,...maketh report:...They do find that the first writ and return, both in manner and form, was perfect and also duly executed, and the second writ not so...; They understood by the...Clerk of the Crown...that the Lord Chancellor and the Judges had resolved, That the said first writ should be returned as that which was in all parts duly and rightly executed, and not the second....One of the committees, assenting with the residue in opinion of [the] validity of the said first writ and return and of the invalidity of the said second, and also in resolution that the explanation and ordering of the case as it standeth appertaineth only to the censure of this House, moved notwithstanding in the Committee, That two of the committees might be sent to the said Lord Chancellor to understand what his Lordship had done in the matter; which the residue thought not convenient, first, for that they were sufficiently satisfied therein by divers of themselves, but principally in respect they thought it very prejudicial and injurious to the privilege and liberties of this House to have the said cause decided or dealt in in any sort by any others than only by such as are members of this House; and that albeit they thought very reverently (as becometh them) of the said Lord Chancellor and Judges, and know them to be competent judges in their places, yet in this case they took them not for judges in Parliament in this House; and so further required that (if it were so thought good) Mr Farmer and Mr Gresham might take their oaths, and be allowed of and received into this House by force of the said first writ, as so allowed and admitted only by the censure of this House and not as allowed of by the said Lord Chancellor or Judges. Which was agreed unto accordingly by the whole House, and so ordered also to be set down and entered by the Clerk...(p. 398).   D'Ewes, *Journal*, pp. 393–8.

Finance

Although in the Tudor period the control of Parliament over taxation was clearly recognised, only a fraction of the royal revenue was provided by taxation; by far the greater part of it came from sources over which Parliament had no control. The royal exchequer was continuously fed (1) by the permanent hereditary revenue, and (2) by indirect taxation upon commodities. With respect to the first of these, the King was independent in theory as well as in practice; with respect to the second, he was dependent as a matter of form, but as a matter of form only, upon a Parliamentary vote, passed at the beginning of each reign, by which this branch of revenue was assigned to the Sovereign for life. This was the King's 'own,' and the ancient tradition of the constitution required him to 'live of his own.' But as during the Tudor period the productiveness of this revenue tended to decline and the expenses of government as a purchaser of commodities and an employer of labour tended to increase, it was necessary to fall back upon other ways of obtaining money, and among these other ways a place may be assigned to parliamentary grants.

§ 1. Permanent Revenue

(1) *Income from Crown lands.* The Crown lands were large and the Dissolution of the Monasteries increased them, but from the point of view of the royal revenue they were not very productive. When the King was in need of ready money the most convenient expedient for raising it was by alienating Crown lands—usually by granting for money down a long lease at a low or even a nominal rent. A good many of Henry VIII's leases fell in to Elizabeth, but the need of money led to the same process being repeated, and at the end of the 16th century the yield to this branch of revenue was reckoned at only £32,000 a year[1].

(2) *Feudal incidents,* including reliefs, escheats, the profits of wardships and marriages, and the rarely recurring right to an aid. This last fell due once only during the Tudor period—in 1504, when Henry VII claimed the aids in respect of the knighting of his eldest son Arthur and the marriage of his eldest daughter Margaret, and by a bargain with his Parliament accepted a grant of £30,000 in lieu thereof [p. 600]. At the time when the negotiation was carried through, Margaret had been already married for two years; and Arthur, who had been actually knighted in 1489 at the age of three, had in 1504 been dead for two years.

(3) *Purveyance and preemption.* Purveyance was the ancient royal right of demanding horses and carts and personal services from the districts through which the royal progresses passed, at prices to be fixed by the royal officers, and paid for by Exchequer tallies entitling the victim to deduct what was due to him from the next taxes which he had to pay. Preemption was the

---

[1] By the reign of William III it had fallen as low as £6000 a year (Anson, II, ii, 134).

same right applied to the purchase of provisions, but 'purveyance' is often used to cover both. These rights had come to be used as a source of revenue, although one of spasmodic productiveness. Thus Elizabeth for a time victualled her navy by means of warrants of purveyance; and twice in her reign she purveyed beer upon her own terms and then sold it abroad at a profit[1].

(4) *Ecclesiastical firstfruits and tenths*, originally paid to the Papacy, were annexed to the Crown by statute[2] in 1534, and remained part of the royal revenue until the establishment of Queen Anne's Bounty in 1703, when they were assigned to the augmentation of poor livings. The firstfruits and tenths were under Henry VIII, and still continue to be, assessed according to the valuations of livings set down in the *Valor Ecclesiasticus*[3].

(5) *Proceeds of justice.* In earlier times justice had been administered mainly for the sake of the profits, but by the 16th century it had ceased to be a very lucrative source of revenue. At the beginning of the Tudor period, however, Empson and Dudley had greatly increased the yield to revenue under this head, both by compositions for outlawry and fines for breaches of the law. Under this head should be noticed also the fines levied in the Court of Star Chamber, although these were not always intended to be paid in full[4].

(6) *Customs, tonnage, and poundage.* The ancient customs on wool, wool-fells, and leather had been levied since the reign of Edward I; and the taxes on each tun of imported wines and every pound of imported or exported merchandise other than the staple commodities, date from Edward III. Since the reign of Edward IV it had been usual for Parliament to grant tonnage and poundage to the Sovereign for life at the beginning of his reign[5]. The revenue from this kind of taxation upon trade was not very productive, although it improved towards the end of the reign of Elizabeth. In 1585 the customs were farmed out at £24,000 a year[6]; but in 1590 they were raised to £50,000[7]. The earlier unproductiveness was partly due to a bad system of administration, which allowed on the one hand of pilfering on the part of those engaged in the collection of revenue, and on the other of smuggling by those who were trying to evade the payment of it. For this the business capacity of the Tudor officials supplied a remedy. In 1559 the old method of assessing taxes upon the value sworn to by the merchant [p. 602], which gave opportunity for small frauds, was abandoned, and the amounts to be charged on the various kinds of goods were determined by statute[8]. In the same year also a stringent Act [p. 602] was passed against smuggling and other frauds upon the revenue.

(7) *Impositions.* These were additional customs, over and above those granted to the Crown at the beginning of a reign, imposed in virtue of the

---

[1] Sinclair, pt. i, pp. 127–8.   [2] 26 Henr. VIII, c. 3.

[3] Under modern conditions the burden of firstfruits and tenths is not a heavy one. Thus the living of Hockwold in Norfolk, with a net income in 1920 of £500, is valued in the *Valor Ecclesiasticus* at £9. 13*s*. 11½*d*. The Rector at his institution pays £9. 13*s*. 11*d*. as firstfruits, and thereafter 19*s*. 4*d*. a year as tenths.

[4] See p. 256 above.   [5] Prothero, p. lxxii.

[6] *Ib.* p. lxxiii.   [7] Sinclair, pt. i, p. 128.

[8] 1 Eliz. c. 20, printed in Prothero, p. 26.

royal prerogative over trade, but imposed not primarily to raise a revenue but to protect the native merchant against the alien. Such a policy was not unpopular, and in order to give better facilities for carrying it out an Act of 1534[1] authorised Henry VIII during his life not only to regulate trade by proclamation, which was already within his power, but to repeal or revive any statutes passed since the beginning of that Parliament concerning the import or export of any merchandise[2].

(1) Act for the Feudal Aid, 1504

De auxilio concesso et forma ejusdem

Forasmuch as the King our Sovereign Lord is rightfully entitled to have two reasonable aids according to the laws of this land, the one aid for the making knight of the right noble Prince his first begotten son Arthur, late Prince of Wales deceased, whose soul God pardon, and the other aid for the marriage of the right noble Princess his first begotten daughter Margaret, now married unto the King of Scots; and also that his Highness hath sustained and borne great and inestimable charges for the defence of this his realm, and for a firm and a perpetual peace with the realm of Scotland and many other countries and regions, to the great weal, comfort, and quietness of all his subjects; The Commons in this present Parliament assembled, considering the premises, and that if the same aids should be either of them levied and had by reason of their tenures according to the ancient laws of this land, should be to them doubtful, uncertain, and great inquietness for the search and none knowledge of their several tenures and of their lands chargeable to the same, have made humble petition to his Highness graciously to accept and take of them the sum of £40,000...upon the which petition and offer so made his Grace benignly considering the good and loving mind of his subjects...of his mere motion and abundant grace, and for the tender zeal and love that his Highness beareth to his said nobles and subjects,...by this present Act doth remit, pardon, and release...all his right, title, and interest which his Grace hath...by reason of the said aids or either of them; And also his Grace holdeth him right well pleased with the said loving offer and grant of his subjects by them so made...and over this of his more ample grace and pity, for that the porail[3] of his Commons of this his land should not in any wise be contributory or chargeable to any part of the said sum of £40,000, but to be thereof discharged, hath pardoned, remitted, and released the

---

[1] 26 Henr. VIII, c. 10.   [2] Prothero, p. lxxiii.

[3] 'Porail' or 'poverail' was used of the poor as a class.

sum of £10,000, parcel of the said sum of £40,000, and is content to accept and take of them the sum of £30,000 only in full recompence and satisfaction of and for all the premises; which sum of £30,000 it is enacted, ordained, and established by the authority of this present Parliament to be ordered, assessed, levied, paid, and had after the manner and form ensuing, that is to say. . .

The £30,000 was to be assessed upon real and personal estate in each county, city, and borough, by commissioners named in the Act.

* * * * * *

XIII. Provided alway that no lands nor tenements nor other hereditaments nor possessions mortised[1], appropried[2], or belonging to any College, Hospital, Hall, or House of Scholars in any of the Universities of Oxenford or Cambridge, the Charterhouses in all England, the House of Syon, or to the College of our Blessed Lady of Eton, or the College of our Blessed Lady of Winchester beside Winchester, or any goods or chattels of the said Colleges or to any of them belonging, be charged or chargeable to or for the satisfaction of the said sum of £30,000 or any parcel of the same. . . .

* * * * * *

19 Henr. VII, c. 32; *Statutes of the Realm*, ii, 675.

(2) Tonnage and Poundage Act, 1510

An Act for a Subsidy to be granted to the King

To the worship of God: We your poor Commons by your high commandment coming to this your present Parliament for the shires, cities, and boroughs of this your noble realm, by the assent of all the Lords spiritual and temporal in this present Parliament assembled, grant by this present indenture to you our Sovereign Lord, for the defence of this your said realm and in especial for the safeguard and keeping of the sea, a subsidy called tonnage, to be taken in manner and form following, that is to say; 3s. of every tun of wine coming into this your said realm; and of every tun of sweet wine coming into the same your realm, by every merchant alien. . . . 3s. over the said 3s. afore granted, to have and to perceive[3] yearly the said subsidy from the first day of this present Parliament for time of your life natural. And over that, we your said Commons, by the assent afore, grant to you our said Sovereign Lord for the safeguard and keeping of the sea another subsidy called poundage, that is to say; of all manner

[1] Amortised, *i.e.* alienated in mortmain to a corporation.
[2] Annexed to a religious corporation; used here in a special sense.
[3] Receive.

merchandises of every merchant, denizen and alien...carried out
of this your said realm or brought into the same by way of merchandise, of the value of every 20s., 12d., Except tin, whereof the
merchants strangers to pay for subsidy of the value of every 20s.,
2s. and the merchants denizens 12d.: And all such manner merchandises of every merchant denizen to be valued after that they
cost at their first buying...by their oaths, or of their servants
buyers of the said merchandises in their absence, or by their
letters the which the same merchants have of such buying from
their factors; all manner woollen cloth made and wrought within
this your realm and by any merchant denizen not born alien to be
carried out of the same realm within the time of this grant except;
And all manner wool, wool fells, and hides, and every manner of
corn flour, every manner of fresh fish, bestial[1], and wine into this
realm coming also except; And beer, ale, and all manner victual
going out of this your said realm for the victualling of your town
of Calais and the marches there under your obeisance out of this
grant alway except: To have and perceive yearly the said subsidy
of poundage from the first day of your most noble reign during
your life natural....

*   *   *   *   *   *

1 Henr. VIII, c. 20; *Statutes of the Realm*, iii, 21.

(3) Act against Smuggling, 1559

*An Act limiting the times for laying on Land Merchandise from
beyond the Seas...*

Most humbly shewing, Beseechen your Highness your Lords
and Commons in this present Parliament assembled, That where
the sums of money paid in the name of customs...is an
ancient revenue annexed and united to your imperial Crown, and
hath...amounted to great and notable sums of money, till of
late years many greedy and covetous persons, respecting more
their private gain and commodity than their duty and allegiance
or the common profit of the realm, have and do daily, as well by
conveying the same their wares and merchandises out of creeks
and places where no customer is resident, as also by or through
the negligence or corruption of the customer, searcher, or other
officer where they be resident, as by divers other fraudulent,
undue, and subtle practices and devices, convey their goods and
merchandises, as well brought from the parties beyond the sea as
transported out of this your realm of England, without payment

---

[1] A collective term for domestic animals kept for food or tillage.

...of the customs...therefor due; whereby the yearly revenue aforesaid is very much impaired and diminished.... That it may therefore be enacted.... That it shall not be lawful to or for any person or persons whatsoever...to lade or put, or cause to be laden or put, of or from any wharf, quay, or other place on the land, into any ship...any goods, wares, or merchandises whatsoever (fish taken by your Highness's subjects only excepted) to be transported into any place of the parties beyond the sea, or into the realm of Scotland, or to take up, discharge, and lay on land...out of any...ship...any goods, wares, or merchandises whatsoever (fish taken by any your Highness's subjects and salt only excepted) to be brought from any the parties beyond the sea or the realm of Scotland by way of merchandises, but only in the daylight...and in...some...open place, quay, or wharf...where a customer, controller, and searcher...or the servants of any of them have by the space of ten years last past been accustomably resident or hereafter shall be resident; upon pain of forfeiture of all such goods, wares, or merchandises so laden or discharged contrary to the true meaning of this Act, or the value thereof.

[II. Penalty on masters of vessels whose goods are unduly laden or discharged, £100.]

[III. Masters of ships exporting goods to give notice 'to the customer of the port where he ladeth and other officers there in the open Custom House' 'that he intendeth to lade, and to what place he intendeth to pass,' and to answer truly questions put to him by the customer concerning his cargo, under a penalty of £100.]

[IV. Similar clause with regard to unlading for masters of ships importing goods.]

[V. Goods imported or exported to be entered in the names of the true owners under penalty of forfeiture.]

[VI. Penalty on 'any wharfinger, crane-keeper, searcher, lighterman, weigher,' 'or other officer pertaining to the subsidy, custom, or Custom House' concealing offences against the Act, £100.]

[VII. Customers to appoint deputies in the several ports, and they and their deputies and servants to attend diligently under a penalty of £100 and loss of office.]   1 Eliz. c. 11; *Statutes of the Realm*, iv, 372.

§ 2. PARLIAMENTARY REVENUE

At the beginning of the Tudor period the most usual form of Parliamentary grant was by the tenth and fifteenth—taxation by fractional parts of moveables dating back to the Saladin tithe. The method was defective, because (1) it did not cover all kinds of property; (2) the traditional method of collection was unsatisfactory, since the collectors in each district were appointed by the member of Parliament for the district—a relic of the time when the members who voted for a tax were themselves responsible for collecting it—and there was no superintendence by the central authority or any protection against fraud or evasion; (3) the assessment was governed by a fixed bargain made with the localities in 1334, and there was no means of dealing adequately with districts which had subsequently increased in wealth. Thus there was every reason why government should be willing to try experiments, and to supplement the tenth and fifteenth by some method which should tax all kinds of property and spread a wider net.

An experiment which failed was the poll-tax of 1512 [p. 606], levied on a scale which ranged from £6. 13s. 4d. for a duke, down to 4d. for a labourer receiving less than 20s. a year in wages. This tax was estimated at £160,000, but its actual yield was only £50,000; it was therefore proposed to make up the deficiency partly by a simplification of the poll-tax scale, and partly by an additional levy upon personal property, and the principle was introduced of making aliens pay double. In the Subsidy Act of 1514[1] the special treatment of the nobility was abandoned in favour of a graduated scale varying according to wealth. The King's native-born subjects receiving yearly wages of not less than 20s. or more than 40s. were to pay 6d., and another 6d. for each additional 20s.; aliens paying 12d. Natives receiving no wages and having no goods or lands or 'other substance' sufficient to bring them within the graduated scale were to pay 4d.; and aliens 8d. In addition to the taxation of wages, personal property was taxed at the rate of 6d. for every £1 value above 40s.; aliens paying 12d. Rents also were taxed at the rate of 6d. in the £; aliens paying 12d. To this additional levy the term 'subsidy,' hitherto loosely used[2], came to be applied; and as a tax at so much in the £ could easily be brought to bear upon lands as well as goods, the subsidy was adopted as a permanent form of direct taxation supplementary to the tenth and fifteenth. It covered all kinds of property; the new assessment was flexible and not a fixed bargain; the collectors of subsidy in each district were appointed by a committee of great officers of state, and so came under the control of the central government; and aliens paid double. The Acts of 1601 for a lay subsidy [p. 610] and a clerical subsidy [p. 616] are printed below.

It is curious that the tendency towards a fixed bargain, so characteristic of English finance in its earlier developments, proved too strong for the subsidy as it had proved too strong for the tenth and fifteenth[3]. A subsidy soon came to be a fixed tax of 4s. in the £ on the annual value of land, and 2s. 8d. in the £ on the value of goods [pp. 614, 615]; and although the assessment was never formally fixed as in 1334, the practice grew up of assessing each subsidy upon the basis of the last. Thus, just as a tenth and fifteenth had come to be a mere fiscal expression for £30,000, so a subsidy became a mere fiscal expression, at first for £100,000, and by the end of the reign of Elizabeth, for about £80,000. This decline in productiveness was due to the disappearance of names from the subsidy books by death, and the difficulty of getting the new names on to the books at adequate rates of as-

---

[1] 5 Henr. VIII, c. 17.
[2] It had been applied in 1510 to tonnage and poundage (p. 601), and in 1512 to the poll-tax (p. 608).
[3] For a fuller discussion of these financial questions see Dowell, vol. i.

sessment which ought to be there[1]. A clerical subsidy granted in Convocation was worth about £20,000.

Lest it should be thought that a despotic sovereign like Henry VIII could raise what money he liked by taxation, reference should be made to the Parliamentary subsidy of 1523. Parliament met on April 15, and on April 29 Wolsey went down to the House of Commons, attended by 'divers Lords,'[2] and demanded a subsidy of 4s. in the £ on all men's goods and lands, which he estimated to produce the unprecedented sum of £800,000[3]. Sir Thomas More, as Speaker, in a speech delivered after the Cardinal had withdrawn, supported his demand, but it met with fierce opposition in the House. The Cardinal came to the House again and desired to reason with the members, but he was informed that 'the fashion of the Nether House was to hear, and not to reason but among themselves' [p. 609]. In the course of the debate which followed, the county members carried a motion for taxing their own lands on which the borough members declined to vote. The Subsidy Act[4] in its final shape gave the King a sum not far short of what he demanded, but it was to be raised in a way entirely different to that proposed by the Cardinal. Instead of a single levy of 4s. in the £ on lands and goods, there was to be a graduated tax spread over four years:—In the first and second years, 5 per cent. on lands and goods of the value of £20 and upwards, 2½ per cent. on goods between £20 and £2, 1⅔ per cent. on goods of 40s. or yearly wages averaging 20s.; in the third year, 5 per cent. on all land of £50 and upwards; in the fourth year 5 per cent. on personal property of £50 and upwards. Hall's account of the proceedings is printed on p. 608 below, where the unpopularity of the tax is clearly brought out. The episode shews (1) that although the House was not strong enough altogether to refuse an unpopular grant, it exercised full control over the form which taxation was to take; and (2) that although it was not unconstitutional for the Lord Chancellor to appear in the House of Commons and address the members on the King's behalf, it was against the privilege of Parliament for him to remain and take part in a debate.

The Parliamentary grants of the Tudor period are almost entirely to meet exceptional expenditure, for the tradition still held, that the King should 'live of his own.' Thus, the subsidy of 1534 was demanded for the expenses of the war with Scotland, for fortifying the Northern border, for rebuilding the defences of Dover and Calais; and to meet the King's desire 'to bring the wilful, wild, unreasonable, and savage people of his said land of Ireland and his whole dominion of the same to such conformity, rule, order, and obedience as the same for ever hereafter shall be much utile and profitable to the Kings of this realm, and a great surety and quietness to the subjects and inhabitants of the same.'[5] Again, when in 1548 the government of Edward VI found itself in financial difficulties, it applied to Parliament for

---

[1] In the debate on the Subsidy Bill of 1601 Sir Walter Raleigh is reported as saying: 'our estates that be £30 or £40 in the Queen's books are not the hundredth part of our wealth' (D'Ewes, p. 633).

[2] Brewer, i, 473.

[3] It is not known on what data this estimate was based, and the figure is probably excessive.

[4] 14 & 15 Henr. VIII, c. 16.   [5] 26 Henr. VIII, c. 19.

a tax upon sheep and cloth, for the purpose of making 'a mass of money' for the defence of the realm[1]. The tax on sheep and cloth was granted, with a prayer from God's 'poor servants and little flock' that He would 'take to His charge and defence' their 'little shepherd' till years and strength make him better able to 'bicker with his enemies'; but it was found convenient afterwards to substitute for it a subsidy of the ordinary kind[2].

In the Tudor period the Commons, although they were feeling their way towards it, did not claim the exclusive right of originating money bills. In 1523 the Lords undoubtedly enjoyed equal rights [p. 609] and in the debate of 1593 [p. 610], when the Lords proposed to increase to three the two subsidies which the Commons were offering, the point of privilege taken was that the Lower House ought not to confer with the Lords and accept an amendment from them; their right to initiate and send down to the Commons a separate Subsidy Bill was fully recognised in the debate. Throughout the Tudor period also the Lords and Commons concur in granting subsidies; it was not until 1625 that these grants came from the Commons alone.

(1) Poll Tax Act of 1512

De Subsidio Regi concesso

Forasmuch as it is openly and notoriously known unto all persons of Christ's Religion, That Lewis the French King, adversary unto our most dread Sovereign and natural liege lord King Harry the VIIIth and to this his realm of England, hath moved and stirred and daily moveth and stirreth by all the subtle means to his power to set and bring schism, variance, and as much as in him lieth studieth the mean of continual error to be had in the Church of Christ. Taking of late upon him against the will and mind of our Holy Father the Pope, the whole Court of Rome, and Holy Church, to summon and call a Council... And without ground, cause, or authority, in the same Council caused to be decreed, That our said Holy Father should from thenceforth be sequestered of and from all jurisdiction and administration Papal, with other great, terrible decrees.... And howbeit our said Holy Father, for the charitable reformation of the said French King, willing the health of the soul of the said French King, hath for his said presumptions and divers other his manifest offences as be foresaid, declared and published the whole realm of France... to be interdicted and so under that interdiction yet remain, The said French King that not regarding, but alway abiding in his said indurate and pervert opinions and erroneous mind, And, the decree of the interdiction despising, will not thereby reform himself, but alway erroneously defending and maintaining his said obstinate opinions against the unity of the Holy Church; And also

---

[1] 2 & 3 Edw. VI, c. 36.   [2] 3 & 4 Edw. VI, c. 23.

hath moved and daily moveth and maintaineth war and battle against our said Holy Father and the universal Christ's Church in such manner that our said Holy Father for the succour, maintenance, and defence of his person and of our Mother, Holy Church, And for the ceasing of the said schism and errors, hath written and sent for aid and assistance unto our said Sovereign Lord and to many other Christian princes, Which schismatic demeanour of the said French King is and hath been perilous and terrible example to all Christian faith: For reformation whereof our said Sovereign Lord the King, of his blessed and godly disposition, for the true faith that his Highness beareth unto Almighty God and to our Mother, Holy Church, as well for resisting the said prepensed malice and errors of his said adversary by the same adversary against our said Holy Father the Pope and Holy Church borne and maintained, as for that his said adversary hath of late attempted divers enterprises of war, as well by sea as by land, against his Highness and his subjects ..., hath prepared and ordained, and purposeth in all hasty speed to prepare and make ready, as well by land as by water, divers and sundry great armies and navies for the intents and defences beforesaid... Which... cannot be supported, maintained, and borne without right great costs and charges: In consideration whereof, and also for that our said Sovereign Lord many other divers and great charges for defence of this his realm in divers sundry wise of late hath borne and sustained, and for the goodness, bounteousness, liberality, favour, and tender zeal by his Highness shewed to his said Commons, as evidently is known, The same loving Commons in this present Parliament assembled, with the assent of the Lords spiritual and temporal in the same Parliament in like manner assembled, have granted unto our said Sovereign Lord the King one whole fifteenth and tenth to be had, taken, perceived[1], and levied of goods, moveables, chattels, and other things to such fifteenth and tenth usually contributory and chargeable within counties, cities, boroughs, and towns, and other places of this realm of England in manner and form aforetime used....

* * * * * *

IV. And for that the said one fifteenth and tenth... extendeth but unto a small sum toward the said great charges, The said loving Commons after to[2] their powers willing a greater sum toward the said charges... as well in shorter time as in more easy, universal, and indifferent manner to be levied than such common tax of fifteenth and tenth hath or can be according to

---

[1] Received.   [2] According to.

the ancient use thereof...have by the assent of the Lords...
granted...one subsidy to be taken and paid of every person underwritten within this realm of England in manner and form as
followeth, that is to say, of every duke, £6. 13s. 4d.; of every
marquis, earl, marchioness, and countess, £4; of every baron,
baronet[1], and baroness, 40s.; of every other knight not being
Lord of the Parliament, 30s.; of every person, man or woman,
having lands, tenements, or rents [etc.]....to the yearly value of
£40 or above, 20s.;...of £20 or above,...10s.;...of £10 or
above,...5s.;...of 40s. or above,...2s.;...under 40s., 12d.
Of every person, man or woman,...having goods or chattels
moveable to the value of £800 or above, 80s. 4d.;...£400 or
above,...40s.;...£200 or above,...26s. 8d.;...£100 or above,
...13s. 4d.;...£40 or above,...6s. 8d.;...£20 or above,...
3s. 4d.;...£10 or above,...20d.;...40s. or above,...12d....
Of every labourer, journeyman, artificer, handicraftman, and
servant, as well men and women, above the age of 15 years,
taking wages or other profits for wages to the value of 40s. by
the year or above...12d.;...20s....or above...6d. Of every
servant taking any wages or other profits under the value of 20s.
...and also of every apprentice and of every other person...4d.

For the rating, collection, and payment of this subsidy the Commons
were to appoint commissioners for each county, city, and town.

*　　　*　　　*　　　*　　　*　　　*

4 Henr. VIII, c. 19; *Statutes of the Realm*, iii, 74.

(2) Subsidy of 1523

The Parliament being begun,...the Cardinal, accompanied
with divers Lords, as well of the spiritualty as of the temporalty,
came the 29th day of April into the Common House, where he
eloquently declared to the Commons how...the King of necessity
was driven to war and defence, which in no wise could be maintained without great sums of money, and he thought no less than
£800,000, to be raised of the fifth part of every man's goods and
lands, that is to say, 4s. of every £, for he said that the year
following the King and the Emperor should make such war in
France as hath not been seen.

After that he had declared his matter at length, exhorting
the Commons to aid their Prince in time of necessity, he departed out of the Common House....

After long reasoning, there were certain appointed to
declare the impossibility of this demand to the Cardinal, which,

[1] Lesser baron.

according to their commission, declared to him substantially the poverty and scarceness of the realm; all which reasons and demonstrations he little regarded, and then the said persons most meekly beseeched his Grace to move the King's Highness to be content with a more easier sum, to the which he currishly answered, that he would rather have his tongue plucked out of his head with a pair of pinsons than to move the King to take any less sum: with which answer they, almost dismayed, came and made report to the Common House, where every day was reasoning, but nothing concluded.

Wherefore the Cardinal came again to the Common House and desired to be reasoned withal, to whom it was answered that the fashion of the Nether House was to hear, and not to reason but among themselves. Then he shewed the realm to be of great riches; first, because the King's customs were greater now than they were beforetime; also he alleged sumptuous buildings, plate, rich apparel of men, women, children, and servants, fat feasts and delicate dishes, which things were all tokens of great abundance; with which repeating of men's substance, as though he had repined or disdained that any man should fare well or be well clothed but himself, the Commons greatly grudged. And when he was departed out of the House, it was proved that honest apparel of the commodities of this realm, abundance of plain and honest viands, were profitable to the realm and not prodigal.

After long debating, the Commons concluded to grant 2s. of the £ of every man's lands or goods that was worth £20 or might dispend £20, to be taken for the King, and so upward of every 20s., 2s.; and from 40s. to £20 of every 20s., 12d.; and under 40s. of every head 16 years and upward, 4d., to be paid in two years. This grant was reported to the Cardinal, which therewith was sore discontent, and said that the Lords had granted 4s. of the £, which was proved untrue, for indeed they had granted nothing, but hearkened[1] all upon the Commons....

After this grant made[2] the 21st day of May, because of Whitsuntide the Parliament was prorogued to the 10th day of June: During which prorogation the common people said to the burgesses, 'Sirs, we hear say you will grant 4s. of the £; we advise you to do so that you may go home'; with many evil words and threatenings....   Hall, *Chronicle* (edn. of 1809), p. 655.

---

[1] In the now obsolete sense of 'attended upon,' *i.e.* 'waited for.'
[2] Hall's account of the grant does not agree with the Subsidy Act of 1523. See p. 605 above.

(3) Subsidy Debate of 1593

This also throws some light on the method of taking a division.

[2 March, 1593]...Sir Robert Cecil, one of the committees appointed by this House for conference with the committees of the Lords, shewed...that...their Lordships, weighing the great present necessity of greater and more speedy supply of treasure to be had than two entire subsidies and four fifteenths, do negatively affirm, That their Lordships will not give in any wise their assents to pass any Act in their House of less than three entire subsidies....

...Mr Francis Bacon...spake next, and yielded to the subsidy, but misliked that this House should join with the Upper House in the granting of it. For the custom and privilege of this House hath always been, first to make offer of the subsidies from hence, then to the Upper House, except it were that they present a bill unto this House with desire of our assent thereto, and then to send it up again. And reason it is that we should stand upon our privilege, seeing the burden resteth upon us as the greatest number; nor is it reason the thanks should be theirs. And in joining with them in this motion, we shall derogate from ours; for the thanks will be theirs and the blame ours, they being the first movers. Wherefore I wish that in this action we should proceed, as heretofore we have done, apart by ourselves, and not join with their Lordships....Whereupon the House, well approving the said Mr Bacon's opinion...(pp. 483–4).

...And then the question being urged and by the order of the House propounded, whether conference should be had with the Lords,...the number of them which were for the said conference, and said Aye, went out of the said House and were found to be in number but 128, whereas those that were against the said conference, and said No, sat still in the House, being in number 217...(p. 486).

The question came up again on 5 March, and it was then agreed to hold a general conference with the Lords, without naming a subsidy (p. 488).

D'Ewes, *Journal*, pp. 483–6.

(4) Lay Subsidy Act of 1601

The preamble of this Statute, with its sustained and eloquent patriotism, seems worth printing in full.

An Act for the Grant of Four entire Subsidies and Eight
Fifteenths and Tenths granted by the Temporalty

Most excellent and most gracious Sovereign, Where we your Majesty's humble, faithful, and loving subjects being here (by your authority) assembled in your High Court of Parliament, have entered into due consideration of the great and weighty causes which ought at this time, more than at any other time, to stir up the hearts of all that are either well affected in religion towards God, loyalty towards you their dear Sovereign, or care of their own safety and their posterities, to consult timely and provide effectually for all such means as are or may be necessary to preserve both you and us from those apparent dangers whereinto this State may fall through lack of so much care and providence as agreeth with the rules of Nature and common reason, and therefore much more to be challenged at our hands, to whom your Majesty hath vouchsafed to give so great light of your inward knowledge and judicial foresight of your enemies' implacable malice and their dangerous plots contrived against this flourishing kingdom, which is and long hath been the principal obstacle against that swelling ambition which hath so blinded their understanding as they do not only greedily seek but vainly hope to attain to their unjust pretensions, coloured with false and vain pretexts and insinuations, as far from truth as light from darkness: Forasmuch as in this time of our advised and mature deliberation we have sufficiently perceived how great and inestimable charges your Majesty hath sustained many years, in seeking (by way of prevention) to hinder all such foreign attempts as others (not provided for) might long since have proved perilous to the whole estate of this Commonwealth; And where it is apparent to all the world that if your Majesty had not exhausted the greatest portion of your private treasures, besides all other means derived from our dutiful affections, as well in making timely provision of all things necessary for your navy and army royal, as in maintaining and using the same (at times convenient), that we should long before this day have been exposed to the danger of many sudden and dangerous attempts of our enemies, and failed in all those happy successes which have accompanied your royal actions taken in hand for the defence of this Estate; And seeing also that at this present time your Highness hath been put to inestimable charge in the necessary prosecution of an unnatural rebellion within your Highness's realm of Ireland, daily fed by foreign enemies, whose actions have not only tended to the subversion of God's true religion planted amongst us, and to the bereaving of that realm from your imperial Crown of England to which it hath been so many years joined and annexed, but consequently to the ruin and spoil of this most flourishing Kingdom of England; For the better effecting whereof the King of Spain hath now openly invaded the realm of Ireland with an army already landed in the Province of Munster, having not forborne to publish there his resolute purpose to usurp to himself that Crown, even by a plain conquest (in case of resistance), though coloured with a vain pretext of an illusory donation from the see of Rome, whose usurped authority we have abandoned (as becometh all good subjects to do that mean no less in deed than they profess in name): Forasmuch as we do seriously consider that your Majesty and we your faithful and obedient subjects are but one Body Politic, and that your Highness is the head and we the members, and that no good or felicity, peril or adversity, can come to the one but the other shall partake thereof, We have thought it a matter incident to the natural care and sense we ought to feel of our present and future condition, seeing your enemies are strengthened by combination with other states, and do receive from their confederates great contributions of treasure for advancement of this and such-like enterprises, whilst we do see on the other side that your Majesty's expenses only tend to the advancement of the true glory of God, and defence of the liberty and felicity of the imperial Crown of this realm and of the kingdoms and dominions thereof, and are neither supported by any other Prince or State, nor carried on in yourself with any vain ambition or wasteful humour of consuming the treasure of this kingdom, to offer to your Majesty the disposition of such means as God has given us, to be employed for preservation of God's cause, for maintenance of your own dignity, and all such rights and titles as be annexed to your imperial Crown; being fully resolved to leave both lands, goods, and whatsoever else that is dearest unto us (yea, and this mortal life) rather than we would suffer your royal estate to be in any part diminished, or the imperial Crown of this realm deprived of any honour, title, right, or interest thereunto belonging, or suffer any foreign power to grow on further, or to continue so long unremoved, as thereby to leave them any ground to presume of good successes, either in this action now begun, or in any future enterprise, which may tend to the dishonour or peril of any your Majesty's kingdoms: In which consideration, and many other needless to repeat, we have thought ourselves bound in thankfulness to God for you, and to your Majesty for ourselves, who feel the happiness of your most gracious clemency and justice at home, under your happy and politic government daily multiplied unto us (beyond the example of all ages), to prepare and make not only our persons ready to withstand, resist, and subdue the force and puissance of our enemies (be they never so potent), but also to present unto you four subsidies and eight fifteenths and tenths, thereby to make up some such portion of treasure as may (in some sort) supply the great and inestimable charges which you our most gracious and dread Sovereign have and daily must sustain: All which, notwithstanding it be much less than may be sufficient for this present, and urgent necessities, yet being a plain demonstration of our due consideration of all those necessary causes and important reasons which we have heard delivered by your royal direction, We have thought meet not only to make it one of our first works to consult of that matter, which in other sessions of Parliament hath usually succeeded many other acts and consultations, but so to enlarge and improve the measure of this oblation which we shall offer to your royal person, as it may give your Majesty an assured testimony of our internal zeals and duties, to be further manifested hereafter by the hazard of our lives and fortunes at all time for your Majesty's service, whereof we beseech you to vouchsafe (at this present) the gracious acceptation, as proceeding from those loving and faithful subjects of yours, who do desire to testify (both in the extraordinary form and substance of our present offer), that though there liveth (and ever shall) in the hearts of your most humble and obedient subjects an extraordinary zeal to your Majesty's person, yet that we desire and intend that this which is done to you at this time shall be no otherwise interpreted than as a lively monument of those great duties and affections which we do contentedly and comfortably strain[1] for your Majesty, and in a manner far exceeding any former precedent, because no age either hath or can produce the like precedent of so much happiness under any Prince's reign, nor of so continual gracious care for our preservation as your Majesty hath shewed in all your actions, having never stuck to hazard, or rather neglect, for our preservation any part of those worldly blessings wherewith Almighty God hath so plentifully endued you in this time of your most happy government: And therefore we do, with all duty and humble affections that heart can conceive or tongue can utter, present to your sacred Majesty four entire subsidies and eight fifteenths and tenths toward your Highness's great charges for our defence: And we do most humbly beseech your Majesty that it may be enacted by the authority of this present Parliament in manner and form following, that is to say: That your Majesty shall have eight whole fifteenths and tenths, to be paid, taken, and levied of the

---

[1] In the sense of making the utmost possible demand upon.

moveable goods, chattels, and other things usual to such fifteenths
and tenths to be contributory and chargeable, within the shires,
cities, boroughs, towns, and other places of this your Majesty's
realm, in manner and form aforetime used....

II. And be it further enacted by the authority aforesaid, That
the knights elected and returned of and for the shires within this
realm for this present Parliament, citizens of cities, burgesses of
boroughs and towns, where Collectors have been used to be
named and appointed for the collection of any fifteenth and tenth
before this time granted, shall name and appoint...sufficient
and able persons to be Collectors...the said persons so to be
named and appointed...then having lands, tenements, and
other hereditaments in their own right of an estate of inheritance
of the yearly value of £40, or in goods worth £400 at the least,
each of them, after such rate and value as he or they shall be
assessed and rated at in the Subsidy Book...And the names and
surnames of every of the said Collectors...together with the
places allotted to their collection and charge, the said knights [etc.]
...shall certify before the Queen's Majesty in Chancery....

* * * * * *

IV. And furthermore for the great and weighty considerations aforesaid, We the Lords spiritual and temporal, and the
Commons of this present Parliament assembled, do by our like
assent and authority of this Parliament, give and grant to your
Highness...four entire subsidies, to be rated, taxed, levied, and
paid...of every person spiritual and temporal...in manner and
form following, that is to say; As well that every person born
within...the Queen's dominions, as all and every fraternity,
guild, corporation, mystery, brotherhood, and commonalty, corporated or not corporated,...being worth £3, for every £1 as
well in coin...as also plate, stock of merchandise, all manner of
corn and grain, household stuff, and all other goods moveable, as
well within this realm as without, and of all such sums of money
as to him or them is or shall be owing, whereof he or they trust
in his or their conscience surely to be paid (Except and out of the
premises deducted such sums of money as he or they owe and in
his or their consciences intendeth truly to pay, And except also
the apparel of every such person their wives and children belonging to their own bodies, saving jewels, gold, silver, stone, and
pearl), shall pay [*for each of the four subsidies*, 2s. 8d. *in the £*]....

V. And be it further enacted by the authority aforesaid, That
every person born under the Queen's obeisance, and every corporation, fraternity, guild, mystery, brotherhood, and common-

alty, corporate or not corporate, for every pound that every of the same...hath in fee simple, fee tail, for term of life, term of years, by execution, wardship, or by copy of court roll, of and in any honours, castles, manors, lands, tenements, rents, services, hereditaments, annuities, fees, corrodies, or other yearly profits of the yearly value of 20*s*., as well within ancient demesne and other places privileged as elsewhere, and so upward, shall pay [*for each of the four subsidies* 4s. *in the* £]....

* * * * * *

VIII. And be it further enacted by the authority aforesaid, That for the assessing and ordering of the said four subsidies to be duly had, the Lord Chancellor of England or the Lord Keeper of the Great Seal, the Lord Treasurer of England, the Lord Steward of the Queen's Majesty's Household, the Lord Admiral of England, the Lord Chamberlain of the Queen's most honourable Household for the time being, or two of them at the least, whereof the Lord Chancellor of England or Keeper of the Great Seal for the time being to be one, shall and may name and appoint of and for every shire...such certain number of persons of every of the same shires...as they shall think convenient to be Commissioners of and within the same place whereof they be inhabitants...And...in like manner may name and appoint of every...borough and towns corporate,...as they shall think requisite, six, five, four, three, or two of the head officers and other honest inhabitants of every the said cities, boroughs, and towns corporate, according to the number and multitude of the people being in the same....And the Lord Chancellor...shall make and direct out of the Court of Chancery...commissions...for every shire...city, town, borough, isle, and household...for the... levying of the said four subsidies....Provided always, That no person be or shall be compelled to be any Commissioner to and for the execution of this present Act but only in the shire where he dwelleth and inhabiteth....

* * * * * *

XVIII. And further be it enacted by the said authority, That the said Commissioners...shall for every of the said payments of the said subsidies, name such sufficient and able persons which then shall have and possess lands and other hereditaments in their own right of the clear yearly value of £40, or goods to the value of £400 at the least, as he shall be taxed in the Subsidy Book, if any such be in the said limits, and for want of such so assessed, then those to be appointed Collectors that then shall be sufficient, and rated and taxed in the Subsidy Books in lands or goods nearest to the values aforesaid, as by their discretion shall be thought good, in shires... cities, towns corporate, and other whatsoever places... to be High Collectors....

      *   *   *   *   *   *

43 Eliz. c. 18; *Statutes of the Realm*, iv, 991.

(5) Clerical Subsidy Act of 1601

An Act for the Confirmation of the Subsidies granted by the Clergy

Where the prelates and clergy of the Province of Canterbury have for certain considerations lovingly and liberally given and granted to the Queen's most excellent Majesty four subsidies of four shillings in the pound, to be taken and levied of all and singular their promotions spiritual within the same Province, at such days and times and in such certain manner and form, and with such exceptions and provisions, as be specified and declared in a certain instrument by them thereof made, and delivered to the Queen's Highness, under the seal of the most Reverend Father in God, John[1], now Archbishop of Canterbury and Primate of all England, which instrument is now exhibited in this present Parliament to be ratified and confirmed: The tenor whereof ensueth in these words:

Illustrissimae et serenissimae in Christo Principi et Dominae nostrae clementissimae, Dominae Elizabethae, Dei gratia Angliae, Franciae, et Hiberniae Reginae, Fidei Defensori, &c., Johannes, divina providentia Cantuariensis Archiepiscopus, totius Angliae Primas et Metropolitanus, omnimodam obedientiam et subjectionem, ac felicitatem et salutem, in eo per quem Reges regnant et Principes dominantur: Vestrae serenissimae Regiae sublimitati per presens publicum Instrumentum, sive has literas nostras testimoniales, significamus et notum facimus, quod prelati et clerus nostrae Cantuariensis Provinciae, in sacra synodo provinciali sive convocatione, vigore et aucthoritate brevis Regii vestri in ea parte nobis directi, in domo capitulari Ecclesiae vestrae Cathedralis Sancti Pauli Londinensis, vicesimo octavo die mensis Octobris, Anno Domini millesimo sexcentesimo primo, jam currente, inchoata et celebrata, ac de die in diem et loco in locum usque ad et in decimum octavum diem presentis mensis Novembris continuata et prorogata, in Ecclesia collegiata divi Petri Westm̃ legittime congregati, pro quibusdam magnis arduis et urgentibus causis per nos eis propositis, ac inter eos matura deliberatione ponderatis, pro defensione regnorum et dominiorum vestrorum, necnon

[1] Archbishop Whitgift.

et pro eorum erga vestram Regiam sublimitatem officio, quatuor ultronea ac spontanea et voluntaria Subsidia vestrae Regiae munificentiae unanimi eorum consensu et assensu dederunt et concesserunt, prout tenore presentis publici Instrumenti (seriem concessionis hujusmodi in se continentis) plenius liquet et apparet; Humiliter et obnixe vestrae Regiae Majestati supplicantes quatenus haec eorum quatuor Subsidia pro vestra solita clementia benigne accipiatis, ac bene consulere gratiose dignemini: Tenor vero dictae concessionis de verbo in verbum sequitur, et est talis.

Most excellent and most gracious Sovereign, Your Majesty's most humble subjects the prelates and clergy of the Province of Canterbury, called together by your Highness's authority and now lawfully assembled and met together in a Convocation or Synod, acknowledging themselves of all other your loyal subjects most bounden, and yet of all other least able to do your Majesty that acceptable service which they are willing to do, have nevertheless by your gracious favour entered into a due consideration by what means in this general inclination of all sorts of your loving subjects they might best declare their devotions and duties to your Highness, wherein though they find no better means in themselves to further and advance your royal estate than by the diligent discharge of their function, that is by their earnest prayers unto God for your Majesty's peaceable and prosperous reign with long and happy life, and by their faithful instruction of your people in their subjection and allegiance, yet remembering on the one side the number and importance of those benefits which your Majesty's wise and godly government hath yielded to all degrees and sorts, and in a special manner unto them (for who hath or should have a livelier sense or better remembrance of your Majesty's princely courage and constancy in advancing and protecting the free profession of the Gospel within and without your Majesty's dominions against so many and mighty adversaries thereof, or your most Christian care to maintain peace within your kingdom and amongst your people, than your clergy); And on the other side considering that for the procuring and continuing of these inestimable benefits unto us, your Majesty's most sacred person hath been often in hazard and danger, your Crown and dignity maliciously envied and undermined, your kingdoms and dominions troubled and invaded, your royal treasure much wasted, the revenues of your Crown greatly diminished, your subjects (saving in cases of extreme necessity) graciously spared and forborne, and that at this present an army of Spaniards (the implacable enemies of your realm) have with great violence entered into some part of your Majesty's Kingdom of Ireland, whence without great and excessive charges they will not be expulsed: Wherefore your said prelates and clergy have thought it their duties, besides their continual intercession unto God for your Highness's prosperity and safety, to offer unto your Majesty some such aid and contribution of money toward the supportation of your charges, as they are persuaded the present expelling of this proud attempt of the Spaniards and other your Majesty's most weighty and princely affairs do necessarily and speedily require: May it therefore please your most excellent Majesty to understand that your said prelates and clergy, with one uniform consent, accord, and agreement, have given and granted and by these presents do give and grant to your Highness, your heirs and successors, four whole and entire subsidies in manner and form following, that is to say; That every archbishop, bishop, dean, archdeacon, provost, master of college, prebendary, parson, and vicar, and every other person and persons of whatsoever name and degree he or they be within the Province of Canterbury, having and enjoying any spiritual promotion or other temporal possession to the same spiritual promotion annexed, now not divided or separated by Act of Parliament or otherwise from the possession of the clergy, shall pay to your Highness, your heirs and successors, for every pound that he may yearly dispend by reason of the said spiritual promotion, the sum of four shillings for every of the said four subsidies: And for the true and certain value of all the promotions and every of them (whereof the payments of these four subsidies shall be made) the rate, taxation, valuation, and estimation now remaining of record in your Majesty's Court of Exchequer for the payment of a perpetual disme or tenth granted unto your Majesty's most noble Father, in the six and twenty year of his reign[1], concerning such promotions as now be in the possession of the clergy, shall only be followed and observed, without making any valuation, rate, taxation, or estimation other than in the said record is comprised: Provided always, That forasmuch as the tenth part of the said rate and valuation before mentioned is yearly paid to your Highness for the said perpetual disme, so as there remaineth only nine parts yearly to the incumbent clear, these four subsidies of four shillings the pound shall be understanded and meant only of every full pound of the said nine parts and of no more;...

* * * * * *

[1] 26 Henr. VIII, c. 3.

...Item, your said prelates and clergy do grant, that every archbishop and bishop...shall be collectors of these subsidies within their proper diocese...and...shall certify into your Majesty's Court of Exchequer under their seals the names and surnames of all such stipendiary priests, deacons, and ministers within their diocese as be chargeable by this Act....

* * * * * *

...Wherefore for the true and sure payment of the said subsidies granted by the said prelates and clergy of the said Province of Canterbury according to the tenor, effect, and true meaning of the said instrument, Be it enacted by the Queen's most excellent Majesty, with the assent of the Lords spiritual and temporal and the Commons in this present Parliament assembled, and by the authority of the same, That the said gift, grant, and every matter, sum of money, petition, provision, clause, and sentence in the same instrument contained. shall stand and be ratified, established, and confirmed by the authority of this present Parliament.

* * * * * *

V. And be it further enacted by the authority aforesaid, That all and every grant and grants of all and every sum and sums of money granted, or which hereafter shall be granted, to the Queen's Majesty by the clergy of the Province of York, shall be of the same strength, force, and effect in all things as the said grant made by the said Province of Canterbury; and shall be taxed, certified, collected, levied, gathered, and paid according to the tenor, form, and effect of this present Act of Parliament, to all intents, constructions, and purposes, in such manner and form as though it were specially, plainly, and particularly expressed and rehearsed in this present Act, by express words, terms, and sentences in their several natures and kinds.

* * * * * *

43 Eliz. c. 17; *Statutes of the Realm*, iv, 984.

§ 3. EXTRAORDINARY REVENUE

Extraordinary revenue, obtained for exceptional purposes or in exceptional need, by methods which were unusual but not necessarily illegal, takes the form in the Tudor period either of benevolences or loans. There should also be included under this head the great windfall which came to Henry VIII and his successor by the dissolution of the monasteries and chantries.

(1) *Benevolences* had been first raised by Edward IV, who obtained them as free gifts more especially from the wealthier members of the trading classes, with whom he was very popular. He applied in person or by letter

to 'the wealthiest sort of people in his realm,' and 'used such gentle fashions toward them, with friendly prayer of their assistance in his necessity,...that they could not otherwise do but frankly and freely yield and give him a reasonable and competent sum.'[1] The citizens of London enjoyed the largest share of his attention, and there was a royal entertainment for them at Waltham, with hunting and dining, 'a tun of wine' for the aldermen's wives, and presumably arrangements for benevolences after dinner. In the reign of Richard III benevolences were made illegal by statute[2]; but they re-appear in the reign of Henry VII, and now without the appearance of generosity and free will which had been imparted to them by Edward IV. They are now levied systematically, by what was practically compulsion on the part of the Council. In 1491 a benevolence was raised from 'the more able sort' [p. 621], and in 1495 this was legalised by what Bacon calls a 'shoring or underpropping Act,'[3] which made persons who had promised benevolence legally liable for any arrears which they had not yet paid. Henry VIII levied two benevolences, one in 1528 and another in 1545, and on the latter occasion it is said that a London alderman who refused to pay was sent to serve as a common soldier on the Scottish border, although the story has not passed unquestioned[4]. With the doubtful exception of 1586, when the clergy were called upon for an aid not granted by Convocation[5], Elizabeth did not adopt the benevolence as a means of raising money, but she was accustomed to receive considerable sums as presents from the towns which she visited upon her royal progresses.

(2) *Loans.* In earlier times an English king in need of ready money would have gone to the Jews, but the Jews had been driven from the kingdom, so the Tudor sovereigns were thrown back upon their subjects. The usual method of raising a loan was for the Privy Council to obtain from the Lords Lieutenant of counties lists of the wealthier persons of the shire, with a note of such sums as they might be reasonably expected to advance. Letters were then sent to them, sealed with the privy seal, requiring them to lend to the King a sum named in the letter, upon the security of the royal promise to pay after the next subsidy granted by Parliament. This method of raising money was twice indirectly sanctioned by statute, by the Acts of 1529[6] and 1544[7] absolving the King from repaying the loans then outstanding. Elizabeth used loans on privy seal largely, but she repaid them punctually and her credit was therefore good.

The loan that is most important from the constitutional point of view is the 'Amicable Loan' of 1525, because it proved to the King and Wolsey 'the existence of definite limitations to the monarchical power.'[8] In its first form it was an attempt to exploit the feudal obligation to contribute to the King's needs when he led an invasion in person[9]. On the pretext that Henry VIII, like Henry V, was about to 'lead his forces into France,' Wolsey demanded a sixth of lay and a third of ecclesiastical property. This met with vehement opposition throughout England. Riots broke out in

[1] Holinshed, iii, 330, 349.
[2] 1 Rich. III, c. 2.
[4] Hallam, i, 25.
[6] 21 Henr. VIII, c. 24.
[8] Traill, iii, 16.

[3] 11 Henr. VII, c. 10; Bacon, vi, 160.
[5] *Ib.* i, 244.
[7] 35 Henr. VIII, c. 12.
[9] Brewer, ii, 48.

Suffolk among the clothworkers which were not easily suppressed[1]; in the diocese of Salisbury every secular priest refused to pay[2]; and the men of Kent assaulted one of the commissioners charged with the duty of levying the contribution[3]. 'When this matter was opened through England,' says Hall[4], 'how the great men took it was marvel; the poor cursed; the rich repugned; the light wits railed—but in conclusion all people cursed the Cardinal and his co-adherents as subversor of the laws and liberty of England[5]. For they said if men should give their goods by a commission, then were it worse than the taxes of France, and so England should be bond and not free.' This opposition, led by London, was successful, and the 'amicable loan' levied on a definite assessment was abandoned for a benevolence. This was scarcely less unpopular than the first proposal, and in the end the scheme was withdrawn, and it was left to every man to 'grant privily what he would.' For the methods of the Amicable Loan and the opposition which it aroused, see pp. 621–4 below.

The methods adopted in the case of the Forced Loan of 1556 are illustrated by the extracts from the Acts of the Privy Council printed below [pp. 624–5]. Privy seals demanding a loan of £100 were sent to all persons of means, either directly or through some important person in the county. As many ignored them, 'Commissioners for the Loan' with local knowledge were appointed in each county, and a larger number of persons were included from whom smaller sums could be demanded. Those who refused were summoned before the Council or the Commissioners, and bound over in recognisances, and in the last resort were imprisoned in the Fleet[6].

(1) The Benevolence of 1491

There is a tradition of a *dilemma* that Bishop Morton (the Chancellor) used, to raise up the Benevolence to higher rates; and some called it his fork and some his crotch[7]. For he had couched an article in the instructions to the Commissioners who were to levy the Benevolence, That if they met with any that were sparing, they should tell them that they must needs have because they laid up; and if they were spenders, they must needs have because it was seen in their port and manner of living; so neither kind came amiss. Bacon, *History of King Henry VII* (Spedding's edn.) vi, 121.

(2) The Amicable Loan, 1525

[April, 1525]

Instructions to the Archbishop of Canterbury for practising an amicable and loving grant with the spiritual persons and clergy of the diocese of Canterbury, for the conservation of the honour

---

[1] *D.N.B.* xxvi, 82.   [2] Fisher, p. 254.   [3] *Ib.* p. 255.   [4] p. 696.
[5] Hall is violently hostile to the Cardinal, and exaggerates where he is concerned; but there is plenty of other evidence of general opposition to the contribution; see Brewer, ii, 51–4.   [6] Dasent, vi, p. xiii.   [7] Fork; used figuratively of a dilemma.

of the realm, and the recovery of the realm and crown of France, with other dominions rightfully appertaining to the King...

...The King...intends personally to invade France, which has thus long been unjustly withheld from the Crown of England, in the beginning of this summer; and another army will be set upon the sea, the expense of which will be too great for the King to support unless his subjects well contribute. He has therefore commissioned the Archbishop of Canterbury to practise an amicable grant by the spiritual persons of his diocese, including monasteries and other houses of religion, exempt and not exempt, collegiate churches, hospitals, chantries, parish churches, etc. First, the Archbishop shall repair to his diocese, summon before himself or his commissaries spiritual persons of all degrees, except those whose names are contained in the enclosed schedule, declare to them the above preamble, and shew them that after long discussion and consultation with the nobles and clergy it has been decided that the rate for the spiritualty must be the third part of yearly revenues of lands, benefices, salaries, or wages, or the value of moveable goods from £10 upwards, and the fourth part from £10 downwards. Though these sums seem great, they will not amount to as much as the first loan[1].

To the persons whose names are enclosed, the King has directed letters requesting the advance of certain sums; which letters the Archbishop must deliver, exhorting them to comply with his request. If any of these are not taxed to the third part of their goods, he shall assess them at that rate. It is advisable to circulate the report of the destruction of the French army in Italy, and the capture of the King, the King of Navarre, and the rest of his nobility, and to make solemn processions, fires, and other tokens of joy and comfort, a few days before assembling the clergy, that this consolation may be fresh in their memory. The shortness of time will not allow the trial and examination of the values, and therefore every person will be assessed as he was at the last loan, unless he has been newly promoted or his salary increased. The Archbishop must take order that some part of the money may be paid at once, and the whole of the rest may be paid to the Treasurer of the Chamber by Midsummer next. A certificate of the sums to be paid must be sent to Wolsey as soon as possible. If the French King recompenses the King, or if a profitable peace is made before the voyage is commenced, the King will restore to his subjects as much of the money as he can.

Letters and Papers, Foreign and Domestic, Henry VIII, vol. iv, pt. iii, App. 34.

[1] See note on p. 623 below.

Archbishop Warham to Wolsey, 5 April, 1525

...It will be hard to raise the money, specially as other Parliamentary grants are now payable. Reports, for the secret ear of the Cardinal, the dissatisfaction now prevailing: 1. That the people speak cursedly[1], saying they shall never have rest of payments as long as some[2] liveth. 2. That some of the Commissioners, through fear of the people, will only announce the King's command without pressing it further, leaving the obnoxious portion to the Archbishop. 3. That complaint is made that the loan[3] is not repaid, nor will this grant be. 4. They would give, but cannot; and will not at any other than the King's appointment. 5. That too much coin of the realm is exported already into Flanders. 6. That it would be the greatest means of enriching France to have all his money spent there, out of the realm; and if the King win France, he will be obliged to spend his time and revenues there.... Would have been glad if the time had allowed 'that this practising with the people for so great sums might have been spared to the cuckoo time, and the hot weather (at which time mad brains be most busy) had been...passed.'

Letters and Papers, Foreign and Domestic, Henry VIII,
vol. iv, pt. i, No. 1243.

Archbishop Warham to Wolsey, 15 April, 1525

Is informed by those whom he has 'secretly caused to make privy espials amongst the clergy of my diocese' that there is great untowardness among the clergy 'to make contribution of the third part of their goods,' saying they have now to pay the subsidy granted at the last Convocation, which they are not able to do. If they pay this third they will be utterly destitute....They complain that they cannot support their fathers and mothers, or dispense hospitality....'The Church was never so continually charged'...if the laity oppose the grant, they of the clergy have greater reason to do so....

Letters and Papers, Foreign and Domestic, Henry VIII,
vol. iv, pt. i, No. 1267.

[8 May, 1525]

...King Henry, pretending an expedition into France, to which the Emperor invited him, desired of his subjects an aid (which he called an amicable grant), and to that purpose sent Commissioners (which were the chief noblemen) into the shires,

---

[1] Ill-temperedly. [2] *I.e.* Wolsey.

[3] Loans had been already granted to the King, particularly one of 4*s.* in the £ by the clergy (Brewer, i, 474).

to assemble and move the people. But the commons plead their poverty, and that they have no money, so that they will not grant anything by letters missives but only by Act of Parliament; which King Henry in a letter to the Commissioners...takes unkindly, yet wills them to proceed doulcely rather than by violence, to reform them, if it be possible. In some places the people arose up in arms against the Commissioners; and in others those who condescended to[1] the grant were threatened by their neighbours; and some recalled their grant....

...It seems this amicable grant was the moderation of a greater grant, which the Commons first condescended to, but after got it in part released.

> *Letters and Papers, Foreign and Domestic, Henry VIII*,
> vol. iv, pt. i, No. 1318.

[13 August, 1525]

The saying of George Cobb to William Woodall of Rugby, being petty collector; when the said William came to ask the King's money the said George made him answer, and said he had no justice to pay his money and was not agreeable to it, and then the said collector said to him he would not be driven no longer from day to day for it; and the said George made him answer that it was a great robbing of money out of the country, but an he must needs pay it he would, and so would pay no money to him at that time....

> *Letters and Papers, Foreign and Domestic, Henry VIII*,
> vol. iv, pt. i, No. 1567.

(3) The Loan of 1556

[At St James's, 5 October, 1556]

A letter to Thomas Mildmay, esquire, of thanks for his diligence and travail in the delivery of a privy seal sent unto him touching the Loan, and where he signifyeth that there be certain that have refused to pay and yet keep their privy seals with them, he is willed to deliver such letters as are addressed unto them and sent herewith, and for the rest that have not paid and be not hitherto discharged he is also willed to keep a note in his book of their names, and to travail with them between this and his coming up for to make payments of the sums required of them.

> Dasent, *Acts of the Privy Council*, vi, 5.

[At St James's, 19 November, 1556]

It was this day ordered that all such to whom privy seals have been addressed unto for the Loan and have detained the same in

---

[1] Agreed to.

their hands and not paid the sums demanded of them, nor otherwise answered the same, notwithstanding divers of them have been eftsoons[1] written unto herein, should be sent for to answer to their said doings.

Ib. vi, 19.

[At Greenwich, 18 January, 1557]

These persons whose names do follow were ordered either to pay the money that they were heretofore appointed by privy seals to lend in such sort as was prescribed unto them, or else to give their continual attendance upon the Council till further order be taken with them by their Lordships....

Ib. vi, 45.

[At St James's, 21 October, 1557]

This day Alexander Wells, Mayor of Rye, having heretofore been committed to the prison of the Fleet for his refusal to appear before the Commissioners for the Loan in the county of Sussex when they sent for him, was this day discharged of the same imprisonment, having a good lesson given him to beware of the like disobedience hereafter.

Ib. vi, 188.

[At St James's, 24 October, 1557]

Edmund Marshall, having been bound before the Bishop of Lincoln and other Commissioners for the Loan in the county of Lincoln to appear here, made this day his personal appearance.

Ib. vi, 189.

[At St James's, 25 October, 1557]

John Love of Winchelsea, merchant, having refused to receive the Queen's Majesty's privy seal for the Loan, was this day for his disobedience committed to the Fleet.

Ib. vi, 190.

[At St James's, 2 November, 1557]

Henry Summers of Gloucestershire, being heretofore bound by the Commissioners for the Loan in that shire to appear personally before the Lords of the Council, made this day his appearance accordingly and desired to have the same recorded, being contented to lend the sum required of him by the Queen's Highness's privy seal.

Ib. vi, 194.

§ 4. EXPENDITURE

In the Tudor period the royal expenditure was entirely under the control of the King, for Parliamentary control over expenditure belongs to a later age. Henry VII reorganised the King's Chamber[2], and Henry VIII ob-

[1] A second time.
[2] For an account of this reorganisation see Mr A. P. Newton's article on *The King's Chamber under the Early Tudors* in *E.H.R.* xxxii, 348.

tained statutory authority for the arrangements which his father had made by his personal authority. The traditional Chamber had been a minor department of the Court; it now became a financial organisation of great importance, handling large sums of money which were removed from the control of the Exchequer. The Chamber now received the profits of Crown lands; customs on the staple commodities; the profits of lands forfeited for treason or felony; the profits of the mints and the Exchanges; and sometimes subsidies granted by Parliament, although these were, as a rule, paid into the Exchequer. Fines and compositions levied by commission were also paid into the Chamber, and 'they were a source that yielded to Henry VII a very material part of his wealth.'[1]

To the accumulations of revenue in the Chamber the King had direct access, without any external control. Under Henry VII the verbal command of the sovereign was sufficient for the issue of his treasure, and there was no other audit than the King's frequent inspection of the accounts. Under Henry VIII, as the volume of business grew, the signed warrant began to displace the verbal order, but it was still within the power of the sovereign to give his instructions by word of mouth; and this system continued until the Exchequer in Mary's reign 'was again set up as the supreme financial machine of the realm.'[2]

The disturbing factor in Tudor finance under the head of expenditure was Ireland. Calais was a source of revenue, as it was an important staple town, and the customs levied there on the staple commodities were productive. It would have been a lucrative source of revenue but for the necessity of spending large sums upon the fortifications. The Scottish Border was expensive, as the inhabitants of the Border counties were exempted from subsidy because they were so much exposed to forays from the other side. But Ireland cost five times as much to govern in time of peace as it produced in the way of revenue, and if a rebellion broke out the expenditure ran into very high figures[3]. 'The Irish action,' says Naunton[4], writing concerning Elizabeth, 'we may call a malady and consumption of her times, for it accompanied her to her end; and it was of so profuse and vast an expense that it drew near a distemperature of state.' How near, a modern writer suggests to us. 'Since 1596,' says Seeley[5], 'Ireland had been in rebellion, and the task of pacifying the island was imposed upon Elizabeth. A military operation of such magnitude was almost beyond the resources of our state, such as it then was. It opened the redoubtable financial problem which involved, as the sequel shewed, a constitutional revolution.' Thus the Irish finance of Elizabeth appears among the causes which were to lead in the next century to civil war.

[1] E.H.R. xxxii, 364.   [2] Ib. p. 350.
[3] It is said that in 1599 £600,000 was spent there in six months (Sinclair, pt. i, p. 124).
[4] Fragmenta Regalia (edn. of 1641), p. 7.   [5] i, 238.

Index

₊ *References to documents are printed in black type*

Abjuration of the realm: after sanctuary, 15; as recusants, 162; as sectaries, 198
Access, right of, 550, 551
Admiralty, Court of, 346; criminal jurisdiction, 347; civil jurisdiction, 347; appeal to delegates, 347; Act of 1536, 347. *See also* 24, 40
'Advertisements' of Archbishop Parker (1566), 166, 191
Aid, feudal: *see* Feudal aid
Ale-houses, licensing of, 500; Licensing Act of 1552, 500, 501
Allen, William, 150
Altar, Ridley's injunction concerning the (1550), 115
Amadas *v.* Williams (court of requests, 1519), 303
'Amicable Loan' of 1525, 620, 621–4
Anabaptists, 186
ANCIENT COURTS, 342: courts of common law, 342; court of admiralty, 346; court of the constable and marshal, 348
Annates: conditional restraint of (1532), 25, 26; absolute restraint of (1534), 29. *See also* Firstfruits
Anonymous writer on the court of requests (*c.* 1600), 311
Apostolic Camera, 34 *n.*
Appeals, Act in restraint of (1533), 40, 41, 532
— reorganisation of: Act of 1357, 343; Act of 1585, 343; Act of 1589, 343, 345
Apprentices, Statute of; *see* Labour, Statute of
Aragon, Queen Catharine of, 25, 40, 380, 384, 390, 422 *n.*
Arbitration, procedure of the Council by, 227, 238
Archbishops, courts of the, 358: court of arches, 358; of audience, 359; of peculiars, 359; prerogative court, 359; chancery court, court of audience, and prerogative court of York, 359. *See also* 192 *n.*

Archdeacons, courts of the, 358
Arches, Court of, 21, 45, 358
Arrest, privilege of freedom from, 578: claimed by the Speaker, 550; did not extend to criminal offences, 578 *n.*; enforced by order of the Houses, 579, 580, 584, 588, 589; members' servants, 580, 583–6; other subsidiary privileges, 580, 586–9
Assistance, writs of, 514 *n.*
Assurance of the Queen's power, Act for (1563), 142
Attainder, 423: of the Duke of Buckingham (1523), 423, 428; of Queen Catherine Howard (1542), 423, 425
Attorney-general, summoned to the House of Lords, 514 and *n.*, 529
— *v.* Parre (star chamber, 1489), 263
Atwyll's case (1477), 579 *n.*
Audience, courts of, 21, 45, 359
Augmentations, Court of, 66, 222, 301, 336; Act for the establishment of (1536), 336; Act of 1540, 336, 339; Act of 1542, 336, 340
Aylmer, John, Bishop of London, 196 *n.*

Babington conspiracy, 443, 447, 448 *n.*
Bacon, Francis (1621): on Henry VII's council, 229; on the star chamber, 288; speech on monopolies (1601), 557, 573; 'Morton's fork,' 621
— Roger, 51
Bail Acts: of 1487, 464; of 1555, 464, 468
Barons of the Exchequer, 342
Barrow, Henry (1590): on Independency, 186
Barton, Elizabeth: attainder of (1534), 423
Beadle, duties of the, 509
Benefit of clergy, 14
Benevolences, 619; benevolence of 1491, 621; benevolence of 1495 legalised by statute, 529
Bible, use of the, 94, 101

'Bill and book,' Mr Cope's (1587), 557, 570

Bills, readings of, 541; impounded by the Queen in 1572, 557, 568; and in 1587, 557, 570

Bishoprics Act (1539), 68

Bishops, Act for the election of (1547), 102

— consistory courts of the, 358

'Black Book,' the, 58 n.

Black Death, 57

Black Rod, gentleman usher of the, 580, 590 n.

Bland's case (right of the Commons to commit, 1586), 594

Boleyn, Queen Anne, 40, 143, 385 ff., 390

'Book of Entries,' 227, 252; see also Liber Intrationum

'Book of the Council,' in 1421, 213; in 1540, 217

Border, Scottish: castles, 314; anarchy of, 315

Borough franchise, 517

'Bouche of Court,' 207, 208

Bownd, Nicholas (1595): on the keeping of the Sabbath, 200

Bowyer's case (privilege of parliament, 1597), 580, 589

Bribery at elections: case of Thomas Long (1571), 520, 526

Bridges, Dr John, 195

Bridges, Statute of (1531), 495

Brownists, 186

Buckingham, Duke of: trial for treason (1521), 421, 428; attainder of (1523), 423. See also 349

Bull of excommunication (1570), 143, 144

Bulls from Rome, Act against (1571), 146

Burges v. Lacy (court of requests, c. 1540), 305

Burghley, Lord: intelligence system, 4; condemns the oath ex officio, 193 n., 373; death of (1598), 558. See also 211, 225

Caesar, Sir Julius (c. 1597): 308, 310, 346 n.; on the court of requests, 308

Caister castle, siege of, 8

Cambridge, 37 n., 106, 112, 166, 230, 280 ff., 284, 289, 384 n., 478, 601; surplice controversy at, 165

Campion, Edmund, 150

Cappis v. Cappis (star chamber, c. 1547), 270

Cartwright, Thomas: his Admonition to Parliament (1572), 166, 167; on reformation in Church government, 167. See also 151, 186

Castle Chamber in Ireland, 228, 240

Cathedral worship, Puritan objection to, 164

Catholics, penal laws against, 141

Cawdrey's case (high commission, 1591), 362, 372

Ceremonies, Puritan objections to, 164

Certiorari, writ of, 268 n.

Chamber: see Duchy Chamber, Exchequer Chamber, King's Chamber, Parliament Chamber, Star Chamber

Chancellor of the diocese, 358

Chancery, 289

Chancery courts: of Durham, 351; of Lancaster, 350, 351; of York, 359

Channel Islands, appeals from the courts of the, 228

Chantries, Act for the dissolution of (1547), 103, 104 n., 535

Chaplain of the House of Commons, 541, 546, 547

Chapter House at Westminster, 542

Chester, county palatine of, 350; palatine courts of, 351; parliamentary incorporation (1543), 514

Church government: controversy with the Puritans, 166

Church Settlements: of Henry VIII, 13; of Edward VI, 99; of Mary, 121; of Elizabeth, 130

Churchwardens: to collect alms, 480; to be overseers of the poor, 488, 509; their other duties, 102, 508, 509

Citations, Act in restraint of (1532), 16

Clergy, submission of the, 16; Act of 1534, 22

Clerical Subsidy Act (1601), 604, 616

Clerk to the Council, 219, 254

— of the Peace, 452, 460, 463

— of the Parliament, 215 n.

— of the Star Chamber, 219, 250, 254, 255, 293

Cleves, Queen Anne of, 380, 395

Coke, Sir Edward (c. 1628): on the star

chamber, 289; on the court of requests, 311; on the council of the north, 318; on the duchy chamber of Lancaster, 351; on treason, 377; on the court of the lord steward, 428; on the election of a Speaker, 527

Colet, John, 51; sermon on clerical abuses (1511), 69

Commissaries of the bishop, 192 n., 359

Commissary Court of London, 362; cases in, 364, 365

Commission of the Peace, 453; revision in 1590, 453, 461

Committees: of Council, 218; of Parliament, 541, 595

Common Law, Courts of, 288, 301, 342
— Pleas, Court of, 289, 342; stipends in, 209
— Prayer, Book of: of 1549, 107, 113, 163; of 1552, 116, 119, 136; of 1559, 136, 137, 141. See also 169, 191, 192, 565

Commons, House of: claimed to be a 'court of record,' 511; increase in power, 512; composition of, 514; franchise, 517; payment of members of, 517; influence of the Crown in, 518, 520–6; independence of, 531, 535; procedure, 541, 546–50. See also Parliament
— petition for ecclesiastical reform (1584), 190, 191
— privilege of: Speaker's claim of privilege, 550, 551–4; right of access, 550; freedom of speech, 554, 558–78; freedom from arrest, 578, 580–3, 584–5, 586–9; right to commit, 589, 590–5; right to determine membership, 595, 596–7

Communion in both kinds, Act for (1547), 102

Confessions of the monks, 89

Congé d'élire, 29, 30 n., 103

Consistory courts: of the archbishop, 358; of the bishop, 358

Constable: see High constable, Petty constable

Constable and marshal, Court of the, 301, 348, 427

Convocation: silenced by the Crown, 16, 22; appeal to, 40, 46
— Puritan articles in (1563), 164

Cook's case (privilege, 1585), 580, 586

Cooper, Thomas, Bishop of Winchester, 196 n.

Cooper v. Gervaux (star chamber, 1493), 276

Cope, Mr, his 'bill and book' (1587), 557, 570

Corporal oath, 130 n.

Corporations, Act concerning (1504), 7

Council, the: history of, 213; composition and procedure, 216; business, 225; cases before (1540–1603), 229–43
— committees of: under Edward VI, 218, 222; under Mary, 218, 224; under Elizabeth, 218, 224
— Fortescue's scheme for a, 213
— memorandum by Dr John Herbert on the distribution of the business of (1600), 228, 247
— oath taken by members of (1570), 218, 225
— president of, 218; clerk to, 219; payments to members of, 219; meeting-place of, 219
— relations of, with the Crown, 215; with the justices of the peace, 507. See also Privy Council

Council Courts, 314: Council of the North, 314; of Wales, 228, 233, 331; of the West, 335
— orders: concerning private suits (1582, 1589), 243; against seditious books (1566), 245
— ordinances: of Henry VIII (1526), 220; of Edward VI (1553), 221
— Register, 212, 213, 217; extracts from (1540–1603), 229–43
— Table, 226, 229, 238, 250, 252, 253, 254, 262, 297

County franchise, 517

Cranmer, Archbishop: trial for treason (1553), 428; his library, 107 n.

Cromwell, Lord: case of privilege (1572), 578, 583
— Thomas, Earl of Essex: attainder (1540), 423

Crown influence in Parliament, 518; interference in elections, 518; in the choice of a Speaker, 527; influence on legislation, 529
— lands, income from, 598

Customs, tonnage, and poundage: revenue from, 599
Custos Rotulorum, 452, 459, 460

Dacre, Lord: case of (1541), 431
Debate, privacy of, 590
Decrees of the Star Chamber, 257
Delegates, to hear appeals from the Admiral's court, 40, 347
— High Court of, 40, 359
Delegations by the Council, 228, 232
Digges's case of privilege (1584), 580, 585
Dispensations Act (1534), 31, 32
Dispensing power, 529
Dissolution of the monasteries; see Monasteries
Dobell *v.* Soley (star chamber, 1533), 269
Douay, English college at, 150
Duchy Chamber of Lancaster, 351
Durham, Bishopric of, 329, 350, 351, 354; courts of the bishopric, 351

ECCLESIASTICAL COURTS, 357: their unpopularity, 192 *n.*; cases in, 362, 363–7
— commission of 1559, 360, 367
— parish, the, 508
— reform: minor measures of Henry VIII, 13; petition of the Commons for (1584), 190, 191; Queen's permission to proceed in (1597), 573
Ecclesiastics: their exclusion from certain high offices, 215 *n.*
EDWARD VI, CHURCH SETTLEMENT OF, 99: injunctions of 1547, 100; statutes of the protectorate, 102; later religious changes, 1550–3, 113
Elections, interference in, 518, 520–6
ELIZABETH, CHURCH SETTLEMENT OF, 130: the Acts of Supremacy and Uniformity, 130; injunctions of 1559, 140; penal laws against the Catholics, 141; the Puritan movement, 163
Eltham, ordinances at (1526), 207, 208 *n.*
Empson and Dudley, 3, 527 *n.*, 599
Erasmus, 69, 82, 101; on monasticism, 73

Essex, Earl of: trial for treason (1601), 433, 448
Exchequer, Court of, 342
— Chamber, 290, 343, 344, 345
Excommunication, 357; bull of (1570), 142, 143, 144
'Exempt' monasteries, 32, 36 *n.*, 51 *n.*
Expenditure, 625
Extraordinary revenue, 619
Eynesham, Abbot of, *v.* Harcourt (star chamber, 1503), 265

'Family of Love,' 186
Fasting, the House of Commons and (1581), 568
Ferrers's case of privilege (1543), 579, 580
Feudal aid, 598; Act for the (1504), 600
— incidents, income from, 598
FINANCE, 598
FINANCIAL COURTS, 336: augmentations, 336; firstfruits and tenths, 340; wards and liveries, 340; surveyors, 341
Finnies, Robert, case of privilege (1584), 580, 585
Firstfruits and tenths, 26 *n.*: annexed to the Crown (1534), 36, 37; court of, 222, 301, 340; income from, 599
Fish, Simon (1528): on clerical abuses, 76
Fisher, Bishop: fictitious speech in Convocation, 63 *n.*; trial of (1535), 433, 440
Fitzherbert's case of privilege (1593), 511, 579, 588, 590
Forced loan of 1556, 621, 624
Forfeiture for treason, 432
Fortescue, Sir John, 1–4; his scheme for a council, 213
FRANCHISE COURTS, 350
Franchise, parliamentary, 517
Freedom of speech; from arrest. *See* Privilege of Parliament

Gascoigne, Thomas, 51
Geneva, 164, 166, 167
Grammar schools, 103, 106
'Great' Bible (1539), 94 *n.*
Grindal, Archbishop: his objection to vestments, 164; his letter to the Queen (1576), 182, 183. *See also* 166, 186, 190, 367

Guilds, legislation against at the dissolution of the chantries (1547), 103, 105, 535
Gunpowder Plot, 151

Hall's case of privilege (1581), 590, 592
Hampden, Dr, 29 *n.*
Henry VII: his policy, 1, 3; his character, 2. *See also* 512
HENRY VIII, CHURCH SETTLEMENT OF, 13: minor ecclesiastical reforms, 13; submission of the clergy, 16; cessation of payments to the see of Rome, 25; prohibition of appeals to Rome, 40; dissolution of the monasteries, 50; injunctions of 1536 and 1538, 93; the Six Articles, 95
— his constitutional position, 5; his relation to Parliament, 512; *et passim*
Herbert, Dr John; his memorandum (1600): duties of the king's secretary, 212; distribution of council business, 228, 247
Heresy: Acts of 1401 and 1414, 95; modification in 1533, 95; Act to revive the heresy laws (1554), 124; repealed by the Act of Supremacy (1559), 132
Hewitt's case (star chamber, 1500), 250 *n.*
High Commission, Court of, 360; commission of 1559, 367; Cawdrey's case (1591), 372; Burghley's criticism of (1584), 373. *See also* 191, 193, 193 *n.*, 246, 281, 283
High constable, 492 *n.*
Highways: first Statute of (1555), 495, 498; second Statute of (1563), 495, 499
— Surveyor of, 495
Hogan's case of privilege (1601), 580, 589
Hooker, Richard: *Ecclesiastical Polity* (1594–7), 170, 171–9
Howard, Queen Catherine: attainder of (1542), 423, 425
Hudson, William (*c.* 1633): on the star chamber, 294

Images: crusade against, 94, 101; Act against (1550), 113
Impeachment, 422, 423

Impositions, 599
Independency, foundation of (1580), 186
Injunction concerning the altar (1550), 115; *see also* Royal Injunctions
Ireland: a disturbing factor in Tudor finance, 626

Jesuit invasion, 142, 150
Jesuits and Seminary priests, Act against (1585), 154
Judges: their tenure, 342; their relative precedence, 342; their salaries, 209, 210, 343; their share in legislation, 529
Justice, income from the proceeds of, 599
Justices Act (1489), 465
Justices of the peace, 452; history of the office, 453; how appointed, 453; property qualification, 453; wages, 453; commission, 453; the 'quorum,' 454, 455, 457, 461; sessions, 454, 459; oath, 455, 458
— judicial functions, 463; vagabonds, beggars and poor relief, 469; roads and bridges, 495; licensing of alehouses, 500; regulation of labour and wages, 502; police duties, 506

King's Bench, Court of, 342; stipends in, 209
— Chamber, 625
KING'S SECRETARY, 202; *see also* Secretary
Kyrle's case of privilege (1585), 580, 586

Labour, Elizabeth's Statute of (1563), 502
— regulation of by the justices of the peace, 502
Lambarde, William: on the star chamber (1591), 285; on the court of requests (1591), 306; on the justices of the peace (1581), 457
Lancaster, Duchy of, 338, 350, 354, 534; courts of, 350; duchy chamber, 339, 351
Lancastrian Council, 213
Latimer, Hugh (1548): on the bishops, 88
Lay Subsidy Act (1601), 604, 610

Legislation: influence of the Crown in, 529; share of the judges and councillors in, 529
Liber Intrationum, 213; see also 'Book of Entries'
Licensing Act of 1552, 500, 501
Litany, the, 102 *n*
Liveries, Statute of (1504), 7, 9, 252
Loans, 620, 623 *n*.: 'amicable loan (1525), 620, 621–4; forced loan of 1556, 621, 624–5
LOCAL GOVERNMENT, 452: the commission of the peace, 453; judicial functions of the justices, 463; vagabonds, beggars, and poor relief, 469; roads and bridges, 495; licensing of alehouses, 500; regulation of labour and wages, 502; miscellaneous police duties, 506; the ecclesiastical parish, 508
Long, Thomas: case of bribery (1571), 526
Lord Chancellor, stipend of the office, 208; he presides in the star chamber, 254; ceases to be an ecclesiastic, 215 *n*.
— Lieutenant, 452
— Steward: court of, 423, 427
Lords, House of: numbers of, 513; composition of, 514; judges, law officers, and privy councillors summoned, 514, 529; proxies, 541, 545
— privilege of: freedom from arrest, 578, 580, 583, 585; right to commit, 590
Lords Triers, 428

'Maintenance,' 8 *n*.
Marches, Council of the; see Wales, Council of
— Warden of the, 212, 314, 315, 316, 331
Marprelate controversy (1588–9), 194, 195, 197
Marriage of priests, Act legalising the (1549), 112
Martin's case (time of privilege, 1587), 579, 587
MARY, CHURCH SETTLEMENT OF, 121
— Queen of Scots, 440, 556; trial of (1586), 433, 443, 444. See also 143, 154, 257 *n*., 448 *n*.
Masters in Chancery: summoned to the House of Lords, 514 *n*.

Masters of Requests; see Requests, Masters of
Merchant Adventurers *v.* Staplers (star chamber, 1504), 251, 260
Misprision of treason, 149 *n*.
Monasteries, dissolution of the, 50: case for, 50; episcopal visitations, 51; royal visitation (1535), 58; first Act of Dissolution (1536), 57, 58, 59, 532 *n*.; second Act (1539), 63, 64; effects of the Dissolution, 67, 598; gives the temporal peers a majority in the House of Lords, 514. See also 432, 481
Money bills: exclusive right to initiate them not yet claimed by the Commons, 606, 609, 610
Monks, confessions of the, 89
Monopolies, debate on (1601), 557, 573; the Queen's speech, 577
More, Cresacre: his *Life* of Sir Thomas More, 433
— Sir Thomas: on clerical abuses (1528), 51, 69, 73; in defence of the Church (1529), 76, 79; his resignation of the chancellorship (1532), 22; his trial (1535), 433. See also 215 *n*.
Morice, Mr: his bills for the reform of the ecclesiastical courts (1593), 557, 572
'Morton's fork,' 621
Mortuaries Act (1529), 13

Nonconformists, 166, 361
Norfolk, case of the county of (1586), 595, 596
— Duke of: his trial for treason (1572), 422, 433, 440
North, Council of the: history, 314–7; commission of 1537, 318; instructions of 1545, 320; mentioned in Subsidy Act (1540), 328; in Tillage Act (1571), 329; stipends, 209. See also 149, 158, 212
Northern Insurrection (1569), 143, 151
Nowell's case (parliament, 1553), 596

Oath, of abjuration, 15, 162, 198
— of allegiance and supremacy, 130, 134, 141, 142, 156–8, 361, 455, 459, 595
— *ex officio*, 193, 357, 360, 362, 572
— of a justice of the peace, 458

Oath of a privy councillor, 218, 225

Officials, stipends and fees of, 208

Ordinances: of Eltham (1526), 207; council ordinances of 1526, 216, 220; of 1553, 217, 221

Ordinaries, Supplication against the (1532), 21; answer of the (1532), 21

'Ordinary councillors,' 216, 217

Ore tenus, 256, 292

Ornaments Rubric, 136, 139

Osborne, Francis (1658): on the star chamber, 296

Outlawry, 579, 588

Oxford, 37 *n.*, 51, 52, 53, 57, 106, 112, 213 *n.*, 228 *n.*, 236, 238, 267, 280 ff., 384 *n.*, 478, 520, 601

Palatine courts, 301, 350; Act of 1536, 351, 352

Papal Authority, Act against the (1536), 48

Pardon of the Clergy, Act for the (1531), 16, 17; of the Laity (1531), 20

Parish, the, 508: parish clerk, duties of the, 509

Parker, Archbishop: 'Advertisements' (1566), 166, 191. *See also* 182, 367

PARLIAMENT, 511; *see also* Commons, Lords, Privilege

Parliament: conceived of as a court, 511; composition, 513; sessions, 515; franchise and qualifications, 517; influence of the Crown on, 518; procedure in, 541; Sir Thomas Smith on, 510, 541, 547

— opening of, 542; conferences between the two Houses, 541; meeting-place, 542; religious questions in, 556, 565; trade questions in, 557, 573

— how far packed, 518; or servile, 531; change of tone in later Parliaments, 558, 578

— Chamber, 205 *n.*, 294, 542

— Privilege of; *see* Privilege

Parliamentary revenue, 603

Parr, Queen Catherine, 397 ff.

Parry, Dr, case of privilege (1584), 590, 593

Parson, the, as a parochial personage, 508

Parsons, Robert, 150

Paulet, Sir William: the Council's letter to (1570), 261

'Peculiars,' 357; Archbishop's Court of, 359

Penal Laws against the Catholics, 141

Penry, John, 195

Permanent revenue of the Crown, 598

Peterson *v.* Frederick (court of requests, 1521), 304

Peter's pence, 31, 32

Petty constable, duties of, 509

— sessions, 454, 455

Pilgrimage of Grace, 64, 217, 316

Plumbers' Hall, conventicle dispersed at (1567), 186

Pluralities, Act in restraint of (1529), 13; bill to amend (1601), 557, 573

Police duties of justices of the peace, 506

Poor relief, 469: Act of 1536, 470, 479; of 1576, 472, 481; of 1598, 472, 488; of 1601, 472, 473

Popish Recusants, Act against (1593), 159

Praemunire, 17, 18 *n.*, 20

Prayer Book: *see* Common Prayer

Preaching, 102, 179

Precedence, Act of (1539), 204

Preemption, 598

Prerogative Courts: of Canterbury, 359; of York, 359

Presbyterian system, 166, 167

President of the Council, 218; of the Council of the North, 316, 317; of the Council of Wales, 331

Principal Secretary, 203, 204 *n.*

Printing: regulated by the Council, 245; by the Star Chamber, 257, 279

Privilege, of Parliament, 550; Speaker's claim of, 550, 551–4; right of access, 550, 551–4; freedom of speech, 550, 551–4, 554, 558–78; freedom from arrest, 551–4, 578, 580–9; right to commit, 589, 590–5; right to determine membership, 595, 596–7

— committees of, 595, 596

— petitions of: in 1542, 551; in 1559, 551; in 1593, 552; in 1601, 553

— time of, 579, 587

PRIVY COUNCIL, 213: origin of the term, 216; use under Henry VIII, 217; interference in elections, 519. *See also* Council

Privy Council, under the Protectorate (1553), 99

Privy Councillors: summoned to the House of Lords, 514

Probate of Wills, Act for (1529), 13

Pro Camera Stellata, 249, 258, 530

Procedure: of the Council, 216; of the Star Chamber, 255; of the Court of Requests, 300; in Parliament, 541

Proclamations, Statute of (1539), 250 *n.*, 530, 532

— breaches of, punished in the Star Chamber, 257

Prophesyings, 179: regulations for the diocese of Lincoln (1574), 179; Grindal's letter (1576), 182, 183; the Queen's letter of suppression (1577), 184

Protector, appointment of (1547), 99; abolition of the Protectorate (1549), 113

Provisors, 18 *n.*

Proxies, 518, 541, 545

Puritan Articles in Convocation (1563), 164

Puritans, the, 163, 558; their criticisms of the Act of Uniformity, 164

Purveyance, 598

Qualifications for members of Parliament, 517

Quarter Sessions, 454

Queen Anne's Bounty, 37, 599

Queen's Person, Act for the Surety of the (1585), 417

Quorum, the, 454, 455, 461

Raleigh, Sir Walter, 574, 605 *n.*

Recognisances, 228, 231

Reconciliation to Rome, Act against (1581), 150, 152

Record, Courts of, 340, 341, 343, 418 *n.*, 454, 511, 590

Reformation Parliament, 13

Regal Power, Act concerning the (1554), 122, 123

Religion, Articles of (1571), 567

Religious questions in Parliament, 556, 565

Repeal, Mary's first Statute of (1553), 121; second Statute (1555), 125

REQUESTS, COURT OF, 299: history, 299; procedure, 300; business, 301;

decline of the court, 301; cases in, 303–6. *See also* White Hall

Requests, Masters of, 248, 300, 301, 302, 307, 308 ff.

Revenue: permanent, 598; parliamentary, 603; extraordinary, 619

Rheims, English college moved from Douay to (1578), 150

Ridley, Bishop: his injunction concerning the altar (1550), 115

Ridolfi plot, 440

Riot: council cases, 232; star chamber cases, 257, 265

Roads and bridges, 495

Roper, William: his *Life* of Sir Thomas More, 433

Royal Household, ordinances for the, 207

Royal Injunctions: of 1536, 93; of 1538, 94; of 1547, 100; of 1554, 122; of 1559, 140, 282

Rushworth, John (1680): on the Star Chamber, 297

Russell's case of privilege (1550), 596

Sabbatarian controversy, 200

St Stephen's Chapel, 542

Saladin tithe, 603

Salisbury, Countess of: attainder (1539), 423

Sanctuary, 15

Sarum, use of, 107, 108 *n.*

Scotland, *see* Border; Marches, Warden of the

Secretary: his status, 204, 207; his relation to the king, 211; warrant for the appointment of two secretaries (1540), 206; Dr John Herbert's memorandum on the duties of a secretary (1600), 212

— of State, 202, 203

— to the Council, 202

Sectaries, Act against (1593), 197

Seditious books, order against (1566), 245

Seminary priests, 150, 154

Serjeant-at-Arms, 579, 580

Serjeants-at-law: summoned to the House of Lords, 514 *n.*, 529

Service-book, controversy concerning the, 164

Sessions of Parliament, 515

Sexton, duties of the, 509

Seymour, Queen Jane, 380, 390 ff., 397

Seymour's case (parliament, 1549), 511, 513

Shute, Robert: his appointment as baron of the exchequer (1579), 342

Six Articles, Statute of (1539), 95, 124, 531

Smalley's case of privilege (1576), 580, 584

Smith, Sir Thomas (1565): on the Star Chamber, 284; on the justices of the peace, 455; on the procedure of the House of Commons, 547; on the Speaker's claim of privilege, 554

Smuggling, Act against (1559), 602

Smyth, Sir John: his letter to Lord Burghley (1597), 262

Solicitor-General: summoned to the House of Lords, 514 n., 529

Spanish Armada, 142, 558

Speaker, the: choice of, 527; procedure at his election, 527; his claim of privilege, 550, 551, 554

— his admonitions to the House (1589), 511, 548, 590, 591

Speech, freedom of, 554: claimed by the Speaker, 550

Stafford's case (treason, 1487), 15, 16, 441

Standish, case of (1515), 46

Stanley, Sir William: case of treason (1495), 376

Stannary Courts, 301, 354, 355; imprisonment of Richard Strode by (1512), 555, 559; Trewynard's case, 355, 356

STAR CHAMBER, 249; see also 10, 206, 213, 220, 245, 247, 301, 361

— history, 249; composition, 254; procedure, 255; business, 257; abolition in 1641, 249

— Act of 1487, 249, 258; Act of 1529, 259; punishments, 256; regulation of printing by (1585), 257, 279; dinners, 254, 263; speeches in, 258, 278

— cases in, 263–78

— clerk of the, 250, 254, 255

— extracts from writers on the: Sir Thomas Smith (1565), 284; William Lambarde (1591), 285; Francis Bacon (1621), 288; Sir Edward Coke (c. 1628), 289;

William Hudson (c. 1633), 294; Francis Osborne (1658), 296; John Rushworth (1680), 297

Starkey, Thomas: on clerical abuses (1535), 51, 82; on monasticism (1536), 86

'Starred Chamber,' 251, 260, 302

Stationers' Company, 279 ff.

'Stellionate,' 289 n.

Stepney v. Flood (court of requests, 1599), 302, 312

Stipends of judges and officials under Elizabeth, 208–10

Strickland, Mr: his bill (1571), 556, 565

Strode's Act (1512), 555, 558

Subsidy, 604: Subsidy Act of 1514, 604; of 1523, 605, 608; of 1534, 605; Acts of 1601, 604, 605 n., 610, 616

Succession Acts: first Act (1534), 380, 382; second Act (1536), 380, 389; Anne of Cleves Act (1540), 380, 395; third Act (1543), 380, 397

Succession question in Parliament, 555: in 1559, 555; in 1563, 555, 559; in 1566, 555, 560, 561; case of Paul Wentworth (1566), 556, 561; in 1567, 562; in 1576, 556, 563; in 1586, 564; in 1593, 564

Supersedeas, writ of, 580, 587

Supremacy, Henry VIII's Act of (1534), 46, 47; Elizabeth's Act of (1559), 130. See also 191

Surplice controversy (1566), 165

Surveyors, Court of, 341

Taxatio of Pope Nicholas IV (1291), 37 n.

Thirty-nine Articles, 191

Throckmorton plot, 154

Tonnage and poundage, 599; Act of 1510, 601

Torture, use of, 228, 241

Tracy's case of privilege (1597), 580, 588

Trade: Act of 1534 for the regulation of, 600; Star Chamber regulation of, 257

— questions in Parliament, 557, 573

Traitorous Words, Act against (1555), 380, 407

TREASON, LAW OF, 375: constructive treasons, 376; statutory treasons, 378; procedure in trials for treason, 421; impeachment, 422; attainder, 422, 423; Court of the Lord Steward, 427; punishment of treason, 432; Council cases, 231; select trials, 433; Sir Edward Coke on treason, 377; petit treason, 402 *n.*
— Statute of Edward III (1352), 375; Statute of 1495, 5, 6; Act of 1531, 379, 381; Treasons Act of 1534, 379, 388; of 1547, 380, 401, 422; of 1552, 380, 405, 422; of 1553, 380, 406; Act against traitorous words (1555), 380, 407; Treasons Act of 1555, 380, 408; of 1559, 381, 411; of 1571, 381, 413; of 1585, 381, 417. *See also* Succession Acts
Trent, Council of, 99, 141, 143
Trewynard's case (stannary court): in the chancery (1562), 355; in the star chamber (1564), 356
Trials for treason: Sir Thomas More (1535), 433; Duke of Norfolk (1572), 422, 433, 440; Mary Queen of Scots (1586), 433, 443, 444; Earl of Essex (1601), 433, 448. *See also* Buckingham, Duke of; Cranmer, Archbishop; Fisher, Bishop; Warwick, Earl of
TUDOR MONARCHY, FOUNDATIONS OF THE, 1

Uniformity: first Act of (1549), 107, 108; second Act of (1552), 116, 117; Elizabeth's Act of (1559), 135, 136

Vagabonds and beggars, 469: Act of 1495, 469, 473; Act of 1531, 470, 475; Act of 1536, 470, 479; Act of 1576, 471, 481; Act of 1598, 471, 484; testimonials for a sturdy beggar, 494
Vale *v.* Broke (star chamber, 1493), 275
Valor Ecclesiasticus (1535), 37, 57, 67, 599
Vernacular, use of in the services of the Church, 101

Vestments, Puritan objections to, 164
Vestry meetings, 508

Wages, regulation of by justices of the peace, 502
— of members of Parliament, 517
Wales, Council of, 233, 328, 329, 331: history, 331; Act of 1534, 331, 333; Act of 1543, 331, 335; stipends in, 209. *See also* 149, 158, 212
— justices of the peace in, 455
— parliamentary incorporation of (1536), 514
Walsingham, Sir Francis: intelligence system, 4; his death (1590), 558. *See also* 211, 225, 447
Walterkyn *v.* Lettice (star chamber, 1503), 272
Wards and Liveries, Court of, 222, 301, 340
Warwick, Earl of: trial for treason (1499), 427
— the Kingmaker, 1, 8 *n.*
Wentworth, Paul, 556, 557, 561, 568
— Peter: in 1571, 548 *n.*; in 1576, 531, 537; in 1587, 557, 571; in 1593, 556, 564, 569
West, Council of the, 319, 328, 335
White Hall: the meeting-place of the court of requests, 289, 300, 302, 303, 307, 308 ff.
Whitehall, fire at (1619), 213 *n.*
Whitgift, Archbishop: articles (1583), 190; interrogatories (1584), 193 *n.* *See also* 170, 279, 373–4, 443
Wickham's case of privilege (1571), 580 *n.*, 583
William the Silent: murder of (1584), 154, 420 *n.* *See also* 141
Wolsey, Cardinal: the subsidy of 1523, 605, 608; the 'amicable loan' of 1525, 620, 621. *See also* 211, 215 *n.*, 217, 225, 285, 300, 302
Wray, Sir Christopher: revised the commission of the justices of the peace (1590), 453, 457
Wyatt's insurrection (1554), 123
Wycliffe, John, 51

Yelverton's speech in Parliament (1571), 557, 566

Printed in Great Britain
by Amazon